VISUAL
dictionary

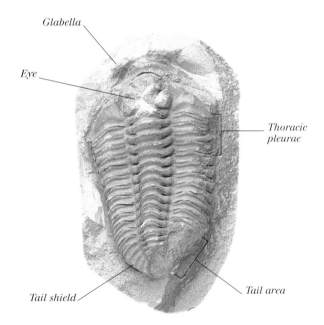

Glabella

Eye

Thoracic
pleurae

Tail shield

Tail area

PREHISTORIC TRILOBITE

DIGITAL VIDEO CAMERA

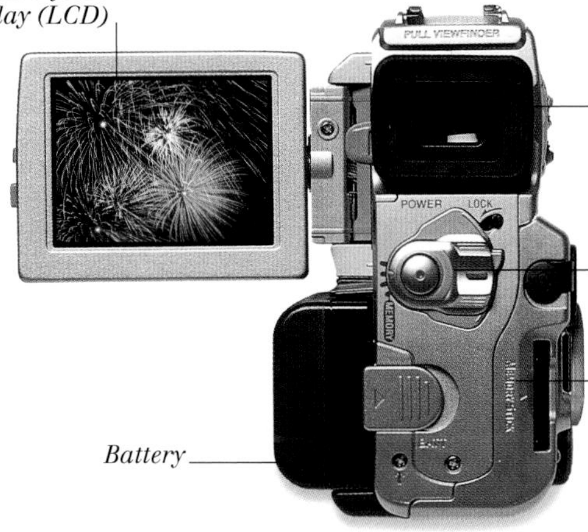

Liquid crystal display (LCD)

Viewfinder

Power switch

Cassette compartment lid

Battery

OVERHEAD VIEW OF OUR GALAXY

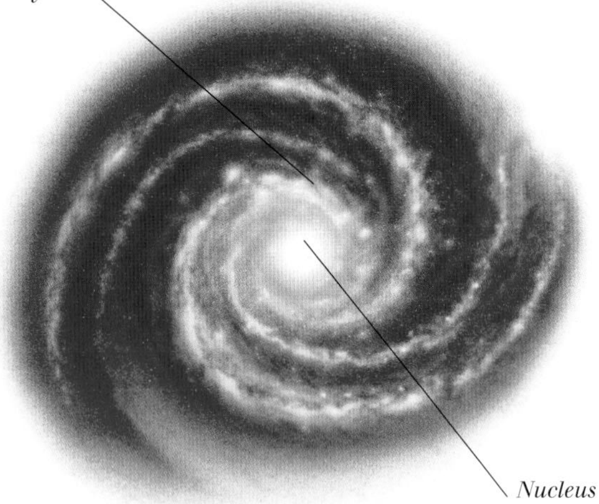

Location of Solar System

Nucleus

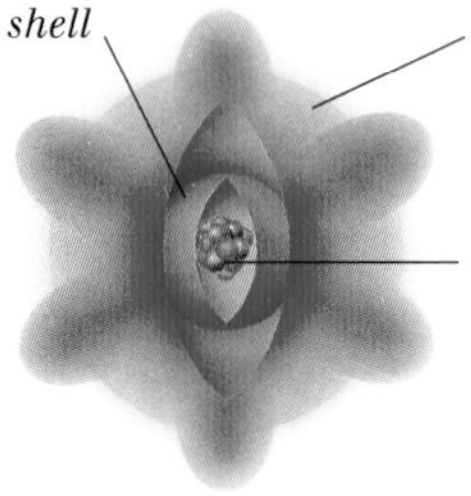

First electron shell

Second electron shell

Nucleus

ANATOMY OF A FLUORINE–19 ATOM

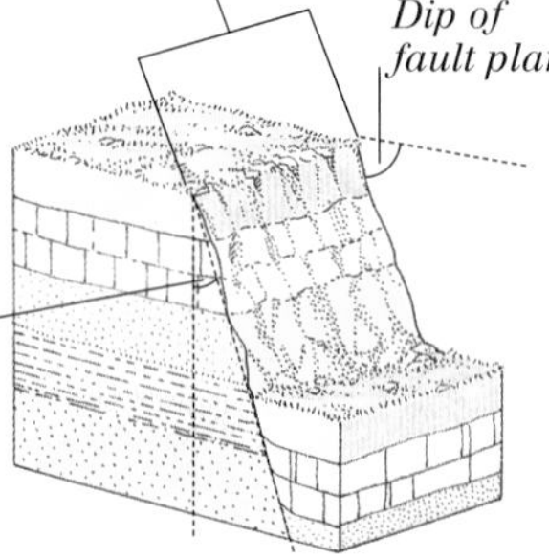

Fault plane

Dip of fault plane

Hade of fault plane

STRUCTURE OF A FAULT

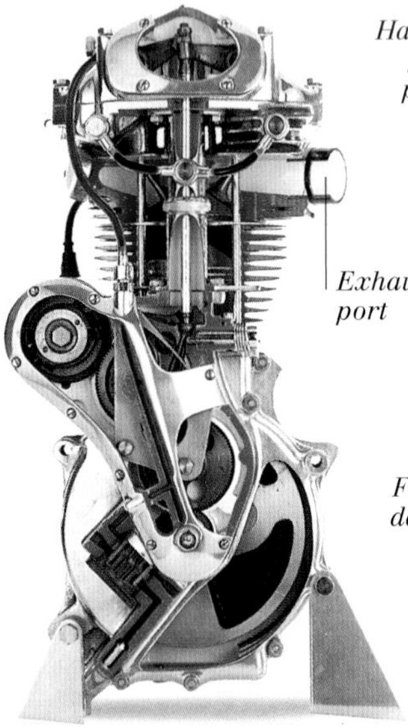

Openable windscreen

Steering wheel

Radiator

Headlamp

Exhaust port

VELOCETTE OHV ENGINE

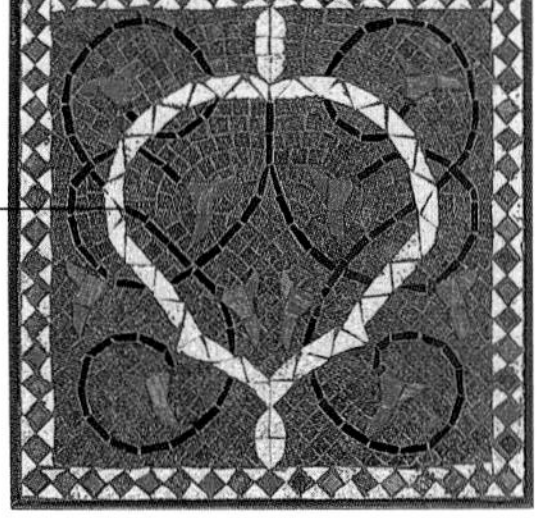

Floral design

MOSAIC DESIGN

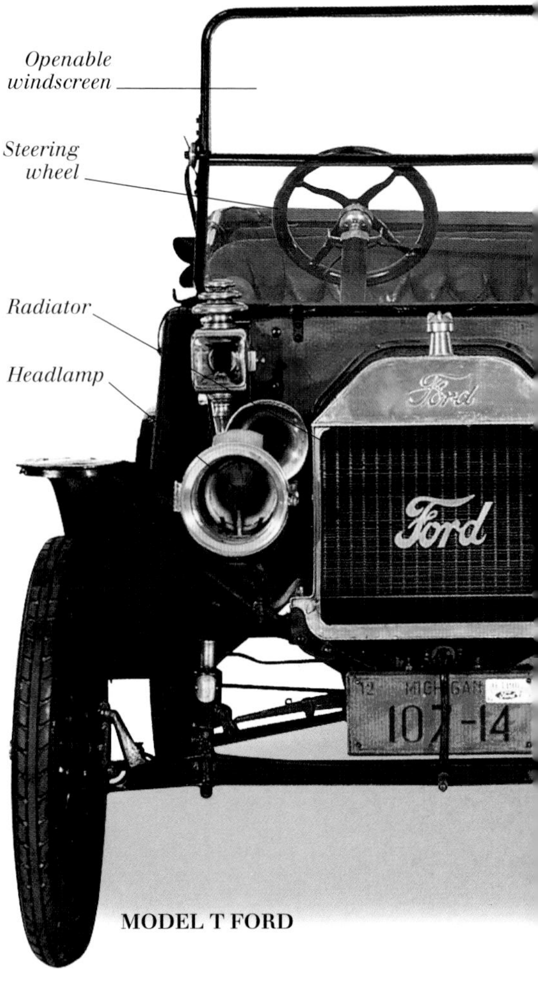

Ford

107-14

MICHIGAN

MODEL T FORD

VISUAL
dictionary

Pedicel
(flower stalk)

Sepal

Achene
(one-seeded
dry fruit)

Remains
of stigma
and style

STRAWBERRY

A DORLING KINDERSLEY BOOK

LONDON, NEW YORK, MUNICH, MELBOURNE, AND DELHI

Revised Editions
Art Editor Hugh Schermuly
Designers Phil Gamble, Simon Oon, Pamela Shiels,
Steve Woosnam-Savage, Lee Riches
Jacket Designer John Dinsdale
Project Editor Cathy Meeus
Editor Paul Docherty
Jacket Editor Beth Apple, Adam Powley
Editorial Consultant Sarah Angliss
Senior Art Editor Ina Stradins
Senior Editor Angeles Gavira
Production Elizabeth Cherry, Tony Phipps
Managing Art Editor Phil Ormerod
Category Publisher Jonathan Metcalf

Anatomical And Botanical Models Supplied By Somso Modelle, Coburg, Germany

Original Edition (*Ultimate Visual Dictionary*)
Project Art Editors Heather McCarry, Johnny Pau, Chris Walker, Kevin Williams
Designer Simon Murrell

Project Editors Luisa Caruso, Peter Jones, Jane Mason, Geoffrey Stalker
Editor Jo Evans

DTP Designer Zirrinia Austin
Picture Researcher Charlotte Bush

Managing Art Editor Toni Kay
Senior Editor Roger Tritton
Managing Editor Sean Moore
Production Manager Hilary Stephens

First published in Great Britain in 1994
under the title *Ultimate Visual Dictionary* by
Dorling Kindersley Limited
80 Strand, London WC2R 0RL
A Penguin Company

This edition published 2008 for Index Books Ltd

Revised editions in 1996, 1997, 1998, 1999, 2000, 2002, 2006

Copyright © 1994, 1996, 1997, 1998, 1999, 2000, 2002, 2006 Dorling Kindersley Limited, London

A CIP catalogue record for this book is available from the British Library

ISBN 978-1-4053-1749-8

Reproduced by Colourscan, Singapore
Printed and bound in Singapore by Star Standard

See our complete catalogue at www.dk.com

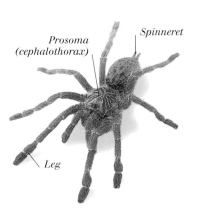

Prosoma (cephalothorax)

Spinneret

Leg

EXTERNAL FEATURES OF A SPIDER

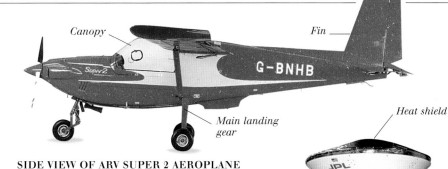

Canopy

Fin

G-BNHB

Main landing gear

SIDE VIEW OF ARV SUPER 2 AEROPLANE

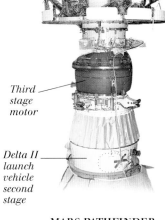

Heat shield

Third stage motor

Delta II launch vehicle second stage

MARS PATHFINDER

Barrel

Permanent black ink

FOUNTAIN PEN AND INK

CONTENTS

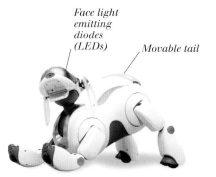

Face light emitting diodes (LEDs)

Movable tail

SONY AIBO ROBOT DOG

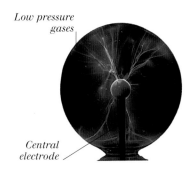

Low pressure gases

Central electrode

BALL CONTAINING HIGH TEMPERATURE GAS (PLASMA)

Parallel bands

ONYX

Non-breakable plastic

Shock absorber

AMERICAN FOOTBALL HELMET

Introduction

THE VISUAL DICTIONARY is a completely new kind of reference book. It provides a link between pictures and words in a way that no ordinary dictionary ever has. Most dictionaries simply tell you what a word means, but the VISUAL DICTIONARY shows you – through a combination of detailed annotations, explicit photographs, and illustrations. In the VISUAL DICTIONARY, pictures define the annotations around them. You do not read definitions of the annotated words, you see them. The highly accessible format of the VISUAL DICTIONARY, the thoroughness of its annotations, and the range of its subject matter make it a unique and helpful reference tool.

How to use the VISUAL DICTIONARY

You will find the VISUAL DICTIONARY simple to use. Instead of being organized alphabetically, it is divided by subject into 14 sections – THE UNIVERSE, PREHISTORIC EARTH, PLANTS, ANIMALS, THE HUMAN BODY, etc. Each section begins with a table of contents listing the major entries within that section. For example, The Visual Arts section has entries on *Drawing, Tempera, Fresco, Oils, Watercolour, Pastels, Acrylics, Calligraphy, Printmaking, Mosaic,* and *Sculpture.* Every entry has a short introduction explaining the purpose of the photographs and illustrations, and the significance of the annotations.

If you know what something looks like, but don't know its name, find the term you need by turning to the annotations surrounding the pictures; if you know a word, but don't know what it refers to, use the comprehensive index to direct you to the appropriate page.

Suppose that you want to know what the bone at the end of your little finger is called. With a standard dictionary, you wouldn't know where to begin. But with the VISUAL DICTIONARY you simply turn to the entry called *Hands* – within THE HUMAN

BODY section – where you will find four fully annotated, colour photographs showing the skin, muscles, and bones of the human hand. In this entry you will quickly find that the bone you are searching for is called the distal phalanx, and for good measure you will discover that it is attached to the middle phalanx by the distal interphalangeal joint.

Perhaps you want to know what a catalytic converter looks like. If you look up "catalytic converter" in an ordinary dictionary, you will be told what it is and possibly what it does – but you will not be able to tell what shape it is or what it is made of. However, if you look up "catalytic converter" in the index of the VISUAL DICTIONARY, you will be directed to the *Modern engines* entry on page 344 – where the introduction gives you basic information about what a catalytic converter is – and to page 350 – where there is a spectacular exploded-view photograph of the mechanics of a Renault Clio. From these pages you will find out not only what a catalytic converter looks like, but also that it is attached at one end to an exhaust downpipe and at the other to a silencer.

Whatever it is that you want to find a name for, or whatever name you want to find a picture for, you will find it quickly and easily in the VISUAL DICTIONARY. Perhaps you need to know where the vamp on a shoe is; or how to tell obovate and lanceolate leaves apart; or what a spiral galaxy looks like; or whether birds have nostrils. With the VISUAL DICTIONARY at hand, the answers to each of these questions, and thousands more, are readily available.

The VISUAL DICTIONARY does not just tell you what the names of the different parts of an object are. The photographs, illustrations, and annotations are all specially arranged to help you understand which parts relate to one another and how objects function.

With the VISUAL DICTIONARY you can find in seconds the words or pictures that you are looking for; or you can simply browse through the pages of the book for your own pleasure. The VISUAL DICTIONARY is not intended to replace a standard dictionary or conventional encyclopedia, but is instead a stimulating and valuable companion to ordinary reference volumes. Giving you instant access to the language that is used by astronomers and architects, musicians and mechanics, scientists and sportspeople, it is the ideal reference book for specialists and generalists of all ages.

Sections of the VISUAL DICTIONARY

The 14 sections of the *VISUAL DICTIONARY* contain a total of more than 30,000 terms, encompassing a wide range of topics:

•In the first section, THE UNIVERSE, spectacular photographs and illustrations are used to show the names of the stars and planets and to explain the structure of solar systems, galaxies, nebulae, comets, and black holes.

•PREHISTORIC EARTH tells the story in annotations of how our own planet has evolved since its formation. It includes examples of prehistoric flora and fauna, and fascinating dinosaur models – some with parts of the body stripped away to show anatomical sections.

•PLANTS covers a huge range of species – from the familiar to the exotic. In addition to the colour photographs of plants included in this section, there is a series of micrographic photographs illustrating plant details – such as pollen grains, spores, and cross-sections of stems and roots – in close-up.

•In the ANIMALS section, skeletons, anatomical diagrams, and different parts of animals' bodies have been meticulously annotated. This section provides a comprehensive guide to the vocabulary of zoological classification and animal physiology.

•The structure of the human body, its parts, and its systems are presented in THE HUMAN BODY. The section includes lifelike, three-dimensional models and the latest false-colour images. Clear and authoritative annotations indicate the correct anatomical terms.

•GEOLOGY, GEOGRAPHY, AND METEOROLOGY describes the structure of the Earth – from the inner core to the exosphere – and the physical phenomena – such as volcanoes, rivers, glaciers, and climate – that shape its surface.

•PHYSICS AND CHEMISTRY is a visual journey through the fundamental principles underlying the physical universe, and provides the essential vocabulary of these sciences.

•In RAIL AND ROAD, a wide range of trains, trams and buses, cars, bicycles, and motorcycles are described. Exploded-view photographs show mechanical details with striking clarity.

•SEA AND AIR gives the names for hundreds of parts of ships and aeroplanes. The section includes civil and fighting craft, both historical and modern.

•THE VISUAL ARTS shows the equipment and materials used by painters, sculptors, printers, and other artists. Well-known compositions have been chosen to illustrate specific artistic techniques and effects.

•ARCHITECTURE includes photographs of exemplary architectural models and illustrates dozens of additional features such as columns, domes, and arches.

•MUSIC provides a visual introduction to the special language of music and musical instruments. It includes clearly annotated photographs of each of the major groups of traditional instruments – brass, woodwind, strings, and percussion – together with modern electronic instruments.

•The SPORTS section is a guide to the playing areas, formations, equipment, and techniques needed for many of today's most popular sports.

•In THE MODERN WORLD, items that are a familiar part of our daily lives are taken apart to reveal their inner workings and give access to the language used by their manufacturers. It also includes systems and concepts, such as the Internet, that increasingly influence our 21st century world.

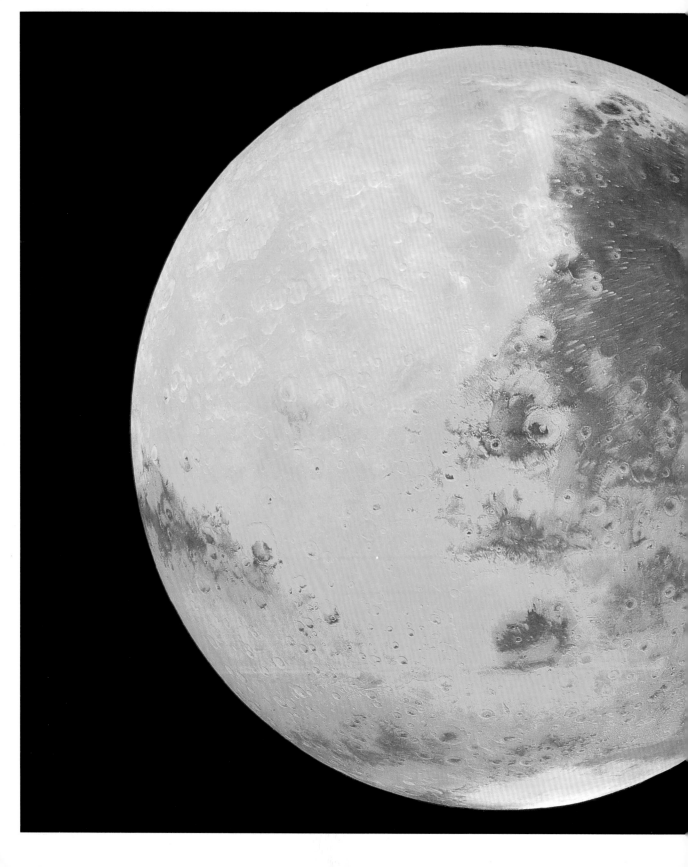

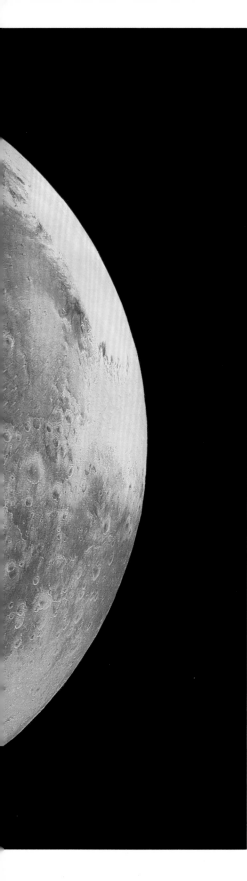

THE UNIVERSE

Anatomy of the Universe

Fireball of rapidly expanding, extremely hot gas lasting about one million years

THE UNIVERSE CONTAINS EVERYTHING that exists, from the tiniest subatomic particles to galactic superclusters (the largest structures known). Nobody knows how big the Universe is, but astronomers estimate that it contains about 100 billion galaxies, each comprising an average of 100 billion stars. The most widely accepted theory about the origin of the Universe is the Big Bang theory, which states that the Universe came into being in a huge explosion – the Big Bang – that took place between 10 and 20 billion years ago. The Universe initially consisted of a very hot, dense fireball of expanding, cooling gas. After about one million years, the gas probably began to condense into localized clumps called protogalaxies. During the next five billion years, the protogalaxies continued condensing, forming galaxies in which stars were being born. Today, billions of years later, the Universe as a whole is still expanding, although there are localized areas in which objects are held together by gravity; for example, many galaxies are found in clusters. The Big Bang theory is supported by the discovery of faint, cool background radiation coming evenly from all directions. This radiation is believed to be the remnant of the radiation produced by the Big Bang. Small "ripples" in the temperature of the cosmic background radiation are thought to be evidence of slight fluctuations in the density of the early Universe, which resulted in the formation of galaxies. Astronomers do not yet know if the Universe is "closed", which means it will eventually stop expanding and begin to contract, or if it is "open", which means it will continue expanding forever.

FALSE-COLOUR MICROWAVE MAP OF COSMIC BACKGROUND RADIATION

Pink indicates "warm ripples" in background radiation

Pale blue indicates "cool ripples" in background radiation

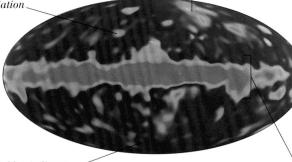

Low-energy microwave radiation corresponding to about -270°C

Deep blue indicates background radiation corresponding to -270.3°C (remnant of the Big Bang)

Red and pink band indicates radiation from our galaxy

High-energy gamma radiation corresponding to about 3,000°C

ORIGIN AND EXPANSION OF THE UNIVERSE

Quasar (probably the centre of a galaxy containing a massive black hole)

Universe one to five billion years after Big Bang

Protogalaxy (condensing gas cloud)

Galaxy spinning and flattening to become spiral shaped

Dark cloud (dust and gas condensing to form a protogalaxy)

Elliptical galaxy in which stars form rapidly

Universe today (10–20 billion years after Big Bang)

Cluster of galaxies held together by gravity

Elliptical galaxy containing old stars and little gas and dust

Irregular galaxy

Spiral galaxy containing gas, dust, and young stars

OBJECTS IN THE UNIVERSE

CLUSTER OF GALAXIES IN VIRGO

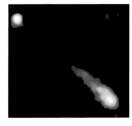

FALSE-COLOUR IMAGE OF 3C273 (QUASAR)

NGC 4406 (ELLIPTICAL GALAXY)

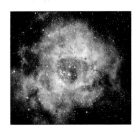

NGC 5236 (SPIRAL GALAXY)

NGC 6822 (IRREGULAR GALAXY)

THE ROSETTE NEBULA (EMISSION NEBULA)

THE JEWEL BOX (STAR CLUSTER)

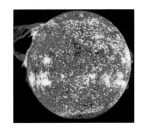

THE SUN (MAIN SEQUENCE STAR)

EARTH

THE MOON

Galaxies

SOMBRERO,
A SPIRAL GALAXY

A GALAXY IS A HUGE MASS OF STARS, nebulae, and interstellar material. The smallest galaxies contain about 100,000 stars, while the largest contain up to 3,000 billion stars. There are three main types of galaxy, classified according to their shape: elliptical, which are oval shaped; spiral, which have arms spiralling outwards from a central bulge; and irregular, which have no obvious shape. Sometimes, the shape of a galaxy is distorted by a collision with another galaxy. Quasars (quasi-stellar objects) are thought to be galactic nuclei but are so far away that their exact nature is still uncertain. They are compact, highly luminous objects in the outer reaches of the known Universe: while the furthest known "ordinary" galaxies are about 10 billion light years away, the furthest known quasar is about 15 billion light years away. Active galaxies, such as Seyfert galaxies and radio galaxies, emit intense radiation. In a Seyfert galaxy, this radiation comes from the galactic nucleus; in a radio galaxy, it also comes from huge lobes on either side of the galaxy. The radiation from active galaxies and quasars is thought to be caused by black holes (see pp. 28-29).

OPTICAL IMAGE OF NGC 4486 (ELLIPTICAL GALAXY)

Globular cluster containing very old red giants

Central region containing old red giants

Less densely populated region

Neighbouring galaxy

OPTICAL IMAGE OF LARGE MAGELLANIC CLOUD (IRREGULAR GALAXY)

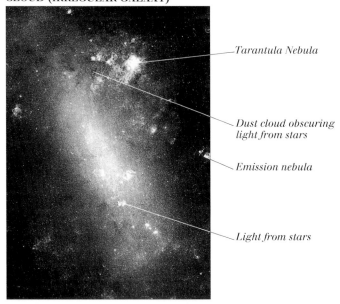

Tarantula Nebula

Dust cloud obscuring light from stars

Emission nebula

Light from stars

OPTICAL IMAGE OF NGC 2997 (SPIRAL GALAXY)

Glowing nebula in spiral arm

Spiral arm containing young stars

Galactic nucleus containing old stars

Dust in spiral arm reflecting blue light from hot young stars

Hot, ionized hydrogen gas emitting red light

Dust lane

OPTICAL IMAGE OF CENTAURUS A
(RADIO GALAXY)

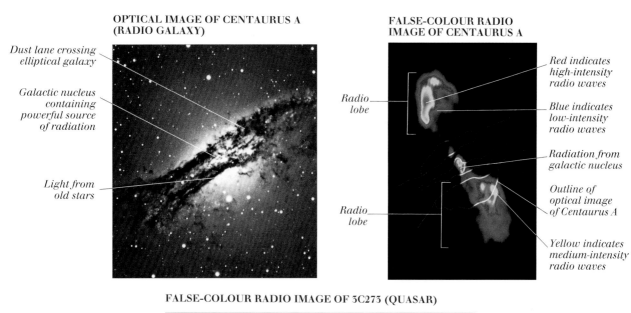

Dust lane crossing
elliptical galaxy

Galactic nucleus
containing
powerful source
of radiation

Light from
old stars

FALSE-COLOUR RADIO
IMAGE OF CENTAURUS A

Radio
lobe

Radio
lobe

Red indicates
high-intensity
radio waves

Blue indicates
low-intensity
radio waves

Radiation from
galactic nucleus

Outline of
optical image
of Centaurus A

Yellow indicates
medium-intensity
radio waves

FALSE-COLOUR RADIO IMAGE OF 3C273 (QUASAR)

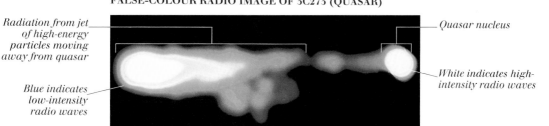

Radiation from jet
of high-energy
particles moving
away from quasar

Blue indicates
low-intensity
radio waves

Quasar nucleus

White indicates high-
intensity radio waves

OPTICAL IMAGE OF NGC 1566
(SEYFERT GALAXY)

Nebula in
spiral arm

Compact nucleus
emitting intense
radiation

Spiral arm

FALSE-COLOUR OPTICAL IMAGE OF NGC 5754
(TWO COLLIDING GALAXIES)

Blue indicates low-
intensity radiation

Red indicates
medium-intensity
radiation

Spiral arm
distorted by
gravitational
influence of
smaller galaxy

Large spiral
galaxy

Smaller galaxy
colliding with
larger galaxy

Yellow indicates
high-intensity
radiation

The Milky Way

VIEW TOWARDS GALACTIC CENTRE

THE MILKY WAY IS THE NAME GIVEN TO THE FAINT BAND OF LIGHT that stretches across the night sky. This light comes from stars and nebulae in our galaxy, known as the Milky Way Galaxy or simply as "the Galaxy". The Galaxy is shaped like a spiral, with a dense central bulge that is encircled by four arms spiralling outwards and surrounded by a less dense halo. We cannot see the spiral shape because the Solar System is in one of the spiral arms, the Orion Arm (also called the Local Arm). From our position, the centre of the Galaxy is completely obscured by dust clouds; as a result, optical maps give only a limited view of the Galaxy. However, a more complete picture can be obtained by studying radio, infra-red, and other radiation. The central bulge of the Galaxy is a relatively small, dense sphere that contains mainly older red and yellow stars. The halo is a less dense region in which the oldest stars are situated; some of these stars may be as old as the Galaxy itself (possibly 15 billion years). The spiral arms contain mainly hot, young, blue stars, as well as nebulae (clouds of dust and gas inside which stars are born). The Galaxy is vast, about 100,000 light years across (a light year is about 9,460 billion kilometres); in comparison, the Solar System seems small, at about 12 light hours across (about 13 billion kilometres). The entire Galaxy is rotating in space, although the inner stars travel faster than those further out. The Sun, which is about two-thirds out from the centre, completes one lap of the Galaxy about every 220 million years.

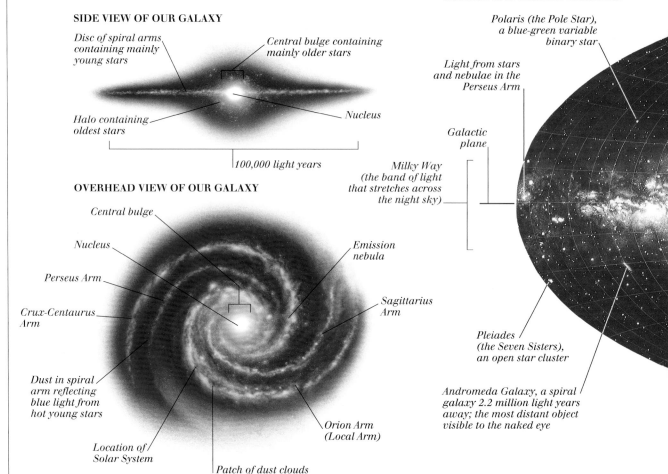

SIDE VIEW OF OUR GALAXY

Disc of spiral arms containing mainly young stars

Central bulge containing mainly older stars

Halo containing oldest stars

Nucleus

100,000 light years

OVERHEAD VIEW OF OUR GALAXY

Central bulge

Nucleus

Perseus Arm

Crux-Centaurus Arm

Dust in spiral arm reflecting blue light from hot young stars

Location of Solar System

Patch of dust clouds

Emission nebula

Sagittarius Arm

Orion Arm (Local Arm)

PANORAMIC OPTICAL MAP OF OUR GALAXY AND NEARBY GALAXIES

Polaris (the Pole Star), a blue-green variable binary star

Light from stars and nebulae in the Perseus Arm

Galactic plane

Milky Way (the band of light that stretches across the night sky)

Pleiades (the Seven Sisters), an open star cluster

Andromeda Galaxy, a spiral galaxy 2.2 million light years away; the most distant object visible to the naked eye

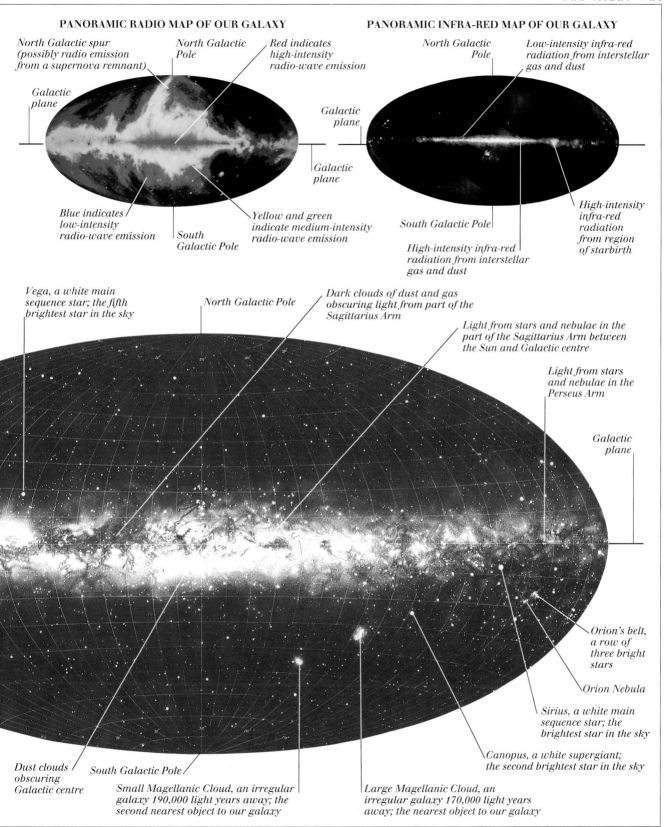

PANORAMIC RADIO MAP OF OUR GALAXY

North Galactic spur (possibly radio emission from a supernova remnant)

North Galactic Pole

Red indicates high-intensity radio-wave emission

Galactic plane

Blue indicates low-intensity radio-wave emission

South Galactic Pole

Yellow and green indicate medium-intensity radio-wave emission

PANORAMIC INFRA-RED MAP OF OUR GALAXY

North Galactic Pole

Low-intensity infra-red radiation from interstellar gas and dust

Galactic plane

Galactic plane

South Galactic Pole

High-intensity infra-red radiation from interstellar gas and dust

High-intensity infra-red radiation from region of starbirth

Vega, a white main sequence star; the fifth brightest star in the sky

North Galactic Pole

Dark clouds of dust and gas obscuring light from part of the Sagittarius Arm

Light from stars and nebulae in the part of the Sagittarius Arm between the Sun and Galactic centre

Light from stars and nebulae in the Perseus Arm

Galactic plane

Orion's belt, a row of three bright stars

Orion Nebula

Sirius, a white main sequence star; the brightest star in the sky

Canopus, a white supergiant; the second brightest star in the sky

Dust clouds obscuring Galactic centre

South Galactic Pole

Small Magellanic Cloud, an irregular galaxy 190,000 light years away; the second nearest object to our galaxy

Large Magellanic Cloud, an irregular galaxy 170,000 light years away; the nearest object to our galaxy

15

Nebulae and star clusters

**HODGE 11, A
GLOBULAR CLUSTER**

A NEBULA IS A CLOUD OF DUST AND GAS inside a galaxy. Nebulae become visible if the gas glows, or if the cloud reflects starlight or obscures light from more distant objects. Emission nebulae shine because their gas emits light when it is stimulated by radiation from hot young stars. Reflection nebulae shine because their dust reflects light from stars in or around the nebula. Dark nebulae appear as silhouettes because they block out light from shining nebulae or stars behind them. Two types of nebula are associated with dying stars: planetary nebulae and supernova remnants. Both consist of expanding shells of gas that were once the outer layers of a star. A planetary nebula is a gas shell drifting away from a dying stellar core. A supernova remnant is a gas shell moving away from a stellar core at great speed following a violent explosion called a supernova (see pp. 26-27). Stars are often found in groups known as clusters. Open clusters are loose groups of a few thousand young stars that were born in the same cloud and are drifting apart. Globular clusters are densely packed, roughly spherical groups of hundreds of thousands of older stars.

TRIFID NEBULA (EMISSION NEBULA)

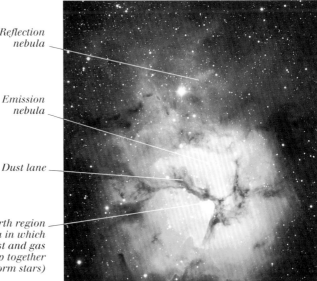

Reflection
nebula

Emission
nebula

Dust lane

Starbirth region
(area in which
dust and gas
clump together
to form stars)

**PLEIADES (OPEN STAR CLUSTER)
WITH A REFLECTION NEBULA**

Wisps of dust and
hydrogen gas
remaining from
cloud in which
stars formed

Young star in an
open cluster of
300–500 stars

Reflection nebula

HORSEHEAD NEBULA (DARK NEBULA)

Glowing filament
of hot, ionized
hydrogen gas

Alnitak (star in
Orion's belt)

Dust lane

Emission nebula

Star near southern
end of Orion's belt

Emission nebula

Horsehead Nebula

Reflection nebula

Dark nebula
obscuring light
from distant stars

ORION NEBULA (DIFFUSE EMISSION NEBULA)

Glowing cloud of dust and hydrogen gas forming part of Orion Nebula

Gas cloud emitting light due to ultraviolet radiation from the four young Trapezium stars

Dust cloud

Trapezium (group of four young stars)

Green light from hot, ionized oxygen gas

Red light from hot, ionized hydrogen gas

Glowing filament of hot, ionized hydrogen gas

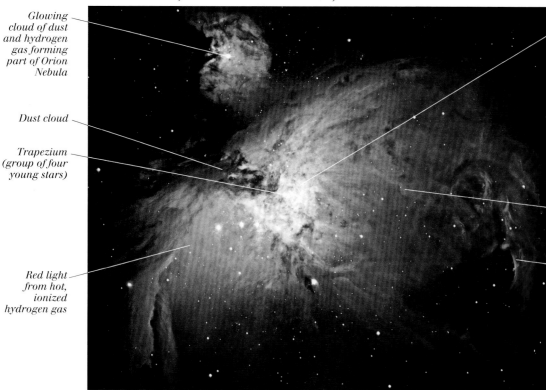

VELA SUPERNOVA REMNANT

Supernova remnant (gas shell consisting of outer layers of star thrown off in supernova explosion)

Hydrogen gas emitting red light due to being heated by supernova explosion

Glowing filament of hot, ionized hydrogen gas

HELIX NEBULA (PLANETARY NEBULA)

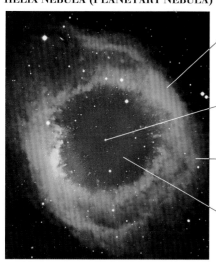

Planetary nebula (gas shell expanding outwards from dying stellar core)

Stellar core at a temperature of about 100,000°C

Red light from hot, ionized hydrogen gas

Blue-green light from hot, ionized oxygen and nitrogen gases

Stars of northern skies

WHEN YOU LOOK AT THE NORTHERN SKY, you look away from the densely populated Galactic centre, so the northern sky generally appears less bright than the southern sky (see pp. 20-21). Among the best-known sights in the northern sky are the constellations Ursa Major (the Great Bear) and Orion. Some ancient civilizations believed that the stars were fixed to a celestial sphere surrounding the Earth, and modern maps of the sky are based on a similar idea. The North and South Poles of this imaginary celestial sphere are directly above the North and South Poles of the Earth, at the points where the Earth's axis of rotation intersects the sphere. The celestial North Pole is at the centre of the map shown here, and Polaris (the Pole Star) lies very close to it. The celestial equator marks a projection of the Earth's equator on the sphere. The ecliptic marks the path of the Sun across the sky as the Earth orbits the Sun. The Moon and planets move against the background of the stars because the stars are much more distant; the nearest star outside the Solar System (Proxima Centauri) is more than 50,000 times further away than the planet Jupiter.

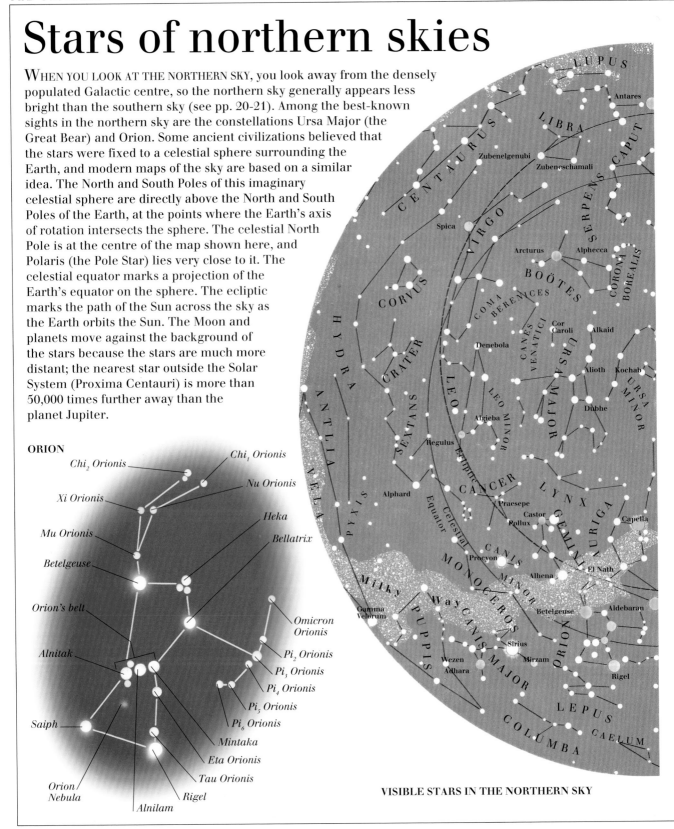

ORION

VISIBLE STARS IN THE NORTHERN SKY

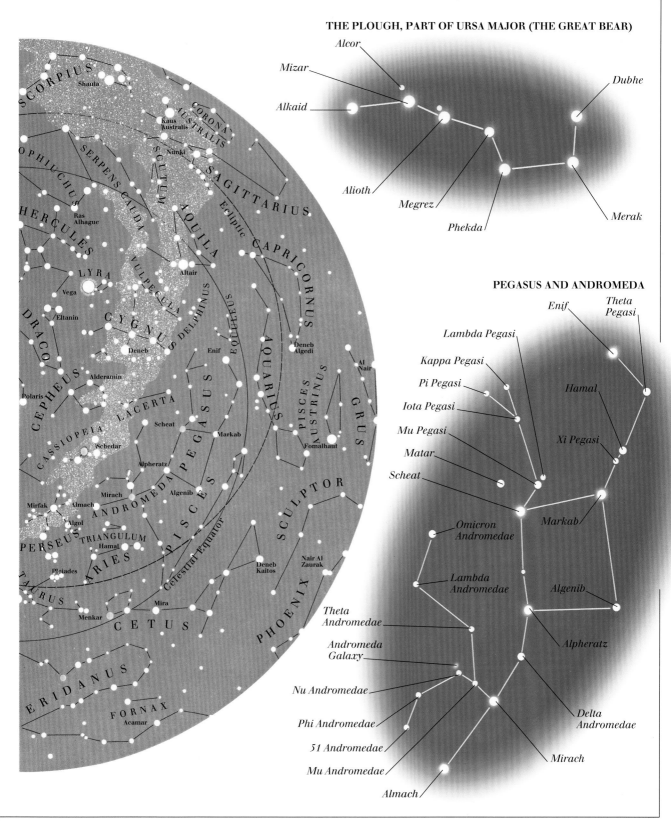

THE PLOUGH, PART OF URSA MAJOR (THE GREAT BEAR)

Alcor
Mizar
Alkaid
Alioth
Megrez
Phekda
Dubhe
Merak

PEGASUS AND ANDROMEDA

Enif
Theta Pegasi
Lambda Pegasi
Kappa Pegasi
Pi Pegasi
Iota Pegasi
Mu Pegasi
Matar
Scheat
Hamal
Xi Pegasi
Markab
Omicron Andromedae
Lambda Andromedae
Algenib
Alpheratz
Theta Andromedae
Andromeda Galaxy
Nu Andromedae
Phi Andromedae
51 Andromedae
Mu Andromedae
Almach
Delta Andromedae
Mirach

Main star map labels:

SCORPIUS
Shaula
CORONA AUSTRALIS
Kaus Australis
Nunki
OPHIUCHUS
SERPENS CAUDA
SCUTUM
SAGITTARIUS
AQUILA
Ecliptic
CAPRICORNUS
Ras Alhague
HERCULES
VULPECULA
Altair
LYRA
Vega
DELPHINUS
Deneb Algedi
Al Nair
DRACO
Eltanin
CYGNUS
Deneb
EQUULEUS
AQUARIUS
Enif
PISCES AUSTRINUS
GRUS
CEPHEUS
Alderamin
LACERTA
PEGASUS
Scheat
Markab
Fomalhaut
Polaris
CASSIOPEIA
Schedar
Alpheratz
ANDROMEDA
Algenib
SCULPTOR
Mirfak
Mirach
Almach
PERSEUS
Algol
TRIANGULUM
Hamal
PISCES
Deneb Kaitos
Nair Al Zaurak
Pleiades
ARIES
PHOENIX
TAURUS
Menkar
Mira
CETUS
ERIDANUS
FORNAX
Acamar
Celestial Equator

Stars of southern skies

Wʜᴇɴ ʏᴏᴜ ʟᴏᴏᴋ ᴀᴛ ᴛʜᴇ sᴏᴜᴛʜᴇʀɴ sᴋʏ, you look towards the Galactic centre, which has a huge population of stars. As a result, the Milky Way appears brighter in the southern sky than in the northern sky (see pp. 18-19). The southern sky is rich in nebulae and star clusters. It contains the Large and Small Magellanic Clouds, which are the two nearest galaxies to our own. Stars make fixed patterns in the sky called constellations. However, the constellations are only apparent groupings of stars, since the distances to the stars in a constellation may vary enormously. The shapes of constellations may change over many thousands of years due to the relative motions of stars. The movement of the constellations across the sky is due to the Earth's motion in space. The daily rotation of the Earth causes the constellations to move across the sky from east to west, and the orbit of the Earth around the Sun causes different areas of sky to be visible in different seasons. The visibility of areas of sky also depends on the location of the observer. For instance, stars near the celestial equator may be seen from either hemisphere at some time during the year, whereas stars close to the celestial poles (the celestial South Pole is at the centre of the map shown here) can never be seen from the opposite hemisphere.

HYDRUS (THE WATER SNAKE) AND MENSA (THE TABLE)

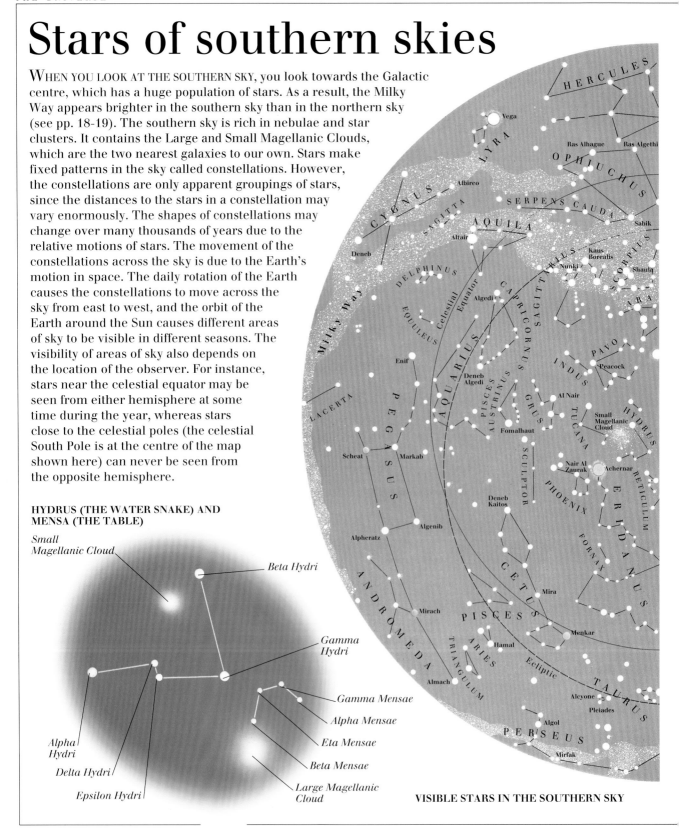

VISIBLE STARS IN THE SOUTHERN SKY

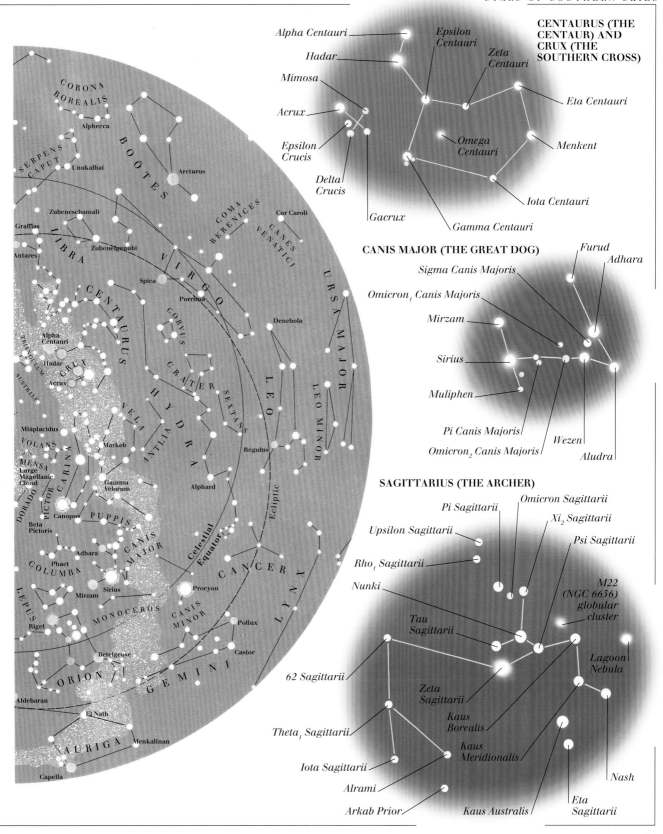

CENTAURUS (THE CENTAUR) AND CRUX (THE SOUTHERN CROSS)

Alpha Centauri
Epsilon Centauri
Hadar
Zeta Centauri
Mimosa
Eta Centauri
Acrux
Epsilon Crucis
Omega Centauri
Menkent
Delta Crucis
Iota Centauri
Gacrux
Gamma Centauri

CANIS MAJOR (THE GREAT DOG)

Furud
Adhara
Sigma Canis Majoris
Omicron$_1$ Canis Majoris
Mirzam
Sirius
Muliphen
Pi Canis Majoris
Wezen
Omicron$_2$ Canis Majoris
Aludra

SAGITTARIUS (THE ARCHER)

Pi Sagittarii
Omicron Sagittarii
Upsilon Sagittarii
Xi$_2$ Sagittarii
Psi Sagittarii
Rho$_1$ Sagittarii
Nunki
M22 (NGC 6656) globular cluster
Tau Sagittarii
Lagoon Nebula
62 Sagittarii
Zeta Sagittarii
Kaus Borealis
Theta$_1$ Sagittarii
Kaus Meridionalis
Iota Sagittarii
Alrami
Arkab Prior
Kaus Australis
Eta Sagittarii
Nash

(Star map labels)

CORONA BOREALIS
Alphecca
SERPENS CAPUT
Unukalhai
BOÖTES
Arcturus
Zubeneschamali
Graffias
COMA BERENICES
Cor Caroli
CANES VENATICI
LIBRA
Zubenelgenubi
Antares
VIRGO
Spica
URSA MAJOR
Porrima
Denebola
CENTAURUS
CORVUS
LEO
Alpha Centauri
Hadar
CRUX
Acrux
TRIANGULUM AUSTRALE
CRATER
SEXTANS
LEO MINOR
HYDRA
VELA
ANTLIA
Regulus
Ecliptic
Miaplacidus
Markeb
VOLANS
MENSA
Large Magellanic Cloud
Gamma Velorum
Alphard
Celestial Equator
DORADO
PICTOR
CARINA
Canopus
PUPPIS
CANCER
LYNX
Beta Pictoris
Adhara
CANIS MAJOR
Phaet
COLUMBA
Mirzam
Sirius
Procyon
Pollux
LEPUS
Rigel
MONOCEROS
CANIS MINOR
Castor
GEMINI
Betelgeuse
ORION
Aldebaran
El Nath
AURIGA
Menkalinan
Capella

21

Stars

OPEN STAR CLUSTER AND DUST CLOUD

STARS ARE BODIES of hot, glowing gas that are born in nebulae (see pp. 24-27). They vary enormously in size, mass, and temperature: diameters range from about 450 times smaller to over 1,000 times bigger than that of the Sun; masses range from about a twentieth to over 50 solar masses; and surface temperatures range from about 3,000°C to over 50,000°C. The colour of a star is determined by its temperature: the hottest stars are blue and the coolest are red. The Sun, with a surface temperature of 5,500°C, is between these extremes and appears yellow. The energy emitted by a shining star is produced by nuclear fusion in the star's core. The brightness of a star is measured in magnitudes – the brighter the star, the lower its magnitude. There are two types of magnitude: apparent magnitude, which is the brightness seen from Earth, and absolute magnitude, which is the brightness that would be seen from a standard distance of 10 parsecs (32.6 light years). The light emitted by a star may be split to form a spectrum containing a series of dark lines (absorption lines). The patterns of lines indicate the presence of particular chemical elements, enabling astronomers to deduce the composition of the star's atmosphere. The magnitude and spectral type (colour) of stars may be plotted on a graph called a Hertzsprung-Russell diagram, which shows that stars tend to fall into several well-defined groups. The principal groups are main sequence stars (those which are fusing hydrogen to form helium), giants, supergiants, and white dwarfs.

STAR SIZES

Red giant (diameters between about 15 million and 150 million km)

The Sun (main sequence star with diameter about 1.4 million km)

White dwarf (diameters between about 3,000 and 50,000 km)

ENERGY EMISSION FROM THE SUN

Nuclear fusion in core produces gamma rays and neutrinos

Neutrinos travel to Earth directly from Sun's core in about 8 minutes

Lower-energy radiation travels to Earth in about 8 minutes

Earth

Sun

High-energy radiation (gamma rays) loses energy while travelling to surface over 2 million years

Lower-energy radiation (mainly ultraviolet, infra-red, and light rays) leaves surface

STAR MAGNITUDES

APPARENT MAGNITUDE

ABSOLUTE MAGNITUDE

Brighter stars

-9

0

+9

Fainter stars

Sirius: apparent magnitude of -1.46

Rigel: apparent magnitude of +0.12

Objects of magnitude higher than about +5.5 cannot be seen by the naked eye

Rigel: absolute magnitude of -7.1

Sirius: absolute magnitude of +1.4

NUCLEAR FUSION IN MAIN SEQUENCE STARS LIKE THE SUN

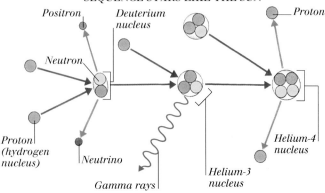

Positron

Deuterium nucleus

Proton

Neutron

Proton (hydrogen nucleus)

Neutrino

Gamma rays

Helium-3 nucleus

Helium-4 nucleus

HERTZSPRUNG-RUSSELL DIAGRAM

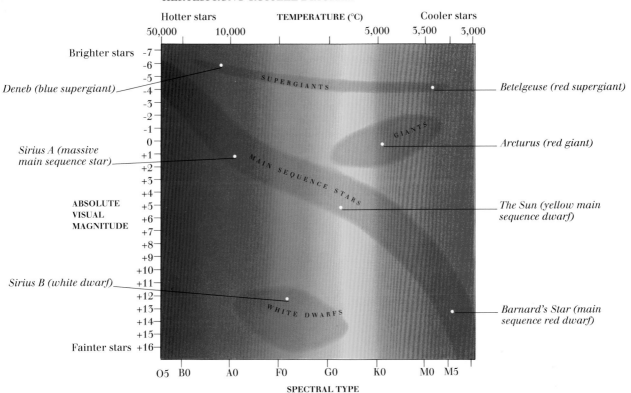

Hotter stars   TEMPERATURE (°C)   Cooler stars

50,000   10,000   5,000   3,500   3,000

Brighter stars

Deneb (blue supergiant)

SUPERGIANTS

Betelgeuse (red supergiant)

GIANTS

Arcturus (red giant)

Sirius A (massive main sequence star)

MAIN SEQUENCE STARS

The Sun (yellow main sequence dwarf)

ABSOLUTE VISUAL MAGNITUDE

Sirius B (white dwarf)

WHITE DWARFS

Barnard's Star (main sequence red dwarf)

Fainter stars

O5   B0   A0   F0   G0   K0   M0   M5

SPECTRAL TYPE

STELLAR SPECTRAL ABSORPTION LINES

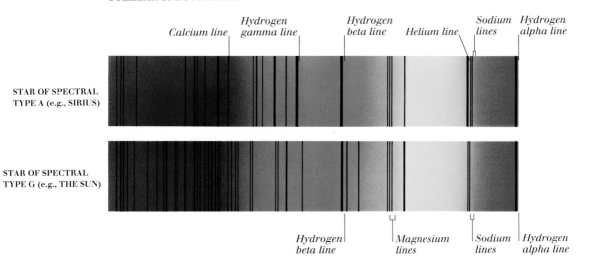

Calcium line   Hydrogen gamma line   Hydrogen beta line   Helium line   Sodium lines   Hydrogen alpha line

STAR OF SPECTRAL TYPE A (e.g., SIRIUS)

STAR OF SPECTRAL TYPE G (e.g., THE SUN)

Hydrogen beta line   Magnesium lines   Sodium lines   Hydrogen alpha line

Small stars

SMALL STARS HAVE A MASS of up to about one and a half times that of the Sun. They begin to form when a region of higher density in a nebula condenses into a huge globule of gas and dust that contracts under its own gravity. Within a globule, regions of condensing matter heat up and begin to glow, forming protostars. If a protostar contains enough matter, the central temperature reaches about 15 million °C. At this temperature, nuclear reactions in which hydrogen fuses to form helium can start. This process releases energy, which prevents the star from contracting further and also causes it to shine; it is now a main sequence star. A star of about one solar mass remains in the main sequence for about 10 billion years, until the hydrogen in the star's core has been converted into helium. The helium core then contracts again, and nuclear reactions continue in a shell around the core. The core becomes hot enough for helium to fuse to form carbon, while the outer layers of the star expand, cool, and shine less brightly. The expanding star is known as a red giant. When the helium in the core runs out, the outer layers of the star may drift off as an expanding gas shell called a planetary nebula. The remaining core (about 80 per cent of the original star) is now in its final stages. It becomes a white dwarf star that gradually cools and dims. When it finally stops shining altogether, the dead star will become a black dwarf.

STRUCTURE OF A MAIN SEQUENCE STAR

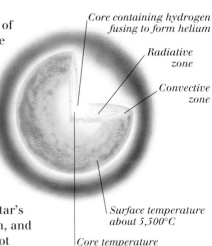

Core containing hydrogen fusing to form helium

Radiative zone

Convective zone

Surface temperature about 5,500°C

Core temperature about 15 million °C

STRUCTURE OF A NEBULA

Young main sequence star

Dense region of dust and gas (mainly hydrogen) condensing under gravity to form globules

Hot, ionized hydrogen gas emitting red light due to being stimulated by radiation from hot young stars

Dark globule of dust and gas (mainly hydrogen) contracting to form protostars

LIFE OF A SMALL STAR OF ABOUT ONE SOLAR MASS

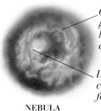

Cool cloud of gas (mainly hydrogen) and dust

Dense globule condensing to form protostars

NEBULA

Glowing ball of gas (mainly hydrogen)

Natal cocoon (shell of dust blown away by radiation from protostar)

PROTOSTAR
Duration: 50 million years

About 1.4 million km

Star producing energy by nuclear fusion in core

MAIN SEQUENCE STAR
Duration: 10 billion years

STRUCTURE OF A RED GIANT

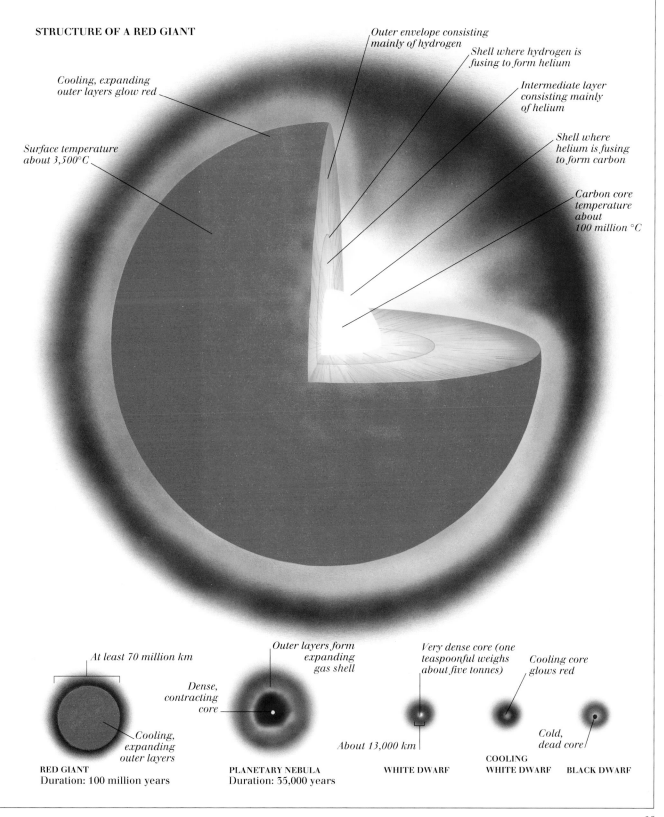

Cooling, expanding outer layers glow red

Surface temperature about 3,500°C

Outer envelope consisting mainly of hydrogen

Shell where hydrogen is fusing to form helium

Intermediate layer consisting mainly of helium

Shell where helium is fusing to form carbon

Carbon core temperature about 100 million °C

At least 70 million km

Cooling, expanding outer layers

RED GIANT
Duration: 100 million years

Outer layers form expanding gas shell

Dense, contracting core

PLANETARY NEBULA
Duration: 35,000 years

Very dense core (one teaspoonful weighs about five tonnes)

About 13,000 km

WHITE DWARF

Cooling core glows red

COOLING WHITE DWARF

Cold, dead core

BLACK DWARF

Massive stars

MASSIVE STARS HAVE A MASS AT LEAST THREE TIMES that of the Sun, and some stars are as massive as about 50 Suns. A massive star evolves in a similar way to a small star until it reaches the main sequence stage (see pp. 24-25). During the main sequence, a star shines steadily until the hydrogen in its core has fused to form helium. This process takes billions of years in a small star, but only millions of years in a massive star. A massive star then becomes a red supergiant, which initially consists of a helium core surrounded by outer layers of cooling, expanding gas. Over the next few million years, a series of nuclear reactions form different elements in shells around an iron core. The core eventually collapses in less than a second, causing a massive explosion called a supernova, in which a shock wave blows away the outer layers of the star. Supernovae shine brighter than an entire galaxy for a short time. Sometimes, the core survives the supernova explosion. If the surviving core is between about one and a half and three solar masses, it contracts to become a tiny, dense neutron star. If the core is considerably greater than three solar masses, it contracts to become a black hole (see pp. 28-29).

SUPERNOVA

TARANTULA NEBULA BEFORE SUPERNOVA

STRUCTURE OF A RED SUPERGIANT

Outer envelope consisting mainly of hydrogen

Layer consisting mainly of helium

Layer consisting mainly of carbon

Layer consisting mainly of oxygen

Layer consisting mainly of silicon

Shell of hydrogen fusing to form helium

Shell of helium fusing to form carbon

Shell of carbon fusing to form oxygen

Shell of oxygen fusing to form silicon

Shell of silicon fusing to form iron core

Surface temperature about 3,000°C

Cooling, expanding outer layers glow red

Core of mainly iron at a temperature of 3–5 billion °C

LIFE OF A MASSIVE STAR OF ABOUT 10 SOLAR MASSES

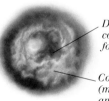

Dense globule condensing to form protostars

Cool cloud of gas (mainly hydrogen) and dust

NEBULA

Glowing ball of gas (mainly hydrogen)

Natal cocoon (shell of dust blown away by radiation from protostar)

PROTOSTAR
Duration: a few hundred thousand years

About 3 million km

Star producing energy by nuclear fusion in core

MAIN SEQUENCE STAR
Duration: 10 million years

FEATURES OF A SUPERNOVA

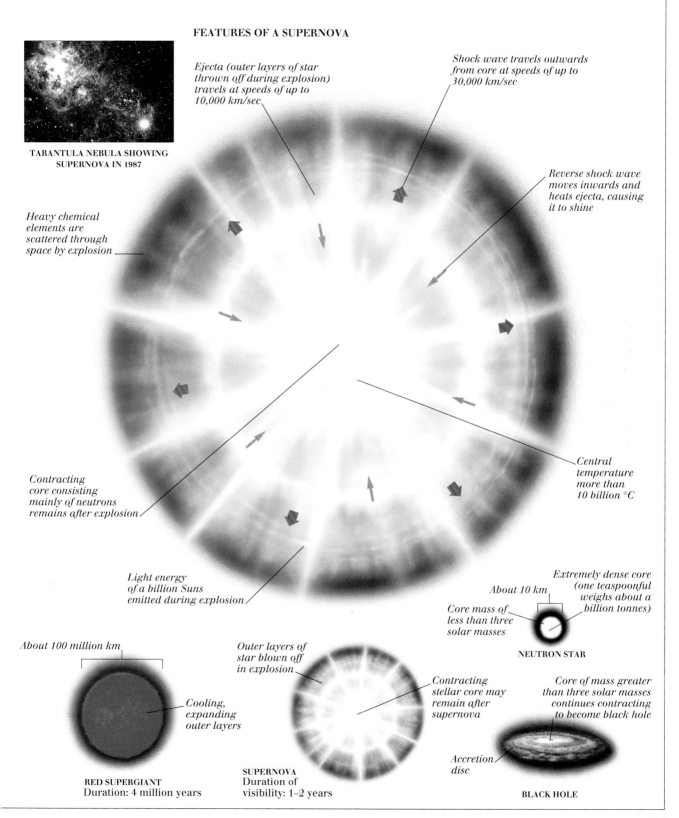

**TARANTULA NEBULA SHOWING
SUPERNOVA IN 1987**

*Ejecta (outer layers of star
thrown off during explosion)
travels at speeds of up to
10,000 km/sec*

*Shock wave travels outwards
from core at speeds of up to
30,000 km/sec*

*Reverse shock wave
moves inwards and
heats ejecta, causing
it to shine*

*Heavy chemical
elements are
scattered through
space by explosion*

*Contracting
core consisting
mainly of neutrons
remains after explosion*

*Central
temperature
more than
10 billion °C*

*Light energy
of a billion Suns
emitted during explosion*

*Extremely dense core
(one teaspoonful
weighs about a
billion tonnes)*

About 10 km

*Core mass of
less than three
solar masses*

NEUTRON STAR

About 100 million km

*Outer layers of
star blown off
in explosion*

*Contracting
stellar core may
remain after
supernova*

*Core of mass greater
than three solar masses
continues contracting
to become black hole*

*Cooling,
expanding
outer layers*

*Accretion
disc*

RED SUPERGIANT
Duration: 4 million years

SUPERNOVA
Duration of
visibility: 1–2 years

BLACK HOLE

Neutron stars and black holes

NEUTRON STARS AND BLACK HOLES form from the stellar cores that remain after stars have exploded as supernovae (see pp. 26-27). If the remaining core is between about one and a half and three solar masses, it contracts to form a neutron star. If the remaining core is greater than about three solar masses, it contracts to form a black hole. Neutron stars are typically only about 10 kilometres in diameter and consist almost entirely of subatomic particles called neutrons. Such stars are so dense that a teaspoonful would weigh about a billion tonnes. Neutron stars are observed as pulsars, so-called because they rotate rapidly and emit two beams of radio waves, which sweep across the sky and are detected as short pulses. Black holes are characterized by their extremely strong gravity, which is so powerful that not even light can escape; as a result, black holes are invisible. However, they may be detected if they have a close companion star. The gravity of the black hole pulls gas from the other star, forming an accretion disc that spirals around the black hole at high speed, heating up and emitting radiation. Eventually, the matter spirals in to cross the event horizon (the boundary of the black hole), thereby disappearing from the visible Universe.

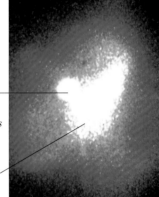

X-ray emission from pulsar (neutron star rotating 30 times each second)

X-ray emission from centre of nebula

X-RAY IMAGE OF THE CRAB NEBULA (SUPERNOVA REMNANT)

PULSAR (ROTATING NEUTRON STAR)

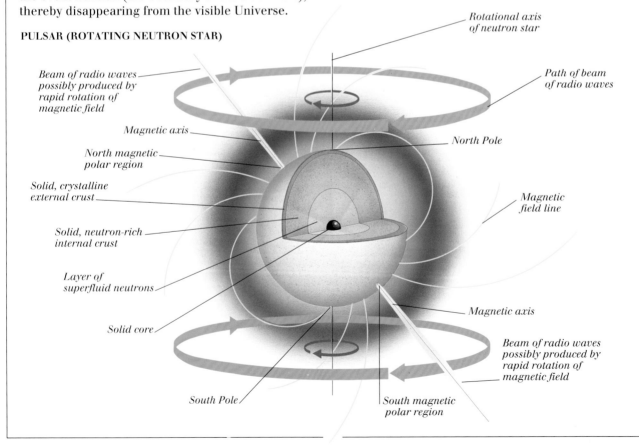

Rotational axis of neutron star

Beam of radio waves possibly produced by rapid rotation of magnetic field

Path of beam of radio waves

Magnetic axis

North Pole

North magnetic polar region

Solid, crystalline external crust

Magnetic field line

Solid, neutron-rich internal crust

Layer of superfluid neutrons

Solid core

Magnetic axis

Beam of radio waves possibly produced by rapid rotation of magnetic field

South Pole

South magnetic polar region

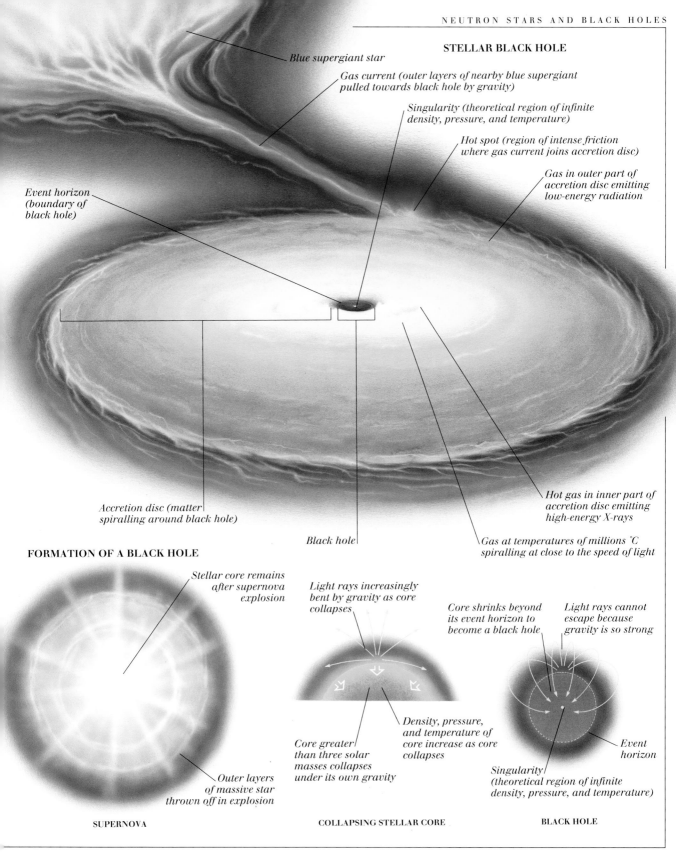

STELLAR BLACK HOLE

Blue supergiant star

Gas current (outer layers of nearby blue supergiant pulled towards black hole by gravity)

Singularity (theoretical region of infinite density, pressure, and temperature)

Hot spot (region of intense friction where gas current joins accretion disc)

Gas in outer part of accretion disc emitting low-energy radiation

Event horizon (boundary of black hole)

Accretion disc (matter spiralling around black hole)

Black hole

Hot gas in inner part of accretion disc emitting high-energy X-rays

Gas at temperatures of millions °C spiralling at close to the speed of light

FORMATION OF A BLACK HOLE

Stellar core remains after supernova explosion

Light rays increasingly bent by gravity as core collapses

Core shrinks beyond its event horizon to become a black hole

Light rays cannot escape because gravity is so strong

Outer layers of massive star thrown off in explosion

Core greater than three solar masses collapses under its own gravity

Density, pressure, and temperature of core increase as core collapses

Event horizon

Singularity (theoretical region of infinite density, pressure, and temperature)

SUPERNOVA

COLLAPSING STELLAR CORE

BLACK HOLE

The Solar System

THE SOLAR SYSTEM consists of a central star (the Sun) and the bodies that orbit it. These bodies include nine planets and their 61 known moons; asteroids; comets; and meteoroids. The Solar System also contains interplanetary gas and dust. Most of the planets fall into two groups: four small rocky planets near the Sun (Mercury, Venus, Earth, and Mars); and four planets further out, the gas giants (Jupiter, Saturn, Uranus, and Neptune). Pluto belongs to neither group but is very small, solid, and icy. Pluto is the outermost planet, except when it passes briefly inside Neptune's orbit. Between the rocky planets and gas giants is the asteroid belt, which contains thousands of chunks of rock orbiting the Sun. Most of the bodies in the Solar System move around the Sun in elliptical orbits located in a thin disc around the Sun's equator. All the planets orbit the Sun in the same direction (anticlockwise when viewed from above) and all but Venus, Uranus, and Pluto also spin about their axes in this direction. Moons also spin as they, in turn, orbit their planets. The entire Solar System orbits the centre of our galaxy, the Milky Way (see pp. 14-15).

THE SUN

PLANETARY ORBIT

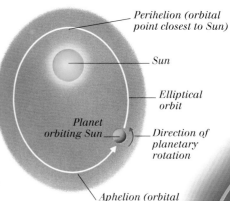

Perihelion (orbital point closest to Sun)

Sun

Elliptical orbit

Planet orbiting Sun

Direction of planetary rotation

Aphelion (orbital point furthest from Sun)

Aphelion of Neptune: 4,537 million km

ORBITS OF INNER PLANETS

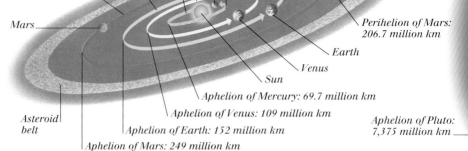

Mercury

Perihelion of Mercury: 45.9 million km
Perihelion of Venus: 107.4 million km
Perihelion of Earth: 147 million km

Average orbital speed of Venus: 35.03 km/sec
Average orbital speed of Mercury: 47.89 km/sec
Average orbital speed of Earth: 29.79 km/sec
Average orbital speed of Mars: 24.13 km/sec

Mars

Perihelion of Mars: 206.7 million km

Earth

Venus

Sun

Asteroid belt

Aphelion of Mercury: 69.7 million km
Aphelion of Venus: 109 million km
Aphelion of Earth: 152 million km
Aphelion of Mars: 249 million km

Aphelion of Pluto: 7,375 million km

MERCURY
Year: 87.97 Earth days
Mass: 0.06 Earth masses
Diameter: 4,878 km

VENUS
Year: 224.7 Earth days
Mass: 0.81 Earth masses
Diameter: 12,103 km

EARTH
Year: 365.26 days
Mass: 1 Earth mass
Diameter: 12,756 km

MARS
Year: 1.88 Earth years
Mass: 0.11 Earth masses
Diameter: 6,786 km

JUPITER
Year: 11.86 Earth years
Mass: 317.94 Earth masses
Diameter: 142,984 km

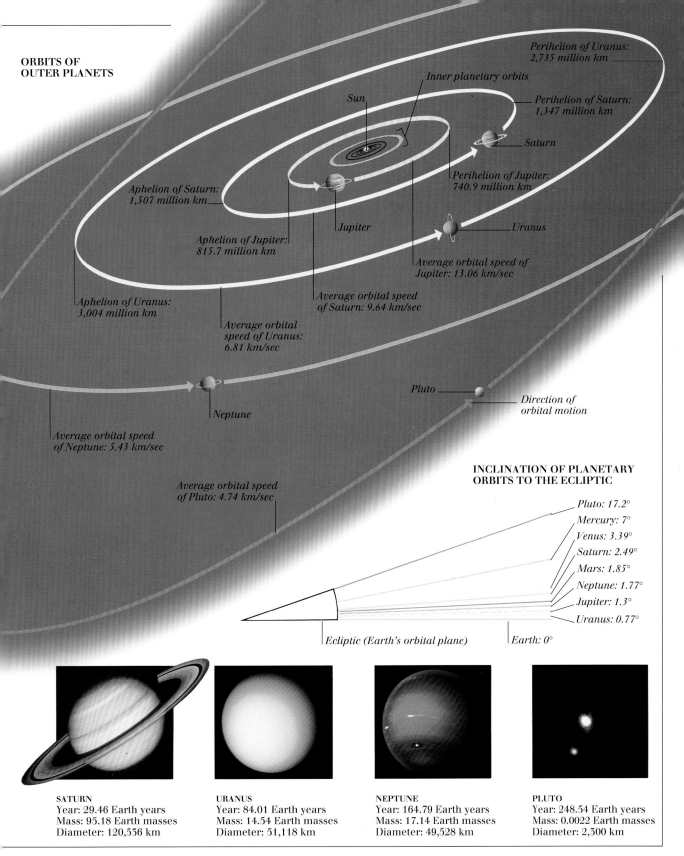

ORBITS OF OUTER PLANETS

Perihelion of Uranus: 2,735 million km

Inner planetary orbits

Sun

Perihelion of Saturn: 1,347 million km

Saturn

Perihelion of Jupiter: 740.9 million km

Aphelion of Saturn: 1,507 million km

Aphelion of Jupiter: 815.7 million km

Jupiter

Uranus

Average orbital speed of Jupiter: 13.06 km/sec

Aphelion of Uranus: 3,004 million km

Average orbital speed of Saturn: 9.64 km/sec

Average orbital speed of Uranus: 6.81 km/sec

Average orbital speed of Neptune: 5.43 km/sec

Neptune

Pluto

Direction of orbital motion

Average orbital speed of Pluto: 4.74 km/sec

INCLINATION OF PLANETARY ORBITS TO THE ECLIPTIC

Pluto: 17.2°
Mercury: 7°
Venus: 3.39°
Saturn: 2.49°
Mars: 1.85°
Neptune: 1.77°
Jupiter: 1.3°
Uranus: 0.77°

Ecliptic (Earth's orbital plane)

Earth: 0°

SATURN
Year: 29.46 Earth years
Mass: 95.18 Earth masses
Diameter: 120,536 km

URANUS
Year: 84.01 Earth years
Mass: 14.54 Earth masses
Diameter: 51,118 km

NEPTUNE
Year: 164.79 Earth years
Mass: 17.14 Earth masses
Diameter: 49,528 km

PLUTO
Year: 248.54 Earth years
Mass: 0.0022 Earth masses
Diameter: 2,300 km

The Sun

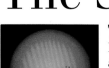

SOLAR
PHOTOSPHERE

THE SUN IS THE STAR AT THE CENTRE of the Solar System. It is about five billion years old and will continue to shine as it does now for about another five billion years. The Sun is a yellow main sequence star (see pp. 22-23) about 1.4 million kilometres in diameter. It consists almost entirely of hydrogen and helium. In the Sun's core, hydrogen is converted to helium by nuclear fusion, releasing energy in the process. The energy travels from the core, through the radiative and convective zones, to the photosphere (visible surface), where it leaves the Sun in the form of heat and light. On the photosphere there are often dark, relatively cool areas called sunspots, which usually appear in pairs or groups and are thought to be caused by magnetic fields. Other types of solar activity are flares, which are usually associated with sunspots, and prominences. Flares are sudden discharges of high-energy radiation and atomic particles. Prominences are huge loops or filaments of gas extending into the solar atmosphere; some last for hours, others for months. Beyond the photosphere is the chromosphere (inner atmosphere) and the extremely rarified corona (outer atmosphere), which extends millions of kilometres into space. Tiny particles that escape from the corona give rise to the solar wind, which streams through space at hundreds of kilometres per second. The chromosphere and corona can be seen from Earth when the Sun is totally eclipsed by the Moon.

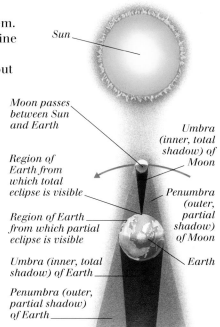

Sun

Moon passes between Sun and Earth

Umbra (inner, total shadow) of Moon

Region of Earth from which total eclipse is visible

Region of Earth from which partial eclipse is visible

Penumbra (outer, partial shadow) of Moon

Umbra (inner, total shadow) of Earth

Earth

Penumbra (outer, partial shadow) of Earth

SURFACE FEATURES

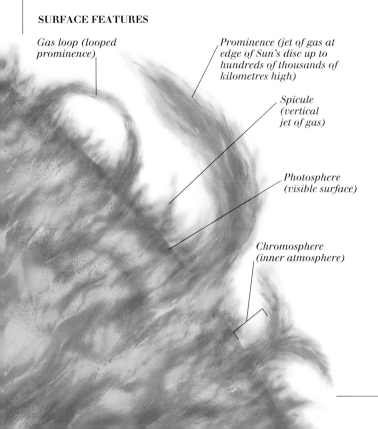

Gas loop (looped prominence)

Prominence (jet of gas at edge of Sun's disc up to hundreds of thousands of kilometres high)

Spicule (vertical jet of gas)

Photosphere (visible surface)

Chromosphere (inner atmosphere)

TOTAL SOLAR ECLIPSE

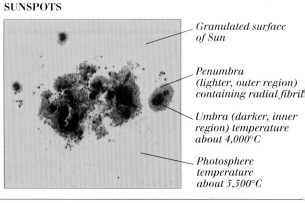

Corona (outer atmosphere of extremely hot, diffuse gas)

Moon covers Sun's disc

SUNSPOTS

Granulated surface of Sun

Penumbra (lighter, outer region) containing radial fibril

Umbra (darker, inner region) temperature about 4,000°C

Photosphere temperature about 5,500°C

**EXTERNAL FEATURES AND
INTERNAL STRUCTURE OF THE SUN**

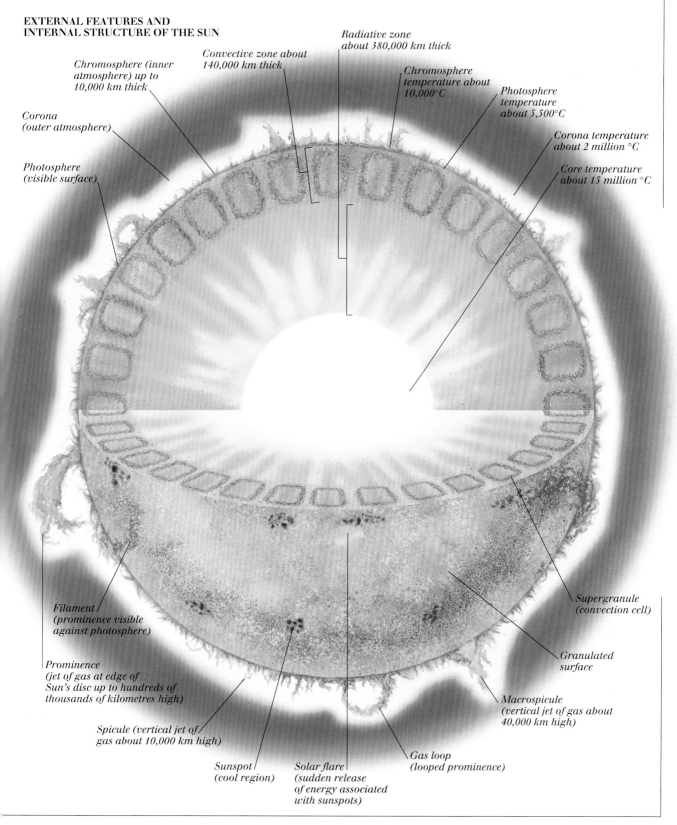

Chromosphere (inner
atmosphere) up to
10,000 km thick

Convective zone about
140,000 km thick

Radiative zone
about 380,000 km thick

Chromosphere
temperature about
10,000°C

Photosphere
temperature
about 5,500°C

Corona
(outer atmosphere)

Corona temperature
about 2 million °C

Core temperature
about 15 million °C

Photosphere
(visible surface)

Supergranule
(convection cell)

Granulated
surface

Filament
(prominence visible
against photosphere)

Macrospicule
(vertical jet of gas about
40,000 km high)

Prominence
(jet of gas at edge of
Sun's disc up to hundreds of
thousands of kilometres high)

Gas loop
(looped prominence)

Spicule (vertical jet of
gas about 10,000 km high)

Sunspot
(cool region)

Solar flare
(sudden release
of energy associated
with sunspots)

Mercury

MERCURY

MERCURY IS THE NEAREST PLANET to the Sun, orbiting at an average distance of about 58 million kilometres. Because Mercury is the closest planet to the Sun, it moves faster than any other planet, travelling at an average speed of nearly 48 kilometres per second and completing an orbit in just under 88 days. Mercury is very small (only Pluto is smaller) and rocky. Most of the surface has been heavily cratered by the impact of meteorites, although there are also smooth, sparsely cratered plains. The Caloris Basin is the largest crater, measuring about 1,300 kilometres across. It is thought to have been formed when a rock the size of an asteroid hit the planet, and is surrounded by concentric rings of mountains thrown up by the impact. The surface also has many ridges (called rupes) that are thought to have been formed when the hot core of the young planet cooled and shrank about four billion years ago, buckling the planet's surface in the process. The planet rotates about its axis very slowly, taking nearly 59 Earth days to complete one rotation. As a result, a solar day (sunrise to sunrise) on Mercury is about 176 Earth days – twice as long as the 88-day Mercurian year. Mercury has extreme surface temperatures, ranging from a maximum of 430°C on the sunlit side to -170°C on the dark side. At nightfall, the temperature drops very quickly because the planet's atmosphere is almost non-existent. It consists only of minute amounts of helium and hydrogen captured from the solar wind, plus traces of other gases.

TILT AND ROTATION OF MERCURY

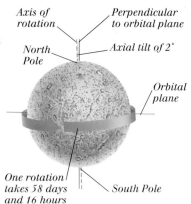

Axis of rotation

Perpendicular to orbital plane

North Pole

Axial tilt of 2°

Orbital plane

One rotation takes 58 days and 16 hours

South Pole

DEGAS AND BRONTË (RAY CRATERS)

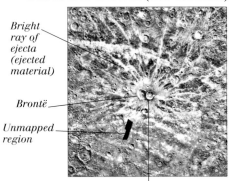

Bright ray of ejecta (ejected material)

Brontë

Unmapped region

Degas with central peak

FORMATION OF A RAY CRATER

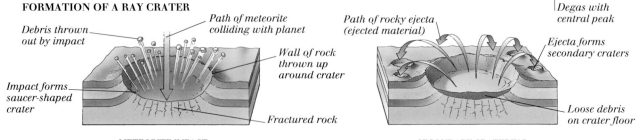

Debris thrown out by impact

Path of meteorite colliding with planet

Wall of rock thrown up around crater

Impact forms saucer-shaped crater

Fractured rock

METEORITE IMPACT

Path of rocky ejecta (ejected material)

Ejecta forms secondary craters

Loose debris on crater floor

SECONDARY CRATERING

Small secondary crater

Wall of rock forms ring of mountains

Ray of ejecta (ejected material)

Loose ejected rock

Central mountain rings form if floor of large crater recoils from meteorite impact

Falling debris forms ridges on side of wall

RAY CRATER

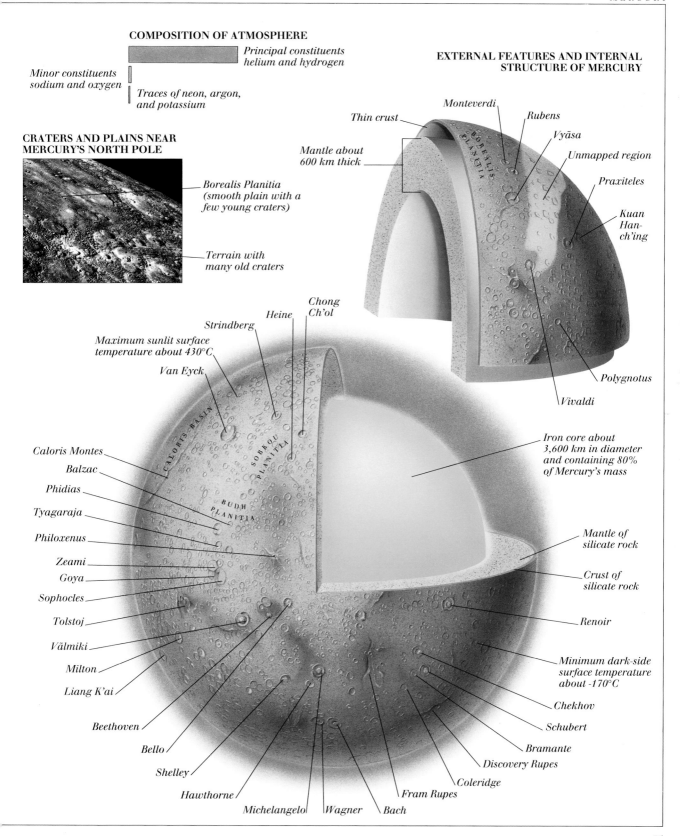

COMPOSITION OF ATMOSPHERE

Principal constituents
helium and hydrogen

Minor constituents
sodium and oxygen

Traces of neon, argon,
and potassium

**CRATERS AND PLAINS NEAR
MERCURY'S NORTH POLE**

Borealis Planitia
(smooth plain with a
few young craters)

Terrain with
many old craters

**EXTERNAL FEATURES AND INTERNAL
STRUCTURE OF MERCURY**

Monteverdi

Thin crust

Rubens

Vyāsa

Mantle about
600 km thick

Unmapped region

Praxiteles

BOREALIS PLANITIA

Kuan
Han-
ch'ing

Polygnotus

Vivaldi

Chong
Ch'ol

Heine

Strindberg

Maximum sunlit surface
temperature about 430°C

Van Eyck

CALORIS BASIN

SOBKOU PLANITIA

BUDH PLANITIA

Caloris Montes

Balzac

Phidias

Tyagaraja

Philoxenus

Zeami

Goya

Sophocles

Tolstoj

Vālmiki

Milton

Liang K'ai

Beethoven

Bello

Shelley

Hawthorne

Michelangelo

Wagner

Bach

Iron core about
3,600 km in diameter
and containing 80%
of Mercury's mass

Mantle of
silicate rock

Crust of
silicate rock

Renoir

Minimum dark-side
surface temperature
about -170°C

Chekhov

Schubert

Bramante

Discovery Rupes

Coleridge

Fram Rupes

35

Venus

RADAR IMAGE OF VENUS

VENUS IS A ROCKY PLANET and the second planet from the Sun. Venus spins slowly backwards as it orbits the Sun, causing its rotational period to be the longest in the Solar System, at about 243 Earth days. It is slightly smaller than Earth and probably has a similar internal structure, consisting of a semi-solid metal core, surrounded by a rocky mantle and crust. Venus is the brightest object in the sky after the Sun and Moon because its atmosphere reflects sunlight strongly. The main component of the atmosphere is carbon dioxide, which traps heat in a greenhouse effect far stronger than that on Earth. As a result, Venus is the hottest planet, with a maximum surface temperature of about 480°C. The thick cloud layers contain droplets of sulphuric acid and are driven around the planet by winds at speeds of up to 360 kilometres per hour. Although the planet takes 243 Earth days to rotate once, the high-speed winds cause the clouds to circle the planet in only four Earth days. The high temperature, acidic clouds, and enormous atmospheric pressure (about 90 times greater at the surface than that on Earth) make the environment extremely hostile. However, space probes have managed to land on Venus and photograph its dry, dusty surface. The Venusian surface has also been mapped by probes with radar equipment that can "see" through the cloud layers. Such radar maps reveal a terrain with craters, mountains, volcanoes, and areas where craters have been covered by plains of solidified volcanic lava. There are two large highland regions called Aphrodite Terra and Ishtar Terra.

TILT AND ROTATION OF VENUS

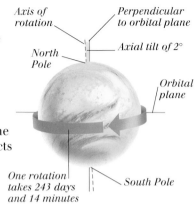

Axis of rotation

Perpendicular to orbital plane

North Pole

Axial tilt of 2°

Orbital plane

One rotation takes 243 days and 14 minutes

South Pole

CLOUD FEATURES

Polar hood

Dark, mid-latitude band

Cloud features swept around planet by winds of up to 360 km/h

Dirty yellow hue due to sulphuric acid in atmosphere

Bright polar band

VENUSIAN CRATERS

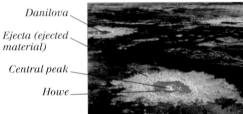

Danilova

Ejecta (ejected material)

Central peak

Howe

FALSE-COLOUR RADAR MAP OF THE SURFACE OF VENUS

Metis Regio

Maxwell Montes

Bell Regio

Tethus Regio

Atalanta Planitia

Sedna Planitia

Leda Planitia

Eisila Regio

Tellus Regio

Guinevere Planitia

Niobe Planitia

Phoebe Regio

Alpha Regio

Ovda Regio

Themis Regio

Thetis Regio

Lavinia Planitia

Aino Planitia

Helen Planitia

Lada Terra

ISHTAR TERRA

APHRODITE TERRA

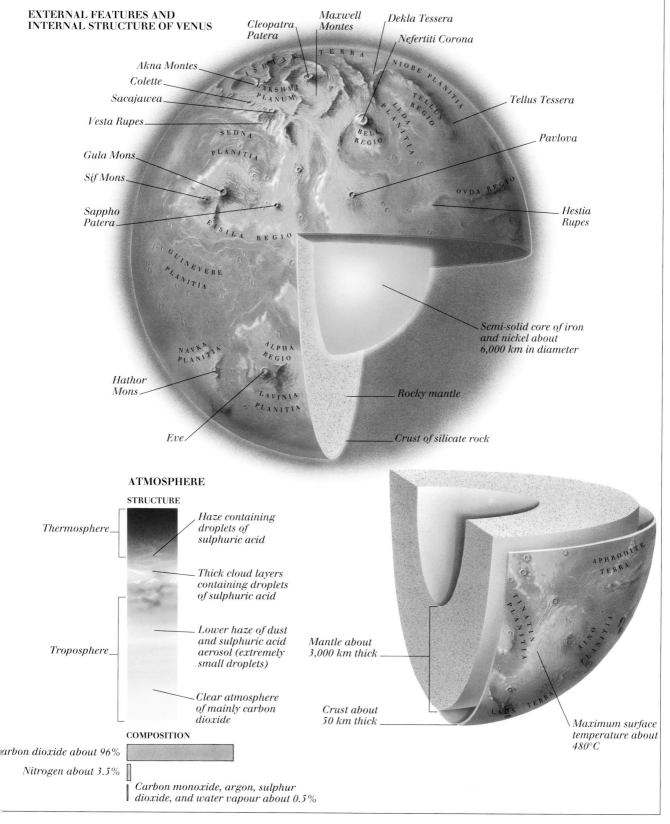

**EXTERNAL FEATURES AND
INTERNAL STRUCTURE OF VENUS**

Cleopatra Patera

Maxwell Montes

Dekla Tessera

Nefertiti Corona

Akna Montes

Colette

Sacajawea

Tellus Tessera

Vesta Rupes

Gula Mons

Pavlova

Sif Mons

Sappho Patera

Hestia Rupes

Semi-solid core of iron and nickel about 6,000 km in diameter

Hathor Mons

Rocky mantle

Eve

Crust of silicate rock

ISHTAR TERRA

LAKSHMI PLANUM

NIOBE PLANITIA

TELLUS REGIO

LEDA PLANITIA

BELL REGIO

SEDNA PLANITIA

OVDA REGIO

EISILA REGIO

GUINEVERE PLANITIA

NAVKA PLANITIA

ALPHA REGIO

LAVINIA PLANITIA

ATMOSPHERE

STRUCTURE

Thermosphere

Haze containing droplets of sulphuric acid

Thick cloud layers containing droplets of sulphuric acid

Troposphere

Lower haze of dust and sulphuric acid aerosol (extremely small droplets)

Clear atmosphere of mainly carbon dioxide

Mantle about 3,000 km thick

Crust about 50 km thick

APHRODITE TERRA

TINATIN PLANITIA

AINO PLANITIA

LADA TERRA

Maximum surface temperature about 480°C

COMPOSITION

Carbon dioxide about 96%

Nitrogen about 3.5%

Carbon monoxide, argon, sulphur dioxide, and water vapour about 0.5%

The Earth

THE EARTH

THE EARTH IS THE THIRD of the nine planets that orbit the Sun. It is the largest and densest rocky planet, and the only one known to support life. About 70 per cent of the Earth's surface is covered by water, which is not found in liquid form on the surface of any other planet. There are four main layers: the inner core, the outer core, the mantle, and the crust. At the heart of the planet the solid inner core has a temperature of about 4,000°C. The heat from this inner core causes material in the molten outer core and mantle to circulate in convection currents. It is thought that these convection currents generate the Earth's magnetic field, which extends into space as the magnetosphere. The Earth's atmosphere helps screen out some of the harmful radiation from the Sun, stops meteorites from reaching the planet's surface, and traps enough heat to prevent extremes of cold. The Earth has one natural satellite, the Moon, which is large enough for both bodies to be considered a double-planet system.

TILT AND ROTATION OF THE EARTH

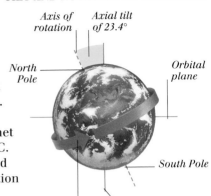

Axis of rotation

Axial tilt of 23.4°

North Pole

Orbital plane

South Pole

Perpendicular to orbital plane

One rotation takes 23 hours and 56 minutes

THE FORMATION OF THE EARTH

The heat of the collisions caused the planet to glow red

The cloud broke up into particles of ice and rock, which stuck together to form planets

Micro-organisms began to photosynthesize, creating a build up of oxygen

4,600 MILLION YEARS AGO, THE SOLAR SYSTEM FORMED FROM A CLOUD OF GAS AND DUST

THE EARTH WAS FORMED FROM COLLIDING ROCKS

4,500 MILLION YEARS AGO THE SURFACE COOLED TO FORM THE CRUST

THE CONTINENTS BROKE UP AND REFORMED, GRADUALLY TAKING THEIR PRESENT POSITIONS

Solar wind enters atmosphere and produces aurora

Magnetosphere (magnetic field)

Solar wind (stream of electrically charged particles)

THE EARTH'S MAGNETOSPHERE

Van Allen radiation belt

Earth

Axis of geographic poles

Axis of magnetic poles

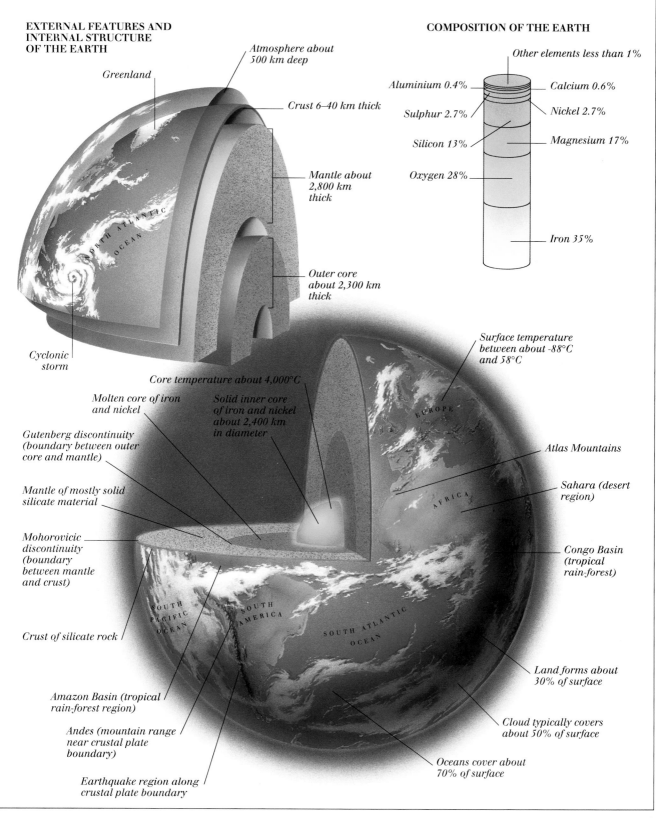

EXTERNAL FEATURES AND INTERNAL STRUCTURE OF THE EARTH

Greenland

Atmosphere about 500 km deep

Crust 6–40 km thick

Mantle about 2,800 km thick

Outer core about 2,300 km thick

Cyclonic storm

COMPOSITION OF THE EARTH

Other elements less than 1%

Aluminium 0.4%

Calcium 0.6%

Sulphur 2.7%

Nickel 2.7%

Silicon 13%

Magnesium 17%

Oxygen 28%

Iron 35%

Core temperature about 4,000°C

Molten core of iron and nickel

Solid inner core of iron and nickel about 2,400 km in diameter

Gutenberg discontinuity (boundary between outer core and mantle)

Mantle of mostly solid silicate material

Mohorovicic discontinuity (boundary between mantle and crust)

Crust of silicate rock

Amazon Basin (tropical rain-forest region)

Andes (mountain range near crustal plate boundary)

Earthquake region along crustal plate boundary

Surface temperature between about -88°C and 58°C

EUROPE

AFRICA

Atlas Mountains

Sahara (desert region)

Congo Basin (tropical rain-forest)

SOUTH PACIFIC OCEAN

SOUTH AMERICA

SOUTH ATLANTIC OCEAN

Land forms about 30% of surface

Cloud typically covers about 50% of surface

Oceans cover about 70% of surface

NORTH ATLANTIC OCEAN

The Moon

THE MOON FROM EARTH

THE MOON IS THE EARTH'S only natural satellite. It is relatively large for a moon, with a diameter of about 3,470 kilometres – just over a quarter that of the Earth. The Moon takes the same time to rotate on its axis as it takes to orbit the Earth (27.3 days), and so the same side (the near side) always faces us. However, the amount of the surface we can see – the phase of the Moon – depends on how much of the near side is in sunlight. The Moon is dry and barren, with no atmosphere or water. It consists mainly of solid rock, although its core may contain molten rock or iron. The surface is dusty, with highlands covered in craters caused by meteorite impacts, and lowlands in which large craters have been filled by solidified lava to form dark areas called maria or "seas". Maria occur mainly on the near side, which has a thinner crust than the far side. Many of the craters are rimmed by mountain ranges that form the crater walls and can be thousands of metres high.

TILT AND ROTATION OF THE MOON

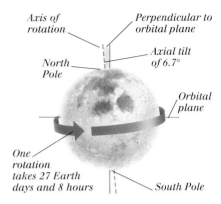

Axis of rotation

Perpendicular to orbital plane

Axial tilt of 6.7°

North Pole

Orbital plane

One rotation takes 27 Earth days and 8 hours

South Pole

CRATERS ON OCEANUS PROCELLARUM

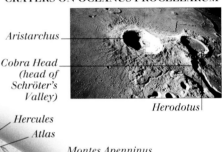

Aristarchus

Cobra Head (head of Schröter's Valley)

Herodotus

NEAR SIDE OF THE MOON

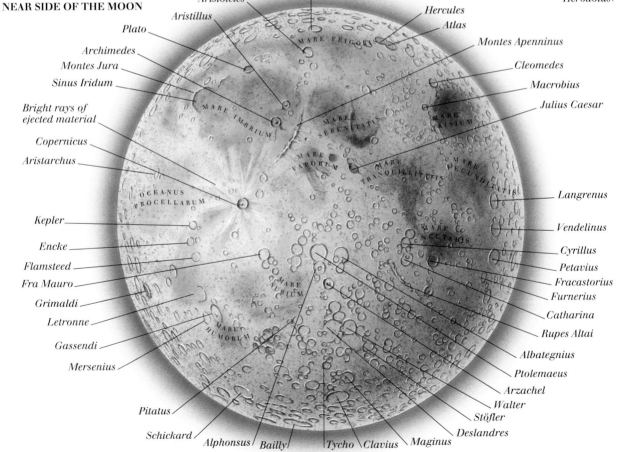

De la Rue

Aristoteles

Aristillus

Plato

Archimedes

Montes Jura

Sinus Iridum

Bright rays of ejected material

Copernicus

Aristarchus

Kepler

Encke

Flamsteed

Fra Mauro

Grimaldi

Letronne

Gassendi

Mersenius

Pitatus

Schickard

Alphonsus

Bailly

Tycho

Clavius

Maginus

Deslandres

Stöfler

Walter

Arzachel

Ptolemaeus

Albategnius

Rupes Altai

Catharina

Furnerius

Fracastorius

Petavius

Cyrillus

Vendelinus

Langrenus

Julius Caesar

Macrobius

Cleomedes

Montes Apenninus

Atlas

Hercules

MARE FRIGORIS

MARE IMBRIUM

MARE SERENITATIS

MARE CRISIUM

MARE VAPORUM

MARE TRANQUILLITATIS

MARE FECUNDITATIS

OCEANUS PROCELLARUM

MARE NECTARIS

MARE NUBIUM

MARE HUMORUM

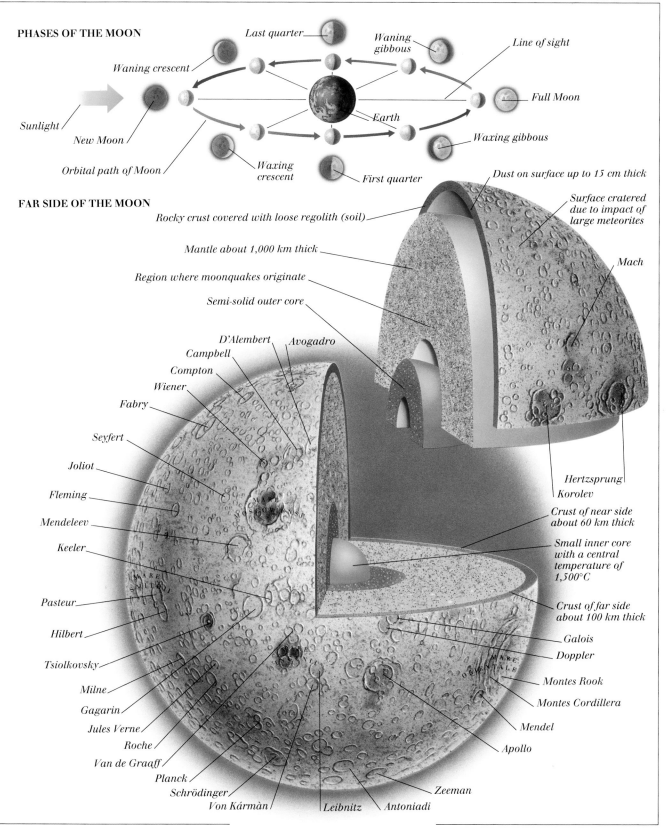

PHASES OF THE MOON

Last quarter

Waning gibbous

Waning crescent

Line of sight

Sunlight

Full Moon

New Moon

Earth

Orbital path of Moon

Waxing gibbous

Waxing crescent

First quarter

Dust on surface up to 15 cm thick

FAR SIDE OF THE MOON

Rocky crust covered with loose regolith (soil)

Surface cratered due to impact of large meteorites

Mantle about 1,000 km thick

Mach

Region where moonquakes originate

Semi-solid outer core

D'Alembert

Avogadro

Campbell

Compton

Wiener

Fabry

Seyfert

Joliot

Fleming

Mendeleev

Keeler

Hertzsprung

Korolev

Crust of near side about 60 km thick

Small inner core with a central temperature of 1,500°C

Pasteur

Hilbert

Crust of far side about 100 km thick

Tsiolkovsky

Galois

Milne

Doppler

Gagarin

Montes Rook

Jules Verne

Montes Cordillera

Roche

Mendel

Van de Graaff

Apollo

Planck

Schrödinger

Zeeman

Von Kármàn

Leibnitz

Antoniadi

41

Mars

MARS

MARS, KNOWN AS THE RED PLANET, is the fourth planet from the Sun and the outermost rocky planet. In the 19th century, astronomers first observed what were thought to be signs of life on Mars. These signs included apparent canal-like markings on the surface, and dark patches that were thought to be vegetation. It is now known that the "canals" are an optical illusion, and the dark patches are areas where the red dust that covers most of the planet has been blown away. The fine dust particles are often whipped up by winds into dust storms that occasionally obscure almost all the surface. Residual dust in the atmosphere gives the Martian sky a pinkish hue. The northern hemisphere of Mars has many large plains formed of solidified volcanic lava, whereas the southern hemisphere has many craters and large impact basins. There are also several huge, extinct volcanoes, including Olympus Mons, which, at 600 kilometres across and 25 kilometres high, is the largest known volcano in the Solar System. The surface also has many canyons and branching channels. The canyons were formed by movements of the surface crust, but the channels are thought to have been formed by flowing water that has now dried up. The Martian atmosphere is much thinner than Earth's, with only a few clouds and morning mists. Mars has two tiny, irregularly shaped moons called Phobos and Deimos. Their small size indicates that they may be asteroids that have been captured by the gravity of Mars.

TILT AND ROTATION OF MARS

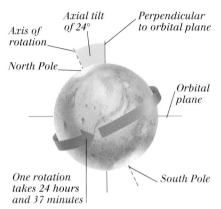

Axis of rotation

Axial tilt of 24°

Perpendicular to orbital plane

North Pole

Orbital plane

One rotation takes 24 hours and 37 minutes

South Pole

SURFACE FEATURES OF MARS

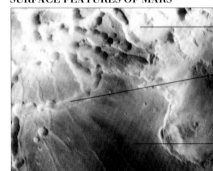

Bright water-ice fog

Fog in canyon about 20 km wide at end of Valles Marineris

Syria Planum

NOCTIS LABYRINTHUS (CANYON SYSTEM)

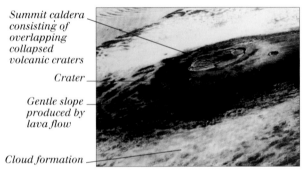

Summit caldera consisting of overlapping collapsed volcanic craters

Crater

Gentle slope produced by lava flow

Cloud formation

OLYMPUS MONS (EXTINCT SHIELD VOLCANO)

THE SURFACE OF MARS

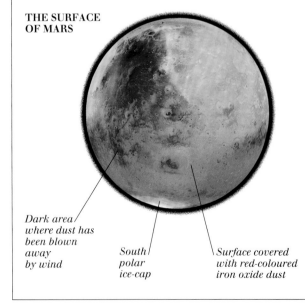

Dark area where dust has been blown away by wind

South polar ice-cap

Surface covered with red-coloured iron oxide dust

MOONS OF MARS

PHOBOS
Average diameter: 22 km
Average distance from planet: 9,400 km

DEIMOS
Average diameter: 13 km
Average distance from planet: 23,500 km

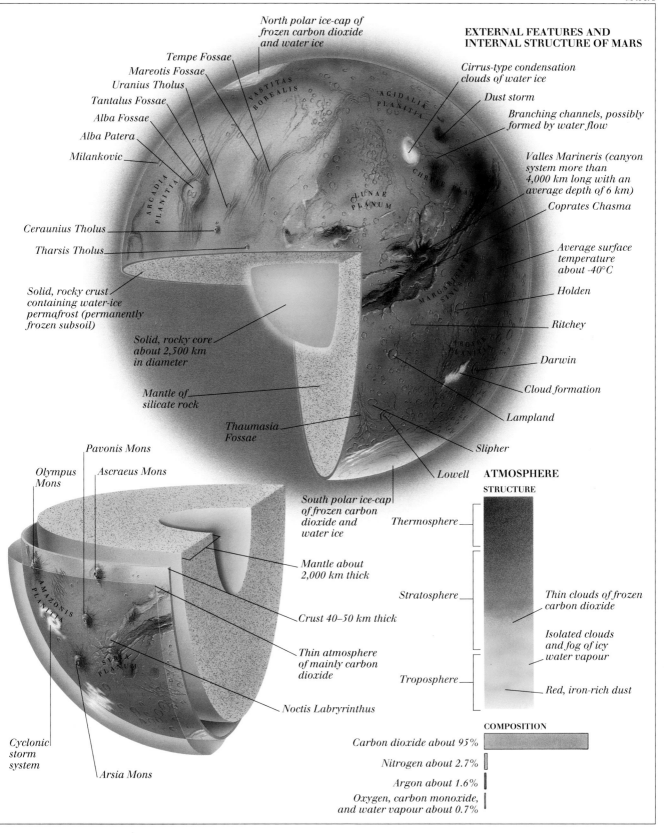

EXTERNAL FEATURES AND INTERNAL STRUCTURE OF MARS

North polar ice-cap of frozen carbon dioxide and water ice

Tempe Fossae

Mareotis Fossae

Uranius Tholus

Tantalus Fossae

Alba Fossae

Alba Patera

Milankovic

Ceraunius Tholus

Tharsis Tholus

Solid, rocky crust containing water-ice permafrost (permanently frozen subsoil)

Solid, rocky core about 2,500 km in diameter

Mantle of silicate rock

Thaumasia Fossae

Cirrus-type condensation clouds of water ice

Dust storm

Branching channels, possibly formed by water flow

Valles Marineris (canyon system more than 4,000 km long with an average depth of 6 km)

Coprates Chasma

Average surface temperature about -40°C

Holden

Ritchey

Darwin

Cloud formation

Lampland

Slipher

Lowell

South polar ice-cap of frozen carbon dioxide and water ice

Olympus Mons

Pavonis Mons

Ascraeus Mons

Mantle about 2,000 km thick

Crust 40–50 km thick

Thin atmosphere of mainly carbon dioxide

Noctis Labyrinthus

Cyclonic storm system

Arsia Mons

ATMOSPHERE

STRUCTURE

Thermosphere

Stratosphere

Troposphere

Thin clouds of frozen carbon dioxide

Isolated clouds and fog of icy water vapour

Red, iron-rich dust

COMPOSITION

Carbon dioxide about 95%

Nitrogen about 2.7%

Argon about 1.6%

Oxygen, carbon monoxide, and water vapour about 0.7%

Jupiter

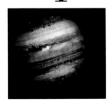

JUPITER

JUPITER IS THE FIFTH PLANET from the Sun and the first of the four gas giants. It is the largest and the most massive planet, with a diameter about 11 times that of the Earth and a mass about 2.5 times the combined mass of the eight other planets. Jupiter is thought to have a small rocky core surrounded by an inner mantle of metallic hydrogen (liquid hydrogen that acts like a metal). Outside the inner mantle is an outer mantle of liquid hydrogen and helium that merges into the gaseous atmosphere. Jupiter's rapid rate of rotation causes the clouds in its atmosphere to form belts and zones that encircle the planet parallel to the equator. Belts are dark, low-lying, relatively warm cloud layers, and zones are bright, high-altitude, cooler cloud layers. Within the belts and zones, turbulence causes the formation of cloud features such as white ovals and red spots, both of which are huge storm systems. The most prominent cloud feature is a storm called the Great Red Spot, which consists of a spiralling column of clouds three times wider than the Earth that rises about eight kilometres above the upper cloud layer. Jupiter has one thin, faint, main ring, inside which is a tenuous halo ring of tiny particles extending towards the planet. There are 16 known Jovian moons. The four largest moons (called the Galileans) are Ganymede, Callisto, Io, and Europa. Ganymede and Callisto are cratered and probably icy. Europa is smooth and icy and may contain water. Io is covered in bright red, orange, and yellow splotches. This colouring is caused by sulphurous material from active volcanoes that shoot plumes of lava hundreds of kilometres above the surface.

TILT AND ROTATION OF JUPITER

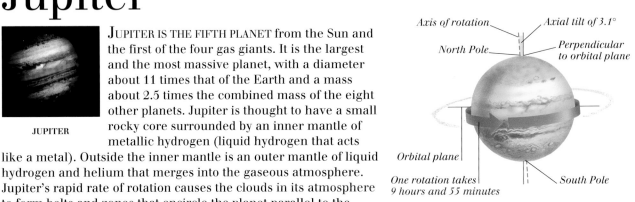

Axis of rotation

Axial tilt of 3.1°

North Pole

Perpendicular to orbital plane

Orbital plane

One rotation takes 9 hours and 55 minutes

South Pole

GREAT RED SPOT AND WHITE OVAL

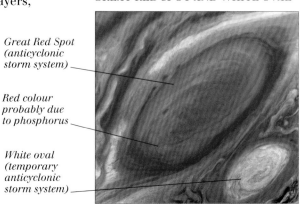

Great Red Spot (anticyclonic storm system)

Red colour probably due to phosphorus

White oval (temporary anticyclonic storm system)

RINGS OF JUPITER

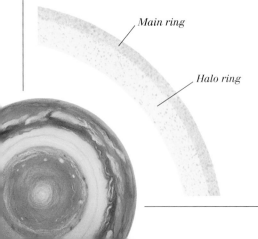

Main ring

Halo ring

GALILEAN MOONS OF JUPITER

EUROPA
Diameter: 3,138 km
Average distance from planet: 670,900 km

CALLISTO
Diameter: 4,800 km
Average distance from planet: 1,880,000 km

GANYMEDE
Diameter: 5,262 km
Average distance from planet: 1,070,000 km

IO
Diameter: 3,642 km
Average distance from planet: 421,800 km

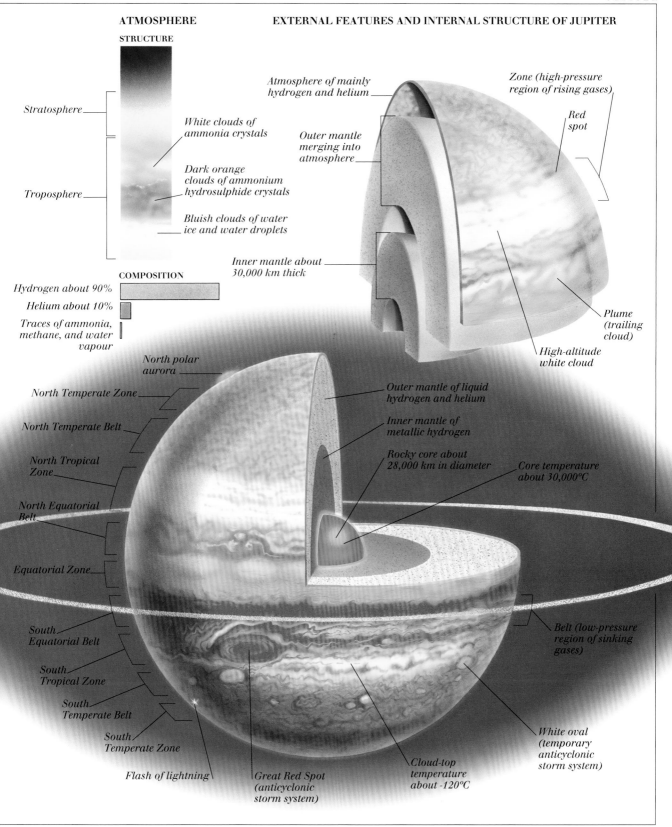

ATMOSPHERE

STRUCTURE

EXTERNAL FEATURES AND INTERNAL STRUCTURE OF JUPITER

Stratosphere

Troposphere

White clouds of
ammonia crystals

Dark orange
clouds of ammonium
hydrosulphide crystals

Bluish clouds of water
ice and water droplets

Atmosphere of mainly
hydrogen and helium

Outer mantle
merging into
atmosphere

Inner mantle about
30,000 km thick

Zone (high-pressure
region of rising gases)

Red
spot

Plume
(trailing
cloud)

High-altitude
white cloud

COMPOSITION

Hydrogen about 90%

Helium about 10%

Traces of ammonia,
methane, and water
vapour

North polar
aurora

North Temperate Zone

North Temperate Belt

North Tropical
Zone

North Equatorial
Belt

Equatorial Zone

South
Equatorial Belt

South
Tropical Zone

South
Temperate Belt

South
Temperate Zone

Flash of lightning

Great Red Spot
(anticyclonic
storm system)

Cloud-top
temperature
about -120°C

Outer mantle of liquid
hydrogen and helium

Inner mantle of
metallic hydrogen

Rocky core about
28,000 km in diameter

Core temperature
about 30,000°C

Belt (low-pressure
region of sinking
gases)

White oval
(temporary
anticyclonic
storm system)

Saturn

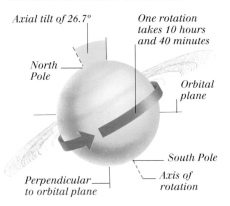

TILT AND ROTATION OF SATURN

Axial tilt of 26.7°

One rotation takes 10 hours and 40 minutes

North Pole

Orbital plane

South Pole

Axis of rotation

Perpendicular to orbital plane

FALSE-COLOUR IMAGE OF SATURN

SATURN IS THE SIXTH PLANET from the Sun. It is a gas giant almost as big as Jupiter, with an equatorial diameter of about 120,500 kilometres. Saturn is thought to consist of a small core of rock and ice surrounded by an inner mantle of metallic hydrogen (liquid hydrogen that acts like a metal). Outside the inner mantle is an outer mantle of liquid hydrogen that merges into a gaseous atmosphere. Saturn's clouds form belts and zones similar to those on Jupiter, but obscured by overlying haze. Storms and eddies, seen as red or white ovals, occur in the clouds. Saturn has an extremely thin but wide system of rings that is less than one kilometre thick but extends outwards to about 420,000 kilometres from the planet's surface. The main rings comprise thousands of narrow ringlets, each made of icy lumps that range in size from tiny particles to chunks several metres across. The D, E, and G rings are very faint, the F ring is brighter, and the A, B, and C rings are bright enough to be seen from Earth with binoculars. Saturn has 18 known moons, some of which orbit inside the rings and are thought to exert a gravitational influence on the shapes of the rings. Unusually, seven of the moons are co-orbital – they share an orbit with another moon. Astronomers believe that such co-orbital moons may have originated from a single satellite that broke up.

FALSE-COLOUR IMAGE OF SATURN'S CLOUD FEATURES

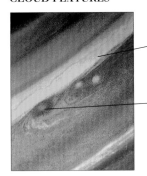

Ribbon-shaped striation caused by winds of up to 540 km/h

Oval (rotating storm system)

INNER RINGS OF SATURN

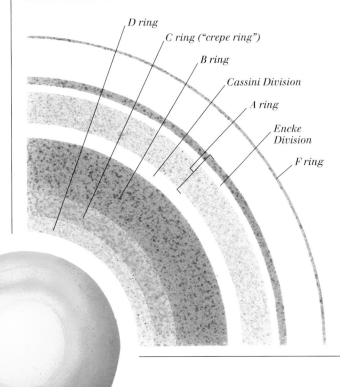

D ring

C ring ("crepe ring")

B ring

Cassini Division

A ring

Encke Division

F ring

MOONS OF SATURN

ENCELADUS
Diameter: 498 km
Average distance from planet: 238,000 km

TETHYS
Diameter: 1,050 km
Average distance from planet: 295,000 km

DIONE
Diameter: 1,118 km
Average distance from planet: 377,000 km

MIMAS
Diameter: 397 km
Average distance from planet: 186,000 km

EXTERNAL FEATURES AND INTERNAL STRUCTURE OF SATURN

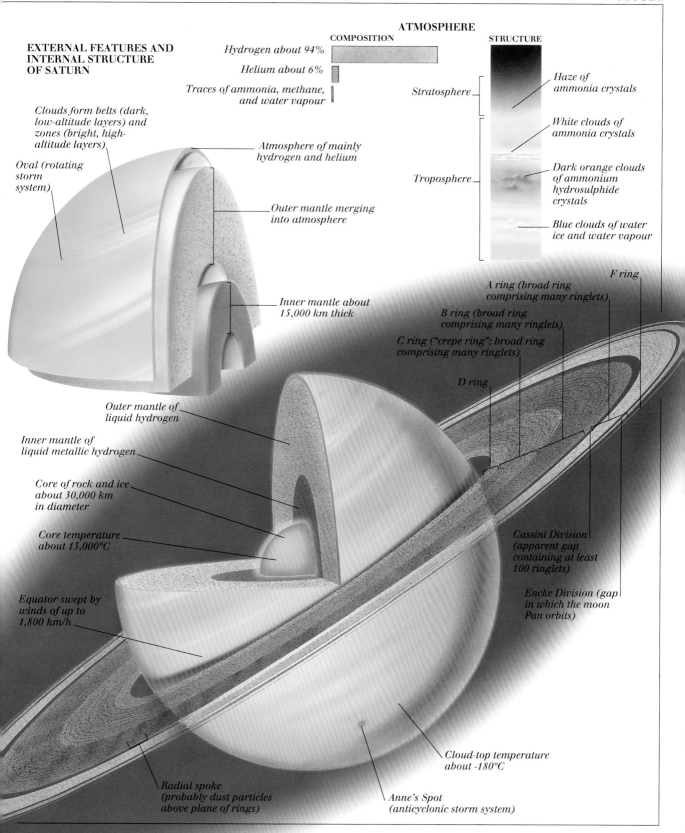

ATMOSPHERE

COMPOSITION

Hydrogen about 94%

Helium about 6%

Traces of ammonia, methane, and water vapour

STRUCTURE

Stratosphere

Troposphere

Haze of ammonia crystals

White clouds of ammonia crystals

Dark orange clouds of ammonium hydrosulphide crystals

Blue clouds of water ice and water vapour

Clouds form belts (dark, low-altitude layers) and zones (bright, high-altitude layers)

Oval (rotating storm system)

Atmosphere of mainly hydrogen and helium

Outer mantle merging into atmosphere

Inner mantle about 15,000 km thick

Outer mantle of liquid hydrogen

Inner mantle of liquid metallic hydrogen

Core of rock and ice about 30,000 km in diameter

Core temperature about 15,000°C

Equator swept by winds of up to 1,800 km/h

F ring

A ring (broad ring comprising many ringlets)

B ring (broad ring comprising many ringlets)

C ring ("crepe ring"; broad ring comprising many ringlets)

D ring

Cassini Division (apparent gap containing at least 100 ringlets)

Encke Division (gap in which the moon Pan orbits)

Cloud-top temperature about -180°C

Radial spoke (probably dust particles above plane of rings)

Anne's Spot (anticyclonic storm system)

47

Uranus

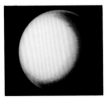

FALSE-COLOUR
IMAGE OF URANUS

URANUS IS THE SEVENTH PLANET from the Sun
and the third largest, with a diameter of about
51,000 kilometres. It is thought to consist of
a dense mixture of different types of ice and
gas around a solid core. Its atmosphere contains
traces of methane, giving the planet a blue-green
hue, and the temperature at the cloud tops is
about -210°C. Uranus is the most featureless
planet to have been closely observed: only a
few icy clouds of methane have been seen so far. Uranus is unique
among the planets in that its axis of rotation lies close to its orbital
plane. As a result of its strongly tilted rotational axis, Uranus rolls on
its side along its orbital path around the Sun, whereas other planets spin
more or less upright. Uranus is encircled by 11 rings that consist of rocks
interspersed with dust lanes. The rings contain some of the darkest matter
in the Solar System and are extremely narrow, making them difficult to detect:
nine of them are less than 10 kilometres wide, whereas most of Saturn's rings
are thousands of kilometres in width. There are 15 known Uranian moons, all
of which are icy and most of which are further out than the rings. The 10 inner
moons are small and dark, with diameters of less than 160 kilometres, and the
five outer moons are between about 470 and 1,600 kilometres in diameter.
The outer moons have a wide variety of surface features. Miranda has the
most varied surface, with cratered areas broken up by huge ridges and
cliffs 20 kilometres high.

TILT AND ROTATION OF URANUS

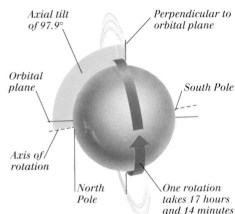

Axial tilt
of 97.9°

Perpendicular to
orbital plane

Orbital
plane

South Pole

Axis of
rotation

North
Pole

One rotation
takes 17 hours
and 14 minutes

OUTER MOONS

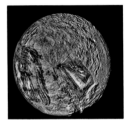

MIRANDA
Diameter: 472 km
Average distance from
planet: 129,800 km

RINGS OF URANUS

Epsilon ring

Ring 1986 U1R

Delta ring

Gamma
ring

Eta ring

Beta ring

Alpha ring

Rings 4 and 5

Ring 6

Ring 1986 U2R

RINGS AND DUST LANES

ARIEL
Diameter: 1,158 km
Average distance from
planet: 191,200 km

TITANIA
Diameter: 1,578 km
Average distance from
planet: 435,900 km

UMBRIEL
Diameter: 1,169 km
Average distance from
planet: 266,000 km

OBERON
Diameter: 1,523 km
Average distance from
planet: 582,600 km

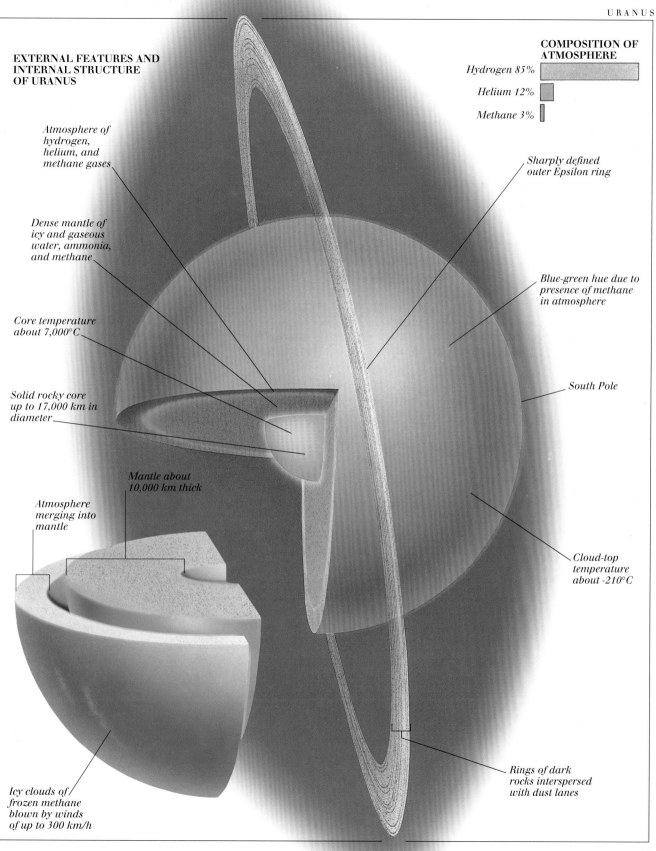

**EXTERNAL FEATURES AND
INTERNAL STRUCTURE
OF URANUS**

**COMPOSITION OF
ATMOSPHERE**

Hydrogen 85%

Helium 12%

Methane 3%

*Atmosphere of
hydrogen,
helium, and
methane gases*

*Dense mantle of
icy and gaseous
water, ammonia,
and methane*

*Core temperature
about 7,000°C*

*Solid rocky core
up to 17,000 km in
diameter*

*Mantle about
10,000 km thick*

*Atmosphere
merging into
mantle*

*Icy clouds of
frozen methane
blown by winds
of up to 300 km/h*

*Sharply defined
outer Epsilon ring*

*Blue-green hue due to
presence of methane
in atmosphere*

South Pole

*Cloud-top
temperature
about -210°C*

*Rings of dark
rocks interspersed
with dust lanes*

49

Neptune and Pluto

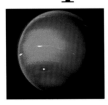

FALSE-COLOUR
IMAGE OF NEPTUNE

NEPTUNE AND PLUTO are the two furthest planets from the Sun, at an average distance of about 4,500 million kilometres and 5,900 million kilometres respectively. Neptune is a gas giant and is thought to consist of a small rocky core surrounded by a mixture of liquids and gases. The atmosphere contains several prominent cloud features. The largest of these are the Great Dark Spot, which is as wide as the Earth, the Small Dark Spot, and the Scooter. The Great and Small Dark Spots are huge storms that are swept around the planet by winds of about 2,000 kilometres per hour. The Scooter is a large area of cirrus cloud. Neptune has four tenuous rings and eight known moons. Triton is the largest Neptunian moon and the coldest object in the Solar System, with a temperature of -235°C. Unlike most moons in the Solar System, Triton orbits its mother planet in the opposite direction to the planet's rotation. Pluto is usually the outermost planet but its elliptical orbit causes it to pass inside the orbit of Neptune for 20 years of its 248-year orbit. Pluto is so small and far away that little is known about it. It is a rocky planet, probably covered with ice and frozen methane. Pluto's only known moon, Charon, is large for a moon, at half the size of its parent planet. Because of the small difference in their sizes, Pluto and Charon are sometimes considered to be a double-planet system.

TILT AND ROTATION OF NEPTUNE

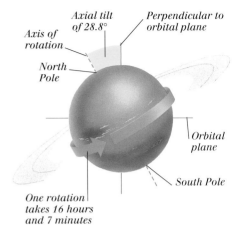

Axial tilt
of 28.8°

Perpendicular to
orbital plane

Axis of
rotation

North
Pole

Orbital
plane

South Pole

One rotation
takes 16 hours
and 7 minutes

CLOUD FEATURES OF NEPTUNE

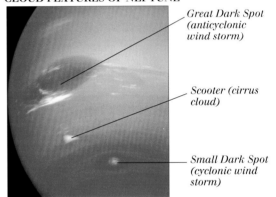

Great Dark Spot
(anticyclonic
wind storm)

Scooter (cirrus
cloud)

Small Dark Spot
(cyclonic wind
storm)

HIGH-ALTITUDE CLOUDS

Methane cirrus clouds
40 km above main
cloud deck

Cloud shadow

Main cloud deck
blown by winds
at speeds of about
2,000 km/h

RINGS OF NEPTUNE

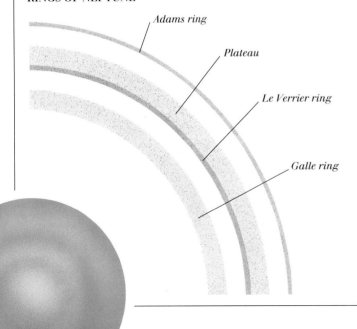

Adams ring

Plateau

Le Verrier ring

Galle ring

MOONS OF NEPTUNE

TRITON
Diameter: 2,705 km
Average distance from
planet: 354,800 km

PROTEUS
Diameter: 416 km
Average distance from
planet: 117,600 km

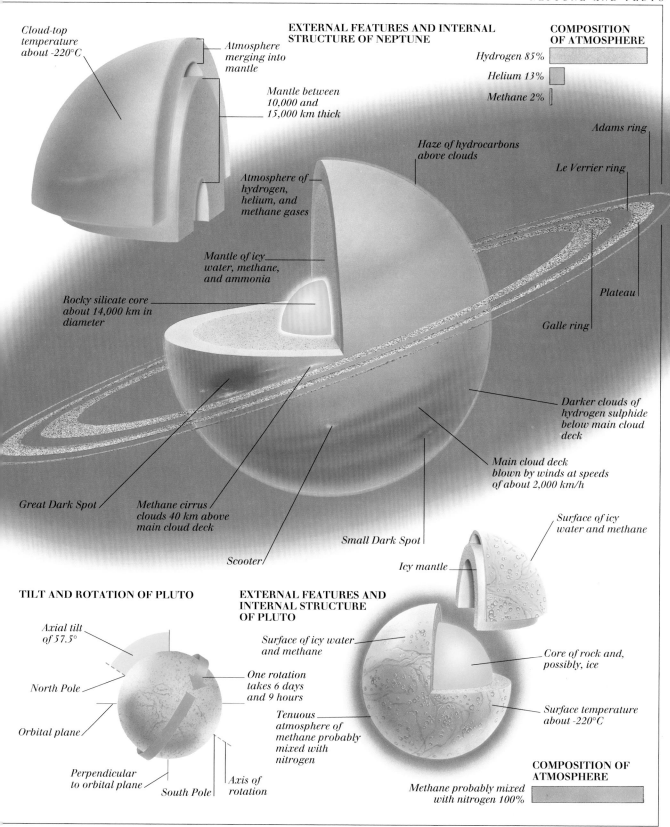

EXTERNAL FEATURES AND INTERNAL STRUCTURE OF NEPTUNE

COMPOSITION OF ATMOSPHERE

Hydrogen 85%

Helium 13%

Methane 2%

Cloud-top temperature about -220°C

Atmosphere merging into mantle

Mantle between 10,000 and 15,000 km thick

Haze of hydrocarbons above clouds

Adams ring

Le Verrier ring

Atmosphere of hydrogen, helium, and methane gases

Mantle of icy water, methane, and ammonia

Plateau

Rocky silicate core about 14,000 km in diameter

Galle ring

Darker clouds of hydrogen sulphide below main cloud deck

Main cloud deck blown by winds at speeds of about 2,000 km/h

Great Dark Spot

Methane cirrus clouds 40 km above main cloud deck

Small Dark Spot

Surface of icy water and methane

Icy mantle

Scooter

TILT AND ROTATION OF PLUTO

EXTERNAL FEATURES AND INTERNAL STRUCTURE OF PLUTO

Axial tilt of 57.5°

Surface of icy water and methane

Core of rock and, possibly, ice

North Pole

One rotation takes 6 days and 9 hours

Orbital plane

Surface temperature about -220°C

Perpendicular to orbital plane

Tenuous atmosphere of methane probably mixed with nitrogen

South Pole

Axis of rotation

COMPOSITION OF ATMOSPHERE

Methane probably mixed with nitrogen 100%

Asteroids, comets, and meteoroids

ASTEROID 951 GASPRA

ASTEROIDS, COMETS, AND METEOROIDS are all debris remaining from the nebula in which the Solar System formed 4.6 billion years ago. Asteroids are rocky bodies up to about 1,000 kilometres in diameter, although most are much smaller. Most of them orbit the Sun in the asteroid belt, which lies between the orbits of Mars and Jupiter. Comets may originate in a huge cloud (called the Oort Cloud) that is thought to surround the Solar System. They are made of frozen gases and dust, and are a few kilometres in diameter. Occasionally, a comet is deflected from the Oort Cloud to orbit the Sun in a long, elliptical path. As the comet approaches the Sun, the comet's surface starts to vaporize in the heat, producing a brightly shining coma (a huge sphere of gas and dust around the nucleus), a gas tail, and a dust tail. Meteoroids are small chunks of stone or stone and iron, some of which are fragments of asteroids or comets. Meteoroids range in size from tiny dust particles to objects tens of metres across. If a meteoroid enters the Earth's atmosphere, it is heated by friction and appears as a glowing streak of light called a meteor (also known as a shooting star). Meteor showers occur when the Earth passes through the trail of dust particles left by a comet. Most meteors burn up in the atmosphere. The few that are large enough to reach the Earth's surface are termed meteorites.

FALSE-COLOUR IMAGE
OF HALLEY'S COMET

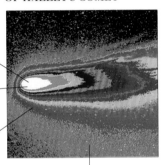

High-intensity light emission

Nucleus

Medium-intensity light emission

Low-intensity light emission

FALSE-COLOUR IMAGE OF A LEONID METEOR SHOWER

METEORITES

DEVELOPMENT OF COMET TAILS

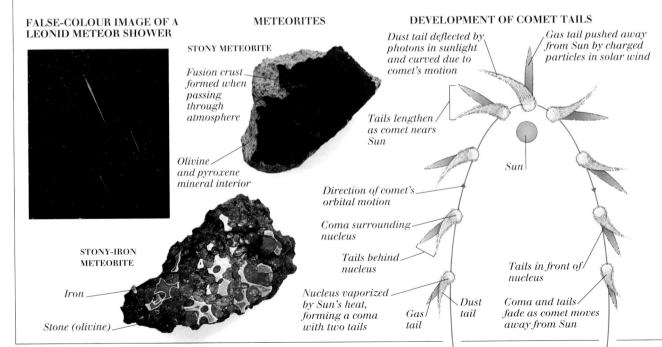

STONY METEORITE

Fusion crust formed when passing through atmosphere

Olivine and pyroxene mineral interior

STONY-IRON METEORITE

Iron

Stone (olivine)

Dust tail deflected by photons in sunlight and curved due to comet's motion

Tails lengthen as comet nears Sun

Direction of comet's orbital motion

Coma surrounding nucleus

Tails behind nucleus

Nucleus vaporized by Sun's heat, forming a coma with two tails

Gas tail

Dust tail

Gas tail pushed away from Sun by charged particles in solar wind

Sun

Tails in front of nucleus

Coma and tails fade as comet moves away from Sun

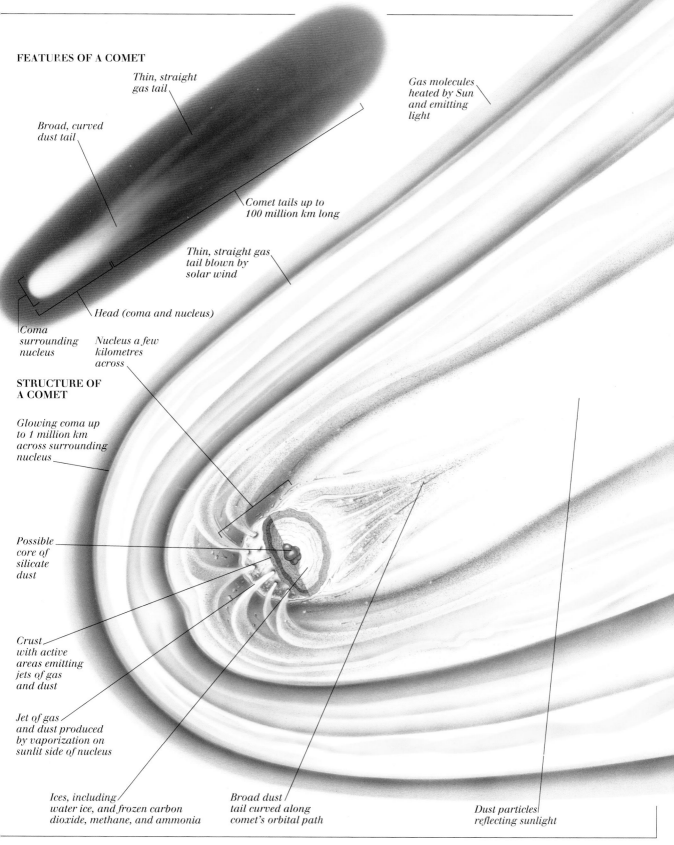

FEATURES OF A COMET

Thin, straight gas tail

Broad, curved dust tail

Gas molecules heated by Sun and emitting light

Comet tails up to 100 million km long

Thin, straight gas tail blown by solar wind

Head (coma and nucleus)

Coma surrounding nucleus

Nucleus a few kilometres across

STRUCTURE OF A COMET

Glowing coma up to 1 million km across surrounding nucleus

Possible core of silicate dust

Crust with active areas emitting jets of gas and dust

Jet of gas and dust produced by vaporization on sunlit side of nucleus

Ices, including water ice, and frozen carbon dioxide, methane, and ammonia

Broad dust tail curved along comet's orbital path

Dust particles reflecting sunlight

PREHISTORIC EARTH

The changing Earth

THE EARTH FORMED FROM A CLOUD OF DUST and gas drifting through space about 4,600 million years ago. Dense minerals sank to the centre while lighter ones formed a thin rocky crust. However, the first known life-forms – bacteria and blue-green algae – did not appear until about 3,400 million years ago, and it was only about 700 million years ago that more complex plants and animals began to develop. Since then, thousands of animal and plant species have evolved; some, such as the dinosaurs, survived for many millions of years, while others died out quickly. The Earth itself is continually changing. Although continents neared their present locations about 50 million years ago, they are still drifting slowly over the planet's surface, and mountain ranges such as the Himalayas – which began to form 40 million years ago – are continually being built up and worn away. Climate is also subject to change: the Earth has undergone a series of ice ages interspersed with warmer periods (the most recent glacial period was at its height about 20,000 years ago).

Small mammals appeared (e.g., Crusafontia)

Dinosaurs became extinct

Global mountain building occurred

Multicellular soft-bodied animals appeared (e.g., worms and jellyfish)

Shelled invertebrates appeared (e.g., trilobites)

Marine plants flourished

Land plants appeared (e.g., Cooksonia)

Unicellular organisms appeared (e.g., blue-green algae)

Earth formed

Coral reefs appeared

Vertebrates appeared (e.g., Hemicyclaspis)

More complex types of algae appeared

Amphibians appeared (e.g., Ichthyostega)

CRETACEO

ORDOVICIAN

CAMBRIAN

PRECAMBRIAN TIME

SILURIAN

DEVONIAN

GEOLOGICAL TIMESCALE

MILLIONS OF
YEARS AGO (MYA)

4,600	570	510	439	409	363	323	29

					MISSISSIPPIAN (NORTH AMERICA)	PENNSYLVANIAN (NORTH AMERICA)	
	CAMBRIAN	ORDOVICIAN	SILURIAN	DEVONIAN	CARBONIFEROUS		
PRECAMBRIAN TIME	PALAEOZOIC						

EVOLUTION OF THE EARTH

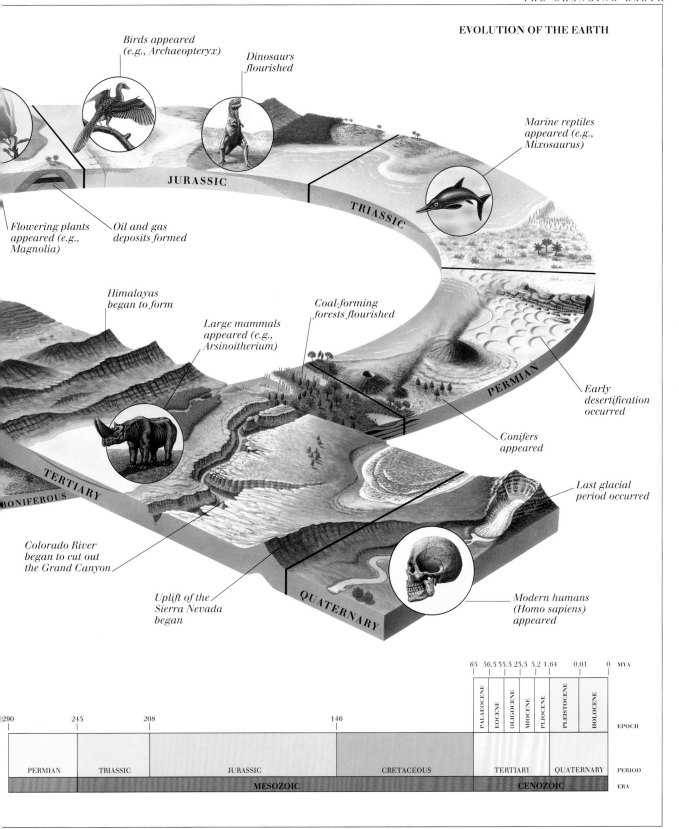

Birds appeared
(e.g., Archaeopteryx)

Dinosaurs
flourished

Marine reptiles
appeared (e.g.,
Mixosaurus)

JURASSIC

TRIASSIC

Flowering plants
appeared (e.g.,
Magnolia)

Oil and gas
deposits formed

Himalayas
began to form

Large mammals
appeared (e.g.,
Arsinoitherium)

Coal-forming
forests flourished

Early
desertification
occurred

PERMIAN

Conifers
appeared

TERTIARY

BONIFEROUS

Last glacial
period occurred

Colorado River
began to cut out
the Grand Canyon

Uplift of the
Sierra Nevada
began

QUATERNARY

Modern humans
(Homo sapiens)
appeared

	65	56.5	35.5	23.5	5.2	1.64	0.01	0	MYA
	PALAEOCENE	EOCENE	OLIGOCENE	MIOCENE	PLIOCENE	PLEISTOCENE	HOLOCENE		EPOCH

290	245	208	146			
PERMIAN	TRIASSIC	JURASSIC	CRETACEOUS	TERTIARY	QUATERNARY	PERIOD
	MESOZOIC			CENOZOIC		ERA

The Earth's crust

THE EARTH'S CRUST IS THE SOLID outer shell of the Earth. It includes continental crust (about 40 kilometres thick) and oceanic crust (about six kilometres thick). The crust and the topmost layer of the mantle form the lithosphere. The lithosphere consists of semi-rigid plates that move relative to each other on the underlying asthenosphere (a partly molten layer of the mantle). This process is known as plate tectonics and helps explain continental drift. Where two plates move apart, there are rifts in the crust. In mid-ocean, this movement results in sea-floor spreading and the formation of ocean ridges; on continents, crustal spreading can form rift valleys. When plates move towards each other, one may be subducted beneath (forced under) the other. In mid-ocean, this causes ocean trenches, seismic activity, and arcs of volcanic islands. Where oceanic crust is subducted beneath continental crust or where continents collide, land may be uplifted and mountains formed (see pp. 62–63). Plates may also slide past each other – along the San Andreas fault, for example. Crustal movement on continents may result in earthquakes, while movement under the seabed can lead to tidal waves.

ELEMENTS IN THE EARTH'S CRUST

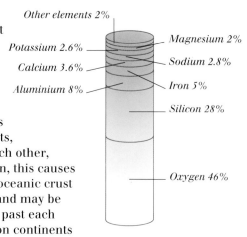

Other elements 2%
Potassium 2.6%
Calcium 3.6%
Aluminium 8%
Magnesium 2%
Sodium 2.8%
Iron 5%
Silicon 28%
Oxygen 46%

FEATURES OF PLATE MOVEMENTS

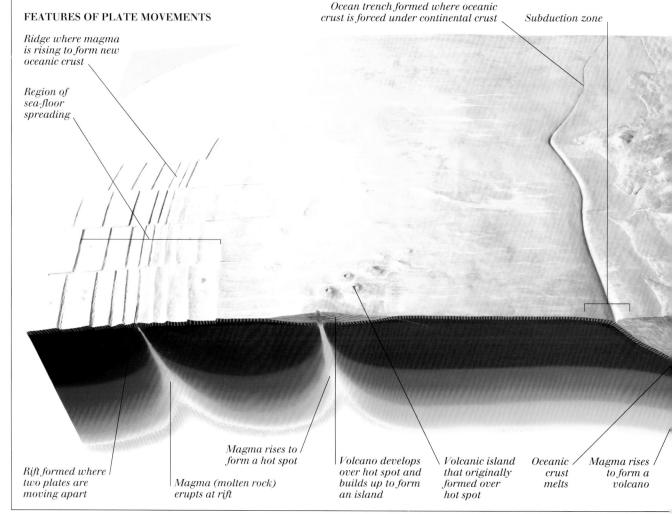

Ridge where magma is rising to form new oceanic crust

Region of sea-floor spreading

Ocean trench formed where oceanic crust is forced under continental crust

Subduction zone

Rift formed where two plates are moving apart

Magma (molten rock) erupts at rift

Magma rises to form a hot spot

Volcano develops over hot spot and builds up to form an island

Volcanic island that originally formed over hot spot

Oceanic crust melts

Magma rises to form a volcano

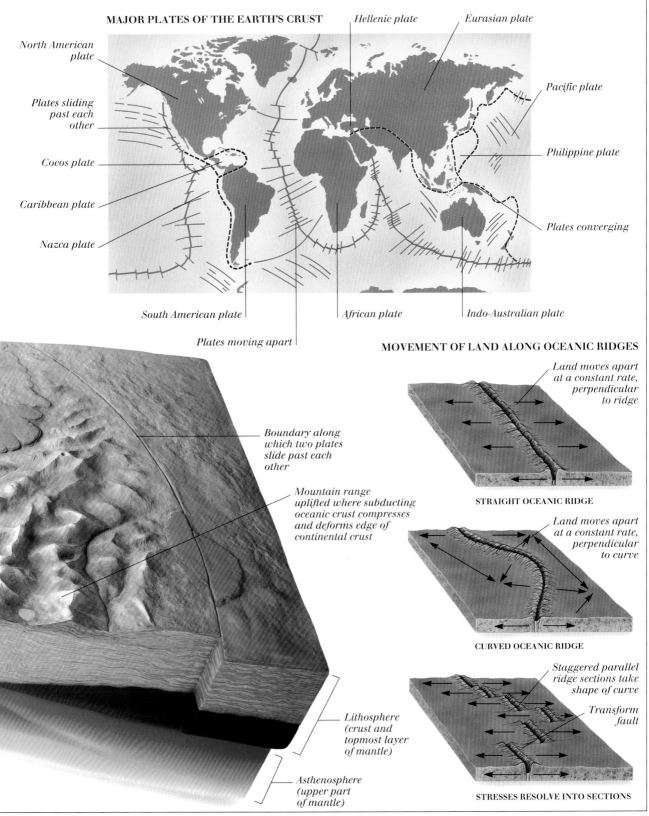

MAJOR PLATES OF THE EARTH'S CRUST

Hellenic plate

Eurasian plate

North American plate

Plates sliding past each other

Cocos plate

Caribbean plate

Nazca plate

Pacific plate

Philippine plate

Plates converging

South American plate

African plate

Indo-Australian plate

Plates moving apart

Boundary along which two plates slide past each other

Mountain range uplifted where subducting oceanic crust compresses and deforms edge of continental crust

Lithosphere (crust and topmost layer of mantle)

Asthenosphere (upper part of mantle)

MOVEMENT OF LAND ALONG OCEANIC RIDGES

Land moves apart at a constant rate, perpendicular to ridge

STRAIGHT OCEANIC RIDGE

Land moves apart at a constant rate, perpendicular to curve

CURVED OCEANIC RIDGE

Staggered parallel ridge sections take shape of curve

Transform fault

STRESSES RESOLVE INTO SECTIONS

Faults and folds

THE CONTINUOUS MOVEMENT of the Earth's crustal plates (see pp. 58–59) can squeeze, stretch, or break rock strata, deforming them and producing faults and folds. A fault is a fracture in a rock along which there is movement of one side relative to the other. The movement can be vertical, horizontal, or oblique (vertical and horizontal). Faults develop when rocks are subjected to compression or tension. They tend to occur in hard, rigid rocks, which are more likely to break than bend. The smallest faults occur in single mineral crystals and are microscopically small, whereas the largest – the Great Rift Valley in Africa, which formed between 5 million and 100,000 years ago – is more than 9,000 kilometres long. A fold is a bend in a rock layer caused by compression. Folds occur in elastic rocks, which tend to bend rather than break. The two main types of fold are anticlines (upfolds) and synclines (downfolds). Folds vary in size from a few millimetres long to folded mountain ranges hundreds of kilometres long, such as the Himalayas (see pp. 62–63) and the Alps, which are repeatedly folding. In addition to faults and folds, other features associated with rock deformations include boudins, mullions, and *en échelon* fractures.

STRUCTURE OF A FOLD

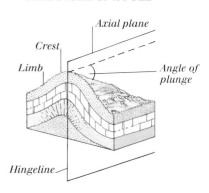

Axial plane
Crest
Limb
Angle of plunge
Hingeline

STRUCTURE OF A FAULT

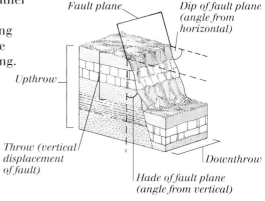

Fault plane
Dip of fault plane (angle from horizontal)
Upthrow
Throw (vertical displacement of fault)
Downthrow
Hade of fault plane (angle from vertical)

STRUCTURE OF A SLOPE

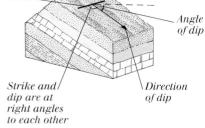

Strike
Angle of dip
Strike and dip are at right angles to each other
Direction of dip

FOLDED ROCK

Crest of anticline
Steeply dipping limbs
Plunge

SECTION THROUGH FOLDED ROCK STRATA THAT HAVE BEEN ERODED

Dipping bed
Anticlinal fold
Monoclinal fold
Mineral-filled fault
Upper Carboniferous Millstone Grit
Lower Carboniferous Limestone

EXAMPLES OF FOLDS

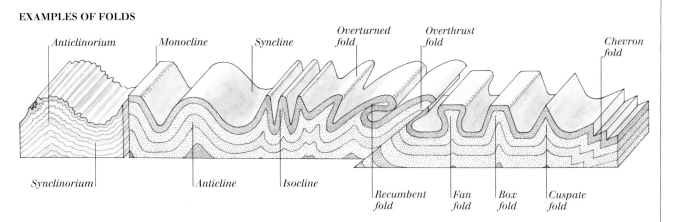

Anticlinorium

Monocline

Syncline

Overturned fold

Overthrust fold

Chevron fold

Synclinorium

Anticline

Isocline

Recumbent fold

Fan fold

Box fold

Cuspate fold

EXAMPLES OF FAULTS

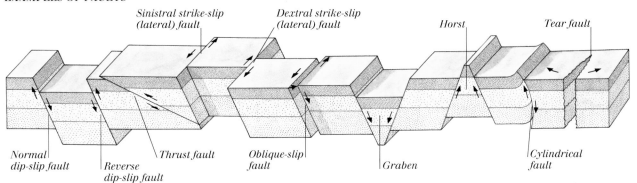

Sinistral strike-slip (lateral) fault

Dextral strike-slip (lateral) fault

Horst

Tear fault

Normal dip-slip fault

Reverse dip-slip fault

Thrust fault

Oblique-slip fault

Graben

Cylindrical fault

SMALL-SCALE ROCK DEFORMATIONS

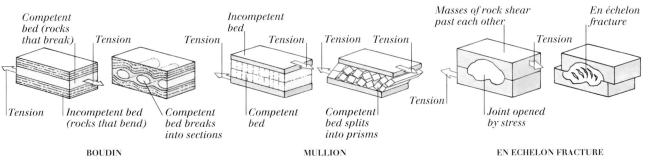

Competent bed (rocks that break)

Tension

Tension

Incompetent bed

Tension

Tension

Tension

Masses of rock shear past each other

Tension

En échelon fracture

Tension

Incompetent bed (rocks that bend)

Competent bed breaks into sections

Competent bed

Competent bed splits into prisms

Joint opened by stress

BOUDIN

MULLION

EN ECHELON FRACTURE

Mineral-filled fault

Dipping bed

Gently folded bed

Horizontal bed

Mineral-filled fault

Dipping bed

Upper Carboniferous Millstone Grit

Upper Carboniferous Coal Measures

61

Mountain building

THE PROCESSES INVOLVED in mountain building – termed orogenesis – occur as a result of the movement of the Earth's crustal plates (see pp. 58–59). There are three main types of mountains: volcanic mountains, fold mountains, and block mountains. Most volcanic mountains have been formed along plate boundaries where plates have come together or moved apart and lava and other debris have been ejected onto the Earth's surface. The lava and debris may have built up to form a dome around the vent of a volcano. Fold mountains are formed where plates push together and cause the rock to buckle upwards. Where oceanic crust meets less dense continental crust, the oceanic crust is forced under the continental crust. The continental crust is buckled by the impact. This is how folded mountain ranges, such as the Appalachian Mountains in North America, were formed. Fold mountains are also formed where two areas of continental crust meet. The Himalayas, for example, began to form when India collided with Asia, buckling the sediments and parts of the oceanic crust between them. Block mountains are formed when a block of land is uplifted between two faults as a result of compression or tension in the Earth's crust (see pp. 60–61). Often, the movement along faults has taken place gradually over millions of years. However, two plates may cause an earthquake by suddenly sliding past each other along a faultline.

BHAGIRATHI PARBAT, HIMALAYAS

FORMATION OF THE HIMALAYAS

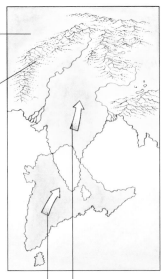

Asia

Himalayas formed by buckling of sediment and part of the oceanic crust between two colliding continents

India moves north

India collides with Asia about 40 million years ago

EXAMPLES OF MOUNTAINS

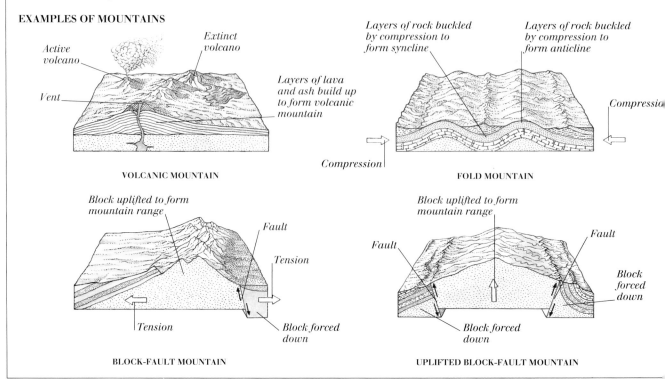

Active volcano

Extinct volcano

Vent

Layers of lava and ash build up to form volcanic mountain

Compression

VOLCANIC MOUNTAIN

Layers of rock buckled by compression to form syncline

Layers of rock buckled by compression to form anticline

Compressio

Compression

FOLD MOUNTAIN

Block uplifted to form mountain range

Fault

Tension

Tension

Block forced down

BLOCK-FAULT MOUNTAIN

Block uplifted to form mountain range

Fault

Fault

Block forced down

Block forced down

UPLIFTED BLOCK-FAULT MOUNTAIN

STAGES IN THE FORMATION OF THE HIMALAYAS

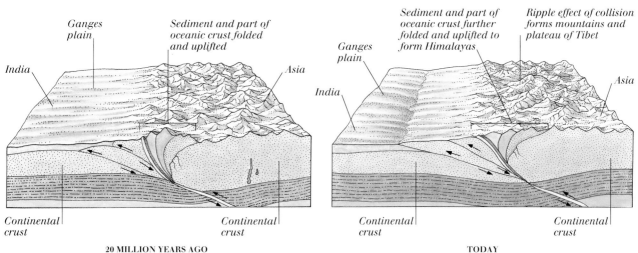

Sediment

Ocean area becomes smaller as plates converge

India moves towards Asia

Sediment

Asia

Volcano

Continental crust

Continental crust

Oceanic crust forced under continental crust

Magma rises to form volcanoes

60 MILLION YEARS AGO

Sediment and part of oceanic crust folded by continental collision

India

Asia

Continental crust

Oceanic crust forced further under continental crust

Continental crust

40 MILLION YEARS AGO

Ganges plain

Sediment and part of oceanic crust folded and uplifted

India

Asia

Continental crust

Continental crust

20 MILLION YEARS AGO

Sediment and part of oceanic crust further folded and uplifted to form Himalayas

Ripple effect of collision forms mountains and plateau of Tibet

Ganges plain

India

Asia

Continental crust

Continental crust

TODAY

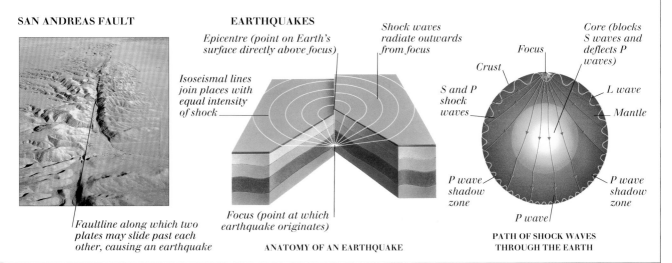

SAN ANDREAS FAULT

Faultline along which two plates may slide past each other, causing an earthquake

EARTHQUAKES

Epicentre (point on Earth's surface directly above focus)

Shock waves radiate outwards from focus

Isoseismal lines join places with equal intensity of shock

Focus (point at which earthquake originates)

ANATOMY OF AN EARTHQUAKE

Core (blocks S waves and deflects P waves)

Focus

Crust

L wave

S and P shock waves

Mantle

P wave shadow zone

P wave shadow zone

P wave

PATH OF SHOCK WAVES THROUGH THE EARTH

Precambrian to Devonian periods

WHEN THE EARTH FORMED about 4,600 million years ago, its atmosphere consisted of volcanic gases with little oxygen, making it hostile to most forms of life. One large supercontinent, Gondwanaland, was situated over the southern polar region, while other smaller continents were spread over the rest of the world. Constant movement of the earth's crustal plates carried continents across the earth's surface. The first primitive life-forms emerged around 3,400 million years ago in shallow, warm seas. The build up of oxygen began to form a shield of ozone around the earth, protecting living organisms from the sun's harmful rays and helping to establish an atmosphere in which life could sustain itself. The first vertebrates appeared about 470 million years ago, during the Ordovician period (510–439 million years ago), the first land plants appeared around 400 million years ago during the Devonian period (409–363 million years ago), and the first land animals about 30 million years later.

North America
South America
Greenland
China
Australia
South Africa
Africa
Scandinavia
Europe
Siberia
India
North East Africa
Central Asia

EXAMPLES OF PRECAMBRIAN TO DEVONIAN PLANT GROUPS

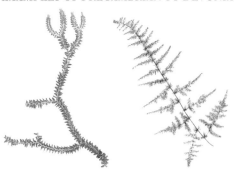

A PRESENT-DAY CLUBMOSS
(*Lycopodium sp.*)

A PRESENT-DAY LAND PLANT
(*Asparagus setaceous*)

FOSSIL OF AN EXTINCT LAND PLANT
(*Cooksonia hemisphaerica*)

FOSSIL OF AN EXTINCT SWAMP PLANT
(*Zosterophyllum llanoveranum*)

EXAMPLES OF PRECAMBRIAN TO DEVONIAN TRILOBITES

ACADAGNOSTUS
Family: Agnostidae
Length: 8 mm (⅓ in)

PHACOPS
Family: Phacopidae
Length: 4.5 cm (1¾ in)

OLENELLUS
Family: Olenellidae
Length: 6 cm (2½ in)

ELRATHIA
Family: Ptychopariidae
Length: 2 cm (¾ in)

THE EARTH DURING THE MIDDLE ORDOVICIAN PERIOD

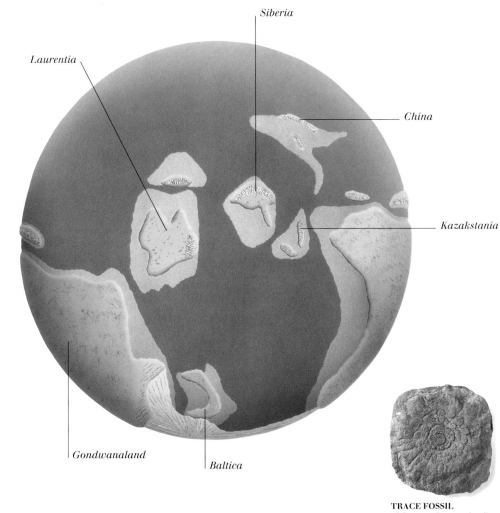

Siberia

Laurentia

China

Kazakstania

Gondwanaland

Baltica

FOSSIL NAUTILOID
(*Estonioceras
perforatum*)

FOSSIL BRACHIOPOD
(*Dicoelosia bilobata*)

TRACE FOSSIL
(*Mawsonites spriggi*)

FOSSIL GRAPTOLITE
(*Monograptus
convolutus*)

EXAMPLES OF DEVONIAN FISH

RHAMPHODOPSIS
Family: Ptyctodontidae
Length: 15 cm (6 in)

PTERASPIS
Family: Pteraspidae
Length: 25 cm (10 in)

COCCOSTEUS
Family: Coccosteidae
Length: 35 cm (14 in)

BOTHRIOLEPIS
Family: Bothriolepidae
Length: 40 cm (16 in)

CHEIRACANTHUS
Family: Acanthodidae
Length: 30 cm (12 in)

PTERICHTHYODES
Family: Asterolepidae
Length: 15 cm (6 in)

CHEIROLEPIS
Family: Cheirolepidae
Length: 17 cm (6¾ in)

CEPHALASPIS
Family: Cephalaspidae
Length: 22 cm (8¾ in)

Carboniferous to Permian periods

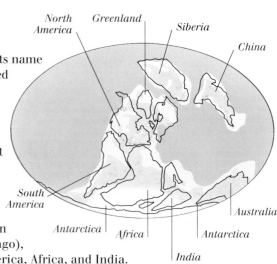

North America

Greenland

Siberia

China

South America

Antarctica

Africa

India

Australia

Antarctica

THE CARBONIFEROUS PERIOD (363–290 million years ago) takes its name from the thick, carbon-rich layers – now coal – that were produced during this period as swampy tropical forests were repeatedly drowned by shallow seas. The humid climate across northern and equatorial continents throughout Carboniferous times produced the first dense plant cover on Earth. During the early part of this period, the first reptiles appeared. Their development of a waterproof egg with a protective internal structure ended animal life's dependence on an aquatic environment. Towards the end of Carboniferous times, the earth's continents Laurasia and Gondwanaland collided, resulting in the huge land-mass of Pangaea. Glaciers smothered much of the southern hemisphere during the Permian period (290–245 million years ago), covering Antarctica, parts of Australia, and much of South America, Africa, and India. Ice locked up much of the world's water and large areas of the northern hemisphere experienced a drop in sea-level. Away from the poles, deserts and a hot dry climate predominated. As a result of these conditions, the Permian period ended with the greatest mass extinction of life on earth ever.

EXAMPLES OF CARBONIFEROUS AND PERMIAN PLANT GROUPS

A PRESENT-DAY FIR
(Abies concolor)

FOSSIL OF AN EXTINCT FERN
(Zeilleria frenzlii)

FOSSIL OF AN EXTINCT HORSETAIL
(Equisetites sp.)

FOSSIL OF AN EXTINCT CLUBMOSS
(Lepidodendron sp.)

EXAMPLES OF CARBONIFEROUS AND PERMIAN TREES

PECOPTERIS
Family: Marattiaceae
Height: 4 m (13 ft)

PARIPTERIS
Family: Medullosaceae
Height: 5 m (16 ft 6 in)

MARIOPTERIS
Family: Unclassified
Height: 5 m (16 ft 6 in)

MEDULLOSA
Family: Medullosaceae
Height: 5 m (16 ft 6 in)

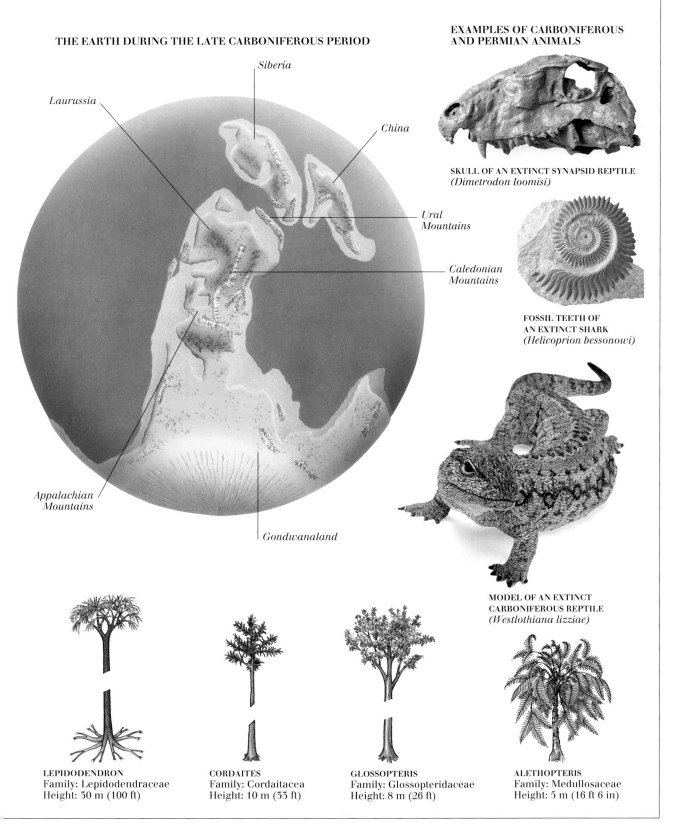

THE EARTH DURING THE LATE CARBONIFEROUS PERIOD

Siberia

Laurussia

China

Ural Mountains

Caledonian Mountains

Appalachian Mountains

Gondwanaland

EXAMPLES OF CARBONIFEROUS AND PERMIAN ANIMALS

SKULL OF AN EXTINCT SYNAPSID REPTILE
(*Dimetrodon loomisi*)

FOSSIL TEETH OF AN EXTINCT SHARK
(*Helicoprion bessonowi*)

MODEL OF AN EXTINCT CARBONIFEROUS REPTILE
(*Westlothiana lizziae*)

LEPIDODENDRON
Family: Lepidodendraceae
Height: 30 m (100 ft)

CORDAITES
Family: Cordaitacea
Height: 10 m (33 ft)

GLOSSOPTERIS
Family: Glossopteridaceae
Height: 8 m (26 ft)

ALETHOPTERIS
Family: Medullosaceae
Height: 5 m (16 ft 6 in)

Triassic period

THE TRIASSIC PERIOD (245–208 million years ago) marked the beginning of what is known as the Age of the Dinosaurs (the Mesozoic era). During this period, the present-day continents were massed together, forming one huge continent known as Pangaea. This land-mass experienced extremes of climate, with lush green areas around the coast or by lakes and rivers, and arid deserts in the interior. The only forms of plant life were non-flowering plants, such as conifers, ferns, cycads, and ginkgos; flowering plants had not yet evolved. The principal forms of animal life included primitive amphibians, rhynchosaurs ("beaked lizards"), and primitive crocodilians. Dinosaurs first appeared about 230 million years ago, at the beginning of the Late Triassic period. The earliest known dinosaurs were the carnivorous (flesh-eating) herrerasaurids and staurikosaurids, such as *Herrerasaurus* and *Staurikosaurus*. Early herbivorous (plant-eating) dinosaurs first appeared in Late Triassic times and included *Plateosaurus* and *Technosaurus*. By the end of the Triassic period, dinosaurs dominated Pangaea, possibly contributing to the extinction of many other reptiles.

TRIASSIC POSITIONS OF PRESENT-DAY LAND-MASSES

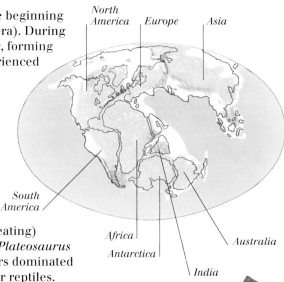

North America
Europe
Asia
South America
Africa
Antarctica
India
Australia

EXAMPLES OF TRIASSIC PLANT GROUPS

A PRESENT-DAY CYCAD
(*Cycas revoluta*)

A PRESENT-DAY GINKGO
(*Ginkgo biloba*)

A PRESENT-DAY CONIFER
(*Araucaria araucana*)

FOSSIL OF AN EXTINCT FERN
(*Pachypteris sp.*)

FOSSIL LEAF OF AN EXTINCT CYCAD
(*Cycas sp.*)

EXAMPLES OF TRIASSIC DINOSAURS

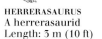

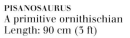

MELANOROSAURUS
A melanorosaurid
Length: 12.2 m (40 ft)

MUSSAURUS
A plateosaurid
Length: 2–3 m (6 ft 6 in–10 ft)

HERRERASAURUS
A herrerasaurid
Length: 3 m (10 ft)

PISANOSAURUS
A primitive ornithischian
Length: 90 cm (3 ft)

THE EARTH DURING THE TRIASSIC PERIOD

EXAMPLES OF TRIASSIC ANIMALS

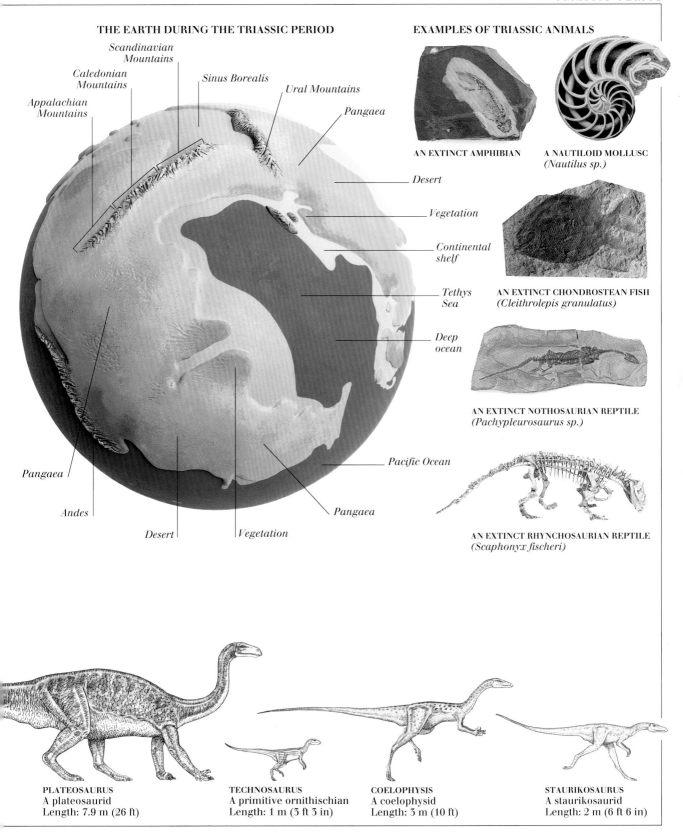

Scandinavian
Mountains

Caledonian
Mountains

Appalachian
Mountains

Sinus Borealis

Ural Mountains

Pangaea

Desert

Vegetation

Continental
shelf

Tethys
Sea

Deep
ocean

Pacific Ocean

Pangaea

Andes

Desert

Vegetation

Pangaea

AN EXTINCT AMPHIBIAN

A NAUTILOID MOLLUSC
(Nautilus sp.)

AN EXTINCT CHONDROSTEAN FISH
(Cleithrolepis granulatus)

AN EXTINCT NOTHOSAURIAN REPTILE
(Pachypleurosaurus sp.)

AN EXTINCT RHYNCHOSAURIAN REPTILE
(Scaphonyx fischeri)

PLATEOSAURUS
A plateosaurid
Length: 7.9 m (26 ft)

TECHNOSAURUS
A primitive ornithischian
Length: 1 m (3 ft 3 in)

COELOPHYSIS
A coelophysid
Length: 3 m (10 ft)

STAURIKOSAURUS
A staurikosaurid
Length: 2 m (6 ft 6 in)

Jurassic period

THE JURASSIC PERIOD, the middle part of the Mesozoic era, lasted from 208 to 146 million years ago. During Jurassic times, the land-mass of Pangaea broke up into the continents of Gondwanaland and Laurasia, and sea-levels rose, flooding areas of lower land. The Jurassic climate was warm and moist. Plants such as ginkgos, horsetails, and conifers thrived, and giant redwood trees appeared, as did the first flowering plants. The abundance of plant food coincided with the proliferation of herbivorous (plant-eating) dinosaurs, such as the large sauropods (e.g., *Diplodocus*) and stegosaurs (e.g., *Stegosaurus*). Carnivorous (flesh-eating) dinosaurs, such as *Compsognathus* and *Allosaurus*, also flourished by hunting the many animals that existed – among them other dinosaurs. Further Jurassic animals included shrew-like mammals, and pterosaurs (flying reptiles), as well as plesiosaurs and ichthyosaurs (both marine reptiles).

JURASSIC POSITIONS OF PRESENT-DAY LAND-MASSES

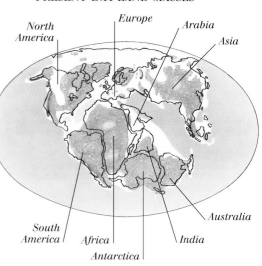

North America
Europe
Arabia
Asia
Australia
India
Antarctica
Africa
South America

EXAMPLES OF JURASSIC PLANT GROUPS

A PRESENT-DAY FERN
(*Dicksonia antarctica*)

A PRESENT-DAY HORSETAIL
(*Equisetum arvense*)

A PRESENT-DAY CONIFER
(*Taxus baccata*)

FOSSIL LEAF OF AN EXTINCT CONIFER
(*Taxus sp.*)

FOSSIL LEAF OF AN EXTINCT REDWOOD
(*Sequoiadendron affinis*)

EXAMPLES OF JURASSIC DINOSAURS

DIPLODOCUS
A diplodocid
Length: 26.8 m (88 ft)

CAMPTOSAURUS
A camptosaurid
Length: 4.9–7 m (16–23 ft)

DRYOSAURUS
A dryosaurid
Length: 3–4 m (10–13 ft)

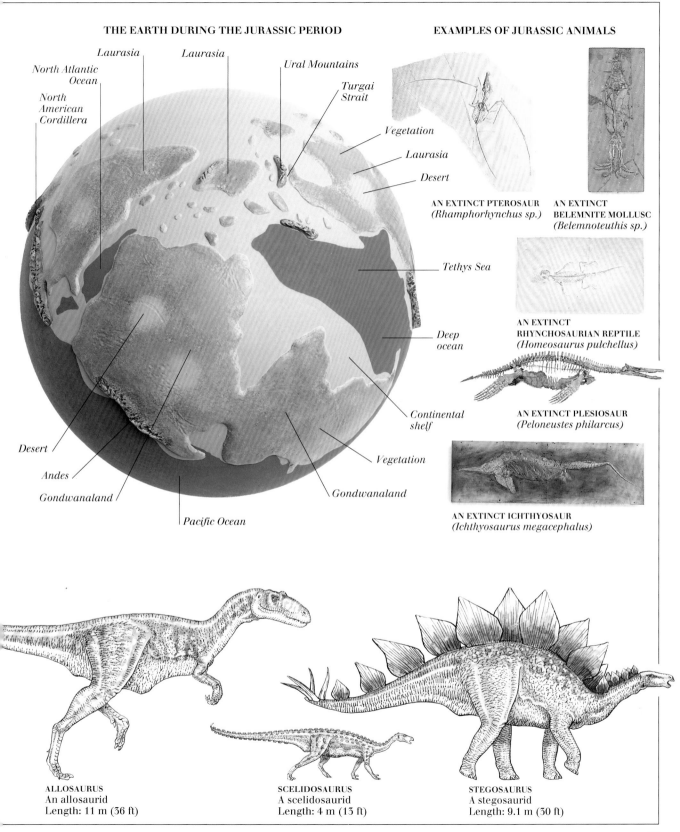

THE EARTH DURING THE JURASSIC PERIOD

North Atlantic Ocean

Laurasia

Laurasia

Ural Mountains

Turgai Strait

North American Cordillera

Vegetation

Laurasia

Desert

Tethys Sea

Deep ocean

Continental shelf

Desert

Vegetation

Andes

Gondwanaland

Gondwanaland

Pacific Ocean

EXAMPLES OF JURASSIC ANIMALS

AN EXTINCT PTEROSAUR
(*Rhamphorhynchus sp.*)

AN EXTINCT BELEMNITE MOLLUSC
(*Belemnoteuthis sp.*)

AN EXTINCT RHYNCHOSAURIAN REPTILE
(*Homeosaurus pulchellus*)

AN EXTINCT PLESIOSAUR
(*Peloneustes philarcus*)

AN EXTINCT ICHTHYOSAUR
(*Ichthyosaurus megacephalus*)

ALLOSAURUS
An allosaurid
Length: 11 m (36 ft)

SCELIDOSAURUS
A scelidosaurid
Length: 4 m (13 ft)

STEGOSAURUS
A stegosaurid
Length: 9.1 m (30 ft)

Cretaceous period

THE MESOZOIC ERA ENDED WITH the Cretaceous period, which lasted from 146 to 65 million years ago. During this period, Gondwanaland and Laurasia were breaking up into smaller land-masses that more closely resembled those of the modern continents. The climate remained mild and moist but the seasons became more marked. Flowering plants, including deciduous trees, replaced many cycads, seed ferns, and conifers. Animal species became more varied, with the evolution of new mammals, insects, fish, crustaceans, and turtles. Dinosaurs evolved into a wide variety of species during Cretaceous times; more than half of all known dinosaurs – including *Iguanodon*, *Deinonychus*, *Tyrannosaurus*, and *Hypsilophodon* – lived during this period. At the end of the Cretaceous period, however, dinosaurs became extinct. The reason for this mass extinction is unknown but it is thought to have been caused by climatic changes due to either a catastrophic meteor impact with the Earth or extensive volcanic eruptions.

CRETACEOUS POSITIONS OF PRESENT-DAY LAND-MASSES

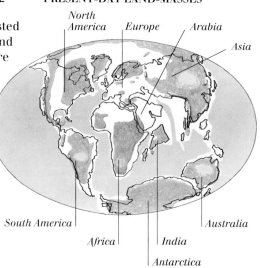

North America
Europe
Arabia
Asia
South America
Africa
India
Antarctica
Australia

EXAMPLES OF CRETACEOUS PLANT GROUPS

A PRESENT-DAY CONIFER
(*Pinus muricata*)

A PRESENT-DAY DECIDUOUS TREE
(*Magnolia sp.*)

FOSSIL OF AN EXTINCT FERN
(*Sphenopteris latiloba*)

FOSSIL OF AN EXTINCT GINKGO
(*Ginkgo pluripartita*)

FOSSIL LEAVES OF AN EXTINCT DECIDUOUS TREE
(*Cercidyphyllum sp.*)

EXAMPLES OF CRETACEOUS DINOSAURS

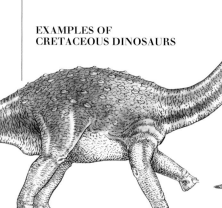

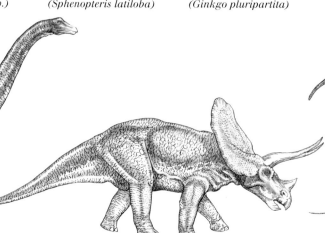

SALTASAURUS
A titanosaurid
Length: 12.2 m (40 ft)

TOROSAURUS
A ceratopsid
Length: 7.6 m (25 ft)

HYPSILOPHODON
A hypsilophodontid
Length: 1.4–2.3 m (4 ft 6 in–7 ft 6 in)

THE EARTH DURING THE CRETACEOUS PERIOD

EXAMPLES OF CRETACEOUS ANIMALS

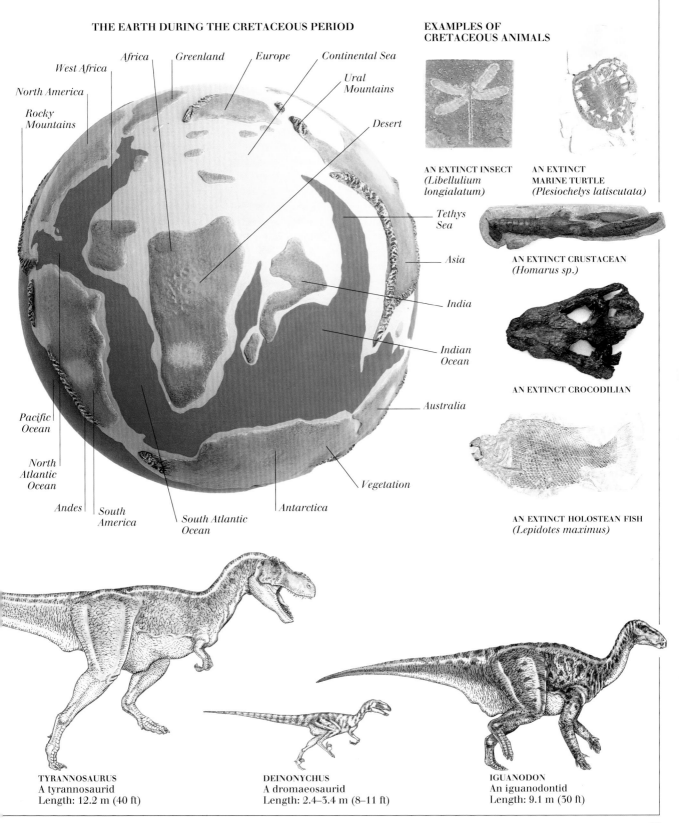

West Africa

Africa

Greenland

Europe

Continental Sea

North America

Ural Mountains

Rocky Mountains

Desert

Tethys Sea

Asia

India

Indian Ocean

Pacific Ocean

Australia

North Atlantic Ocean

Andes

South America

South Atlantic Ocean

Antarctica

Vegetation

AN EXTINCT INSECT
(*Libellulium longialatum*)

AN EXTINCT MARINE TURTLE
(*Plesiochelys latiscutata*)

AN EXTINCT CRUSTACEAN
(*Homarus sp.*)

AN EXTINCT CROCODILIAN

AN EXTINCT HOLOSTEAN FISH
(*Lepidotes maximus*)

TYRANNOSAURUS
A tyrannosaurid
Length: 12.2 m (40 ft)

DEINONYCHUS
A dromaeosaurid
Length: 2.4–3.4 m (8–11 ft)

IGUANODON
An iguanodontid
Length: 9.1 m (30 ft)

Tertiary period

FOLLOWING THE DEMISE OF THE DINOSAURS at the end of the Cretaceous period, the Tertiary period (65–1.6 million years ago), which formed the first part of the Cenozoic era (65 million years ago–present), was characterized by a huge expansion of mammal life. Placental mammals nourish and maintain the young in the mother's uterus; only three orders of placental mammals existed during Cretaceous times, compared with 25 orders during the Tertiary period. One of these 25 included the first hominid (see pp.108–109), *Australopithecus*, which appeared in Africa. By the beginning of the Tertiary period, the continents had almost reached their present position. The Tethys Sea, which had separated the northern continents from Africa and India, began to close up, forming the Mediterranean Sea and allowing the migration of terrestrial animals between Africa and western Europe. India's collision with Asia led to the formation of the Himalayas. During the middle part of the Tertiary period, the forest-dwelling and browsing mammals were replaced by mammals such as the horse, better suited to grazing the open savannahs that began to dominate. Repeated cool periods throughout the Tertiary period established the Antarctic as an icy island continent.

TERTIARY POSITIONS OF PRESENT-DAY LAND-MASSES

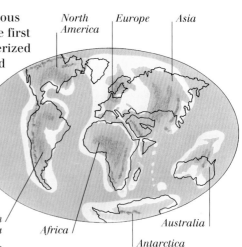

North America

Europe

Asia

South America

Africa

Australia

Antarctica

EXAMPLES OF TERTIARY PLANT GROUPS

A PRESENT-DAY OAK
(*Quercus palustris*)

A PRESENT-DAY BIRCH
(*Betula grossa*)

FOSSIL LEAF OF AN EXTINCT BIRCH
(*Betulites sp.*)

FOSSILIZED STEM OF AN EXTINCT PALM
(*Palmoxylon sp.*)

EXAMPLES OF TERTIARY ANIMAL GROUPS

HYAENODON
An hyaenodontid
Length: 2 m (6 ft 6 in)

TITANOHYRAX
A pliohyracid
Length: 2 m (6 ft 6 in)

PHORUSRHACUS
A phorusrhacid
Length: 1.5 m (5 ft)

SAMOTHERIUM
A giraffid
Length: 3 m (10 ft)

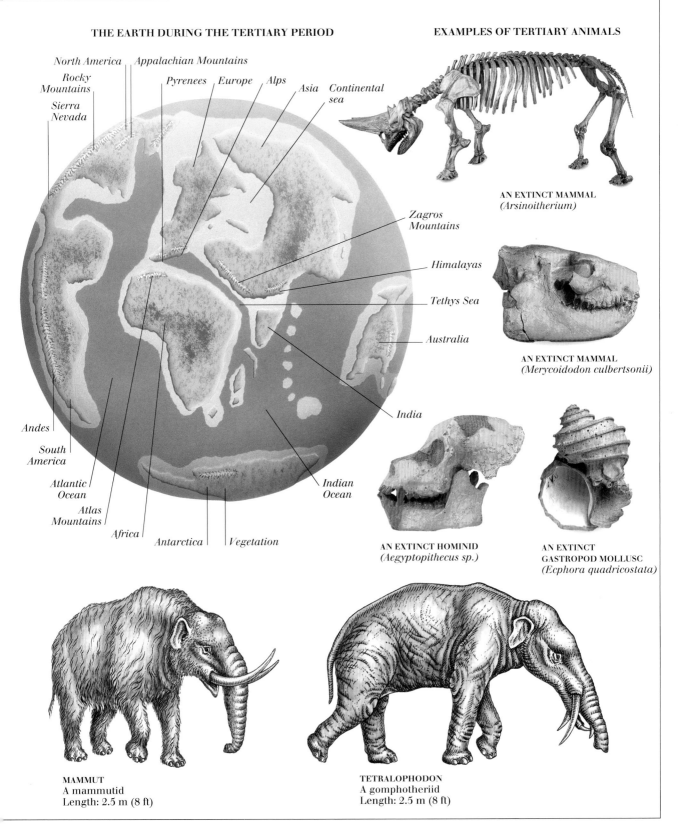

THE EARTH DURING THE TERTIARY PERIOD

North America
Appalachian Mountains
Rocky Mountains
Pyrenees
Europe
Alps
Asia
Continental sea
Sierra Nevada
Zagros Mountains
Himalayas
Tethys Sea
Australia
India
Andes
South America
Atlantic Ocean
Atlas Mountains
Africa
Antarctica
Vegetation
Indian Ocean

EXAMPLES OF TERTIARY ANIMALS

AN EXTINCT MAMMAL
(Arsinoitherium)

AN EXTINCT MAMMAL
(Merycoidodon culbertsonii)

AN EXTINCT HOMINID
(Aegyptopithecus sp.)

AN EXTINCT
GASTROPOD MOLLUSC
(Ecphora quadricostata)

MAMMUT
A mammutid
Length: 2.5 m (8 ft)

TETRALOPHODON
A gomphotheriid
Length: 2.5 m (8 ft)

Quaternary period

THE QUATERNARY PERIOD (1.6 million years ago–present) forms the second part of the Cenozoic era (65 million years ago–present): it has been characterized by alternating cold (glacial) and warm (interglacial) periods. During cold periods, ice sheets and glaciers have formed repeatedly on northern and southern continents. The cold environments in North America and Eurasia, and to a lesser extent in southern South America and parts of Australia, have caused the migration of many life forms towards the Equator. Only the specialized ice age mammals such as *Mammuthus* and *Coelodonta*, with their thick wool and fat insulation, were suited to life in very cold climates. Humans developed throughout the Pleistocene period (1.6 million–10,000 years ago) in Africa and migrated northward into Europe and Asia. Modern humans, *Homo sapiens*, lived on the cold European continent 30,000 years ago and hunted mammals. The end of the last ice age and the climatic changes that occurred about 10,000 years ago brought extinction to many Pleistocene mammals, but enabled humans to flourish.

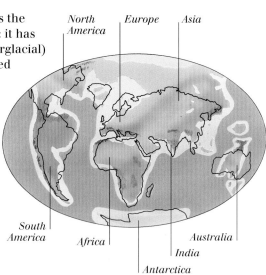

North America
Europe
Asia
South America
Africa
India
Antarctica
Australia

EXAMPLES OF QUATERNARY PLANT GROUPS

A PRESENT-DAY BIRCH
(*Betula lenta*)

A PRESENT-DAY SWEETGUM
(*Liquidambar styraciflua*)

FOSSIL LEAF OF A SWEETGUM
(*Liquidambar europeanum*)

FOSSIL LEAF OF A BIRCH
(*Betula sp.*)

EXAMPLES OF QUATERNARY ANIMAL GROUPS

PROCOPTODON
A macropodid
Length: 3 m (10 ft)

DIPROTODON
A diprotodontid
Length: 3 m (10 ft)

TOXODON
A toxodontid
Length: 3 m (10 ft)

MAMMUTHUS
An elephantid
Length: 3 m (10 ft)

THE EARTH DURING THE QUATERNARY PERIOD

EXAMPLES OF QUATERNARY ANIMALS

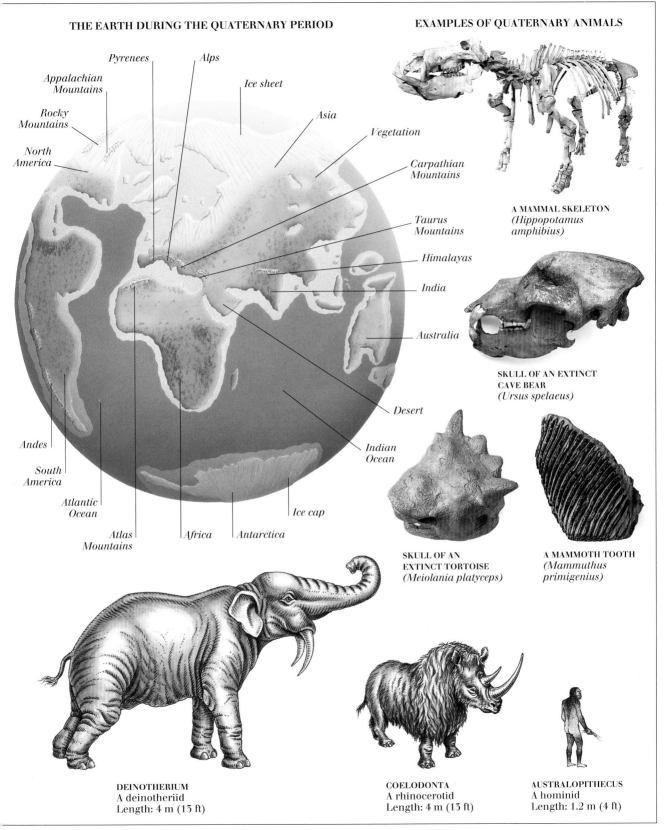

Appalachian Mountains

Rocky Mountains

North America

Pyrenees

Alps

Ice sheet

Asia

Vegetation

Carpathian Mountains

Taurus Mountains

Himalayas

India

Australia

Desert

Indian Ocean

Andes

South America

Atlantic Ocean

Atlas Mountains

Africa

Antarctica

Ice cap

A MAMMAL SKELETON
(Hippopotamus amphibius)

SKULL OF AN EXTINCT CAVE BEAR
(Ursus spelaeus)

SKULL OF AN EXTINCT TORTOISE
(Meiolania platyceps)

A MAMMOTH TOOTH
(Mammuthus primigenius)

DEINOTHERIUM
A deinotheriid
Length: 4 m (13 ft)

COELODONTA
A rhinocerotid
Length: 4 m (13 ft)

AUSTRALOPITHECUS
A hominid
Length: 1.2 m (4 ft)

Early signs of life

FOR ALMOST A THOUSAND MILLION YEARS after its formation, there was no known life on Earth. The first simple, sea-dwelling organic structures appeared about 3,500 million years ago; they may have formed when certain chemical molecules joined together. Prokaryotes, single-celled micro-organisms such as blue-green algae, were able to photosynthesize (see pp. 138–139), and thus produce oxygen. A thousand million years later, sufficient oxygen had built up in the earth's atmosphere to allow multicellular organisms to proliferate in the Precambrian seas (before 570 million years ago). Soft-bodied jellyfish, corals, and seaworms flourished about 700 million years ago. Trilobites, the first animals with hard body frames, developed during the Cambrian period (570–510 million years ago). However, it was not until the beginning of the Devonian period (409–363 million years ago) that early land plants, such as *Asteroxylon*, formed a water-retaining cuticle, which ended their dependence on an aquatic environment. About 360 million years ago, the first amphibians (see pp. 80–81) crawled onto the land, although they still returned to the water to lay their soft eggs. Not until the emergence of the first reptiles would animals with backbones appear that were independent of water in this way.

STROMATOLITIC LIMESTONE

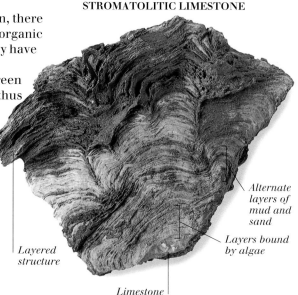

Alternate layers of mud and sand

Layers bound by algae

Layered structure

Limestone

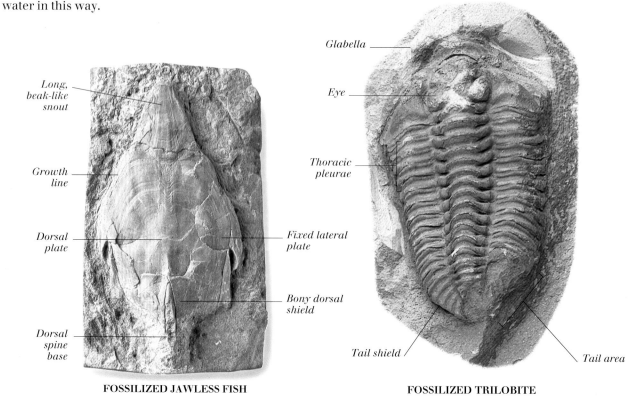

Long, beak-like snout

Growth line

Dorsal plate

Dorsal spine base

FOSSILIZED JAWLESS FISH

Glabella

Eye

Thoracic pleurae

Fixed lateral plate

Bony dorsal shield

Tail shield

Tail area

FOSSILIZED TRILOBITE

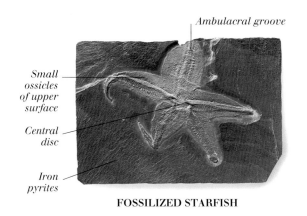

Ambulacral groove

Small ossicles of upper surface

Central disc

Iron pyrites

FOSSILIZED STARFISH

Row of ossicles

Broad disc

Row of ossicles

Short arm

UPPER SURFACE OF FOSSILIZED STARFISH

LOWER SURFACE OF FOSSILIZED STARFISH

Jointed leg

Chelicera (jointed pincer)

Jointed leg with oar-shaped paddle

Segmented abdomen

UNDERSIDE OF FOSSILIZED EURYPTERID

Telson (tail spine)

Shell contains eight somites (thoracic segments)

Abdominal segments

Hingeless, bivalved shell

FOSSIL OF AN EXTINCT SHRIMP

Growing tip

Disc-shaped sporangium (spore-case)

Leaf-like scale

Stem

RECONSTRUCTION OF ASTEROXYLON

Amphibians and reptiles

THE EARLIEST KNOWN AMPHIBIANS, such as *Acanthostega* and *Ichthyostega*, lived about 363 million years ago at the end of the Devonian period (409–363 million years ago). Their limbs may have evolved from the muscular fins of lungfish-like creatures. These fish can use their fins to push themselves along the bottom of lakes and some can breathe at the water's surface. While amphibians (see pp. 182–183) can exist on land, they are dependent on a wet environment because their skin does not retain moisture and they must return to the water to lay their eggs. Evolving from amphibians, reptiles (see pp. 184–187) first appeared during the Carboniferous period (363–290 million years ago): *Westlothiana*, a possible early reptile, lived on land 338 million years ago. The development of the amniotic egg, with an embryo enclosed in its own wet environment (the amnion) and protected by a waterproof shell, freed reptiles from the amphibian's dependence on a wet habitat. A scaly skin protected the reptile from desiccation on land and enabled it to exploit ways of life closed to its amphibian ancestors. Reptiles include the dinosaurs, which came to dominate life on land during the Mesozoic era (245–65 million years ago).

FOSSIL SKULL OF ACANTHOSTEGA

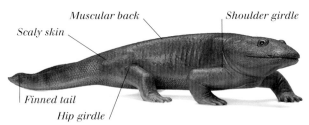

MODEL OF ICHTHYOSTEGA

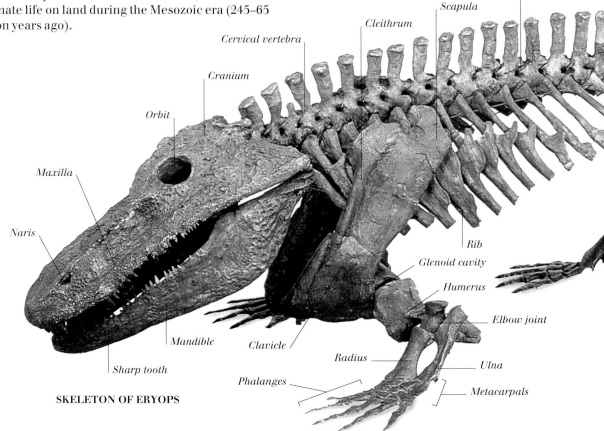

SKELETON OF ERYOPS

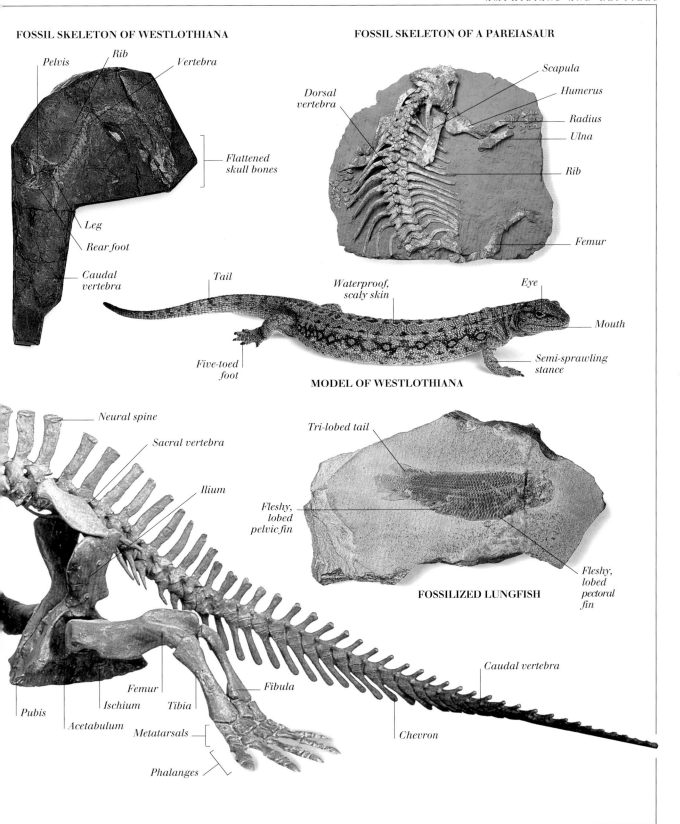

FOSSIL SKELETON OF WESTLOTHIANA

Pelvis

Rib

Vertebra

Flattened
skull bones

Leg

Rear foot

Caudal
vertebra

FOSSIL SKELETON OF A PAREIASAUR

Scapula

Humerus

Radius

Ulna

Rib

Dorsal
vertebra

Femur

Tail

Waterproof,
scaly skin

Eye

Mouth

Semi-sprawling
stance

Five-toed
foot

MODEL OF WESTLOTHIANA

Neural spine

Sacral vertebra

Ilium

Tri-lobed tail

Fleshy,
lobed
pelvic fin

Fleshy,
lobed
pectoral
fin

FOSSILIZED LUNGFISH

Pubis

Acetabulum

Femur

Ischium

Tibia

Metatarsals

Phalanges

Fibula

Chevron

Caudal vertebra

The dinosaurs

THE DINOSAURS WERE A LARGE GROUP of reptiles that were the dominant land vertebrates (animals with backbones) for most of the Mesozoic era (245–65 million years ago). They appeared some 230 million years ago and were distinguished from other scaly, egg-laying reptiles by an important feature: dinosaurs had an erect limb stance. This enabled them to keep their bodies well above the ground, unlike the sprawling and semi-sprawling stance of other reptiles. The head of the dinosaur's femur (thigh-bone) fitted into a socket in its pelvis (hip-bone), producing efficient and mobile locomotion. Dinosaurs are categorized into two groups according to the structure of their pelvis: saurischian (lizard-hipped) and ornithischian (bird-hipped) dinosaurs. In the case of most saurischians, the pubis (part of the pelvis) jutted forward, while in ornithischians it slanted back, parallel to the ischium (another part of the pelvis). Dinosaurs ranged in size from smaller than a domestic cat to the biggest land animals ever known. The Dinosauria were the most successful land vertebrates ever, and survived for 165 million years, until their extinction 65 million years ago.

STRUCTURE OF SAURISCHIAN PELVIS

Ilium
Postacetabular process
Ilio-ischial joint
Ischium
Hook of preacetabular process
Ilio-pubic joint
Acetabulum
Pubis
Pubic foot

GALLIMIMUS
A saurischian dinosaur

POSITION OF PELVIS IN A SAURISCHIAN DINOSAUR

STRUCTURE OF ORNITHISCHIAN PELVIS

Ilium
Postacetabular process
Ilio-ischial joint
Ischium
Pubis
Acetabulum
Preacetabular process
Ilio-pubic joint
Prepubis

HYPSILOPHODON
An ornithischian dinosaur

POSITION OF PELVIS IN AN ORNITHISCHIAN DINOSAUR

BAROSAURUS
A saurischian dinosaur

COMPARISON OF ANIMAL STANCES

SPRAWLING STANCE
The thighs and upper arms project straight out from the body so that the knees and elbows are bent at right angles.

COMMON IGUANA
(Iguana iguana)
A present-day reptile

ERECT STANCE
The thighs and upper arms project straight down from the body so that the knees and elbows are straight.

SEMI-SPRAWLING STANCE
The thighs and upper arms project downwards and outwards so that the knees and elbows are slightly bent.

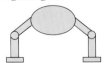

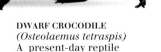

DWARF CROCODILE
(Osteolaemus tetraspis)
A present-day reptile

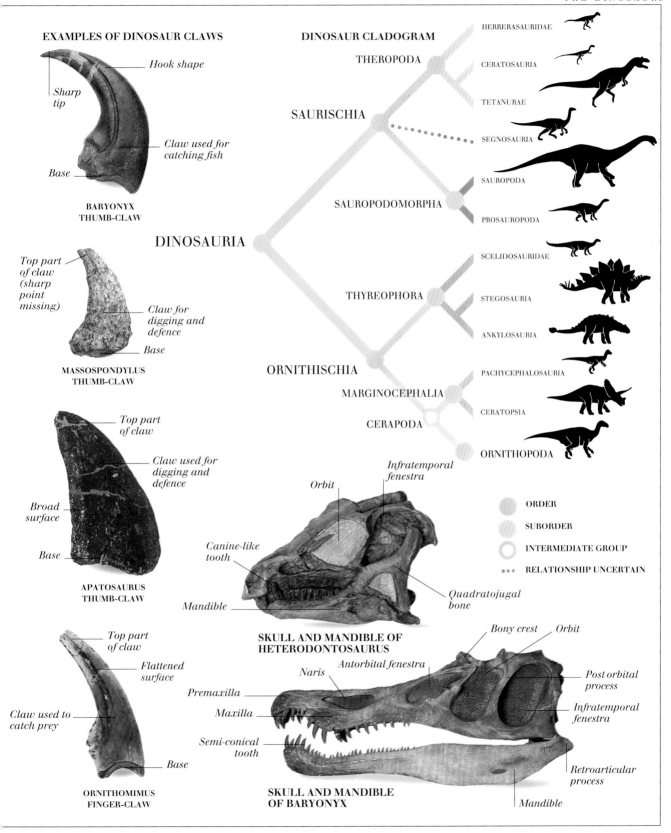

EXAMPLES OF DINOSAUR CLAWS

BARYONYX THUMB-CLAW

- Hook shape
- Sharp tip
- Claw used for catching fish
- Base

MASSOSPONDYLUS THUMB-CLAW

- Top part of claw (sharp point missing)
- Claw for digging and defence
- Base

APATOSAURUS THUMB-CLAW

- Top part of claw
- Claw used for digging and defence
- Broad surface
- Base

ORNITHOMIMUS FINGER-CLAW

- Top part of claw
- Flattened surface
- Claw used to catch prey
- Base

DINOSAUR CLADOGRAM

HERRERASAURIDAE

THEROPODA
- CERATOSAURIA
- TETANURAE

SAURISCHIA
- SEGNOSAURIA

SAUROPODOMORPHA
- SAUROPODA
- PROSAUROPODA

DINOSAURIA

THYREOPHORA
- SCELIDOSAURIDAE
- STEGOSAURIA
- ANKYLOSAURIA

ORNITHISCHIA

MARGINOCEPHALIA
- PACHYCEPHALOSAURIA
- CERATOPSIA

CERAPODA

ORNITHOPODA

- ORDER
- SUBORDER
- INTERMEDIATE GROUP
- ••• RELATIONSHIP UNCERTAIN

SKULL AND MANDIBLE OF HETERODONTOSAURUS

- Infratemporal fenestra
- Orbit
- Canine-like tooth
- Mandible
- Quadratojugal bone

SKULL AND MANDIBLE OF BARYONYX

- Bony crest
- Orbit
- Antorbital fenestra
- Naris
- Premaxilla
- Maxilla
- Semi-conical tooth
- Post orbital process
- Infratemporal fenestra
- Retroarticular process
- Mandible

Theropods 1

AN ENORMOUSLY SUCCESSFUL SUBORDER of the Saurischia, the bipedal (two-footed) theropods ("beast feet") emerged 230 million years ago in Late Triassic times; the oldest known example comes from South America. Theropods spanned the whole of the Age of the Dinosaurs (230–65 million years ago) and included most of the known predatory dinosaurs. The typical theropod had small arms with sharp, clawed fingers; powerful jaws lined with sharp teeth; an S-shaped neck; long, muscular hind limbs; and clawed, usually four-toed feet. Many theropods may have been warm-blooded; most were exclusively carnivorous. Theropods ranged from animals no larger than a chicken to huge creatures, such as Tyrannosaurus and Baryonyx. The group also included ostrich-like omnivores and herbivores with toothless beaks, such as Struthiomimus and Gallimimus. Many scientists believe that birds are the closest living relatives to the dinosaurs, and share a common ancestor with the theropods. Archaeopteryx, small and feathered, was the first known bird and lived alongside its dinosaur relatives.

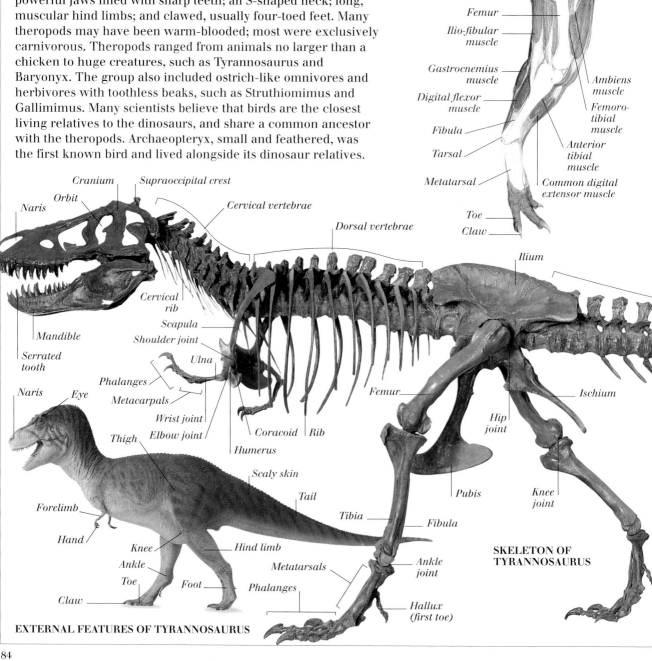

INTERNAL ANATOMY OF ALBERTOSAURUS LEG

Ilio-tibial muscle
Ilio-femoral muscle
Femoro-tibial muscle
Internal tibial flexor muscle
Femur
Ilio-fibular muscle
Gastrocnemius muscle
Digital flexor muscle
Fibula
Tarsal
Metatarsal
Ambiens muscle
Femoro-tibial muscle
Anterior tibial muscle
Common digital extensor muscle
Toe
Claw

Cranium
Orbit
Naris
Supraoccipital crest
Cervical vertebrae
Dorsal vertebrae
Ilium
Cervical rib
Scapula
Mandible
Shoulder joint
Serrated tooth
Ulna
Phalanges
Metacarpals
Wrist joint
Elbow joint
Coracoid
Rib
Humerus
Femur
Ischium
Hip joint
Naris
Eye
Thigh
Scaly skin
Tail
Forelimb
Hand
Knee
Ankle
Toe
Hind limb
Tibia
Fibula
Pubis
Knee joint
Foot
Metatarsals
Phalanges
Ankle joint
Claw
Hallux (first toe)

SKELETON OF TYRANNOSAURUS

EXTERNAL FEATURES OF TYRANNOSAURUS

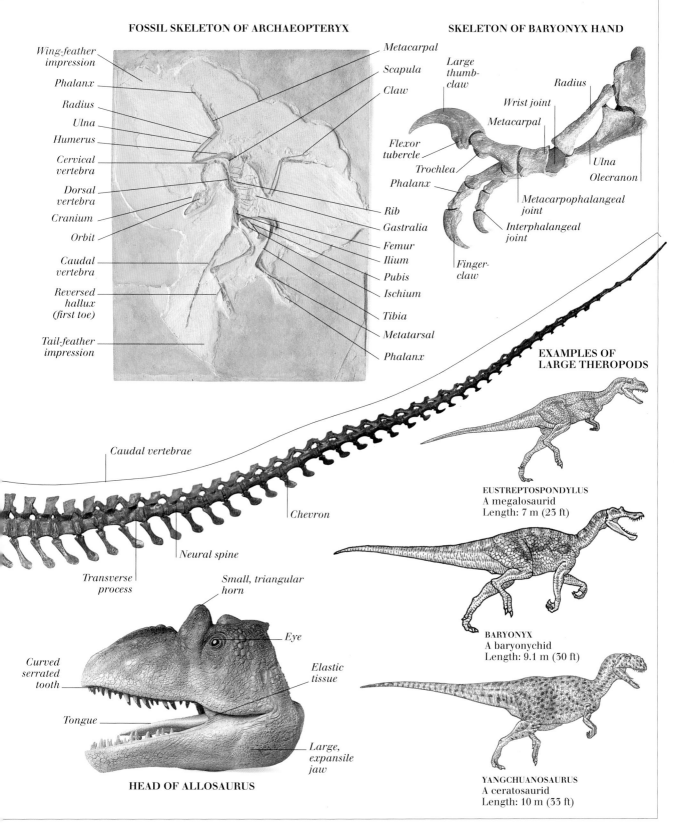

FOSSIL SKELETON OF ARCHAEOPTERYX

Wing-feather impression
Phalanx
Radius
Ulna
Humerus
Cervical vertebra
Dorsal vertebra
Cranium
Orbit
Caudal vertebra
Reversed hallux (first toe)
Tail-feather impression

Metacarpal
Scapula
Claw

Rib
Gastralia
Femur
Ilium
Pubis
Ischium
Tibia
Metatarsal
Phalanx

SKELETON OF BARYONYX HAND

Large thumb-claw
Flexor tubercle
Trochlea
Phalanx
Finger-claw

Wrist joint
Metacarpal
Radius
Ulna
Olecranon
Metacarpophalangeal joint
Interphalangeal joint

Caudal vertebrae
Chevron
Neural spine
Transverse process

EXAMPLES OF LARGE THEROPODS

EUSTREPTOSPONDYLUS
A megalosaurid
Length: 7 m (23 ft)

BARYONYX
A baryonychid
Length: 9.1 m (30 ft)

YANGCHUANOSAURUS
A ceratosaurid
Length: 10 m (33 ft)

Small, triangular horn
Eye
Curved serrated tooth
Elastic tissue
Tongue
Large, expansile jaw

HEAD OF ALLOSAURUS

Theropods 2

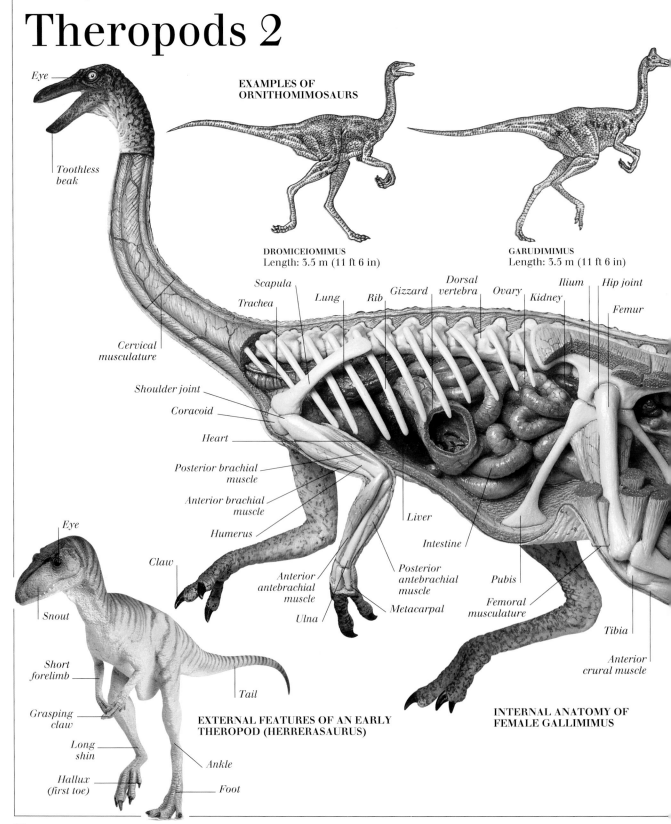

Eye

Toothless beak

EXAMPLES OF ORNITHOMIMOSAURS

DROMICEIOMIMUS
Length: 3.5 m (11 ft 6 in)

GARUDIMIMUS
Length: 3.5 m (11 ft 6 in)

Cervical musculature

Scapula

Trachea

Lung

Rib

Gizzard

Dorsal vertebra

Ovary

Kidney

Ilium

Hip joint

Femur

Shoulder joint

Coracoid

Heart

Posterior brachial muscle

Anterior brachial muscle

Humerus

Liver

Intestine

Anterior antebrachial muscle

Posterior antebrachial muscle

Ulna

Metacarpal

Pubis

Femoral musculature

Tibia

Anterior crural muscle

Eye

Snout

Short forelimb

Grasping claw

Long shin

Hallux (first toe)

Claw

Tail

Ankle

Foot

EXTERNAL FEATURES OF AN EARLY THEROPOD (HERRERASAURUS)

INTERNAL ANATOMY OF FEMALE GALLIMIMUS

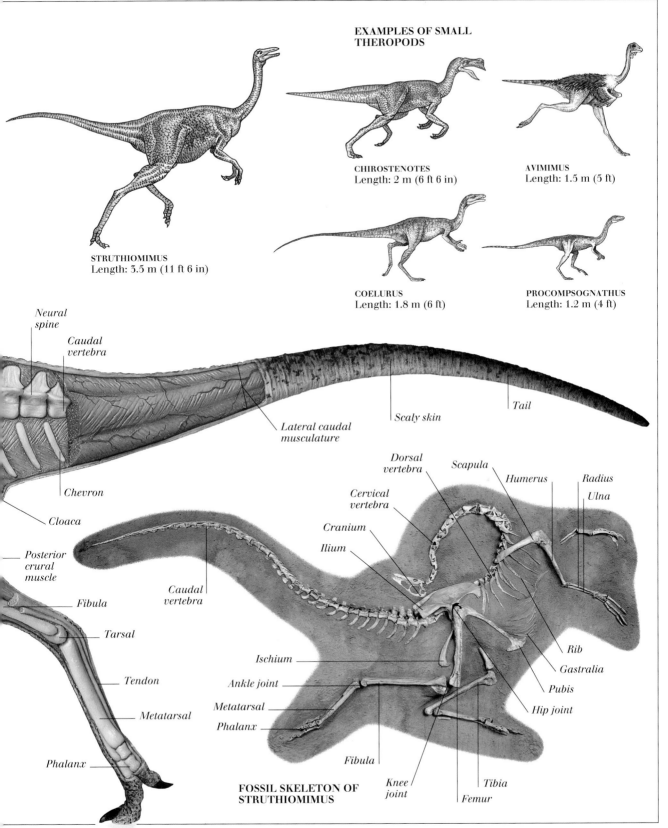

EXAMPLES OF SMALL THEROPODS

CHIROSTENOTES
Length: 2 m (6 ft 6 in)

AVIMIMUS
Length: 1.5 m (5 ft)

STRUTHIOMIMUS
Length: 3.5 m (11 ft 6 in)

COELURUS
Length: 1.8 m (6 ft)

PROCOMPSOGNATHUS
Length: 1.2 m (4 ft)

Neural spine

Caudal vertebra

Lateral caudal musculature

Scaly skin

Tail

Chevron

Cloaca

Dorsal vertebra

Scapula

Humerus

Radius

Cervical vertebra

Ulna

Cranium

Ilium

Posterior crural muscle

Caudal vertebra

Fibula

Rib

Tarsal

Gastralia

Ischium

Pubis

Tendon

Ankle joint

Hip joint

Metatarsal

Metatarsal

Phalanx

Phalanx

Fibula

Tibia

Knee joint

Femur

FOSSIL SKELETON OF STRUTHIOMIMUS

Sauropodomorphs 1

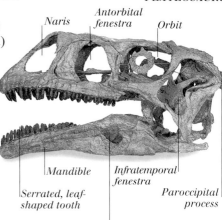

THE SAUROPODOMORPHA ("lizard-feet forms") were herbivorous, usually quadrupedal (four-footed) dinosaurs. A suborder of the Saurischia, they were characterized by small heads, bulky bodies, and long necks and tails. There were two infraorders: prosauropods and sauropods.

THECODONTOSAURUS

Prosauropods lived from Late Triassic to Early Jurassic times (225–180 million years ago) and included beasts such as the small *Anchisaurus* and one of the first very large dinosaurs, *Plateosaurus*. By Middle Jurassic times (about 165 million years ago), sauropods had replaced prosauropods and spread worldwide. They included the heaviest and longest land animals ever, such as *Diplodocus* and *Brachiosaurus*. Sauropods persisted to the end of the Cretaceous period (65 million years ago). Many of these dinosaurs moved in herds, protected from predatory theropods by their huge bulk and powerful tails, which they could use to lash out at attackers. Sauropodomorphs were the most common large herbivores until Late Jurassic times (about 145 million years ago), and appear to have survived in southern continents long after they had disappeared from the north.

SKELETON OF PLATEOSAURUS

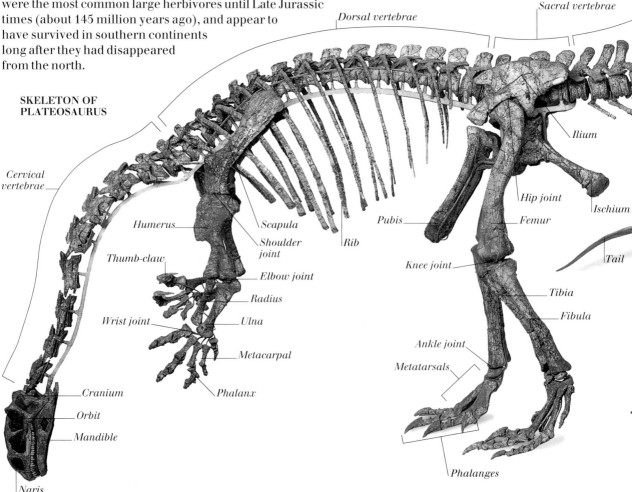

Skull and mandible labels: Naris, Antorbital fenestra, Orbit, Mandible, Serrated, leaf-shaped tooth, Infratemporal fenestra, Paroccipital process, Mandibular fenestra

Skeleton labels: Dorsal vertebrae, Sacral vertebrae, Cervical vertebrae, Humerus, Scapula, Shoulder joint, Rib, Ilium, Hip joint, Ischium, Pubis, Femur, Tail, Thumb-claw, Elbow joint, Knee joint, Radius, Tibia, Wrist joint, Ulna, Fibula, Metacarpal, Ankle joint, Metatarsals, Cranium, Phalanx, Orbit, Mandible, Phalanges, Naris

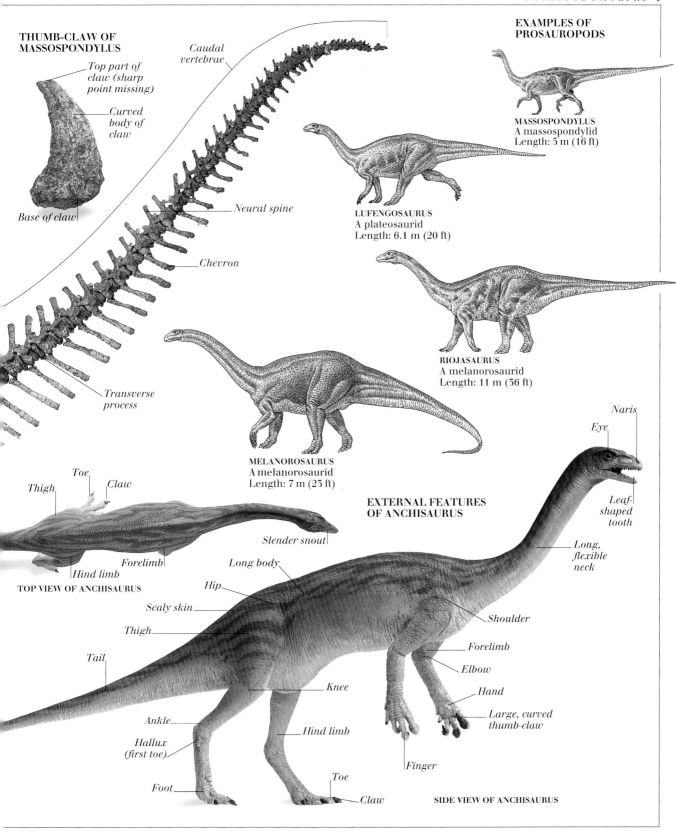

THUMB-CLAW OF MASSOSPONDYLUS

Top part of claw (sharp point missing)

Curved body of claw

Base of claw

Caudal vertebrae

Neural spine

Chevron

Transverse process

EXAMPLES OF PROSAUROPODS

MASSOSPONDYLUS
A massospondylid
Length: 5 m (16 ft)

LUFENGOSAURUS
A plateosaurid
Length: 6.1 m (20 ft)

RIOJASAURUS
A melanorosaurid
Length: 11 m (36 ft)

MELANOROSAURUS
A melanorosaurid
Length: 7 m (23 ft)

EXTERNAL FEATURES OF ANCHISAURUS

Naris

Eye

Leaf-shaped tooth

Long, flexible neck

Shoulder

Forelimb

Elbow

Hand

Large, curved thumb-claw

Finger

Hind limb

Knee

Hip

Long body

Scaly skin

Thigh

Tail

Ankle

Hallux (first toe)

Foot

Toe

Claw

SIDE VIEW OF ANCHISAURUS

Toe

Claw

Thigh

Forelimb

Hind limb

Slender snout

TOP VIEW OF ANCHISAURUS

Sauropodomorphs 2

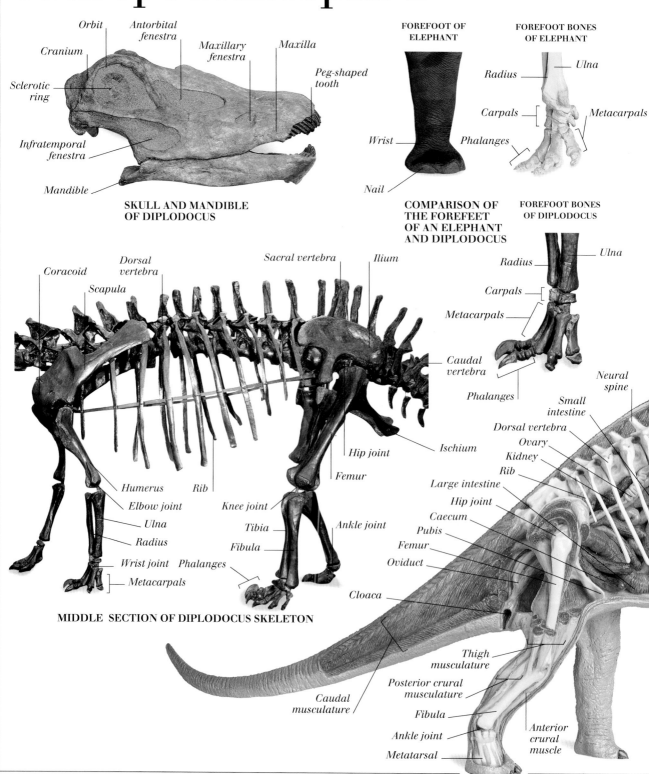

SKULL AND MANDIBLE OF DIPLODOCUS

Orbit

Cranium

Antorbital fenestra

Maxillary fenestra

Maxilla

Peg-shaped tooth

Sclerotic ring

Infratemporal fenestra

Mandible

FOREFOOT OF ELEPHANT

Wrist

Nail

FOREFOOT BONES OF ELEPHANT

Radius

Ulna

Carpals

Metacarpals

Phalanges

COMPARISON OF THE FOREFEET OF AN ELEPHANT AND DIPLODOCUS

FOREFOOT BONES OF DIPLODOCUS

Radius

Ulna

Carpals

Metacarpals

Phalanges

Coracoid

Dorsal vertebra

Scapula

Sacral vertebra

Ilium

Caudal vertebra

Hip joint

Ischium

Femur

Humerus

Rib

Elbow joint

Knee joint

Ulna

Tibia

Ankle joint

Radius

Fibula

Wrist joint

Phalanges

Metacarpals

MIDDLE SECTION OF DIPLODOCUS SKELETON

Neural spine

Small intestine

Dorsal vertebra

Ovary

Kidney

Rib

Large intestine

Hip joint

Caecum

Pubis

Femur

Oviduct

Cloaca

Caudal musculature

Thigh musculature

Posterior crural musculature

Fibula

Ankle joint

Anterior crural muscle

Metatarsal

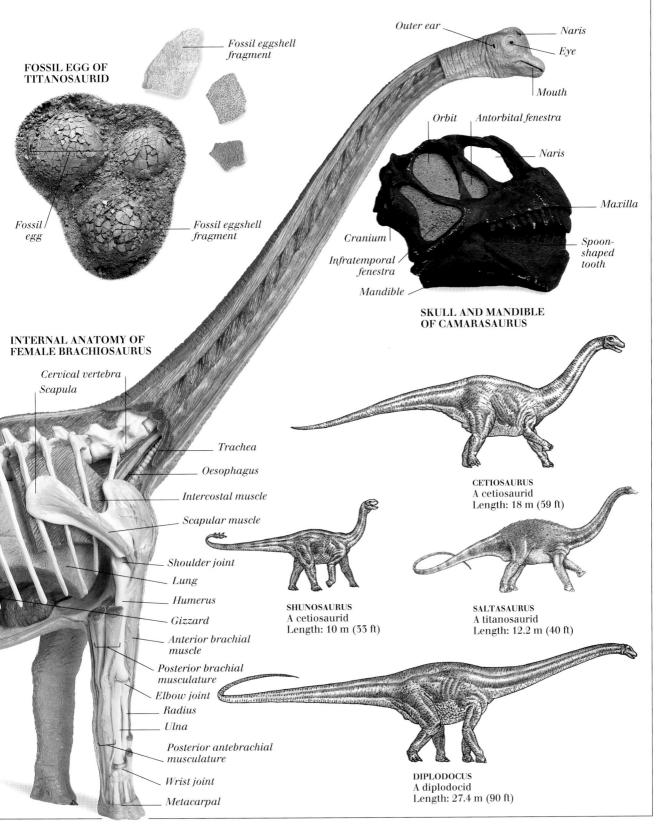

FOSSIL EGG OF TITANOSAURID

Fossil eggshell fragment

Fossil egg

Fossil eggshell fragment

Outer ear

Naris

Eye

Mouth

Orbit

Antorbital fenestra

Naris

Maxilla

Cranium

Spoon-shaped tooth

Infratemporal fenestra

Mandible

SKULL AND MANDIBLE OF CAMARASAURUS

INTERNAL ANATOMY OF FEMALE BRACHIOSAURUS

Cervical vertebra

Scapula

Trachea

Oesophagus

Intercostal muscle

Scapular muscle

Shoulder joint

Lung

Humerus

Gizzard

Anterior brachial muscle

Posterior brachial musculature

Elbow joint

Radius

Ulna

Posterior antebrachial musculature

Wrist joint

Metacarpal

CETIOSAURUS
A cetiosaurid
Length: 18 m (59 ft)

SHUNOSAURUS
A cetiosaurid
Length: 10 m (33 ft)

SALTASAURUS
A titanosaurid
Length: 12.2 m (40 ft)

DIPLODOCUS
A diplodocid
Length: 27.4 m (90 ft)

Thyreophorans 1

THYREOPHORANS ("SHIELD BEARERS") were a group of quadrupedal armoured dinosaurs. A sub-order of the Ornithischia (bird-hipped dinosaurs), they were characterized by rows of bony studs, plates, or spikes along the back, which protected some from predators and may have helped others regulate body temperature. Up to 9m (30ft) long, with a small head and small cheek teeth, Thyreophorans had shorter forelimbs than hind limbs and probably browsed on low-level vegetation. The earliest thyreophorans were small and lived in Early Jurassic times (about 200 million years ago) in Europe, North America, and China. Stegosaurs, such as Stegosaurus and Kentrosaurus, replaced these older forms. The earliest stegosaur remains come mainly from China. Several genera of stegosaurs survived into the Early Cretaceous period (146–100 million years ago), but only in India did they persist into Late Cretaceous times (97–65 million years ago). Ankylosaurs, with their toothless beaks and cheek teeth adapted for cropping vegetation, appeared later than stegosaurs. They originated in the Late Jurassic period (155 million years ago) and in North America survived until 65 million years ago.

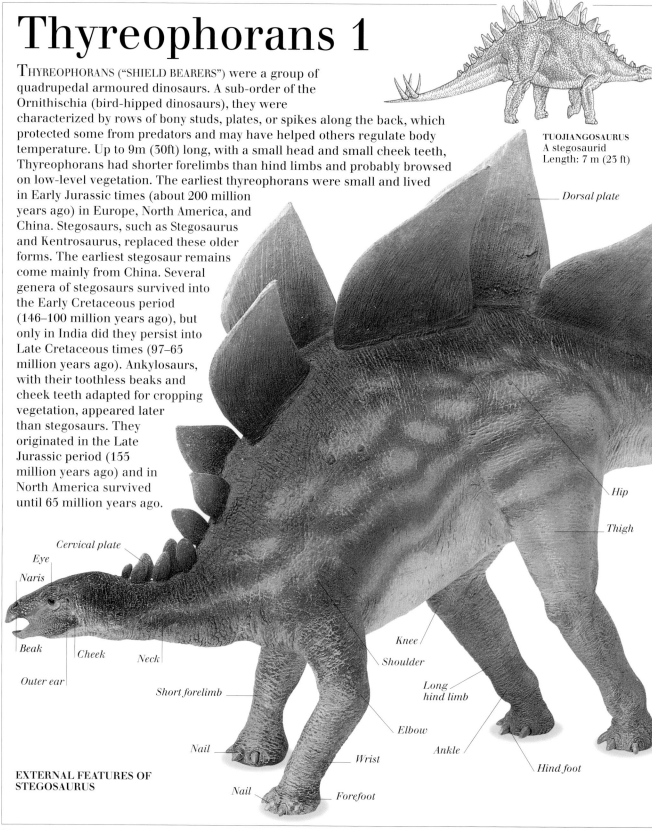

TUOJIANGOSAURUS
A stegosaurid
Length: 7 m (23 ft)

Dorsal plate

Hip

Thigh

Cervical plate

Eye

Naris

Knee

Shoulder

Beak

Cheek

Neck

Long
hind limb

Outer ear

Short forelimb

Elbow

Ankle

Nail

Wrist

Hind foot

**EXTERNAL FEATURES OF
STEGOSAURUS**

Nail

Forefoot

EXAMPLES OF STEGOSAURS

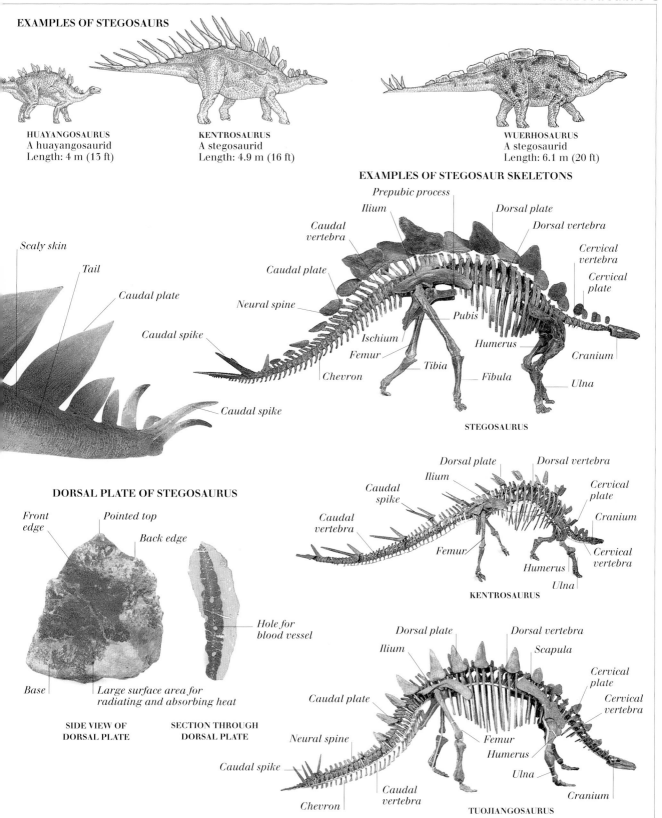

HUAYANGOSAURUS
A huayangosaurid
Length: 4 m (13 ft)

KENTROSAURUS
A stegosaurid
Length: 4.9 m (16 ft)

WUERHOSAURUS
A stegosaurid
Length: 6.1 m (20 ft)

EXAMPLES OF STEGOSAUR SKELETONS

Scaly skin

Tail

Caudal plate

Caudal spike

Caudal spike

Prepubic process

Ilium

Caudal vertebra

Caudal plate

Neural spine

Ischium

Femur

Tibia

Pubis

Chevron

Dorsal plate

Dorsal vertebra

Cervical vertebra

Cervical plate

Humerus

Fibula

Cranium

Ulna

STEGOSAURUS

DORSAL PLATE OF STEGOSAURUS

Front edge

Pointed top

Back edge

Hole for blood vessel

Base

Large surface area for radiating and absorbing heat

SIDE VIEW OF DORSAL PLATE

SECTION THROUGH DORSAL PLATE

Dorsal plate

Dorsal vertebra

Ilium

Caudal spike

Caudal vertebra

Femur

Humerus

Cervical plate

Cranium

Cervical vertebra

Ulna

KENTROSAURUS

Dorsal plate

Dorsal vertebra

Ilium

Scapula

Cervical plate

Caudal plate

Cervical vertebra

Neural spine

Femur

Humerus

Caudal spike

Ulna

Chevron

Caudal vertebra

Cranium

TUOJIANGOSAURUS

Thyreophorans 2

EXAMPLES OF ANKYLOSAUR SKULLS

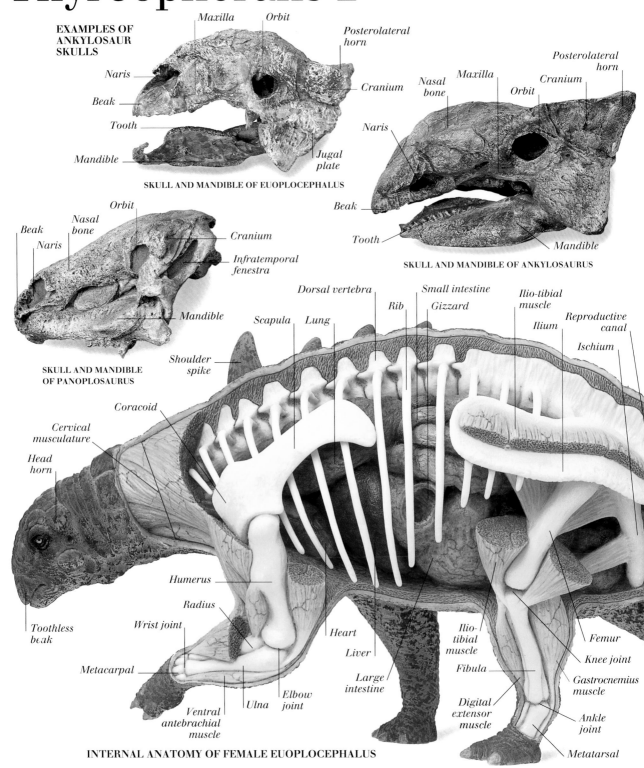

Maxilla
Orbit
Posterolateral horn
Naris
Cranium
Beak
Tooth
Mandible
Jugal plate

SKULL AND MANDIBLE OF EUOPLOCEPHALUS

Posterolateral horn
Nasal bone
Maxilla
Cranium
Orbit
Naris
Beak
Tooth
Mandible

SKULL AND MANDIBLE OF ANKYLOSAURUS

Orbit
Nasal bone
Beak
Naris
Cranium
Infratemporal fenestra
Mandible

SKULL AND MANDIBLE OF PANOPLOSAURUS

Dorsal vertebra
Small intestine
Ilio-tibial muscle
Rib
Gizzard
Ilium
Reproductive canal
Scapula
Lung
Ischium
Shoulder spike
Coracoid
Cervical musculature
Head horn
Toothless beak
Humerus
Radius
Wrist joint
Metacarpal
Ventral antebrachial muscle
Ulna
Elbow joint
Heart
Liver
Large intestine
Ilio-tibial muscle
Fibula
Digital extensor muscle
Femur
Knee joint
Gastrocnemius muscle
Ankle joint
Metatarsal

INTERNAL ANATOMY OF FEMALE EUOPLOCEPHALUS

EXTERNAL FEATURES OF EDMONTONIA

EXAMPLES OF ANKYLOSAURS

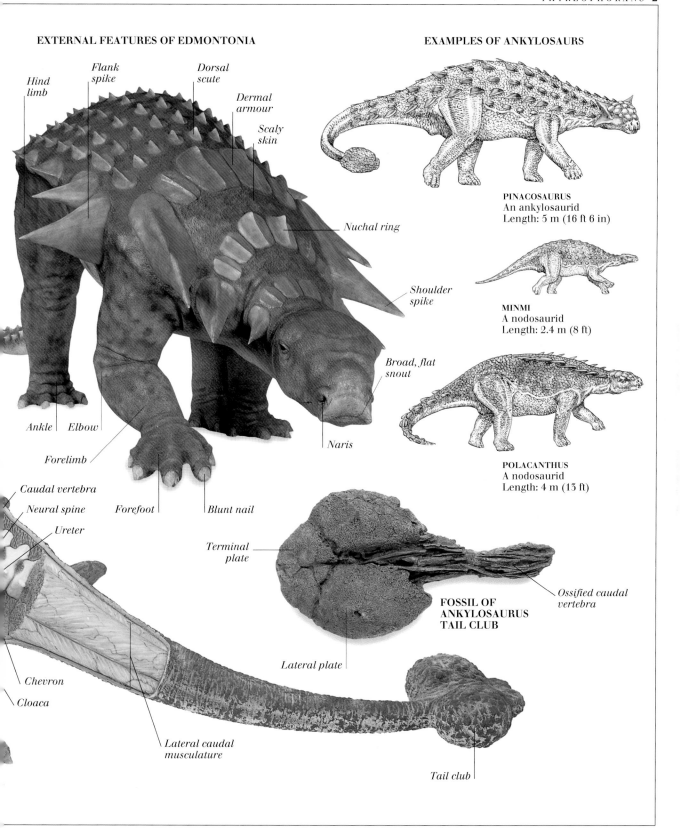

Hind
limb

Flank
spike

Dorsal
scute

Dermal
armour

Scaly
skin

Nuchal ring

Shoulder
spike

Broad, flat
snout

Ankle Elbow

Forelimb

Naris

Caudal vertebra

Neural spine

Ureter

Forefoot Blunt nail

Terminal
plate

Chevron

Cloaca

Lateral caudal
musculature

Lateral plate

PINACOSAURUS
An ankylosaurid
Length: 5 m (16 ft 6 in)

MINMI
A nodosaurid
Length: 2.4 m (8 ft)

POLACANTHUS
A nodosaurid
Length: 4 m (13 ft)

Ossified caudal
vertebra

**FOSSIL OF
ANKYLOSAURUS
TAIL CLUB**

Tail club

Ornithopods 1

IGUANODON TOOTH

ORNITHOPODS ("BIRD FEET") were a group of ornithischian ("bird-hipped") dinosaurs. These bipedal and quadrupedal herbivores had a horny beak, plant-cutting or grinding cheek teeth, and a pelvic and tail region stiffened by bony tendons. They evolved teeth and jaws adapted to pulping vegetation and flourished from the Middle Jurassic to the Late Cretaceous period (165–65 million years ago) in North America, Europe, Africa, China, Australia, and Antarctica. Some ornithopods were no larger than a dog, while others were immense creatures up to 15 m (49 ft) long. Iguanodonts, an ornithopod group, had a broad, toothless beak at the end of a long snout, large jaws with long rows of ridged, closely packed teeth for grinding vegetation, a bulky body, and a heavy tail. *Iguanodon* and some other iguanodonts had large thumb-spikes that were strong enough to stab attackers. Another group, the hadrosaurs, such as *Gryposaurus* and *Hadrosaurus,* lived in Late Cretaceous times (97–65 million years ago) and with their broad beaks are sometimes known as "duckbills". They were characterized by their deep skulls and closely packed rows of teeth, while some, such as *Corythosaurus* and *Lambeosaurus,* had tall, hollow, bony head crests.

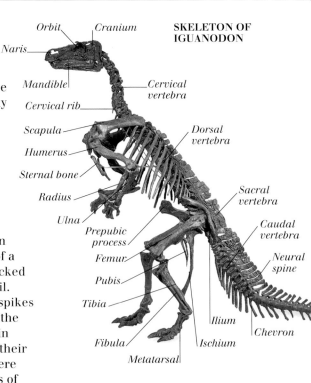

SKELETON OF IGUANODON

Orbit
Cranium
Naris
Mandible
Cervical vertebra
Cervical rib
Scapula
Dorsal vertebra
Humerus
Sternal bone
Radius
Sacral vertebra
Ulna
Caudal vertebra
Prepubic process
Neural spine
Femur
Pubis
Tibia
Ilium
Chevron
Fibula
Ischium
Metatarsal

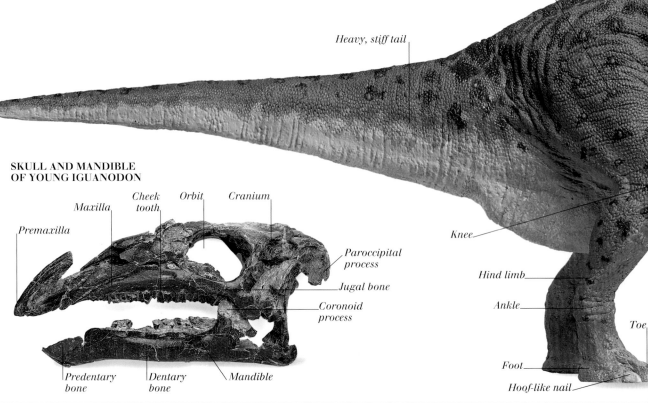

Thigh
Heavy, stiff tail
Knee
Hind limb
Ankle
Toe
Foot
Hoof-like nail

SKULL AND MANDIBLE OF YOUNG IGUANODON

Maxilla
Cheek tooth
Orbit
Cranium
Premaxilla
Paroccipital process
Jugal bone
Coronoid process
Predentary bone
Dentary bone
Mandible

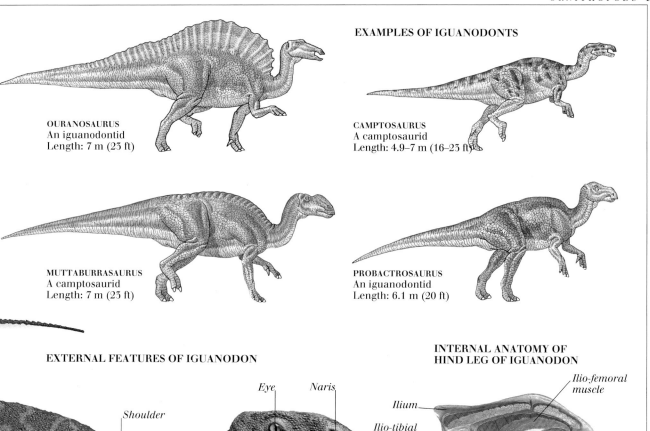

EXAMPLES OF IGUANODONTS

OURANOSAURUS
An iguanodontid
Length: 7 m (23 ft)

CAMPTOSAURUS
A camptosaurid
Length: 4.9–7 m (16–23 ft)

MUTTABURRASAURUS
A camptosaurid
Length: 7 m (23 ft)

PROBACTROSAURUS
An iguanodontid
Length: 6.1 m (20 ft)

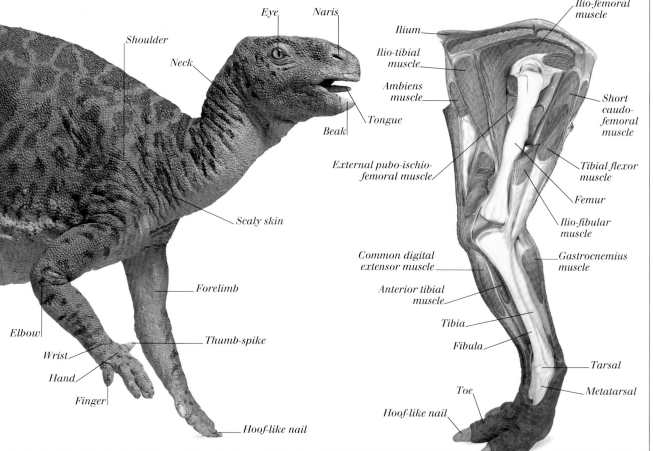

EXTERNAL FEATURES OF IGUANODON

Eye
Naris
Shoulder
Neck
Tongue
Beak
Scaly skin
External pubo-ischio-
femoral muscle
Forelimb
Common digital
extensor muscle
Anterior tibial
muscle
Elbow
Wrist
Thumb-spike
Hand
Finger
Hoof-like nail

**INTERNAL ANATOMY OF
HIND LEG OF IGUANODON**

Ilio-femoral
muscle
Ilium
Ilio-tibial
muscle
Ambiens
muscle
Short
caudo-
femoral
muscle
Tibial flexor
muscle
Femur
Ilio-fibular
muscle
Gastrocnemius
muscle
Tibia
Fibula
Tarsal
Metatarsal
Toe
Hoof-like nail

Ornithopods 2

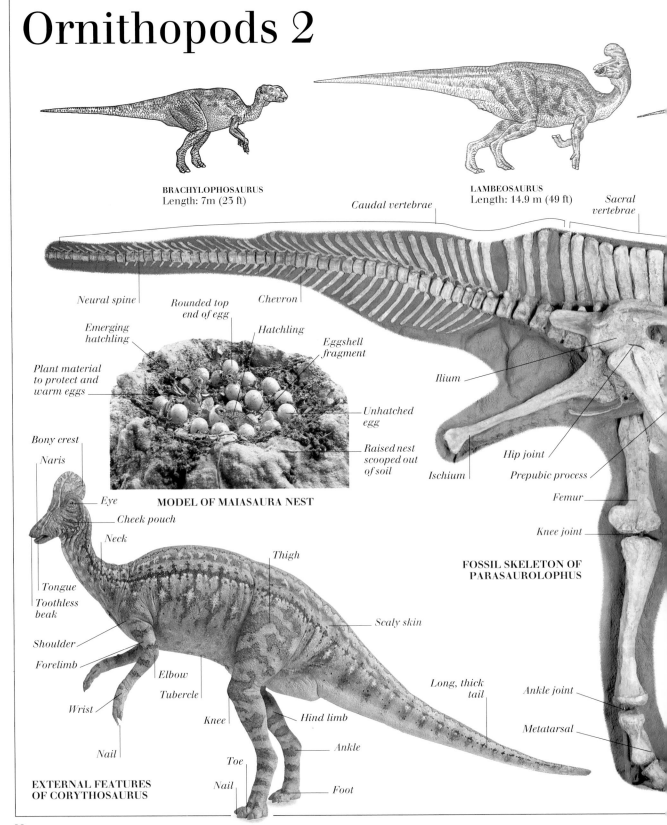

BRACHYLOPHOSAURUS
Length: 7m (23 ft)

LAMBEOSAURUS
Length: 14.9 m (49 ft)

Caudal vertebrae

Sacral vertebrae

Neural spine

Rounded top end of egg

Chevron

Emerging hatchling

Hatchling

Eggshell fragment

Plant material to protect and warm eggs

Ilium

Unhatched egg

Raised nest scooped out of soil

Bony crest

Naris

Eye

Hip joint

Ischium

Prepubic process

MODEL OF MAIASAURA NEST

Cheek pouch

Femur

Neck

Thigh

Knee joint

Tongue

Toothless beak

Scaly skin

FOSSIL SKELETON OF PARASAUROLOPHUS

Shoulder

Forelimb

Elbow

Tubercle

Long, thick tail

Ankle joint

Wrist

Knee

Hind limb

Metatarsal

Nail

Ankle

Toe

EXTERNAL FEATURES OF CORYTHOSAURUS

Nail

Foot

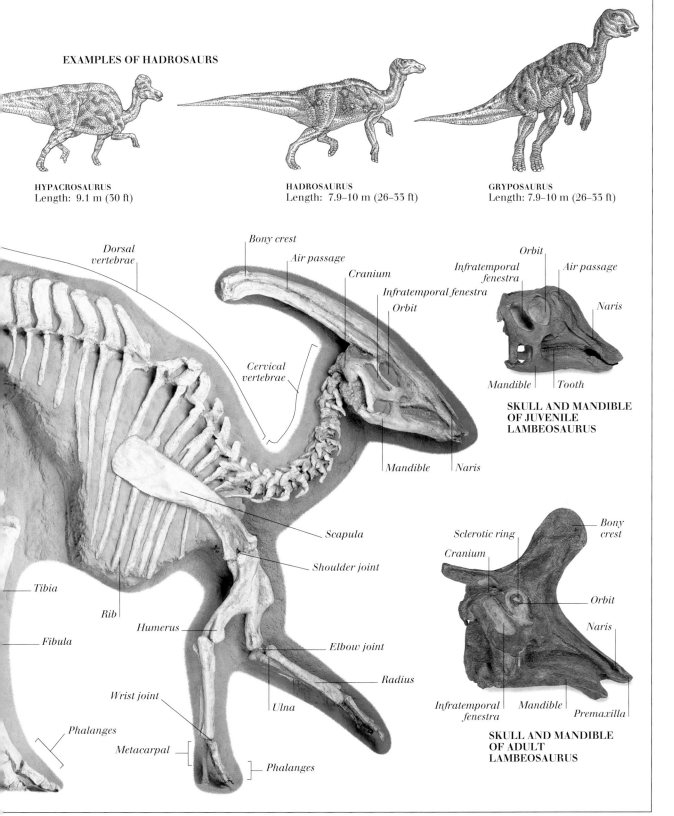

EXAMPLES OF HADROSAURS

HYPACROSAURUS
Length: 9.1 m (30 ft)

HADROSAURUS
Length: 7.9–10 m (26–33 ft)

GRYPOSAURUS
Length: 7.9–10 m (26–33 ft)

Dorsal vertebrae

Bony crest

Air passage

Cranium

Infratemporal fenestra

Orbit

Cervical vertebrae

Mandible

Naris

Orbit

Infratemporal fenestra

Air passage

Naris

Mandible

Tooth

SKULL AND MANDIBLE OF JUVENILE LAMBEOSAURUS

Scapula

Shoulder joint

Tibia

Rib

Humerus

Fibula

Elbow joint

Radius

Wrist joint

Ulna

Phalanges

Metacarpal

Phalanges

Sclerotic ring

Cranium

Bony crest

Orbit

Naris

Infratemporal fenestra

Mandible

Premaxilla

SKULL AND MANDIBLE OF ADULT LAMBEOSAURUS

Marginocephalians 1

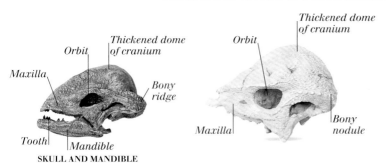

HEAD-BUTTING PRENOCEPHALES

MARGINOCEPHALIA ("margined heads") were a group of bipedal and quadrupedal ornithischian dinosaurs with a narrow shelf or deep, bony frill at the back of the skull. Marginocephalians were probably descended from the same ancestor as the ornithopods and lived in what are now North America, Africa, Asia, and Europe during the Cretaceous period (146–65 million years ago). They were divided into two infraorders: Pachycephalosauria ("thick-headed lizards"), such as *Pachycephalosaurus* and *Stegoceras*, and Ceratopsia ("horned faces"), such as *Triceratops* and *Psittacosaurus*. The thick skulls of Pachycephalosauria protected their brains during head-butting contests fought to win territory and mates; their hips and spines were also strengthened to withstand the shock. The bony frill of Ceratopsia would have added to their frightening appearance when charging; the neck was strengthened for impact and to support the huge head, with its snipping beak and powerful slicing toothed jaws. A charging ceratops would have been a formidable opponent for even the largest predators. Ceratopsia were among the most abundant herbivorous dinosaurs of the Late Cretaceous period (97–65 million years ago).

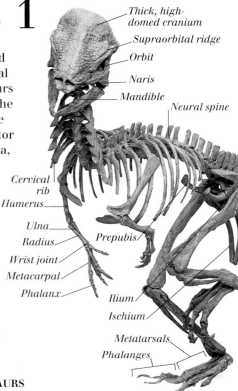

Thick, high-domed cranium
Supraorbital ridge
Orbit
Naris
Mandible
Neural spine
Cervical rib
Humerus
Ulna
Radius
Prepubis
Wrist joint
Metacarpal
Phalanx
Ilium
Ischium
Metatarsals
Phalanges

EXAMPLES OF SKULLS OF PACHYCEPHALOSAURS

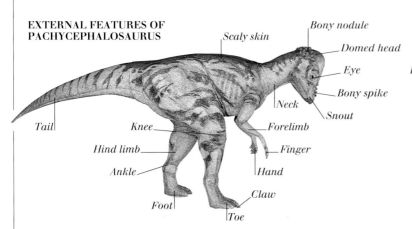

Orbit
Thickened dome of cranium
Maxilla
Bony ridge
Tooth
Mandible

SKULL AND MANDIBLE OF STEGOCERAS

Thickened dome of cranium
Orbit
Maxilla
Bony nodule

SKULL OF PRENOCEPHALE

Thickened dome of cranium
Bony spike
Maxilla
Orbit
Bony nodule

SKULL OF PACHYCEPHALOSAURUS

EXTERNAL FEATURES OF PACHYCEPHALOSAURUS

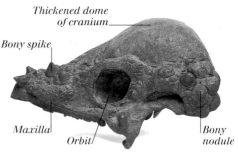

Scaly skin
Bony nodule
Domed head
Eye
Bony spike
Neck
Snout
Tail
Knee
Forelimb
Hind limb
Finger
Ankle
Hand
Claw
Foot
Toe

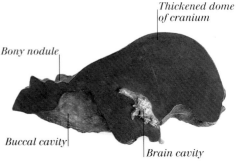

Thickened dome of cranium
Bony nodule
Buccal cavity
Brain cavity

SECTION THROUGH SKULL OF PACHYCEPHALOSAURUS

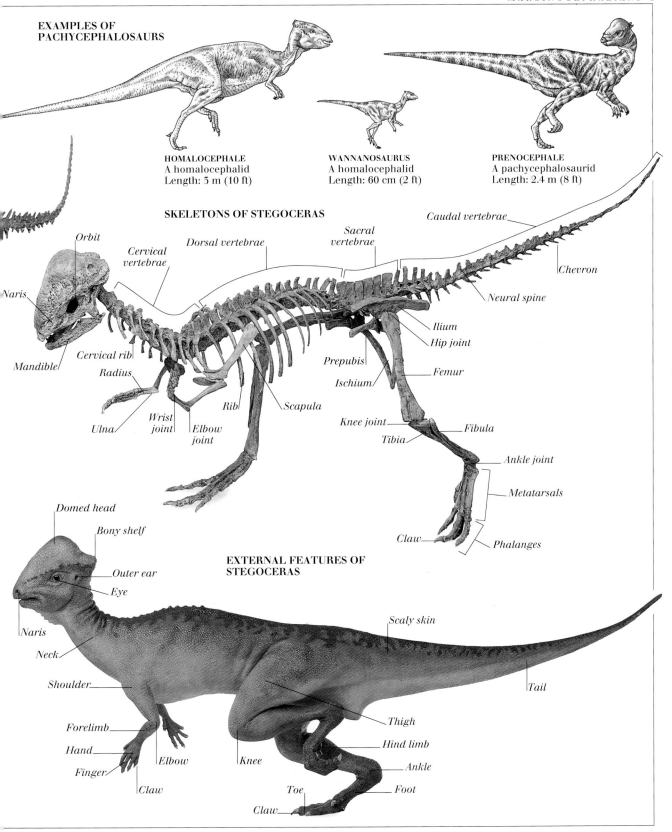

EXAMPLES OF PACHYCEPHALOSAURS

HOMALOCEPHALE
A homalocephalid
Length: 3 m (10 ft)

WANNANOSAURUS
A homalocephalid
Length: 60 cm (2 ft)

PRENOCEPHALE
A pachycephalosaurid
Length: 2.4 m (8 ft)

SKELETONS OF STEGOCERAS

Orbit

Cervical vertebrae

Dorsal vertebrae

Sacral vertebrae

Caudal vertebrae

Chevron

Naris

Neural spine

Ilium

Hip joint

Mandible

Cervical rib

Prepubis

Ischium

Femur

Radius

Rib

Scapula

Ulna

Wrist joint

Elbow joint

Knee joint

Tibia

Fibula

Ankle joint

Metatarsals

Claw

Phalanges

EXTERNAL FEATURES OF STEGOCERAS

Domed head

Bony shelf

Outer ear

Eye

Scaly skin

Naris

Neck

Shoulder

Thigh

Forelimb

Hand

Elbow

Knee

Hind limb

Ankle

Finger

Claw

Toe

Foot

Tail

Claw

Marginocephalians 2

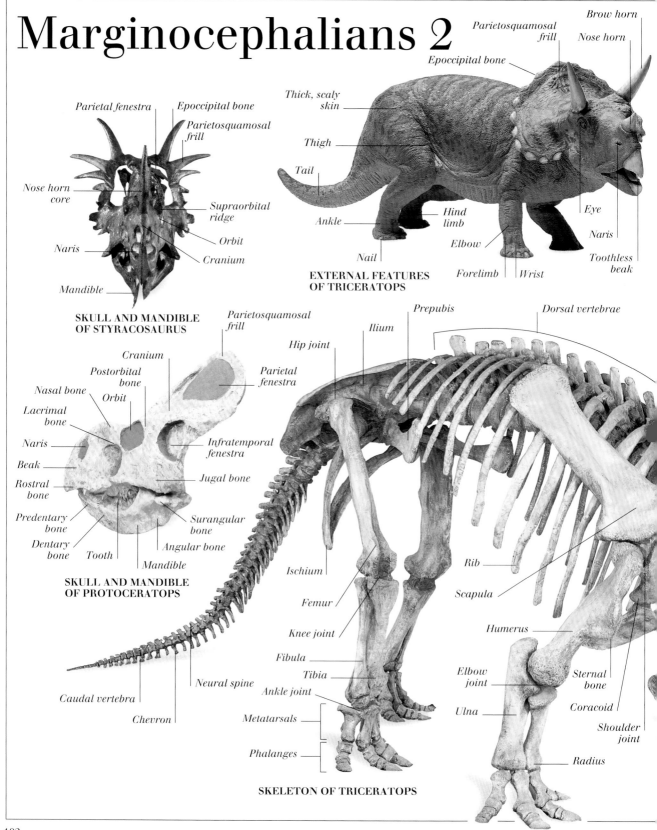

Parietosquamosal frill

Brow horn

Nose horn

Epoccipital bone

Thick, scaly skin

Thigh

Tail

Ankle

Nail

Hind limb

Elbow

Forelimb

Wrist

Eye

Naris

Toothless beak

EXTERNAL FEATURES OF TRICERATOPS

Parietal fenestra

Epoccipital bone

Parietosquamosal frill

Nose horn core

Supraorbital ridge

Naris

Orbit

Cranium

Mandible

SKULL AND MANDIBLE OF STYRACOSAURUS

Parietosquamosal frill

Cranium

Postorbital bone

Nasal bone

Orbit

Lacrimal bone

Naris

Beak

Rostral bone

Predentary bone

Dentary bone

Tooth

Mandible

Parietal fenestra

Infratemporal fenestra

Jugal bone

Surangular bone

Angular bone

SKULL AND MANDIBLE OF PROTOCERATOPS

Prepubis

Ilium

Hip joint

Dorsal vertebrae

Ischium

Femur

Knee joint

Fibula

Tibia

Ankle joint

Metatarsals

Phalanges

Caudal vertebra

Chevron

Neural spine

Rib

Scapula

Humerus

Elbow joint

Ulna

Sternal bone

Coracoid

Shoulder joint

Radius

SKELETON OF TRICERATOPS

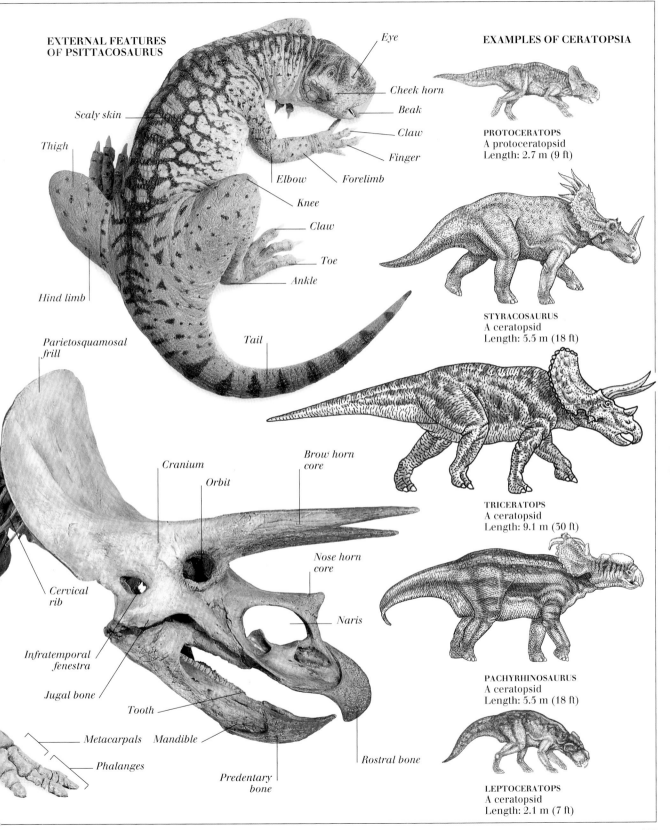

**EXTERNAL FEATURES
OF PSITTACOSAURUS**

Eye

Cheek horn

Beak

Claw

Finger

Scaly skin

Thigh

Forelimb

Elbow

Knee

Claw

Toe

Ankle

Hind limb

Parietosquamosal
frill

Tail

Cranium

Orbit

Brow horn
core

Nose horn
core

Cervical
rib

Naris

Infratemporal
fenestra

Jugal bone

Tooth

Metacarpals

Mandible

Phalanges

Predentary
bone

Rostral bone

EXAMPLES OF CERATOPSIA

PROTOCERATOPS
A protoceratopsid
Length: 2.7 m (9 ft)

STYRACOSAURUS
A ceratopsid
Length: 5.5 m (18 ft)

TRICERATOPS
A ceratopsid
Length: 9.1 m (30 ft)

PACHYRHINOSAURUS
A ceratopsid
Length: 5.5 m (18 ft)

LEPTOCERATOPS
A ceratopsid
Length: 2.1 m (7 ft)

Mammals 1

**TETRALOPHODON
CHEEK TEETH**

SINCE THE EXTINCTION of the dinosaurs 65 million years ago, mammals have been the dominant vertebrates on land. This class includes terrestrial, aerial, and aquatic forms. Having developed from the reptilian Therapsids, the first true mammals – small, nocturnal, shrew-like creatures, such as *Megazostrodon* – appeared over 200 million years ago during the Triassic period (245–208 million years ago). Mammals had several features that improved on those of their reptilian ancestors: an efficient four-chambered heart allowed these warm-blooded animals to sustain high levels of activity; a covering of hair helped them maintain a constant body temperature; an improved limb structure gave them more efficient locomotion; and the birth of live young and the immediate supply of food from the mother's milk aided their rapid growth. Since the end of the Mesozoic era (65 million years ago), the number of different mammal orders and the abundance of species in each order have varied dramatically. For example, the Perissodactyla (the order that includes *Coelodonta* and modern horses) was a common group during the Early Tertiary period (about 54 million years ago). Today, the mammalian orders with the most species include the Rodentia (rats and mice), the Chiroptera (bats), the Primates (monkeys and apes), the Carnivora (bears, cats, and dogs), and the Artiodactyla (cattle, deer, and pigs), while the Proboscidea order, which formerly included many genera, such as *Phiomia, Moeritherium, Tetralophodon,* and *Mammuthus*, now has only three species of elephant. In Australia and South America, millions of years of continental isolation led to increased diversity of the marsupials, a group of mammals distinct from the placentals (see p. 74) that existed elsewhere.

*Long tail aids
balance*

*Insulating
hair*

*Neural
spine*

Scapula

*Cervical
vertebra*

Humerus

Nasal horn

Naris

Orbit

*Predentary
bone*

Mandible

Radius

Ulna

*Chisel-edged
molar*

Metacarpal

Phalanx

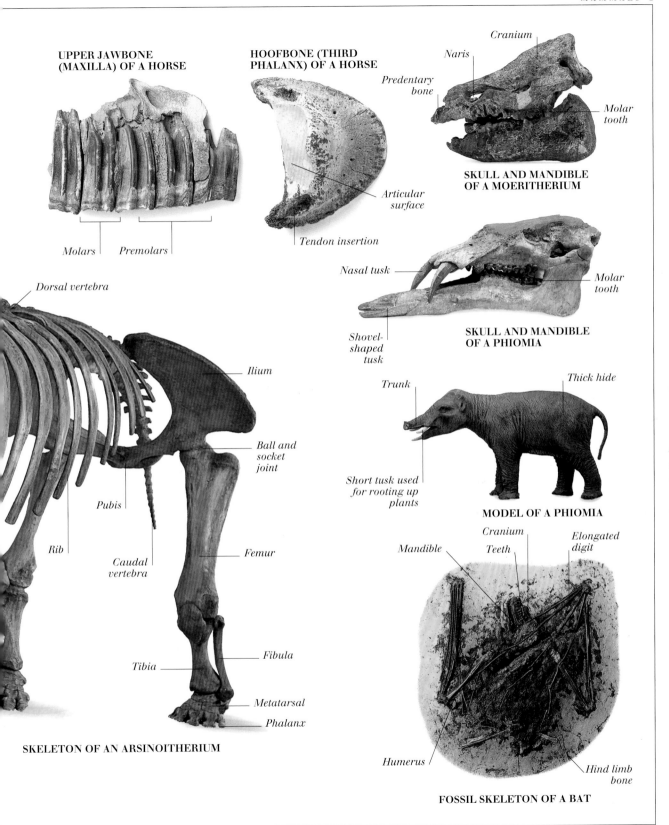

**UPPER JAWBONE
(MAXILLA) OF A HORSE**

Molars | *Premolars*

**HOOFBONE (THIRD
PHALANX) OF A HORSE**

*Articular
surface*

Tendon insertion

Cranium

Naris

*Predentary
bone*

*Molar
tooth*

**SKULL AND MANDIBLE
OF A MOERITHERIUM**

Nasal tusk

*Molar
tooth*

*Shovel-
shaped
tusk*

**SKULL AND MANDIBLE
OF A PHIOMIA**

Trunk

Thick hide

*Short tusk used
for rooting up
plants*

MODEL OF A PHIOMIA

Dorsal vertebra

Ilium

*Ball and
socket
joint*

Pubis

Rib

Femur

*Caudal
vertebra*

Tibia

Fibula

Metatarsal

Phalanx

SKELETON OF AN ARSINOITHERIUM

Mandible

Cranium

Teeth

*Elongated
digit*

Humerus

*Hind limb
bone*

FOSSIL SKELETON OF A BAT

Mammals 2

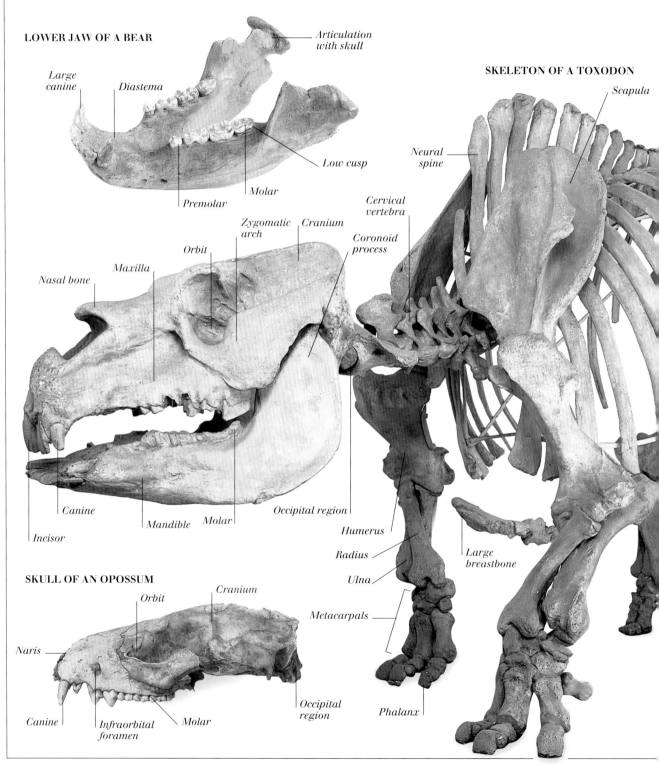

LOWER JAW OF A BEAR

Articulation with skull

Large canine

Diastema

Low cusp

Molar

Premolar

Zygomatic arch

Cranium

Orbit

Coronoid process

Maxilla

Nasal bone

Canine

Incisor

Mandible

Molar

Occipital region

SKULL OF AN OPOSSUM

Orbit

Cranium

Naris

Occipital region

Canine

Infraorbital foramen

Molar

SKELETON OF A TOXODON

Scapula

Neural spine

Cervical vertebra

Humerus

Radius

Ulna

Metacarpals

Large breastbone

Phalanx

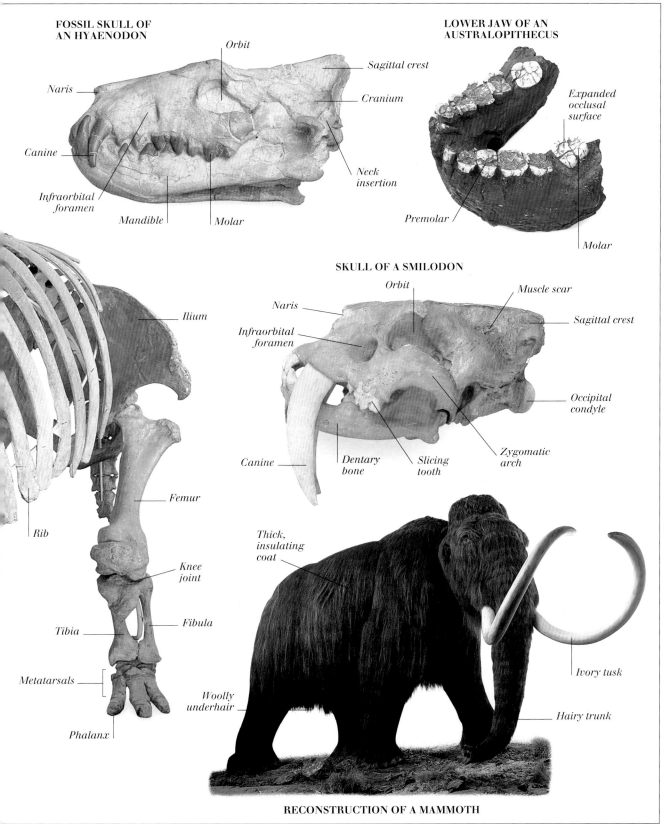

FOSSIL SKULL OF AN HYAENODON

Orbit

Sagittal crest

Cranium

Naris

Canine

Neck insertion

Infraorbital foramen

Mandible

Molar

LOWER JAW OF AN AUSTRALOPITHECUS

Expanded occlusal surface

Premolar

Molar

SKULL OF A SMILODON

Orbit

Muscle scar

Naris

Sagittal crest

Infraorbital foramen

Occipital condyle

Canine

Dentary bone

Slicing tooth

Zygomatic arch

Ilium

Femur

Rib

Knee joint

Tibia

Fibula

Metatarsals

Phalanx

Thick, insulating coat

Woolly underhair

Ivory tusk

Hairy trunk

RECONSTRUCTION OF A MAMMOTH

The first hominids

MODERN HUMANS BELONG TO THE MAMMALIAN order of primates (see pp. 202–203), which originated about 55 million years ago; they comprise the only extant hominid species. The earliest hominid was *Australopithecus* ("southern ape"), a small-brained intermediate between apes and humans that was capable of standing and walking upright. *Homo habilis*, the first known human appeared at least 2 million years ago. This larger-brained "handy man" began making tools for hunting. *Homo erectus* first appeared in Africa about 1.8 million years ago and spread into Asia about 800,000 years later. Smaller-toothed than *Homo habilis*, it developed fire as a tool, which enabled it to cook food. Neanderthals, a near relative of modern humans, originated about 200,000 years ago, and *Homo sapiens* (modern humans) appeared in Africa about 100,000 years later. The two co-existed for thousands of years, but by 30,000 years ago, *Homo sapiens* had become dominant and the Neanderthals had died out. Classification of *Homo sapiens* in relation to its ancestors is enormously problematic: modern humans must be classified not only by bone structure, but also by specific behaviour – the ability to plan future action; to follow traditions; and to use symbolic communication, including complex language and the ability to use and recognize symbols.

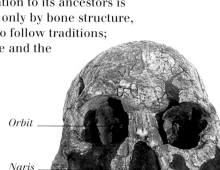

JAWBONE OF AUSTRALOPITHECUS (SOUTHERN APE)

Larger jawbone than modern human

Large back tooth

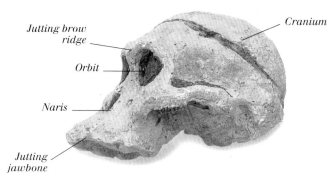

Jutting brow ridge

Cranium

Orbit

Naris

Jutting jawbone

SKULL OF AUSTRALOPITHECUS (SOUTHERN APE)

Orbit

Naris

SKULL OF HOMO HABILIS (FIRST KNOWN HUMAN)

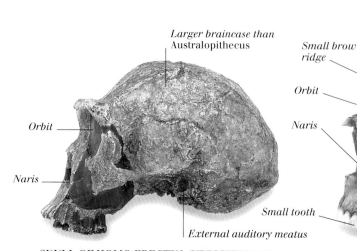

Larger braincase than Australopithecus

Orbit

Naris

External auditory meatus

SKULL OF HOMO ERECTUS (UPRIGHT MAN)

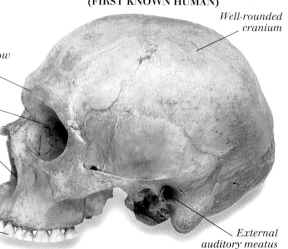

Well-rounded cranium

Small brow ridge

Orbit

Naris

Small tooth

External auditory meatus

SKULL OF HOMO SAPIENS (MODERN HUMAN)

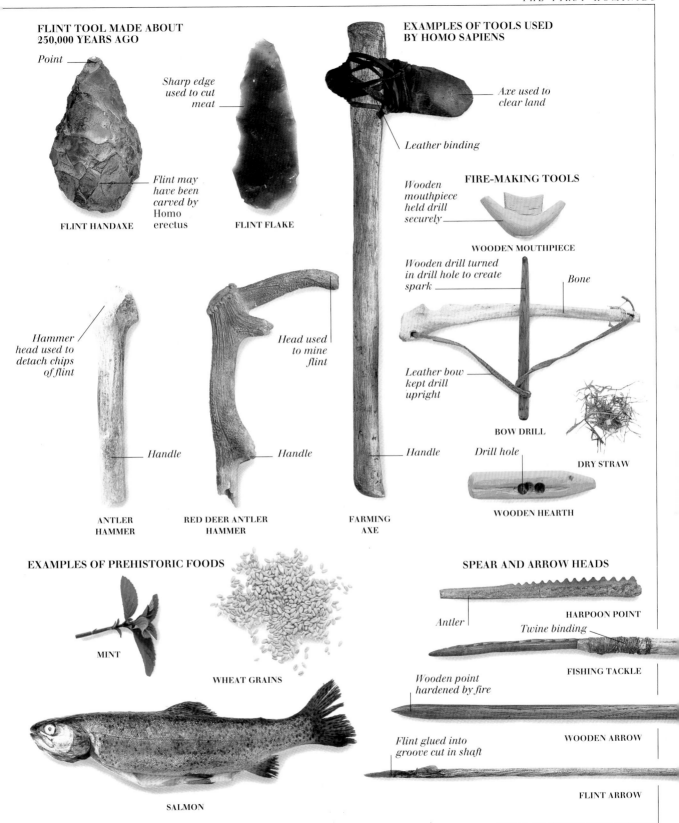

FLINT TOOL MADE ABOUT 250,000 YEARS AGO

Point

Sharp edge used to cut meat

Flint may have been carved by Homo erectus

FLINT HANDAXE

FLINT FLAKE

Hammer head used to detach chips of flint

Handle

ANTLER HAMMER

Head used to mine flint

Handle

RED DEER ANTLER HAMMER

EXAMPLES OF TOOLS USED BY HOMO SAPIENS

Axe used to clear land

Leather binding

FIRE-MAKING TOOLS

Wooden mouthpiece held drill securely

WOODEN MOUTHPIECE

Wooden drill turned in drill hole to create spark

Bone

Leather bow kept drill upright

BOW DRILL

Drill hole

DRY STRAW

WOODEN HEARTH

Handle

FARMING AXE

EXAMPLES OF PREHISTORIC FOODS

MINT

WHEAT GRAINS

SALMON

SPEAR AND ARROW HEADS

Antler

HARPOON POINT

Twine binding

FISHING TACKLE

Wooden point hardened by fire

WOODEN ARROW

Flint glued into groove cut in shaft

FLINT ARROW

PLANTS

Plant variety

THERE ARE MORE THAN 300,000 SPECIES of plants. They
show a wide diversity of forms and life-styles, ranging, for example, from delicate
liverworts, adapted for life in a damp habitat, to cacti, capable of surviving in the desert, and
from herbaceous plants, such as corn, which completes its life-cycle in one year, to the giant redwood tree,
which can live for thousands of years. This diversity reflects the adaptations of plants to survive in a wide
range of habitats. This is seen most clearly in the flowering plants (phylum Angiospermophyta), which are
the most numerous, with over 250,000 species, and the most widespread, being found from the tropics to the
poles. Despite their diversity, plants share certain characteristics: typically, plants are green, and make their
food by photosynthesis; and most plants live in or on a substrate, such as soil, and do not actively move. Algae
(kingdom Protista) and fungi (kingdom Fungi) have some plant-like characteristics and are
often studied alongside plants, although they are not true plants.

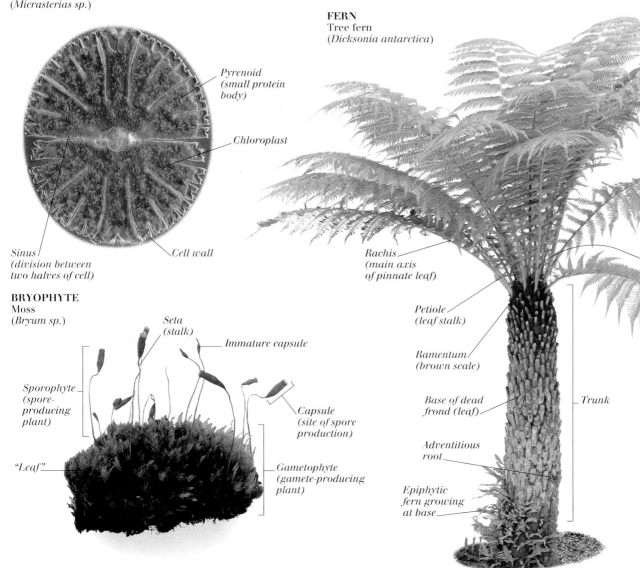

FLOWERING PLANT
Bromeliad
(*Acanthostachys strobilacea*)

Leaf

GREEN ALGA
Micrograph of desmid
(*Micrasterias sp.*)

*Pyrenoid
(small protein
body)*

Chloroplast

*Sinus
(division between
two halves of cell)*

Cell wall

FERN
Tree fern
(*Dicksonia antarctica*)

*Rachis
(main axis
of pinnate leaf)*

*Petiole
(leaf stalk)*

*Ramentum
(brown scale)*

*Base of dead
frond (leaf)*

*Adventitious
root*

*Epiphytic
fern growing
at base*

Trunk

BRYOPHYTE
Moss
(*Bryum sp.*)

*Seta
(stalk)*

Immature capsule

*Sporophyte
(spore-
producing
plant)*

*Capsule
(site of spore
production)*

"Leaf"

*Gametophyte
(gamete-producing
plant)*

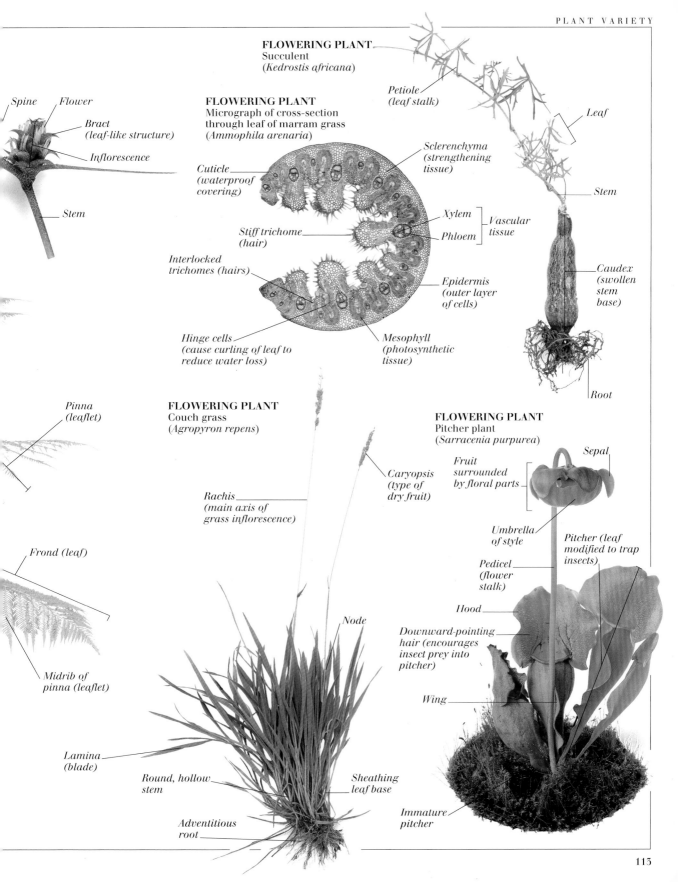

FLOWERING PLANT
Succulent
(*Kedrostis africana*)

Petiole
(leaf stalk)

Leaf

Spine

Flower

Bract
(leaf-like structure)

Inflorescence

Stem

FLOWERING PLANT
Micrograph of cross-section
through leaf of marram grass
(*Ammophila arenaria*)

Sclerenchyma
(strengthening
tissue)

Cuticle
(waterproof
covering)

Stiff trichome
(hair)

Interlocked
trichomes (hairs)

Xylem

Phloem

Vascular
tissue

Epidermis
(outer layer
of cells)

Hinge cells
(cause curling of leaf to
reduce water loss)

Mesophyll
(photosynthetic
tissue)

Stem

Caudex
(swollen
stem
base)

Root

Pinna
(leaflet)

FLOWERING PLANT
Couch grass
(*Agropyron repens*)

Rachis
(main axis of
grass inflorescence)

Caryopsis
(type of
dry fruit)

FLOWERING PLANT
Pitcher plant
(*Sarracenia purpurea*)

Sepal

Fruit
surrounded
by floral parts

Umbrella
of style

Pitcher (leaf
modified to trap
insects)

Pedicel
(flower
stalk)

Frond (leaf)

Node

Hood

Downward-pointing
hair (encourages
insect prey into
pitcher)

Midrib of
pinna (leaflet)

Wing

Lamina
(blade)

Round, hollow
stem

Sheathing
leaf base

Adventitious
root

Immature
pitcher

113

Fungi and lichens

FUNGI WERE ONCE THOUGHT OF AS PLANTS but are now classified as a separate kingdom. This kingdom includes not only the familiar mushrooms, puffballs, stinkhorns, and moulds, but also yeasts, smuts, rusts, and lichens. Most fungi are multicellular, consisting of a mass of thread-like hyphae that together form a mycelium. However, the simpler fungi (e.g., yeasts) are microscopic, single-celled organisms. Typically, fungi reproduce by means of spores. Most fungi feed on dead or decaying matter, or on living organisms. A few fungi obtain their food from plants or algae, with which they have a symbiotic (mutually advantageous) relationship. Lichens are a symbiotic partnership between algae and fungi. Of the six types of lichens the three most common are crustose (flat and crusty), foliose (leafy), and fruticose (shrub-like). Some lichens (e.g., *Cladonia floerkeana*) are a combination of types. Lichens reproduce by means of spores or soredia (powdery vegetative fragments).

EXAMPLES OF FUNGI

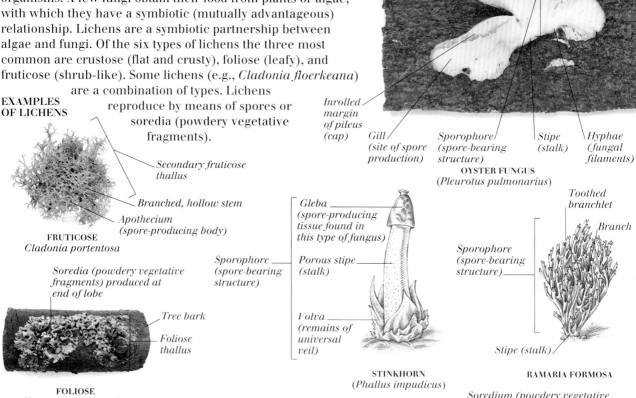

Emerging sporophore (spore-bearing structure)

Pileus (cap) continuous with stipe (stalk)

Bark of dead beech tree

Inrolled margin of pileus (cap)

Gill (site of spore production)

Sporophore (spore-bearing structure)

Stipe (stalk)

Hyphae (fungal filaments)

OYSTER FUNGUS
(*Pleurotus pulmonarius*)

EXAMPLES OF LICHENS

Secondary fruticose thallus

Branched, hollow stem

Apothecium (spore-producing body)

FRUTICOSE
Cladonia portentosa

Soredia (powdery vegetative fragments) produced at end of lobe

Tree bark

Foliose thallus

FOLIOSE
Hypogymnia physodes

Gleba (spore-producing tissue found in this type of fungus)

Sporophore (spore-bearing structure)

Porous stipe (stalk)

Volva (remains of universal veil)

STINKHORN
(*Phallus impudicus*)

Toothed branchlet

Branch

Sporophore (spore-bearing structure)

Stipe (stalk)

RAMARIA FORMOSA

Soredia (powdery vegetative fragments) released onto surface of squamulose thallus

Apothecium (spore-producing body)

Basal scale of primary squamulose thallus

Moss

Podetium (granular stalk) of secondary fruticose thallus

SQUAMULOSE (SCALY) AND FRUTICOSE THALLUS
Cladonia floerkeana

SECTION THROUGH FOLIOSE LICHEN SHOWING REPRODUCTION BY SOREDIA

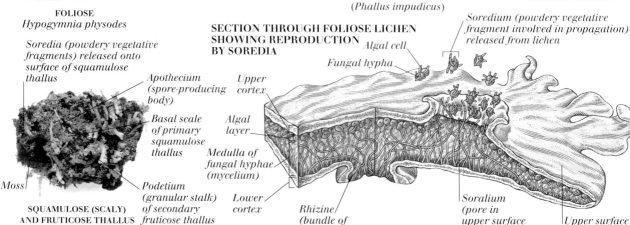

Algal cell

Fungal hypha

Upper cortex

Algal layer

Medulla of fungal hyphae (mycelium)

Lower cortex

Rhizine (bundle of absorptive hyphae)

Soredium (powdery vegetative fragment involved in propagation) released from lichen

Soralium (pore in upper surface of thallus)

Upper surface of thallus

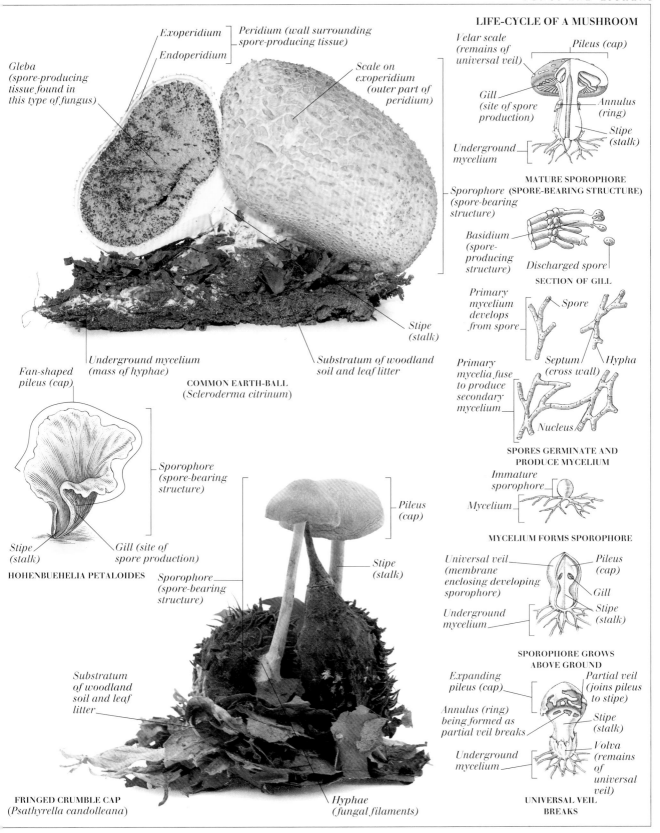

LIFE-CYCLE OF A MUSHROOM

Exoperidium

Endoperidium

Peridium (wall surrounding spore-producing tissue)

Gleba (spore-producing tissue found in this type of fungus)

Scale on exoperidium (outer part of peridium)

Velar scale (remains of universal veil)

Pileus (cap)

Gill (site of spore production)

Annulus (ring)

Stipe (stalk)

Underground mycelium

MATURE SPOROPHORE (SPORE-BEARING STRUCTURE)

Sporophore (spore-bearing structure)

Basidium (spore-producing structure)

Discharged spore

SECTION OF GILL

Primary mycelium develops from spore

Spore

Primary mycelia fuse to produce secondary mycelium

Septum (cross wall)

Hypha

Nucleus

SPORES GERMINATE AND PRODUCE MYCELIUM

Immature sporophore

Mycelium

MYCELIUM FORMS SPOROPHORE

Stipe (stalk)

Substratum of woodland soil and leaf litter

Underground mycelium (mass of hyphae)

COMMON EARTH-BALL (Scleroderma citrinum)

Fan-shaped pileus (cap)

Sporophore (spore-bearing structure)

Stipe (stalk)

Gill (site of spore production)

HOHENBUEHELIA PETALOIDES

Sporophore (spore-bearing structure)

Pileus (cap)

Stipe (stalk)

Universal veil (membrane enclosing developing sporophore)

Pileus (cap)

Gill

Underground mycelium

Stipe (stalk)

SPOROPHORE GROWS ABOVE GROUND

Expanding pileus (cap)

Partial veil (joins pileus to stipe)

Annulus (ring) being formed as partial veil breaks

Stipe (stalk)

Substratum of woodland soil and leaf litter

Underground mycelium

Volva (remains of universal veil)

FRINGED CRUMBLE CAP (Psathyrella candolleana)

Hyphae (fungal filaments)

UNIVERSAL VEIL BREAKS

Algae and seaweeds

ALGAE ARE NOT TRUE PLANTS. They form a diverse group
of plant-like organisms that belong to the kingdom Protista.
Like plants, algae possess the green pigment chlorophyll
and make their own food by photosynthesis (see pp. 138-139).
Many algae also possess other pigments by which they can be
classified; for example, the brown pigment fucoxanthin is
found in the brown algae. Some of the ten phyla of algae are
exclusively unicellular (single-celled); others also contain
aggregates of cells in filaments or colonies. Three phyla –
the Chlorophyta (green algae), Rhodophyta (red algae),
and Phaeophyta (brown algae) – contain larger, multicellular,
thalloid (flat), marine organisms commonly known as seaweeds.
Most algae can reproduce sexually. For
example, in the brown seaweed
Fucus vesiculosus, gametes
(sex cells) are produced in
conceptacles (chambers) in
the receptacles (fertile tips
of fronds); after their release
into the sea, antherozoids
(male gametes) and oospheres
(female gametes) fuse; the
resulting zygote settles on a rock
and develops into a new seaweed.

BROWN SEAWEED
Channelled wrack
(*Pelvetia canaliculata*)

Receptacle
(fertile tip
of frond)

Thallus
(plant
body)

Apical
notch

Margin of
lamina (blade)
rolled inwards
to form channel

Hapteron (holdfast)

BROWN SEAWEED
Spiral wrack
(*Fucus spiralis*)

Apical notch

Conceptacle
(chamber)

Receptacle
(fertile tip
of frond)

Thallus
(plant
body)

Lamina
(blade)

Smooth margin

Midrib

Hapteron (holdfast)

EXAMPLES OF ALGAE

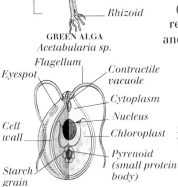

Reproductive
chamber

Cap

Sterile whorl

Cell wall

Stalk

Rhizoid

GREEN ALGA
Acetabularia sp.

Flagellum

Eyespot

Contractile
vacuole

Cytoplasm

Nucleus

Cell
wall

Chloroplast

Pyrenoid
(small protein
body)

Starch
grain

GREEN ALGA
Chlamydomonas sp.

Coenobium
(colony of cells)

Daughter
coenobium

Gelatinous
sheath

Nucleus

Biflagellate cell

GREEN ALGA
Volvox sp.

Spine

Cytoplasm

Girdle

Vacuole

Plastid
(photosynthetic
organelle)

Nucleus

DIATOM
Thalassiosira sp.

Apical notch

Receptacle
(fertile tip
of frond)

Conceptacle
(chamber)
containing
reproductive
structures)

Lamina
(blade)

Midrib

RECEPTACLE
Spiral wrack
(*Fucus spiralis*)

BROWN SEAWEED
Oarweed
(*Laminaria digitata*)

Thallus (plant body)

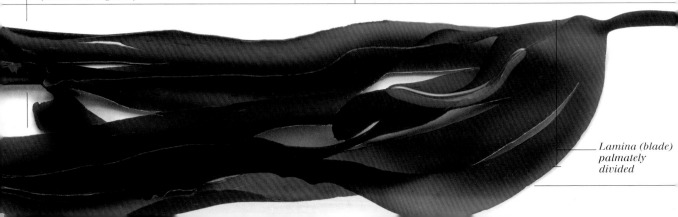

Lamina (blade)
palmately
divided

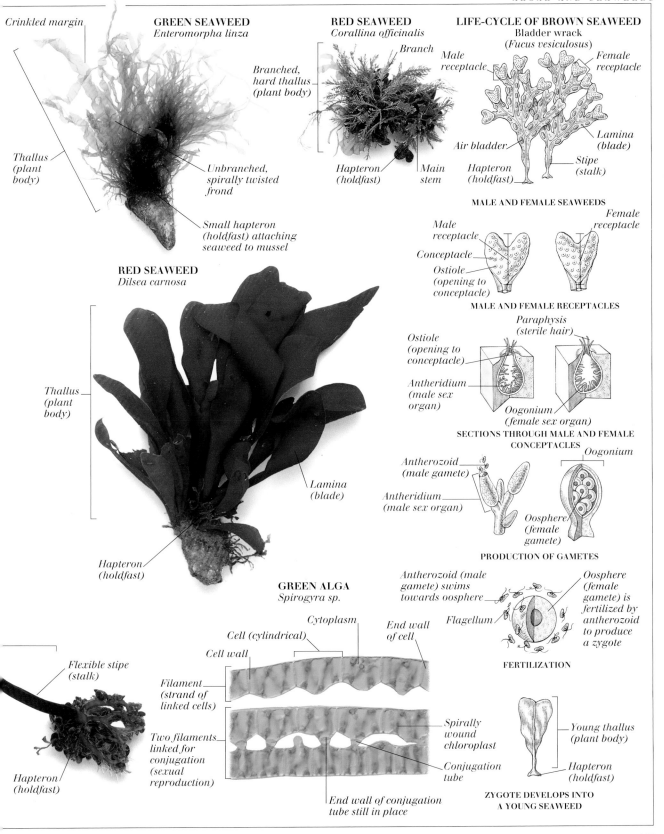

GREEN SEAWEED
Enteromorpha linza

Crinkled margin

Thallus
(plant
body)

Unbranched,
spirally twisted
frond

Small hapteron
(holdfast) attaching
seaweed to mussel

RED SEAWEED
Corallina officinalis

Branch

Branched,
hard thallus
(plant body)

Hapteron
(holdfast)

Main
stem

LIFE-CYCLE OF BROWN SEAWEED
Bladder wrack
(*Fucus vesiculosus*)

Male
receptacle

Female
receptacle

Air bladder

Lamina
(blade)

Hapteron
(holdfast)

Stipe
(stalk)

MALE AND FEMALE SEAWEEDS

Male
receptacle

Conceptacle

Ostiole
(opening to
conceptacle)

Female
receptacle

MALE AND FEMALE RECEPTACLES

Ostiole
(opening to
conceptacle)

Antheridium
(male sex
organ)

Paraphysis
(sterile hair)

Oogonium
(female sex organ)

**SECTIONS THROUGH MALE AND FEMALE
CONCEPTACLES**

Antherozoid
(male gamete)

Antheridium
(male sex organ)

Oogonium

Oosphere
(female
gamete)

PRODUCTION OF GAMETES

RED SEAWEED
Dilsea carnosa

Thallus
(plant
body)

Lamina
(blade)

Hapteron
(holdfast)

GREEN ALGA
Spirogyra sp.

Cytoplasm

Cell (cylindrical)

Cell wall

Filament
(strand of
linked cells)

Two filaments
linked for
conjugation
(sexual
reproduction)

End wall
of cell

Spirally
wound
chloroplast

Conjugation
tube

End wall of conjugation
tube still in place

Antherozoid (male
gamete) swims
towards oosphere

Flagellum

Oosphere
(female
gamete) is
fertilized by
antherozoid
to produce
a zygote

FERTILIZATION

Young thallus
(plant body)

Hapteron
(holdfast)

**ZYGOTE DEVELOPS INTO
A YOUNG SEAWEED**

Flexible stipe
(stalk)

Hapteron
(holdfast)

Liverworts and mosses

LIVERWORTS AND MOSSES ARE SMALL, LOW-GROWING PLANTS that belong to the phylum Bryophyta. Bryophytes do not have true stems, leaves, or roots (they are anchored to the ground by rhizoids), nor do they have the vascular tissues (xylem and phloem) that transport water and nutrients in higher plants. With no outer, waterproof cuticle, bryophytes are susceptible to drying out, and most grow in moist habitats. The bryophyte life-cycle has two stages. In stage one, the green plant (gametophyte) produces male and female gametes (sex cells), which fuse to form a zygote. In stage two, the zygote develops into a sporophyte that remains attached to the gametophyte. The sporophyte produces spores, which are released and germinate into new green plants. Liverworts (class Hepaticae) grow horizontally and may be thalloid (flat and ribbon-like) or "leafy". Mosses (class Musci) typically have an upright "stem" with spirally arranged "leaves".

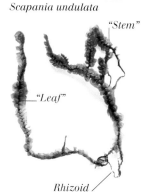

A LEAFY LIVERWORT
Scapania undulata

"Stem"

"Leaf"

Rhizoid

A THALLOID LIVERWORT
Marchantia polymorpha

Gemma cup

Gemma (detachable tissue that produces new plants)

Thallus (plant body)

Toothed margin of cup

DETAIL OF GEMMA CUP

Archegoniophore (stalked structure carrying archegonia)

Disc

Lobe

Stalk

Thallus (plant body)

Apical notch

Rhizoid

FEMALE GAMETOPHYTE

Disc

Lobe

Stalk

SIDE VIEW OF ARCHEGONIOPHORE

Lobe

Disc

Ray (radial groove)

Stalk

ARCHEGONIOPHORE FROM BELOW

Pore

Ray (radial groove)

MICROGRAPH OF LOBE

MICROGRAPH OF THALLUS
Conocephalum conicum

Position of air chamber

Pore for exchange of gases

Upper surface

Rhizoid

Gemma cup

Thallus (plant body)

Midrib

Archegoniophore (stalked structure carrying archegonia)

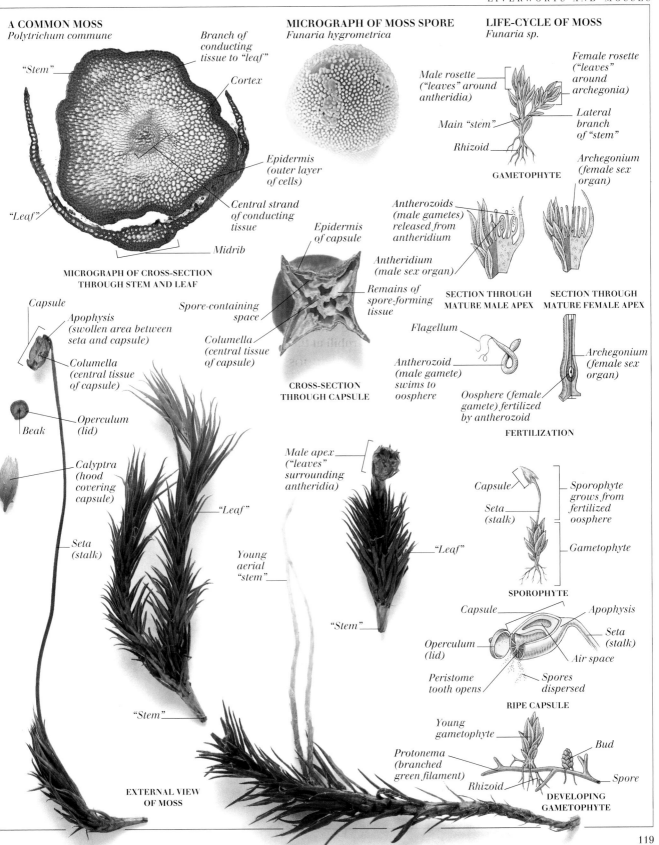

A COMMON MOSS
Polytrichum commune

"Stem"

Branch of conducting tissue to "leaf"

Cortex

Epidermis (outer layer of cells)

Central strand of conducting tissue

"Leaf"

Midrib

MICROGRAPH OF CROSS-SECTION THROUGH STEM AND LEAF

MICROGRAPH OF MOSS SPORE
Funaria hygrometrica

LIFE-CYCLE OF MOSS
Funaria sp.

Male rosette ("leaves" around antheridia)

Female rosette ("leaves" around archegonia)

Main "stem"

Lateral branch of "stem"

Rhizoid

GAMETOPHYTE

Archegonium (female sex organ)

Antherozoids (male gametes) released from antheridium

Antheridium (male sex organ)

SECTION THROUGH MATURE MALE APEX

SECTION THROUGH MATURE FEMALE APEX

Flagellum

Antherozoid (male gamete) swims to oosphere

Archegonium (female sex organ)

Oosphere (female gamete) fertilized by antherozoid

FERTILIZATION

Capsule

Apophysis (swollen area between seta and capsule)

Columella (central tissue of capsule)

Operculum (lid)

Beak

Calyptra (hood covering capsule)

Seta (stalk)

Epidermis of capsule

Spore-containing space

Remains of spore-forming tissue

Columella (central tissue of capsule)

CROSS-SECTION THROUGH CAPSULE

"Leaf"

Male apex ("leaves" surrounding antheridia)

"Leaf"

Young aerial "stem"

"Stem"

Capsule

Seta (stalk)

Sporophyte grows from fertilized oosphere

Gametophyte

SPOROPHYTE

Capsule

Operculum (lid)

Peristome tooth opens

Apophysis

Seta (stalk)

Air space

Spores dispersed

RIPE CAPSULE

Young gametophyte

Protonema (branched green filament)

Rhizoid

Bud

Spore

DEVELOPING GAMETOPHYTE

"Stem"

EXTERNAL VIEW OF MOSS

119

Horsetails, clubmosses, and ferns

HORSETAILS, CLUBMOSSES, AND FERNS are primitive land plants, which, like higher plants, have stems, roots, and leaves, and vascular systems that transport water, minerals, and food. However, unlike higher plants, they do not produce seeds when reproducing. Their life-cycles involve two stages. In stage one, the sporophyte (green plant) produces spores in sporangia. In stage two, the spores germinate, developing into small, short-lived gametophyte plants that produce male and female gametes (sex cells); the gametes fuse to form a zygote from which a new sporophyte plant develops. Horsetails (phylum Sphenophyta) have erect, green stems with branches arranged in whorls; some stems are fertile and have a single spore-producing strobilus (group of sporangia) at the tip. Clubmosses (phylum Lycopodophyta) typically have small leaves arranged spirally around the stem, with spore-producing strobili at the tip of some stems. Ferns (phylum Filicinophyta) typically have large, pinnate fronds (leaves); sporangia, grouped together in sori, develop on the underside of fertile fronds.

FROND
Male fern
(*Dryopteris filix-mas*)

CLUBMOSS
Lycopodium sp.

Stem with spirally arranged leaves

Branch

Strobilus (group of sporangia)

CLUBMOSS
Selaginella sp.

Epidermis (outer layer of cells)

Cortex (layer between epidermis and vascular tissue)

Shoot apex

Branch

Rhizophore (leafless branch)

Vascular tissue — Phloem / Xylem

Lacuna (air space)

Root

Creeping stem with spirally arranged leaves

MICROGRAPH OF CROSS-SECTION THROUGH CLUBMOSS STEM

HORSETAIL
Common horsetail
(*Equisetum arvense*)

Apex of sterile shoot

Sporangiophore (structure carrying sporangia)

Strobilus (group of sporangia)

Non-photosynthetic fertile stem

Young shoot

Collar of small brown leaves

Lateral branch

Photosynthetic sterile stem

Node

Internode

Node

Tuber

Rhizome

Adventitious root

Endodermis (inner layer of cortex)

Vascular tissue

Sclerenchyma (strengthening tissue)

Chlorenchyma (photosynthetic tissue)

Epidermis (outer layer of cells)

Parenchyma (packing tissue)

Cortex (layer between epidermis and vascular tissue)

Hollow pith cavity

Vallecular canal (longitudinal channel)

Carinal canal (longitudinal channel)

MICROGRAPH OF CROSS-SECTION THROUGH HORSETAIL STEM

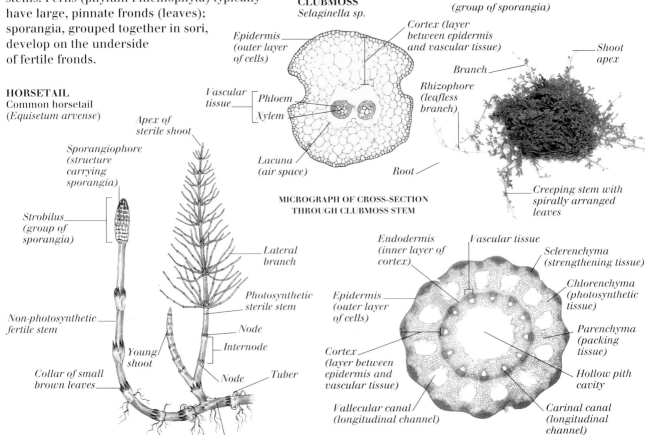

120

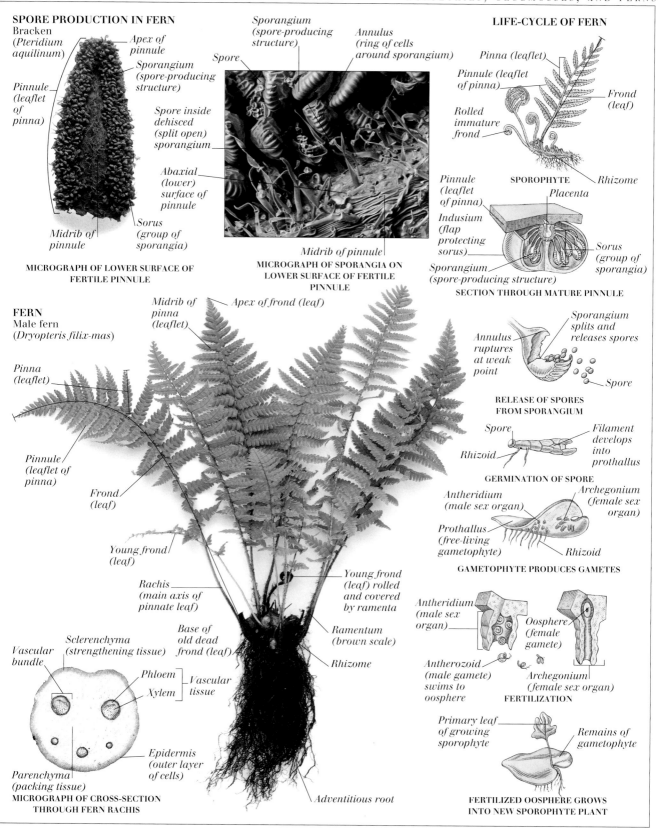

SPORE PRODUCTION IN FERN
Bracken
(*Pteridium aquilinum*)

Apex of pinnule

Sporangium (spore-producing structure)

Pinnule (leaflet of pinna)

Spore

Sporangium (spore-producing structure)

Annulus (ring of cells around sporangium)

Spore inside dehisced (split open) sporangium

Abaxial (lower) surface of pinnule

Midrib of pinnule

Sorus (group of sporangia)

MICROGRAPH OF LOWER SURFACE OF FERTILE PINNULE

Midrib of pinnule
MICROGRAPH OF SPORANGIA ON LOWER SURFACE OF FERTILE PINNULE

LIFE-CYCLE OF FERN

Pinna (leaflet)

Pinnule (leaflet of pinna)

Rolled immature frond

Frond (leaf)

SPOROPHYTE

Rhizome

Pinnule (leaflet of pinna)

Placenta

Indusium (flap protecting sorus)

Sorus (group of sporangia)

Sporangium (spore-producing structure)

SECTION THROUGH MATURE PINNULE

Sporangium splits and releases spores

Annulus ruptures at weak point

Spore

RELEASE OF SPORES FROM SPORANGIUM

Spore

Filament develops into prothallus

Rhizoid

GERMINATION OF SPORE

Antheridium (male sex organ)

Archegonium (female sex organ)

Prothallus (free-living gametophyte)

Rhizoid

GAMETOPHYTE PRODUCES GAMETES

Antheridium (male sex organ)

Oosphere (female gamete)

Antherozoid (male gamete) swims to oosphere

Archegonium (female sex organ)

FERTILIZATION

Primary leaf of growing sporophyte

Remains of gametophyte

FERTILIZED OOSPHERE GROWS INTO NEW SPOROPHYTE PLANT

FERN
Male fern
(*Dryopteris filix-mas*)

Midrib of pinna (leaflet)

Apex of frond (leaf)

Pinna (leaflet)

Pinnule (leaflet of pinna)

Frond (leaf)

Young frond (leaf)

Rachis (main axis of pinnate leaf)

Base of old dead frond (leaf)

Young frond (leaf) rolled and covered by ramenta

Ramentum (brown scale)

Rhizome

Vascular bundle

Sclerenchyma (strengthening tissue)

Phloem

Xylem

Vascular tissue

Epidermis (outer layer of cells)

Parenchyma (packing tissue)

MICROGRAPH OF CROSS-SECTION THROUGH FERN RACHIS

Adventitious root

121

Gymnosperms 1

THE GYMNOSPERMS ARE FOUR RELATED PHYLA of seed-producing plants; their seeds, however, lack the protective, outer covering which surrounds the seeds of flowering plants. Typically, gymnosperms are woody, perennial shrubs or trees, with stems, leaves, and roots, and a well-developed vascular (transport) system. The reproductive structures in most gymnosperms are cones: male cones produce microspores in which male gametes (sex cells) develop; female cones produce megaspores in which female gametes develop. Microspores are blown by the wind to female cones, male and female gametes fuse during fertilization, and a seed develops. The four gymnosperm phyla are the conifers (phylum Coniferophyta), mostly tall trees; cycads (phylum Cycadophyta), small palm-like trees; the ginkgo or maidenhair tree (phylum Ginkgophyta), a tall tree with bilobed leaves; and gnetophytes (phylum Gnetophyta), a diverse group of plants, mainly shrubs, but also including the horizontally growing welwitschia.

LIFE-CYCLE OF SCOTS PINE
(*Pinus sylvestris*)

Needle
(*foliage
leaf*)

Cone

Ovuliferous scale
(*ovule- then seed-
bearing structure*)

MALE CONES   **YOUNG FEMALE CONE**

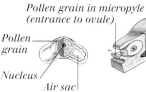

Pollen grain in micropyle
(*entrance to ovule*)   Ovuliferous
scale

Pollen
grain

Ovule
(*contains
female
gamete*)

Nucleus

Air sac

POLLINATION

Integument
(*outer part
of ovule*)

Archegonium
(*containing
female
gamete*)

Pollen tube
(*carries male
gamete from
pollen grain
to ovum*)   **FERTILIZATION**

SCALE AND SEEDS
Pine
(*Pinus sp.*)

Ovuliferous scale
(*ovule- then seed-
bearing structure*)

Wing
scar

Wing of seed
derived from
ovuliferous scale

Seed

Seed

Point of attachment
to axis of cone

Seed scar

**OVULIFEROUS SCALE FROM
THIRD-YEAR FEMALE CONE**

Microsporangium
(*structure in which
pollen grains are
formed*)

Ovuliferous
scale
(*ovule- then
seed-bearing
structure*)

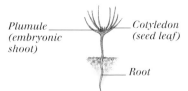

Seed

Seed

Wing

**MATURE FEMALE CONE AND
WINGED SEED**

Microsporophyll
(*modified leaf
carrying
microsporangia*)

Ovule
(*contains
female
gametes*)

Bract
scale

Plumule
(*embryonic
shoot*)

Cotyledon
(*seed leaf*)

Root

**GERMINATION OF
PINE SEEDLING**

Axis
of cone

Scale leaf

Ovuliferous scale
(*ovule- then seed-
bearing structure*)

Axis
of cone

**MICROGRAPH OF LONGITUDINAL
SECTION THROUGH YOUNG
MALE CONE**

**MICROGRAPH OF LONGITUDINAL
SECTION THROUGH SECOND-YEAR
FEMALE CONE**

WELWITSCHIA
(*Welwitschia mirabilis*)

Frayed end of leaf

SMOOTH CYPRESS
(*Cupressus glabra*)

Immature female cone

Ovuliferous scale (ovule- then seed-bearing structure)

Ovuliferous scale

Ovule (contains female gamete)

CROSS-SECTION THROUGH IMMATURE CONE

Scale-like leaf

Seed

Ovuliferous scale (ovule- then seed-bearing structure)

CROSS-SECTION THROUGH MATURE CONE

Mature female cone

Immature male cone

Woody scale

Opening between woody scales through which seeds are released

DISCARDED CONE

Stem

YEW
(*Taxus baccata*)

Single ovule (contains female gamete)

Scale

Female "cone"

Scale

Developing seed

Scale

FEMALE "CONES" AT VARIOUS STAGES OF DEVELOPMENT

Seed

Aril (fleshy outgrowth from seed)

Stem

Needle (foliage leaf)

CYCAD
Sago palm
(*Cycas revoluta*)

Pinnate leaf

Scale leaf

Pinna (leaflet)

Old leaf base

Stem covered by scale leaves

Continuously growing leaf

MAIDENHAIR TREE
(*Ginkgo biloba*)

Stem

Girdle scar

Petiole (leaf stalk)

Bilobed leaf

Site of cone growth

Adaxial (upper) surface of leaf

Abaxial (lower) surface of leaf

Frayed end of leaf

Immature cone

Stalk scar

Woody stem

123

Gymnosperms 2

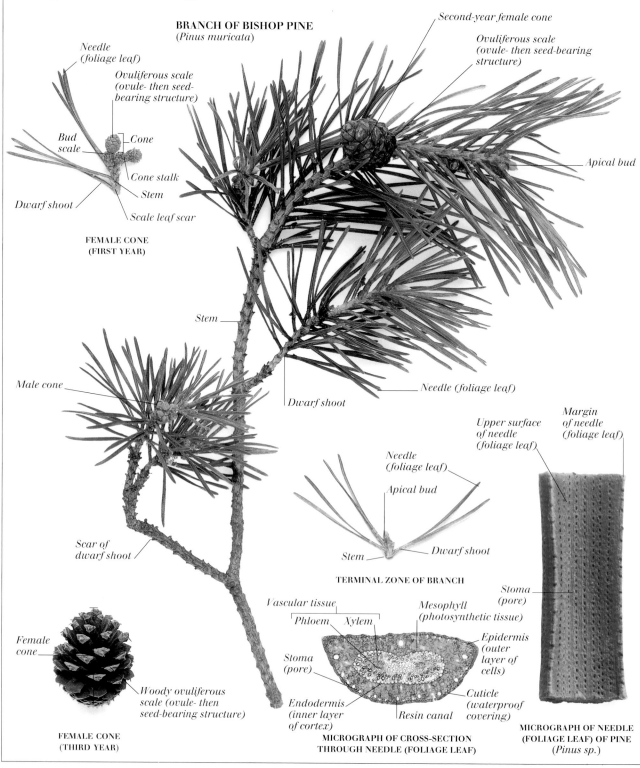

BRANCH OF BISHOP PINE
(*Pinus muricata*)

*Needle
(foliage leaf)*

*Ovuliferous scale
(ovule- then seed-
bearing structure)*

*Bud
scale*

Cone

Cone stalk

Stem

Dwarf shoot

Scale leaf scar

**FEMALE CONE
(FIRST YEAR)**

Second-year female cone

*Ovuliferous scale
(ovule- then seed-bearing
structure)*

Apical bud

Stem

Dwarf shoot

Needle (foliage leaf)

Male cone

*Scar of
dwarf shoot*

*Female
cone*

*Woody ovuliferous
scale (ovule- then
seed-bearing structure)*

**FEMALE CONE
(THIRD YEAR)**

*Needle
(foliage leaf)*

Apical bud

Stem

Dwarf shoot

TERMINAL ZONE OF BRANCH

*Upper surface
of needle
(foliage leaf)*

*Margin
of needle
(foliage leaf)*

*Stoma
(pore)*

**MICROGRAPH OF NEEDLE
(FOLIAGE LEAF) OF PINE
(*Pinus sp.*)**

Vascular tissue

Phloem   *Xylem*

*Mesophyll
(photosynthetic tissue)*

*Stoma
(pore)*

*Epidermis
(outer
layer of
cells)*

*Endodermis
(inner layer
of cortex)*

Resin canal

*Cuticle
(waterproof
covering)*

**MICROGRAPH OF CROSS-SECTION
THROUGH NEEDLE (FOLIAGE LEAF)**

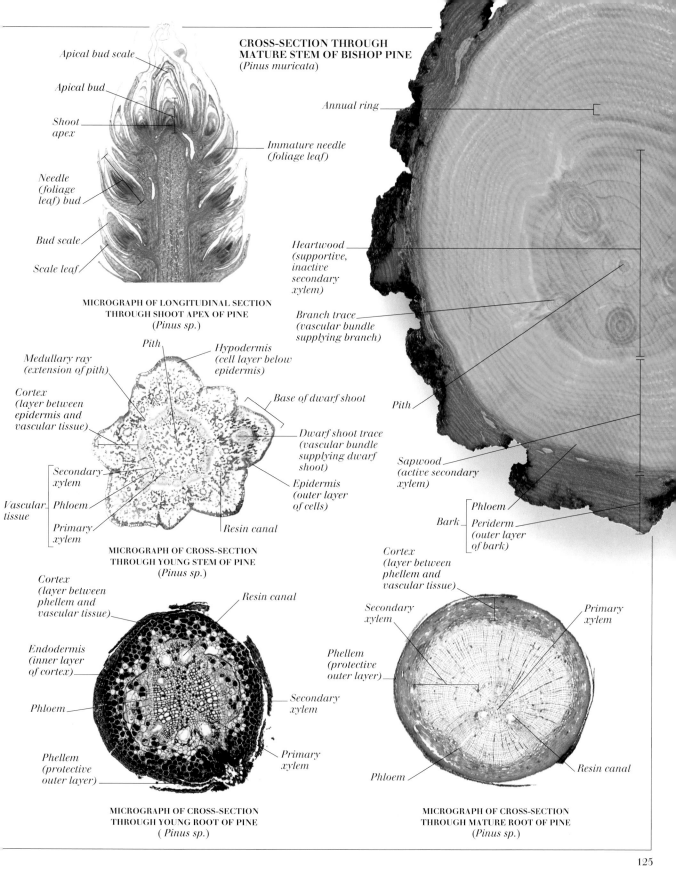

CROSS-SECTION THROUGH MATURE STEM OF BISHOP PINE
(*Pinus muricata*)

Apical bud scale

Apical bud

Shoot apex

Needle (foliage leaf) bud

Bud scale

Scale leaf

Annual ring

Immature needle (foliage leaf)

MICROGRAPH OF LONGITUDINAL SECTION THROUGH SHOOT APEX OF PINE
(*Pinus sp.*)

Heartwood (supportive, inactive secondary xylem)

Branch trace (vascular bundle supplying branch)

Pith

Medullary ray (extension of pith)

Cortex (layer between epidermis and vascular tissue)

Pith

Hypodermis (cell layer below epidermis)

Base of dwarf shoot

Dwarf shoot trace (vascular bundle supplying dwarf shoot)

Epidermis (outer layer of cells)

Secondary xylem

Vascular tissue

Phloem

Primary xylem

Resin canal

Sapwood (active secondary xylem)

Phloem

Bark

Periderm (outer layer of bark)

MICROGRAPH OF CROSS-SECTION THROUGH YOUNG STEM OF PINE
(*Pinus sp.*)

Cortex (layer between phellem and vascular tissue)

Resin canal

Endodermis (inner layer of cortex)

Phloem

Phellem (protective outer layer)

Secondary xylem

Primary xylem

Cortex (layer between phellem and vascular tissue)

Secondary xylem

Phellem (protective outer layer)

Primary xylem

Phloem

Resin canal

MICROGRAPH OF CROSS-SECTION THROUGH YOUNG ROOT OF PINE
(*Pinus sp.*)

MICROGRAPH OF CROSS-SECTION THROUGH MATURE ROOT OF PINE
(*Pinus sp.*)

Monocotyledons and dicotyledons

FLOWERING PLANTS (PHYLUM ANGIOSPERMOPHYTA) are divided into two classes: monocotyledons (class Monocotyledoneae) and dicotyledons (class Dicotyledoneae). Typically, monocotyledons have seeds with one cotyledon (seed leaf); their foliage leaves are narrow with parallel veins; the flower components occur in multiples of three; sepals and petals are indistinguishable and are known as tepals; vascular (transport) tissues are scattered in random bundles throughout the stem; and, since they lack stem cambium (actively dividing cells that produce wood), most monocotyledons are herbaceous (see pp. 128-129). Dicotyledons have seeds with two cotyledons; leaves are broad with a central midrib and branched veins; flower parts occur in multiples of four or five; sepals are generally small and green; petals are large and colourful; vascular bundles are arranged in a ring around the edge of the stem; and, because many dicotyledons possess wood-producing stem cambium, there are woody forms (see pp. 130-131) as well as herbaceous ones.

CROSS-SECTION THROUGH MONOCOTYLEDONOUS LEAF BASES

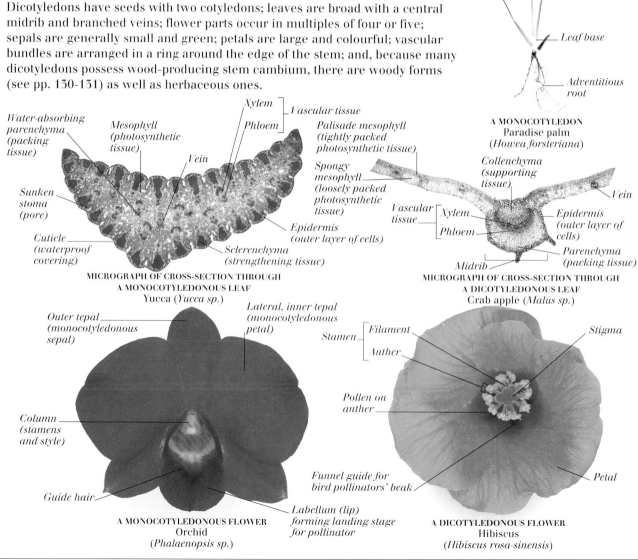

Vein (parallel venation)

Leaflet

Petiole (leaf stalk)

Emerging leaf

Leaf base

Adventitious root

A MONOCOTYLEDON
Paradise palm
(*Howea forsteriana*)

Water-absorbing parenchyma (packing tissue)

Mesophyll (photosynthetic tissue)

Xylem

Phloem

Vascular tissue

Vein

Sunken stoma (pore)

Cuticle (waterproof covering)

Epidermis (outer layer of cells)

Sclerenchyma (strengthening tissue)

MICROGRAPH OF CROSS-SECTION THROUGH A MONOCOTYLEDONOUS LEAF
Yucca (*Yucca sp.*)

Palisade mesophyll (tightly packed photosynthetic tissue)

Spongy mesophyll (loosely packed photosynthetic tissue)

Collenchyma (supporting tissue)

Vascular tissue

Xylem

Phloem

Vein

Epidermis (outer layer of cells)

Parenchyma (packing tissue)

Midrib

MICROGRAPH OF CROSS-SECTION THROUGH A DICOTYLEDONOUS LEAF
Crab apple (*Malus sp.*)

Outer tepal (monocotyledonous sepal)

Lateral, inner tepal (monocotyledonous petal)

Stamen

Filament

Anther

Stigma

Pollen on anther

Column (stamens and style)

Guide hair

Funnel guide for bird pollinators' beak

Labellum (lip) forming landing stage for pollinator

Petal

A MONOCOTYLEDONOUS FLOWER
Orchid
(*Phalaenopsis sp.*)

A DICOTYLEDONOUS FLOWER
Hibiscus
(*Hibiscus rosa-sinensis*)

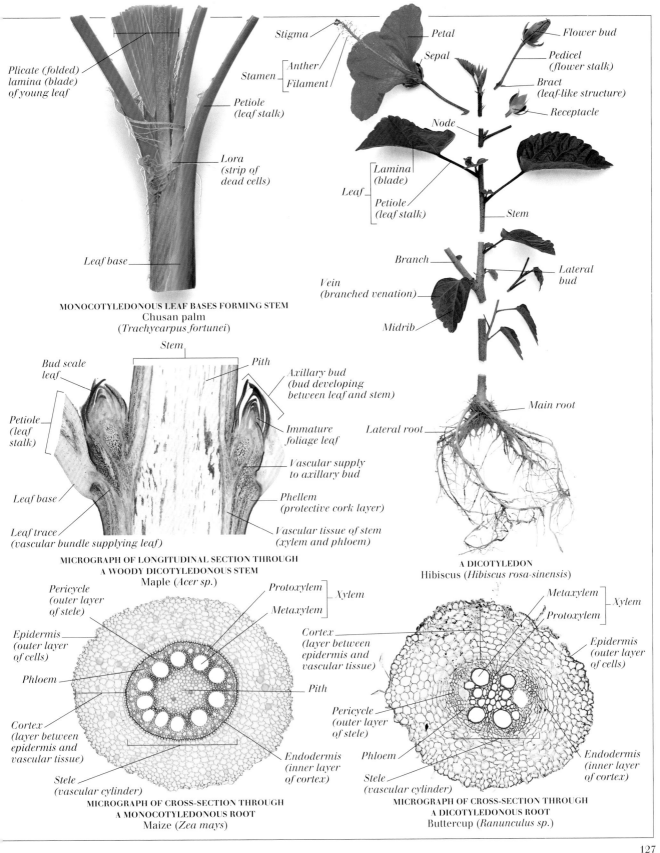

Plicate (folded) lamina (blade) of young leaf

Stigma

Petal

Flower bud

Sepal

Stamen — **Anther** / **Filament**

Pedicel (flower stalk)

Petiole (leaf stalk)

Bract (leaf-like structure)

Lora (strip of dead cells)

Node

Receptacle

Lamina (blade)

Leaf — **Petiole (leaf stalk)**

Stem

Leaf base

Branch

Lateral bud

Vein (branched venation)

Midrib

MONOCOTYLEDONOUS LEAF BASES FORMING STEM
Chusan palm
(*Trachycarpus fortunei*)

Bud scale leaf

Stem

Pith

Axillary bud (bud developing between leaf and stem)

Petiole (leaf stalk)

Immature foliage leaf

Vascular supply to axillary bud

Main root

Lateral root

Leaf base

Leaf trace (vascular bundle supplying leaf)

Phellem (protective cork layer)

Vascular tissue of stem (xylem and phloem)

MICROGRAPH OF LONGITUDINAL SECTION THROUGH
A WOODY DICOTYLEDONOUS STEM
Maple (*Acer sp.*)

A DICOTYLEDON
Hibiscus (*Hibiscus rosa-sinensis*)

Pericycle (outer layer of stele)

Protoxylem — **Xylem**
Metaxylem

Metaxylem — **Xylem**
Protoxylem

Epidermis (outer layer of cells)

Cortex (layer between epidermis and vascular tissue)

Epidermis (outer layer of cells)

Phloem

Pith

Cortex (layer between epidermis and vascular tissue)

Pericycle (outer layer of stele)

Endodermis (inner layer of cortex)

Stele (vascular cylinder)

Endodermis (inner layer of cortex)

Phloem

Stele (vascular cylinder)

MICROGRAPH OF CROSS-SECTION THROUGH
A MONOCOTYLEDONOUS ROOT
Maize (*Zea mays*)

MICROGRAPH OF CROSS-SECTION THROUGH
A DICOTYLEDONOUS ROOT
Buttercup (*Ranunculus sp.*)

Herbaceous flowering plants

HERBACEOUS FLOWERING PLANTS TYPICALLY HAVE GREEN, NON-WOODY STEMS, and tend to be relatively short-lived. Many herbaceous plants live for only one or two years. Annuals (e.g., sweet peas) grow from seed, produce flowers and then seeds, and die within a single year. Biennials (e.g., carrots) have a two-year life cycle. In the first year, seeds grow into plants, which produce leaves and store food in underground storage organs; the stems and foliage then die back in winter. In the second year, new stems grow from the storage organs, produce leaves, flowers, and seeds, and then die. Some herbaceous plants (e.g., potatoes) are perennial. They grow back year after year, producing shoots and flowers in spring, storing food in underground tubers or rhizomes during summer, dying back in autumn, and surviving underground during winter.

Young plant forming

Petiole (stalk) of young leaf

Lateral root

Stipule (structure at base of leaf)

Trifoliate leaf

Node

Simple ovate leaflet

Root nodule

Main root

SWEET PEA
(*Lathyrus odoratus*)

STRAWBERRY
(*Fragaria* x *ananassa*)

Runner (creeping stem)

Remains of leaves

Lateral root scar

Leaf scar

Stem

Rib

Lateral root

Tap root

Leaf scar

Leaf base

CARROT
(*Daucus carota*)

Petiole (leaf stalk)

Spine (modified leaf)

Slender rhizome

Stem tuber

Adventitious root

Stem

Simple deltoid leaf

Narrow, succulent leaf

ROCK STONECROP
(*Sedum rupestre*)

POTATO
(*Solanum tuberosum*)

Adventitious root

PARTS OF HERBACEOUS FLOWERING PLANTS

Succulent, simple ovate leaf

Midrib

Bract (leaf-like structure)

Bracteole (small bract)

Cyme (type of inflorescence)

Inner, tubular disc floret

Outer, ligulate ray floret

Node

Dentate margin

Flower bud

Peduncle (inflorescence stalk)

Internode

LIVE-FOR-EVER OR ICE PLANT
(Sedum spectabile)

Simple lobed leaf

Petiole (leaf stalk)

Leaf base

Prickle

FLORISTS' CHRYSANTHEMUM
(Chrysanthemum morifolium)

Capitulum (type of inflorescence)

Leaf

Peduncle (inflorescence stalk)

Petiole (leaf stalk)

Stem

Flower bud

Linear leaf

Succulent stem

Leaf scar

Lateral bud

CEREOID CACTUS

BEGONIA
(Begonia x tuberhybrida)

Bract (leaf-like structure)

Spinose-dentate margin

Capitulum (type of inflorescence)

Hollow stem

Sheath formed from leaf base

TOADFLAX
(Linaria sp.)

SLENDER THISTLE
(Carduus tenuiflorus)

Dentate margin

Unwinged rachis (main axis of pinnate leaf)

Rachis (main axis of pinnate leaf)

Winged stem

Stipule (structure at base of leaf)

Tendril

Pinna (leaflet)

Petiole (leaf stalk)

Peduncle (inflorescence stalk)

Stem segment

Winged rachis (main axis of pinnate leaf)

HOGWEED
(Heracleum sphondylium)

Peduncle (inflorescence stalk)

Flower bud

Bract (leaf-like structure)

Tepal

PERUVIAN LILY
(Alstroemeria aurea)

Margin of cladode

Toothed notch

Cladode (flattened stem)

Stem branch

Raceme (type of inflorescence)

Petal

Sepal

EVERLASTING PEA
(Lathyrus latifolius)

CRAB CACTUS
(Schlumbergera truncata)

Woody flowering plants

WOODY FLOWERING PLANTS ARE PERENNIAL, that is, they continue to grow and reproduce for many years. They have one or more permanent stems above ground, and numerous smaller branches. The stems and branches have a strong woody core that supports the plant and contains vascular tissue for transporting water and nutrients. Outside the woody core is a layer of tough, protective bark, which has lenticels (tiny pores) in it to enable gases to pass through. Woody flowering plants may be shrubs, which have several stems arising from the soil; bushes, which are shrubs with dense branching and foliage; or trees, which typically have a single upright stem (the trunk) that bears branches. Deciduous woody plants (e.g., roses) shed all their leaves once a year and remain leafless during winter. Evergreen woody plants (e.g., ivy) shed their leaves gradually, so retaining full leaf cover throughout the year.

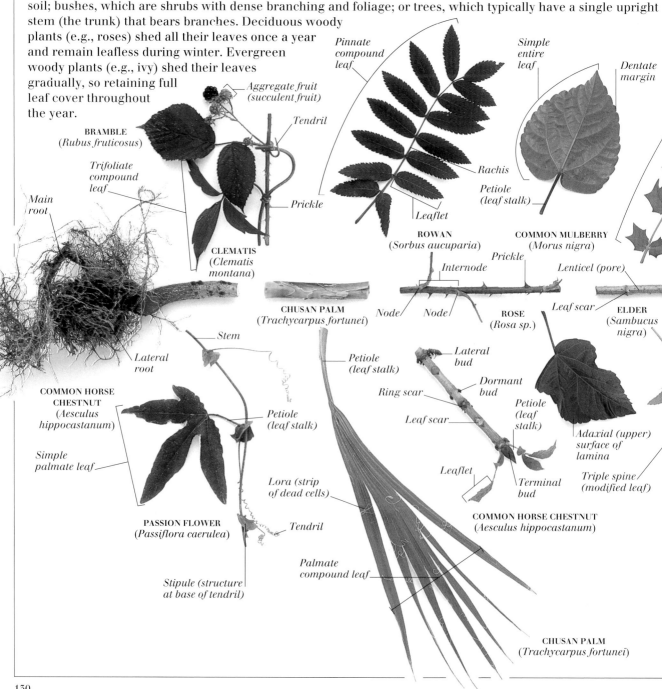

Aggregate fruit (succulent fruit)

BRAMBLE (Rubus fruticosus)

Trifoliate compound leaf

Tendril

Prickle

CLEMATIS (Clematis montana)

Main root

Lateral root

Pinnate compound leaf

Rachis

Leaflet

Petiole (leaf stalk)

ROWAN (Sorbus aucuparia)

Simple entire leaf

Dentate margin

COMMON MULBERRY (Morus nigra)

Prickle

Internode

Node

Node

ROSE (Rosa sp.)

Lenticel (pore)

Leaf scar

ELDER (Sambucus nigra)

CHUSAN PALM (Trachycarpus fortunei)

Stem

COMMON HORSE CHESTNUT (Aesculus hippocastanum)

Simple palmate leaf

Petiole (leaf stalk)

PASSION FLOWER (Passiflora caerulea)

Lora (strip of dead cells)

Tendril

Stipule (structure at base of tendril)

Petiole (leaf stalk)

Palmate compound leaf

Lateral bud

Dormant bud

Ring scar

Leaf scar

Leaflet

Terminal bud

Petiole (leaf stalk)

Adaxial (upper) surface of lamina

Triple spine (modified leaf)

COMMON HORSE CHESTNUT (Aesculus hippocastanum)

CHUSAN PALM (Trachycarpus fortunei)

PARTS OF WOODY FLOWERING PLANTS

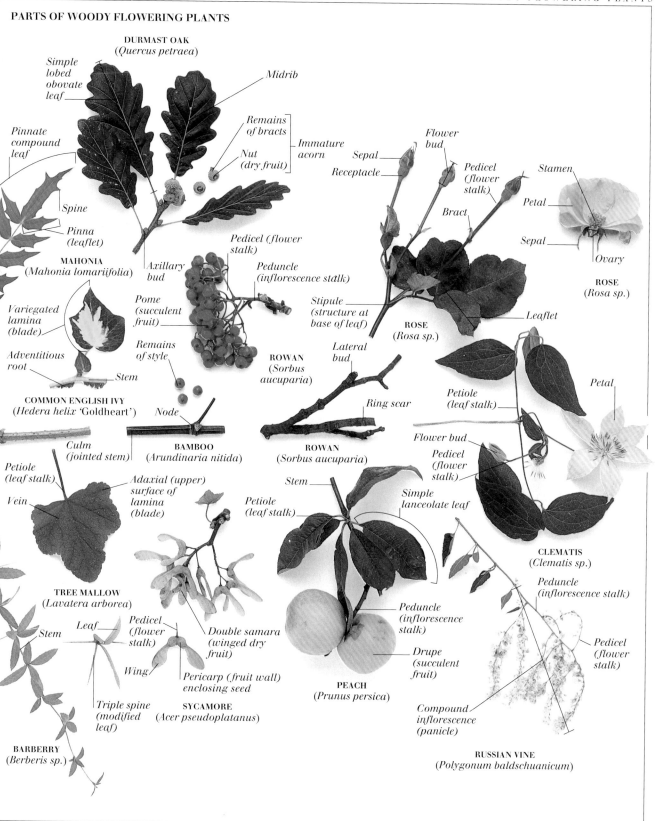

DURMAST OAK
(*Quercus petraea*)

Simple lobed obovate leaf

Midrib

Pinnate compound leaf

Remains of bracts

Immature acorn

Nut (dry fruit)

Flower bud

Sepal

Receptacle

Pedicel (flower stalk)

Stamen

Petal

Sepal

Spine

Pinna (leaflet)

Bract

Ovary

MAHONIA
(*Mahonia lomariifolia*)

Axillary bud

Pedicel (flower stalk)

Peduncle (inflorescence stalk)

ROSE
(*Rosa sp.*)

Variegated lamina (blade)

Pome (succulent fruit)

Stipule (structure at base of leaf)

ROSE
(*Rosa sp.*)

Leaflet

Adventitious root

Remains of style

Stem

Lateral bud

Petiole (leaf stalk)

Petal

COMMON ENGLISH IVY
(*Hedera helix* 'Goldheart')

Node

Ring scar

Flower bud

Pedicel (flower stalk)

ROWAN
(*Sorbus aucuparia*)

ROWAN
(*Sorbus aucuparia*)

Culm (jointed stem)

BAMBOO
(*Arundinaria nitida*)

Petiole (leaf stalk)

Vein

Adaxial (upper) surface of lamina (blade)

Stem

Petiole (leaf stalk)

Simple lanceolate leaf

CLEMATIS
(*Clematis sp.*)

TREE MALLOW
(*Lavatera arborea*)

Pedicel (flower stalk)

Double samara (winged dry fruit)

Peduncle (inflorescence stalk)

Peduncle (inflorescence stalk)

Stem

Leaf

Wing

Pericarp (fruit wall) enclosing seed

Drupe (succulent fruit)

Pedicel (flower stalk)

Triple spine (modified leaf)

SYCAMORE
(*Acer pseudoplatanus*)

PEACH
(*Prunus persica*)

Compound inflorescence (panicle)

BARBERRY
(*Berberis sp.*)

RUSSIAN VINE
(*Polygonum baldschuanicum*)

Roots

ROOTS ARE THE UNDERGROUND PARTS OF PLANTS. They have three main functions. First, they anchor the plant in the soil. Second, they absorb water and minerals from the spaces between soil particles; the roots' absorptive properties are increased by root hairs, which grow behind the root tip, allowing maximum uptake of vital substances. Third, the root is part of the plant's transport system: xylem carries water and minerals from the roots to the stem and leaves, and phloem carries nutrients from the leaves to all parts of the root system. In addition, some roots (e.g., carrots) are food stores. Roots have an outer epidermis covering a cortex of parenchyma (packing tissue), and a central cylinder of vascular tissue. This arrangement helps the roots resist the forces of compression as they grow through the soil.

CARROT
(*Daucus carota*)

MICROGRAPH OF PRIMARY ROOT DEVELOPMENT
Cabbage (*Brassica sp.*)

Split in testa
as seed
germinates

Cotyledon
(seed leaf)

Primary root

Testa
(seed coat)

Root hair

Root tip
(region of
cell division)

FEATURES OF A TYPICAL ROOT
Buttercup
(*Ranunculus sp.*)

Stele
(vascular cylinder)

Phloem sieve tube
(through which
nutrients are
transported)

Pericycle
(outer layer
of stele)

Companion cell
(cell associated
with phloem
sieve tube)

Root hair

Cortex
(layer between
epidermis and
vascular tissue)

Air space
(allowing gas
diffusion in
the root)

Root hair

Epidermis
(outer layer
of cells)

Xylem vessel
(through which water
and minerals are transported)

Endodermis
(inner layer
of cortex)

Cell wall

Nucleus

Cytoplasm

Parenchyma
(packing) cell

PRIMARY ROOT AND MICROGRAPHS OF SECTIONS THROUGH ROOTS

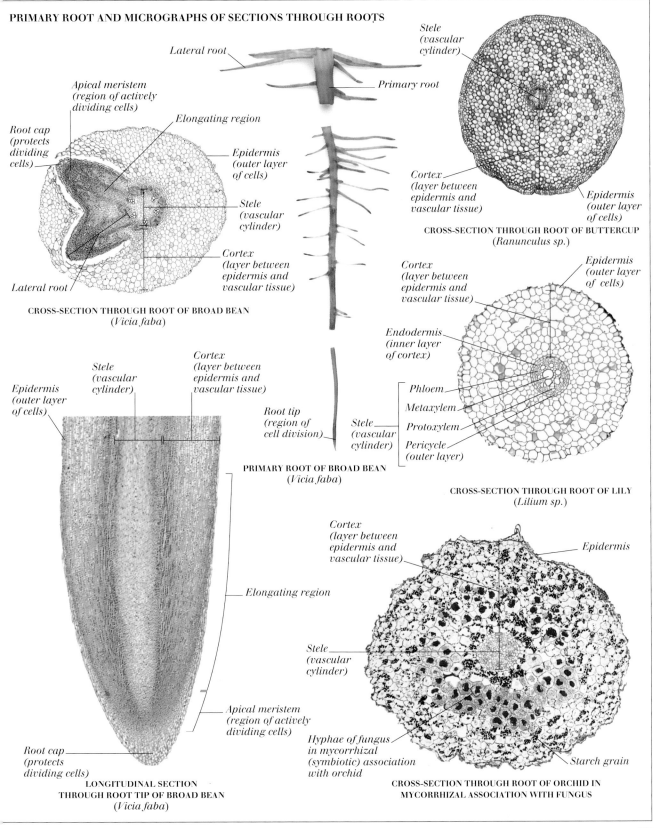

Lateral root

Primary root

Apical meristem (region of actively dividing cells)

Elongating region

Root cap (protects dividing cells)

Epidermis (outer layer of cells)

Stele (vascular cylinder)

Cortex (layer between epidermis and vascular tissue)

Lateral root

CROSS-SECTION THROUGH ROOT OF BROAD BEAN
(*Vicia faba*)

Stele (vascular cylinder)

Cortex (layer between epidermis and vascular tissue)

Epidermis (outer layer of cells)

CROSS-SECTION THROUGH ROOT OF BUTTERCUP
(*Ranunculus sp.*)

Cortex (layer between epidermis and vascular tissue)

Epidermis (outer layer of cells)

Endodermis (inner layer of cortex)

Phloem

Metaxylem

Protoxylem

Pericycle (outer layer)

Stele (vascular cylinder)

CROSS-SECTION THROUGH ROOT OF LILY
(*Lilium sp.*)

Stele (vascular cylinder)

Cortex (layer between epidermis and vascular tissue)

Epidermis (outer layer of cells)

Root tip (region of cell division)

Stele (vascular cylinder)

PRIMARY ROOT OF BROAD BEAN
(*Vicia faba*)

Elongating region

Apical meristem (region of actively dividing cells)

Root cap (protects dividing cells)

**LONGITUDINAL SECTION
THROUGH ROOT TIP OF BROAD BEAN**
(*Vicia faba*)

Cortex (layer between epidermis and vascular tissue)

Epidermis

Stele (vascular cylinder)

Hyphae of fungus in mycorrhizal (symbiotic) association with orchid

Starch grain

**CROSS-SECTION THROUGH ROOT OF ORCHID IN
MYCORRHIZAL ASSOCIATION WITH FUNGUS**

Stems

THE STEM IS THE MAIN SUPPORTIVE PART OF A PLANT that grows above ground. Stems bear leaves (organs of photosynthesis), which grow at nodes; buds (shoots covered by protective scales), which grow at the stem tip (apical or terminal buds) and in the angle between a leaf and the stem (axillary or lateral buds); and flowers (reproductive structures). The stem forms part of the plant's transport system: xylem tissue in the stem transports water and minerals from the roots to the aerial parts of the plant, and phloem tissue transports nutrients manufactured in the leaves to other parts of the plant. Stem tissues are also used for storing water and food. Herbaceous (non-woody) stems have an outer protective epidermis covering a cortex that consists mainly of parenchyma (packing tissue) but also has some collenchyma (supporting tissue). The vascular tissue of such stems is arranged in bundles, each of which consists of xylem, phloem, and sclerenchyma (strengthening tissue). Woody stems have an outer protective layer of tough bark, which is perforated with lenticels (pores) to allow gas exchange. Inside the bark is a ring of secondary phloem, which surrounds an inner core of secondary xylem.

MICROGRAPH OF LONGITUDINAL SECTION THROUGH APEX OF STEM
Coleus sp.

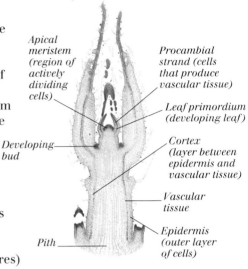

Apical meristem (region of actively dividing cells)

Procambial strand (cells that produce vascular tissue)

Leaf primordium (developing leaf)

Developing bud

Cortex (layer between epidermis and vascular tissue)

Vascular tissue

Pith

Epidermis (outer layer of cells)

YOUNG WOODY STEM
Lime
(*Tilia sp.*)

Secondary phloem

Pith

Phellem (protective cork layer)

Cortex (layer between phellem and vascular tissue)

Xylem vessel (through which water and minerals are transported)

Xylem fibre (supporting tissue)

Ray (parenchyma cells)

Phloem sieve tube (through which nutrients are transported)

Phloem fibre (supporting tissue)

Lenticel (pore)

Vascular cambium (actively dividing cells that produce xylem and phloem)

Autumn wood

Spring wood

Secondary xylem

Companion cell (cell associated with phloem sieve tube)

EMERGENT BUDS
London plane
(*Platanus x acerifolia*)

Young leaves emerging

Terminal bud

Lateral bud

Node

Internode

Inner bud scale

Outer bud scale

Node

Leaf scar

Lenticel (pore)

Woody stem

MICROGRAPHS OF CROSS-SECTIONS THROUGH VARIOUS STEMS

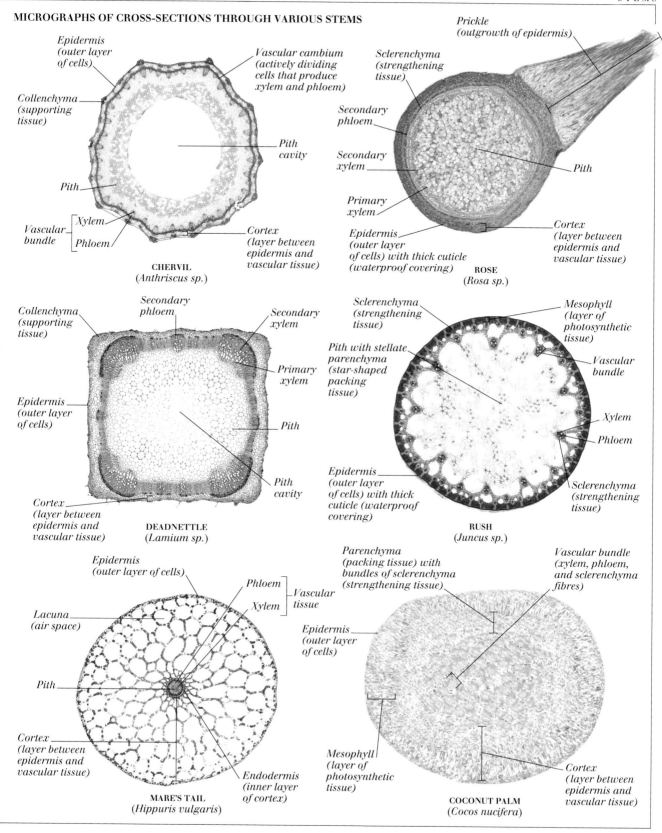

Epidermis (outer layer of cells)

Collenchyma (supporting tissue)

Pith

Vascular bundle — Xylem / Phloem

Vascular cambium (actively dividing cells that produce xylem and phloem)

Pith cavity

Cortex (layer between epidermis and vascular tissue)

CHERVIL (*Anthriscus sp.*)

Prickle (outgrowth of epidermis)

Sclerenchyma (strengthening tissue)

Secondary phloem

Secondary xylem

Primary xylem

Epidermis (outer layer of cells) with thick cuticle (waterproof covering)

Pith

Cortex (layer between epidermis and vascular tissue)

ROSE (*Rosa sp.*)

Collenchyma (supporting tissue)

Secondary phloem

Secondary xylem

Primary xylem

Epidermis (outer layer of cells)

Pith

Pith cavity

Cortex (layer between epidermis and vascular tissue)

DEADNETTLE (*Lamium sp.*)

Sclerenchyma (strengthening tissue)

Pith with stellate parenchyma (star-shaped packing tissue)

Epidermis (outer layer of cells) with thick cuticle (waterproof covering)

Mesophyll (layer of photosynthetic tissue)

Vascular bundle

Xylem

Phloem

Sclerenchyma (strengthening tissue)

RUSH (*Juncus sp.*)

Epidermis (outer layer of cells)

Lacuna (air space)

Pith

Cortex (layer between epidermis and vascular tissue)

Phloem / Xylem — Vascular tissue

Endodermis (inner layer of cortex)

MARE'S TAIL (*Hippuris vulgaris*)

Parenchyma (packing tissue) with bundles of sclerenchyma (strengthening tissue)

Epidermis (outer layer of cells)

Mesophyll (layer of photosynthetic tissue)

Vascular bundle (xylem, phloem, and sclerenchyma fibres)

Cortex (layer between epidermis and vascular tissue)

COCONUT PALM (*Cocos nucifera*)

135

Leaves

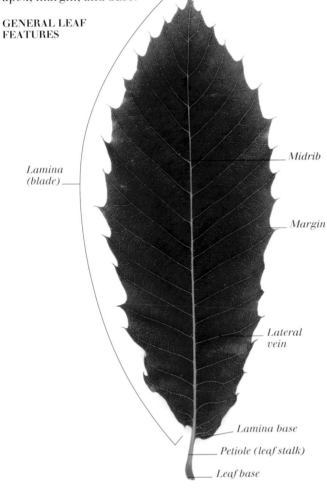

LEAVES ARE THE MAIN SITES OF PHOTOSYNTHESIS (see pp. 138-139) and transpiration (water loss by evaporation) in plants. A typical leaf consists of a thin, flat lamina (blade) supported by a network of veins; a petiole (leaf stalk); and a leaf base, where the petiole joins the stem. Leaves can be classified as simple, in which the lamina is a single unit, or compound, in which the lamina is divided into separate leaflets. Compound leaves may be pinnate, with pinnae (leaflets) on both sides of a rachis (main axis), or palmate, with leaflets arising from a single point at the tip of the petiole. Leaves can be classified further by the overall shape of the lamina, and by the shape of the lamina's apex, margin, and base.

CHECKERBLOOM
(*Sidalcea malviflora*)

SIMPLE LEAF SHAPES

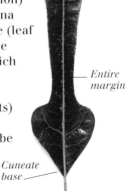

Subacute apex

Acuminate apex

Entire margin

Cuneate base

PANDURIFORM
Croton
(*Codiaeum variegatum*)

Entire margin

Cordate base

LANCEOLATE
Sea buckthorn
(*Hippophae rhamnoides*)

GENERAL LEAF FEATURES

Apex

Midrib

Lamina (blade)

Margin

Lateral vein

Lamina base

Petiole (leaf stalk)

Leaf base

Sweet chestnut
(*Castanea sativa*)

COMPOUND LEAF SHAPES

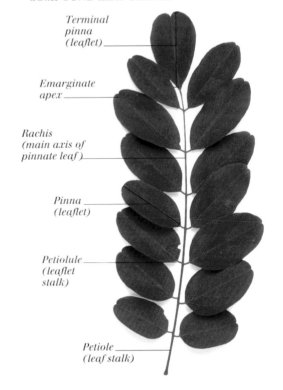

Terminal pinna (leaflet)

Emarginate apex

Rachis (main axis of pinnate leaf)

Pinna (leaflet)

Petiolule (leaflet stalk)

Petiole (leaf stalk)

ODD PINNATE
False acacia
(*Robinia pseudoacacia*)

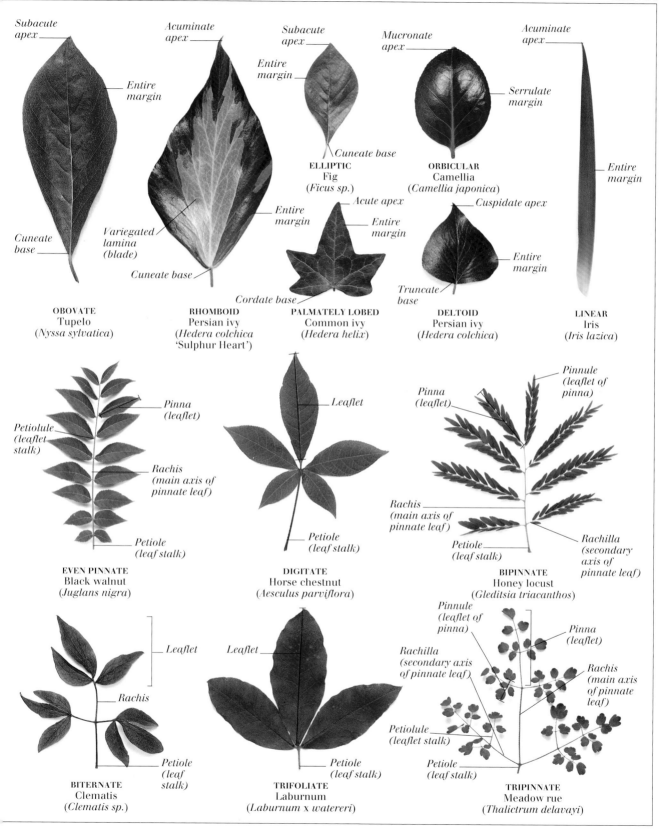

Subacute apex

Entire margin

Cuneate base

OBOVATE
Tupelo
(*Nyssa sylvatica*)

Acuminate apex

Entire margin

Variegated lamina (blade)

Cuneate base

RHOMBOID
Persian ivy
(*Hedera colchica* 'Sulphur Heart')

Subacute apex

Entire margin

Cuneate base

ELLIPTIC
Fig
(*Ficus sp.*)

Acute apex

Entire margin

Cordate base

PALMATELY LOBED
Common ivy
(*Hedera helix*)

Mucronate apex

Serrulate margin

ORBICULAR
Camellia
(*Camellia japonica*)

Cuspidate apex

Entire margin

Truncate base

DELTOID
Persian ivy
(*Hedera colchica*)

Acuminate apex

Entire margin

LINEAR
Iris
(*Iris lazica*)

Pinna (leaflet)

Petiolule (leaflet stalk)

Rachis (main axis of pinnate leaf)

Petiole (leaf stalk)

EVEN PINNATE
Black walnut
(*Juglans nigra*)

Leaflet

Petiole (leaf stalk)

DIGITATE
Horse chestnut
(*Aesculus parviflora*)

Pinnule (leaflet of pinna)

Pinna (leaflet)

Rachis (main axis of pinnate leaf)

Petiole (leaf stalk)

Rachilla (secondary axis of pinnate leaf)

BIPINNATE
Honey locust
(*Gleditsia triacanthos*)

Leaflet

Rachis

Petiole (leaf stalk)

BITERNATE
Clematis
(*Clematis sp.*)

Leaflet

Petiole (leaf stalk)

TRIFOLIATE
Laburnum
(*Laburnum* x *watereri*)

Pinnule (leaflet of pinna)

Rachilla (secondary axis of pinnate leaf)

Petiolule (leaflet stalk)

Petiole (leaf stalk)

Pinna (leaflet)

Rachis (main axis of pinnate leaf)

TRIPINNATE
Meadow rue
(*Thalictrum delavayi*)

Photosynthesis

PHOTOSYNTHESIS IS THE PROCESS by which plants make their food using sunlight, water, and carbon dioxide. It takes place inside special structures in leaf cells called chloroplasts. The chloroplasts contain chlorophyll, a green pigment that absorbs energy from sunlight. During photosynthesis, the absorbed energy is used to join together carbon dioxide and water to form the sugar glucose, which is the energy source for the whole plant; oxygen, a waste product, is released into the air. Leaves are the main sites of photosynthesis, and have various adaptations for that purpose: flat laminae (blades) provide a large surface for absorbing sunlight; stomata (pores) in the lower surface of the laminae allow gases (carbon dioxide and oxygen) to pass into and out of the leaves; and an extensive network of veins brings water into the leaves and transports the glucose produced by photosynthesis to the rest of the plant.

MICROGRAPH OF LEAF
Lily (*Lilium sp.*)

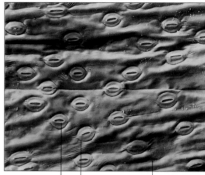

Stoma (pore) *Guard cell (controls opening and closing of stoma)* *Lower surface of lamina (blade)*

THE PROCESS OF PHOTOSYNTHESIS

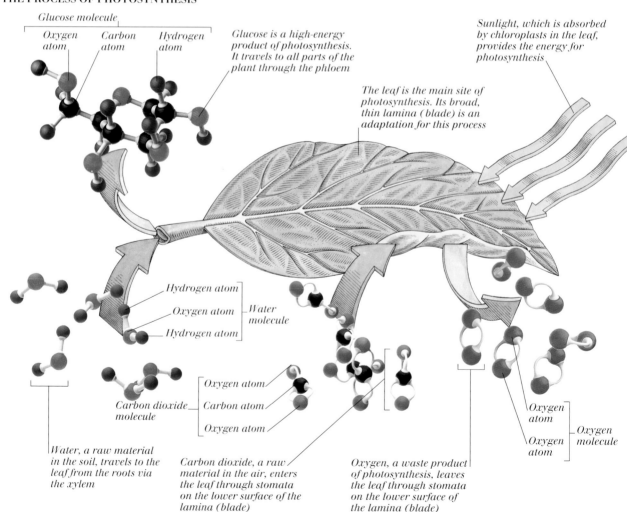

Glucose molecule

Oxygen atom *Carbon atom* *Hydrogen atom*

Glucose is a high-energy product of photosynthesis. It travels to all parts of the plant through the phloem

Sunlight, which is absorbed by chloroplasts in the leaf, provides the energy for photosynthesis

The leaf is the main site of photosynthesis. Its broad, thin lamina (blade) is an adaptation for this process

Hydrogen atom
Oxygen atom *Water molecule*
Hydrogen atom

Carbon dioxide molecule

Oxygen atom
Carbon atom
Oxygen atom

Oxygen atom
Oxygen molecule
Oxygen atom

Water, a raw material in the soil, travels to the leaf from the roots via the xylem

Carbon dioxide, a raw material in the air, enters the leaf through stomata on the lower surface of the lamina (blade)

Oxygen, a waste product of photosynthesis, leaves the leaf through stomata on the lower surface of the lamina (blade)

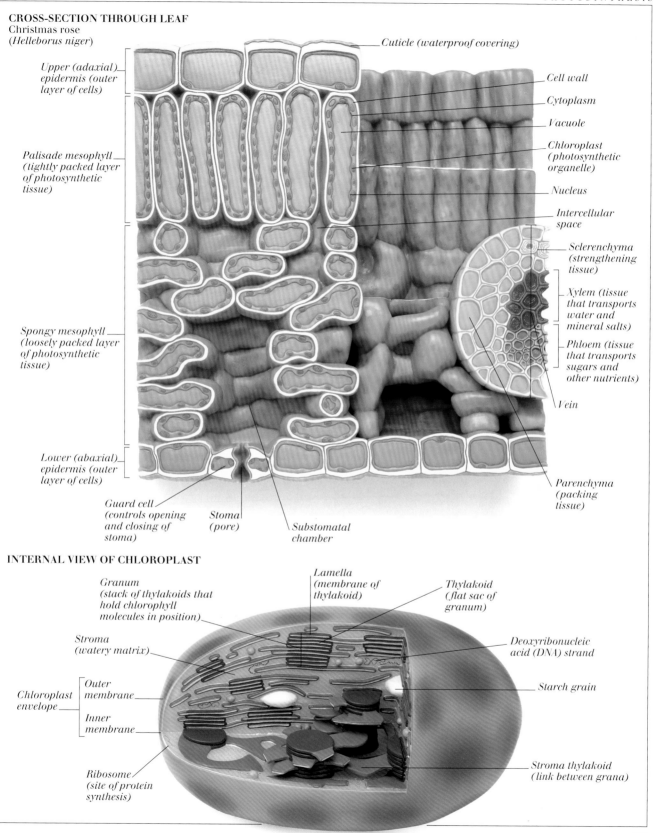

CROSS-SECTION THROUGH LEAF
Christmas rose
(*Helleborus niger*)

Cuticle (waterproof covering)

Upper (adaxial) epidermis (outer layer of cells)

Cell wall

Cytoplasm

Vacuole

Chloroplast (photosynthetic organelle)

Palisade mesophyll (tightly packed layer of photosynthetic tissue)

Nucleus

Intercellular space

Sclerenchyma (strengthening tissue)

Xylem (tissue that transports water and mineral salts)

Phloem (tissue that transports sugars and other nutrients)

Spongy mesophyll (loosely packed layer of photosynthetic tissue)

Vein

Lower (abaxial) epidermis (outer layer of cells)

Parenchyma (packing tissue)

Guard cell (controls opening and closing of stoma)

Stoma (pore)

Substomatal chamber

INTERNAL VIEW OF CHLOROPLAST

Granum (stack of thylakoids that hold chlorophyll molecules in position)

Lamella (membrane of thylakoid)

Thylakoid (flat sac of granum)

Stroma (watery matrix)

Deoxyribonucleic acid (DNA) strand

Chloroplast envelope

Outer membrane

Inner membrane

Starch grain

Ribosome (site of protein synthesis)

Stroma thylakoid (link between grana)

Flowers 1

FLOWERS ARE THE SITES OF SEXUAL REPRODUCTION in flowering plants. Their component parts are arranged in whorls around the receptacle (tip of the flower stalk). The sepals (collectively called the calyx) are outermost; typically small and green, they protect the developing flower. The petals (collectively called the corolla) are typically large and brightly coloured; they are found inside the sepals. In monocotyledonous flowers (see pp. 126-127), sepals and petals are indistinguishable; individually they are called tepals (collectively called the perianth). The petals surround the male and female reproductive structures (androecium and gynoecium). The androecium consists of stamens (male organs); each stamen is made up of a filament (stalk) and anther. The gynoecium has one or more carpels (female organs); each carpel consists of an ovary, style, and stigma. Some flowers (e.g., lily) occur singly on a pedicel (flower stalk); others (e.g., elder, sunflower) are arranged in a group (inflorescence) on a peduncle (inflorescence stalk).

Inner tepal (monocotyledonous petal)
Honey guide
Groove secreting nectar
Filament
Style
Outer tepal (monocotyledonous sepal)
Stigma
Anther

EXTERNAL VIEW

A MONOCOTYLEDONOUS FLOWER
Lily
(Lilium sp.)

Syncarpous (fused carpels) gynoecium
Ovary
Stigma
Style

Inner tepal (monocotyledonous petal)
Honey guide
Outer tepal (monocotyledonous sepal)

Tepal scar
Receptacle

Stamen
Anther
Filament

Pollen on anther

Ovary wall
Ovule

Pedicel (flower stalk)

Papilla (fleshy hair)

Outer tepal sheath
Style
Folded inner tepal (monocotyledonous petal)
Stigma
Ovary
Receptacle
Anther
Pedicel (flower stalk)
Filament

LONGITUDINAL SECTION THROUGH FLOWER BUD

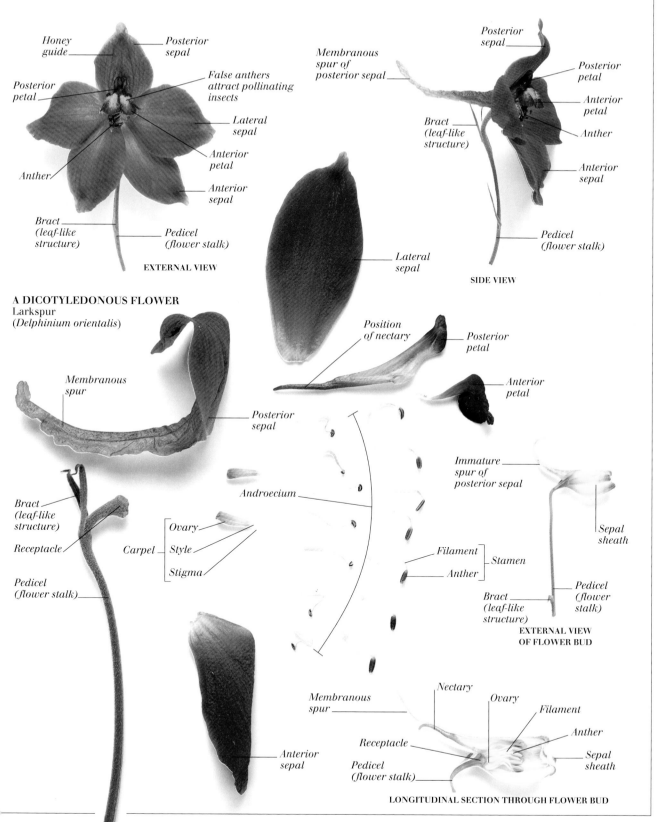

Honey guide

Posterior sepal

Posterior petal

False anthers attract pollinating insects

Lateral sepal

Anterior petal

Anterior sepal

Anther

Bract (leaf-like structure)

Pedicel (flower stalk)

EXTERNAL VIEW

Membranous spur of posterior sepal

Posterior sepal

Posterior petal

Anterior petal

Anther

Bract (leaf-like structure)

Anterior sepal

Pedicel (flower stalk)

SIDE VIEW

Lateral sepal

A DICOTYLEDONOUS FLOWER
Larkspur
(*Delphinium orientalis*)

Membranous spur

Posterior sepal

Position of nectary

Posterior petal

Anterior petal

Immature spur of posterior sepal

Sepal sheath

Bract (leaf-like structure)

Receptacle

Pedicel (flower stalk)

Carpel
- Ovary
- Style
- Stigma

Androecium

Filament

Anther

Stamen

Bract (leaf-like structure)

Pedicel (flower stalk)

EXTERNAL VIEW OF FLOWER BUD

Anterior sepal

Membranous spur

Nectary

Ovary

Filament

Anther

Sepal sheath

Receptacle

Pedicel (flower stalk)

LONGITUDINAL SECTION THROUGH FLOWER BUD

Flowers 2

COMPOUND INFLORESCENCE (CAPITULUM)
Sunflower
(*Helianthus annulus*)

Disc florets

Ray floret

Florets (small flowers) are grouped together to resemble a single large flower

Sterile ray floret to attract pollinating insects

Outer fertilized floret

Two-lobed stigma

Florets with anthers ready to shed pollen

Style

Pollen

Anther

Corolla tube (fused petals)

Inner, immature florets

Pappus (modified sepal)

Ovary

Corolla tube (fused petals)

Ovary

FLORETS FROM SUNFLOWER

Pollen

Anther

Nectar

Disc floret

Ray floret

Stigma

Style

Ovary

Corolla tube (fused petals)

Bract (leaf-like structure)

Hair

Pappus (modified sepal)

Domed receptacle (flattened top of inflorescence stalk)

Pith

Epidermis (outer layer of cells) of peduncle (inflorescence stalk)

Peduncle (inflorescence stalk)

LONGITUDINAL SECTION THROUGH SUNFLOWER INFLORESCENCE

ARRANGEMENT OF FLOWERS ON STEM

Bract
(leaf-like
structure)

Flower

Ovary

Peduncle
(inflorescence
stalk)

Remains of tepals
(monocotyledonous
petals and sepals)

INFLORESCENCE (SPIKE)
Heliconia peruviana

Flower

Petal

Peduncle
(inflorescence
stalk)

Pedicel
(flower
stalk)

**INFLORESCENCE
(COMPOUND UMBEL)**
Common elder
(*Sambucus nigra*)

Spathe
(large bract) to
attract pollinating
insects

Spadix (fleshy
axis) carrying
male and female
flowers

Peduncle
(inflorescence
stalk)

INFLORESCENCE (SPADIX)
Painter's palette
(*Anthurium andreanum*)

Stigma

Anther

Style

Filament

Stamen

Flower
bud

Pedicel
(flower
stalk)

Bract
(leaf-like
structure)

Peduncle
(inflorescence
stalk) fused
to bract

**INFLORESCENCE
(DICHASIAL CYME)**
Common lime
(*Tilia x europaea*)

Three-lobed
stigma

Inner tepal
(monocotyledonous
petal)

Style

Ovary

Filament

Anther

Stamen

Outer tepal
(monocotyledonous
sepal)

Pedicel
(flower stalk)

SINGLE FLOWER
Glory lily
(*Gloriosa superba*)

Flower

Corolla

Calyx

Bract
(leaf-like
structure)

**SINGLE
FLOWER**

Peduncle
(inflorescence
stalk)

**INFLORESCENCE
(SPHERICAL UMBEL)**
Allium sp.

Pollination

POLLINATION IS THE TRANSFER OF POLLEN (which contains the male sex cells) from an anther (part of the male reproductive organ) to a stigma (part of the female reproductive organ). This process precedes fertilization (see pp. 146-147). Pollination may occur within the same flower (self-pollination), or between flowers on separate plants of the same species (cross-pollination). In most plants, pollination is carried out either by insects (entomophilous pollination) or by the wind (anemophilous pollination). Less commonly, birds, bats, or water are the agents of pollination. Insect-pollinated flowers are typically brightly coloured, scented, and produce nectar, on which insects feed. Such flowers also tend to have patterns that are visible only in ultraviolet light, which many insects can see but which humans cannot. These features attract insects, which become covered with the sticky or hooked pollen grains when they visit one flower, and then transfer the pollen to the next flower they visit. Wind-pollinated flowers are generally small, relatively inconspicuous, and unscented. They produce large quantities of light pollen grains that are easily blown by the wind to other flowers.

REPRODUCTIVE STRUCTURES IN WIND-POLLINATED PLANT
Sweet chestnut
(*Castanea sativa*)

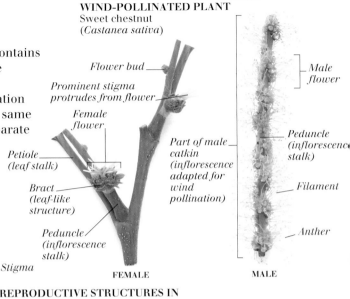

Flower bud

Prominent stigma protrudes from flower

Female flower

Petiole (leaf stalk)

Bract (leaf-like structure)

Peduncle (inflorescence stalk)

Male flower

Peduncle (inflorescence stalk)

Filament

Anther

FEMALE

MALE

REPRODUCTIVE STRUCTURES IN INSECT-POLLINATED PLANTS

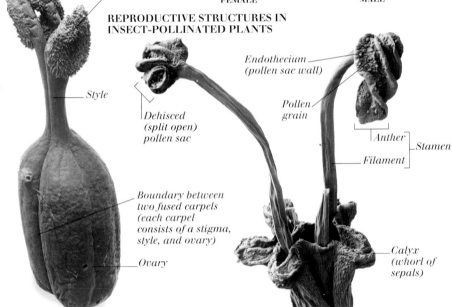

Stigma

Style

Dehisced (split open) pollen sac

Boundary between two fused carpels (each carpel consists of a stigma, style, and ovary)

Ovary

Endothecium (pollen sac wall)

Pollen grain

Anther

Filament

Stamen

Calyx (whorl of sepals)

MICROGRAPH OF STAMENS (MALE ORGANS)
Common centaury
(*Centaurium erythraea*)

MICROGRAPHS OF POLLEN GRAINS

Exine (outer coat of pollen grain)

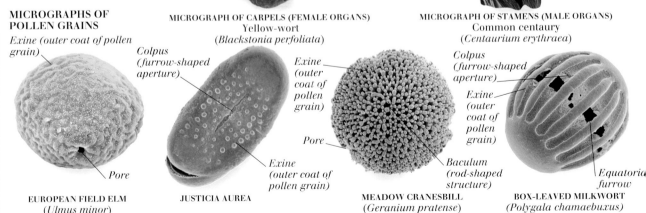

Colpus (furrow-shaped aperture)

Pore

EUROPEAN FIELD ELM
(*Ulmus minor*)

MICROGRAPH OF CARPELS (FEMALE ORGANS)
Yellow-wort
(*Blackstonia perfoliata*)

Exine (outer coat of pollen grain)

JUSTICIA AUREA

Exine (outer coat of pollen grain)

Pore

Baculum (rod-shaped structure)

MEADOW CRANESBILL
(*Geranium pratense*)

Colpus (furrow-shaped aperture)

Exine (outer coat of pollen grain)

Equatorial furrow

BOX-LEAVED MILKWORT
(*Polygala chamaebuxus*)

INSECT POLLINATION OF MEADOW SAGE

Sepal

Immature, unreceptive stigma

Anther pushed on to bee's hairy abdomen

Labellum (lip) forming landing stage for bee

Pollen grains from anther stick to bee's abdomen

1. BEE VISITS FLOWER WITH MATURE ANTHERS BUT IMMATURE STIGMA

Pollen grains attached to hairy abdomen

Long style curves downwards when bee enters flower

Sepal

Mature, receptive stigma touches bee's abdomen, picking up pollen

Labellum (lip) forming landing stage for bee

2. BEE FLIES TO OTHER FLOWERS

3. BEE VISITS FLOWER WHERE THE ANTHERS HAVE WITHERED AND THE STIGMA IS MATURE

SUNFLOWER UNDER NORMAL AND ULTRAVIOLET LIGHT

Central area of disc florets

Ray floret

NORMAL LIGHT

Petal

Ovary

Stigma

Stamen { Filament

Anther

NORMAL LIGHT

ST JOHN'S WORT UNDER NORMAL AND ULTRAVIOLET LIGHT

Honey guide directs insects to dark, central part of flower

Paler, outer part of ray floret

Darker, inner part of ray floret

Insects attracted to darkest, central part of flower, which contains nectaries, anthers, and stigmas

Dark central area containing nectaries, anthers, and stigmas

ULTRAVIOLET LIGHT

ULTRAVIOLET LIGHT

Pore

Exine (outer coat of pollen grain)

Exine (outer coat of pollen grain)

MIMULOPSIS SOLMSII

Trilete mark (development scar)

Exine (outer coat of pollen grain)

THESIUM ALPINIUM

Columella (small column-shaped structure)

Exine (outer coat of pollen grain)

RUELLIA GRANDIFLORA

Colpus (furrow-shaped aperture)

Exine (outer coat of pollen grain)

Tricolpate (three colpae) pollen grain

CROSSANDRA NILOTICA

Fertilization

FERTILIZATION IS THE FUSION of male and female gametes (sex cells) to produce a zygote (embryo). Following pollination (see pp. 144-145), the pollen grains that contain the male gametes are on the stigma, some distance from the female gamete (ovum) inside the ovule. To enable the gametes to meet, the pollen grain germinates and produces a pollen tube, which grows down and enters the embryo sac (the inner part of the ovule that contains the ovum). Two male gametes, travelling at the tip of the pollen tube, enter the embryo sac. One gamete fuses with the ovum to produce a zygote that will develop into an embryo plant. The other male gamete fuses with two polar nuclei to produce the endosperm, which acts as a food store for the developing embryo. Fertilization also initiates other changes: the integument (outer part of ovule) forms a testa (seed coat) around the embryo and endosperm; the petals fall off; the stigma and style wither; and the ovary wall forms a layer (called the pericarp) around the seed. Together, the pericarp and seed form the fruit, which may be succulent (see pp. 148-149) or dry (see pp. 150-151). In some species (e.g., blackberry), apomixis can occur: the seed develops without fertilization of the ovum by a male gamete but endosperm formation and fruit development take place as in other species.

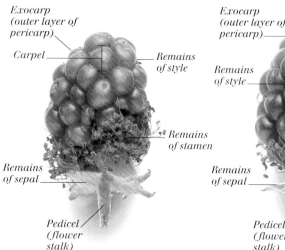

BANANA
(*Musa 'lacatan'*)

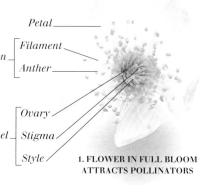

DEVELOPMENT OF A SUCCULENT FRUIT
Blackberry
(*Rubus fruticosus*)

Petal

Stamen
— Filament
— Anther

Carpel
— Ovary
— Stigma
— Style

1. FLOWER IN FULL BLOOM
ATTRACTS POLLINATORS

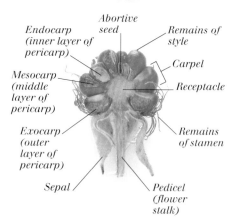

Endocarp
(inner layer of
pericarp)

Abortive
seed

Remains of
style

Carpel

Mesocarp
(middle
layer of
pericarp)

Receptacle

Exocarp
(outer
layer of
pericarp)

Remains
of stamen

Sepal

Pedicel
(flower
stalk)

4. PERICARP FORMS
FLESH, SKIN, AND A HARD INNER
LAYER (SHOWN IN CROSS-SECTION)

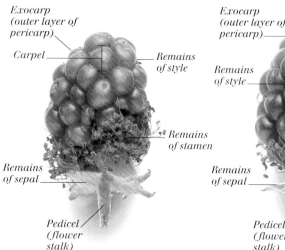

Exocarp
(outer layer of
pericarp)

Carpel

Remains
of style

Remains
of stamen

Remains
of sepal

Pedicel
(flower
stalk)

7. MESOCARP (FLESHY PART OF PERICARP)
OF EACH CARPEL STARTS TO
CHANGE COLOUR

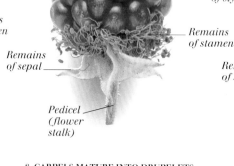

Exocarp
(outer layer of
pericarp)

Drupelet

Remains
of style

Remains
of stamen

Remains
of sepal

Pedicel
(flower
stalk)

8. CARPELS MATURE INTO DRUPELETS
(SMALL FLESHY FRUITS WITH SINGLE SEEDS
SURROUNDED BY HARD ENDOCARP)

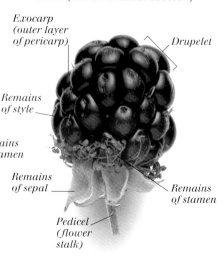

Exocarp
(outer layer
of pericarp)

Drupelet

Remains
of style

Remains
of sepal

Remains
of stamen

Pedicel
(flower
stalk)

9. MESOCARP OF DRUPELET BECOMES
DARKER AND SWEETER

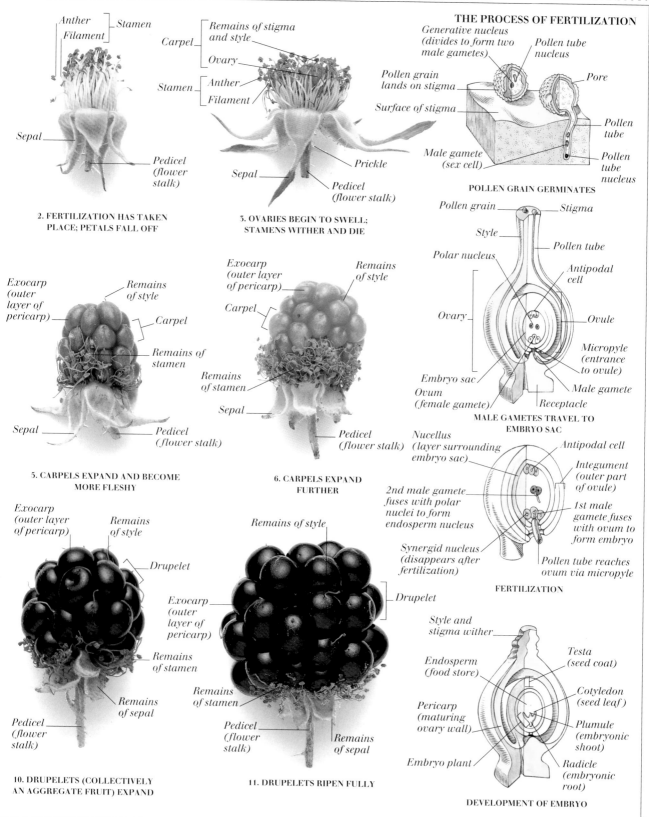

THE PROCESS OF FERTILIZATION

2. FERTILIZATION HAS TAKEN PLACE; PETALS FALL OFF

3. OVARIES BEGIN TO SWELL; STAMENS WITHER AND DIE

POLLEN GRAIN GERMINATES

5. CARPELS EXPAND AND BECOME MORE FLESHY

6. CARPELS EXPAND FURTHER

MALE GAMETES TRAVEL TO EMBRYO SAC

FERTILIZATION

10. DRUPELETS (COLLECTIVELY AN AGGREGATE FRUIT) EXPAND

11. DRUPELETS RIPEN FULLY

DEVELOPMENT OF EMBRYO

Succulent fruits

A FRUIT IS A FULLY DEVELOPED and ripened ovary (seed-producing part of a plant's female reproductive organs). Fruits may be succulent or dry (see pp. 150-151). Succulent fruits are fleshy and brightly coloured, making them attractive to animals, which eat them and so disperse the seeds away from the parent plant. The wall (pericarp) of a succulent fruit has three layers: an outer exocarp, a middle mesocarp, and an inner endocarp. These three layers vary in thickness and texture in different types of fruits and may blend into each other. Succulent fruits can be classed as simple (derived from one ovary) or compound (derived from several ovaries). Simple succulent fruits include berries, which typically have many seeds, and drupes, which typically have a single stone or pip (e.g., cherry and peach). Compound succulent fruits include aggregate fruits, which are formed from many ovaries in one flower, and multiple fruits, which develop from the ovaries of many flowers. Some fruits, known as false fruits or pseudocarps, develop from parts of the flower in addition to the ovaries. For example, the flesh of the apple is formed from the receptacle (the upper end of the flower stalk).

BERRY
Cocoa
(*Theobroma cacao*)

HESPERIDIUM (A TYPE OF BERRY)
Lemon
(*Citrus limon*)

Pedicel (flower stalk)

Leathery exocarp

Remains of style

EXTERNAL VIEW OF FRUIT

Endocarp

Mesocarp

Oil gland

Remains of style

Pedicel (flower stalk)

Exocarp

Seed

Vesicle (juice sac)

Placenta

LONGITUDINAL SECTION THROUGH FRUIT

Hilum (point of attachment to ovary)

Testa (seed coat)

Embryo

Cotyledon (seed leaf)

EXTERNAL VIEW AND SECTION THROUGH SEED

Seed

Carpel wall

Carpel

Placenta

CROSS-SECTION THROUGH FRUIT

SYCONIUM (A TYPE OF FALSE FRUIT)
Fig
(*Ficus carica*)

Peduncle (inflorescence stalk)

Skin

EXTERNAL VIEW OF FRUIT

Remains of female flowers

Pip (seed surrounded by endocarp)

Fleshy infolded receptacle

Remains of male flowers

Pore closed by scales

LONGITUDINAL SECTION THROUGH FRUIT

FRUIT WITH FLESHY ARIL
Lychee
(*Litchi chinensis*)

Pedicel (flower stalk)

Pericarp (fruit wall)

EXTERNAL VIEW OF FRUIT

Pedicel (flower stalk)

Seed

Aril (fleshy outgrowth from seed stalk)

Pericarp (fruit wall)

LONGITUDINAL SECTION THROUGH FRUIT

Remains of style

Drupelet

Pedicel (flower stalk)

REMAINS OF A SINGLE FEMALE FLOWER

Pip

Endocarp

EXTERNAL VIEW AND SECTION THROUGH PIP

Endocarp

Embryo

Cotyledon (seed leaf)

Testa (seed coat)

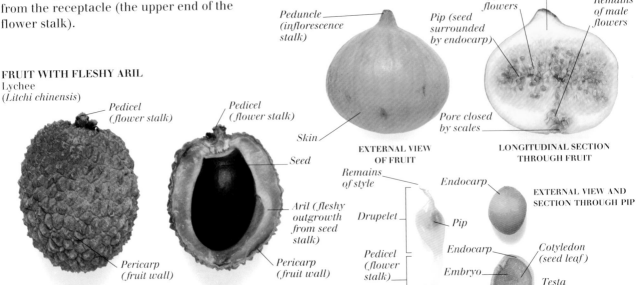

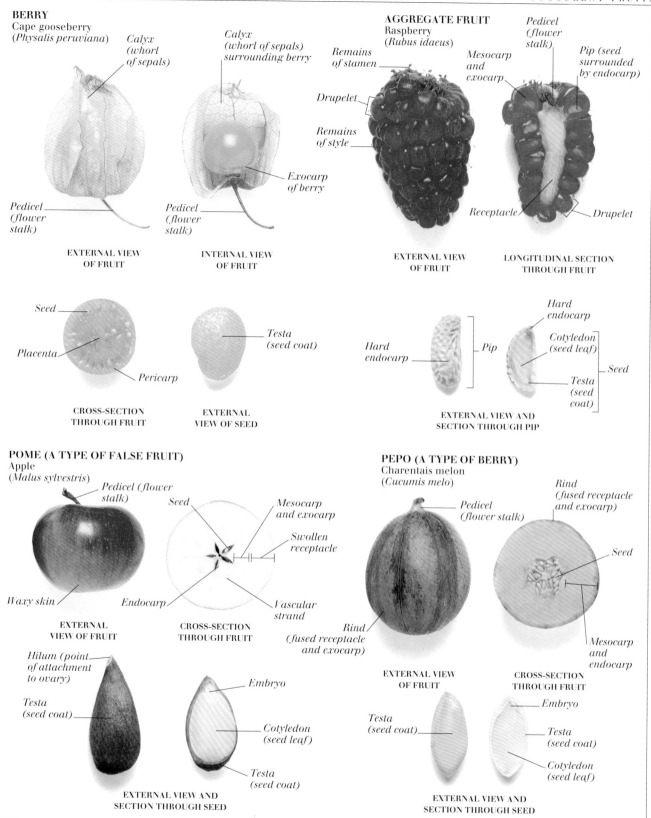

BERRY
Cape gooseberry
(*Physalis peruviana*)

Calyx (whorl of sepals)

Calyx (whorl of sepals) surrounding berry

Pedicel (flower stalk)

Pedicel (flower stalk)

Exocarp of berry

EXTERNAL VIEW OF FRUIT

INTERNAL VIEW OF FRUIT

Seed

Placenta

Pericarp

Testa (seed coat)

CROSS-SECTION THROUGH FRUIT

EXTERNAL VIEW OF SEED

AGGREGATE FRUIT
Raspberry
(*Rubus idaeus*)

Remains of stamen

Drupelet

Remains of style

Mesocarp and exocarp

Pedicel (flower stalk)

Pip (seed surrounded by endocarp)

Receptacle

Drupelet

EXTERNAL VIEW OF FRUIT

LONGITUDINAL SECTION THROUGH FRUIT

Hard endocarp

Pip

Hard endocarp

Cotyledon (seed leaf)

Seed

Testa (seed coat)

EXTERNAL VIEW AND SECTION THROUGH PIP

POME (A TYPE OF FALSE FRUIT)
Apple
(*Malus sylvestris*)

Pedicel (flower stalk)

Seed

Mesocarp and exocarp

Swollen receptacle

Waxy skin

Endocarp

Vascular strand

EXTERNAL VIEW OF FRUIT

CROSS-SECTION THROUGH FRUIT

Hilum (point of attachment to ovary)

Testa (seed coat)

Embryo

Cotyledon (seed leaf)

Testa (seed coat)

EXTERNAL VIEW AND SECTION THROUGH SEED

PEPO (A TYPE OF BERRY)
Charentais melon
(*Cucumis melo*)

Pedicel (flower stalk)

Rind (fused receptacle and exocarp)

Seed

Rind (fused receptacle and exocarp)

Mesocarp and endocarp

EXTERNAL VIEW OF FRUIT

CROSS-SECTION THROUGH FRUIT

Testa (seed coat)

Embryo

Testa (seed coat)

Cotyledon (seed leaf)

EXTERNAL VIEW AND SECTION THROUGH SEED

Dry fruits

DRY FRUITS HAVE A HARD, DRY PERICARP (fruit wall) around their seeds unlike succulent fruits, which have fleshy pericarps (see pp. 148-149). Dry fruits are divided into three types: dehiscent, in which the pericarp splits open to release the seeds; indehiscent, which do not split open; and schizocarpic, in which the fruit splits but the seeds are not exposed. Dehiscent dry fruits include capsules (e.g., love-in-a-mist), follicles (e.g., delphinium), legumes (e.g., pea), and siliquas (e.g., honesty). Typically, the seeds of dehiscent fruits are dispersed by the wind. Indehiscent dry fruits include nuts (e.g., sweet chestnut), nutlets (e.g., goosegrass), achenes (e.g., strawberry), caryopses (e.g., wheat), samaras (e.g., elm), and cypselas (e.g., dandelion). Some indehiscent dry fruits are dispersed by the wind, assisted by "wings" (e.g., elm) or "parachutes" (e.g., dandelion); others (e.g., goosegrass) have hooked pericarps to aid dispersal on animals' fur. Schizocarpic dry fruits include cremocarps (e.g., hogweed), and double samaras (e.g., sycamore); these are dispersed by the wind.

NUTLET
Goosegrass
(*Galium aparine*)

LEGUME
Pea
(*Pisum sativum*)

Pedicel (flower stalk)
Receptacle
Remains of sepal
Remains of stamen
Placenta
Pericarp (fruit wall)
Remains of style and stigma

EXTERNAL VIEW OF FRUIT

Pedicel (flower stalk)
Receptacle
Remains of sepal
Funicle (stalk attaching seed to placenta)
Pericarp (fruit wall)
Seed
Remains of style and stigma

INTERNAL VIEW OF FRUIT

Funicle (stalk attaching seed to placenta)
Micropyle (pore for water absorption)
Testa (seed coat)

Cotyledon (seed leaf)
Radicle (embryonic root)
Testa (seed coat)
Plumule (embryonic shoot)

EXTERIOR VIEW AND SECTION THROUGH SEED

NUT
Sweet chestnut
(*Castanea sativa*)

Line of splitting between valves of cupule

Peduncle (inflorescence stalk)
Remains of male inflorescence
Nut (indehiscent fruit)
Spiky cupule (husk around fruit formed from bracts)

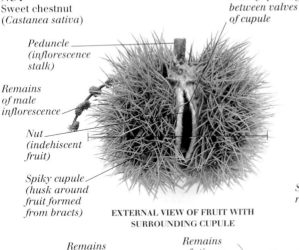

EXTERNAL VIEW OF FRUIT WITH SURROUNDING CUPULE

ACHENE
Strawberry
(*Fragaria* x *ananassa*)

Pedicel (flower stalk)
Sepal
Swollen receptacle
Remains of stigma and style
Achene (one-seeded dry fruit)

EXTERNAL VIEW OF FRUIT

Sepal
Pedicel (flower stalk)
Swollen fleshy tissues of receptacle

LONGITUDINAL SECTION THROUGH FRUIT

Remains of stigma
Remains of style
Remains of stigma
Remains of style
Embryo
Cotyledon (seed leaf)
Testa (seed coat)
Woody pericarp (fruit wall)
Nut (indehiscent fruit)
Woody pericarp (fruit wall)

EXTERNAL VIEW AND SECTION THROUGH FRUIT

Pericarp (fruit wall)
Pericarp (fruit wall)
Cotyledon (seed leaf)
Testa (seed coat)

EXTERNAL VIEW AND SECTION THROUGH SEED

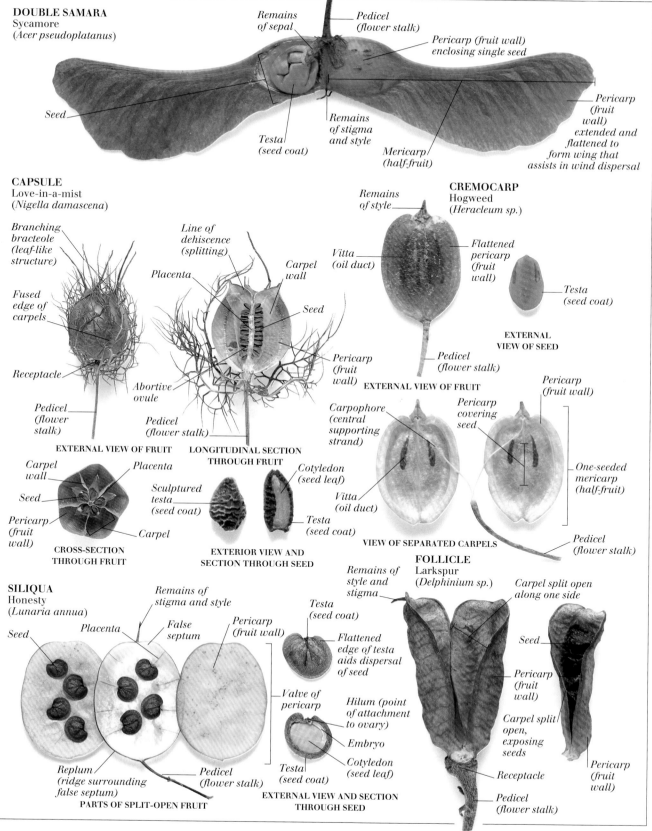

DOUBLE SAMARA
Sycamore
(*Acer pseudoplatanus*)

Remains of sepal

Pedicel (flower stalk)

Pericarp (fruit wall) enclosing single seed

Seed

Testa (seed coat)

Remains of stigma and style

Mericarp (half-fruit)

Pericarp (fruit wall) extended and flattened to form wing that assists in wind dispersal

CAPSULE
Love-in-a-mist
(*Nigella damascena*)

Branching bracteole (leaf-like structure)

Line of dehiscence (splitting)

Placenta

Carpel wall

Seed

Fused edge of carpels

Receptacle

Abortive ovule

Pedicel (flower stalk)

Pedicel (flower stalk)

Pericarp (fruit wall)

EXTERNAL VIEW OF FRUIT

LONGITUDINAL SECTION THROUGH FRUIT

Carpel wall

Placenta

Seed

Pericarp (fruit wall)

Carpel

CROSS-SECTION THROUGH FRUIT

Sculptured testa (seed coat)

Cotyledon (seed leaf)

Testa (seed coat)

EXTERIOR VIEW AND SECTION THROUGH SEED

CREMOCARP
Hogweed
(*Heracleum sp.*)

Remains of style

Vitta (oil duct)

Flattened pericarp (fruit wall)

Testa (seed coat)

EXTERNAL VIEW OF SEED

Pedicel (flower stalk)

EXTERNAL VIEW OF FRUIT

Pericarp (fruit wall)

Carpophore (central supporting strand)

Pericarp covering seed

Vitta (oil duct)

One-seeded mericarp (half-fruit)

VIEW OF SEPARATED CARPELS

Pedicel (flower stalk)

FOLLICLE
Larkspur
(*Delphinium sp.*)

Remains of style and stigma

Carpel split open along one side

Seed

Pericarp (fruit wall)

Carpel split open, exposing seeds

Receptacle

Pericarp (fruit wall)

Pedicel (flower stalk)

SILIQUA
Honesty
(*Lunaria annua*)

Seed

Placenta

Remains of stigma and style

False septum

Pericarp (fruit wall)

Testa (seed coat)

Flattened edge of testa aids dispersal of seed

Valve of pericarp

Hilum (point of attachment to ovary)

Embryo

Testa (seed coat)

Cotyledon (seed leaf)

Replum (ridge surrounding false septum)

Pedicel (flower stalk)

PARTS OF SPLIT-OPEN FRUIT

EXTERNAL VIEW AND SECTION THROUGH SEED

Germination

GERMINATION IS THE GROWTH OF SEEDS INTO SEEDLINGS. It starts when seeds become active below ground, and ends when the first foliage leaves appear above ground. A seed consists of an embryo and its food store, surrounded by a testa (seed coat). The embryo is made up of one or two cotyledons (seed leaves) attached to a central axis. The upper part of the axis consists of an epicotyl, which has a plumule (embryonic shoot) at its tip. The lower part of the axis consists of a hypocotyl and a radicle (embryonic root). After dispersal from the parent plant, the seeds dehydrate and enter a period of dormancy. Following this dormant period, germination begins, provided that the seeds have enough water, oxygen, warmth, and, in some cases, light. In the first stages of germination, the seed takes in water; the embryo starts to use its food store; and the radicle swells, breaks through the testa, and grows downwards. Germination then proceeds in one of two ways, depending on the type of seed. In epigeal germination, the hypocotyl lengthens, pulling the plumule and its protective cotyledons out of the soil. In hypogeal germination, the cotyledons remain below ground and the epicotyl lengthens, pushing the plumule upwards.

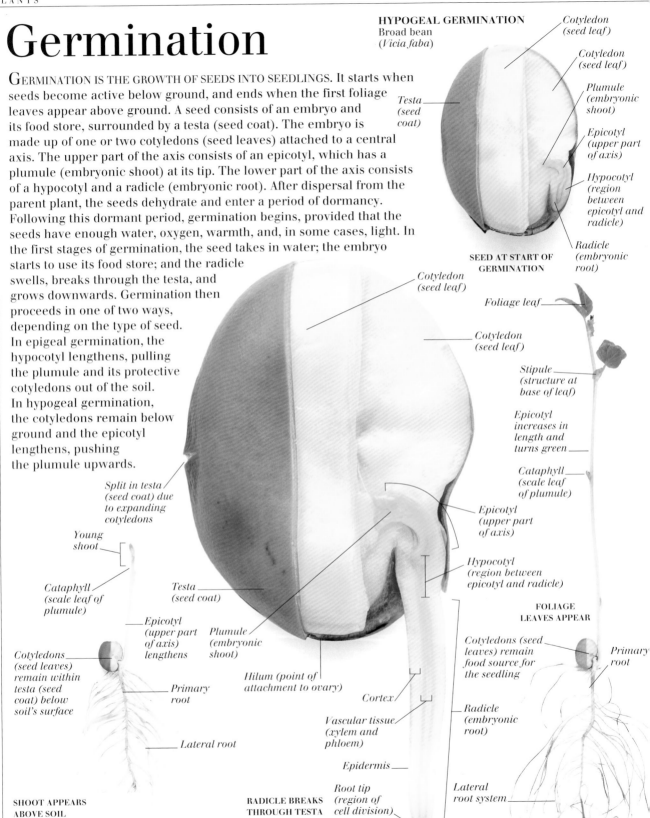

HYPOGEAL GERMINATION
Broad bean
(*Vicia faba*)

Cotyledon (seed leaf)

Cotyledon (seed leaf)

Plumule (embryonic shoot)

Testa (seed coat)

Epicotyl (upper part of axis)

Hypocotyl (region between epicotyl and radicle)

Radicle (embryonic root)

SEED AT START OF GERMINATION

Cotyledon (seed leaf)

Foliage leaf

Cotyledon (seed leaf)

Stipule (structure at base of leaf)

Epicotyl increases in length and turns green

Cataphyll (scale leaf of plumule)

Epicotyl (upper part of axis)

Hypocotyl (region between epicotyl and radicle)

FOLIAGE LEAVES APPEAR

Split in testa (seed coat) due to expanding cotyledons

Young shoot

Cataphyll (scale leaf of plumule)

Cotyledons (seed leaves) remain within testa (seed coat) below soil's surface

Testa (seed coat)

Epicotyl (upper part of axis) lengthens

Plumule (embryonic shoot)

Primary root

Lateral root

Hilum (point of attachment to ovary)

Cortex

Vascular tissue (xylem and phloem)

Epidermis

Root tip (region of cell division)

Cotyledons (seed leaves) remain food source for the seedling

Primary root

Radicle (embryonic root)

Lateral root system

SHOOT APPEARS ABOVE SOIL

RADICLE BREAKS THROUGH TESTA

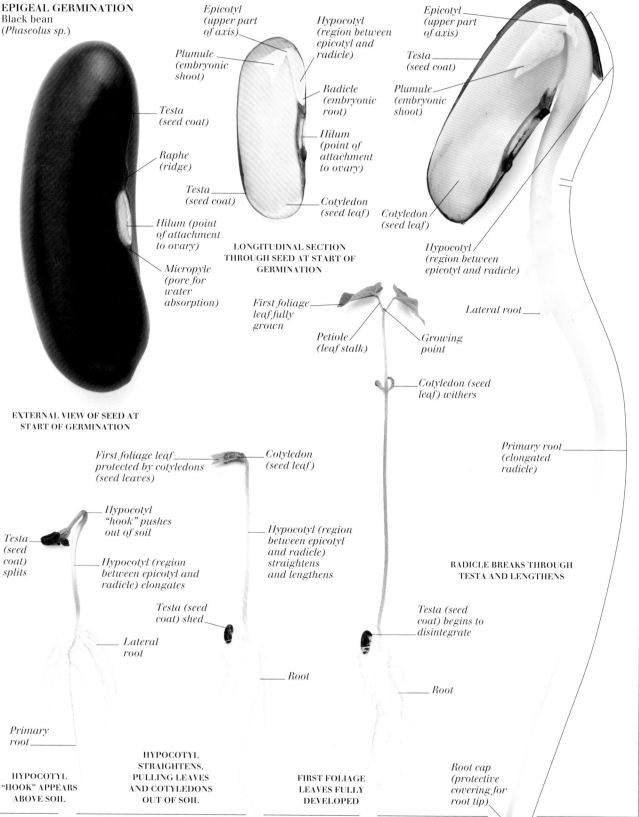

EPIGEAL GERMINATION
Black bean
(*Phaseolus sp.*)

Epicotyl (upper part of axis)

Plumule (embryonic shoot)

Hypocotyl (region between epicotyl and radicle)

Radicle (embryonic root)

Testa (seed coat)

Hilum (point of attachment to ovary)

Testa (seed coat)

Cotyledon (seed leaf)

LONGITUDINAL SECTION THROUGH SEED AT START OF GERMINATION

Epicotyl (upper part of axis)

Testa (seed coat)

Plumule (embryonic shoot)

Cotyledon (seed leaf)

Hypocotyl (region between epicotyl and radicle)

Testa (seed coat)

Raphe (ridge)

Hilum (point of attachment to ovary)

Micropyle (pore for water absorption)

EXTERNAL VIEW OF SEED AT START OF GERMINATION

First foliage leaf fully grown

Petiole (leaf stalk)

Growing point

Lateral root

Cotyledon (seed leaf) withers

Primary root (elongated radicle)

First foliage leaf protected by cotyledons (seed leaves)

Cotyledon (seed leaf)

Testa (seed coat) splits

Hypocotyl "hook" pushes out of soil

Hypocotyl (region between epicotyl and radicle) elongates

Testa (seed coat) shed

Lateral root

Hypocotyl (region between epicotyl and radicle) straightens and lengthens

RADICLE BREAKS THROUGH TESTA AND LENGTHENS

Testa (seed coat) begins to disintegrate

Root

Root

Primary root

HYPOCOTYL "HOOK" APPEARS ABOVE SOIL

HYPOCOTYL STRAIGHTENS, PULLING LEAVES AND COTYLEDONS OUT OF SOIL

FIRST FOLIAGE LEAVES FULLY DEVELOPED

Root cap (protective covering for root tip)

153

Vegetative reproduction

CORM
Gladiolus
(*Gladiolus sp.*)

MANY PLANTS CAN PROPAGATE THEMSELVES by vegetative reproduction. In this process, part of a plant separates off, takes root, and grows into a new plant. Vegetative reproduction is a type of asexual reproduction; that is, it involves only one parent, and there is no fusion of gametes (sex cells). Plants use various structures to reproduce vegetatively. Some plants use underground storage organs. Such organs include rhizomes (horizontal, underground stems), the branches of which produce new plants; bulbs (swollen leaf bases) and corms (swollen stems), which produce daughter bulbs or corms that separate off from the parent; and stem tubers (thickened underground stems) and root tubers (swollen adventitious roots), which also separate off from the parent. Other propagative structures include runners and stolons, creeping horizontal stems that take root and produce new plants; bulbils, small bulbs that develop on the stem or in the place of flowers, and then drop off and grow into new plants; and adventitious buds, miniature plants that form on leaf margins before dropping to the ground and growing into mature plants.

ADVENTITIOUS BUD
Mexican hat plant
(*Kalanchoe daigremontiana*)

Apex of leaf

Lamina (blade) of leaf

Leaf margin

Notch in leaf margin containing meristematic (actively dividing) cells

Adventitious bud (detachable bud with adventitious roots) drops from leaf

Petiole (leaf stalk)

BULBIL IN PLACE OF FLOWER
Orange lily
(*Lilium bulbiferum*)

Scar left by flower

Leaf

Pedicel (flower stalk)

Terminal bud

Detachable bulbil formed in place of flower

Peduncle (inflorescence stalk)

STOLON
Ground ivy
(*Glechoma hederacea*)

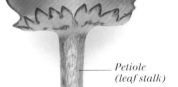

Internode

Parent plant

Stolon (creeping stem)

Node

Node

Adventitious root of daughter plant

Daughter plant developed from lateral bud

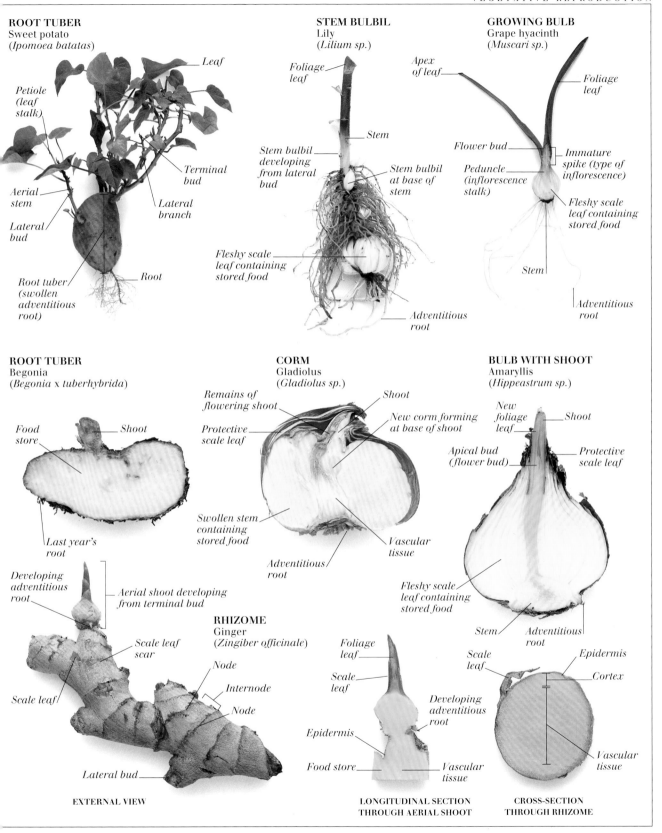

ROOT TUBER
Sweet potato
(*Ipomoea batatas*)

Leaf

Petiole
(leaf
stalk)

Terminal
bud

Aerial
stem

Lateral
branch

Lateral
bud

Root tuber
(swollen
adventitious
root)

Root

STEM BULBIL
Lily
(*Lilium sp.*)

Foliage
leaf

Stem

Stem bulbil
developing
from lateral
bud

Stem bulbil
at base of
stem

Fleshy scale
leaf containing
stored food

Adventitious
root

GROWING BULB
Grape hyacinth
(*Muscari sp.*)

Apex
of leaf

Foliage
leaf

Flower bud

Immature
spike (type of
inflorescence)

Peduncle
(inflorescence
stalk)

Fleshy scale
leaf containing
stored food

Stem

Adventitious
root

ROOT TUBER
Begonia
(*Begonia* x *tuberhybrida*)

Food
store

Shoot

Last year's
root

Developing
adventitious
root

Aerial shoot developing
from terminal bud

Scale leaf
scar

Scale leaf

Lateral bud

EXTERNAL VIEW

CORM
Gladiolus
(*Gladiolus sp.*)

Remains of
flowering shoot

Shoot

Protective
scale leaf

New corm forming
at base of shoot

Swollen stem
containing
stored food

Adventitious
root

Vascular
tissue

RHIZOME
Ginger
(*Zingiber officinale*)

Node

Internode

Node

Foliage
leaf

Scale
leaf

Developing
adventitious
root

Epidermis

Food store

Vascular
tissue

**LONGITUDINAL SECTION
THROUGH AERIAL SHOOT**

BULB WITH SHOOT
Amaryllis
(*Hippeastrum sp.*)

New
foliage
leaf

Shoot

Apical bud
(flower bud)

Protective
scale leaf

Fleshy scale
leaf containing
stored food

Stem

Adventitious
root

Scale
leaf

Epidermis

Cortex

Vascular
tissue

**CROSS-SECTION
THROUGH RHIZOME**

Dryland plants

DRYLAND PLANTS (XEROPHYTES) are able to survive in unfavourable habitats. All are found in places where little water is available; some live in high temperatures that cause excessive loss of water from the leaves. Xerophytes show a number of adaptations to dry conditions; these include reduced leaf area, rolled leaves, sunken stomata, hairs, spines, and thick cuticles. One group, succulent plants, stores water in specially enlarged spongy tissues found in leaves, roots, or stems. Leaf succulents have enlarged, fleshy, water-storing leaves. Root succulents have a large, underground water-storage organ with short-lived stems and leaves above ground. Stem succulents are represented by the cacti (family Cactaceae). Cacti stems are fleshy, green, and photosynthetic; they are typically ribbed or covered by tubercles in rows, with leaves being reduced to spines or entirely absent.

LEAF SUCCULENT
Lithops sp.

STEM SUCCULENT
Golden barrel cactus
(*Echinocactus grusonii*)

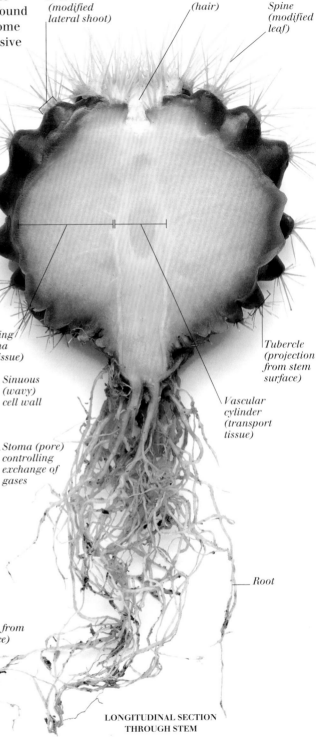

Areole (modified lateral shoot)

Trichome (hair)

Spine (modified leaf)

Tubercle (projection from stem surface)

Vascular cylinder (transport tissue)

Root

LONGITUDINAL SECTION THROUGH STEM

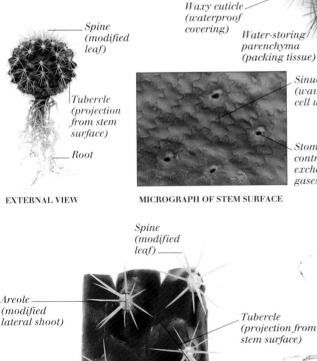

Spine (modified leaf)

Tubercle (projection from stem surface)

Root

EXTERNAL VIEW

Waxy cuticle (waterproof covering)

Water-storing parenchyma (packing tissue)

Sinuous (wavy) cell wall

Stoma (pore) controlling exchange of gases

MICROGRAPH OF STEM SURFACE

Spine (modified leaf)

Areole (modified lateral shoot)

Tubercle (projection from stem surface)

Waxy cuticle (waterproof covering)

DETAIL OF STEM SURFACE

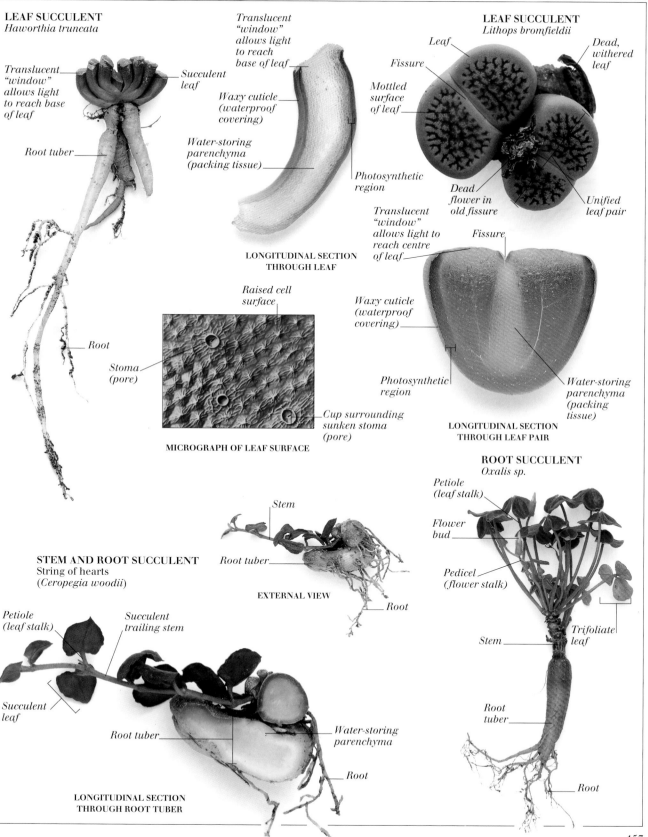

LEAF SUCCULENT
Haworthia truncata

Translucent "window" allows light to reach base of leaf

Succulent leaf

Root tuber

Root

Translucent "window" allows light to reach base of leaf

Waxy cuticle (waterproof covering)

Water-storing parenchyma (packing tissue)

Photosynthetic region

LONGITUDINAL SECTION THROUGH LEAF

Raised cell surface

Stoma (pore)

Cup surrounding sunken stoma (pore)

MICROGRAPH OF LEAF SURFACE

LEAF SUCCULENT
Lithops bromfieldii

Leaf

Fissure

Mottled surface of leaf

Dead, withered leaf

Dead flower in old fissure

Unified leaf pair

Translucent "window" allows light to reach centre of leaf

Fissure

Waxy cuticle (waterproof covering)

Photosynthetic region

Water-storing parenchyma (packing tissue)

LONGITUDINAL SECTION THROUGH LEAF PAIR

ROOT SUCCULENT
Oxalis sp.

Petiole (leaf stalk)

Flower bud

Pedicel (flower stalk)

Stem

Trifoliate leaf

Root tuber

Root

STEM AND ROOT SUCCULENT
String of hearts
(*Ceropegia woodii*)

Stem

Root tuber

Root

EXTERNAL VIEW

Petiole (leaf stalk)

Succulent trailing stem

Succulent leaf

Root tuber

Water-storing parenchyma

Root

LONGITUDINAL SECTION THROUGH ROOT TUBER

Wetland plants

WETLAND PLANTS GROW SUBMERGED IN WATER, either partially (e.g., water hyacinth) or completely (e.g., pond weeds), and show various adaptations to this habitat. Typically, there are numerous air spaces inside the stems, leaves, and roots; these aid gas exchange and buoyancy. Submerged parts generally have no cuticle (waterproof covering), enabling the plants to absorb minerals and gases directly from the water; in addition, being supported by the water, they need little of the supportive tissue found in land plants. Stomata, the gas exchange pores, are absent from plants that are completely submerged; in partially submerged plants with floating leaves (e.g., water lilies), stomata are found on the upper leaf surfaces, where they cannot be flooded.

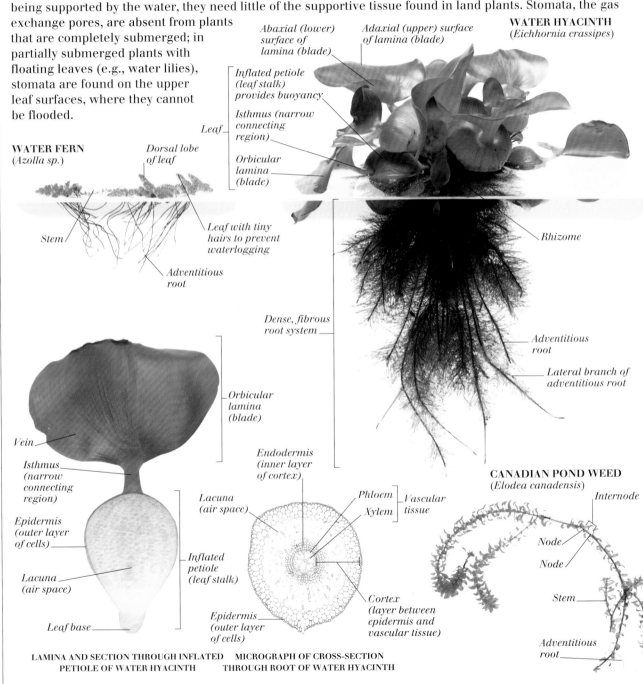

WATER FERN
(*Azolla sp.*)

Dorsal lobe
of leaf

Stem

Adventitious
root

Leaf with tiny
hairs to prevent
waterlogging

Abaxial (lower)
surface of
lamina (blade)

Adaxial (upper) surface
of lamina (blade)

WATER HYACINTH
(*Eichhornia crassipes*)

Inflated petiole
(leaf stalk)
provides buoyancy

Isthmus (narrow
connecting
region)

Leaf

Orbicular
lamina
(blade)

Rhizome

Dense, fibrous
root system

Adventitious
root

Lateral branch of
adventitious root

Vein

Orbicular
lamina
(blade)

Isthmus
(narrow
connecting
region)

Epidermis
(outer layer
of cells)

Lacuna
(air space)

Leaf base

Inflated
petiole
(leaf stalk)

Endodermis
(inner layer
of cortex)

Lacuna
(air space)

Phloem

Xylem

Vascular
tissue

Epidermis
(outer layer
of cells)

Cortex
(layer between
epidermis and
vascular tissue)

CANADIAN POND WEED
(*Elodea canadensis*)

Internode

Node

Node

Stem

Adventitious
root

LAMINA AND SECTION THROUGH INFLATED
PETIOLE OF WATER HYACINTH

MICROGRAPH OF CROSS-SECTION
THROUGH ROOT OF WATER HYACINTH

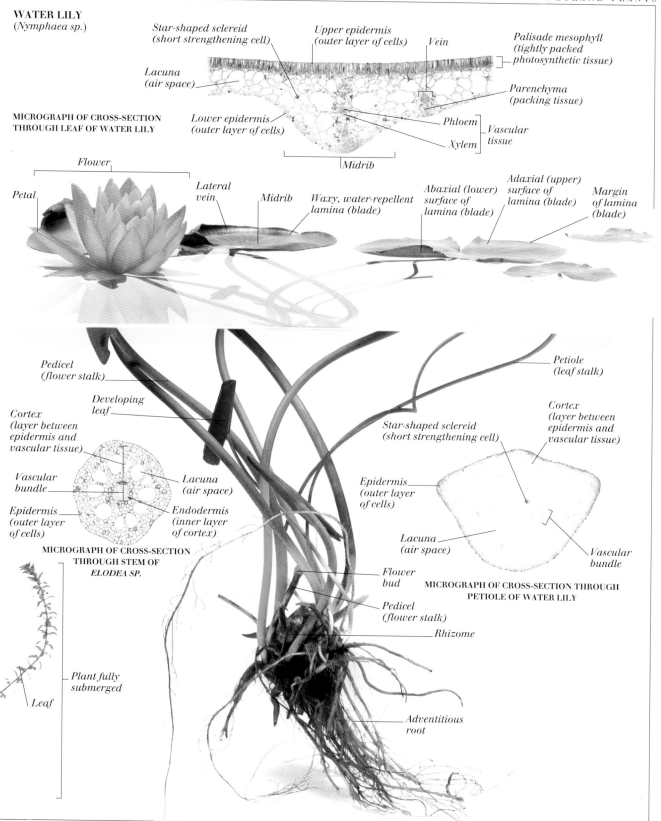

WATER LILY
(*Nymphaea* sp.)

Star-shaped sclereid
(short strengthening cell)

Upper epidermis
(outer layer of cells)

Vein

Palisade mesophyll
(tightly packed
photosynthetic tissue)

Lacuna
(air space)

Parenchyma
(packing tissue)

**MICROGRAPH OF CROSS-SECTION
THROUGH LEAF OF WATER LILY**

Lower epidermis
(outer layer of cells)

Phloem
Vascular
tissue

Xylem

Midrib

Flower

Petal

Lateral
vein

Midrib

Waxy, water-repellent
lamina (blade)

Abaxial (lower)
surface of
lamina (blade)

Adaxial (upper)
surface of
lamina (blade)

Margin
of lamina
(blade)

Pedicel
(flower stalk)

Petiole
(leaf stalk)

Developing
leaf

Cortex
(layer between
epidermis and
vascular tissue)

Star-shaped sclereid
(short strengthening cell)

Cortex
(layer between
epidermis and
vascular tissue)

Vascular
bundle

Lacuna
(air space)

Epidermis
(outer layer
of cells)

Epidermis
(outer layer
of cells)

Endodermis
(inner layer
of cortex)

Lacuna
(air space)

Vascular
bundle

**MICROGRAPH OF CROSS-SECTION
THROUGH STEM OF
ELODEA SP.**

**MICROGRAPH OF CROSS-SECTION THROUGH
PETIOLE OF WATER LILY**

Flower
bud

Pedicel
(flower stalk)

Rhizome

Plant fully
submerged

Leaf

Adventitious
root

Carnivorous plants

CARNIVOROUS (INSECTIVOROUS) PLANTS FEED ON INSECTS and other small animals, in addition to producing food in their leaves by photosynthesis. The nutrients absorbed from trapped insects enable carnivorous plants to thrive in acid, boggy soils that lack essential minerals, especially nitrates, where most other plants could not survive. All carnivorous plants have some leaves modified as traps; many use bright colours and scented nectar to attract prey; and most use enzymes to digest the prey. There are three types of traps. Pitcher plants, such as the monkey cup and cobra lily, have leaves modified as pitcher-shaped pitfall traps, half-filled with water; once lured inside the mouth of the trap, insects lose their footing on the slippery surface, fall into the liquid, and either decompose or are digested. Venus fly traps use a spring-trap mechanism; when an insect touches trigger hairs on the inner surfaces of the leaves, the two lobes of the trap snap shut. Butterworts and sundews entangle prey by sticky droplets on the leaf surface, while the edges of the leaves slowly curl over to envelop and digest the prey.

PITCHER PLANT
Cobra lily (*Darlingtonia californica*)

Areola ("window" of transparent tissue)

Fishtail nectary

Wing

Hood

Pitcher

Tubular petiole (leaf stalk)

Areola ("window" of transparent tissue)

Dome-shaped hood develops

Smooth surface

Nectar roll

Fishtail nectary appears

Mouth

Immature pitcher

Wing

Downward pointing hair

DEVELOPMENT OF MODIFIED LEAF IN COBRA LILY

Immature trap

Interlocked teeth

Closed trap

VENUS FLY TRAP
(*Dionaea muscipula*)

Red colour of trap attracts insects

Phyllode (flattened petiole)

Summer petiole (leaf stalk)

Sensory hinge

Trigger hair

Inner surface of trap

Nectary zone (glands secrete nectar)

Digestive zone (glands secrete digestive enzymes)

Lobe of trap

Trap (twin-lobed leaf blade)

Midrib (hinge of trap)

Tooth

Spring petiole (leaf stalk)

Trigger hair

Digestive gland

MICROGRAPH OF LOBE OF VENUS FLY TRAP

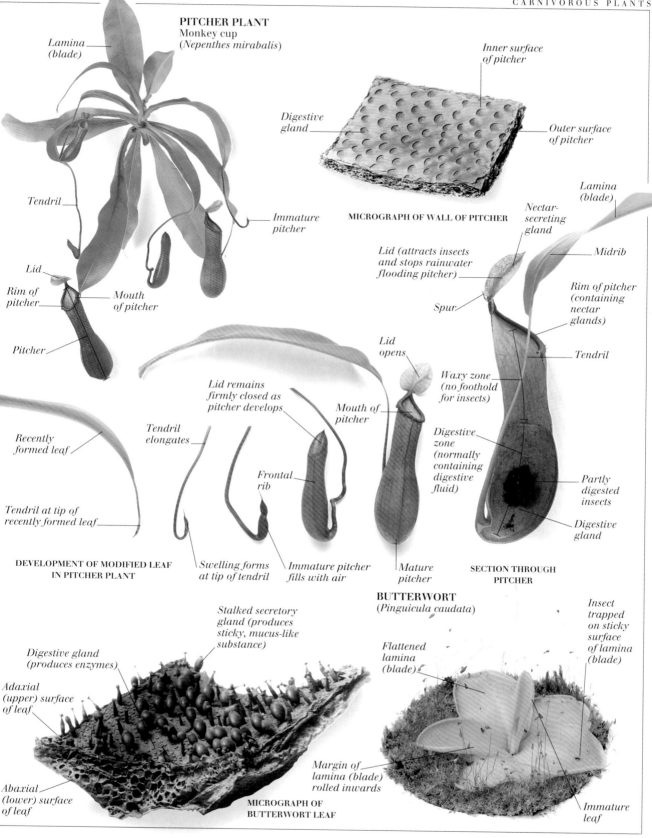

PITCHER PLANT
Monkey cup
(*Nepenthes mirabalis*)

Lamina (blade)

Tendril

Lid

Rim of pitcher

Mouth of pitcher

Pitcher

Immature pitcher

Inner surface of pitcher

Digestive gland

Outer surface of pitcher

MICROGRAPH OF WALL OF PITCHER

Lamina (blade)

Nectar-secreting gland

Midrib

Lid (attracts insects and stops rainwater flooding pitcher)

Spur

Rim of pitcher (containing nectar glands)

Tendril

Waxy zone (no foothold for insects)

Digestive zone (normally containing digestive fluid)

Partly digested insects

Digestive gland

Recently formed leaf

Tendril at tip of recently formed leaf

Tendril elongates

Lid remains firmly closed as pitcher develops

Frontal rib

Lid opens

Mouth of pitcher

DEVELOPMENT OF MODIFIED LEAF IN PITCHER PLANT

Swelling forms at tip of tendril

Immature pitcher fills with air

Mature pitcher

SECTION THROUGH PITCHER

BUTTERWORT
(*Pinguicula caudata*)

Stalked secretory gland (produces sticky, mucus-like substance)

Digestive gland (produces enzymes)

Adaxial (upper) surface of leaf

Abaxial (lower) surface of leaf

MICROGRAPH OF BUTTERWORT LEAF

Insect trapped on sticky surface of lamina (blade)

Flattened lamina (blade)

Margin of lamina (blade) rolled inwards

Immature leaf

Epiphytic and parasitic plants

EPIPHYTIC AND PARASITIC PLANTS GROW ON OTHER LIVING PLANTS. Typically, epiphytic plants are not rooted in the soil; instead, they live above ground level on the stems and branches of other plants. Epiphytes obtain water from trapped rainwater and from moisture in the air, and minerals from organic matter that has accumulated on the surface of the plant on which they are growing. Like other green plants, epiphytes produce their food by photosynthesis. Epiphytes include tropical orchids and bromeliads (air plants), and some mosses that live in temperate regions. Parasitic plants obtain all their nutrient requirements from the host plants on which they grow. The parasites produce haustoria, root-like organs that penetrate the stem or roots of the host and grow inwards to merge with the host's vascular tissue, from which the parasite extracts water, minerals, and manufactured nutrients. As they have no need to produce their own food, parasitic plants lack chlorophyll, the green photosynthetic pigment, and they have no foliage leaves. Partial parasitic plants (e.g., mistletoe) obtain water and minerals from the host plant but have green leaves and stems and are therefore able to produce their own food by photosynthesis.

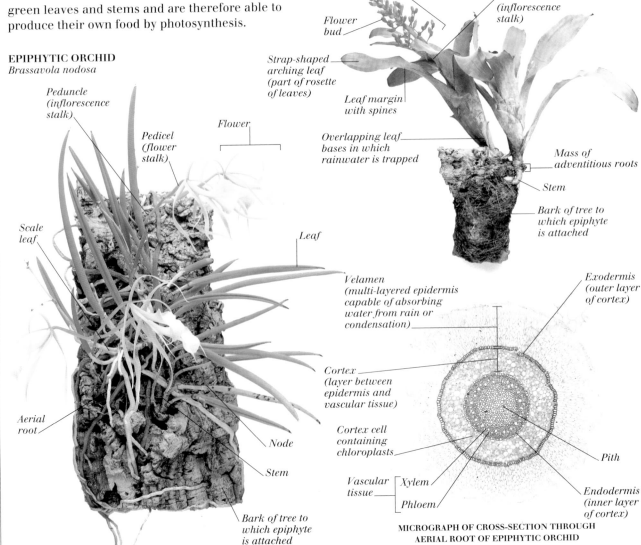

EPIPHYTIC BROMELIAD
Aechmea miniata

Inflorescence (spike)

Peduncle (inflorescence stalk)

Flower bud

Strap-shaped arching leaf (part of rosette of leaves)

Leaf margin with spines

Overlapping leaf bases in which rainwater is trapped

Mass of adventitious roots

Stem

Bark of tree to which epiphyte is attached

EPIPHYTIC ORCHID
Brassavola nodosa

Peduncle (inflorescence stalk)

Pedicel (flower stalk)

Flower

Scale leaf

Leaf

Velamen (multi-layered epidermis capable of absorbing water from rain or condensation)

Cortex (layer between epidermis and vascular tissue)

Cortex cell containing chloroplasts

Vascular tissue — Xylem / Phloem

Aerial root

Node

Stem

Bark of tree to which epiphyte is attached

Exodermis (outer layer of cortex)

Pith

Endodermis (inner layer of cortex)

MICROGRAPH OF CROSS-SECTION THROUGH AERIAL ROOT OF EPIPHYTIC ORCHID

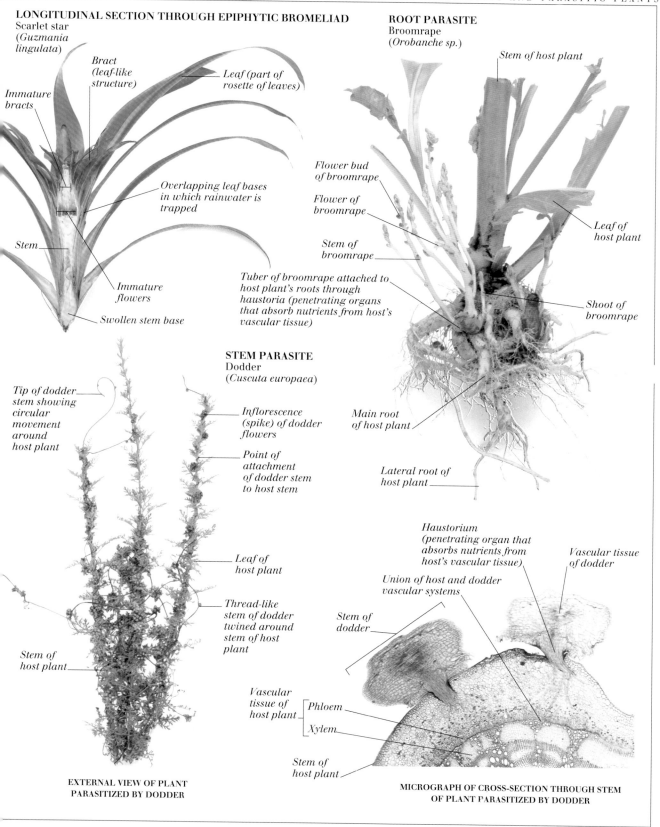

LONGITUDINAL SECTION THROUGH EPIPHYTIC BROMELIAD
Scarlet star
(*Guzmania lingulata*)

Bract (leaf-like structure)

Leaf (part of rosette of leaves)

Immature bracts

Overlapping leaf bases in which rainwater is trapped

Stem

Immature flowers

Swollen stem base

ROOT PARASITE
Broomrape
(*Orobanche sp.*)

Stem of host plant

Flower bud of broomrape

Flower of broomrape

Stem of broomrape

Tuber of broomrape attached to host plant's roots through haustoria (penetrating organs that absorb nutrients from host's vascular tissue)

Leaf of host plant

Shoot of broomrape

Main root of host plant

Lateral root of host plant

STEM PARASITE
Dodder
(*Cuscuta europaea*)

Tip of dodder stem showing circular movement around host plant

Inflorescence (spike) of dodder flowers

Point of attachment of dodder stem to host stem

Leaf of host plant

Thread-like stem of dodder twined around stem of host plant

Stem of host plant

Haustorium (penetrating organ that absorbs nutrients from host's vascular tissue)

Vascular tissue of dodder

Union of host and dodder vascular systems

Stem of dodder

Vascular tissue of host plant

Phloem

Xylem

Stem of host plant

EXTERNAL VIEW OF PLANT PARASITIZED BY DODDER

MICROGRAPH OF CROSS-SECTION THROUGH STEM OF PLANT PARASITIZED BY DODDER

163

ANIMALS

Sponges, jellyfish, and sea anemones

SPONGES ARE MAINLY MARINE animals that make up the phylum Porifera. They are among the simplest of all animals, having no tissues or organs. Their bodies consist of two layers of cells separated by a jelly-like layer (mesohyal) that is strengthened by mineral spicules or protein fibres. The body is perforated by a system of pores and water channels called the aquiferous system. Special cells (choanocytes) with whip-like structures (flagella) draw water through the aquiferous system, thereby bringing tiny food particles to the sponge's cells. Jellyfish (class Scyphozoa), sea anemones (class Anthozoa), and corals (also class Anthozoa) belong to the phylum Cnidaria, also known as Coelenterata. More complex than sponges, coelenterates have simple tissues, such as nervous tissue; a radially symmetrical body; and a mouth surrounded by tentacles with unique stinging cells (cnidocytes).

INTERNAL ANATOMY OF A SPONGE

Amoebocyte

Osculum (excurrent pore)

Choanocyte (collar cell)

Ostium (incurrent pore)

Porocyte (pore cell)

Mesohyal

Spongocoel (atrium; paragaster)

Spicule

Pinacocyte (epidermal cell)

Ostium (incurrent pore)

SKELETON OF A SPONGE

Protein matrix

Pore

EXTERNAL FEATURES OF A SEA ANEMONE

Tentacle

EXAMPLES OF SEA ANEMONES

JEWEL ANEMONE (Corynactis viridis)

PARASITIC ANEMONE (Calliactis parasitica)

PLUMOSE ANEMONE (Metridium senile)

MEDITERRANEAN SEA ANEMONE (Condylactis sp.)

GREEN SNAKELOCK ANEMONE (Anemonia viridis)

BEADLET ANEMONE (Actinia equina)

GHOST ANEMONE (Actinothoe sphyrodeta)

Sagartia elegans

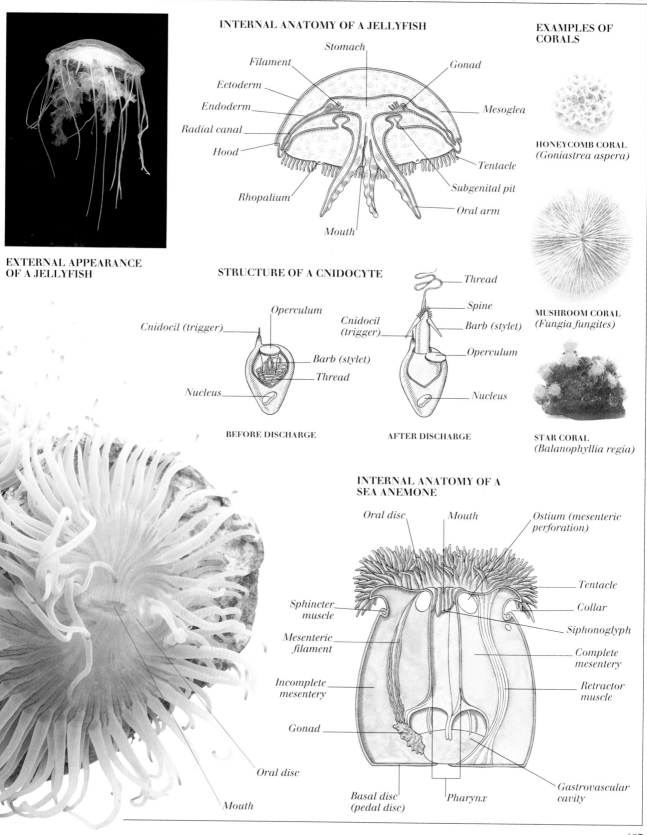

INTERNAL ANATOMY OF A JELLYFISH

Stomach

Filament

Gonad

Ectoderm

Endoderm

Mesoglea

Radial canal

Hood

Tentacle

Subgenital pit

Rhopalium

Oral arm

Mouth

EXTERNAL APPEARANCE OF A JELLYFISH

EXAMPLES OF CORALS

HONEYCOMB CORAL
(Goniastrea aspera)

MUSHROOM CORAL
(Fungia fungites)

STAR CORAL
(Balanophyllia regia)

STRUCTURE OF A CNIDOCYTE

Operculum

Cnidocil (trigger)

Barb (stylet)

Thread

Nucleus

Thread

Spine

Cnidocil (trigger)

Barb (stylet)

Operculum

Nucleus

BEFORE DISCHARGE

AFTER DISCHARGE

INTERNAL ANATOMY OF A SEA ANEMONE

Oral disc

Mouth

Ostium (mesenteric perforation)

Tentacle

Sphincter muscle

Collar

Siphonoglyph

Mesenteric filament

Complete mesentery

Incomplete mesentery

Retractor muscle

Gonad

Oral disc

Mouth

Basal disc (pedal disc)

Pharynx

Gastrovascular cavity

167

Insects

**PUPA
(CHRYSALIS)**

THE WORD INSECT REFERS to small invertebrate creatures, especially those with bodies divided into sections. Insects, including beetles, ants, bees, butterflies, and moths, belong to various orders in the class Insecta, which is a division of the phylum Arthropoda. Features common to all insects are an exoskeleton (external skeleton); three pairs of jointed legs; three body sections (head, thorax, and abdomen); and one pair of sensory antennae. Beetles (order Coleoptera) are the biggest group of insects, with about 300,000 species (about 30 per cent of all known insects). They have a pair of hard elytra (wing cases), which are modified front wings. The principal function of the elytra is to protect the hind wings, which are used for flying. Ants, together with bees and wasps, form the order Hymenoptera, which contains about 200,000 species. This group is characterized by a marked narrowing between the thorax and abdomen. Butterflies and moths form the order Lepidoptera, which has about 150,000 species. They have wings covered with tiny scales, hence the name of their order (Lepidoptera means "scale wings"). The separation of lepidopterans into butterflies and moths is largely artificial as there are no features that categorically distinguish one group from the other. In general, however, most butterflies fly by day, whereas most moths are night-flyers. Some insects, including butterflies and moths, undergo complete metamorphosis (transformation) during their life-cycle. A butterfly metamorphoses from an egg to a larva (caterpillar), then to a pupa (chrysalis), and finally to an imago (adult).

EXAMPLES OF INSECTS

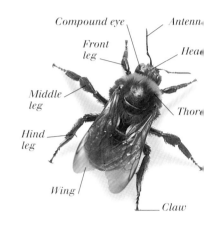

Compound eye
Antenn
Front
leg
Hea
Middle
leg
Thor
Hind
leg
Wing
Claw

BUMBLEBEE

Compound
eye
Stigma
(spot)
Vein
Abdomen

DAMSELFLY

**EXTERNAL FEATURES
OF A BEETLE**

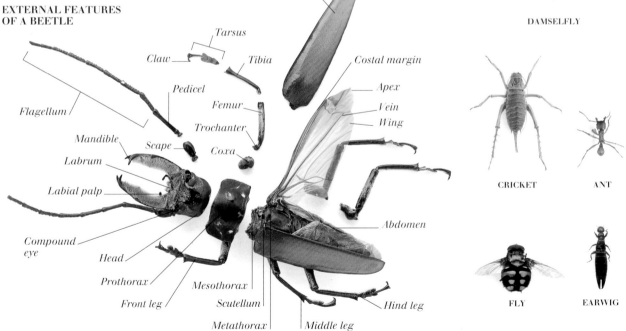

Elytron
Tarsus
Claw
Tibia
Costal margin
Pedicel
Apex
Flagellum
Femur
Vein
Trochanter
Wing
Mandible
Scape
Coxa
Labrum
Labial palp
Abdomen
Compound
eye
Head
Prothorax
Mesothorax
Front leg
Scutellum
Hind leg
Metathorax
Middle leg

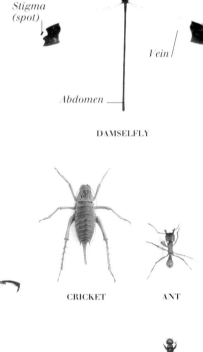

CRICKET

ANT

FLY

EARWIG

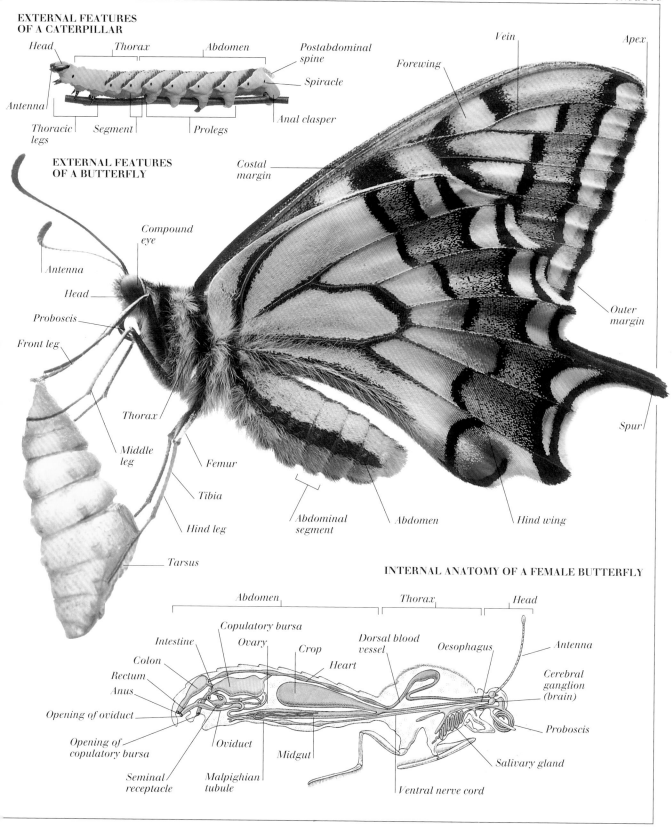

EXTERNAL FEATURES OF A CATERPILLAR

Head

Thorax

Abdomen

Postabdominal spine

Antenna

Spiracle

Thoracic legs

Segment

Prolegs

Anal clasper

EXTERNAL FEATURES OF A BUTTERFLY

Vein

Apex

Forewing

Costal margin

Compound eye

Antenna

Head

Proboscis

Front leg

Outer margin

Thorax

Middle leg

Femur

Tibia

Hind leg

Tarsus

Abdominal segment

Abdomen

Hind wing

Spur

INTERNAL ANATOMY OF A FEMALE BUTTERFLY

Abdomen

Thorax

Head

Copulatory bursa

Ovary

Crop

Dorsal blood vessel

Oesophagus

Antenna

Intestine

Heart

Cerebral ganglion (brain)

Colon

Rectum

Anus

Proboscis

Opening of oviduct

Opening of copulatory bursa

Oviduct

Midgut

Salivary gland

Seminal receptacle

Malpighian tubule

Ventral nerve cord

Arachnids

THE CLASS ARACHNIDA INCLUDES SPIDERS (order Araneae) and
scorpions (order Scorpiones). The class is part of the phylum
Arthropoda, which also includes insects and crustaceans.
Spiders and scorpions are characterized by having four pairs of
walking legs; a pair of pincer-like mouthparts called chelicerae; another
pair of frontal appendages called pedipalps, which are sensory in spiders
but used for grasping in scorpions; and a body divided into two
sections (a combined head and thorax called a cephalothorax
or prosoma, and an abdomen or opisthosoma).
Unlike other arthropods, spiders and
scorpions lack antennae. Spiders
and scorpions are carnivorous.
Spiders poison prey by biting
with the fanged chelicerae,
scorpions by stinging
with the end of the
metasoma (tail).

**MEXICAN TRUE RED-
LEGGED TARANTULA**
(Euathlus emilia)

INTERNAL ANATOMY OF A FEMALE SPIDER

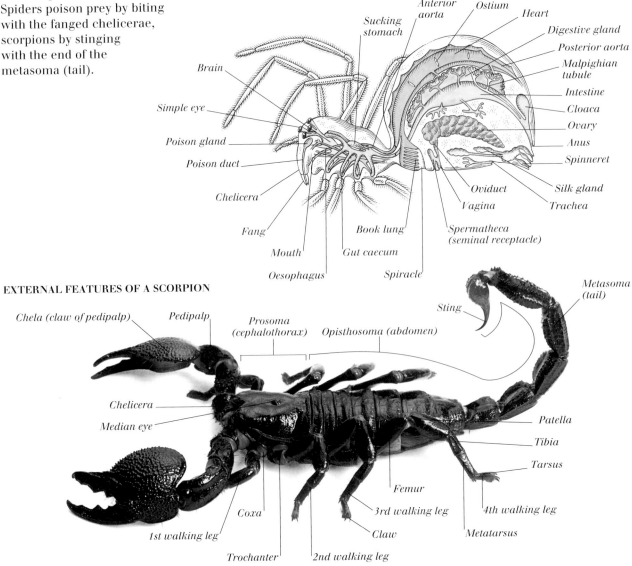

Anterior aorta
Ostium
Heart
Digestive gland
Posterior aorta
Malpighian tubule
Intestine
Cloaca
Ovary
Anus
Spinneret
Silk gland
Trachea
Oviduct
Vagina
Spermatheca (seminal receptacle)
Spiracle
Gut caecum
Book lung
Oesophagus
Mouth
Fang
Chelicera
Poison duct
Poison gland
Simple eye
Brain
Sucking stomach

EXTERNAL FEATURES OF A SCORPION

Chela (claw of pedipalp)
Pedipalp
Prosoma (cephalothorax)
Opisthosoma (abdomen)
Sting
Metasoma (tail)
Chelicera
Median eye
Patella
Tibia
Tarsus
Femur
4th walking leg
Coxa
3rd walking leg
Metatarsus
1st walking leg
Claw
Trochanter
2nd walking leg

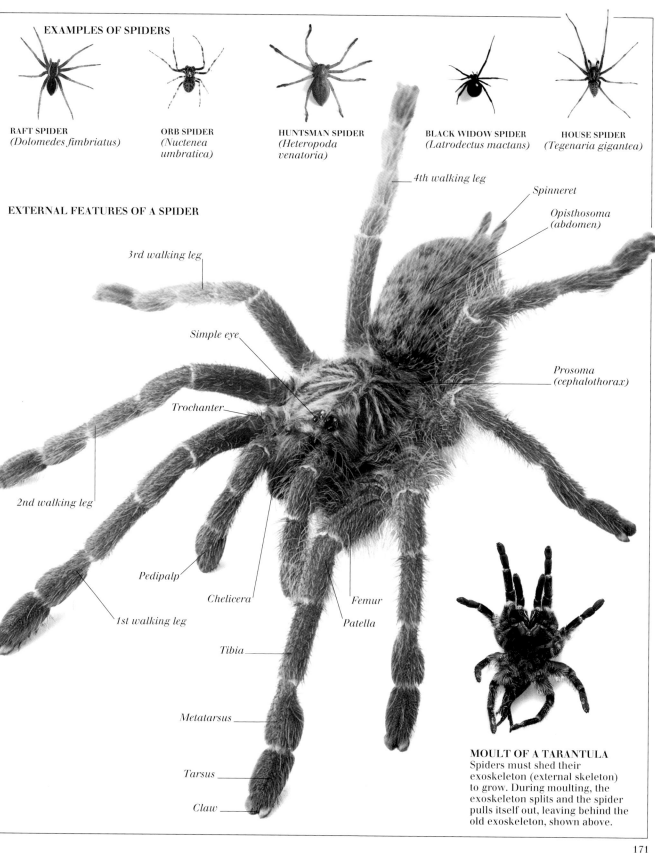

EXAMPLES OF SPIDERS

RAFT SPIDER
(Dolomedes fimbriatus)

ORB SPIDER
(Nuctenea umbratica)

HUNTSMAN SPIDER
(Heteropoda venatoria)

BLACK WIDOW SPIDER
(Latrodectus mactans)

HOUSE SPIDER
(Tegenaria gigantea)

EXTERNAL FEATURES OF A SPIDER

4th walking leg

Spinneret

Opisthosoma
(abdomen)

3rd walking leg

Simple eye

Prosoma
(cephalothorax)

Trochanter

2nd walking leg

Pedipalp

Chelicera

Femur

Patella

1st walking leg

Tibia

Metatarsus

Tarsus

Claw

MOULT OF A TARANTULA
Spiders must shed their
exoskeleton (external skeleton)
to grow. During moulting, the
exoskeleton splits and the spider
pulls itself out, leaving behind the
old exoskeleton, shown above.

Crustaceans

THE SUBPHYLUM CRUSTACEA is one of the largest groups
in the phylum Arthropoda. The subphylum is divided
into several classes, the most important of which
are Malacostraca and Cirripedia. The class
Malacostraca includes crayfish, crabs,
lobsters, and shrimps. Typical features of
malacostracans include a body divided
into two sections (a combined head
and thorax called a cephalothorax,
and an abdomen); an exoskeleton
(external skeleton) with a large
plate (carapace) covering the
cephalothorax; stalked,
compound eyes; and two
pairs of antennae. The class
Cirripedia includes barnacles,
which, unlike other
crustaceans, spend their
adult lives attached to a
surface, such as a rock. Other
characteristics of cirripedes
include an exoskeleton of
overlapping calcareous plates;
a body consisting almost entirely
of thorax (the abdomen and head
are minute); and six pairs of thoracic
appendages (cirri) used for filter feeding.

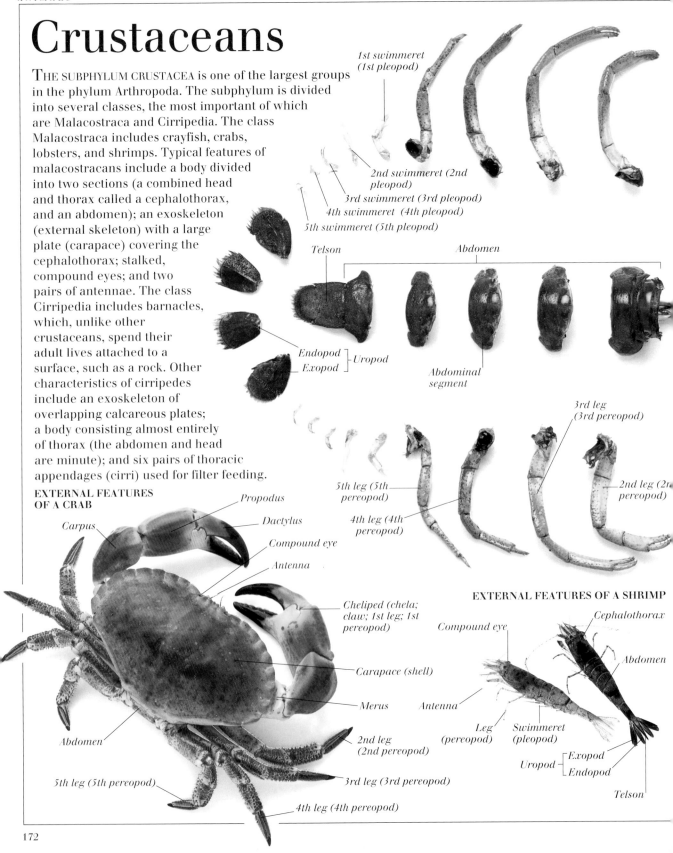

1st swimmeret
(1st pleopod)

2nd swimmeret (2nd
pleopod)

3rd swimmeret (3rd pleopod)

4th swimmeret (4th pleopod)

5th swimmeret (5th pleopod)

Telson

Abdomen

Endopod
Exopod
} Uropod

Abdominal
segment

3rd leg
(3rd pereopod)

5th leg (5th
pereopod)

4th leg (4th
pereopod)

2nd leg (2n
pereopod)

**EXTERNAL FEATURES
OF A CRAB**

Propodus

Carpus

Dactylus

Compound eye

Antenna

Cheliped (chela;
claw; 1st leg; 1st
pereopod)

Carapace (shell)

Merus

Abdomen

2nd leg
(2nd pereopod)

5th leg (5th pereopod)

3rd leg (3rd pereopod)

4th leg (4th pereopod)

EXTERNAL FEATURES OF A SHRIMP

Cephalothorax

Compound eye

Abdomen

Antenna

Leg
(pereopod)

Swimmeret
(pleopod)

Uropod

Exopod
Endopod

Telson

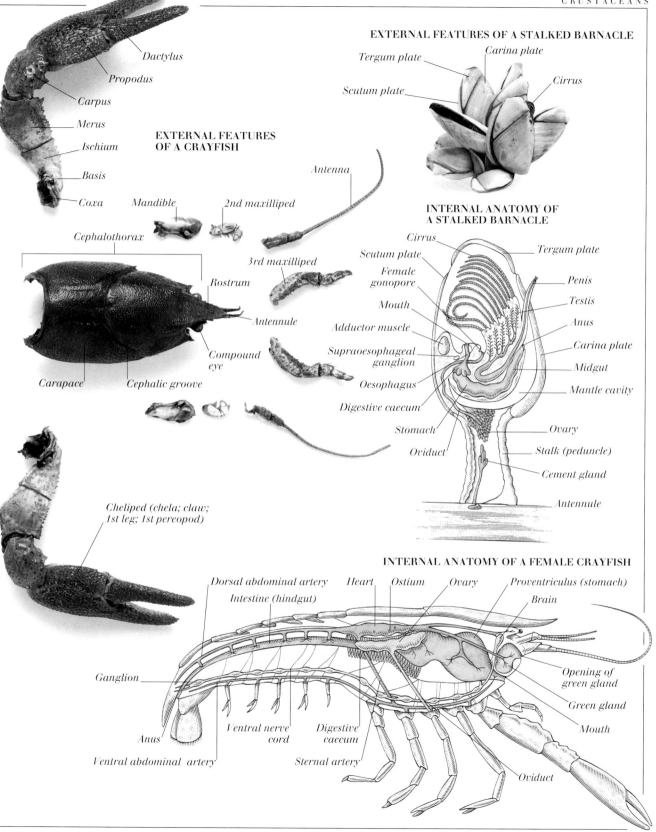

EXTERNAL FEATURES OF A STALKED BARNACLE

Tergum plate

Carina plate

Scutum plate

Cirrus

Dactylus

Propodus

Carpus

EXTERNAL FEATURES OF A CRAYFISH

Merus

Ischium

Basis

Coxa

Mandible

2nd maxilliped

Antenna

INTERNAL ANATOMY OF A STALKED BARNACLE

3rd maxilliped

Cephalothorax

Rostrum

Antennule

Compound eye

Carapace

Cephalic groove

Cirrus

Scutum plate

Female gonopore

Mouth

Adductor muscle

Supraoesophageal ganglion

Oesophagus

Digestive caecum

Stomach

Oviduct

Tergum plate

Penis

Testis

Anus

Carina plate

Midgut

Mantle cavity

Ovary

Stalk (peduncle)

Cement gland

Antennule

Cheliped (chela; claw; 1st leg; 1st pereopod)

INTERNAL ANATOMY OF A FEMALE CRAYFISH

Dorsal abdominal artery

Heart

Ostium

Ovary

Proventriculus (stomach)

Intestine (hindgut)

Brain

Ganglion

Opening of green gland

Green gland

Anus

Ventral nerve cord

Digestive caecum

Mouth

Ventral abdominal artery

Sternal artery

Oviduct

Starfish and sea urchins

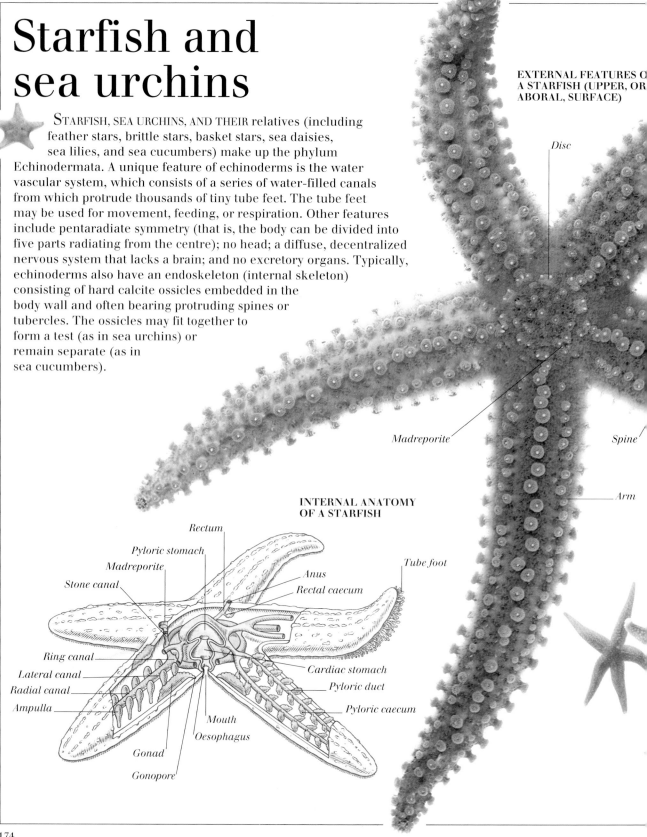

STARFISH, SEA URCHINS, AND THEIR relatives (including feather stars, brittle stars, basket stars, sea daisies, sea lilies, and sea cucumbers) make up the phylum Echinodermata. A unique feature of echinoderms is the water vascular system, which consists of a series of water-filled canals from which protrude thousands of tiny tube feet. The tube feet may be used for movement, feeding, or respiration. Other features include pentaradiate symmetry (that is, the body can be divided into five parts radiating from the centre); no head; a diffuse, decentralized nervous system that lacks a brain; and no excretory organs. Typically, echinoderms also have an endoskeleton (internal skeleton) consisting of hard calcite ossicles embedded in the body wall and often bearing protruding spines or tubercles. The ossicles may fit together to form a test (as in sea urchins) or remain separate (as in sea cucumbers).

EXTERNAL FEATURES OF A STARFISH (UPPER, OR ABORAL, SURFACE)

Disc

Madreporite

Spine

Arm

INTERNAL ANATOMY OF A STARFISH

Rectum

Pyloric stomach

Madreporite

Stone canal

Ring canal

Lateral canal

Radial canal

Ampulla

Gonad

Gonopore

Mouth

Oesophagus

Anus

Rectal caecum

Tube foot

Cardiac stomach

Pyloric duct

Pyloric caecum

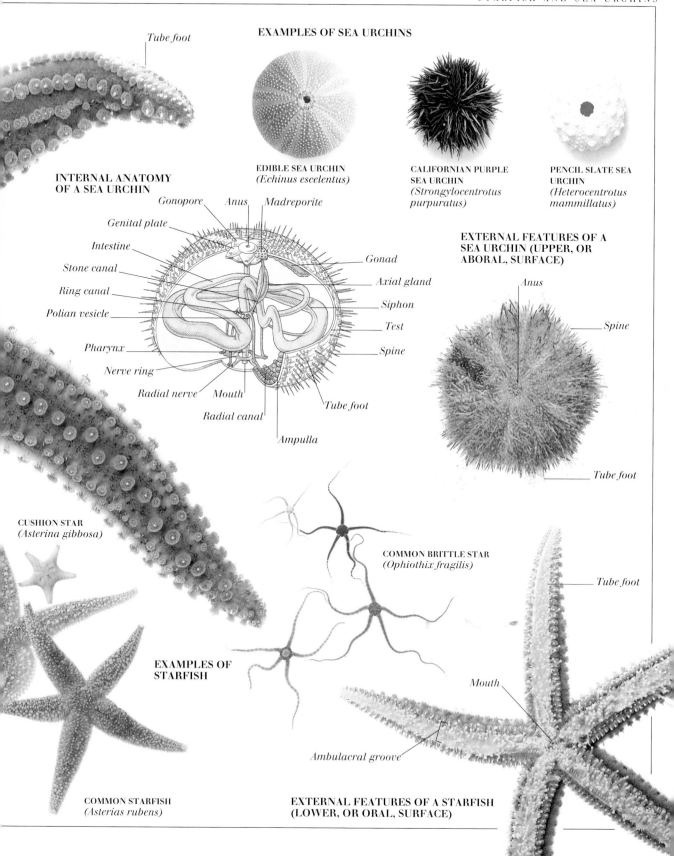

Tube foot

EXAMPLES OF SEA URCHINS

EDIBLE SEA URCHIN
(Echinus escelentus)

**CALIFORNIAN PURPLE
SEA URCHIN**
*(Strongylocentrotus
purpuratus)*

**PENCIL SLATE SEA
URCHIN**
*(Heterocentrotus
mammillatus)*

**INTERNAL ANATOMY
OF A SEA URCHIN**

Gonopore   *Anus*   *Madreporite*

Genital plate

Intestine

Stone canal

Ring canal

Polian vesicle

Pharynx

Nerve ring

Radial nerve   *Mouth*

Radial canal

Ampulla

Gonad

Axial gland

Siphon

Test

Spine

Tube foot

**EXTERNAL FEATURES OF A
SEA URCHIN (UPPER, OR
ABORAL, SURFACE)**

Anus

Spine

Tube foot

CUSHION STAR
(Asterina gibbosa)

COMMON BRITTLE STAR
(Ophiothix fragilis)

Tube foot

**EXAMPLES OF
STARFISH**

Mouth

Ambulacral groove

COMMON STARFISH
(Asterias rubens)

**EXTERNAL FEATURES OF A STARFISH
(LOWER, OR ORAL, SURFACE)**

Molluscs

THE PHYLUM MOLLUSCA (MOLLUSCS) is a large group of animals that includes octopuses, snails, and scallops. Octopuses and their relatives —including squid and cuttlefish—form the class Cephalopoda. Cephalopods typically have a head with a radula (a file-like feeding organ) and beak; a well-developed nervous system; sucker-bearing tentacles; a muscular mantle (part of the body wall) that can expel water through the siphon, enabling movement by jet propulsion; and a small shell or no shell. Snails and their relatives—including slugs, limpets, and abalones—make up the class Gastropoda. Gastropods typically have a coiled external shell, although some, such as slugs, have a small internal shell or no shell; a flat foot; and a head with tentacles and a radula. Scallops and their relatives—including clams, mussels, and oysters—make up the class Bivalvia (also called Pelecypoda). Features of bivalves include a shell with two halves (valves); large gills that are used for breathing and filter feeding; and no radula.

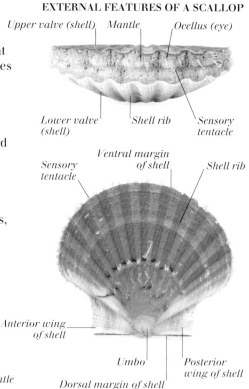

EXTERNAL FEATURES OF A SCALLOP

Upper valve (shell)
Mantle
Ocellus (eye)
Lower valve (shell)
Shell rib
Sensory tentacle

Sensory tentacle
Ventral margin of shell
Shell rib

Anterior wing of shell
Umbo
Posterior wing of shell
Dorsal margin of shell

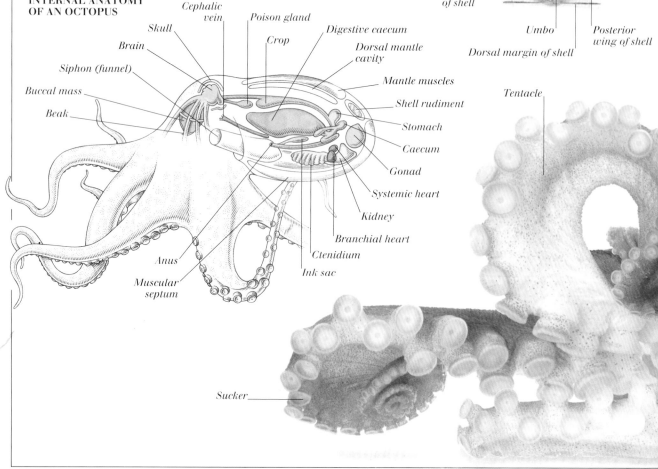

INTERNAL ANATOMY OF AN OCTOPUS

Cephalic vein
Poison gland
Digestive caecum
Skull
Crop
Dorsal mantle cavity
Brain
Mantle muscles
Siphon (funnel)
Shell rudiment
Buccal mass
Stomach
Beak
Caecum
Gonad
Systemic heart
Kidney
Branchial heart
Ctenidium
Anus
Ink sac
Muscular septum

Tentacle

Sucker

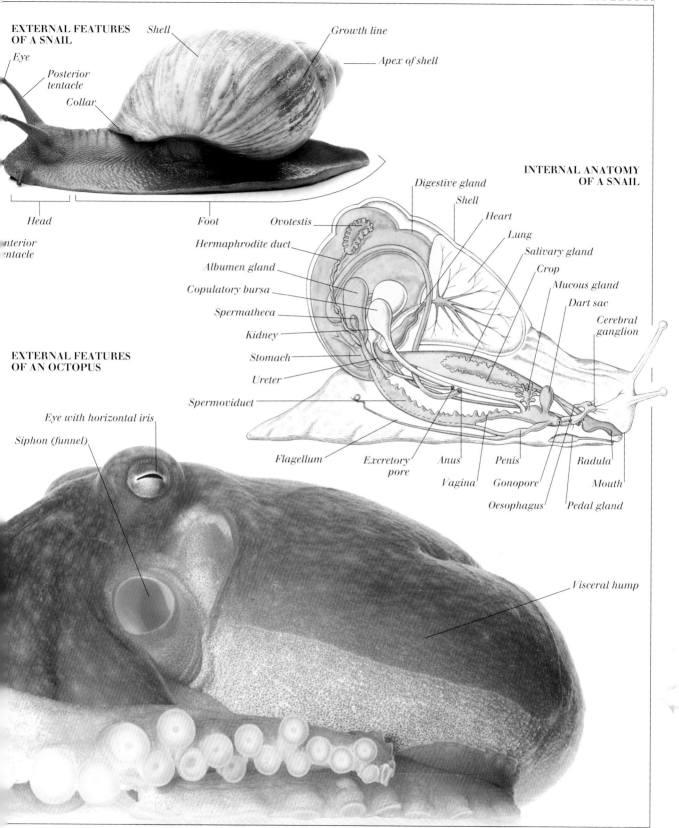

EXTERNAL FEATURES OF A SNAIL

Shell
Growth line
Eye
Apex of shell
Posterior tentacle
Collar
Head
Foot

nterior
entacle

INTERNAL ANATOMY OF A SNAIL

Digestive gland
Shell
Heart
Lung
Salivary gland
Crop
Mucous gland
Dart sac
Cerebral ganglion
Ovotestis
Hermaphrodite duct
Albumen gland
Copulatory bursa
Spermatheca
Kidney
Stomach
Ureter
Spermoviduct
Flagellum
Excretory pore
Anus
Penis
Radula
Vagina
Gonopore
Mouth
Oesophagus
Pedal gland

EXTERNAL FEATURES OF AN OCTOPUS

Eye with horizontal iris
Siphon (funnel)
Visceral hump

Sharks and jawless fish

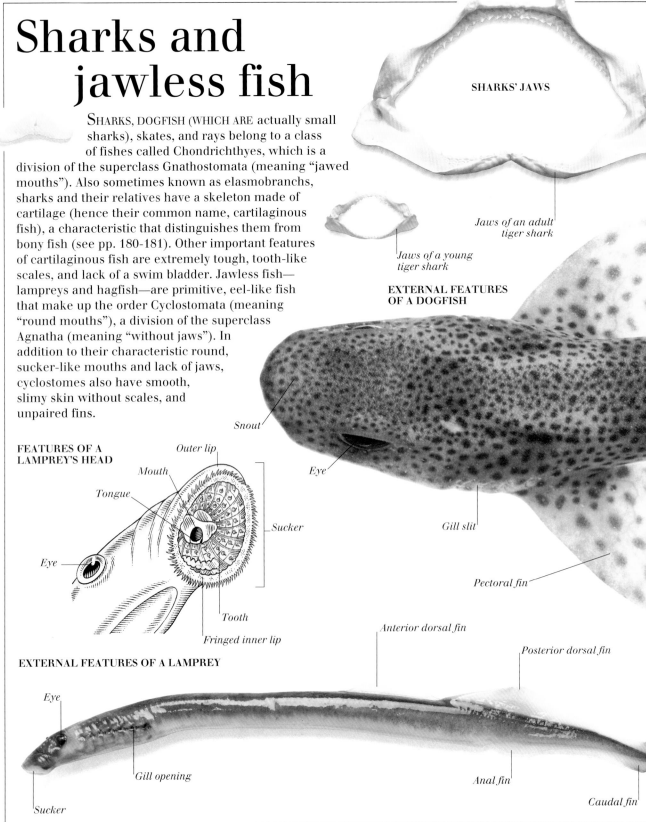

SHARKS, DOGFISH (WHICH ARE actually small sharks), skates, and rays belong to a class of fishes called Chondrichthyes, which is a division of the superclass Gnathostomata (meaning "jawed mouths"). Also sometimes known as elasmobranchs, sharks and their relatives have a skeleton made of cartilage (hence their common name, cartilaginous fish), a characteristic that distinguishes them from bony fish (see pp. 180-181). Other important features of cartilaginous fish are extremely tough, tooth-like scales, and lack of a swim bladder. Jawless fish—lampreys and hagfish—are primitive, eel-like fish that make up the order Cyclostomata (meaning "round mouths"), a division of the superclass Agnatha (meaning "without jaws"). In addition to their characteristic round, sucker-like mouths and lack of jaws, cyclostomes also have smooth, slimy skin without scales, and unpaired fins.

SHARKS' JAWS

Jaws of an adult tiger shark

Jaws of a young tiger shark

EXTERNAL FEATURES OF A DOGFISH

Snout

Eye

Gill slit

Pectoral fin

FEATURES OF A LAMPREY'S HEAD

Outer lip

Mouth

Tongue

Eye

Sucker

Tooth

Fringed inner lip

EXTERNAL FEATURES OF A LAMPREY

Eye

Gill opening

Sucker

Anterior dorsal fin

Posterior dorsal fin

Anal fin

Caudal fin

EXAMPLES OF CARTILAGINOUS FISH

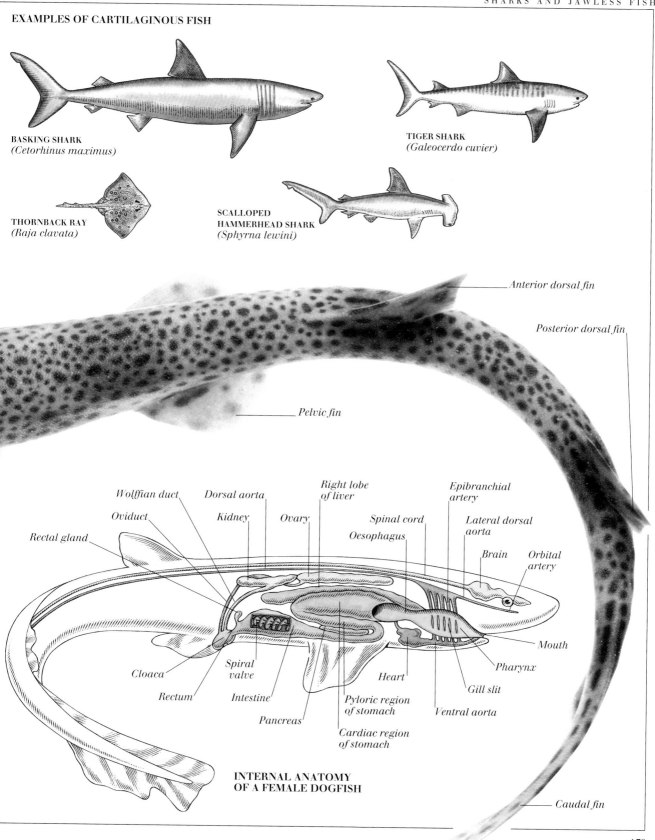

BASKING SHARK
(*Cetorhinus maximus*)

TIGER SHARK
(*Galeocerdo cuvier*)

THORNBACK RAY
(*Raja clavata*)

SCALLOPED HAMMERHEAD SHARK
(*Sphyrna lewini*)

Anterior dorsal fin

Posterior dorsal fin

Pelvic fin

Wolffian duct

Oviduct

Rectal gland

Dorsal aorta

Kidney

Right lobe of liver

Ovary

Spinal cord

Oesophagus

Epibranchial artery

Lateral dorsal aorta

Brain

Orbital artery

Mouth

Pharynx

Gill slit

Ventral aorta

Cardiac region of stomach

Pyloric region of stomach

Heart

Pancreas

Intestine

Rectum

Spiral valve

Cloaca

INTERNAL ANATOMY OF A FEMALE DOGFISH

Caudal fin

179

Bony fish

BONY FISH, SUCH AS CARP, TROUT, SALMON, perch, and cod, are by far the best known and largest group of fish, with more than 20,000 species (over 95 per cent of all known fish). As their name suggests, bony fish have skeletons made of bone, in contrast to the cartilaginous skeletons of sharks, jawless fish, and their relatives (see pp. 178-179). Other typical features of bony fish include a swim bladder, which functions as a variable-buoyancy organ, enabling a fish to remain effortlessly at whatever depth it is swimming; relatively thin, bone-like scales; a flap (called an operculum) covering the gills; and paired pelvic and pectoral fins. Scientifically, bony fish belong to the class Osteichthyes, which is a division of the superclass Gnathostomata (meaning "jawed mouths").

HOW FISH BREATHE

Fish "breathe" by extracting oxygen from water through their gills. Water is sucked in through the mouth; simultaneously, the opercula close to prevent the water from escaping. The mouth is then closed, and muscles in the walls of the mouth, pharynx, and opercular cavity contract to pump the water inside over the gills and out through the opercula. Some fish rely on swimming with their mouths open to keep water flowing over the gills.

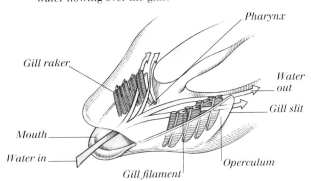

Pharynx

Gill raker

Water out

Gill slit

Mouth

Water in

Gill filament

Operculum

EXAMPLES OF BONY FISH

MANDARINFISH
(Synchiropus splendidus)

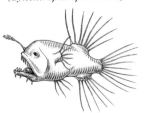

ANGLERFISH
(Caulophryne jordani)

LIONFISH
(Pterois volitans)

OCEANIC SEAHORSE
(Hippocampus kuda)

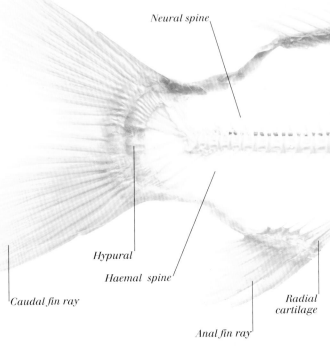

Vertebra

Neural spine

Hypural

Haemal spine

Caudal fin ray

Radial cartilage

Anal fin ray

STURGEON
(Acipenser sturio)

SNOWFLAKE MORAY EEL
(Echidna nebulosa)

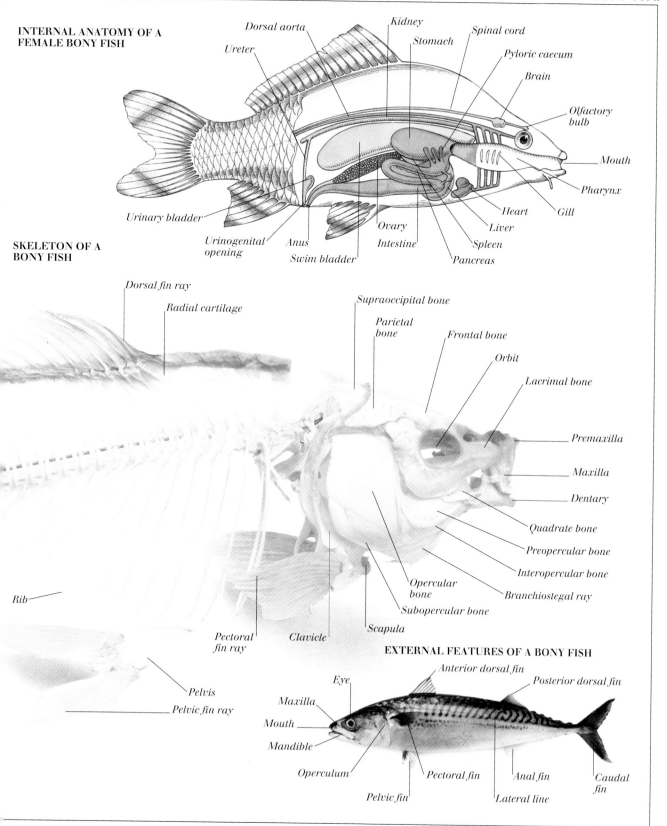

INTERNAL ANATOMY OF A FEMALE BONY FISH

Dorsal aorta

Ureter

Kidney

Stomach

Spinal cord

Pyloric caecum

Brain

Olfactory bulb

Mouth

Pharynx

Gill

Heart

Liver

Spleen

Pancreas

Intestine

Swim bladder

Ovary

Anus

Urinogenital opening

Urinary bladder

SKELETON OF A BONY FISH

Dorsal fin ray

Radial cartilage

Supraoccipital bone

Parietal bone

Frontal bone

Orbit

Lacrimal bone

Premaxilla

Maxilla

Dentary

Quadrate bone

Preopercular bone

Interopercular bone

Branchiostegal ray

Subopercular bone

Opercular bone

Scapula

Clavicle

Pectoral fin ray

Rib

Pelvis

Pelvic fin ray

EXTERNAL FEATURES OF A BONY FISH

Eye

Maxilla

Mouth

Mandible

Operculum

Pelvic fin

Pectoral fin

Anterior dorsal fin

Posterior dorsal fin

Anal fin

Lateral line

Caudal fin

Amphibians

THE CLASS AMPHIBIA INCLUDES FROGS and toads (which make up the order Anura), and newts and salamanders (which make up the order Urodela). Amphibians typically have moist, scaleless, hairless skin; lungs; and are cold-blooded. They also undergo complete metamorphosis, from eggs laid in water through various water-living larval stages (such as tadpoles) to land-living adults. Typical features of adult frogs and toads include a squat body with no tail; long, powerful hind legs; and large, often bulging, eyes. Adult newts and salamanders typically have a long body with a well-developed tail; and relatively short, equal-sized legs. However, newts and salamanders show considerable variation; for example, in some species the adults have minute legs, external gills rather than lungs, and spend their entire lives in water.

INTERNAL ANATOMY OF A FEMALE FROG

EXTERNAL FEATURES OF A FROG

EXTERNAL FEATURES OF A SALAMANDER

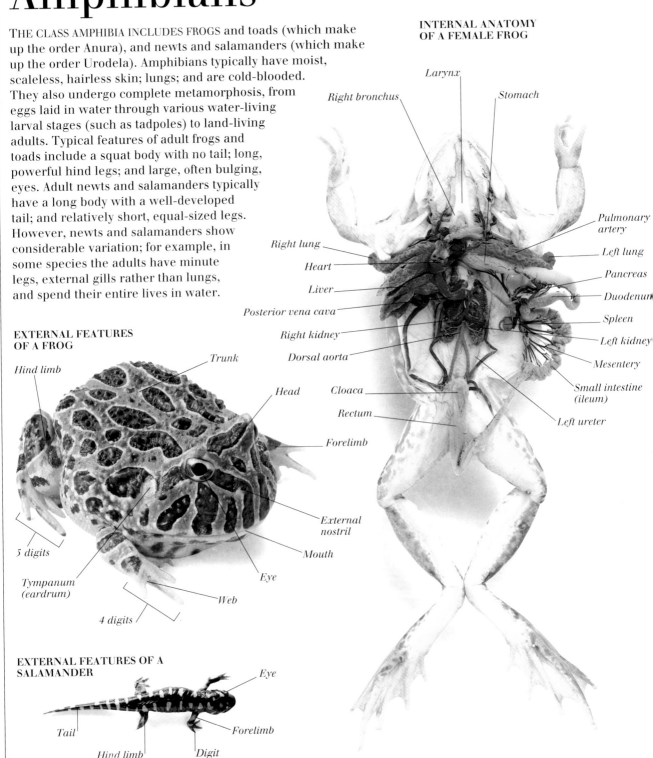

Labels (Internal anatomy of a female frog): Larynx, Right bronchus, Stomach, Pulmonary artery, Right lung, Left lung, Heart, Pancreas, Liver, Duodenum, Posterior vena cava, Spleen, Right kidney, Left kidney, Dorsal aorta, Mesentery, Cloaca, Small intestine (ileum), Rectum, Left ureter

Labels (External features of a frog): Trunk, Head, Hind limb, Forelimb, 5 digits, External nostril, Tympanum (eardrum), Mouth, Eye, Web, 4 digits

Labels (External features of a salamander): Eye, Tail, Forelimb, Hind limb, Digit

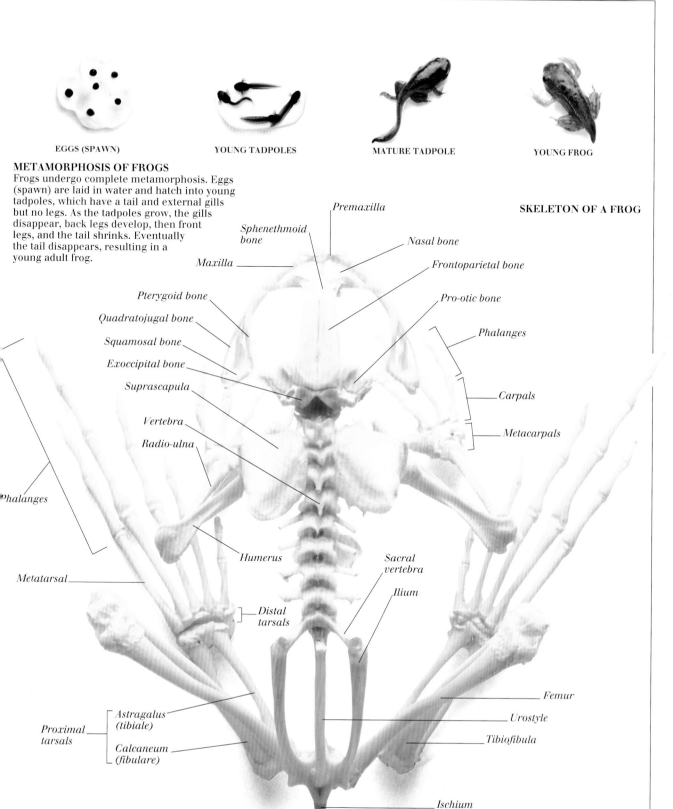

EGGS (SPAWN)　　　　**YOUNG TADPOLES**　　　　**MATURE TADPOLE**　　　　**YOUNG FROG**

METAMORPHOSIS OF FROGS

Frogs undergo complete metamorphosis. Eggs (spawn) are laid in water and hatch into young tadpoles, which have a tail and external gills but no legs. As the tadpoles grow, the gills disappear, back legs develop, then front legs, and the tail shrinks. Eventually the tail disappears, resulting in a young adult frog.

SKELETON OF A FROG

Premaxilla

Sphenethmoid bone

Nasal bone

Maxilla

Frontoparietal bone

Pterygoid bone

Pro-otic bone

Quadratojugal bone

Phalanges

Squamosal bone

Exoccipital bone

Suprascapula

Carpals

Vertebra

Metacarpals

Radio-ulna

Phalanges

Humerus

Metatarsal

Sacral vertebra

Ilium

Distal tarsals

Femur

Astragalus (tibiale)

Urostyle

Proximal tarsals

Tibiofibula

Calcaneum (fibulare)

Ischium

Lizards and snakes

LIZARDS AND SNAKES BELONG to the order Squamata, a division of the class Reptilia. Characteristic reptilian features include scaly skin, lungs, and cold-bloodedness. Most reptiles lay leathery-shelled eggs, although some hatch the eggs inside their bodies and give birth to live young. Lizards belong to the suborder Lacertilia. Typically, they have long tails, and shed their skin in several pieces. Many lizards can regenerate a tail if it is lost; some can change colour; and some are limbless. Snakes make up the suborder Ophidia (also called Serpentes). All snakes have long, limbless bodies; can dislocate their lower jaw to swallow large prey; and have eyelids that are joined together to form a single transparent covering over the front of the eye. Most snakes shed their skin in a single piece. Constrictor snakes kill their prey by squeezing; venomous snakes poison their prey.

EXAMPLES OF SNAKES

MEXICAN MOUNTAIN KING SNAKE (*Lampropeltis triangulum annulata*)

BANDED MILK SNAKE (*Lampropeltis ruthveni*)

EXTERNAL FEATURES OF A LIZARD

Eye

Mouth

Crest

Eardrum

Masseteric scale

Dorsal scale

External nostril

Dewlap

Foreleg

Belly

Ventral scale

SKELETON OF A LIZARD

Skull

Orbit

Scapula

Cervical vertebrae

Phalanges

Carpals

Metacarpal

Humerus

Ulna

Rib

Radius

Thoracolumbar vertebrae

Pelvis

Sacrum

Femur

Tibia

Fibula

Tarsals

Metatarsal

Caudal vertebrae

Phalanges

Toe

Claw

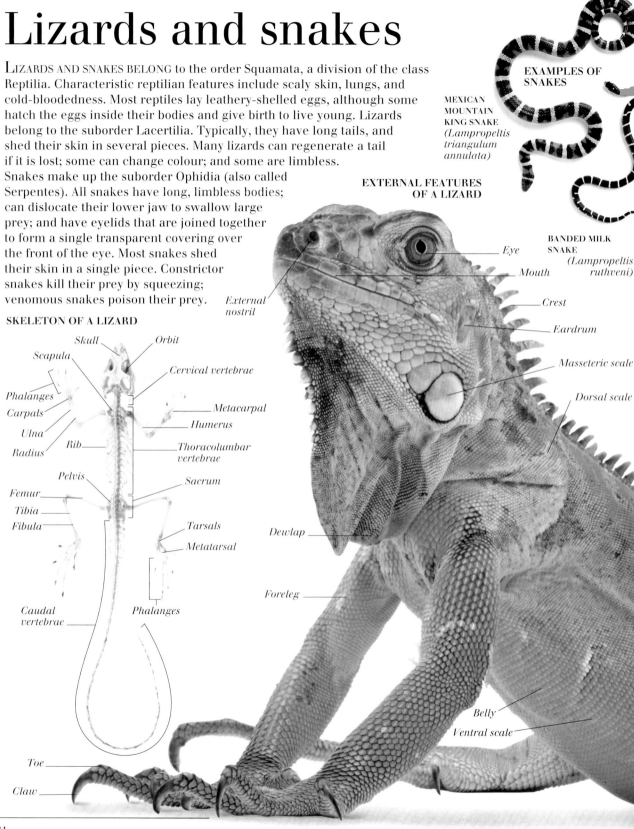

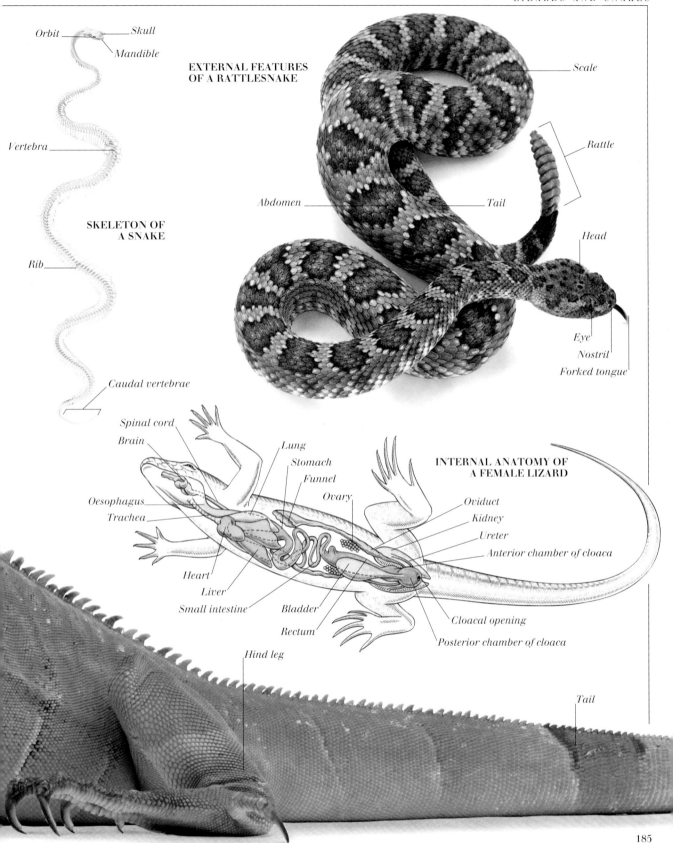

Orbit

Skull

Mandible

**EXTERNAL FEATURES
OF A RATTLESNAKE**

Scale

Vertebra

Rattle

Abdomen

Tail

**SKELETON OF
A SNAKE**

Head

Rib

Eye

Nostril

Forked tongue

Caudal vertebrae

Spinal cord

Brain

Lung

Stomach

Funnel

**INTERNAL ANATOMY OF
A FEMALE LIZARD**

Ovary

Oesophagus

Oviduct

Trachea

Kidney

Ureter

Anterior chamber of cloaca

Heart

Liver

Small intestine

Bladder

Cloacal opening

Rectum

Posterior chamber of cloaca

Hind leg

Tail

Crocodilians and turtles

GHARIAL
(Gavialis gangeticus)

CROCODILIANS AND TURTLES BELONG to different orders in the class Reptilia. The order Crocodilia includes crocodiles, alligators, caimans, and gharials. Typically, crocodilians are carnivores (flesh-eaters), and have a long snout, sharp teeth for gripping prey, and hard, square scales. All crocodilians are adapted to living on land and in water: they have four strong legs for moving on land; a powerful tail for swimming; and their eyes and nostrils are high on the head so that they stay above water while the rest of the body is submerged. The order Chelonia includes marine turtles, terrapins (freshwater turtles), and tortoises (land turtles). Characteristically, chelonians have a short, broad body encased in a bony shell with an outer horny covering, into which the head and limbs can be withdrawn; and a horny beak instead of teeth.

NILE CROCODILE
(Crocodylus niloticus)

AMERICAN ALLIGATOR
(Alligator mississippiensis)

SKELETON OF A CROCODILE

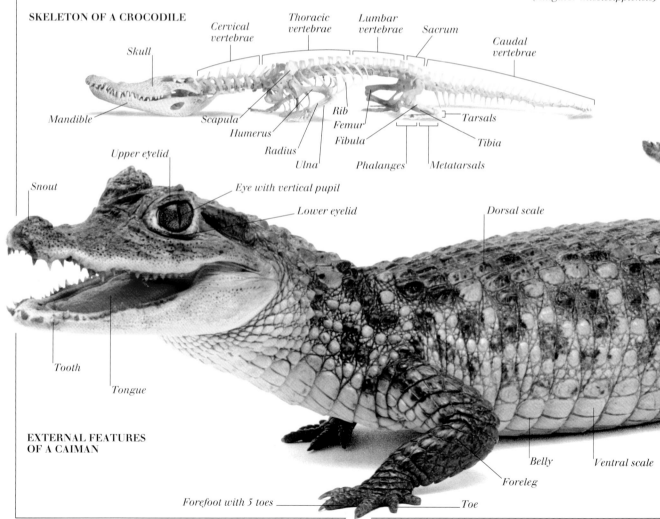

Cervical vertebrae

Thoracic vertebrae

Lumbar vertebrae

Sacrum

Caudal vertebrae

Skull

Mandible

Scapula

Humerus

Radius

Ulna

Rib

Femur

Fibula

Phalanges

Metatarsals

Tarsals

Tibia

Snout

Upper eyelid

Eye with vertical pupil

Lower eyelid

Dorsal scale

Tooth

Tongue

EXTERNAL FEATURES OF A CAIMAN

Belly

Ventral scale

Foreleg

Forefoot with 5 toes

Toe

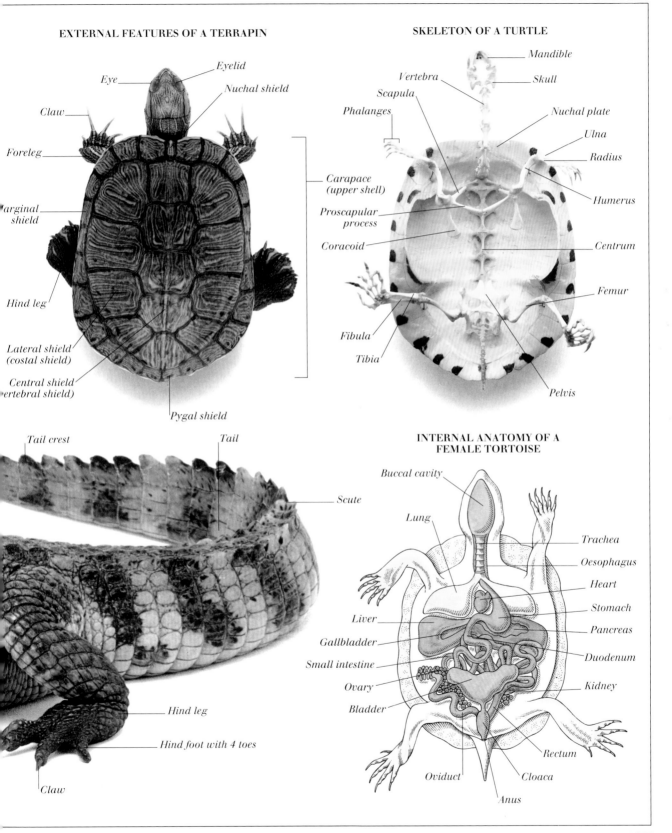

EXTERNAL FEATURES OF A TERRAPIN

Eye

Eyelid

Nuchal shield

Claw

Foreleg

arginal shield

Hind leg

Lateral shield (costal shield)

Central shield ertebral shield)

Pygal shield

Carapace (upper shell)

SKELETON OF A TURTLE

Mandible

Vertebra

Skull

Scapula

Phalanges

Nuchal plate

Ulna

Radius

Humerus

Proscapular process

Coracoid

Centrum

Femur

Fibula

Tibia

Pelvis

Tail crest

Tail

Scute

Hind leg

Hind foot with 4 toes

Claw

INTERNAL ANATOMY OF A FEMALE TORTOISE

Buccal cavity

Lung

Trachea

Oesophagus

Heart

Liver

Stomach

Pancreas

Gallbladder

Duodenum

Small intestine

Kidney

Ovary

Bladder

Rectum

Oviduct

Cloaca

Anus

Birds 1

BIRDS MAKE UP THE CLASS AVES. There are more than 9,000 species, almost all of which can fly (the only flightless birds are penguins, ostriches, rheas, cassowaries, and kiwis). The ability to fly is reflected in the typical bird features: forelimbs modified as wings; a streamlined body; and hollow bones to reduce weight. All birds lay hard-shelled eggs, which the parents incubate. Birds' beaks and feet vary according to diet and way of life. Beaks range from general-purpose types suitable for a mixed diet (those of thrushes, for example), to types specialized for particular foods (such as the large, curved, sieving beaks of flamingos). Feet range from the webbed "paddles" of ducks, to the talons of birds of prey. Plumage also varies widely, and in many species the male is brightly coloured for courtship display whereas the female is drab.

EXTERNAL FEATURES OF A BIRD

Forehead

Eye

Crown

Nostril

Nape

Upper mandible

Beak

Lower mandible

Chin

Throat

EXAMPLES OF BIRDS

MALE TUFTED DUCK
(*Aythya fuligula*)

Minor coverts

Lesser wing coverts

Median wing coverts

Greater wing coverts
(major coverts)

Secondary flight feathers
(secondary remiges)

Primary flight feathers
(primaryremiges)

WHITE STORK
(*Ciconia ciconia*)

Breast

Belly

Flank

Thigh

Under tail coverts

Cla

Toe

Tarsus

Tail feathers (retrices)

MALE OSTRICH
(*Struthio camelus*)

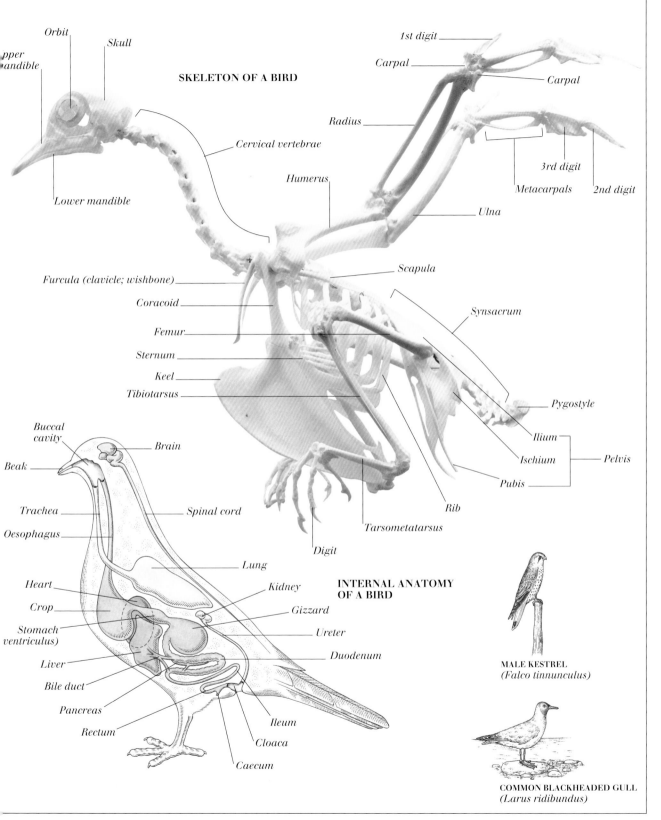

SKELETON OF A BIRD

Orbit

Skull

Upper mandible

1st digit

Carpal

Carpal

Radius

Cervical vertebrae

3rd digit

Humerus

Metacarpals

2nd digit

Lower mandible

Ulna

Furcula (clavicle; wishbone)

Scapula

Coracoid

Synsacrum

Femur

Sternum

Keel

Tibiotarsus

Pygostyle

Ilium

Ischium

Pelvis

Pubis

Rib

Tarsometatarsus

Digit

**INTERNAL ANATOMY
OF A BIRD**

*Buccal
cavity*

Brain

Beak

Trachea

Spinal cord

Oesophagus

Lung

Heart

Kidney

Crop

Gizzard

*Stomach
(ventriculus)*

Ureter

Liver

Duodenum

Bile duct

Pancreas

Ileum

Rectum

Cloaca

Caecum

MALE KESTREL
(Falco tinnunculus)

COMMON BLACKHEADED GULL
(Larus ridibundus)

Birds 2

EXAMPLES OF BIRDS' FEET

KITTIWAKE
(Rissa tridactyla)
The webbed feet are
adapted for paddling
through water.

LITTLE GREBE
(Tachybaptus ruficollis)
The lobed, flattened feet
are adapted for swimming
underwater.

TAWNY OWL
(Strix aluco)
The clawed feet are adapted
for gripping prey.

EXAMPLES OF BIRDS' BEAKS

KING VULTURE
(Sarcorhamphus papa)
The hooked beak is adapted
for pulling apart flesh.

GREATER FLAMINGO
(Phoenicopterus ruber)
In the living bird, the large,
curved beak contains a
cartilaginous "sieve" for
filtering food particles
from water.

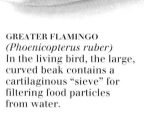

MISTLE THRUSH
(Turdus viscivorus)
The general-purpose beak is
suitable for a wide range of animal
and plant foods.

BLUE-AND-YELLOW MACAW
(Ara ararauna)
The broad, powerful, hooked beak
is adapted for crushing seeds and
eating fruit.

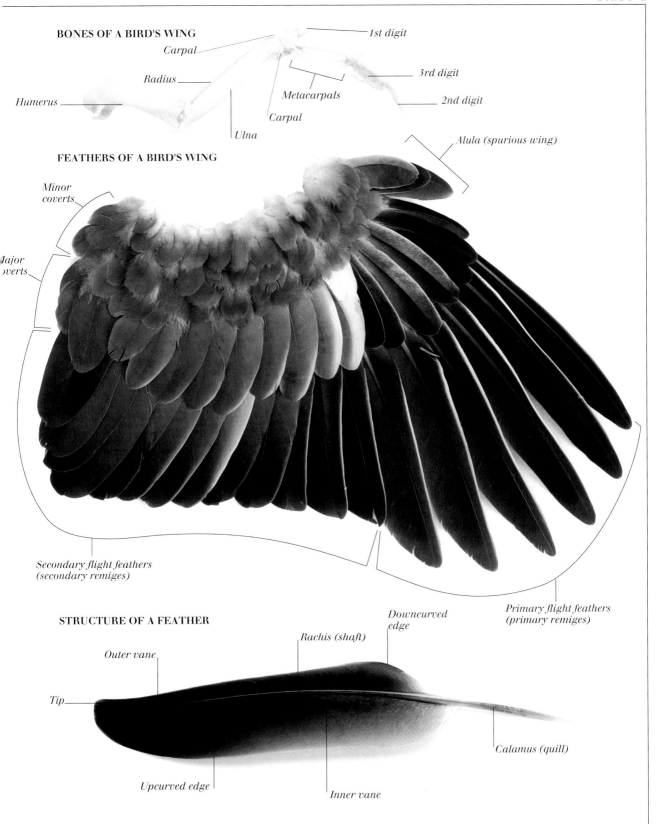

BONES OF A BIRD'S WING

Carpal

1st digit

Radius

3rd digit

Humerus

Metacarpals

2nd digit

Carpal

Ulna

Alula (spurious wing)

FEATHERS OF A BIRD'S WING

Minor
coverts

Major
coverts

Secondary flight feathers
(secondary remiges)

Primary flight feathers
(primary remiges)

STRUCTURE OF A FEATHER

Downcurved
edge

Rachis (shaft)

Outer vane

Tip

Calamus (quill)

Upcurved edge

Inner vane

Eggs

AN EGG IS A SINGLE CELL, produced by the female, with the capacity to develop into a new individual. Development may take place inside the mother's body (as in most mammals) or outside, in which case the egg has a protective covering such as a shell. Egg yolk nourishes the growing young. Eggs developing inside the mother generally have little yolk, because the young are nourished from her body. Eggs developing outside may also have little yolk if they are produced by animals whose young go through a larval stage (such as a caterpillar) that feeds itself while developing into the adult form. The shelled eggs of birds and reptiles contain enough yolk to sustain the young until it hatches into a juvenile version of the adult.

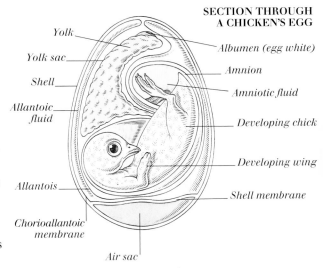

SECTION THROUGH A CHICKEN'S EGG

Yolk
Yolk sac
Shell
Allantoic fluid
Allantois
Chorioallantoic membrane
Air sac
Albumen (egg white)
Amnion
Amniotic fluid
Developing chick
Developing wing
Shell membrane

VARIETY OF EGGS

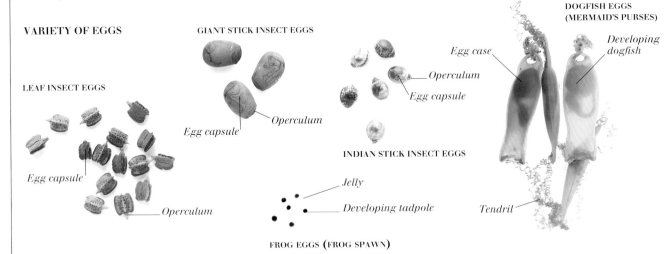

LEAF INSECT EGGS
Egg capsule
Operculum

GIANT STICK INSECT EGGS
Egg capsule
Operculum

INDIAN STICK INSECT EGGS
Operculum
Egg capsule

FROG EGGS (FROG SPAWN)
Jelly
Developing tadpole

DOGFISH EGGS (MERMAID'S PURSES)
Developing dogfish
Egg case
Tendril

HATCHING OF A QUAIL'S EGG

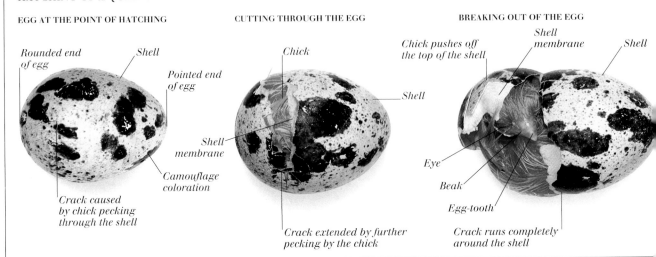

EGG AT THE POINT OF HATCHING
Rounded end of egg
Shell
Pointed end of egg
Shell membrane
Camouflage coloration
Crack caused by chick pecking through the shell

CUTTING THROUGH THE EGG
Chick
Shell
Crack extended by further pecking by the chick

BREAKING OUT OF THE EGG
Chick pushes off the top of the shell
Shell membrane
Shell
Eye
Beak
Egg-tooth
Crack runs completely around the shell

192

EXAMPLES OF BIRDS' EGGS

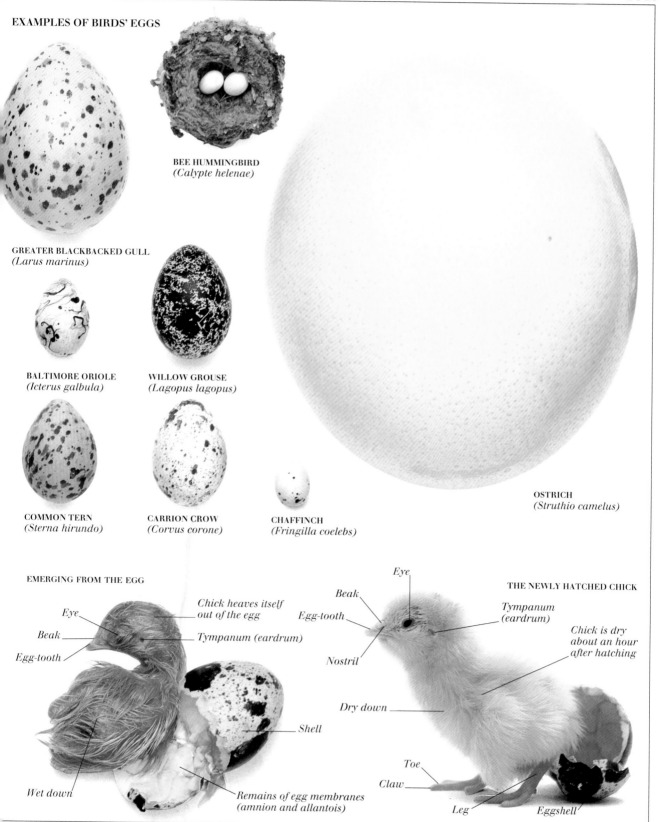

BEE HUMMINGBIRD
(Calypte helenae)

GREATER BLACKBACKED GULL
(Larus marinus)

BALTIMORE ORIOLE
(Icterus galbula)

WILLOW GROUSE
(Lagopus lagopus)

COMMON TERN
(Sterna hirundo)

CARRION CROW
(Corvus corone)

CHAFFINCH
(Fringilla coelebs)

OSTRICH
(Struthio camelus)

EMERGING FROM THE EGG

Eye

Beak

Egg-tooth

Chick heaves itself
out of the egg

Tympanum (eardrum)

Wet down

Remains of egg membranes
(amnion and allantois)

Shell

THE NEWLY HATCHED CHICK

Eye

Beak

Egg-tooth

Nostril

Tympanum
(eardrum)

Chick is dry
about an hour
after hatching

Dry down

Toe

Claw

Leg

Eggshell

Carnivores

THE MAMMALIAN ORDER CARNIVORA includes cats, dogs, bears, raccoons, pandas, weasels, badgers, skunks, otters, civets, mongooses, and hyenas. The order's name is derived from the fact that most of its members are carnivores (flesh-eaters). Typical carnivore features therefore reflect a hunting life-style: speed and agility; sharp claws and well-developed canine teeth for holding and killing prey; carnassial teeth (cheek teeth) for cutting flesh; and forward-facing eyes for good distance judgment. However, some members of the order—bears, badgers, and foxes, for example—have a more mixed diet, and a few are entirely herbivorous (plant-eating), notably pandas. Such animals have no carnassial teeth and tend to be slower-moving than pure flesh-eaters.

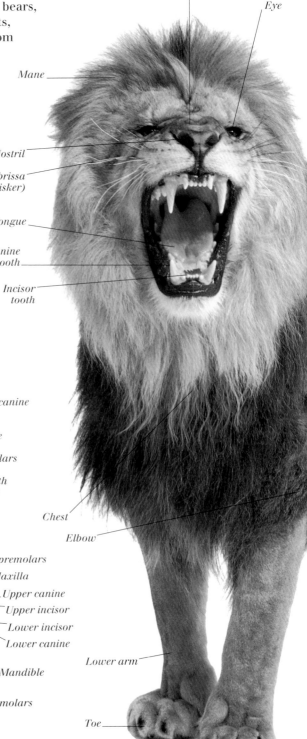

Nose

Eye

Mane

Nostril

Vibrissa
(whisker)

Tongue

Canine
tooth

Incisor
tooth

Chest

Elbow

Lower arm

Toe

SKULL OF A LION

Coronoid process

Zygomatic arch

Sagittal crest

Orbit

Nasal bone

Maxilla

Upper premolars

Upper canine

Lower canine

Mandible

Lower premolars

Occipital
condyle

Tympanic
bulla

Condyle

Angular process

Upper carnassial tooth
(4th upper premolar)

SKULL OF A BEAR

Sagittal crest

Occipital
condyle

Zygomatic arch

Orbit

Upper molars

Nasal bone

Upper premolars

Maxilla

Upper canine

Upper incisor

Lower incisor

Lower canine

Mandible

Tympanic
bulla

Angular
process

Condyle

Lower molars

Lower premolars

EXAMPLES OF CARNIVORES

ALSATIAN DOG
(Canis familiaris)

MANED WOLF
(Chrysocyon brachyurus)

RACCOON
(Procyon lotor)

AMERICAN BLACK BEAR
(Ursus americanus)

SKELETON OF A DOMESTIC CAT

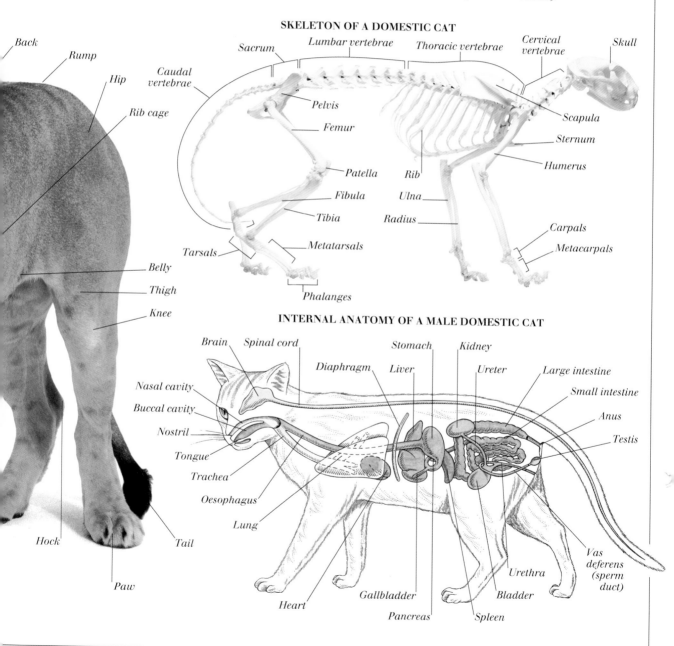

Back

Rump

Hip

Rib cage

Caudal
vertebrae

Sacrum

Lumbar vertebrae

Thoracic vertebrae

Cervical
vertebrae

Skull

Pelvis

Scapula

Femur

Sternum

Humerus

Patella

Rib

Fibula

Ulna

Tibia

Radius

Belly

Carpals

Metacarpals

Tarsals

Metatarsals

Thigh

Knee

Phalanges

Hock

Tail

Paw

INTERNAL ANATOMY OF A MALE DOMESTIC CAT

Brain

Spinal cord

Stomach

Kidney

Diaphragm

Liver

Ureter

Large intestine

Nasal cavity

Small intestine

Buccal cavity

Anus

Nostril

Testis

Tongue

Trachea

Oesophagus

Lung

Vas
deferens
(sperm
duct)

Urethra

Heart

Gallbladder

Bladder

Pancreas

Spleen

Rabbits and rodents

ALTHOUGH RABBITS AND RODENTS belong to
different orders of mammals, they have some
features in common. These features include
chisel-shaped incisor teeth that grow
continually, and eating their faeces to
extract more nutrients from their plant diet. Rabbits and
hares belong to the order Lagomorpha. Characteristically,
they have four incisors in the upper jaw and two in the
lower jaw; powerful hind legs for jumping; forelimbs
adapted for burrowing; long ears; and a small tail. Rodents
make up the order Rodentia. This is the largest order of
mammals, with more than 1,700 species, including
squirrels, beavers, chipmunks, gophers, rats,
mice, lemmings, gerbils, porcupines, cavies,
and the capybara. Typical rodent features
include two incisors in each jaw;
short forelimbs for manipulating
food; and cheek pouches
for storing food.

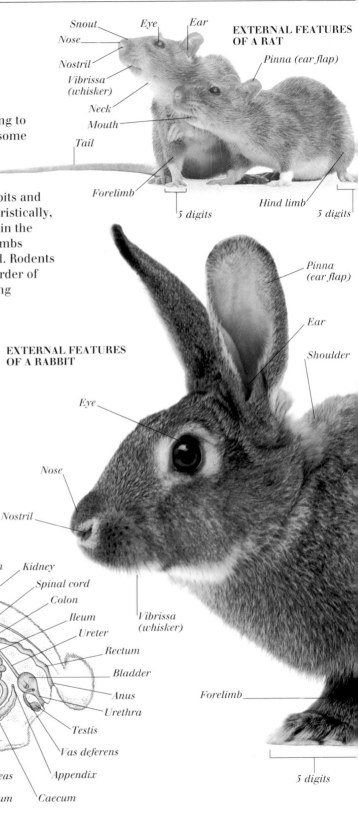

**EXTERNAL FEATURES
OF A RAT**

Snout
Eye
Ear
Pinna (ear flap)
Nose
Nostril
Vibrissa
(whisker)
Neck
Mouth
Tail
Forelimb
5 digits
Hind limb
5 digits

**EXTERNAL FEATURES
OF A RABBIT**

Pinna
(ear flap)
Ear
Shoulder
Eye
Nose
Nostril
Vibrissa
(whisker)
Forelimb
5 digits

**INTERNAL ANATOMY OF
A MALE RABBIT**

Brain
Gallbladder
Liver
Stomach
Kidney
Spinal cord
Colon
Ileum
Ureter
Rectum
Bladder
Anus
Urethra
Testis
Vas deferens
Appendix
Caecum
Duodenum
Pancreas
Heart
Diaphragm
Lung
Trachea
Oesophagus
Tongue
Buccal
cavity
Mouth
Nasal
cavity

196

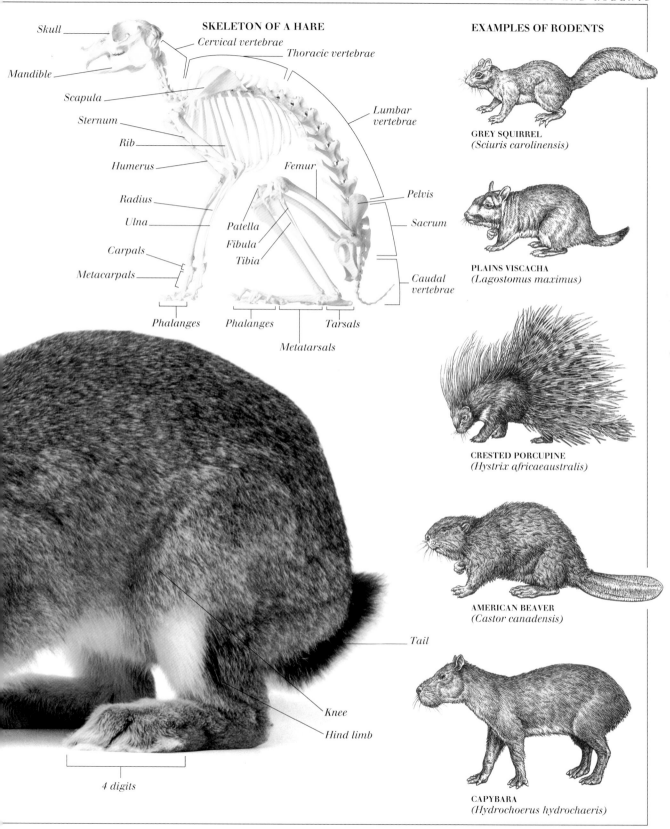

SKELETON OF A HARE

Skull

Mandible

Cervical vertebrae

Thoracic vertebrae

Scapula

Sternum

Rib

Humerus

Radius

Ulna

Carpals

Metacarpals

Lumbar vertebrae

Femur

Pelvis

Sacrum

Patella

Fibula

Tibia

Caudal vertebrae

Phalanges

Phalanges

Tarsals

Metatarsals

Tail

Knee

Hind limb

4 digits

EXAMPLES OF RODENTS

GREY SQUIRREL
(*Sciuris carolinensis*)

PLAINS VISCACHA
(*Lagostomus maximus*)

CRESTED PORCUPINE
(*Hystrix africaeaustralis*)

AMERICAN BEAVER
(*Castor canadensis*)

CAPYBARA
(*Hydrochoerus hydrochaeris*)

Ungulates

UNGULATES IS A GENERAL TERM FOR a large, varied group of mammals that includes horses, cattle, and their relatives. The ungulates are divided into two orders on the basis of the number of toes. Members of the order Perissodactyla (odd-toed ungulates) have one or three toes. Perissodactyls include horses, asses, and zebras (all of which are one-toed), and rhinoceroses and tapirs (which are three-toed). Members of the order Artiodactyla (even-toed ungulates) have two or four toes. Most artiodactyls have two toes, which are typically encased in hooves to give the so-called cloven hoof. Two-toed, cloven-hoofed artiodactyls include cows and other cattle, sheep, goats, antelopes, deer, and giraffes. The other main two-toed artiodactyls are camels and llamas. Most two-toed artiodactyls are ruminants; that is, they have a four-chambered stomach and chew the cud. The principal four-toed artiodactyls are pigs, peccaries, and hippopotamuses.

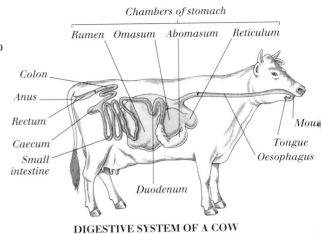

DIGESTIVE SYSTEM OF A COW

COMPARISON OF THE FRONT FEET OF A HORSE AND A COW

SKELETON OF THE LEFT FRONT FOOT OF A HORSE

SKELETON OF THE RIGHT FRONT FOOT OF A COW

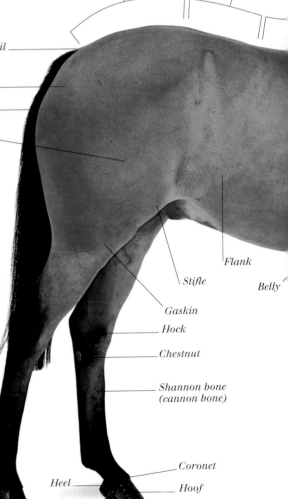

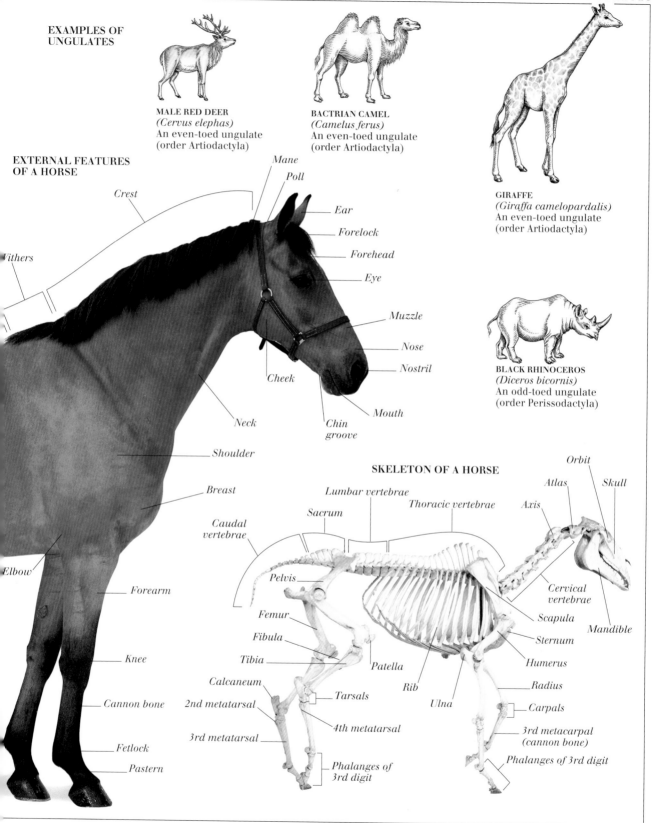

**EXAMPLES OF
UNGULATES**

MALE RED DEER
(*Cervus elephas*)
An even-toed ungulate
(order Artiodactyla)

BACTRIAN CAMEL
(*Camelus ferus*)
An even-toed ungulate
(order Artiodactyla)

GIRAFFE
(*Giraffa camelopardalis*)
An even-toed ungulate
(order Artiodactyla)

BLACK RHINOCEROS
(*Diceros bicornis*)
An odd-toed ungulate
(order Perissodactyla)

**EXTERNAL FEATURES
OF A HORSE**

Mane
Poll
Crest
Ear
Forelock
Withers
Forehead
Eye
Muzzle
Nose
Nostril
Cheek
Mouth
Neck
Chin
groove
Shoulder
Breast
Elbow
Forearm
Knee
Cannon bone
Fetlock
Pastern

SKELETON OF A HORSE

Orbit
Atlas
Skull
Lumbar vertebrae
Thoracic vertebrae
Axis
Sacrum
Caudal
vertebrae
Pelvis
Cervical
vertebrae
Femur
Scapula
Fibula
Sternum
Tibia
Patella
Humerus
Rib
Calcaneum
Radius
2nd metatarsal
Tarsals
Ulna
Carpals
3rd metatarsal
4th metatarsal
3rd metacarpal
(cannon bone)
Phalanges of
3rd digit
Phalanges of 3rd digit

Elephants

THE TWO SPECIES OF elephants—African and Asian—are the only members of the mammalian order Proboscidea. The bigger African elephant is the largest land animal: a fully grown male may be up to 4 m (13 ft) tall and weigh as much as 7 tonnes (6.9 tons). A fully grown male Asian elephant may be 3.3 m (11 ft) tall and weigh 5.4 tonnes (5.3 tons). The trunk—an extension of the nose and upper lip—is the elephant's other most obvious feature. It is used for manipulating and lifting, feeding, drinking and spraying water, smelling, touching, and producing trumpeting sounds. Other characteristic features include a pair of tusks, used for defence and for crushing vegetation; thick, pillar-like legs and broad feet to support the massive body; and large ear flaps that act as radiators to keep the elephant cool.

DIFFERENCES BETWEEN AFRICAN AND ASIAN ELEPHANTS

Flat forehead
Concave back
Very large ears
2 "lips" at the end of the trunk
4 toenails
3 toenails

AFRICAN ELEPHANT
(Loxodonta africana)

Twin-domed forehead
Arched back
Smaller ears
1 "lip" at the end of the trunk
5 toenails
4 toenails

ASIAN ELEPHANT
(Elephas maximus)

INTERNAL ANATOMY OF A FEMALE ELEPHANT

Spinal cord
Heart
Duodenum
Kidney
Ureter
Uterus
Brain
Rectum
Nasal cavity
Stomach
Bladder
Buccal cavity
Anal flap
Mouth
Anus
Vagina
Tongue
Tusk
Hind leg
Epiglottis
Oesophagus
Trachea
Small intestine
Lung
Spleen
Diaphragm
Vulva
Nasal passage
Rump
Nostril
Toenail

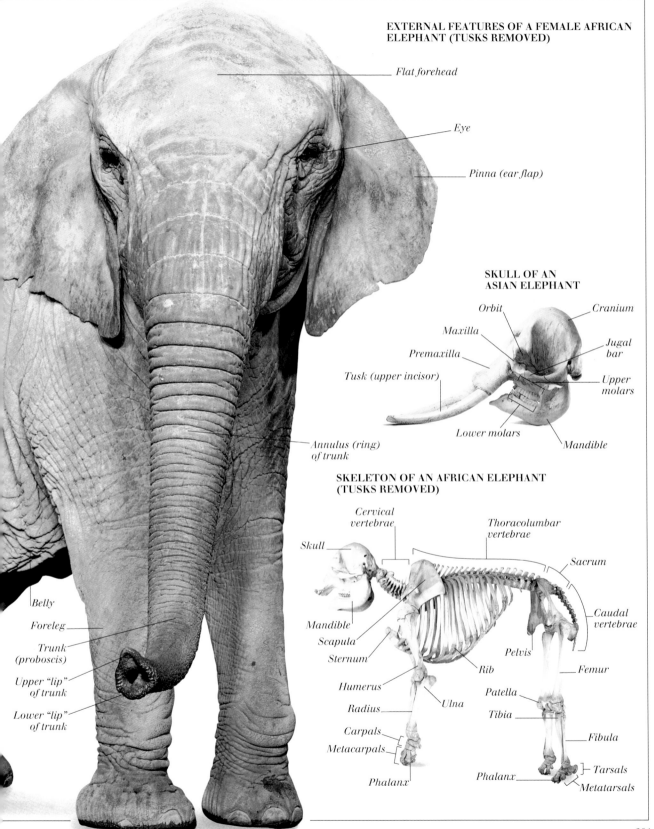

EXTERNAL FEATURES OF A FEMALE AFRICAN ELEPHANT (TUSKS REMOVED)

Flat forehead

Eye

Pinna (ear flap)

Annulus (ring) of trunk

Belly

Foreleg

Trunk (proboscis)

Upper "lip" of trunk

Lower "lip" of trunk

SKULL OF AN ASIAN ELEPHANT

Orbit

Cranium

Maxilla

Jugal bar

Premaxilla

Upper molars

Tusk (upper incisor)

Lower molars

Mandible

SKELETON OF AN AFRICAN ELEPHANT (TUSKS REMOVED)

Cervical vertebrae

Thoracolumbar vertebrae

Skull

Sacrum

Mandible

Caudal vertebrae

Scapula

Sternum

Pelvis

Humerus

Rib

Femur

Radius

Ulna

Patella

Carpals

Tibia

Metacarpals

Fibula

Phalanx

Phalanx

Tarsals

Metatarsals

Primates

THE MAMMALIAN ORDER PRIMATES consists of monkeys, apes, and their relatives (including humans). There are two suborders of primates: Prosimii, the primitive primates, which include lemurs, tarsiers, and lorises; and Anthropoidea, the advanced primates, which include monkeys, apes, and humans. The anthropoids are divided into New World monkeys, Old World monkeys, and hominids. New World monkeys typically have wide-apart nostrils that open to the side; and long tails, which are prehensile (grasping) in some species. This group of monkeys lives in South America, and includes marmosets, tamarins, and howler monkeys. Old World monkeys typically have close-set nostrils that open forwards or downwards; and non-prehensile tails. This group of monkeys lives in Africa and Asia, and includes langurs, mandrills, macaques, and baboons. Hominids typically have large brains, and no tail. This group includes the apes—chimpanzees, gibbons, gorillas, and orangutans—and humans.

INTERNAL ANATOMY OF A FEMALE CHIMPANZEE

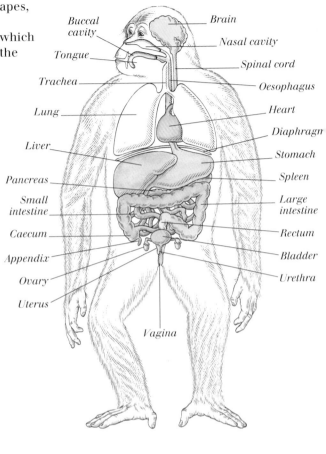

Buccal cavity
Tongue
Trachea
Lung
Liver
Pancreas
Small intestine
Caecum
Appendix
Ovary
Uterus
Vagina
Brain
Nasal cavity
Spinal cord
Oesophagus
Heart
Diaphragm
Stomach
Spleen
Large intestine
Rectum
Bladder
Urethra

SKELETON OF A RHESUS MONKEY

Skull
Cervical vertebrae
Orbit
Thoracic vertebrae
Mandible
Clavicle
Scapula
Rib
Humerus
Lumbar vertebrae
Femur
Radius
Ulna
Sacrum
Patella
Tibia
Carpals
Metacarpals
Fibula
Pelvis
Phalanges
Caudal vertebrae
Tarsals
Metatarsals
Phalanges

SKULL OF A CHIMPANZEE

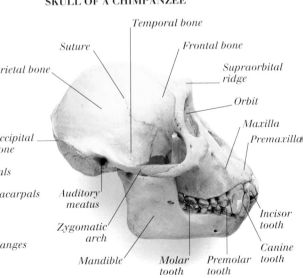

Temporal bone
Suture
Frontal bone
Parietal bone
Supraorbital ridge
Orbit
Occipital bone
Maxilla
Premaxilla
Auditory meatus
Incisor tooth
Zygomatic arch
Mandible
Molar tooth
Premolar tooth
Canine tooth

EXAMPLES OF PRIMATES

RING-TAILED LEMUR
(Lemur catta)
A prosimian

MALE RED HOWLER MONKEY
(Alouatta seniculus)
A New World monkey

MALE MANDRILL
(Mandrillus sphinx)
An Old World monkey

CHIMPANZEE
(Pan troglodytes)
An ape

EXTERNAL FEATURES OF A YOUNG GORILLA

GOLDEN LION TAMARIN
(Leontopithecus rosalia)
A New World monkey

Pinna (ear flap)

Shoulder

Brow ridge

Eye

Nostril

Mouth

Upper arm

Thigh

Forearm

Chest

Elbow

Knee

Lower leg

Hand

Foot

Finger

Toe

Toenail

Dolphins, whales, and seals

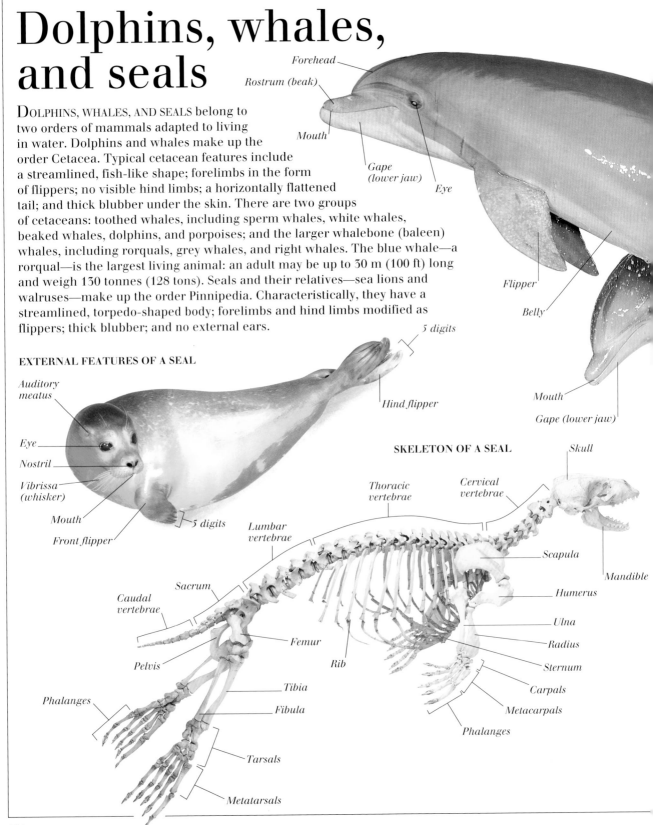

DOLPHINS, WHALES, AND SEALS belong to two orders of mammals adapted to living in water. Dolphins and whales make up the order Cetacea. Typical cetacean features include a streamlined, fish-like shape; forelimbs in the form of flippers; no visible hind limbs; a horizontally flattened tail; and thick blubber under the skin. There are two groups of cetaceans: toothed whales, including sperm whales, white whales, beaked whales, dolphins, and porpoises; and the larger whalebone (baleen) whales, including rorquals, grey whales, and right whales. The blue whale—a rorqual—is the largest living animal: an adult may be up to 30 m (100 ft) long and weigh 130 tonnes (128 tons). Seals and their relatives—sea lions and walruses—make up the order Pinnipedia. Characteristically, they have a streamlined, torpedo-shaped body; forelimbs and hind limbs modified as flippers; thick blubber; and no external ears.

Forehead

Rostrum (beak)

Mouth

Gape (lower jaw)

Eye

Flipper

Belly

Mouth

Gape (lower jaw)

5 digits

Hind flipper

EXTERNAL FEATURES OF A SEAL

Auditory meatus

Eye

Nostril

Vibrissa (whisker)

Mouth

Front flipper

5 digits

SKELETON OF A SEAL

Skull

Thoracic vertebrae

Cervical vertebrae

Lumbar vertebrae

Scapula

Mandible

Sacrum

Caudal vertebrae

Humerus

Ulna

Radius

Pelvis

Femur

Rib

Sternum

Carpals

Phalanges

Tibia

Metacarpals

Fibula

Phalanges

Tarsals

Metatarsals

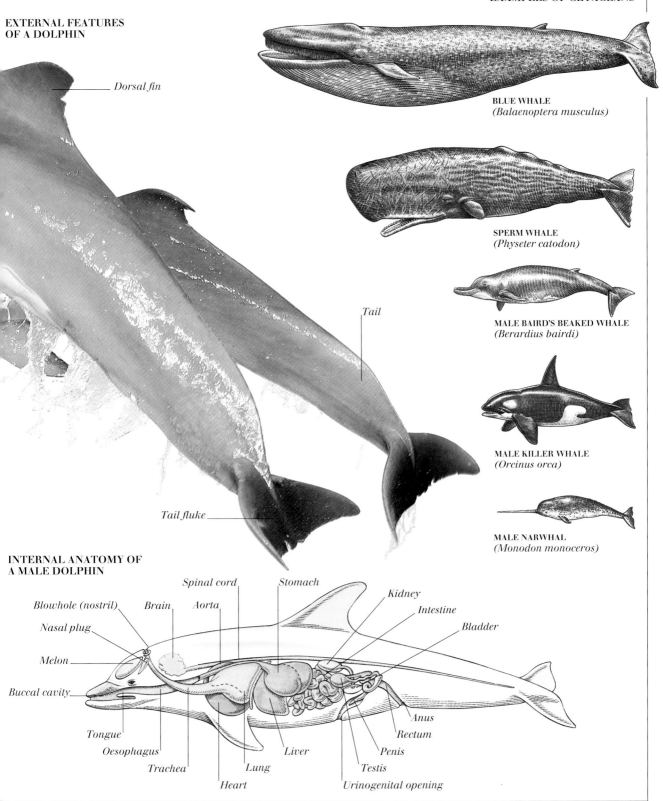

**EXTERNAL FEATURES
OF A DOLPHIN**

Dorsal fin

Tail

Tail fluke

BLUE WHALE
(*Balaenoptera musculus*)

SPERM WHALE
(*Physeter catodon*)

MALE BAIRD'S BEAKED WHALE
(*Berardius bairdi*)

MALE KILLER WHALE
(*Orcinus orca*)

MALE NARWHAL
(*Monodon monoceros*)

**INTERNAL ANATOMY OF
A MALE DOLPHIN**

Spinal cord

Stomach

Kidney

Intestine

Blowhole (nostril)

Brain

Aorta

Bladder

Nasal plug

Melon

Buccal cavity

Anus

Rectum

Tongue

Penis

Oesophagus

Testis

Trachea

Lung

Liver

Urinogenital opening

Heart

205

Marsupials and Monotremes

MARSUPIALS AND MONOTREMES are two orders of mammals that differ from other mammalian groups in the ways that their young develop. The order Marsupalia, the pouched mammals, is made up of kangaroos and their relatives. Typically, marsupials give birth to their young at a very early stage of development. The young then crawls to the mother's pouch (which is on the outside of her abdomen), where it attaches itself to a nipple and remains until fully developed. Most marsupials live in Australia, although the opossums—which are classified as marsupials despite not having a pouch—live in the Americas. The order Monotremata is made up of the platypus and its relatives (the echidnas, or spiny anteaters). The monotremes are primitive mammals that lay eggs, which the mother incubates. The monotremes are found only in Australia and New Guinea.

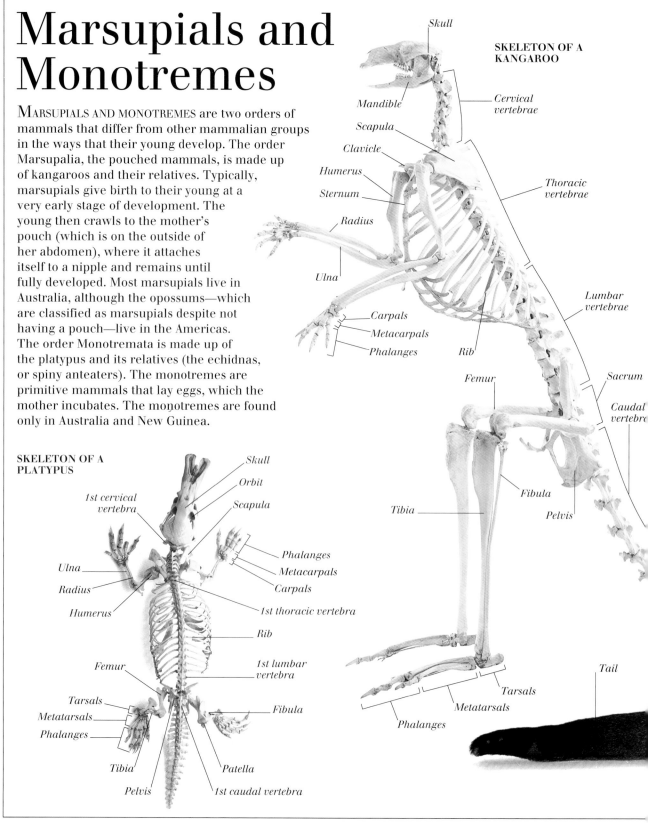

SKELETON OF A KANGAROO

Skull

Mandible

Cervical vertebrae

Scapula

Clavicle

Humerus

Sternum

Radius

Thoracic vertebrae

Ulna

Carpals

Metacarpals

Phalanges

Rib

Lumbar vertebrae

Femur

Sacrum

Caudal vertebra

Tibia

Fibula

Pelvis

Tail

Tarsals

Metatarsals

Phalanges

SKELETON OF A PLATYPUS

Skull

Orbit

Scapula

1st cervical vertebra

Phalanges

Metacarpals

Carpals

1st thoracic vertebra

Ulna

Radius

Humerus

Rib

1st lumbar vertebra

Femur

Fibula

Tarsals

Metatarsals

Phalanges

Tibia

Patella

Pelvis

1st caudal vertebra

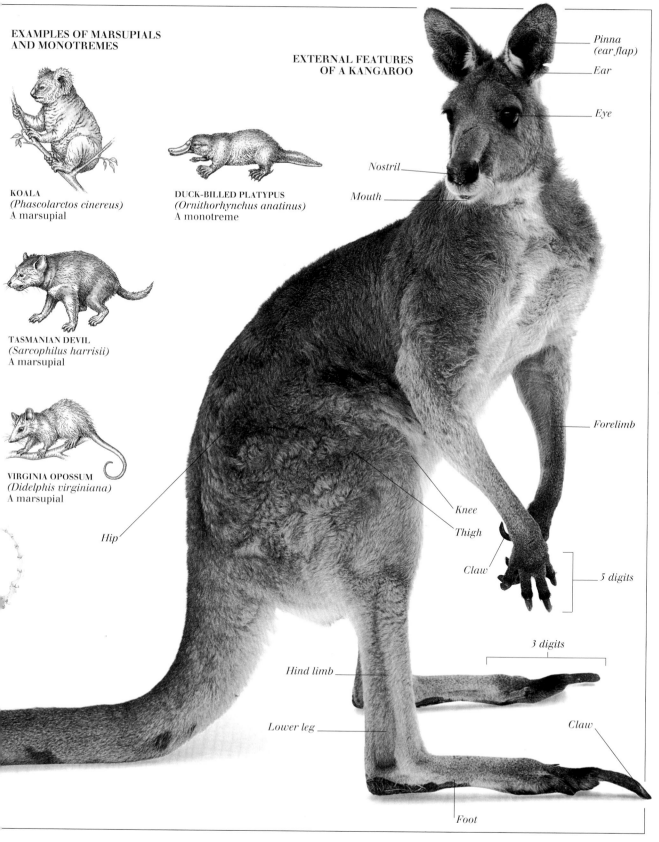

EXAMPLES OF MARSUPIALS AND MONOTREMES

EXTERNAL FEATURES OF A KANGAROO

KOALA
(Phascolarctos cinereus)
A marsupial

DUCK-BILLED PLATYPUS
(Ornithorhynchus anatinus)
A monotreme

TASMANIAN DEVIL
(Sarcophilus harrisii)
A marsupial

VIRGINIA OPOSSUM
(Didelphis virginiana)
A marsupial

Pinna
(ear flap)

Ear

Eye

Nostril

Mouth

Forelimb

Knee

Thigh

Claw

5 digits

Hip

3 digits

Hind limb

Lower leg

Claw

Foot

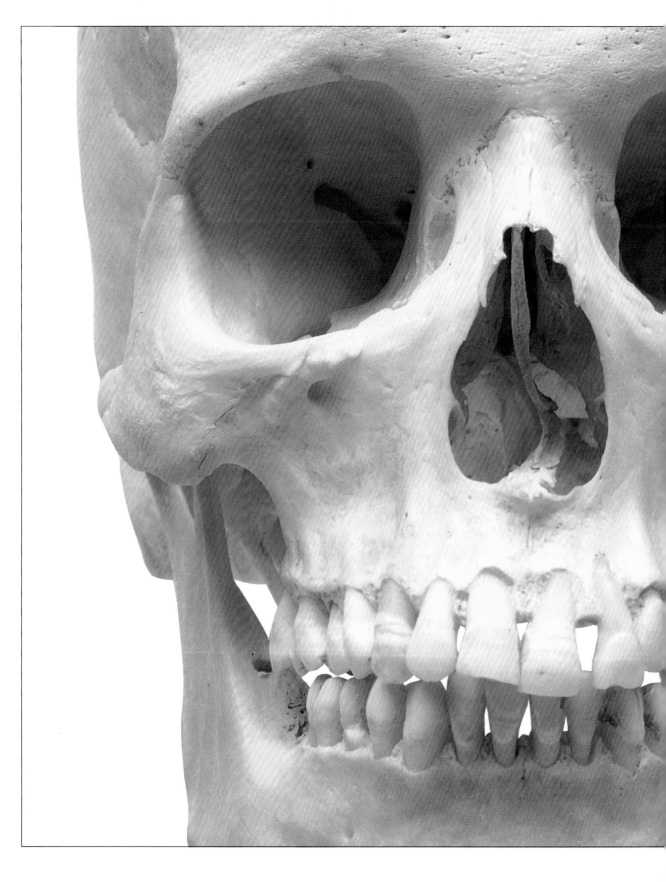

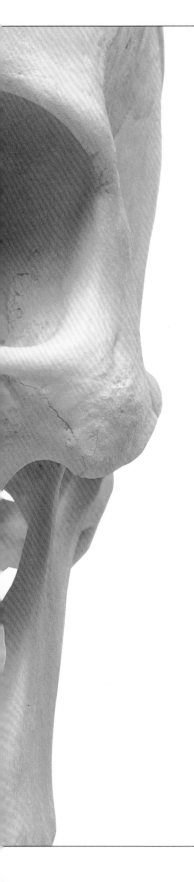

THE HUMAN BODY

Body features

ALTHOUGH THERE IS enormous
variation between the external
appearances of humans, all bodies
contain the same basic features.
The outward form of the
human body depends on the
size of the skeleton, the shape
of the muscles, the thickness
of the fat layer beneath
the skin, the elasticity or
sagginess of the skin, and
the person's age and sex.
Males tend to be taller than
females, with broader
shoulders, more body hair,
and a different pattern of fat
deposits under the skin; the
female body tends to be
less muscular and has
a shallower and wider
pelvis to allow
for childbirth.

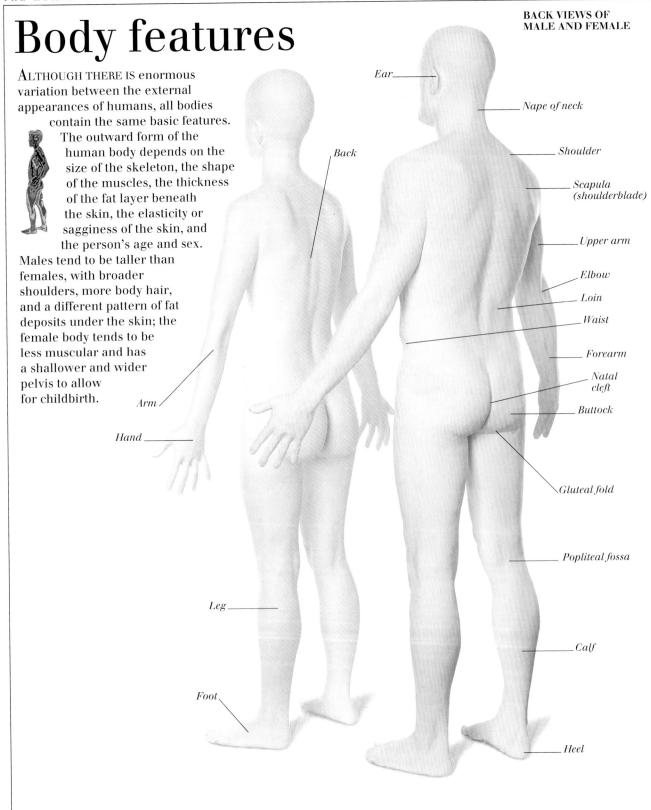

Ear

Nape of neck

Shoulder

Scapula
(shoulderblade)

Upper arm

Elbow

Loin

Waist

Forearm

Natal
cleft

Buttock

Gluteal fold

Popliteal fossa

Calf

Heel

Back

Arm

Hand

Leg

Foot

**FRONT VIEWS OF
MALE AND FEMALE**

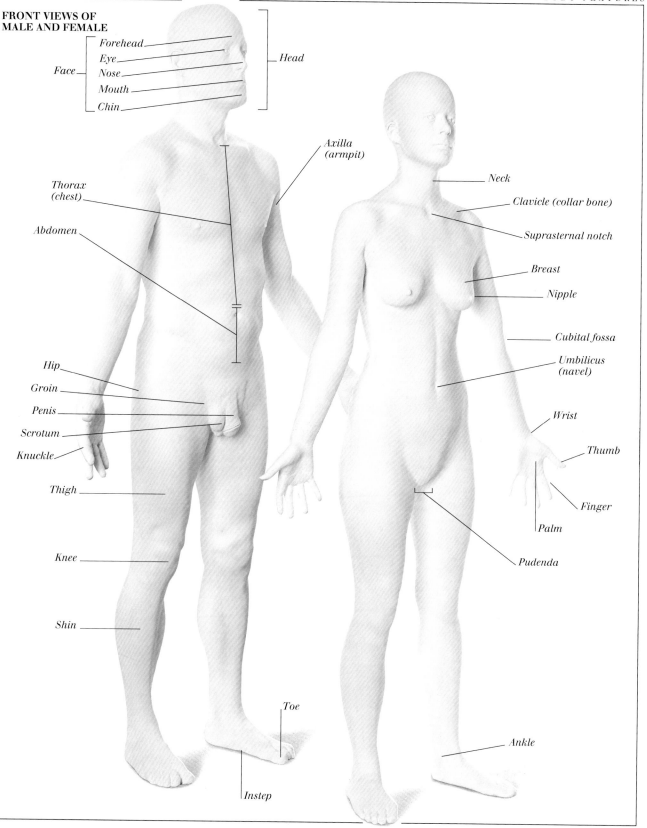

Forehead

Eye

Face —

Nose

Mouth

Chin

Head

Thorax
(chest)

Abdomen

Hip

Groin

Penis

Scrotum

Knuckle

Thigh

Knee

Shin

Toe

Instep

Axilla
(armpit)

Neck

Clavicle (collar bone)

Suprasternal notch

Breast

Nipple

Cubital fossa

Umbilicus
(navel)

Wrist

Thumb

Finger

Palm

Pudenda

Ankle

Head

In a newborn baby, the head accounts for one-quarter of the total body length; by adulthood, the proportion has reduced to one-eighth. Contained in the head are the body's main sense organs: eyes, ears, olfactory nerves that detect smells, and the taste buds of the tongue. Signals from these organs pass to the body's great coordination centre: the brain, housed in the protective, bony dome of the skull. Hair on the head insulates against heat loss, and adult males also grow thick facial hair. The face has three important openings: two nostrils through which air passes, and the mouth, which takes in nourishment and helps form speech. Although all heads are basically similar, differences in the size, shape, and colour of features produce an infinite variety of appearances.

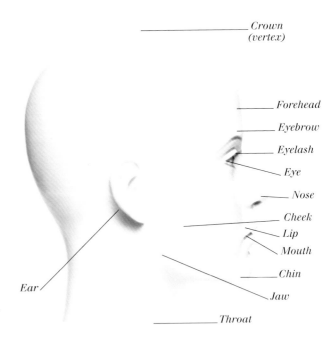

Crown (vertex)

Forehead

Eyebrow

Eyelash

Eye

Nose

Cheek

Lip

Mouth

Chin

Jaw

Ear

Throat

SECTION THROUGH HEAD

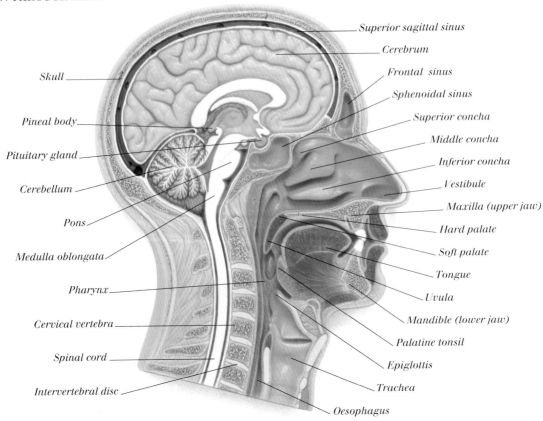

Skull

Pineal body

Pituitary gland

Cerebellum

Pons

Medulla oblongata

Pharynx

Cervical vertebra

Spinal cord

Intervertebral disc

Superior sagittal sinus

Cerebrum

Frontal sinus

Sphenoidal sinus

Superior concha

Middle concha

Inferior concha

Vestibule

Maxilla (upper jaw)

Hard palate

Soft palate

Tongue

Uvula

Mandible (lower jaw)

Palatine tonsil

Epiglottis

Trachea

Oesophagus

**FRONT VIEW OF EXTERNAL
FEATURES OF HEAD**

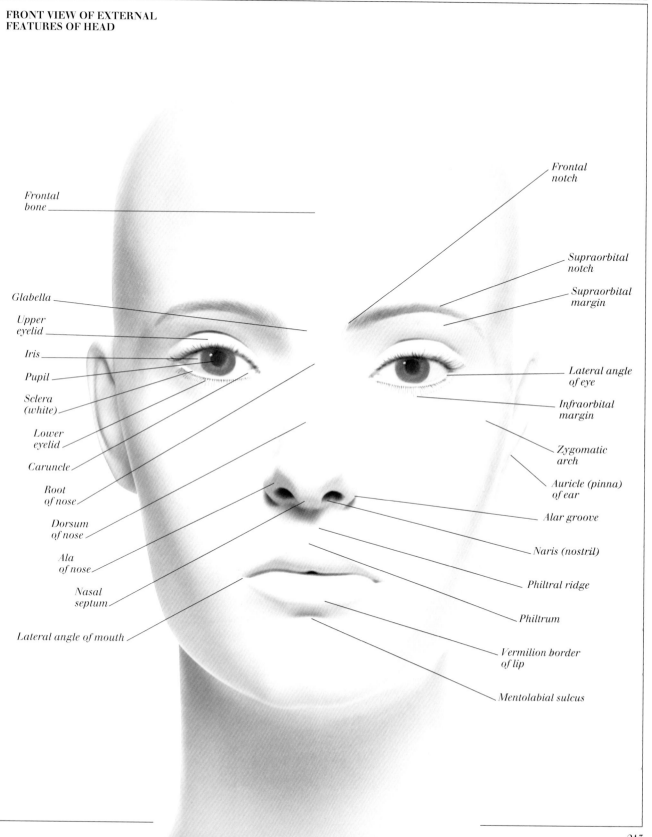

Frontal
notch

Supraorbital
notch

Supraorbital
margin

Frontal
bone

Glabella

Upper
eyelid

Iris

Pupil

Sclera
(white)

Lower
eyelid

Caruncle

Root
of nose

Dorsum
of nose

Ala
of nose

Nasal
septum

Lateral angle of mouth

Lateral angle
of eye

Infraorbital
margin

Zygomatic
arch

Auricle (pinna)
of ear

Alar groove

Naris (nostril)

Philtral ridge

Philtrum

Vermilion border
of lip

Mentolabial sulcus

Body organs

ALL THE VITAL BODY ORGANS except for the brain are enclosed within the trunk or torso (the body apart from the head and limbs). The trunk contains two large cavities separated by a muscular sheet called the diaphragm. The upper cavity, known as the thorax or chest cavity, contains the heart and lungs. The lower cavity, called the abdominal cavity, contains the stomach, intestines, liver, and pancreas, which all play a role in digesting food. Also within the trunk are the kidneys and bladder, which are part of the urinary system, and the reproductive organs, which hold the seeds of new human life. Modern imaging techniques, such as contrast X-rays and different types of scans, make it possible to see and study body organs without the need to cut through their protective coverings of skin, fat, muscle, and bone.

MAJOR INTERNAL STRUCTURES

Thyroid gland

Larynx

Heart

Right lung

Left lung

Diaphragm

Liver

Large intestine

Stomach

Small intestine

Greater omentum

IMAGING THE BODY

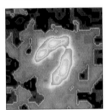

SCINTIGRAM OF HEART CHAMBERS

ANGIOGRAM OF RIGHT LUNG

CONTRAST X-RAY OF GALLBLADDER

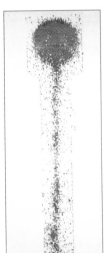

SCINTIGRAM OF NERVOUS SYSTEM

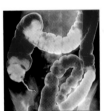

DOUBLE CONTRAST X-RAY OF COLON

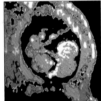

ULTRASOUND SCAN OF TWINS IN UTERUS

ANGIOGRAM OF KIDNEYS

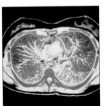

ANGIOGRAM OF ARTERIES OF HEAD

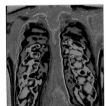

CT SCAN THROUGH FEMALE CHEST

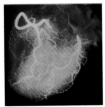

THERMOGRAM OF CHEST REGION

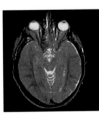

ANGIOGRAM OF ARTERIES OF HEART

MRI SCAN THROUGH HEAD AT EYE LEVEL

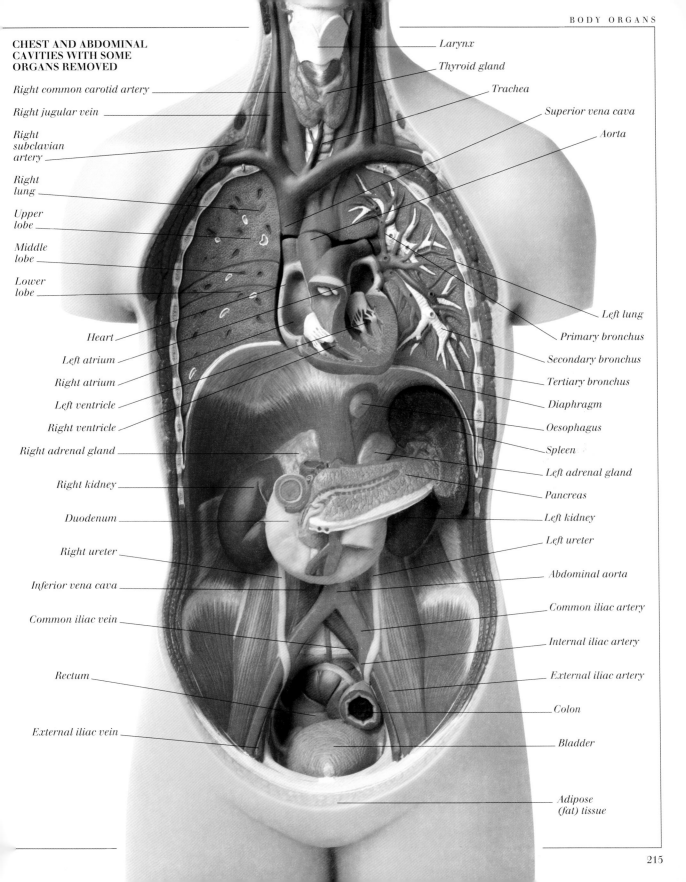

CHEST AND ABDOMINAL CAVITIES WITH SOME ORGANS REMOVED

Right common carotid artery

Right jugular vein

Right subclavian artery

Right lung

Upper lobe

Middle lobe

Lower lobe

Heart

Left atrium

Right atrium

Left ventricle

Right ventricle

Right adrenal gland

Right kidney

Duodenum

Right ureter

Inferior vena cava

Common iliac vein

Rectum

External iliac vein

Larynx

Thyroid gland

Trachea

Superior vena cava

Aorta

Left lung

Primary bronchus

Secondary bronchus

Tertiary bronchus

Diaphragm

Oesophagus

Spleen

Left adrenal gland

Pancreas

Left kidney

Left ureter

Abdominal aorta

Common iliac artery

Internal iliac artery

External iliac artery

Colon

Bladder

Adipose (fat) tissue

Body cells

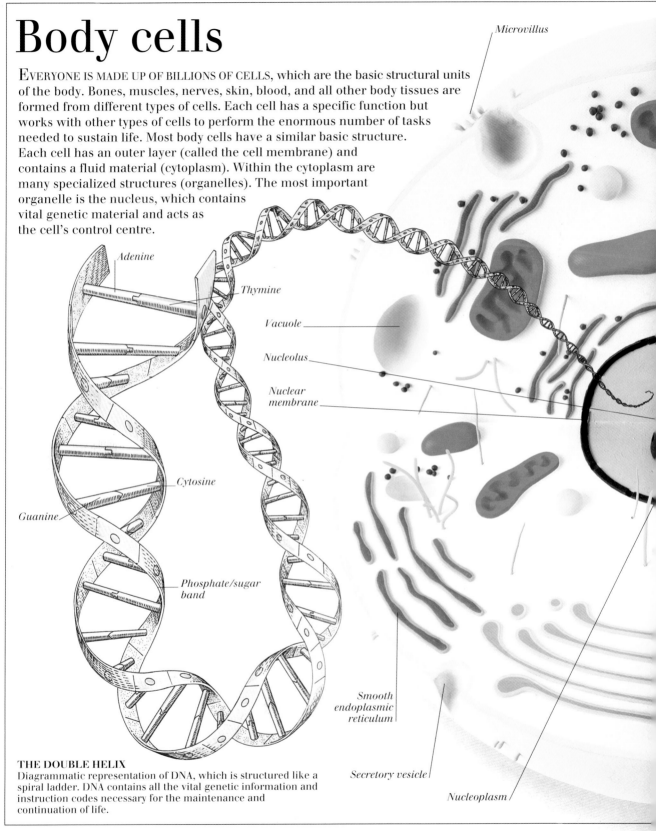

EVERYONE IS MADE UP OF BILLIONS OF CELLS, which are the basic structural units of the body. Bones, muscles, nerves, skin, blood, and all other body tissues are formed from different types of cells. Each cell has a specific function but works with other types of cells to perform the enormous number of tasks needed to sustain life. Most body cells have a similar basic structure. Each cell has an outer layer (called the cell membrane) and contains a fluid material (cytoplasm). Within the cytoplasm are many specialized structures (organelles). The most important organelle is the nucleus, which contains vital genetic material and acts as the cell's control centre.

Microvillus

Adenine

Thymine

Vacuole

Nucleolus

Nuclear membrane

Cytosine

Guanine

Phosphate/sugar band

Smooth endoplasmic reticulum

Secretory vesicle

Nucleoplasm

THE DOUBLE HELIX
Diagrammatic representation of DNA, which is structured like a spiral ladder. DNA contains all the vital genetic information and instruction codes necessary for the maintenance and continuation of life.

GENERALIZED HUMAN CELL

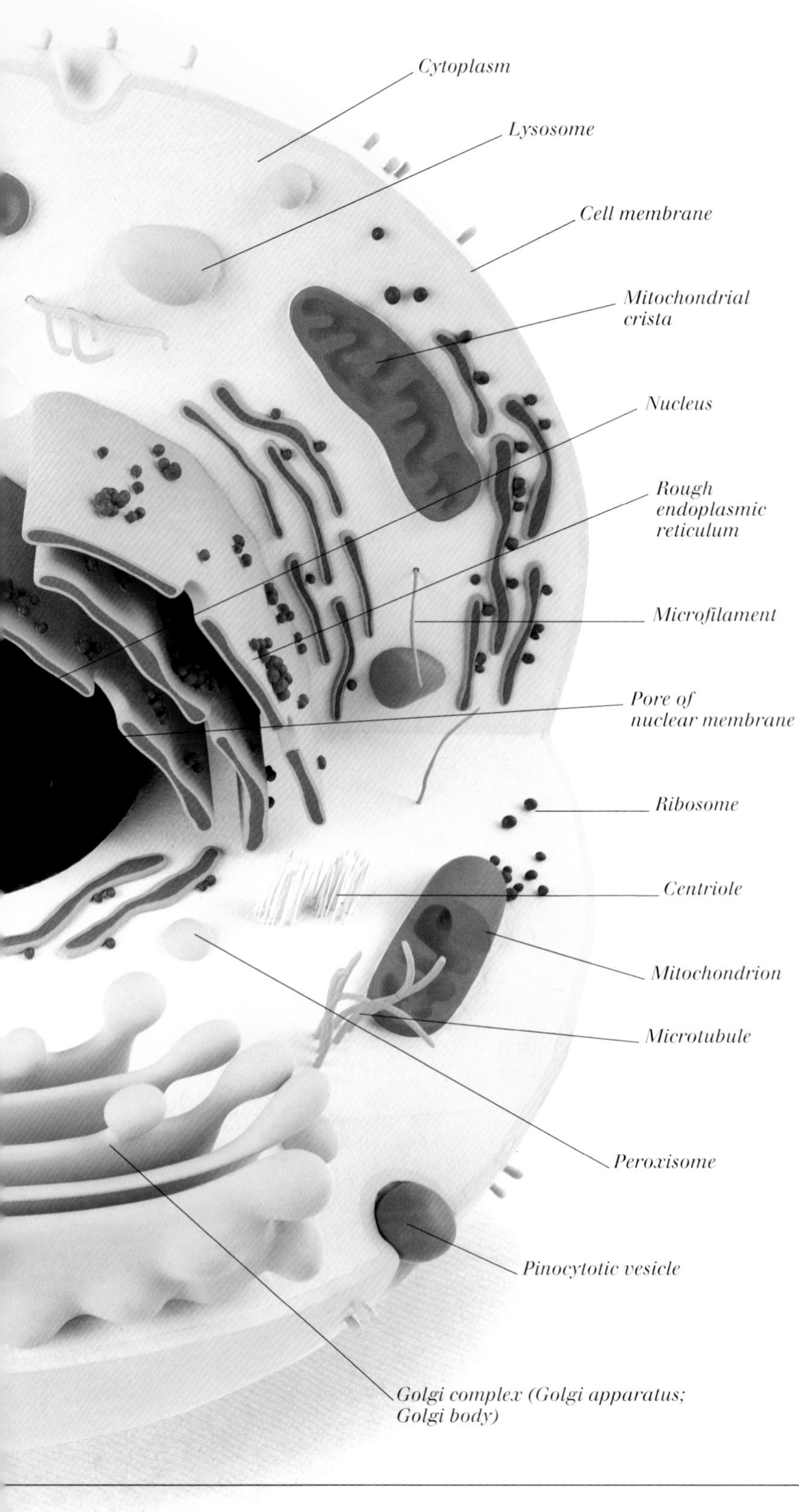

Cytoplasm

Lysosome

Cell membrane

Mitochondrial crista

Nucleus

Rough endoplasmic reticulum

Microfilament

Pore of nuclear membrane

Ribosome

Centriole

Mitochondrion

Microtubule

Peroxisome

Pinocytotic vesicle

Golgi complex (Golgi apparatus; Golgi body)

TYPES OF CELLS

BONE-FORMING CELL

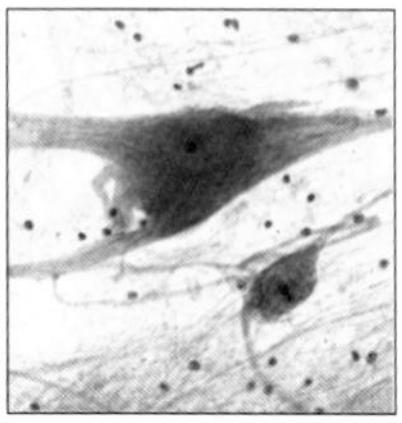

NERVE CELLS IN SPINAL CORD

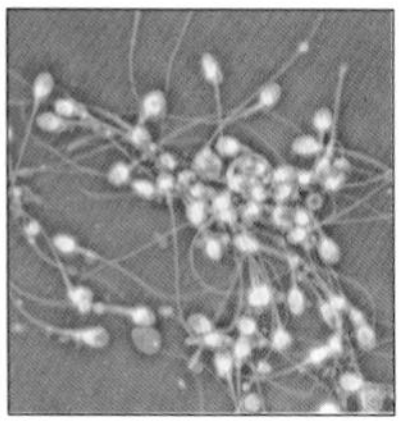

SPERM CELLS IN SEMEN

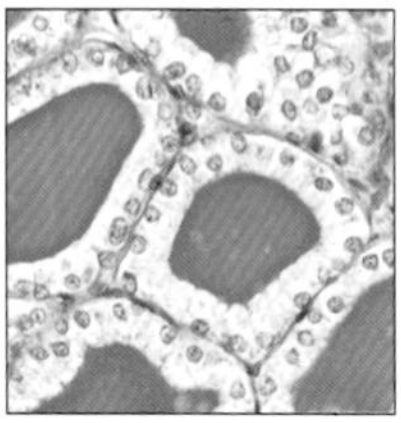

SECRETORY THYROID GLAND CELLS

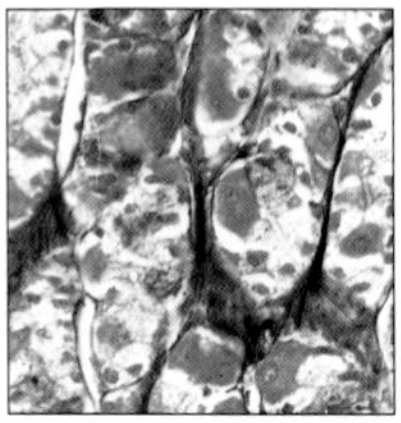

ACID-SECRETING STOMACH CELLS

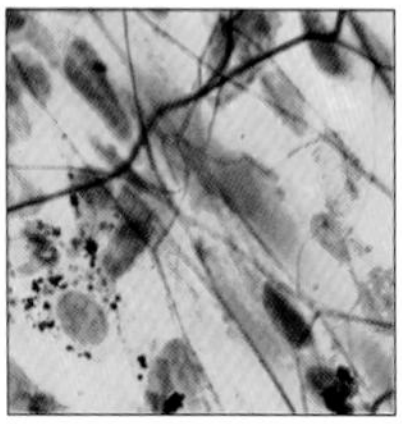

CONNECTIVE TISSUE CELLS

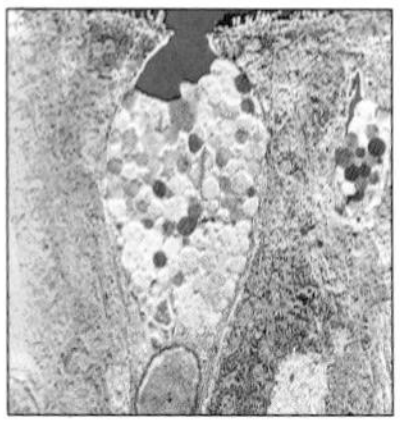

MUCUS-SECRETING DUODENAL CELLS

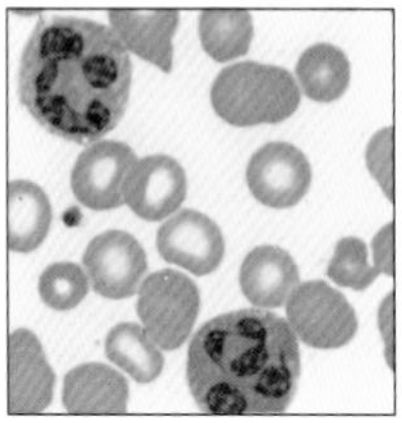

RED AND TWO WHITE BLOOD CELLS

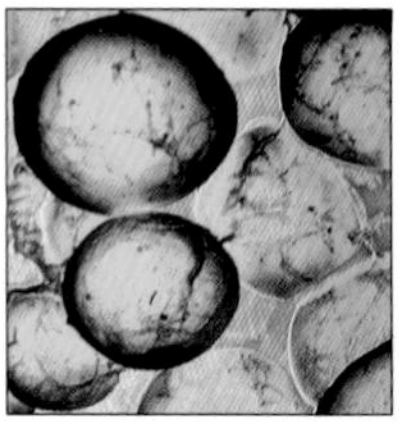

FAT CELLS IN ADIPOSE TISSUE

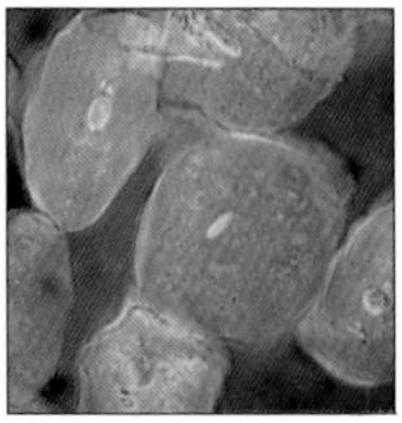

EPITHELIAL CELLS IN CHEEK

Skeleton

The skeleton is a mobile framework made up of 206 bones, approximately half of which are in the hands and feet. Although individual bones are rigid, the skeleton as a whole is remarkably flexible and allows the human body a huge range of movement. The skeleton serves as an anchorage for the skeletal muscles, and as a protective cage for the body's internal organs. Female bones are usually smaller and lighter than male bones, and the female pelvis is shallower and has a wider cavity.

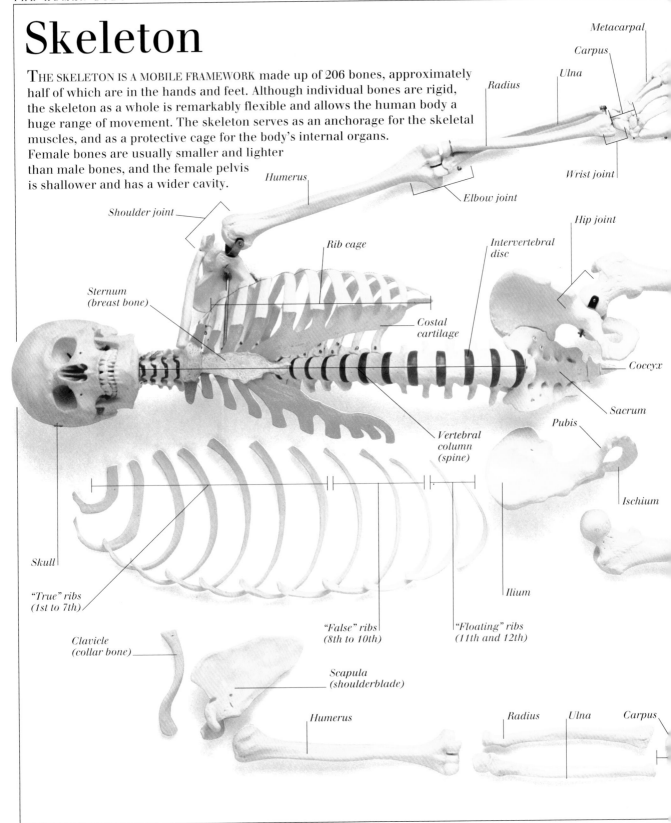

Metacarpal

Carpus

Ulna

Radius

Wrist joint

Humerus

Elbow joint

Shoulder joint

Hip joint

Rib cage

Intervertebral disc

Sternum (breast bone)

Costal cartilage

Coccyx

Vertebral column (spine)

Sacrum

Pubis

Ischium

Skull

Ilium

"True" ribs (1st to 7th)

"False" ribs (8th to 10th)

"Floating" ribs (11th and 12th)

Clavicle (collar bone)

Scapula (shoulderblade)

Humerus

Radius

Ulna

Carpus

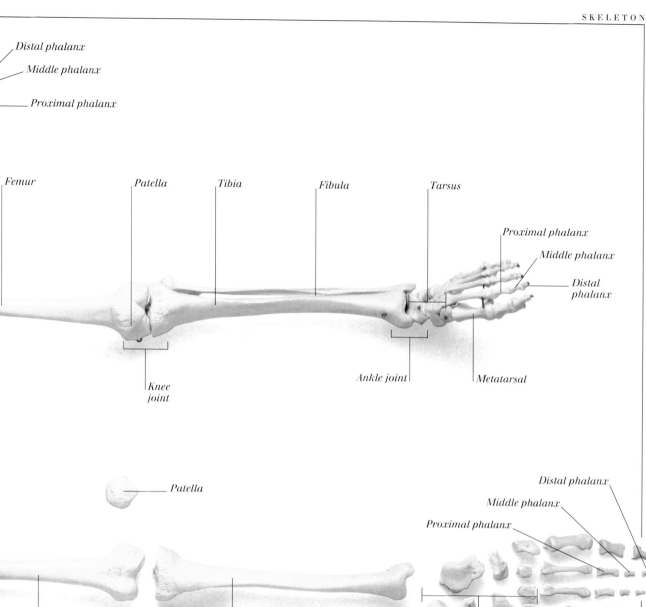

Distal phalanx

Middle phalanx

Proximal phalanx

Femur

Patella

Tibia

Fibula

Tarsus

Proximal phalanx

Middle phalanx

Distal phalanx

Knee joint

Ankle joint

Metatarsal

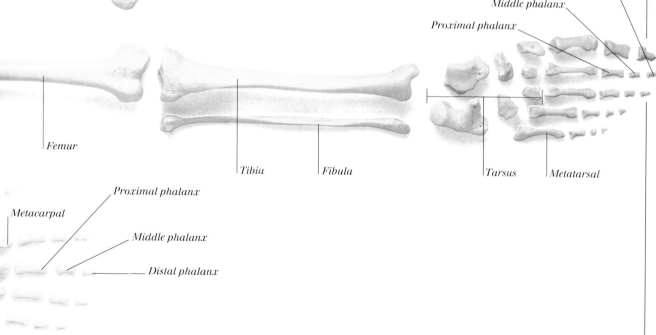

Patella

Distal phalanx

Middle phalanx

Proximal phalanx

Femur

Tibia

Fibula

Tarsus

Metatarsal

Metacarpal

Proximal phalanx

Middle phalanx

Distal phalanx

Skull

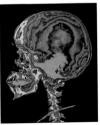

THE SKULL is the most complicated bony structure of the body but every feature serves a purpose. Internally, the main hollow chamber of the skull has three levels that support the brain, with every bump and hollow corresponding to the shape of the brain. Underneath and towards the back of the skull is a large round hole, the foramen magnum, through which the spinal cord passes. To the front of this are many smaller openings through which nerves, arteries, and veins pass to and from the brain. The roof of the skull is formed from four thin, curved bones that are firmly fixed together from the age of about two years. At the front of the skull are the two orbits, which contain the eyeballs, and a central hole for the airway of the nose. The jaw bone hinges on either side at ear level.

RIGHT SIDE VIEW OF A FETAL SKULL

Anterior fontanelle

Parietal bone

Coronal suture

Frontal bone

Nasal bone

Mental symphysis

Lambdoid suture

Occipital bone

Mastoid fontanelle

External auditory meatus

Sphenoidal fontanelle

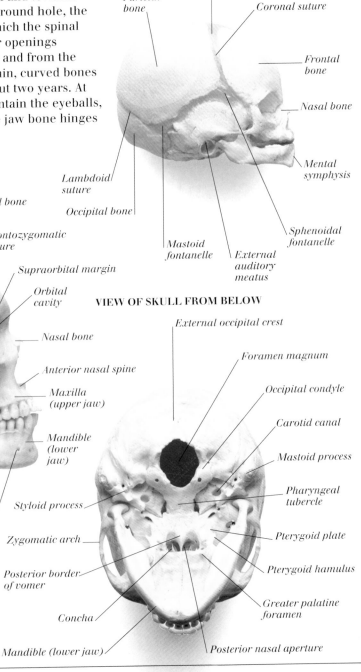

RIGHT SIDE VIEW OF SKULL

Greater wing of sphenoid bone

Coronal suture

Frontal bone

Frontozygomatic suture

Supraorbital margin

Parietal bone

Squamous suture

Orbital cavity

Nasal bone

Anterior nasal spine

Maxilla (upper jaw)

Mandible (lower jaw)

Lambdoid suture

Occipital bone

Temporal bone

External auditory meatus

Mastoid process

Condyle

Coronoid process

Zygomatic bone

Mental foramen

Styloid process

Zygomatic arch

Posterior border of vomer

Concha

Mandible (lower jaw)

VIEW OF SKULL FROM BELOW

External occipital crest

Foramen magnum

Occipital condyle

Carotid canal

Mastoid process

Pharyngeal tubercle

Pterygoid plate

Pterygoid hamulus

Greater palatine foramen

Posterior nasal aperture

FRONT VIEW OF SKULL

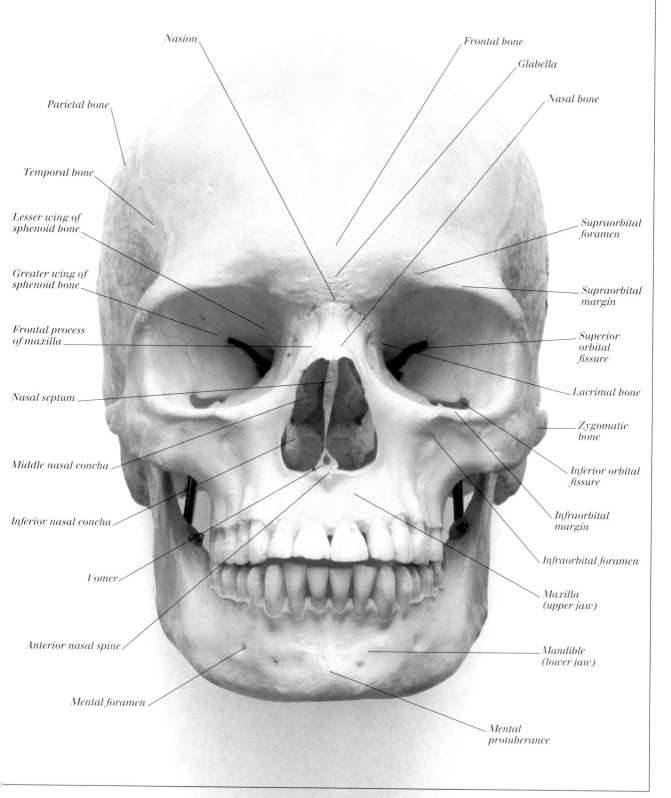

Nasion

Frontal bone

Glabella

Nasal bone

Parietal bone

Temporal bone

Lesser wing of
sphenoid bone

Greater wing of
sphenoid bone

Frontal process
of maxilla

Nasal septum

Middle nasal concha

Inferior nasal concha

Vomer

Anterior nasal spine

Mental foramen

Supraorbital
foramen

Supraorbital
margin

Superior
orbital
fissure

Lacrimal bone

Zygomatic
bone

Inferior orbital
fissure

Infraorbital
margin

Infraorbital foramen

Maxilla
(upper jaw)

Mandible
(lower jaw)

Mental
protuberance

Spine

The spine (or vertebral column) has two main functions: it serves as a protective surrounding for the delicate spinal cord and forms the supporting back bone of the skeleton. The spine consists of 24 separate differently shaped bones (vertebrae) with a curved, triangular bone (the sacrum) at the bottom. The sacrum is made up of fused vertebrae; at its lower end is a small tail-like structure made up of tiny bones collectively called the coccyx. Between each pair of vertebrae is a disc of cartilage that cushions the bones during movement. The top two vertebrae differ in appearance from the others and work as a pair: the first, called the atlas, rotates around a stout vertical peg on the second, the axis. This arrangement allows the skull to move freely up and down, and from side to side.

SPINE DIVIDED INTO VERTEBRAL SECTIONS

FRONT

Cervical vertebrae

Thoracic vertebrae

Lumbar vertebrae

Sacral vertebrae

Coccygeal vertebrae

TYPES OF VERTEBRAE (VIEWED FROM ABOVE)

ATLAS

Lateral mass with superior articular facet

Anterior arch

Posterior arch

Anterior tubercle

Posterior tubercle

Vertebral foramen

Transverse foramen

Transverse process

AXIS

Vertebral foramen

Facet

Dens

Spinous process

Lamina

Transverse process and foramen

CERVICAL VERTEBRA

Superior articular process

Body

Spinous process

Anterior tubercle

Vertebral foramen

Posterior tubercle

Transverse foramen

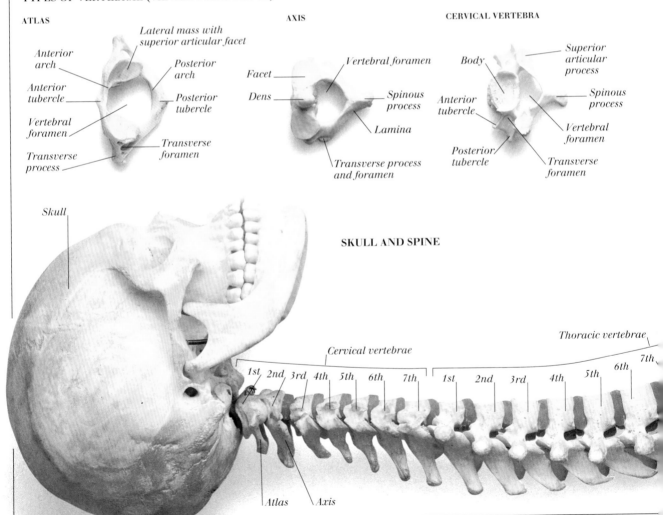

Skull

SKULL AND SPINE

Cervical vertebrae

Thoracic vertebrae

1st 2nd 3rd 4th 5th 6th 7th

1st 2nd 3rd 4th 5th 6th 7th

Atlas Axis

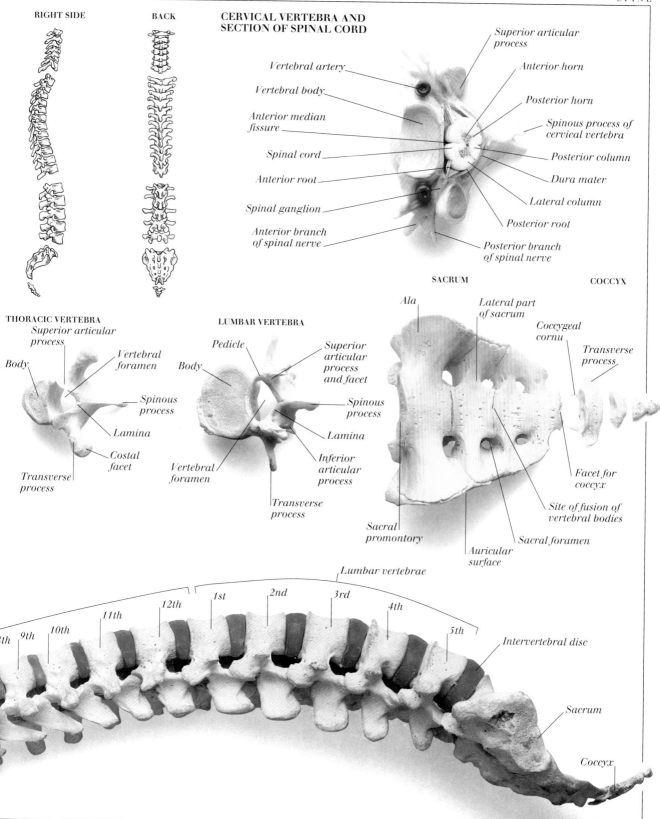

RIGHT SIDE

BACK

CERVICAL VERTEBRA AND SECTION OF SPINAL CORD

Superior articular process

Vertebral artery

Anterior horn

Vertebral body

Posterior horn

Anterior median fissure

Spinous process of cervical vertebra

Spinal cord

Posterior column

Anterior root

Dura mater

Spinal ganglion

Lateral column

Posterior root

Anterior branch of spinal nerve

Posterior branch of spinal nerve

SACRUM

COCCYX

Ala

Lateral part of sacrum

Coccygeal cornu

Transverse process

THORACIC VERTEBRA

Superior articular process

Vertebral foramen

Body

Spinous process

Lamina

Costal facet

Transverse process

LUMBAR VERTEBRA

Pedicle

Superior articular process and facet

Body

Spinous process

Lamina

Inferior articular process

Vertebral foramen

Transverse process

Facet for coccyx

Site of fusion of vertebral bodies

Sacral promontory

Sacral foramen

Auricular surface

Lumbar vertebrae

1st *2nd* *3rd* *4th* *5th*

12th *11th* *10th* *9th* *8th*

Intervertebral disc

Sacrum

Coccyx

Bones and joints

BONES FORM the body's hard, strong skeletal framework. Each bone has a hard, compact exterior surrounding a spongy, lighter interior. The long bones of the arms and legs, such as the femur (thigh bone), have a central cavity containing bone marrow. Bones are composed chiefly of calcium, phosphorus, and a fibrous substance known as collagen. Bones meet at joints, which are of several different types. For example, the hip is a ball-and-socket joint that allows the femur a wide range of movement, whereas finger joints are simple hinge joints that allow only bending and straightening. Joints are held in place by bands of tissue called ligaments. Movement of joints is facilitated by the smooth hyaline cartilage that covers the bone ends and by the synovial membrane that lines and lubricates the joint.

LIGAMENTS SURROUNDING HIP JOINT

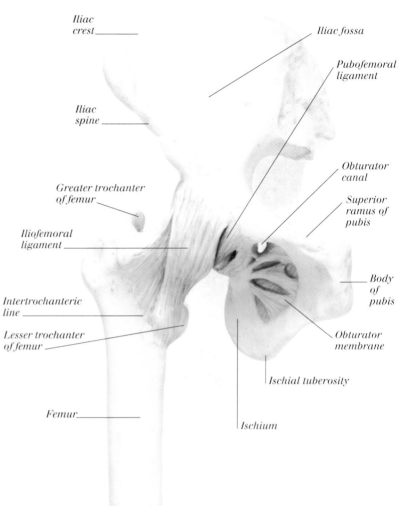

Iliac crest

Iliac fossa

Pubofemoral ligament

Iliac spine

Greater trochanter of femur

Obturator canal

Superior ramus of pubis

Iliofemoral ligament

Intertrochanteric line

Lesser trochanter of femur

Body of pubis

Obturator membrane

Ischial tuberosity

Femur

Ischium

SECTION THROUGH LEFT FEMUR

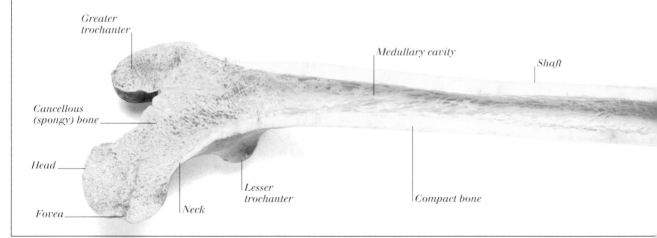

Greater trochanter

Medullary cavity

Shaft

Cancellous (spongy) bone

Head

Fovea

Neck

Lesser trochanter

Compact bone

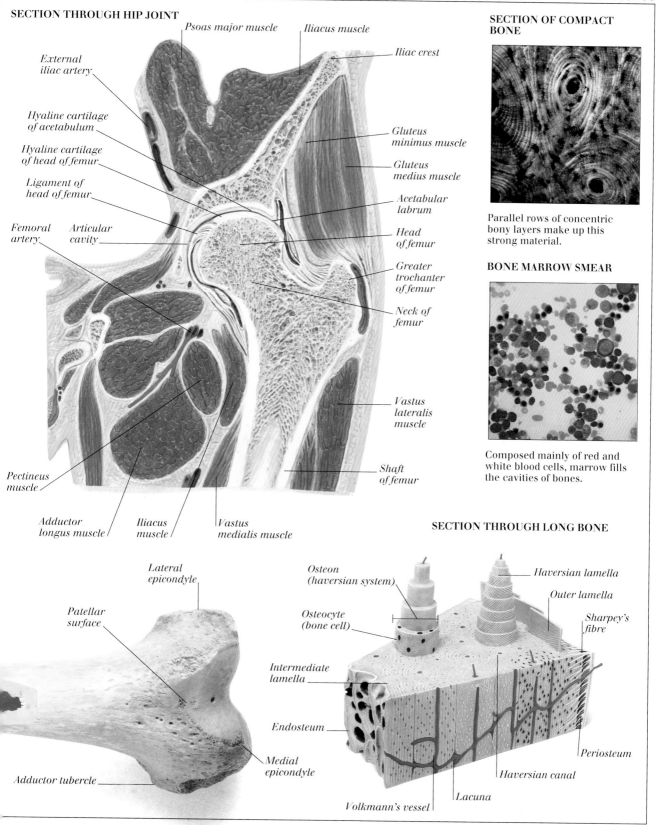

SECTION THROUGH HIP JOINT

Psoas major muscle

Iliacus muscle

External iliac artery

Iliac crest

Hyaline cartilage of acetabulum

Gluteus minimus muscle

Hyaline cartilage of head of femur

Gluteus medius muscle

Ligament of head of femur

Acetabular labrum

Femoral artery

Articular cavity

Head of femur

Greater trochanter of femur

Neck of femur

Pectineus muscle

Vastus lateralis muscle

Adductor longus muscle

Iliacus muscle

Vastus medialis muscle

Shaft of femur

SECTION OF COMPACT BONE

Parallel rows of concentric bony layers make up this strong material.

BONE MARROW SMEAR

Composed mainly of red and white blood cells, marrow fills the cavities of bones.

SECTION THROUGH LONG BONE

Lateral epicondyle

Patellar surface

Adductor tubercle

Medial epicondyle

Osteon (haversian system)

Osteocyte (bone cell)

Intermediate lamella

Endosteum

Volkmann's vessel

Lacuna

Haversian canal

Haversian lamella

Outer lamella

Sharpey's fibre

Periosteum

Muscles 1

THERE ARE THREE MAIN TYPES OF MUSCLE: skeletal muscle (also called voluntary muscle because it can be consciously controlled); smooth muscle (also called involuntary muscle because it is not under voluntary control); and the specialized muscle tissue of the heart. Humans have more than 600 skeletal muscles, which differ in size and shape according to the jobs they do. Skeletal muscles are attached either directly or indirectly (via tendons) to bones, and work in opposing pairs (one muscle in the pair contracts while the other relaxes) to produce body movements as diverse as walking, threading a needle, and an array of facial expressions. Smooth muscles occur in the walls of internal body organs and perform actions such as forcing food through the intestines, contracting the uterus (womb) in childbirth, and pumping blood through the blood vessels.

SOME OTHER MUSCLES IN THE BODY

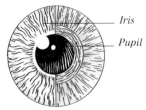

IRIS
The muscle fibres contract and dilate (expand) to alter pupil size.

- Iris
- Pupil

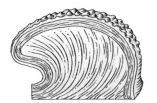

TONGUE
Interlacing layers of muscle allow great mobility.

ILEUM
Opposing muscle layers transport semi-digested food.

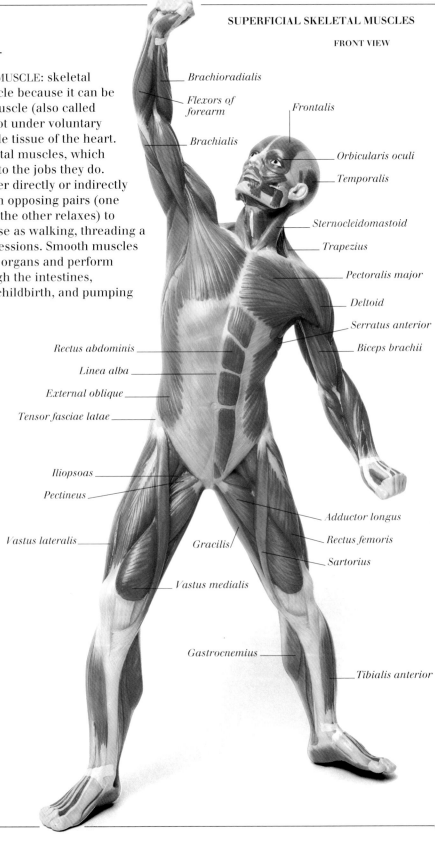

SUPERFICIAL SKELETAL MUSCLES

FRONT VIEW

- Brachioradialis
- Flexors of forearm
- Brachialis
- Frontalis
- Orbicularis oculi
- Temporalis
- Sternocleidomastoid
- Trapezius
- Pectoralis major
- Deltoid
- Serratus anterior
- Biceps brachii
- Rectus abdominis
- Linea alba
- External oblique
- Tensor fasciae latae
- Iliopsoas
- Pectineus
- Adductor longus
- Rectus femoris
- Sartorius
- Vastus lateralis
- Gracilis
- Vastus medialis
- Gastrocnemius
- Tibialis anterior

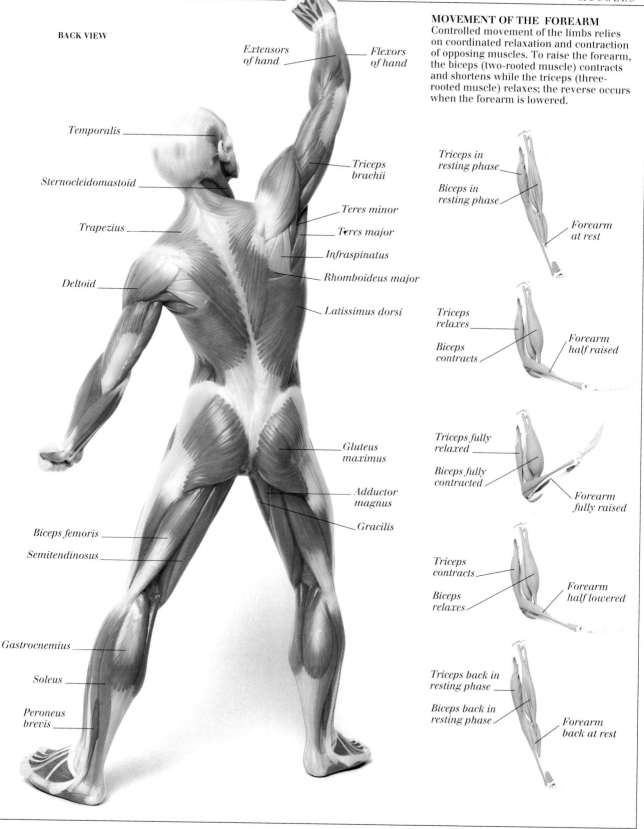

BACK VIEW

Extensors
of hand

Flexors
of hand

Temporalis

Sternocleidomastoid

Trapezius

Deltoid

Triceps
brachii

Teres minor

Teres major

Infraspinatus

Rhomboideus major

Latissimus dorsi

Gluteus
maximus

Adductor
magnus

Gracilis

Biceps femoris

Semitendinosus

Gastrocnemius

Soleus

Peroneus
brevis

MOVEMENT OF THE FOREARM

Controlled movement of the limbs relies on coordinated relaxation and contraction of opposing muscles. To raise the forearm, the biceps (two-rooted muscle) contracts and shortens while the triceps (three-rooted muscle) relaxes; the reverse occurs when the forearm is lowered.

Triceps in
resting phase

Biceps in
resting phase

Forearm
at rest

Triceps
relaxes

Biceps
contracts

Forearm
half raised

Triceps fully
relaxed

Biceps fully
contracted

Forearm
fully raised

Triceps
contracts

Biceps
relaxes

Forearm
half lowered

Triceps back in
resting phase

Biceps back in
resting phase

Forearm
back at rest

Muscles 2

SKELETAL MUSCLE FIBRE

Myofibril

Sarcomere

*Motor
end plate*

Nucleus

*Synaptic
knob*

*Sarcoplasmic
reticulum*

Sarcolemma

*Schwann
cell*

Endomysium

*Motor
neuron*

*Node of
Ranvier*

**MUSCLES OF FACIAL
EXPRESSION**
A single expression
is the result of
movement of many
muscles; the main
muscles of expression
are shown in action
below.

FRONTALIS

CORRUGATOR
SUPERCILII

ORBICULARIS ORIS

ZYGOMATICUS MAJOR

DEPRESSOR ANGULI
ORIS

TYPES OF MUSCLE

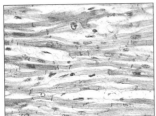

CARDIAC MUSCLE

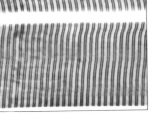

SKELETAL MUSCLE

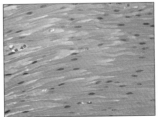

SMOOTH MUSCLE

CONTRACTION OF SKELETAL MUSCLE

RELAXED STATE

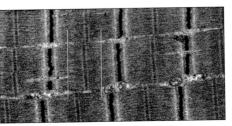

CONTRACTED STATE

**MUSCLES OF
HEAD AND NECK**

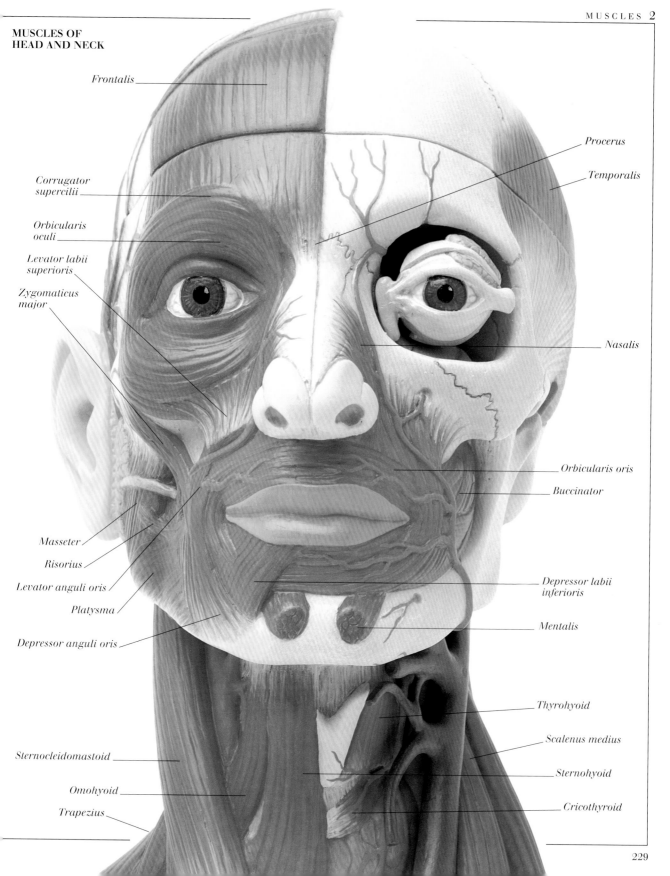

Frontalis

Procerus

Temporalis

Corrugator
supercilii

Orbicularis
oculi

Nasalis

Levator labii
superioris

Zygomaticus
major

Orbicularis oris

Buccinator

Masseter

Risorius

Levator anguli oris

Depressor labii
inferioris

Platysma

Mentalis

Depressor anguli oris

Thyrohyoid

Scalenus medius

Sternocleidomastoid

Sternohyoid

Omohyoid

Cricothyroid

Trapezius

Hands

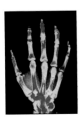

THE HUMAN HAND is an extremely versatile tool, capable of delicate manipulation as well as powerful gripping actions. The arrangement of its 27 small bones, moved by 37 skeletal muscles that are connected to the bones by tendons, allows a wide range of movements. Our ability to bring the tips of our thumbs and fingers together, combined with the extraordinary sensitivity of our fingertips due to their rich supply of nerve endings, makes our hands uniquely dextrous.

X-RAY OF LEFT HAND OF A YOUNG CHILD

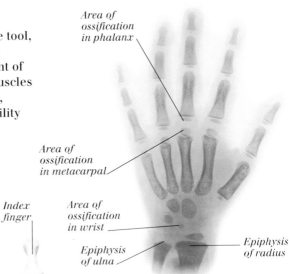

Area of ossification in phalanx

Area of ossification in metacarpal

Area of ossification in wrist

Epiphysis of ulna

Epiphysis of radius

Areas of cartilage in the wrist and at the ends of the finger bones are the sites of growth and have still to ossify.

BONES OF HAND

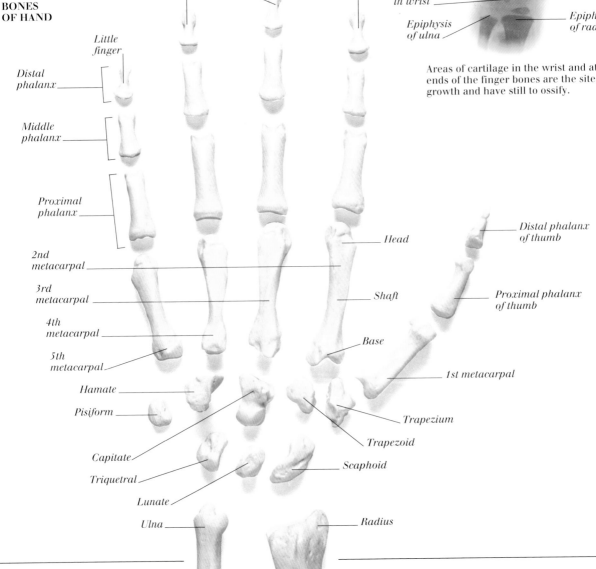

Ring finger

Middle finger

Index finger

Little finger

Distal phalanx

Middle phalanx

Proximal phalanx

2nd metacarpal

3rd metacarpal

4th metacarpal

5th metacarpal

Hamate

Pisiform

Capitate

Triquetral

Lunate

Ulna

Head

Shaft

Base

Trapezium

Trapezoid

Scaphoid

Radius

Distal phalanx of thumb

Proximal phalanx of thumb

1st metacarpal

STRUCTURES UNDERLYING SKIN OF PALM OF HAND

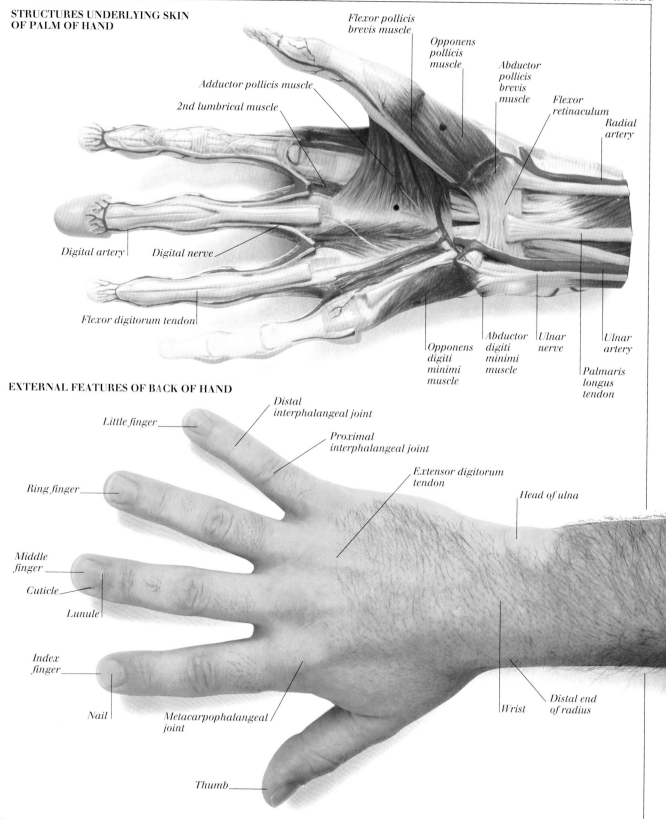

Flexor pollicis brevis muscle

Opponens pollicis muscle

Abductor pollicis brevis muscle

Flexor retinaculum

Radial artery

Adductor pollicis muscle

2nd lumbrical muscle

Digital artery

Digital nerve

Flexor digitorum tendon

Opponens digiti minimi muscle

Abductor digiti minimi muscle

Ulnar nerve

Ulnar artery

Palmaris longus tendon

EXTERNAL FEATURES OF BACK OF HAND

Little finger

Distal interphalangeal joint

Proximal interphalangeal joint

Extensor digitorum tendon

Head of ulna

Ring finger

Middle finger

Cuticle

Lunule

Index finger

Nail

Metacarpophalangeal joint

Wrist

Distal end of radius

Thumb

Feet

The feet and toes are essential elements in body movement. They bear and propel the weight of the body during walking and running, and also help to maintain balance during changes of body position. Each foot has 26 bones, more than 100 ligaments, and 33 muscles, some of which are attached to the lower leg. The heel pad and the arch of the foot act as shock absorbers, providing a cushion against the jolts that occur with every step.

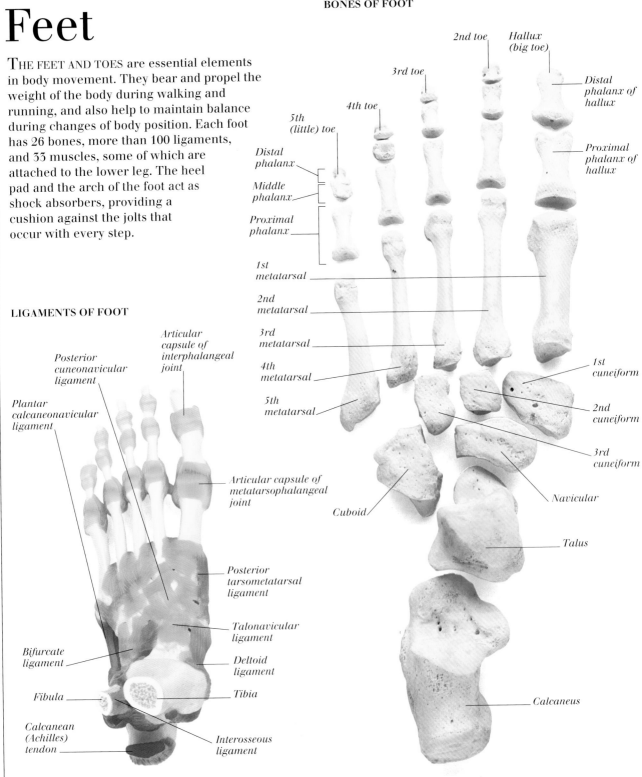

2nd toe

Hallux (big toe)

3rd toe

Distal phalanx of hallux

4th toe

Proximal phalanx of hallux

5th (little) toe

Distal phalanx

Middle phalanx

Proximal phalanx

1st metatarsal

2nd metatarsal

3rd metatarsal

1st cuneiform

4th metatarsal

2nd cuneiform

5th metatarsal

3rd cuneiform

Navicular

Cuboid

Talus

Calcaneus

LIGAMENTS OF FOOT

Posterior cuneonavicular ligament

Articular capsule of interphalangeal joint

Plantar calcaneonavicular ligament

Articular capsule of metatarsophalangeal joint

Posterior tarsometatarsal ligament

Talonavicular ligament

Bifurcate ligament

Deltoid ligament

Fibula

Tibia

Calcanean (Achilles) tendon

Interosseous ligament

STRUCTURES UNDERLYING SKIN OF FOOT

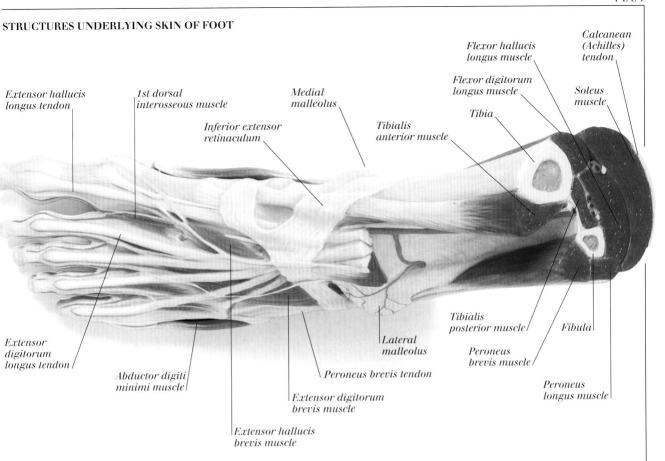

Flexor hallucis
longus muscle

Calcanean
(Achilles)
tendon

Flexor digitorum
longus muscle

Soleus
muscle

Extensor hallucis
longus tendon

1st dorsal
interosseous muscle

Medial
malleolus

Tibia

Tibialis
anterior muscle

Inferior extensor
retinaculum

Tibialis
posterior muscle

Fibula

Extensor
digitorum
longus tendon

Lateral
malleolus

Peroneus
brevis muscle

Abductor digiti
minimi muscle

Peroneus brevis tendon

Peroneus
longus muscle

Extensor digitorum
brevis muscle

Extensor hallucis
brevis muscle

EXTERNAL FEATURES OF FOOT

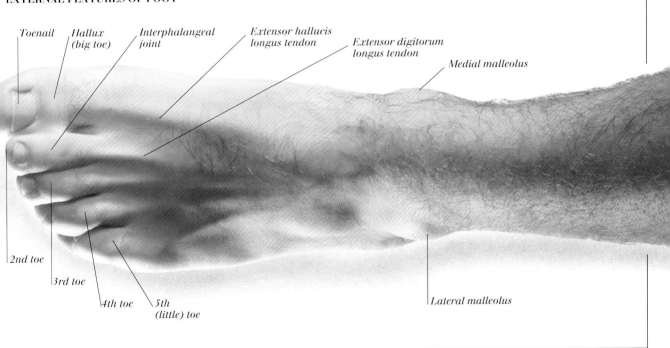

Toenail

Hallux
(big toe)

Interphalangeal
joint

Extensor hallucis
longus tendon

Extensor digitorum
longus tendon

Medial malleolus

2nd toe

3rd toe

4th toe

5th
(little) toe

Lateral malleolus

Skin and hair

SKIN IS THE BODY'S LARGEST ORGAN, a waterproof barrier that protects the internal organs against infection, injury, and harmful sun rays. The skin is also an important sensory organ and helps to control body temperature. The outer layer of the skin, known as the epidermis, is coated with keratin, a tough, horny protein that is also the chief constituent of hair and nails. Dead cells are shed from the skin's surface and are replaced by new cells from the base of the epidermis, the region that also produces the skin pigment, melanin. The dermis contains most of the skin's living structures, and includes nerve endings, blood vessels, elastic fibres, sweat glands that cool the skin, and sebaceous glands that produce oil to keep the skin supple. Beneath the dermis lies the subcutaneous tissue (hypodermis), which is rich in fat and blood vessels. Hair shafts grow from hair follicles situated in the dermis and subcutaneous tissue. Hair grows on every part of the skin apart from the palms of the hands and soles of the feet.

SECTION OF HAIR

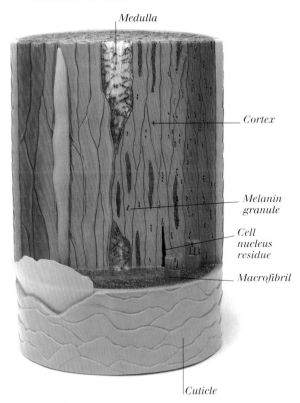

Medulla

Cortex

Melanin granule

Cell nucleus residue

Macrofibril

Cuticle

SECTIONS OF DIFFERENT TYPES OF SKIN

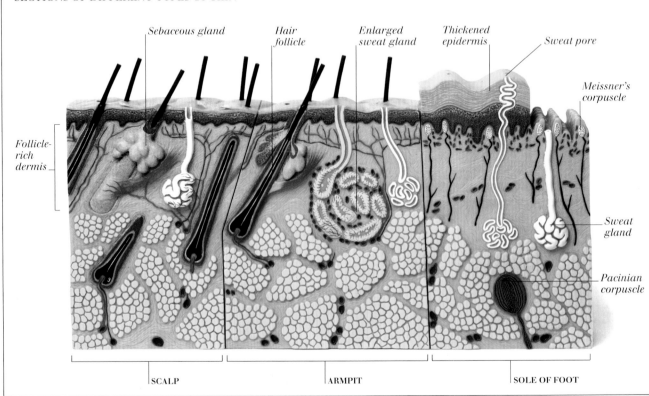

Sebaceous gland

Hair follicle

Enlarged sweat gland

Thickened epidermis

Sweat pore

Meissner's corpuscle

Follicle-rich dermis

Sweat gland

Pacinian corpuscle

SCALP

ARMPIT

SOLE OF FOOT

SECTION OF SKIN

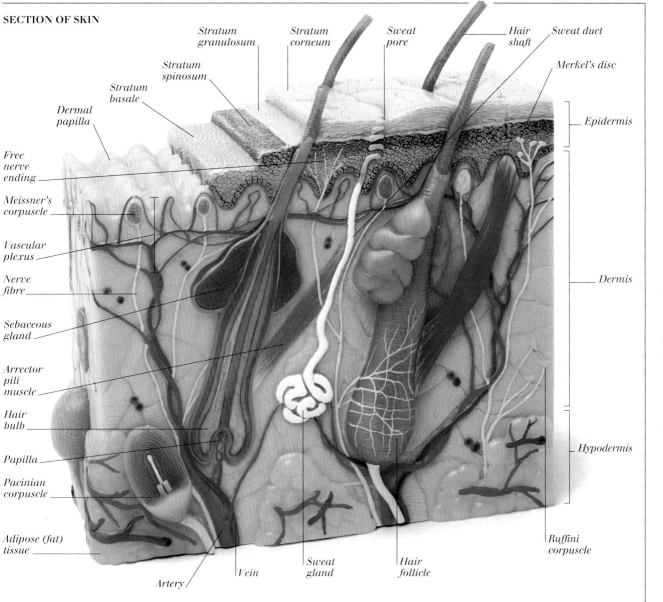

Stratum granulosum

Stratum corneum

Sweat pore

Hair shaft

Sweat duct

Stratum spinosum

Merkel's disc

Stratum basale

Dermal papilla

Epidermis

Free nerve ending

Meissner's corpuscle

Vascular plexus

Dermis

Nerve fibre

Sebaceous gland

Arrector pili muscle

Hair bulb

Papilla

Hypodermis

Pacinian corpuscle

Adipose (fat) tissue

Ruffini corpuscle

Artery

Vein

Sweat gland

Hair follicle

PHOTOMICROGRAPHS OF SKIN AND HAIR

SECTION OF SKIN
The flaky cells at the skin's surface are shed continuously.

SWEAT PORE
This allows loss of fluid as part of temperature control.

SKIN HAIR
Two hairs pushing through the outer layer of skin.

HEAD HAIR
The root and part of the shaft of a hair from the scalp.

Brain

THE BRAIN IS THE MAJOR ORGAN of the central nervous system and the control centre for all the body's voluntary and involuntary activities. It is also responsible for the complexities of thought, memory, emotion, and language. In adults, this complex organ is a mere 1.4 kg (3 lb) in weight, containing over 10 thousand million nerve cells. Three distinct regions can easily be seen – the brainstem, the cerebellum, and the large cerebrum. The brainstem controls vital body functions, such as breathing and digestion. The cerebellum's main functions are the maintenance of posture and the coordination of body movements. The cerebrum, which consists of the right and left cerebral hemispheres joined by the corpus callosum, is the site of most conscious and intelligent activities.

MRI SCAN OF TRANSVERSE SECTION THROUGH BRAIN

White matter

Grey matter

Skull

Scalp

Longitudinal fissure

Lateral ventricle

Sagittal section

Coronal section

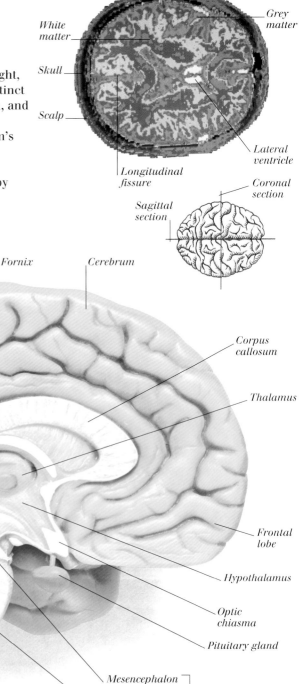

SAGITTAL SECTION THROUGH BRAIN

Central sulcus

Fornix

Cerebrum

Parietal lobe

Corpus callosum

Parieto-occipital sulcus

Thalamus

Pineal body

Occipital lobe

Frontal lobe

Aqueduct

Hypothalamus

Cerebellum

Optic chiasma

4th ventricle

Pituitary gland

Spinal cord

Mesencephalon (midbrain)

Pons

Brainstem

Medulla oblongata

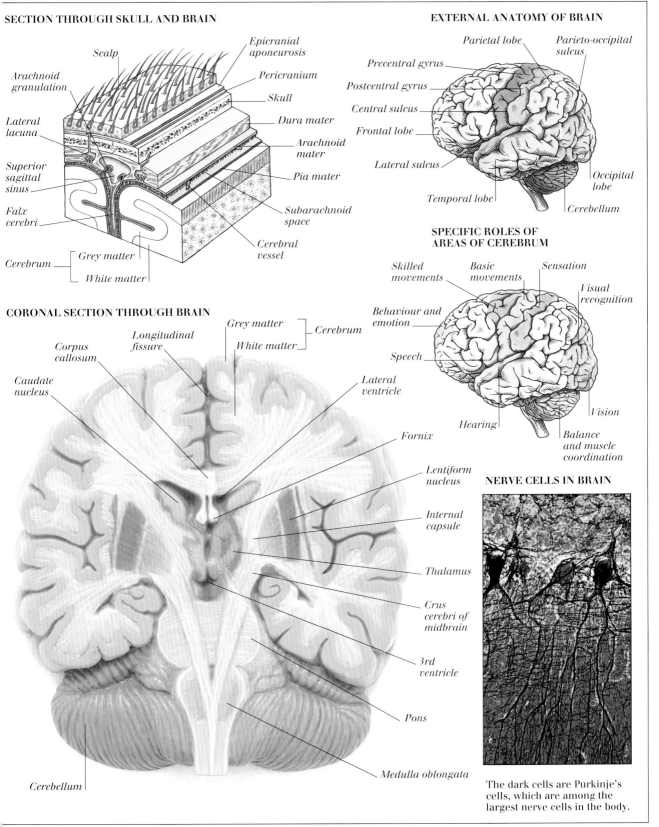

SECTION THROUGH SKULL AND BRAIN

Scalp
Epicranial aponeurosis
Arachnoid granulation
Pericranium
Skull
Lateral lacuna
Dura mater
Arachnoid mater
Superior sagittal sinus
Pia mater
Falx cerebri
Subarachnoid space
Cerebrum
Cerebral vessel
Grey matter
White matter

EXTERNAL ANATOMY OF BRAIN

Parietal lobe
Parieto-occipital sulcus
Precentral gyrus
Postcentral gyrus
Central sulcus
Frontal lobe
Lateral sulcus
Occipital lobe
Temporal lobe
Cerebellum

SPECIFIC ROLES OF AREAS OF CEREBRUM

Skilled movements
Basic movements
Sensation
Visual recognition
Behaviour and emotion
Speech
Hearing
Vision
Balance and muscle coordination

CORONAL SECTION THROUGH BRAIN

Corpus callosum
Longitudinal fissure
Grey matter
White matter
Cerebrum
Caudate nucleus
Lateral ventricle
Fornix
Lentiform nucleus
Internal capsule
Thalamus
Crus cerebri of midbrain
3rd ventricle
Pons
Medulla oblongata
Cerebellum

NERVE CELLS IN BRAIN

The dark cells are Purkinje's cells, which are among the largest nerve cells in the body.

Nervous system

THE NERVOUS SYSTEM IS THE BODY'S internal, electrochemical, communications network. Its main parts are the brain, spinal cord, and nerves. The brain and spinal cord form the central nervous system (CNS), the body's chief controlling and coordinating centres. Billions of long neurons, many grouped as nerves, make up the peripheral nervous system, transmitting nerve impulses between the CNS and other regions of the body. Each neuron has three parts: a cell body, branching dendrites that receive chemical signals from other neurons, and a tube-like axon that conveys these signals as electrical impulses.

CENTRAL AND PERIPHERAL NERVOUS SYSTEMS

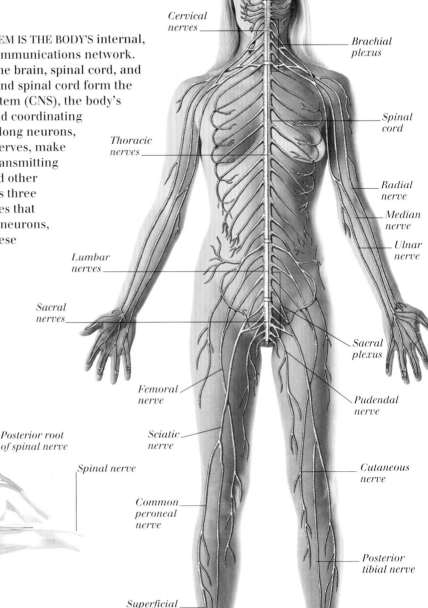

Cranial nerves

Cerebrum

Cerebellum

Cervical nerves

Brachial plexus

Thoracic nerves

Spinal cord

Radial nerve

Median nerve

Ulnar nerve

Lumbar nerves

Sacral nerves

Sacral plexus

Femoral nerve

Pudendal nerve

Sciatic nerve

Cutaneous nerve

Common peroneal nerve

Posterior tibial nerve

Superficial peroneal nerve

Deep peroneal nerve

SECTION THROUGH SPINAL CORD

Spinal ganglion

Grey matter

Central canal

Posterior root of spinal nerve

Spinal nerve

White matter

Anterior median fissure

Anterior root of spinal nerve

STRUCTURE OF A MOTOR NEURON

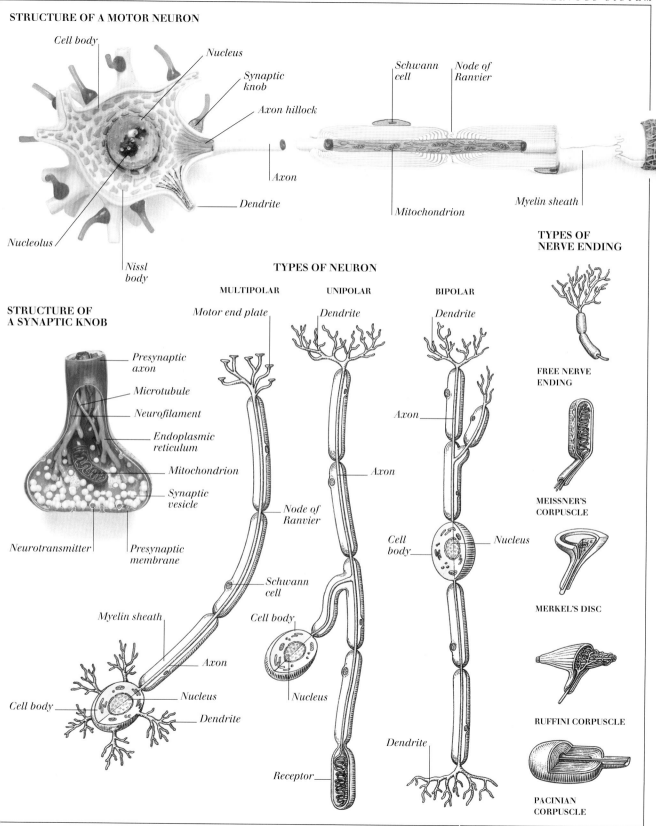

Cell body

Nucleus

Synaptic knob

Axon hillock

Axon

Dendrite

Nucleolus

Nissl body

Schwann cell

Node of Ranvier

Mitochondrion

Myelin sheath

STRUCTURE OF A SYNAPTIC KNOB

Presynaptic axon

Microtubule

Neurofilament

Endoplasmic reticulum

Mitochondrion

Synaptic vesicle

Neurotransmitter

Presynaptic membrane

Myelin sheath

Axon

Cell body

Nucleus

Dendrite

TYPES OF NEURON

MULTIPOLAR

Motor end plate

Node of Ranvier

Schwann cell

Cell body

Nucleus

Receptor

UNIPOLAR

Dendrite

Axon

Nucleus

Dendrite

BIPOLAR

Dendrite

Axon

Cell body

Nucleus

TYPES OF NERVE ENDING

FREE NERVE ENDING

MEISSNER'S CORPUSCLE

MERKEL'S DISC

RUFFINI CORPUSCLE

PACINIAN CORPUSCLE

239

Eye

THE EYE IS THE ORGAN OF SIGHT. The two eyeballs, protected within bony sockets called orbits and on the outside by the eyelids, eyebrows, and tear film, are directly connected to the brain by the optic nerves. Each eye is moved by six muscles, which are attached around the eyeball. Light rays entering the eye through the pupil are focused by the cornea and lens to form an image on the retina. The retina contains millions of light-sensitive cells, called rods and cones, which convert the image into a pattern of nerve impulses. These impulses are transmitted along the optic nerve to the brain. Information from the two optic nerves is processed in the brain to produce a single coordinated image.

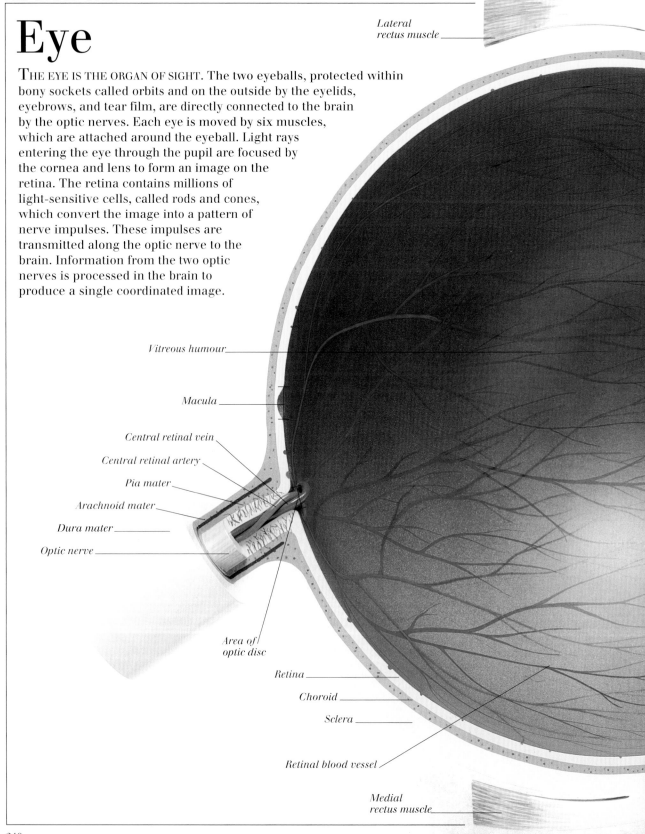

Lateral rectus muscle

Vitreous humour

Macula

Central retinal vein

Central retinal artery

Pia mater

Arachnoid mater

Dura mater

Optic nerve

Area of optic disc

Retina

Choroid

Sclera

Retinal blood vessel

Medial rectus muscle

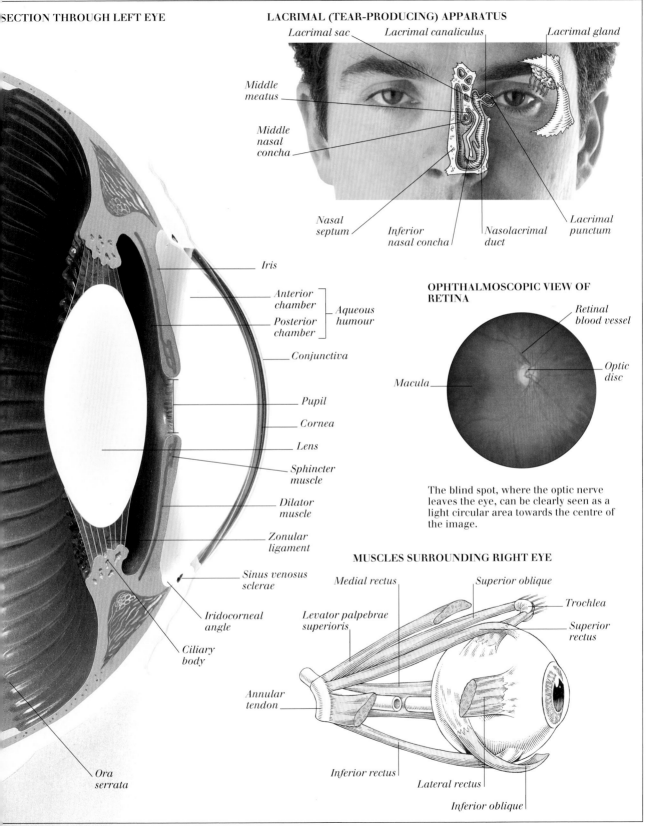

SECTION THROUGH LEFT EYE

Iris

Anterior
chamber

Posterior
chamber

} Aqueous
humour

Conjunctiva

Pupil

Cornea

Lens

Sphincter
muscle

Dilator
muscle

Zonular
ligament

Sinus venosus
sclerae

Iridocorneal
angle

Ciliary
body

Ora
serrata

LACRIMAL (TEAR-PRODUCING) APPARATUS

Lacrimal sac

Lacrimal canaliculus

Lacrimal gland

Middle
meatus

Middle
nasal
concha

Nasal
septum

Inferior
nasal concha

Nasolacrimal
duct

Lacrimal
punctum

OPHTHALMOSCOPIC VIEW OF RETINA

Retinal
blood vessel

Optic
disc

Macula

The blind spot, where the optic nerve
leaves the eye, can be clearly seen as a
light circular area towards the centre of
the image.

MUSCLES SURROUNDING RIGHT EYE

Medial rectus

Superior oblique

Trochlea

Levator palpebrae
superioris

Superior
rectus

Annular
tendon

Inferior rectus

Lateral rectus

Inferior oblique

241

Ear

THE EAR IS THE ORGAN OF HEARING AND BALANCE. The outer ear consists of a flap called the auricle or pinna and the auditory canal. The main functional parts – the middle and inner ears – are enclosed within the skull. The middle ear consists of three tiny bones, known as auditory ossicles, and the eustachian tube, which links the ear to the back of the nose. The inner ear consists of the spiral-shaped cochlea, and also the semicircular canals and the vestibule, which are the organs of balance. Sound waves entering the ear travel through the auditory canal to the tympanic membrane (eardrum), where they are converted to vibrations that are transmitted via the ossicles to the cochlea. Here, the vibrations are converted by millions of microscopic hairs into electrical nerve signals to be interpreted by the brain.

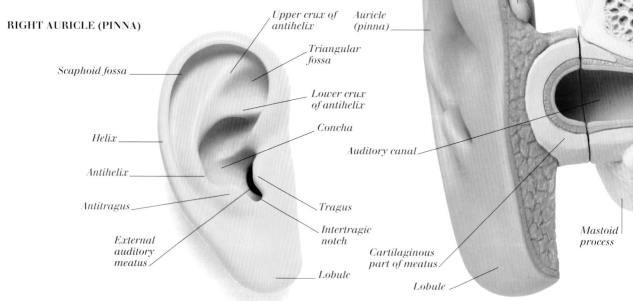

RIGHT AURICLE (PINNA)

Upper crux of antihelix

Triangular fossa

Auricle (pinna)

Scaphoid fossa

Lower crux of antihelix

Concha

Helix

Auditory canal

Antihelix

Temporal bone

Cartilage of auricle

Antitragus

Tragus

Intertragic notch

Mastoid process

External auditory meatus

Cartilaginous part of meatus

Lobule

Lobule

OSSICLES OF MIDDLE EAR

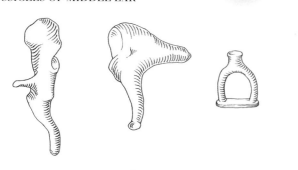

MALLEUS (HAMMER)   **INCUS (ANVIL)**   **STAPES (STIRRUP)**

These three tiny bones connect to form a bridge between the tympanic membrane and the oval window. With a system of membranes they convey sound vibrations to the inner ear.

INTERNAL STRUCTURE OF AMPULLA

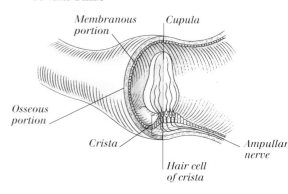

Membranous portion

Cupula

Osseous portion

Crista

Ampullar nerve

Hair cell of crista

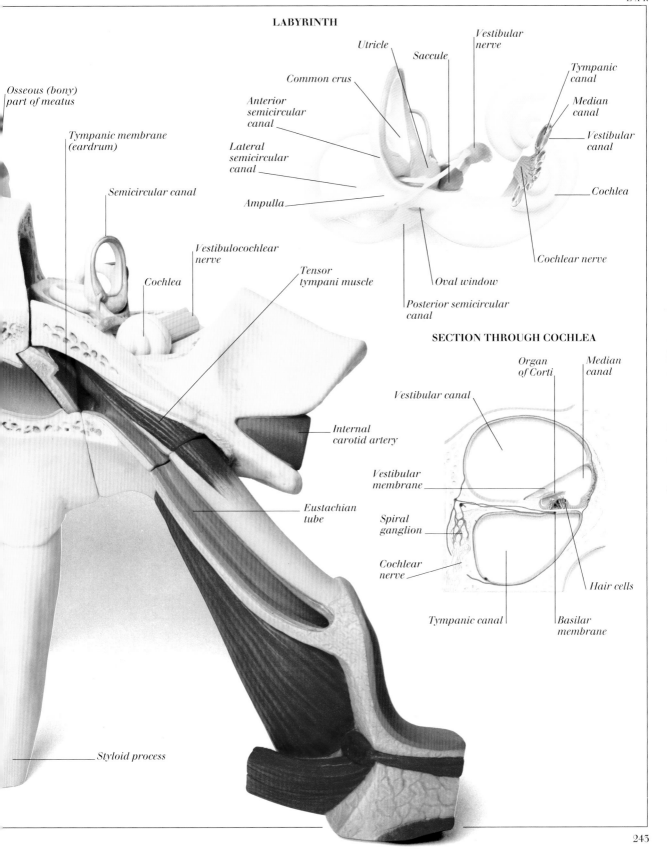

LABYRINTH

Osseous (bony)
part of meatus

Tympanic membrane
(eardrum)

Semicircular canal

Cochlea

Vestibulocochlear
nerve

Tensor
tympani muscle

Utricle

Saccule

Common crus

Vestibular
nerve

Anterior
semicircular
canal

Lateral
semicircular
canal

Ampulla

Tympanic
canal

Median
canal

Vestibular
canal

Cochlea

Cochlear nerve

Oval window

Posterior semicircular
canal

Internal
carotid artery

Eustachian
tube

Styloid process

SECTION THROUGH COCHLEA

Organ
of Corti

Median
canal

Vestibular canal

Vestibular
membrane

Spiral
ganglion

Cochlear
nerve

Tympanic canal

Hair cells

Basilar
membrane

243

Nose, mouth, and throat

WITH EVERY BREATH, air passes through the nasal cavity down the pharynx (throat), larynx ("voice box"), and trachea (windpipe) to the lungs. The nasal cavity warms and moistens air, and the tiny layers in its lining protect the airway against damage by foreign bodies. During swallowing, the tongue moves up and back, the larynx rises, the epiglottis closes off the entrance to the trachea, and the soft palate separates the nasal cavity from the pharynx. Saliva, secreted from three pairs of salivary glands, lubricates food to make swallowing easier; it also begins the chemical breakdown of food, and helps to produce taste. The senses of taste and smell are closely linked. Both depend on the detection of dissolved molecules by sensory receptors in the olfactory nerve endings of the nose and in the taste buds of the tongue.

STRUCTURE OF TONGUE

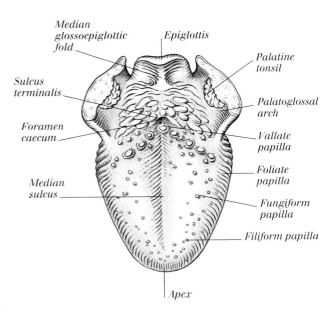

Median glossoepiglottic fold
Epiglottis
Palatine tonsil
Sulcus terminalis
Palatoglossal arch
Foramen caecum
Vallate papilla
Median sulcus
Foliate papilla
Fungiform papilla
Filiform papilla
Apex

STRUCTURES SURROUNDING PHARYNX

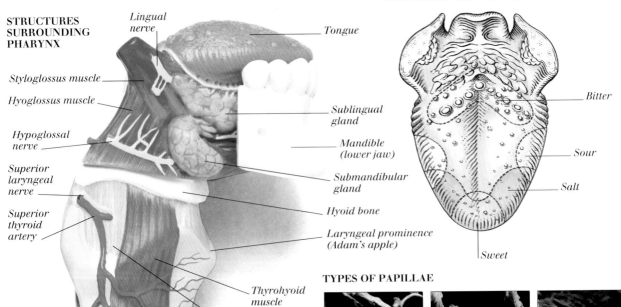

Lingual nerve
Tongue
Styloglossus muscle
Hyoglossus muscle
Sublingual gland
Hypoglossal nerve
Mandible (lower jaw)
Superior laryngeal nerve
Submandibular gland
Superior thyroid artery
Hyoid bone
Laryngeal prominence (Adam's apple)
Thyrohyoid muscle
Thyrohyoid membrane
Cricothyroid muscle
Cricothyroid ligament
Thyroid gland
Trachea

TASTE AREAS ON TONGUE

Bitter
Sour
Salt
Sweet

TYPES OF PAPILLAE

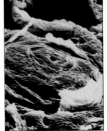

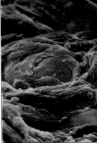

FILIFORM PAPILLAE   FUNGIFORM PAPILLAE   VALLATE PAPILLAE

SECTION THROUGH NOSE, MOUTH, AND THROAT

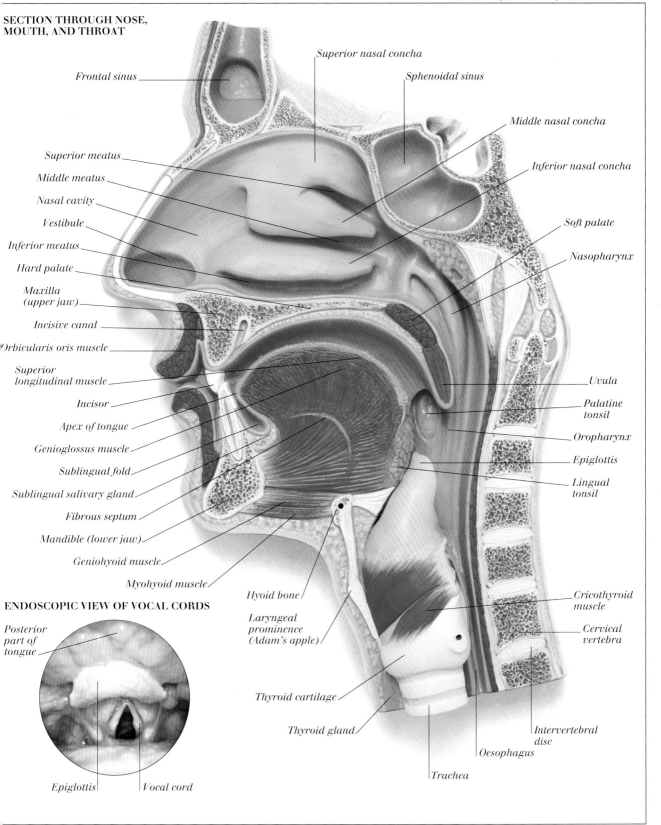

Frontal sinus

Superior nasal concha

Sphenoidal sinus

Middle nasal concha

Inferior nasal concha

Superior meatus

Middle meatus

Nasal cavity

Vestibule

Inferior meatus

Hard palate

Maxilla (upper jaw)

Incisive canal

Orbicularis oris muscle

Superior longitudinal muscle

Incisor

Apex of tongue

Genioglossus muscle

Sublingual fold

Sublingual salivary gland

Fibrous septum

Mandible (lower jaw)

Geniohyoid muscle

Myohyoid muscle

Soft palate

Nasopharynx

Uvula

Palatine tonsil

Oropharynx

Epiglottis

Lingual tonsil

Cricothyroid muscle

Cervical vertebra

Intervertebral disc

Oesophagus

Trachea

Thyroid gland

Thyroid cartilage

Laryngeal prominence (Adam's apple)

Hyoid bone

ENDOSCOPIC VIEW OF VOCAL CORDS

Posterior part of tongue

Epiglottis

Vocal cord

Teeth

THE 20 PRIMARY TEETH (also called deciduous or milk teeth) usually begin to erupt when a baby is about six months old. They start to be replaced by the permanent teeth when the child is about six years old. By the age of 20, most adults have a full set of 32 teeth although the third molars (commonly called wisdom teeth) may never erupt. While teeth help people to speak clearly and give shape to the face, their main function is the chewing of food. Incisors and canines shear and tear the food into pieces; premolars and molars crush and grind it further. Although tooth enamel is the hardest substance in the body, it tends to be eroded and destroyed by acid produced in the mouth during the breakdown of food.

DEVELOPMENT OF TEETH IN A FETUS

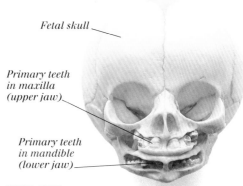

Fetal skull

Primary teeth in maxilla (upper jaw)

Primary teeth in mandible (lower jaw)

FETAL JAWS
By the sixth week of embryonic development areas of thickening occur in each jaw; these areas give rise to tooth buds. By the time the fetus is six months old, enamel has formed on the tooth buds.

DEVELOPMENT OF JAW AND TEETH

Maxilla (upper jaw)

Mandible (lower jaw)

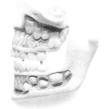

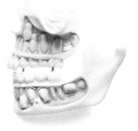

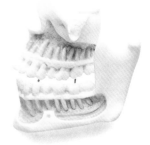

A NEWBORN BABY'S JAWS
The primary teeth can be seen developing in the jaw bones; they begin to erupt around the age of six months.

A FIVE-YEAR-OLD CHILD'S TEETH
There is a full set of 20 erupted primary teeth; the permanent teeth can be seen developing in the upper and lower jaws.

A NINE-YEAR-OLD CHILD'S TEETH
Most of the teeth are primary teeth but the permanent incisors and first molars have now emerged.

AN ADULT'S TEETH
By the age of 20, the full set of 32 permanent teeth (including the wisdom teeth) should be in position.

THE PERMANENT TEETH

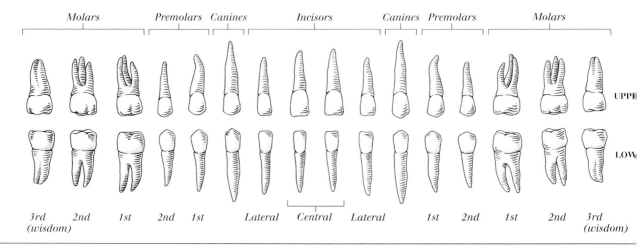

Molars *Premolars* *Canines* *Incisors* *Canines* *Premolars* *Molars*

UPPER

LOWER

3rd (wisdom) 2nd 1st 2nd 1st Lateral Central Lateral 1st 2nd 1st 2nd 3rd (wisdom)

STRUCTURE OF A TOOTH

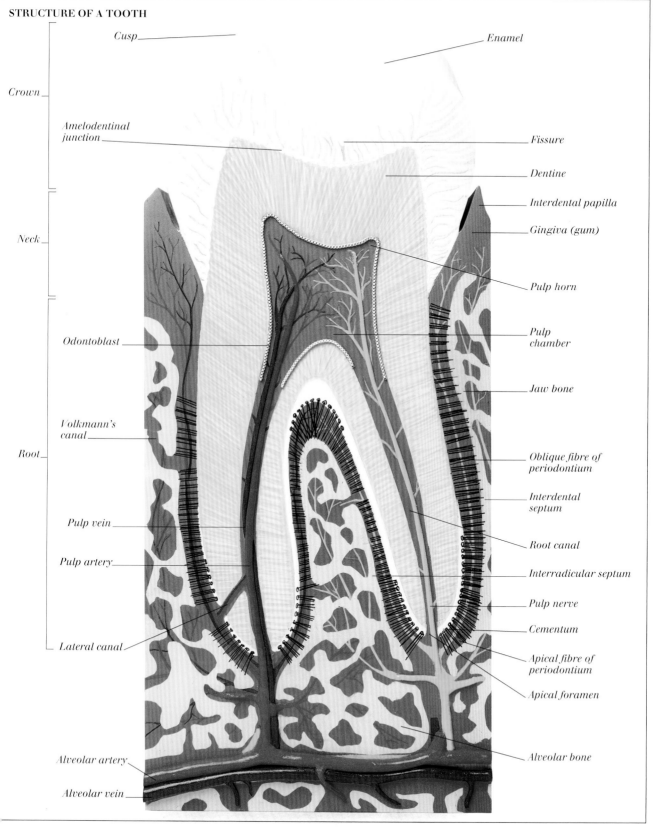

Cusp

Enamel

Crown

Amelodentinal junction

Fissure

Dentine

Interdental papilla

Neck

Gingiva (gum)

Pulp horn

Odontoblast

Pulp chamber

Jaw bone

Volkmann's canal

Oblique fibre of periodontium

Root

Interdental septum

Pulp vein

Root canal

Pulp artery

Interradicular septum

Pulp nerve

Cementum

Lateral canal

Apical fibre of periodontium

Apical foramen

Alveolar artery

Alveolar bone

Alveolar vein

Digestive system

THE DIGESTIVE SYSTEM BREAKS DOWN FOOD into particles so tiny that blood can take nourishment to all parts of the body. The system's main part is a 9 m (30 ft) tube from mouth to rectum; muscles in this alimentary canal force food along. Chewed food first travels through the oesophagus to the stomach, which churns and liquidizes food before it passes through the duodenum, jejunum, and ileum – the three parts of the long, convoluted small intestine. Here, digestive juices from the gallbladder and pancreas break down food particles; many filter out into the blood through tiny fingerlike villi that line the small intestine's inner wall. Undigested food in the colon forms faeces that leave the body through the anus.

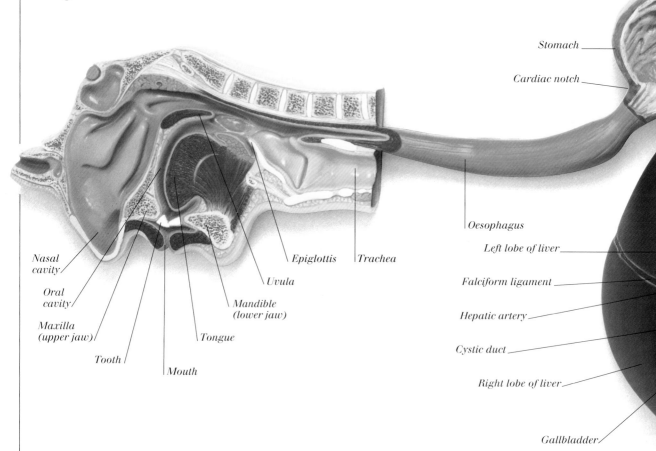

Stomach

Cardiac notch

Oesophagus

Left lobe of liver

Falciform ligament

Hepatic artery

Cystic duct

Right lobe of liver

Gallbladder

Nasal cavity

Oral cavity

Maxilla (upper jaw)

Tooth

Mouth

Tongue

Mandible (lower jaw)

Uvula

Epiglottis

Trachea

ENDOSCOPIC VIEWS INSIDE ALIMENTARY CANAL

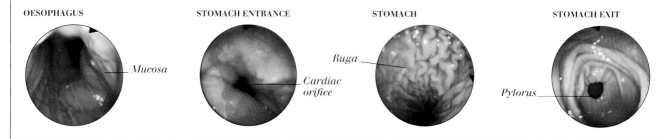

OESOPHAGUS

Mucosa

STOMACH ENTRANCE

Cardiac orifice

STOMACH

Ruga

STOMACH EXIT

Pylorus

ALIMENTARY CANAL

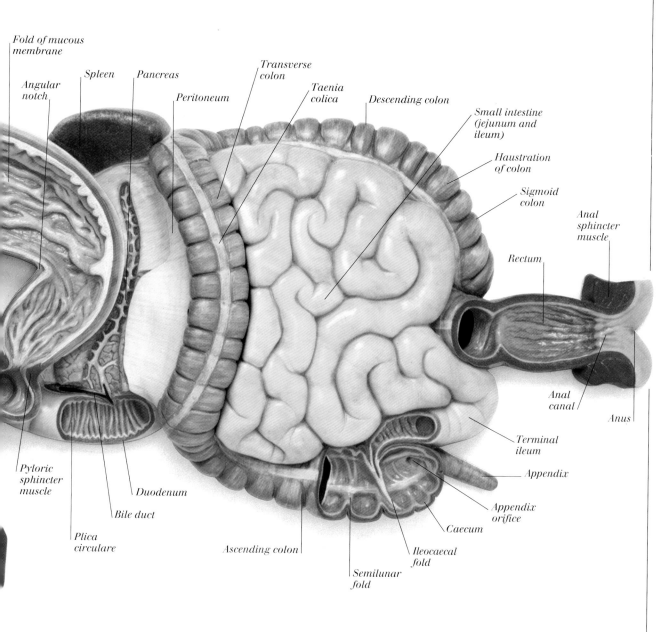

Fold of mucous membrane

Angular notch

Spleen

Pancreas

Peritoneum

Transverse colon

Taenia colica

Descending colon

Small intestine (jejunum and ileum)

Haustration of colon

Sigmoid colon

Anal sphincter muscle

Rectum

Anal canal

Anus

Terminal ileum

Appendix

Appendix orifice

Caecum

Ileocaecal fold

Ascending colon

Semilunar fold

Plica circulare

Bile duct

Duodenum

Pyloric sphincter muscle

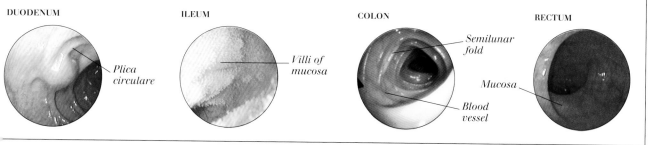

DUODENUM

Plica circulare

ILEUM

Villi of mucosa

COLON

Semilunar fold

Blood vessel

RECTUM

Mucosa

Heart

THE HEART IS A HOLLOW MUSCLE in the middle of the chest that pumps blood around the body, supplying cells with oxygen and nutrients. A muscular wall, called the septum, divides the heart lengthways into left and right sides. A valve divides each side into two chambers: an upper atrium and a lower ventricle. When the heart muscle contracts, it squeezes blood through the atria and then through the ventricles. Oxygenated blood from the lungs flows from the pulmonary veins into the left atrium, through the left ventricle, and then out via the aorta to all parts of the body. Deoxygenated blood returning from the body flows from the vena cava into the right atrium, through the right ventricle, and then out via the pulmonary artery to the lungs for reoxygenation. At rest the heart beats between 60 and 80 times a minute; during exercise or at times of stress or excitement the rate may increase to 200 beats a minute.

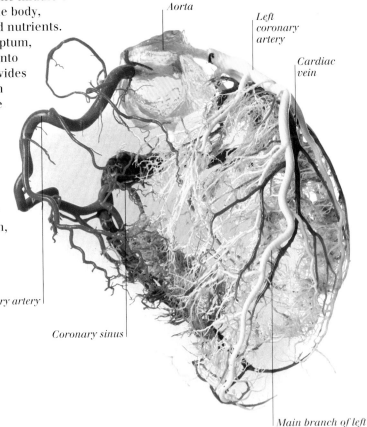

Aorta

Left coronary artery

Cardiac vein

Right coronary artery

Coronary sinus

Main branch of left coronary artery

SECTION THROUGH HEART WALL

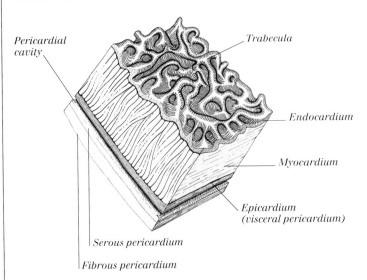

Pericardial cavity

Trabecula

Endocardium

Myocardium

Epicardium (visceral pericardium)

Serous pericardium

Fibrous pericardium

HEARTBEAT SEQUENCE

ATRIAL DIASTOLE

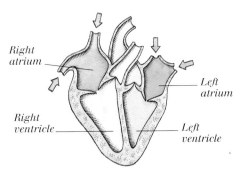

Right atrium

Left atrium

Right ventricle

Left ventricle

Deoxygenated blood enters the right atrium while the left atrium receives oxygenated blood.

STRUCTURE OF HEART

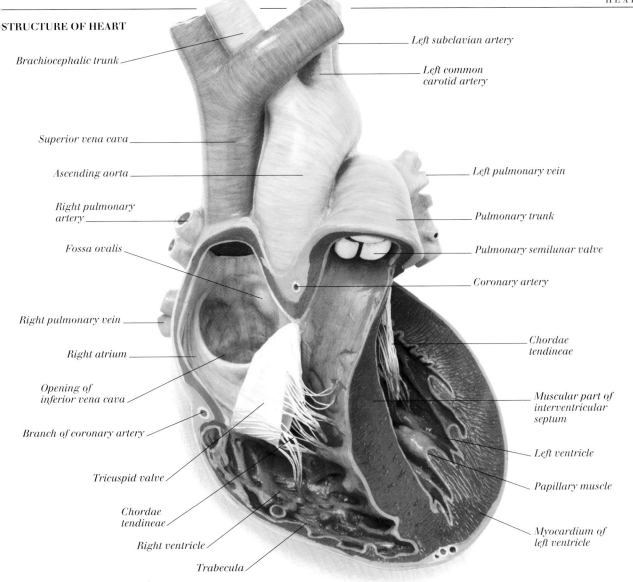

Brachiocephalic trunk

Left subclavian artery

Left common carotid artery

Superior vena cava

Ascending aorta

Left pulmonary vein

Right pulmonary artery

Pulmonary trunk

Fossa ovalis

Pulmonary semilunar valve

Coronary artery

Right pulmonary vein

Right atrium

Chordae tendineae

Opening of inferior vena cava

Muscular part of interventricular septum

Branch of coronary artery

Left ventricle

Tricuspid valve

Papillary muscle

Chordae tendineae

Right ventricle

Myocardium of left ventricle

Trabecula

ATRIAL SYSTOLE (VENTRICULAR DIASTOLE)

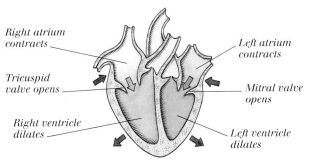

Right atrium contracts

Left atrium contracts

Tricuspid valve opens

Mitral valve opens

Right ventricle dilates

Left ventricle dilates

Left and right atria contract, forcing blood into the relaxed ventricles.

VENTRICULAR SYSTOLE

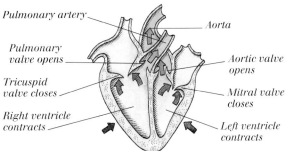

Pulmonary artery

Aorta

Pulmonary valve opens

Aortic valve opens

Tricuspid valve closes

Mitral valve closes

Right ventricle contracts

Left ventricle contracts

Ventricles contract and force blood to the lungs for oxygenation and via the aorta to the rest of the body.

Circulatory system

THE CIRCULATORY SYSTEM consists of the heart and blood vessels, which together maintain a continuous flow of blood around the body. The heart pumps oxygen-rich blood from the lungs to all parts of the body through a network of tubes called arteries, and smaller branches called arterioles. Blood returns to the heart via small vessels called venules, which lead in turn into larger tubes called veins. Arterioles and venules are linked by a network of tiny vessels called capillaries, where the exchange of oxygen and carbon dioxide between blood and body cells takes place. Blood has four main components: red blood cells, white blood cells, platelets, and liquid plasma.

ARTERIAL SYSTEM OF BRAIN

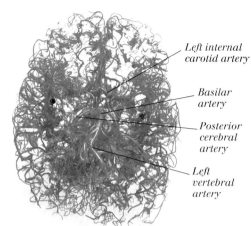

Left internal carotid artery

Basilar artery

Posterior cerebral artery

Left vertebral artery

CIRCULATORY SYSTEM OF LIVER

Inferior vena cava

Portal vein

Common bile duct

Hepatic artery

Gallbladder

CIRCULATORY SYSTEM OF HEART AND LUNGS

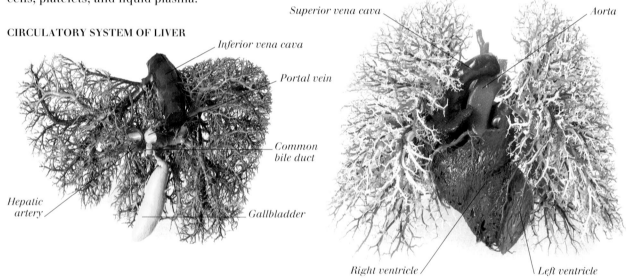

Superior vena cava

Aorta

Right ventricle

Left ventricle

SECTION OF MAIN ARTERY

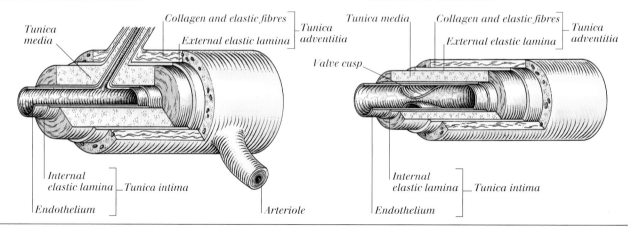

Tunica media

Collagen and elastic fibres

External elastic lamina

Tunica adventitia

Internal elastic lamina

Tunica intima

Endothelium

Arteriole

SECTION OF MAIN VEIN

Tunica media

Collagen and elastic fibres

External elastic lamina

Tunica adventitia

Valve cusp

Internal elastic lamina

Tunica intima

Endothelium

PRINCIPAL ARTERIES AND VEINS OF CIRCULATORY SYSTEM

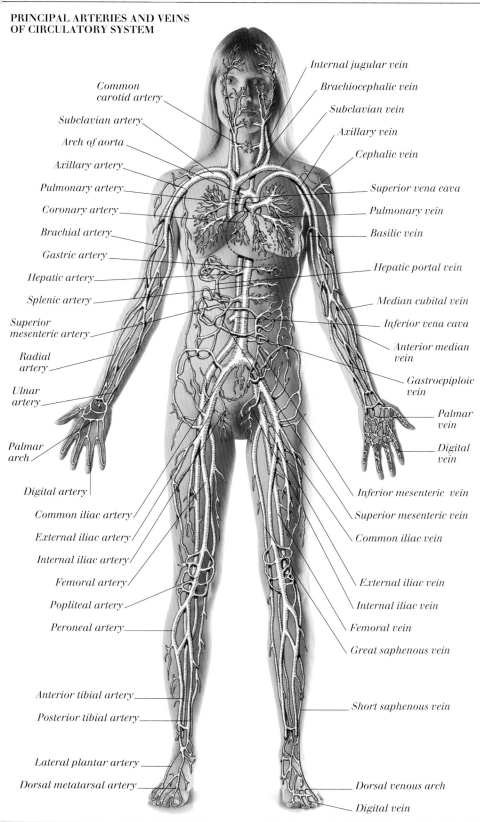

Common carotid artery

Subclavian artery

Arch of aorta

Axillary artery

Pulmonary artery

Coronary artery

Brachial artery

Gastric artery

Hepatic artery

Splenic artery

Superior mesenteric artery

Radial artery

Ulnar artery

Palmar arch

Digital artery

Common iliac artery

External iliac artery

Internal iliac artery

Femoral artery

Popliteal artery

Peroneal artery

Anterior tibial artery

Posterior tibial artery

Lateral plantar artery

Dorsal metatarsal artery

Internal jugular vein

Brachiocephalic vein

Subclavian vein

Axillary vein

Cephalic vein

Superior vena cava

Pulmonary vein

Basilic vein

Hepatic portal vein

Median cubital vein

Inferior vena cava

Anterior median vein

Gastroepiploic vein

Palmar vein

Digital vein

Inferior mesenteric vein

Superior mesenteric vein

Common iliac vein

External iliac vein

Internal iliac vein

Femoral vein

Great saphenous vein

Short saphenous vein

Dorsal venous arch

Digital vein

TYPES OF BLOOD CELLS

RED BLOOD CELLS
These cells are biconcave in shape to maximize their oxygen-carrying capacity.

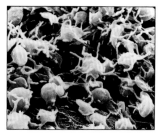

WHITE BLOOD CELLS
Lymphocytes are the smallest white blood cells; they form antibodies against disease.

PLATELETS
Tiny cells that are activated whenever blood clotting or repair to vessels is necessary.

BLOOD CLOTTING

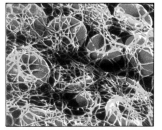

Filaments of fibrin enmesh red blood cells as part of the process of blood clotting.

Respiratory system

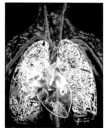

THE RESPIRATORY SYSTEM supplies the oxygen needed by body cells and carries off their carbon dioxide waste. Inhaled air passes via the trachea (windpipe) through two narrower tubes, the bronchi, to the lungs. Each lung comprises many fine, branching tubes called bronchioles that end in tiny clustered chambers called alveoli. Gases cross the thin alveolar walls to and from a network of tiny blood vessels. Intercostal (rib) muscles and the muscular diaphragm below the lungs operate the lungs like bellows, drawing air in and forcing it out at regular intervals.

BRONCHIOLE AND ALVEOLI

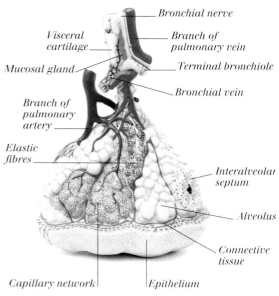

Visceral cartilage

Mucosal gland

Branch of pulmonary artery

Elastic fibres

Bronchial nerve

Branch of pulmonary vein

Terminal bronchiole

Bronchial vein

Interalveolar septum

Alveolus

Connective tissue

Capillary network

Epithelium

SEGMENTS OF BRONCHIAL TREE

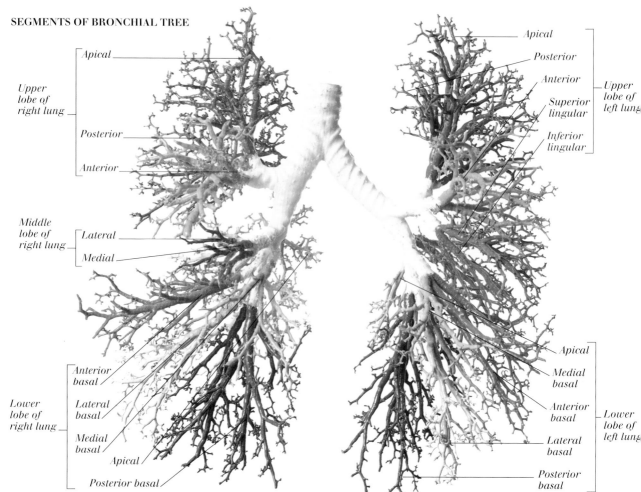

Upper lobe of right lung
- Apical
- Posterior
- Anterior

Middle lobe of right lung
- Lateral
- Medial

Lower lobe of right lung
- Anterior basal
- Lateral basal
- Medial basal
- Apical
- Posterior basal

Upper lobe of left lung
- Apical
- Posterior
- Anterior
- Superior lingular
- Inferior lingular

Lower lobe of left lung
- Apical
- Medial basal
- Anterior basal
- Lateral basal
- Posterior basal

STRUCTURES OF THORACIC CAVITY

GASEOUS EXCHANGE IN ALVEOLUS

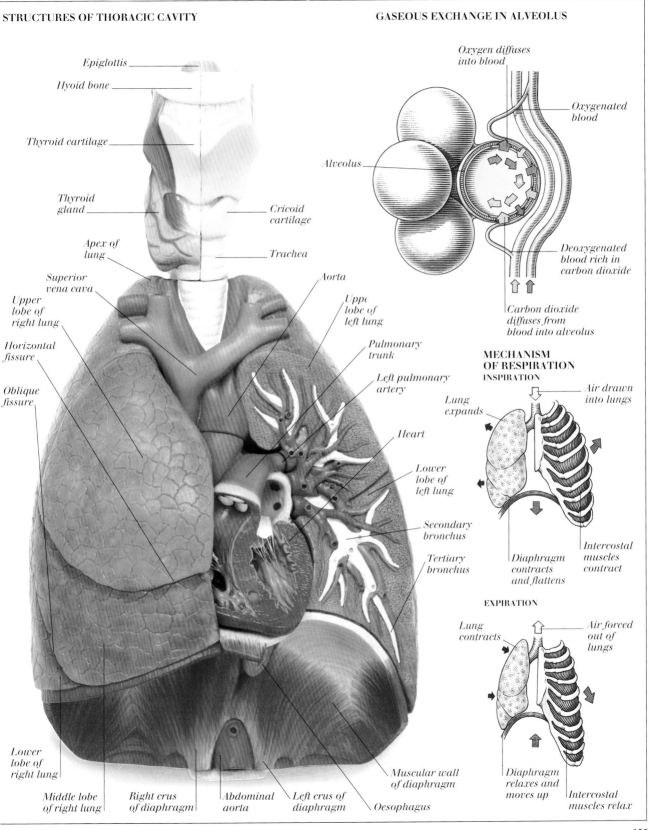

Epiglottis

Hyoid bone

Thyroid cartilage

Thyroid gland

Apex of lung

Superior vena cava

Upper lobe of right lung

Horizontal fissure

Oblique fissure

Cricoid cartilage

Trachea

Aorta

Upper lobe of left lung

Pulmonary trunk

Left pulmonary artery

Heart

Lower lobe of left lung

Secondary bronchus

Tertiary bronchus

Muscular wall of diaphragm

Lower lobe of right lung

Middle lobe of right lung

Right crus of diaphragm

Abdominal aorta

Left crus of diaphragm

Oesophagus

Oxygen diffuses into blood

Oxygenated blood

Alveolus

Deoxygenated blood rich in carbon dioxide

Carbon dioxide diffuses from blood into alveolus

MECHANISM OF RESPIRATION
INSPIRATION

Lung expands

Air drawn into lungs

Diaphragm contracts and flattens

Intercostal muscles contract

EXPIRATION

Lung contracts

Air forced out of lungs

Diaphragm relaxes and moves up

Intercostal muscles relax

Urinary system

THE URINARY SYSTEM FILTERS WASTE PRODUCTS from the blood and removes them from the body via a system of tubes. Blood is filtered in the two kidneys, which are fist-sized, bean-shaped organs. The renal arteries carry blood to the kidneys; the renal veins remove blood after filtering. Each kidney contains about one million tiny units called nephrons. Each nephron is made up of a tubule and a filtering unit called a glomerulus, which consists of a collection of tiny blood vessels surrounded by the hollow Bowman's capsule. The filtering process produces a watery fluid that leaves the kidney as urine. The urine is carried via two tubes called ureters to the bladder, where it is stored until its release from the body through another tube called the urethra.

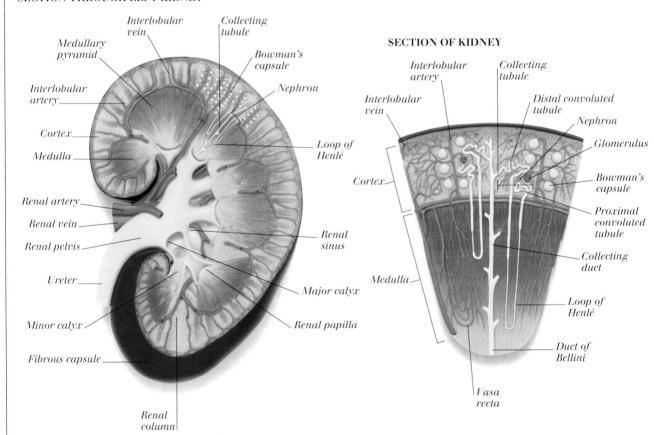

ARTERIAL SYSTEM OF KIDNEYS

Aorta

Coeliac trunk

Superior mesenteric artery

Right renal artery

Left renal artery

Right ureter

Left ureter

SECTION THROUGH LEFT KIDNEY

Medullary pyramid

Interlobular vein

Collecting tubule

Bowman's capsule

Interlobular artery

Nephron

Cortex

Medulla

Loop of Henlé

Renal artery

Renal vein

Renal pelvis

Ureter

Renal sinus

Minor calyx

Major calyx

Fibrous capsule

Renal papilla

Renal column

SECTION OF KIDNEY

Interlobular artery

Collecting tubule

Interlobular vein

Distal convoluted tubule

Nephron

Glomerulus

Cortex

Bowman's capsule

Proximal convoluted tubule

Medulla

Collecting duct

Loop of Henlé

Duct of Bellini

Vasa recta

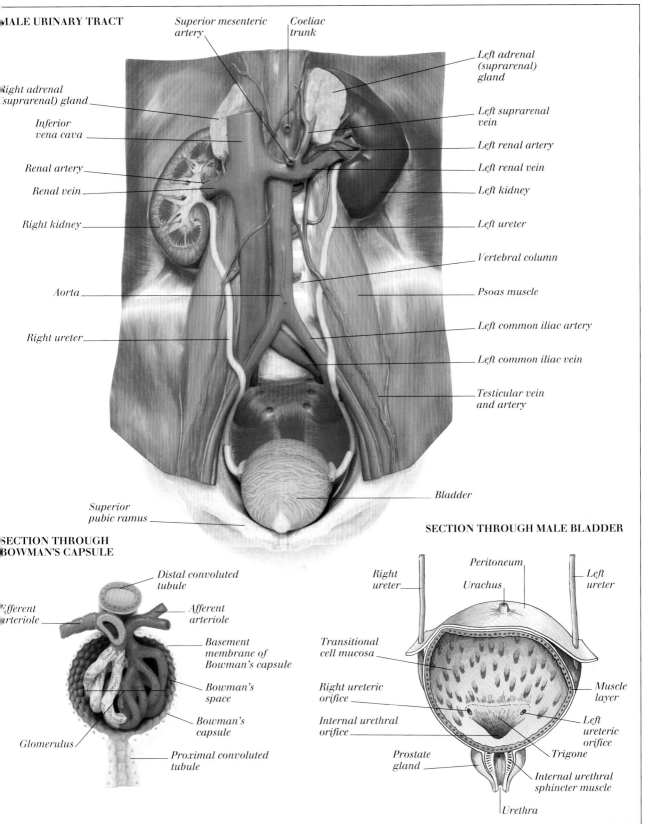

MALE URINARY TRACT

Superior mesenteric artery

Coeliac trunk

Left adrenal (suprarenal) gland

Right adrenal (suprarenal) gland

Inferior vena cava

Left suprarenal vein

Left renal artery

Renal artery

Left renal vein

Renal vein

Left kidney

Right kidney

Left ureter

Vertebral column

Aorta

Psoas muscle

Right ureter

Left common iliac artery

Left common iliac vein

Testicular vein and artery

Bladder

Superior pubic ramus

SECTION THROUGH BOWMAN'S CAPSULE

Distal convoluted tubule

Efferent arteriole

Afferent arteriole

Basement membrane of Bowman's capsule

Bowman's space

Bowman's capsule

Glomerulus

Proximal convoluted tubule

SECTION THROUGH MALE BLADDER

Right ureter

Peritoneum

Urachus

Left ureter

Transitional cell mucosa

Right ureteric orifice

Muscle layer

Internal urethral orifice

Left ureteric orifice

Prostate gland

Trigone

Internal urethral sphincter muscle

Urethra

Reproductive system

SEX ORGANS LOCATED IN THE PELVIS create new human lives. Each month a ripe egg is released from one of the female's ovaries into a fallopian tube leading to the uterus (womb), a muscular pear-sized organ. A male produces minute tadpole-like sperm in two oval glands called testes. When the male is ready to release sperm into the female's vagina, many millions pass into his urethra and leave his body through the fleshy penis. The sperm travel up through the vagina into the uterus and fallopian tubes, and one sperm may enter and fertilize an egg. The fertilized egg becomes embedded in the uterus wall and starts to grow into a new human being.

SECTION THROUGH OVARY

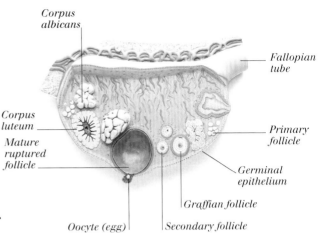

Corpus albicans

Fallopian tube

Corpus luteum

Mature ruptured follicle

Primary follicle

Germinal epithelium

Graffian follicle

Oocyte (egg)

Secondary follicle

SECTION THROUGH FEMALE PELVIC REGION

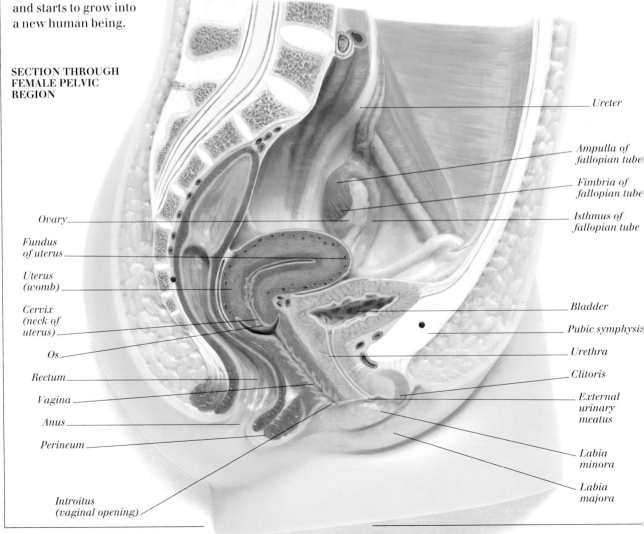

Ureter

Ampulla of fallopian tube

Fimbria of fallopian tube

Isthmus of fallopian tube

Ovary

Fundus of uterus

Uterus (womb)

Cervix (neck of uterus)

Os

Rectum

Vagina

Anus

Perineum

Bladder

Pubic symphysis

Urethra

Clitoris

External urinary meatus

Labia minora

Labia majora

Introitus (vaginal opening)

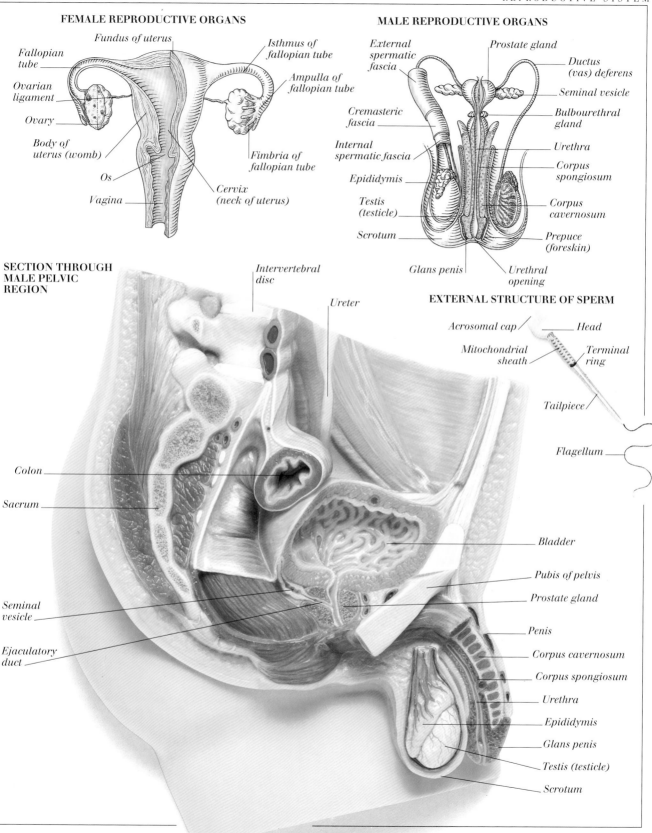

FEMALE REPRODUCTIVE ORGANS

Fundus of uterus

Fallopian tube

Isthmus of fallopian tube

Ovarian ligament

Ampulla of fallopian tube

Ovary

Body of uterus (womb)

Fimbria of fallopian tube

Os

Cervix (neck of uterus)

Vagina

MALE REPRODUCTIVE ORGANS

External spermatic fascia

Prostate gland

Ductus (vas) deferens

Cremasteric fascia

Seminal vesicle

Internal spermatic fascia

Bulbourethral gland

Epididymis

Urethra

Testis (testicle)

Corpus spongiosum

Scrotum

Corpus cavernosum

Glans penis

Prepuce (foreskin)

Urethral opening

SECTION THROUGH MALE PELVIC REGION

Intervertebral disc

Ureter

Colon

Sacrum

Seminal vesicle

Ejaculatory duct

Bladder

Pubis of pelvis

Prostate gland

Penis

Corpus cavernosum

Corpus spongiosum

Urethra

Epididymis

Glans penis

Testis (testicle)

Scrotum

EXTERNAL STRUCTURE OF SPERM

Acrosomal cap

Head

Mitochondrial sheath

Terminal ring

Tailpiece

Flagellum

Development of a baby

A FERTILIZED EGG IS NOURISHED AND PROTECTED as it
develops into an embryo and then a fetus during the 40
weeks of pregnancy. The placenta, a mass of blood vessels
implanted in the uterus lining, delivers nourishment and
oxygen, and removes waste through the umbilical cord.
Meanwhile, the fetus lies snugly in its amniotic sac, a bag of
fluid that protects it against any sudden jolts. In the last
weeks of the pregnancy, the rapidly growing fetus turns
head-down: a baby ready to be born.

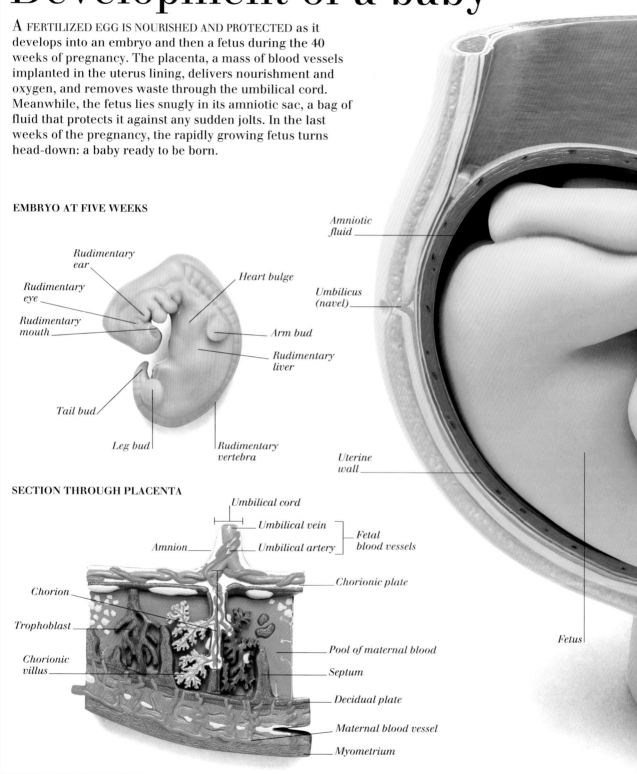

EMBRYO AT FIVE WEEKS

Rudimentary ear

Rudimentary eye

Rudimentary mouth

Heart bulge

Arm bud

Rudimentary liver

Tail bud

Leg bud

Rudimentary vertebra

Amniotic fluid

Umbilicus (navel)

Uterine wall

Fetus

SECTION THROUGH PLACENTA

Umbilical cord

Umbilical vein

Amnion

Umbilical artery

Fetal blood vessels

Chorionic plate

Chorion

Trophoblast

Chorionic villus

Pool of maternal blood

Septum

Decidual plate

Maternal blood vessel

Myometrium

SECTION THROUGH PELVIS IN NINTH MONTH OF PREGNANCY

THE DEVELOPING FETUS

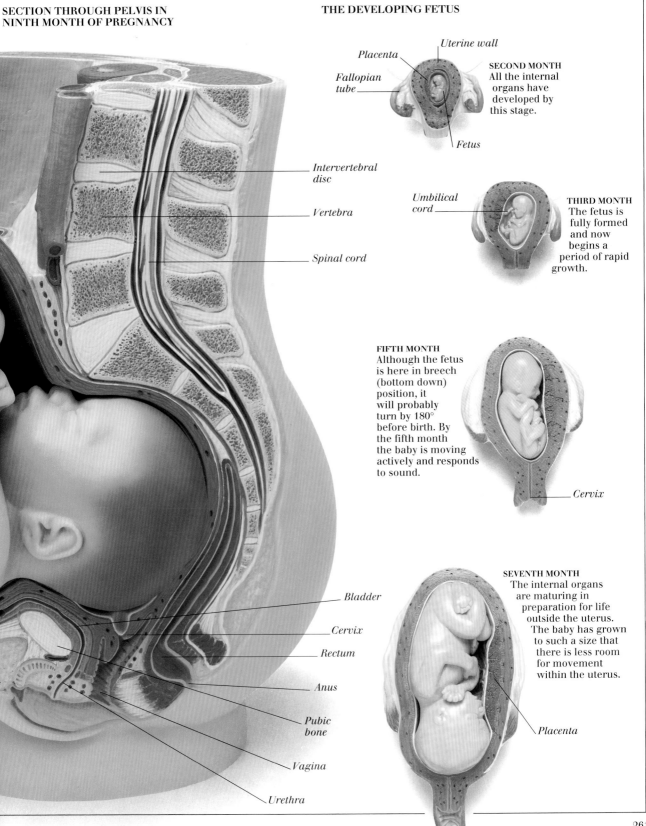

Uterine wall

Placenta

Fallopian tube

SECOND MONTH
All the internal organs have developed by this stage.

Fetus

Umbilical cord

THIRD MONTH
The fetus is fully formed and now begins a period of rapid growth.

FIFTH MONTH
Although the fetus is here in breech (bottom down) position, it will probably turn by 180° before birth. By the fifth month the baby is moving actively and responds to sound.

Cervix

SEVENTH MONTH
The internal organs are maturing in preparation for life outside the uterus. The baby has grown to such a size that there is less room for movement within the uterus.

Placenta

Intervertebral disc

Vertebra

Spinal cord

Bladder

Cervix

Rectum

Anus

Pubic bone

Vagina

Urethra

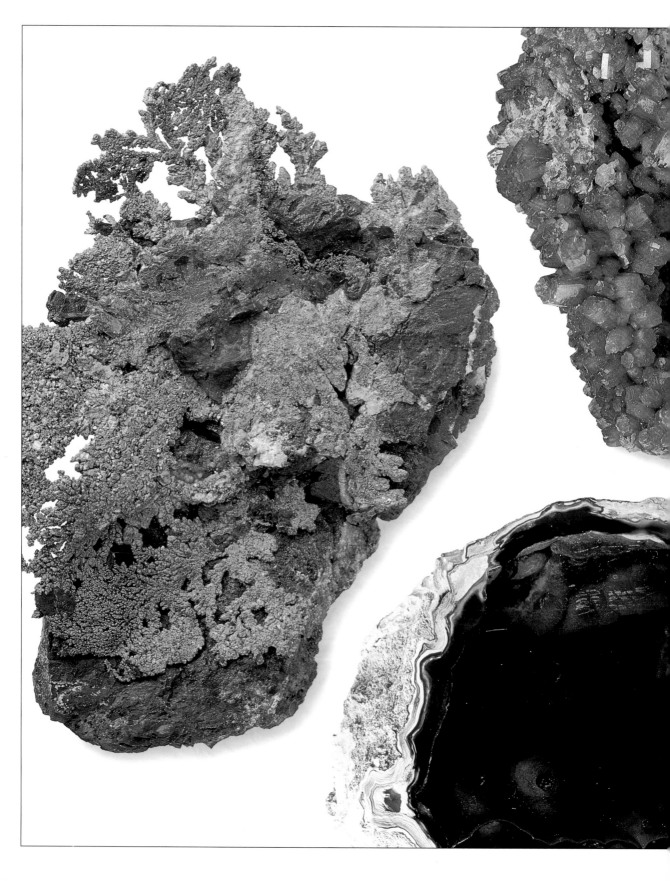

GEOLOGY, GEOGRAPHY, AND METEOROLGY

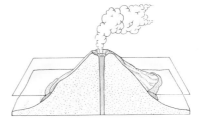

Earth's physical features

MOST OF THE EARTH'S SURFACE (about 70 per cent) is covered with water. The largest single body of water, the Pacific Ocean, alone covers about 30 per cent of the surface. Most of the land is distributed as seven continents; these are (from largest to smallest) Asia, Africa, North America, South America, Antarctica, Europe, and Australasia. The physical features of the land are remarkably varied. Among the most notable are mountain ranges, rivers, and deserts. The largest mountain ranges – the Himalayas in Asia and the Andes in South America – extend for thousands of kilometres. The Himalayas include the world's highest mountain, Mount Everest (8,848 metres). The longest rivers are the River Nile in Africa (6,695 kilometres) and the Amazon River in South America (6,437 kilometres). Deserts cover about 20 per cent of the total land area. The largest is the Sahara, which covers nearly a third of Africa. The Earth's surface features can be represented in various ways. Only a globe can correctly represent areas, shapes, sizes, and directions, because there is always distortion when a spherical surface – the Earth's, for example – is projected on to the flat surface of a map. Each map projection is therefore a compromise: it shows some features accurately but distorts others. Even satellite mapping does not produce completely accurate maps, although they can show physical features with great clarity.

EXAMPLES OF MAP PROJECTIONS

CYLINDRICAL PROJECTION

CYLINDRICAL-PROJECTION MAP

SATELLITE MAPPING OF THE EARTH

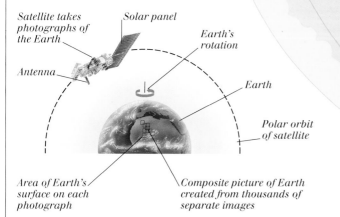

Satellite takes photographs of the Earth

Solar panel

Earth's rotation

Antenna

Earth

Polar orbit of satellite

Area of Earth's surface on each photograph

Composite picture of Earth created from thousands of separate images

180° 160° 120° 80°

Great Slave Lake

Great Bear Lake

Lake Superior

Greenlan

Mackenzie-Peace River

Hudson Bay

Ba Isl

Bering Sea

NORTH AMERICA

Rocky Mountains

Lake Huror

Lake Ontario

Lake Erie

Lake Michigan

Sonoran Desert

Sierra Madre

Appalachian Mountains

Chihuahuan Desert

Gulf of Mexico

ATLAN

OCEA

Mississippi-Missouri River

Caribbean Sea

Guiana Highlands

PACIFIC OCEAN

SOUTH AMERICA

Andes

Atacama Desert

Gran Chaco

Parana River

Pampas

Patagonia

120° 80°

180° 160° WEST OF GREE MERIDIAN

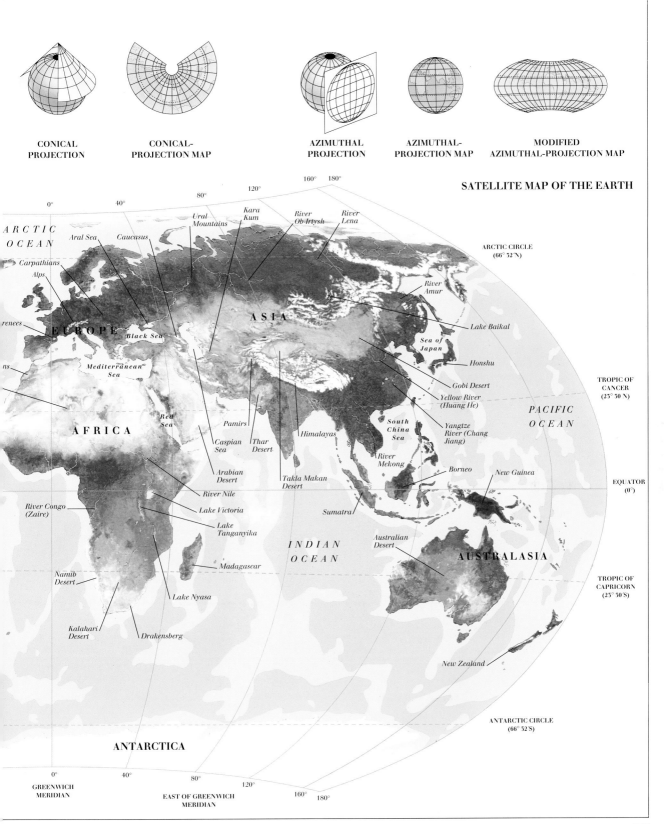

CONICAL
PROJECTION

CONICAL-
PROJECTION MAP

AZIMUTHAL
PROJECTION

AZIMUTHAL-
PROJECTION MAP

MODIFIED
AZIMUTHAL-PROJECTION MAP

SATELLITE MAP OF THE EARTH

160° 180°

120°

80°

40°

0°

Ural Mountains

Kara Kum

River Ob-Irtysh

River Lena

ARCTIC CIRCLE
(66° 52'N)

A R C T I C
O C E A N

Aral Sea

Caucasus

Carpathians

Alps

renees

E U R O P E

Black Sea

A S I A

River Amur

Lake Baikal

Sea of Japan

ns

Mediterranean Sea

Honshu

TROPIC OF
CANCER
(23° 30'N)

Gobi Desert

Yellow River (Huang He)

PACIFIC OCEAN

AFRICA

Red Sea

Pamirs

Thar Desert

Himalayas

Yangtze River (Chang Jiang)

Caspian Sea

South China Sea

Arabian Desert

Takla Makan Desert

River Mekong

Borneo

New Guinea

EQUATOR
(0°)

River Nile

River Congo (Zaire)

Lake Victoria

Lake Tanganyika

Sumatra

INDIAN OCEAN

Australian Desert

AUSTRALASIA

Namib Desert

Madagascar

TROPIC OF
CAPRICORN
(23° 30'S)

Lake Nyasa

Kalahari Desert

Drakensberg

New Zealand

ANTARCTIC CIRCLE
(66° 52'S)

ANTARCTICA

0°

40°

80°

120°

160° 180°

GREENWICH
MERIDIAN

EAST OF GREENWICH
MERIDIAN

The rock cycle

THE ROCK CYCLE IS A CONTINUOUS PROCESS through which old rocks are transformed into new ones. Rocks can be divided into three main groups: igneous, sedimentary, and metamorphic. Igneous rocks are formed when magma (molten rock) from the Earth's interior cools and solidifies (see pp. 274-275). Sedimentary rocks are formed when sediment (rock particles, for example) becomes compressed and cemented together in a process known as lithification (see pp. 276-277). Metamorphic rocks are formed when igneous, sedimentary, or other metamorphic rocks are changed by heat or pressure (see pp. 274-275). Rocks are added to the Earth's surface by crustal movements and volcanic activity. Once exposed on the surface, the rocks are broken down into rock particles by weathering (see pp. 282-283). The particles are then transported by glaciers, rivers, and wind, and deposited as sediment in lakes, deltas, deserts, and on the ocean floor. Some of this sediment undergoes lithification and forms sedimentary rock. This rock may be thrust back to the surface by crustal movements or forced deeper into the Earth's interior, where heat and pressure transform it into metamorphic rock. The metamorphic rock in turn may be pushed up to the surface or may be melted to form magma. Eventually, the magma cools and solidifies – below or on the surface – forming igneous rock. When the sedimentary, igneous, and metamorphic rocks are exposed once more on the Earth's surface, the cycle begins again.

HEXAGONAL BASALT
COLUMNS, ICELAND

THE ROCK CYCLE

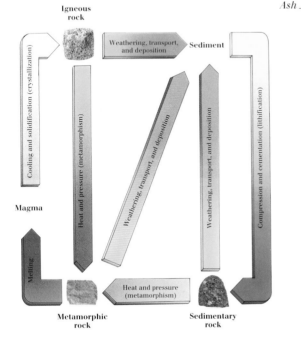

Igneous rock

Cooling and solidification (crystallization)

Weathering, transport, and deposition

Sediment

Heat and pressure (metamorphism)

Weathering, transport, and deposition

Weathering, transport, and deposition

Compression and cementation (lithification)

Magma

Melting

Heat and pressure (metamorphism)

Metamorphic rock

Sedimentary rock

STAGES IN THE ROCK CYCLE

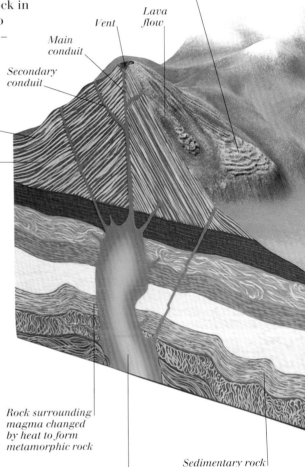

Magma extruded as lava, which solidifies to form igneous rock

Lava flow

Vent

Main conduit

Secondary conduit

Lava

Ash

Rock surrounding magma changed by heat to form metamorphic rock

Intense heat of rising magma melts some of the surrounding rock

Sedimentary rock crushed and folded to form metamorphic rock

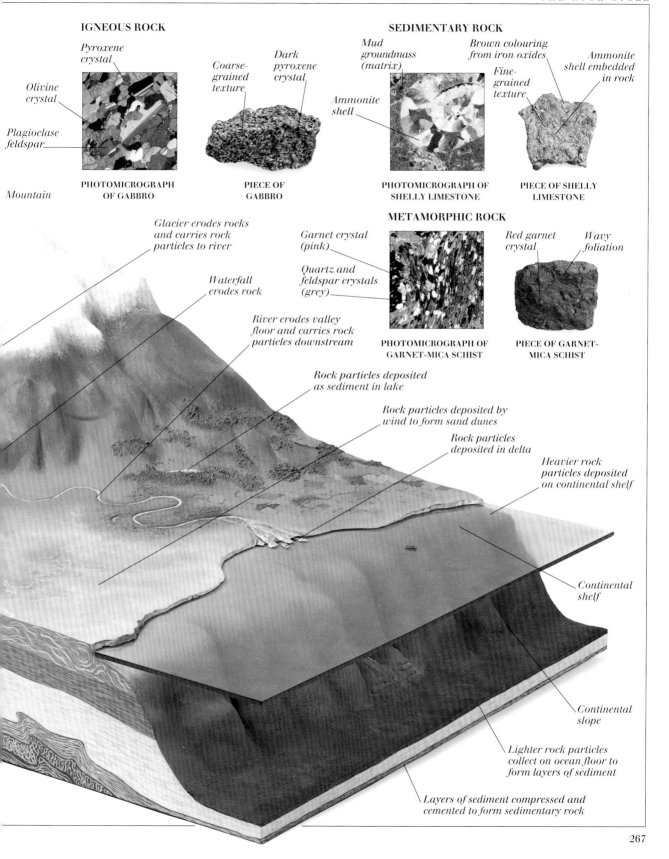

IGNEOUS ROCK

Pyroxene crystal

Olivine crystal

Plagioclase feldspar

Coarse-grained texture

Dark pyroxene crystal

PHOTOMICROGRAPH OF GABBRO

PIECE OF GABBRO

Mountain

SEDIMENTARY ROCK

Mud groundmass (matrix)

Brown colouring from iron oxides

Fine-grained texture

Ammonite shell embedded in rock

Ammonite shell

PHOTOMICROGRAPH OF SHELLY LIMESTONE

PIECE OF SHELLY LIMESTONE

METAMORPHIC ROCK

Garnet crystal (pink)

Quartz and feldspar crystals (grey)

Red garnet crystal

Wavy foliation

PHOTOMICROGRAPH OF GARNET-MICA SCHIST

PIECE OF GARNET-MICA SCHIST

Glacier erodes rocks and carries rock particles to river

Waterfall erodes rock

River erodes valley floor and carries rock particles downstream

Rock particles deposited as sediment in lake

Rock particles deposited by wind to form sand dunes

Rock particles deposited in delta

Heavier rock particles deposited on continental shelf

Continental shelf

Continental slope

Lighter rock particles collect on ocean floor to form layers of sediment

Layers of sediment compressed and cemented to form sedimentary rock

267

Minerals

A MINERAL IS A NATURALLY OCCURRING SUBSTANCE that has a characteristic chemical composition and specific physical properties, such as habit and streak (see pp. 270-271). A rock, by comparison, is an aggregate of minerals and need not have a specific chemical composition. Minerals are made up of elements (substances that cannot be broken down chemically into simpler substances), each of which can be represented by a chemical symbol. Minerals can be divided into two main groups: native elements and compounds. Native elements are made up of a pure element. Examples include gold (chemical symbol Au), silver (Ag), copper (Cu), and carbon (C); carbon occurs as a native element in two forms, diamond and graphite. Compounds are combinations of two or more elements. For example, sulphides are compounds of sulphur (S) and one or more other elements, such as lead (Pb) in the mineral galena, or antimony (Sb) in the mineral stibnite.

NATIVE ELEMENTS

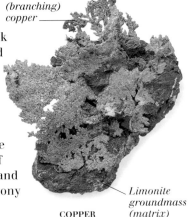

Dendritic (branching) copper

Limonite groundmass (matrix)

COPPER
(Cu)

SULPHIDES

Cubic galena crystal

GALENA
(PbS)

Dendritic (branching) gold

Kimberlite groundmass (matrix)

White diamond

Quartz vein

GOLD
(Au)

DIAMOND
(C)

Hexagonal graphite crystal

GRAPHITE
(C)

OXIDES/HYDROXIDES

Milky quartz groundmass (matrix)

Smoky quartz crystal

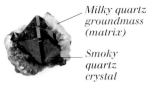

SMOKY QUARTZ
(SiO_2)

Rounded bauxite grains in groundmass (matrix)

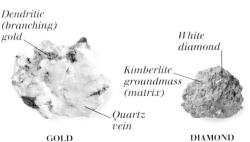

BAUXITE
(FeO(OH) and $Al_2O_3.2H_2O$)

Mass of specular haematite crystals

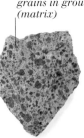

SPECULAR HAEMATITE
(Fe_2O_3)

Prismatic stibnite crystal

Quartz groundmass (matrix)

STIBNITE
(Sb_2S_3)

Perfect octahedral pyrites crystal

Quartz crystal

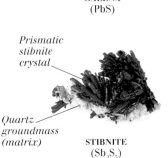

PYRITES
(FeS_2)

Parallel bands of onyx

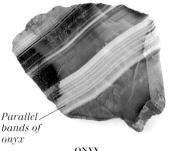

ONYX
(SiO_2)

Kidney ore haematite

Specular crystals of haematite

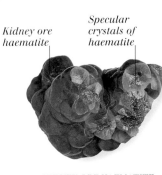

KIDNEY ORE HAEMATITE
(Fe_2O_3)

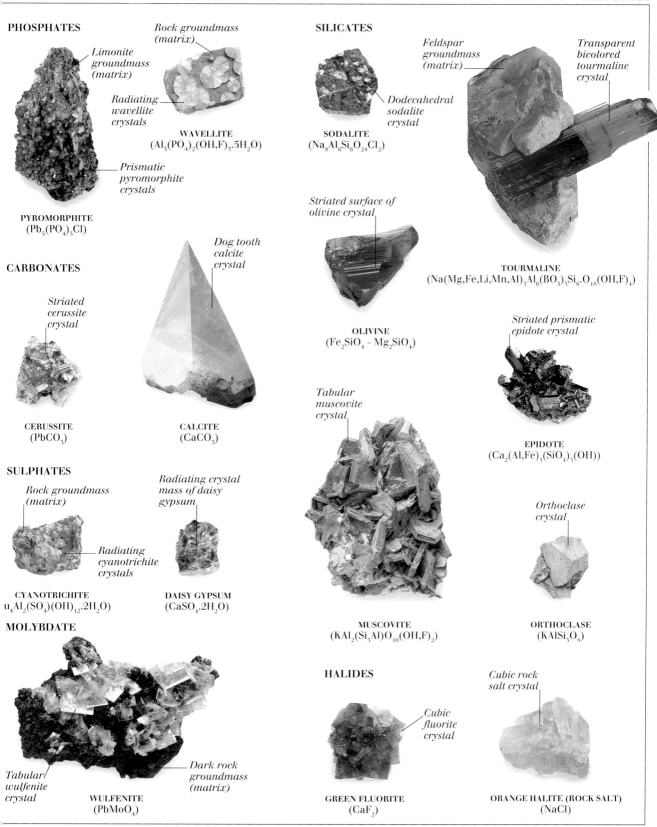

PHOSPHATES

Limonite groundmass (matrix)

Rock groundmass (matrix)

Radiating wavellite crystals

WAVELLITE
$(Al_5(PO_4)_2(OH,F)_5.5H_2O)$

Prismatic pyromorphite crystals

PYROMORPHITE
$(Pb_5(PO_4)_3Cl)$

CARBONATES

Striated cerussite crystal

Dog tooth calcite crystal

CERUSSITE
$(PbCO_3)$

CALCITE
$(CaCO_3)$

SULPHATES

Rock groundmass (matrix)

Radiating crystal mass of daisy gypsum

Radiating cyanotrichite crystals

CYANOTRICHITE
$u_4Al_2(SO_4)(OH)_{12}.2H_2O)$

DAISY GYPSUM
$(CaSO_4.2H_2O)$

MOLYBDATE

Tabular wulfenite crystal

Dark rock groundmass (matrix)

WULFENITE
$(PbMoO_4)$

SILICATES

Feldspar groundmass (matrix)

Transparent bicolored tourmaline crystal

Dodecahedral sodalite crystal

SODALITE
$(Na_8Al_6Si_6O_{24}Cl_2)$

Striated surface of olivine crystal

TOURMALINE
$(Na(Mg,Fe,Li,Mn,Al)_3Al_6(BO_3)_3Si_6.O_{18}(OH,F)_4)$

OLIVINE
$(Fe_2SiO_4 - Mg_2SiO_4)$

Striated prismatic epidote crystal

Tabular muscovite crystal

EPIDOTE
$(Ca_2(Al,Fe)_3(SiO_4)_3(OH))$

Orthoclase crystal

MUSCOVITE
$(KAl_2(Si_3Al)O_{10}(OH,F)_2)$

ORTHOCLASE
$(KAlSi_3O_8)$

HALIDES

Cubic rock salt crystal

Cubic fluorite crystal

GREEN FLUORITE
(CaF_2)

ORANGE HALITE (ROCK SALT)
$(NaCl)$

Mineral features

MINERALS CAN BE IDENTIFIED BY STUDYING features such as fracture, cleavage, crystal system, habit, hardness, colour, and streak. Minerals can break in different ways. If a mineral breaks in an irregular way, leaving rough surfaces, it possesses fracture. If a mineral breaks along well-defined planes of weakness, it possesses cleavage. Specific minerals have distinctive patterns of cleavage; for example, mica cleaves along one plane. Most minerals form crystals, which can be categorized into crystal systems according to their symmetry and number of faces. Within each system, several different but related forms of crystal are possible; for example, a cubic crystal can have six, eight, or twelve sides. A mineral's habit is the typical form taken by an aggregate of its crystals. Examples of habit include botryoidal (like a bunch of grapes) and massive (no definite form). The relative hardness of a mineral may be assessed by testing its resistance to scratching. This property is usually measured using Mohs scale, which increases in hardness from 1 (talc) to 10 (diamond). The colour of a mineral is not a dependable guide to its identity as some minerals have a range of colours. Streak (the colour the powdered mineral makes when rubbed across an unglazed tile) is a more reliable indicator.

CLEAVAGE

Cleavage in one direction

CLEAVAGE ALONG ONE PLANE

Cleavage in three directions, forming a block cube

CLEAVAGE ALONG THREE PLANES

Horizontal cleavage

Vertical cleavage

CLEAVAGE ALONG TWO PLANES

Cleavage in four directions, forming a double-pyramid crystal

CLEAVAGE ALONG FOUR PLANES

CRYSTAL SYSTEMS

Cubic iron pyrites crystal

Tetragonal idocrase crystal

Representation of tetragonal system

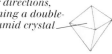

TETRAGONAL SYSTEM

CUBIC SYSTEM

Representation of cubic system

Hexagonal beryl crystal

Representation of hexagonal/trigonal system

HEXAGONAL/TRIGONAL SYSTEM

Orthorhombic barytes crystal

Representation of orthorhombic system

ORTHORHOMBIC SYSTEM

FRACTURE

Fire opal with conchoidal (shell-like) fracture

Nickel-iron with hackly (jagged) fracture

CONCHOIDAL FRACTURE

HACKLY FRACTURE

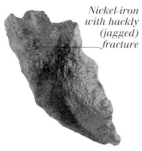

Orpiment with uneven fracture

Garnierite with splintery fracture

UNEVEN FRACTURE

SPLINTERY FRACTURE

Monoclinic selenite crystal

Representation of monoclinic system

MONOCLINIC SYSTEM

Representation of triclinic system

Triclinic axinite crystal

TRICLINIC SYSTEM

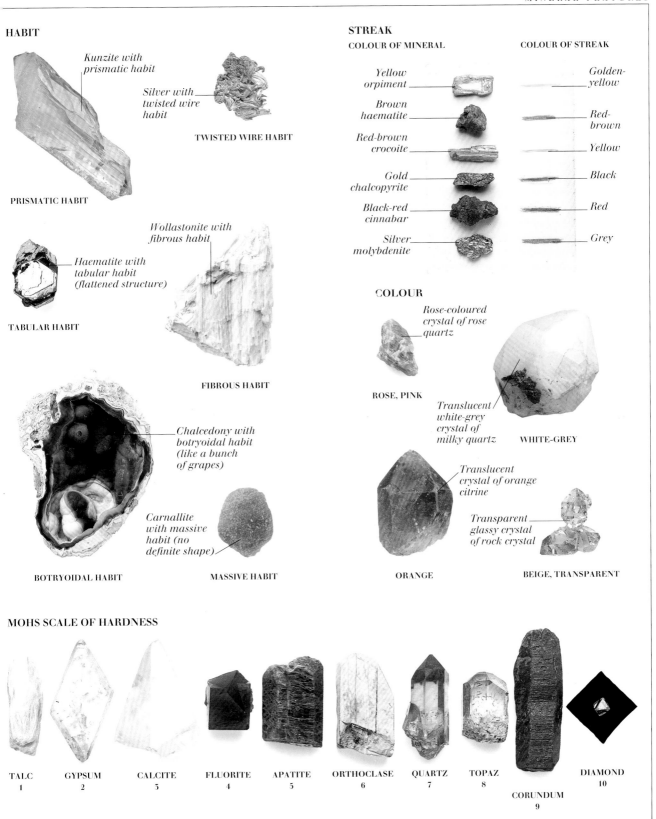

HABIT

Kunzite with prismatic habit

Silver with twisted wire habit

TWISTED WIRE HABIT

PRISMATIC HABIT

Haematite with tabular habit (flattened structure)

Wollastonite with fibrous habit

TABULAR HABIT

FIBROUS HABIT

Chalcedony with botryoidal habit (like a bunch of grapes)

Carnallite with massive habit (no definite shape)

BOTRYOIDAL HABIT

MASSIVE HABIT

STREAK

COLOUR OF MINERAL

Yellow orpiment

Brown haematite

Red-brown crocoite

Gold chalcopyrite

Black-red cinnabar

Silver molybdenite

COLOUR OF STREAK

Golden-yellow

Red-brown

Yellow

Black

Red

Grey

COLOUR

Rose-coloured crystal of rose quartz

ROSE, PINK

Translucent white-grey crystal of milky quartz

WHITE-GREY

Translucent crystal of orange citrine

Transparent glassy crystal of rock crystal

ORANGE

BEIGE, TRANSPARENT

MOHS SCALE OF HARDNESS

TALC
1

GYPSUM
2

CALCITE
3

FLUORITE
4

APATITE
5

ORTHOCLASE
6

QUARTZ
7

TOPAZ
8

CORUNDUM
9

DIAMOND
10

271

Volcanoes

Folded, rope-like surface

PAHOEHOE (ROPY LAVA)

VOLCANOES ARE VENTS OR FISSURES in the Earth's crust through which magma (molten rock that originates from deep beneath the crust) is forced on to the surface as lava. They occur most commonly along the boundaries of crustal plates; most volcanoes lie in a belt called the "Ring of Fire", which runs along the edge of the Pacific Ocean. Volcanoes can be classified according to the violence and frequency of their eruptions. Non-explosive volcanic eruptions generally occur where crustal plates pull apart. These eruptions produce runny basaltic lava that spreads quickly over a wide area to form relatively flat cones. The most violent eruptions take place where plates collide. Such eruptions produce thick rhyolitic lava and may also blast out clouds of dust and pyroclasts (lava fragments). The lava does not flow far before cooling and therefore builds up steep-sided, conical volcanoes. Some volcanoes produce lava and ash eruptions, which build up composite volcanic cones. Volcanoes that erupt frequently are described as active; those that erupt rarely are termed dormant; and those that have stopped erupting altogether are termed extinct. As well as the volcanoes themselves, other features associated with volcanic regions include geysers, hot mineral springs, solfataras, fumaroles, and bubbling mud pools.

HORU GEYSER, NEW ZEALAND

VOLCANO TYPES

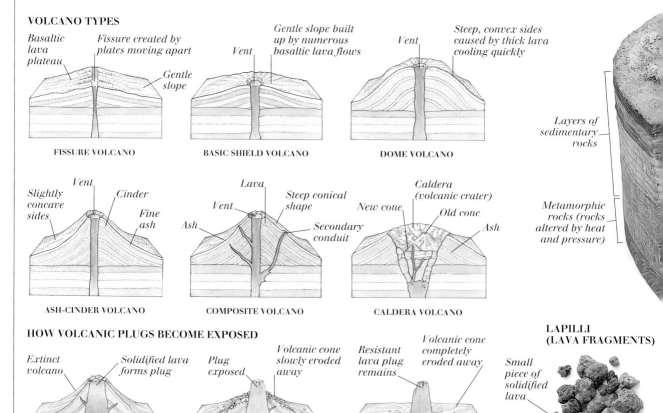

Basaltic lava plateau

Fissure created by plates moving apart

Gentle slope

FISSURE VOLCANO

Gentle slope built up by numerous basaltic lava flows

Vent

BASIC SHIELD VOLCANO

Vent

Steep, convex sides caused by thick lava cooling quickly

DOME VOLCANO

Slightly concave sides

Vent

Cinder

Fine ash

ASH-CINDER VOLCANO

Lava

Vent

Steep conical shape

Ash

Secondary conduit

COMPOSITE VOLCANO

Caldera (volcanic crater)

New cone

Old cone

Ash

CALDERA VOLCANO

Layers of sedimentary rocks

Metamorphic rocks (rocks altered by heat and pressure)

HOW VOLCANIC PLUGS BECOME EXPOSED

Extinct volcano

Solidified lava forms plug

PLUG FORMATION

Plug exposed

Volcanic cone slowly eroded away

INITIAL EROSION AROUND PLUG

Resistant lava plug remains

Volcanic cone completely eroded away

COMPLETE DENUDATION OF PLUG

LAPILLI (LAVA FRAGMENTS)

Small piece of solidified lava

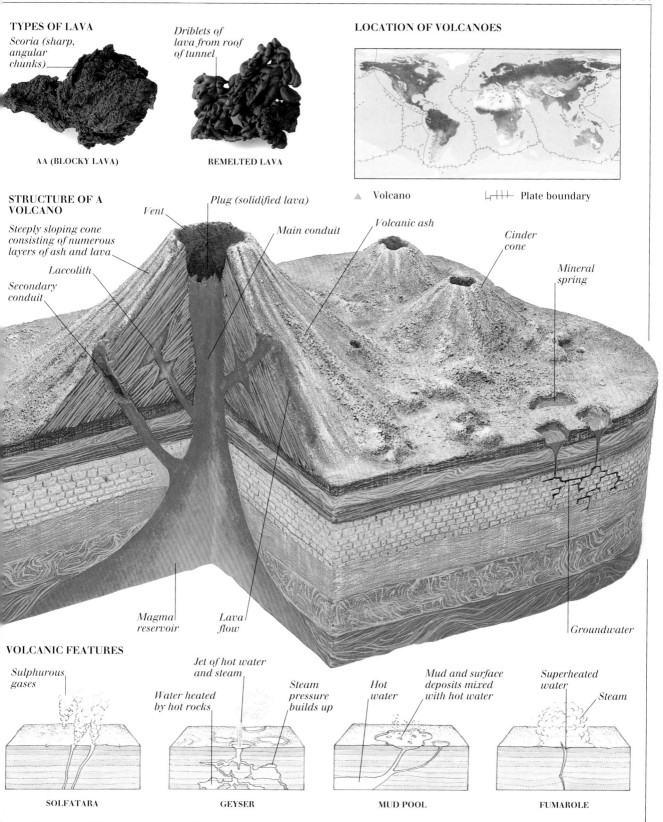

TYPES OF LAVA

Scoria (sharp, angular chunks)

Driblets of lava from roof of tunnel

AA (BLOCKY LAVA)

REMELTED LAVA

LOCATION OF VOLCANOES

▲ Volcano

Plate boundary

STRUCTURE OF A VOLCANO

Steeply sloping cone consisting of numerous layers of ash and lava

Vent

Plug (solidified lava)

Main conduit

Volcanic ash

Cinder cone

Mineral spring

Laccolith

Secondary conduit

Magma reservoir

Lava flow

Groundwater

VOLCANIC FEATURES

Sulphurous gases

Jet of hot water and steam

Water heated by hot rocks

Steam pressure builds up

Hot water

Mud and surface deposits mixed with hot water

Superheated water

Steam

SOLFATARA

GEYSER

MUD POOL

FUMAROLE

Igneous and metamorphic rocks

IGNEOUS ROCKS ARE FORMED WHEN MAGMA (molten rock that originates from deep beneath the Earth's crust) cools and solidifies. There are two main types of igneous rock: intrusive and extrusive. Intrusive rocks are formed deep underground where magma is forced into cracks or between rock layers to form structures such as sills, dykes, and batholiths. The magma cools slowly to form coarse-grained rocks such as gabbro and pegmatite. Extrusive rocks are formed above the Earth's surface from lava (magma that has been ejected in a volcanic eruption). The molten lava cools quickly, producing fine-grained rocks such as rhyolite and basalt. Metamorphic rocks are those that have been altered by intense heat (contact metamorphism) or extreme pressure (regional metamorphism). Contact metamorphism occurs when rocks are changed by heat from, for example, an igneous intrusion or lava flow. Regional metamorphism occurs when rock is crushed in the middle of a folding mountain range. Metamorphic rocks can be formed from igneous rocks, sedimentary rocks, or even from other metamorphic rocks.

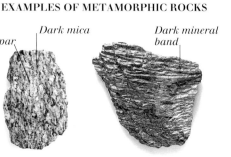

Cinder cone

Large eroded lava flow

Cedar-tree laccolith

Butte

Plug

Cone sheet

Ring dyke

Batholith

Dyke

Sill

Dyke swarm

Lopolith

IGNEOUS ROCK STRUCTURES

CONTACT METAMORPHISM

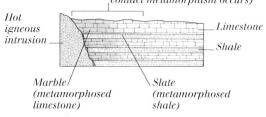

Metamorphic aureole (region where contact metamorphism occurs)

Hot igneous intrusion

Limestone

Shale

Marble (metamorphosed limestone)

Slate (metamorphosed shale)

REGIONAL METAMORPHISM

Mountain range

Slate, formed under low pressure and temperature

Compression

Compression

Schist, formed under medium pressure and temperature

Crust

Gneiss, formed under high pressure and temperature

Mantle

Magma

EXAMPLES OF METAMORPHIC ROCKS

Pale feldspar

Dark mica

Dark mineral band

Pale calcite

GNEISS

FOLDED SCHIST

SKARN

EXAMPLES OF EXTRUSIVE IGNEOUS ROCKS

Porphyritic texture

Fine-grained crystals

Elongated vesicles (gas cavities)

Fine-grained groundmass (matrix)

Conchoidal fracture

Glassy lustre

RHYOLITE

BASALT

PUMICE

PORPHYRITIC ANDESITE

OBSIDIAN

Mesa (flat-topped plateau)

Extinct geyser

Lake

Caldera

Sea

Lava flow

Vent

Active juvenile volcano

Parasitic volcano

Main conduit

Sagging caused by weight of volcano

Batholith

Laccolith

Eroded plug of extinct volcano

Magma reservoir

EXAMPLES OF INTRUSIVE IGNEOUS ROCKS

Dark groundmass (matrix)

KIMBERLITE

Plagioclase feldspar

OLIVINE GABBRO

Amphibole crystals

White feldspar

FELDSPAR PEGMATITE

Fine groundmass (matrix)

Pyrites crystal

Chiastolite crystal

Green calc-silicate mineral

High quartz content

Amphibole crystal

SLATE WITH PYRITES

CHIASTOLITE HORNFELS

GREEN MARBLE

HALLEFLINTA

SYENITE

Sedimentary rocks

SEDIMENTARY ROCKS ARE FORMED BY THE ACCUMULATION and consolidation of sediments (see pp. 266-267). There are three main types of sedimentary rock. Clastic sedimentary rocks, such as breccia or sandstone, are formed from other rocks that have been broken down into fragments by weathering (see pp. 282-283), which have then been transported and deposited elsewhere. Organic sedimentary rocks – for example, coal (see pp. 280-281) – are derived from plant and animal remains. Chemical sedimentary rocks are formed by chemical processes. For example, rock salt is formed when salt dissolved in water is deposited as the water evaporates. Sedimentary rocks are laid down in layers, called beds or strata. Each new layer is laid down horizontally over older ones. There are usually some gaps in the sequence, called unconformities. These represent periods in which no new sediments were being laid down, or when earlier sedimentary layers were raised above sea level and eroded away.

THE GRAND CANYON, USA

see pp. 266-267; see pp. 282-283; see pp. 280-281

EXAMPLES OF UNCONFORMITIES

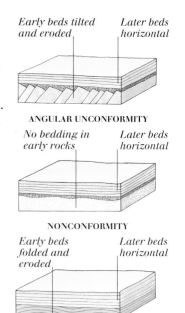

Early beds tilted and eroded   Later beds horizontal

ANGULAR UNCONFORMITY

No bedding in early rocks   Later beds horizontal

NONCONFORMITY

Early beds folded and eroded   Later beds horizontal

DISCONFORMITY

SEDIMENTARY LAYERS OF THE GRAND CANYON REGION

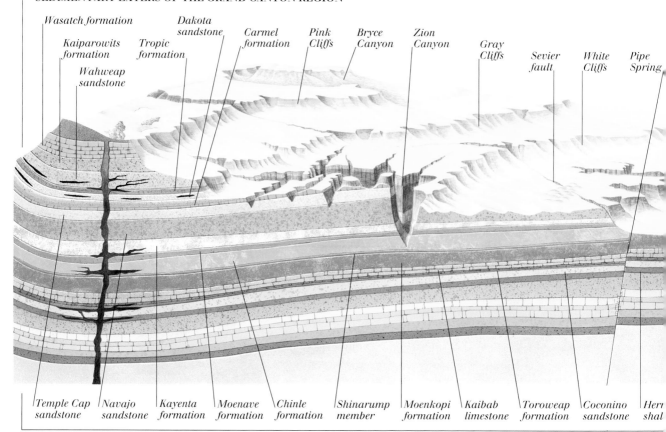

Wasatch formation
Kaiparowits formation
Tropic formation
Dakota sandstone
Carmel formation
Pink Cliffs
Bryce Canyon
Zion Canyon
Gray Cliffs
Sevier fault
White Cliffs
Pipe Spring
Wahweap sandstone

Temple Cap sandstone
Navajo sandstone
Kayenta formation
Moenave formation
Chinle formation
Shinarump member
Moenkopi formation
Kaibab limestone
Toroweap formation
Coconino sandstone
Herr shal

EXAMPLES OF SEDIMENTARY ROCKS

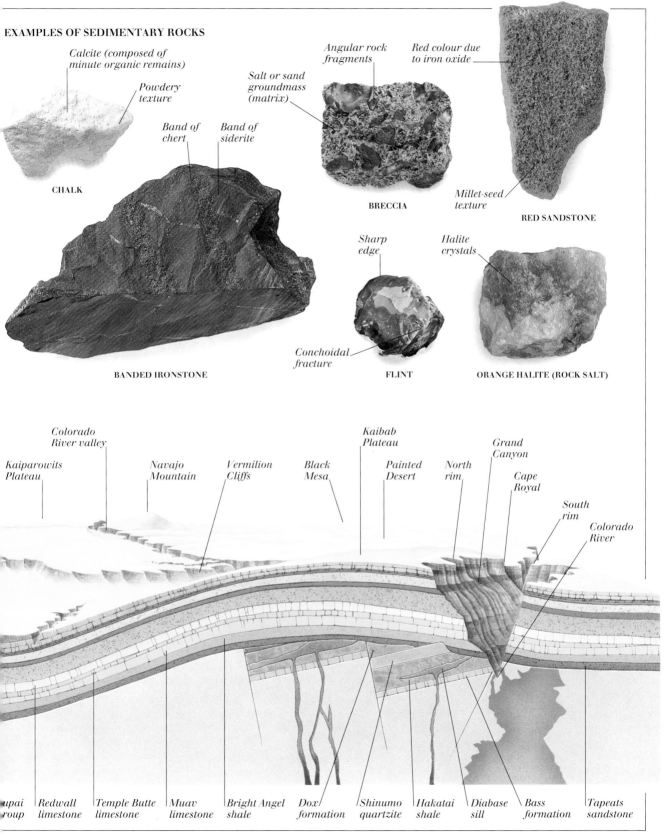

Calcite (composed of minute organic remains)

Powdery texture

CHALK

Band of chert

Band of siderite

BANDED IRONSTONE

Angular rock fragments

Salt or sand groundmass (matrix)

Red colour due to iron oxide

BRECCIA

Millet-seed texture

RED SANDSTONE

Sharp edge

Halite crystals

Conchoidal fracture

FLINT

ORANGE HALITE (ROCK SALT)

Colorado River valley

Kaibab Plateau

Grand Canyon

Kaiparowits Plateau

Navajo Mountain

Vermilion Cliffs

Black Mesa

Painted Desert

North rim

Cape Royal

South rim

Colorado River

upai roup

Redwall limestone

Temple Butte limestone

Muav limestone

Bright Angel shale

Dox formation

Shinumo quartzite

Hakatai shale

Diabase sill

Bass formation

Tapeats sandstone

Fossils

FOSSILS ARE THE REMAINS of plants and animals that have been preserved in rock. A fossil may be the preserved remains of an organism itself, an impression of it in rock, or preserved traces (known as trace fossils) left by an organism while it was alive, such as organic carbon outlines, fossilized footprints, or droppings. Most dead organisms soon rot away or are eaten by scavengers. For fossilization to occur, rapid burial by sediment is necessary. The organism decays, but the harder parts – bones, teeth, and shells, for example – may be preserved and hardened by minerals from the surrounding sediment. Fossilization may also occur even when the hard parts of an organism are dissolved away to leave an impression called a mould. The mould is filled by minerals, thereby creating a cast of the organism. The study of fossils (palaeontology) can not only show how living things have evolved, but can also help to reveal the Earth's geological history – for example, by aiding in the dating of rock strata.

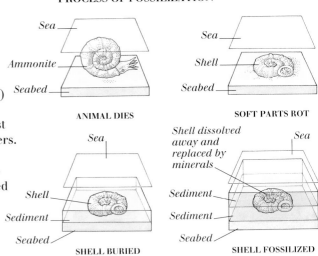

PROCESS OF FOSSILIZATION

Sea — *Ammonite* — *Seabed* —
ANIMAL DIES

Sea — *Shell* — *Seabed* —
SOFT PARTS ROT

Sea — *Shell* — *Sediment* — *Seabed* —
SHELL BURIED

Shell dissolved away and replaced by minerals — *Sea* — *Sediment* — *Sediment* — *Seabed* —
SHELL FOSSILIZED

EXAMPLES OF FOSSILS

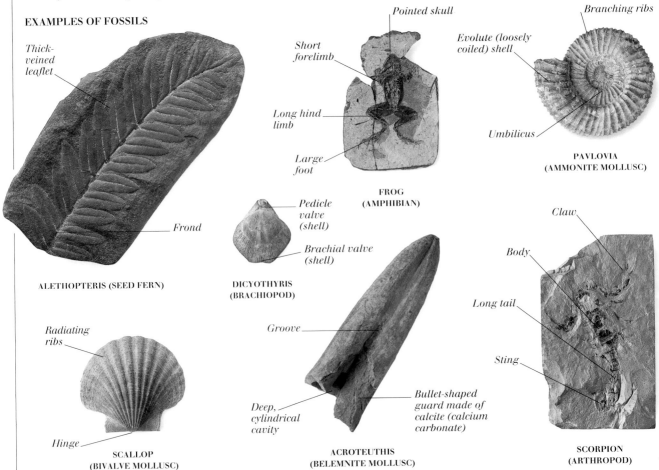

Thick-veined leaflet

Frond

ALETHOPTERIS (SEED FERN)

Radiating ribs

Hinge

SCALLOP (BIVALVE MOLLUSC)

Pointed skull

Short forelimb

Long hind limb

Large foot

FROG (AMPHIBIAN)

Pedicle valve (shell)

Brachial valve (shell)

DICYOTHYRIS (BRACHIOPOD)

Groove

Deep, cylindrical cavity

Bullet-shaped guard made of calcite (calcium carbonate)

ACROTEUTHIS (BELEMNITE MOLLUSC)

Branching ribs

Evolute (loosely coiled) shell

Umbilicus

PAVLOVIA (AMMONITE MOLLUSC)

Claw

Body

Long tail

Sting

SCORPION (ARTHROPOD)

278

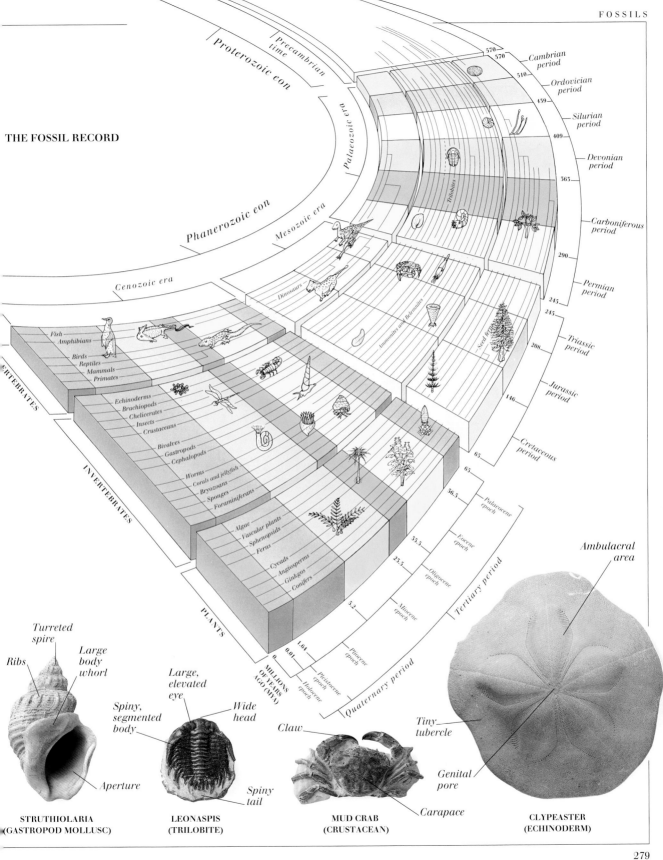

THE FOSSIL RECORD

Precambrian time

Proterozoic eon

Palaeozoic era

Phanerozoic eon

Mesozoic era

Cenozoic era

Cambrian period — 570 — 570
Ordovician period — 510
Silurian period — 439
Devonian period — 409
Carboniferous period — 363
Permian period — 290
Triassic period — 245 — 245
Jurassic period — 208
Cretaceous period — 146 — 65
Tertiary period
Palaeocene epoch — 65
Eocene epoch — 36.5
Oligocene epoch — 55.5
Miocene epoch — 25.5
Pliocene epoch — 5.2
Quaternary period
Pleistocene epoch — 1.64
Holocene epoch — 0.01

Trilobites

Dinosaurs

Ammonites and belemnites

Seed ferns

VERTEBRATES

Fish
Amphibians
Birds
Reptiles
Mammals
Primates

INVERTEBRATES

Echinoderms
Brachiopods
Chelicerates
Insects
Crustaceans
Bivalves
Gastropods
Cephalopods
Worms
Corals and jellyfish
Bryozoans
Sponges
Foraminiferans

PLANTS

Algae
Vascular plants
Sphenopsids
Ferns
Cycads
Angiosperms
Ginkgos
Conifers

MILLIONS OF YEARS AGO (MYA)
0

Turreted spire
Ribs
Large body whorl
Aperture

STRUTHIOLARIA (GASTROPOD MOLLUSC)

Large, elevated eye
Spiny, segmented body
Wide head
Spiny tail

LEONASPIS (TRILOBITE)

Claw
Carapace

MUD CRAB (CRUSTACEAN)

Ambulacral area
Tiny tubercle
Genital pore

CLYPEASTER (ECHINODERM)

279

Mineral resources

Stalk

Leaf

PLANT MATTER

MINERAL RESOURCES CAN BE DEFINED AS naturally occurring substances that can be extracted from the Earth and are useful as fuels and raw materials. Coal, oil, and gas – collectively called fossil fuels – are commonly included in this group, but are not strictly minerals, because they are of organic origin. Coal formation begins when vegetation is buried and partly decomposed to form peat. Overlying sediments compress the peat and transform it into lignite (soft brown coal). As the overlying sediments

OIL RIG, NORTH SEA

accumulate, increasing pressure and temperature eventually transform the lignite into bituminous and hard anthracite coals. Oil and gas are usually formed from organic matter that was deposited in marine sediments. Under the effects of heat and pressure, the compressed organic matter undergoes complex chemical changes to form oil and gas. The oil and gas percolate upwards through water-saturated, permeable rocks and they may rise to the Earth's surface or accumulate below an impermeable layer of rock that has been folded or faulted to form a trap – an anticline (upfold) trap, for example. Minerals are inorganic substances that may consist of a single chemical element, such as gold, silver, or copper, or combinations of elements (see pp. 268-269). Some minerals are concentrated in mineralization zones in rock associated with crustal movements or volcanic activity. Others may be found in sediments as placer deposits – accumulations of high-density minerals that have been weathered out of rocks, transported, and deposited (on river-beds, for example).

Decayed plant matter

About 60% carbon

PEAT

About 70% carbon

Crumbly texture

LIGNITE (BROWN COAL)

Powdery texture

About 80% carbon

BITUMINOUS COAL

About 95% carbon

Shiny surface

HOW COAL IS FORMED

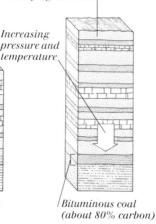

Increasing layers of overlying sediment

Vegetation

Increasing layers of overlying sediment

Increasing pressure and temperature

Increasing pressure and temperature

Increasing pressure and temperature

Peat (about 60% carbon)

PEAT

Lignite (about 70% carbon)

LIGNITE (BROWN COAL)

Bituminous coal (about 80% carbon)

BITUMINOUS COAL

ANTHRACITE COAL

EXAMPLES OF OIL AND GAS TRAPS

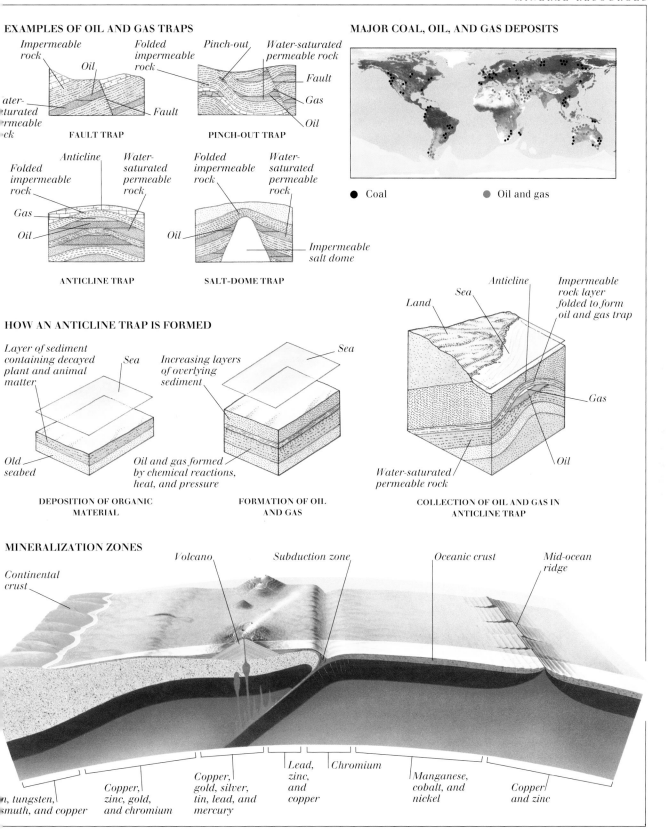

Impermeable rock

Oil

Water-saturated permeable rock

Fault

FAULT TRAP

Pinch-out

Folded impermeable rock

Water-saturated permeable rock

Fault

Gas

Oil

PINCH-OUT TRAP

Folded impermeable rock

Anticline

Water-saturated permeable rock

Gas

Oil

ANTICLINE TRAP

Folded impermeable rock

Water-saturated permeable rock

Oil

Impermeable salt dome

SALT-DOME TRAP

MAJOR COAL, OIL, AND GAS DEPOSITS

● Coal   ● Oil and gas

HOW AN ANTICLINE TRAP IS FORMED

Layer of sediment containing decayed plant and animal matter

Sea

Old seabed

DEPOSITION OF ORGANIC MATERIAL

Increasing layers of overlying sediment

Sea

Oil and gas formed by chemical reactions, heat, and pressure

FORMATION OF OIL AND GAS

Land

Sea

Anticline

Impermeable rock layer folded to form oil and gas trap

Gas

Oil

Water-saturated permeable rock

COLLECTION OF OIL AND GAS IN ANTICLINE TRAP

MINERALIZATION ZONES

Continental crust

Volcano

Subduction zone

Oceanic crust

Mid-ocean ridge

n, tungsten, smuth, and copper

Copper, zinc, gold, and chromium

Copper, gold, silver, tin, lead, and mercury

Lead, zinc, and copper

Chromium

Manganese, cobalt, and nickel

Copper and zinc

281

Weathering and erosion

WEATHERING IS THE BREAKING DOWN of rocks on the Earth's surface. There are two main types: physical (or mechanical) and chemical. Physical weathering may be caused by temperature changes, such as freezing and thawing, or by abrasion from material carried by winds, rivers, or glaciers. Rocks may also be broken down by the actions of animals and plants, such as the burrowing of animals and the growth of roots. Chemical weathering causes rocks to decompose by changing their chemical composition – for example, rainwater may dissolve certain minerals in a rock. Erosion is the wearing away and removal of land surfaces by water, wind, or ice. It is greatest in areas of little or no surface vegetation, such as deserts, where sand dunes may form.

FORMATION OF A HAMADA (ROCK PAVEMENT)

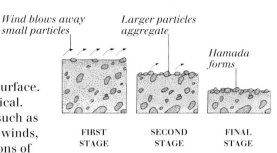

Wind blows away small particles

Larger particles aggregate

Hamada forms

FIRST STAGE

SECOND STAGE

FINAL STAGE

FEATURES OF WEATHERING AND EROSION

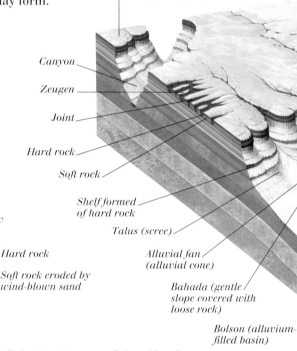

Mesa (flat-topped plateau)

Canyon

Zeugen

Joint

Hard rock

Soft rock

Shelf formed of hard rock

Talus (scree)

Alluvial fan (alluvial cone)

Bahada (gentle slope covered with loose rock)

Bolson (alluvium-filled basin)

FEATURES PRODUCED BY WIND ACTION

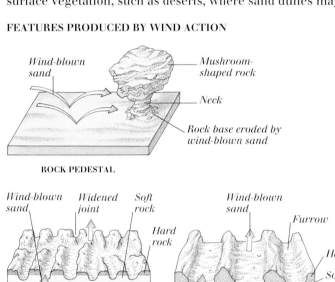

Wind-blown sand

Mushroom-shaped rock

Neck

Rock base eroded by wind-blown sand

ROCK PEDESTAL

Wind-blown sand

Widened joint

Soft rock

Hard rock

ZEUGEN

Wind-blown sand

Furrow

Hard rock

Soft rock eroded by wind-blown sand

YARDANG

EXAMPLES OF PHYSICAL WEATHERING PROCESSES

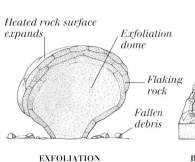

Heated rock surface expands

Exfoliation dome

Flaking rock

Fallen debris

EXFOLIATION (ONION-SKIN WEATHERING)

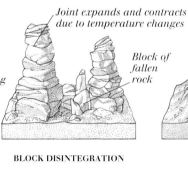

Joint expands and contracts due to temperature changes

Block of fallen rock

BLOCK DISINTEGRATION

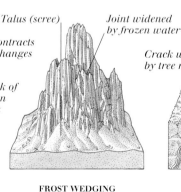

Talus (scree)

Joint widened by frozen water

FROST WEDGING

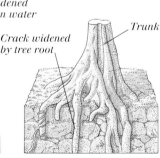

Trunk

Crack widened by tree root

TREE ROOT ACTION

SECTION THROUGH A BARKHAN DUNE

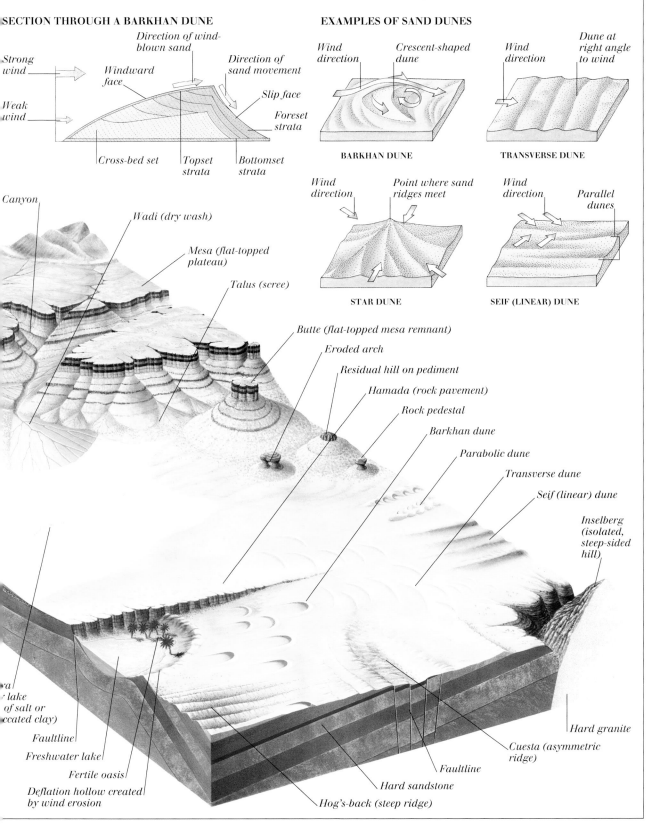

Strong wind

Weak wind

Direction of wind-blown sand

Windward face

Direction of sand movement

Slip face

Foreset strata

Cross-bed set

Topset strata

Bottomset strata

EXAMPLES OF SAND DUNES

Wind direction

Crescent-shaped dune

BARKHAN DUNE

Wind direction

Dune at right angle to wind

TRANSVERSE DUNE

Wind direction

Point where sand ridges meet

STAR DUNE

Wind direction

Parallel dunes

SEIF (LINEAR) DUNE

Canyon

Wadi (dry wash)

Mesa (flat-topped plateau)

Talus (scree)

Butte (flat-topped mesa remnant)

Eroded arch

Residual hill on pediment

Hamada (rock pavement)

Rock pedestal

Barkhan dune

Parabolic dune

Transverse dune

Seif (linear) dune

Inselberg (isolated, steep-sided hill)

Playa (dry lake of salt or desiccated clay)

Faultline

Freshwater lake

Fertile oasis

Deflation hollow created by wind erosion

Hard granite

Cuesta (asymmetric ridge)

Faultline

Hard sandstone

Hog's-back (steep ridge)

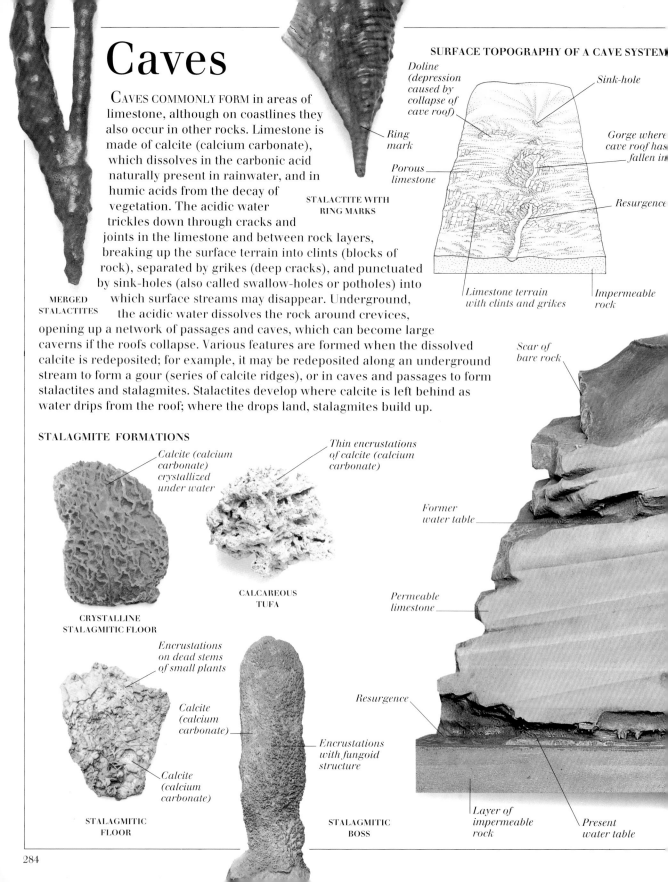

Caves

CAVES COMMONLY FORM in areas of limestone, although on coastlines they also occur in other rocks. Limestone is made of calcite (calcium carbonate), which dissolves in the carbonic acid naturally present in rainwater, and in humic acids from the decay of vegetation. The acidic water trickles down through cracks and joints in the limestone and between rock layers, breaking up the surface terrain into clints (blocks of rock), separated by grikes (deep cracks), and punctuated by sink-holes (also called swallow-holes or potholes) into which surface streams may disappear. Underground, the acidic water dissolves the rock around crevices, opening up a network of passages and caves, which can become large caverns if the roofs collapse. Various features are formed when the dissolved calcite is redeposited; for example, it may be redeposited along an underground stream to form a gour (series of calcite ridges), or in caves and passages to form stalactites and stalagmites. Stalactites develop where calcite is left behind as water drips from the roof; where the drops land, stalagmites build up.

MERGED STALACTITES

STALACTITE WITH RING MARKS

Ring mark

SURFACE TOPOGRAPHY OF A CAVE SYSTEM

Doline (depression caused by collapse of cave roof)

Sink-hole

Gorge where cave roof has fallen in

Porous limestone

Resurgence

Limestone terrain with clints and grikes

Impermeable rock

STALAGMITE FORMATIONS

Calcite (calcium carbonate) crystallized under water

Thin encrustations of calcite (calcium carbonate)

Scar of bare rock

CRYSTALLINE STALAGMITIC FLOOR

CALCAREOUS TUFA

Former water table

Permeable limestone

Encrustations on dead stems of small plants

Calcite (calcium carbonate)

Calcite (calcium carbonate)

Encrustations with fungoid structure

Resurgence

STALAGMITIC FLOOR

STALAGMITIC BOSS

Layer of impermeable rock

Present water table

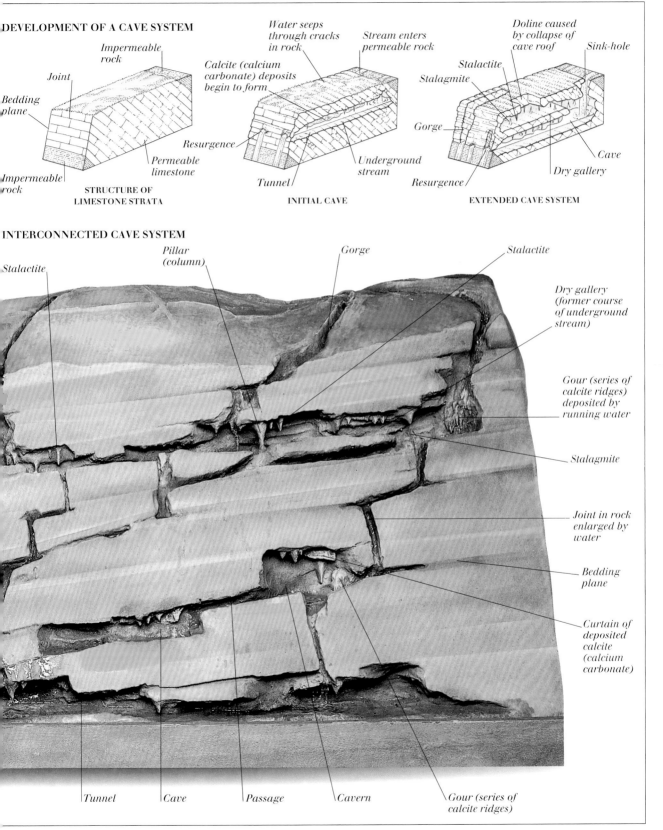

DEVELOPMENT OF A CAVE SYSTEM

STRUCTURE OF LIMESTONE STRATA

Impermeable rock

Joint

Bedding plane

Impermeable rock

Permeable limestone

INITIAL CAVE

Water seeps through cracks in rock

Stream enters permeable rock

Calcite (calcium carbonate) deposits begin to form

Resurgence

Tunnel

Underground stream

EXTENDED CAVE SYSTEM

Doline caused by collapse of cave roof

Sink-hole

Stalactite

Stalagmite

Gorge

Resurgence

Cave

Dry gallery

INTERCONNECTED CAVE SYSTEM

Stalactite

Pillar (column)

Gorge

Stalactite

Dry gallery (former course of underground stream)

Gour (series of calcite ridges) deposited by running water

Stalagmite

Joint in rock enlarged by water

Bedding plane

Curtain of deposited calcite (calcium carbonate)

Tunnel

Cave

Passage

Cavern

Gour (series of calcite ridges)

Glaciers

GLACIER BAY, ALASKA

A VALLEY GLACIER IS A LARGE MASS OF ICE that forms on land and moves slowly downhill under its own weight. It is formed from snow that collects in cirques (mountain hollows also known as corries) and compresses into ice as more and more snow accumulates. The cirque is deepened by frost wedging and abrasion (see pp. 282-283), and arêtes (sharp ridges) develop between adjacent cirques. Eventually, so much ice builds up that the glacier begins to move downhill. As the glacier moves it collects moraine (debris), which may range in size from particles of dust to large boulders. The rocks at the base of the glacier erode the glacial valley, giving it a U-shaped cross-section. Under the glacier, *roches moutonnées* (eroded outcrops of hard rock) and drumlins (rounded mounds of rock and clay) are left behind on the valley floor. The glacier ends at a terminus (the snout), where the ice melts as fast as it arrives. If the temperature increases, the ice melts faster than it arrives, and the glacier retreats. The retreating glacier leaves behind its moraine and also erratics (isolated single boulders). Glacial streams from the melting glacier deposit eskers and kames (ridges and mounds of sand and gravel), but carry away the finer sediment to form a stratified outwash plain. Lumps of ice carried on to this plain melt, creating holes called kettles.

VALLEY GLACIER

POST-GLACIAL VALLEY

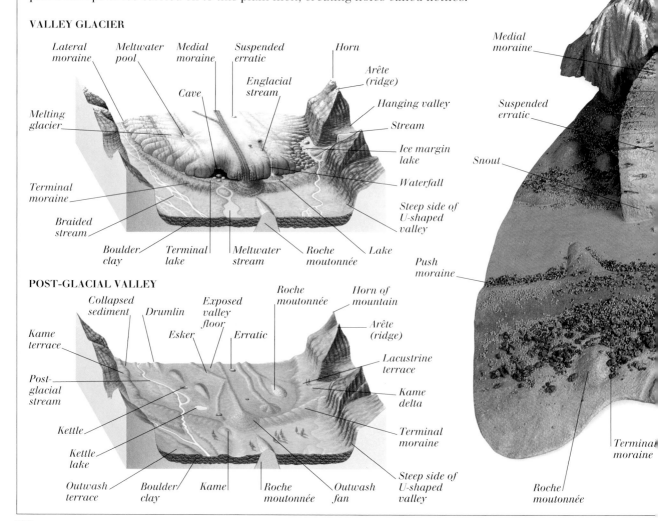

FEATURES OF A GLACIER

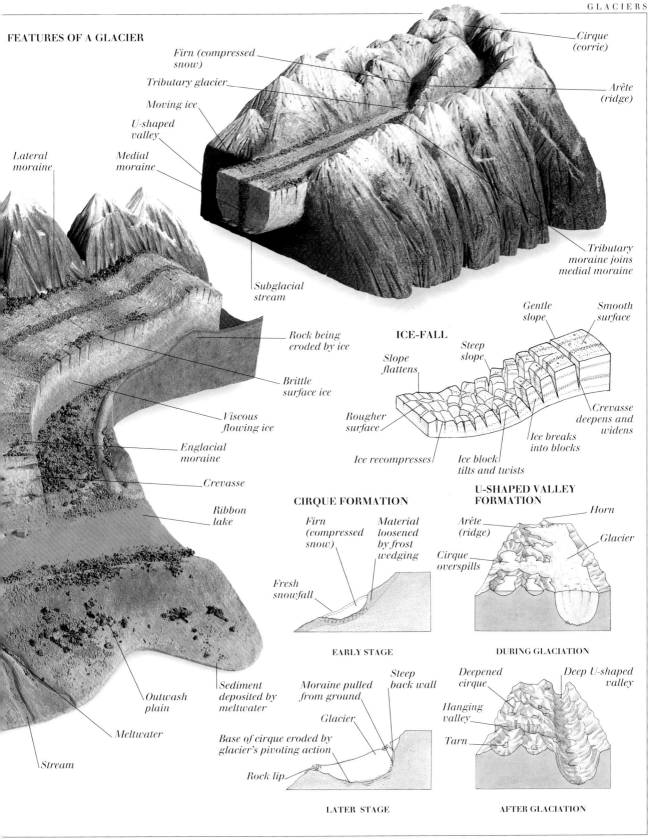

Firn (compressed snow)

Tributary glacier

Moving ice

U-shaped valley

Medial moraine

Lateral moraine

Cirque (corrie)

Arête (ridge)

Tributary moraine joins medial moraine

Subglacial stream

Rock being eroded by ice

Brittle surface ice

Viscous flowing ice

Englacial moraine

Crevasse

Ribbon lake

Outwash plain

Sediment deposited by meltwater

Meltwater

Stream

ICE-FALL

Gentle slope

Smooth surface

Steep slope

Slope flattens

Rougher surface

Ice recompresses

Ice block tilts and twists

Ice breaks into blocks

Crevasse deepens and widens

CIRQUE FORMATION

Firn (compressed snow)

Material loosened by frost wedging

Fresh snowfall

EARLY STAGE

Moraine pulled from ground

Steep back wall

Glacier

Base of cirque eroded by glacier's pivoting action

Rock lip

LATER STAGE

U-SHAPED VALLEY FORMATION

Arête (ridge)

Horn

Glacier

Cirque overspills

DURING GLACIATION

Deepened cirque

Deep U-shaped valley

Hanging valley

Tarn

AFTER GLACIATION

Rivers

RIVERS FORM PART of the water cycle – the continuous circulation of water between the land, sea, and atmosphere. The source of a river may be a mountain spring or lake, or a melting glacier. The course that the river subsequently takes depends on the slope of the terrain and on the rock types and formations over which it flows. In its early, upland stages, a river tumbles steeply over rocks and boulders and cuts a steep-sided V-shaped valley. Farther downstream, it flows smoothly over sediments and forms winding meanders, eroding sideways to create broad valleys and plains. On reaching the coast, the river may deposit sediment to form an estuary or delta (see pp. 290-291).

RIVER CAPTURE

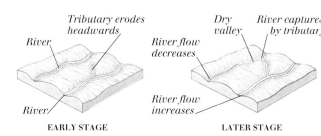

EARLY STAGE

River

Tributary erodes headwards

River

LATER STAGE

Dry valley

River capture by tributar

River flow decreases

River flow increases

THE WATER CYCLE

Precipitatio falls on hig grou

Wind

Wat carri downstrea by riv

Water vapour released into atmosphere by trees and other plants

Wind

Water vapour forms clouds

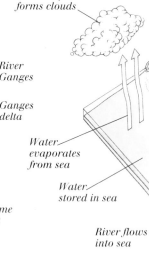

Water evaporates from sea

Water stored in sea

River flows into sea

Water see undergrou and flows to s

Water evaporates from lake

Water seeps underground and flows to sea

SATELLITE IMAGE OF GANGES RIVER DELTA, BANGLADESH

River Ganges

Ganges delta

Infertile swampland

Distributary

Large volume of sediment

RIVER DRAINAGE PATTERNS

RADIAL

CENTRIPETAL

PARALLEL

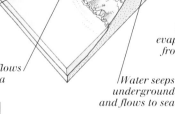

DENDRITIC

DERANGED

TRELLISED

ANNULAR

RECTANGULAR

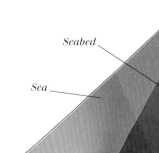

Seabed

Sea

Sediment layers

STAGES IN A RIVER'S DEVELOPMENT

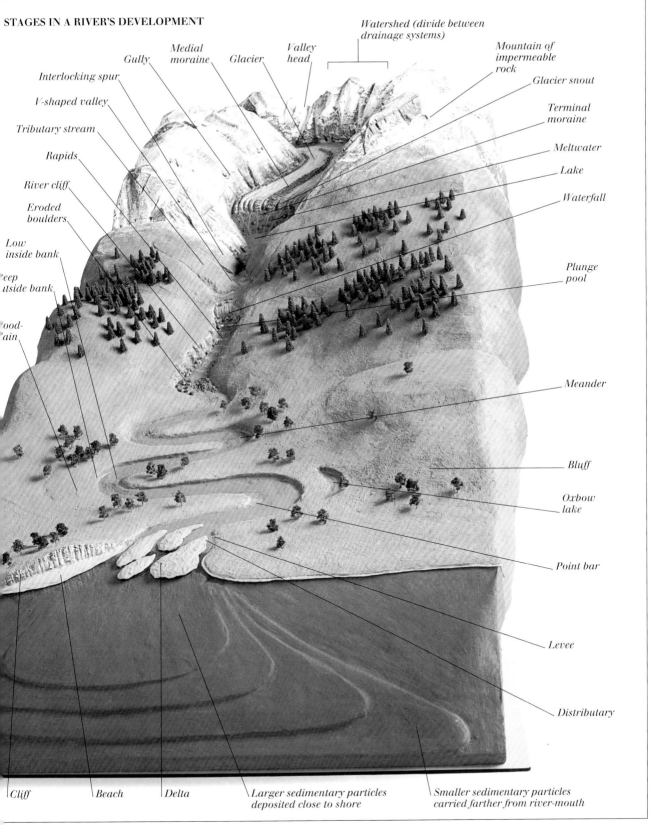

Watershed (divide between drainage systems)

Medial moraine

Gully

Glacier

Valley head

Interlocking spur

Mountain of impermeable rock

Glacier snout

V-shaped valley

Terminal moraine

Tributary stream

Meltwater

Rapids

Lake

River cliff

Waterfall

Eroded boulders

Plunge pool

Low inside bank

eep utside bank

ood- ain

Meander

Bluff

Oxbow lake

Point bar

Levee

Distributary

Cliff

Beach

Delta

Larger sedimentary particles deposited close to shore

Smaller sedimentary particles carried farther from river-mouth

River features

RIVERS ARE ONE OF THE MAJOR FORCES that shape the landscape. Near its source, a river is steep (see pp. 288-289). It erodes downwards, carving out V-shaped valleys and deep gorges. Waterfalls and rapids are formed where the river flows from hard rock to softer, more easily eroded rock. Farther downstream, meanders may form and there is greater sideways erosion, resulting in a broad river valley. The river sometimes erodes through the neck of a meander to form an oxbow lake. Sediment deposited on the valley floor by meandering rivers and during floods helps to create a flood-plain. Floods may also deposit sediment on the banks of the river to form levees. As a river spills into the sea or a lake, it deposits large amounts of sediment, and may form a delta. A delta is an area of sand-bars, swamps, and lagoons through which the river flows in several channels called distributaries – the Mississippi delta, for example. Often, a rise in sea level may have flooded the river-mouth to form a broad estuary, a tidal section where seawater mixes with fresh water.

HOW WATERFALLS AND RAPIDS ARE FORMED

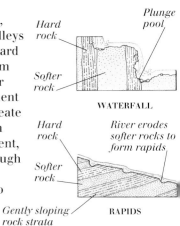

WATERFALL

RAPIDS

A RIVER VALLEY DRAINAGE SYSTEM

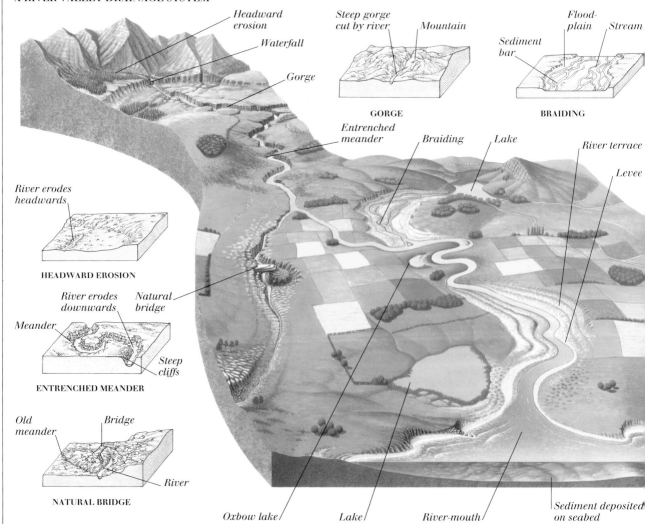

GORGE

BRAIDING

HEADWARD EROSION

ENTRENCHED MEANDER

NATURAL BRIDGE

WATERFALL FEATURES

Hard rock

Island

River

Hard rock

Rock undercut by swirling boulders

Plunge pool

Softer rock

Rock undercut by swirling boulders

Flood-plain

River

Levee formed from sediment deposited by floods

Sediment

LEVEE

River

Present flood-plain

Oldest terrace (remnant of previous flood-plain)

Sediment

RIVER TERRACE

Flood-plain

Bay

Sea-cliff

Sea

THE MISSISSIPPI DELTA

Mississippi River

Levee

Distributary

Point bar

Swamp

Sediment plume

Sea

Levee

Freshwater bay

Spit

Sediment plume

FORMATION OF A DELTA

Distributary

Lagoon

Sediment deposited by river

River

Levee

Sea

EARLY STAGE

Earliest deposit of sediment

Bedrock

Latest deposit of sediment

Sea

SECTION THROUGH DELTA

Distributary

Lagoon

Bar

Sediment deposited by river

River

Sea

Swamp formed by deposition of sediment in lagoon

Levee

Spit

MIDDLE STAGE

River

Sediment deposited by river

Distributary

Lagoon

Levee

Infilled swamp

Lagoon

Sea

LATE STAGE

Lakes and groundwater

NATURAL LAKES OCCUR WHERE a large quantity of water collects in a hollow in impermeable rock, or is prevented from draining away by a barrier, such as moraine (glacial deposits) or solidified lava. Lakes are often relatively short-lived landscape features, as they tend to become silted up by sediment from the streams and rivers that feed them. Some of the more long-lasting lakes are found in deep rift valleys formed by vertical movements of the Earth's crust (see pp. 58-59) – for example, Lake Baikal in Russia, the world's largest freshwater lake, and the Dead Sea in the Middle East, one of the world's saltiest lakes. Where water is able to drain away, it sinks into the ground until it reaches a layer of impermeable rock, then accumulates in the permeable rock above it; this water-saturated permeable rock is called an aquifer. The saturated zone varies in depth according to seasonal and climatic changes. In wet conditions, the water stored underground builds up, while in dry periods it becomes depleted. Where the upper edge of the saturated zone – the water table – meets the ground surface, water emerges as springs. In an artesian basin, where the aquifer is below an aquiclude (layer of impermeable rock), the water table throughout the basin is determined by its height at the rim. In the centre of such a basin, the water table is above ground level. The water in the basin is thus trapped below the water table and can rise under its own pressure along faultlines or well shafts.

LAKE BAIKAL, RUSSIA

EXAMPLES OF SPRINGS

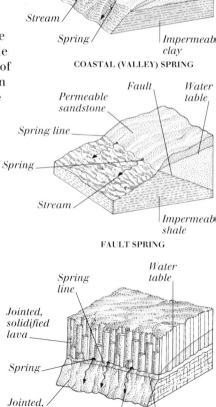

LIMESTONE SPRING

COASTAL (VALLEY) SPRING

FAULT SPRING

LAVA SPRING

STRUCTURE OF AN ARTESIAN BASIN

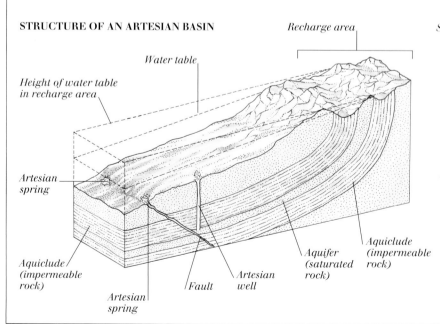

FEATURES OF A GROUNDWATER SYSTEM

Zone of aeration

Lake

Stream

Marsh

Layer of soil moisture

Zone of aeration

Capillary fringe

Water table

Saturated zone

CLOSE-UP OF SURFACE LAYER

Dry-season water table

Present water table (wet season)

Temporarily saturated zone (saturated only in wet season)

Permanently saturated zone (saturated in wet and dry seasons)

EXAMPLES OF LAKES

Glacial deposits

Lake in kettle (former site of ice block)

Oxbow lake (cut-off river meander)

River

KETTLE LAKE

OXBOW LAKE

Caldera (collapsed crater)

Volcanic lake

Movement along strike-slip (lateral) fault

Strike-slip (lateral) fault

Lake in elongated hollow

VOLCANIC LAKE

STRIKE-SLIP (LATERAL) FAULT LAKE

Rift valley

Steep back wall eroded by frost and ice

Moraine or rock lip damming lake

High valley walls

Sinking graben (block fault)

Tarn (circular mountain lake)

GRABEN (BLOCK-FAULT) LAKE

TARN

THE DEAD SEA, ISRAEL/JORDAN

River Jordan

Dead Sea

Steep rift-valley walls

Salt left by evaporation

Israel

Shallow flats

Jordan

293

Coastlines

COASTLINES ARE AMONG THE MOST RAPIDLY changing landscape features. Some are eroded by waves, wind, and rain, causing cliffs to be undercut and caves to be hollowed out of solid rock. Others are built up by waves transporting sand and small rocks in a process known as longshore drift, and by rivers depositing sediment in deltas. Additional influences include the activities of living organisms such as coral, crustal movements, and sea-level variations due to climatic changes. Rising land or a drop in sea level creates an emergent coastline, with cliffs and beaches stranded above the new shoreline. Sinking land or a rise in sea level produces a drowned coastline, typified by fjords (submerged glacial valleys) or submerged river valleys.

FEATURES OF A SEA-CLIFF

Cliff-top
Cliff-face
High tide level
Low tide level
Offshore deposits
Wave-cut platform
Undercut area of cliff

FEATURES OF WAVES

Wave height
Crest
Wavelength
Trough
Shorter wavelength near beach
Circular orbit of water and suspended particles
Orbit deformed into ellipse as water gets shallower

Mature river
Headland
Bedding plane
Sea-cliff
Remnants of former headland
Estuary

LONGSHORE DRIFT

Pebble
Backwash
Movement of material along beach
Build-up of material against groyne
Beach
Groyne
Waves approaching shore at an oblique angle
Swash zone
Swash

DEPOSITIONAL FEATURES OF COASTLINES

Bay-head beach
Wave direction
Headland
Wave direction
Tombolo
Island
Wave direction
Cuspate foreland
Wave direction
Barrier beach
Lagoon

BAY-HEAD BEACH

TOMBOLO

CUSPATE FORELAND

BARRIER BEACH

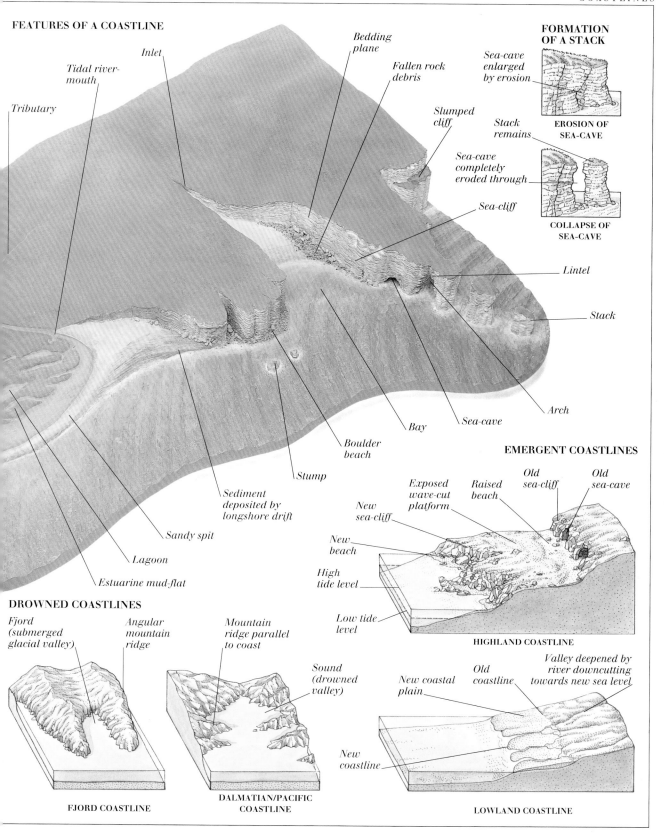

FEATURES OF A COASTLINE

Tributary

Tidal river-mouth

Inlet

Bedding plane

Fallen rock debris

Slumped cliff

Sea-cliff

Lintel

Stack

Arch

Sea-cave

Bay

Boulder beach

Stump

Sediment deposited by longshore drift

Sandy spit

Lagoon

Estuarine mud-flat

FORMATION OF A STACK

Sea-cave enlarged by erosion

EROSION OF SEA-CAVE

Stack remains

Sea-cave completely eroded through

COLLAPSE OF SEA-CAVE

EMERGENT COASTLINES

Exposed wave-cut platform

Raised beach

Old sea-cliff

Old sea-cave

New sea-cliff

New beach

High tide level

Low tide level

HIGHLAND COASTLINE

Valley deepened by river downcutting towards new sea level

New coastal plain

Old coastline

New coastline

LOWLAND COASTLINE

DROWNED COASTLINES

Fjord (submerged glacial valley)

Angular mountain ridge

Mountain ridge parallel to coast

Sound (drowned valley)

FJORD COASTLINE

DALMATIAN/PACIFIC COASTLINE

Oceans and seas

OCEANS AND SEAS COVER ABOUT 70 PER CENT of the Earth's surface and account for about 97 per cent of its total water. These oceans and seas play a crucial role in regulating temperature variations and determining climate. Their waters absorb heat from the Sun, especially in tropical regions, and the surface currents distribute it around the Earth, warming overlying air masses and neighbouring land in winter and cooling them in summer. The oceans are never still. Differences in temperature and salinity drive deep current systems, while surface currents are generated by winds blowing over the oceans. All currents are deflected – to the right in the Northern Hemisphere, to the left in the Southern Hemisphere – as a result of the Earth's rotation. This deflective factor is known as the Coriolis force. A current that begins on the surface is immediately deflected. This current in turn generates a current in the layer of water beneath, which is also deflected. As the movement is transmitted downwards, the deflections form an Ekman spiral. The waters of the oceans and seas are also moved by the constant ebb and flow of tides. These are caused by the gravitational pull of the Moon and Sun. The highest tides (Spring tides) occur at full and new Moon; the lowest tides (neap tides) occur at first and last quarter.

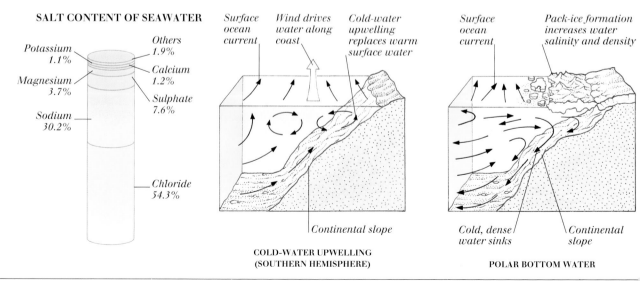

SALT CONTENT OF SEAWATER

Potassium 1.1%
Others 1.9%
Calcium 1.2%
Magnesium 3.7%
Sulphate 7.6%
Sodium 30.2%
Chloride 54.3%

OFFSHORE CURRENTS

Surface ocean current
Wind drives water along coast
Cold-water upwelling replaces warm surface water

Continental slope

COLD-WATER UPWELLING (SOUTHERN HEMISPHERE)

Surface ocean current
Pack-ice formation increases water salinity and density

Cold, dense water sinks
Continental slope

POLAR BOTTOM WATER

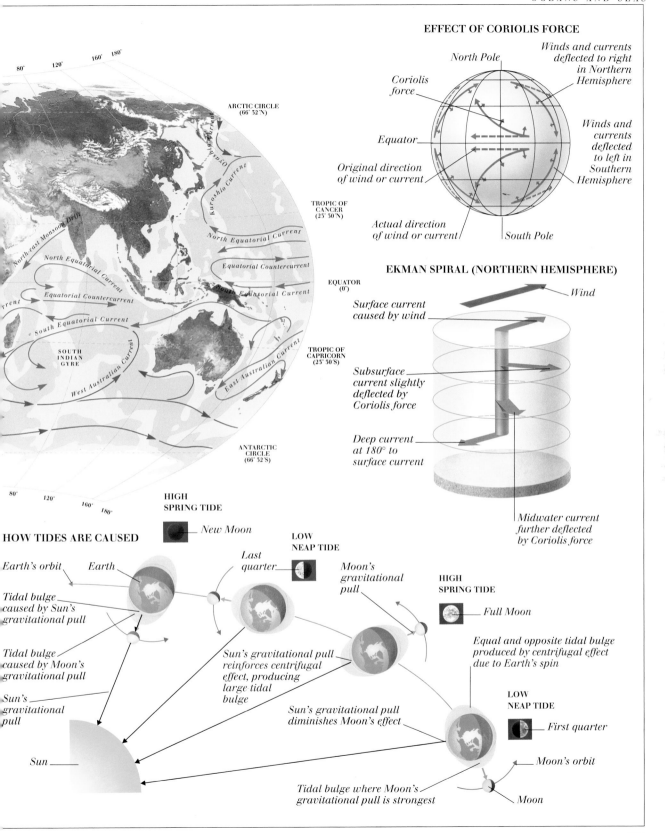

EFFECT OF CORIOLIS FORCE

North Pole

Coriolis
force

Winds and currents
deflected to right
in Northern
Hemisphere

Equator

Winds and
currents
deflected
to left in
Southern
Hemisphere

Original direction
of wind or current

Actual direction
of wind or current

South Pole

EKMAN SPIRAL (NORTHERN HEMISPHERE)

EQUATOR
(0°)

Wind

Surface current
caused by wind

Subsurface
current slightly
deflected by
Coriolis force

Deep current
at 180° to
surface current

Midwater current
further deflected
by Coriolis force

ARCTIC CIRCLE
(66° 52'N)

80° 120° 160° 180°

Oyashio Current

Kuroshio Current

North-east Monsoon Drift

TROPIC OF
CANCER
(23° 30'N)

North Equatorial Current

North Equatorial Current

Equatorial Countercurrent

Equatorial Countercurrent

South Equatorial Current

South Equatorial Current

SOUTH
INDIAN
GYRE

West Australian Current

TROPIC OF
CAPRICORN
(23° 30'S)

East Australian Current

ANTARCTIC
CIRCLE
(66° 52'S)

80° 120° 160° 180°

HOW TIDES ARE CAUSED

HIGH
SPRING TIDE

New Moon

LOW
NEAP TIDE

Last
quarter

Moon's
gravitational
pull

HIGH
SPRING TIDE

Full Moon

Earth's orbit   Earth

Tidal bulge
caused by Sun's
gravitational pull

Tidal bulge
caused by Moon's
gravitational pull

Sun's
gravitational
pull

Sun

Sun's gravitational pull
reinforces centrifugal
effect, producing
large tidal
bulge

Sun's gravitational pull
diminishes Moon's effect

Equal and opposite tidal bulge
produced by centrifugal effect
due to Earth's spin

LOW
NEAP TIDE

First quarter

Moon's orbit

Moon

Tidal bulge where Moon's
gravitational pull is strongest

The ocean floor

THE OCEAN FLOOR COMPRISES TWO SECTIONS: the continental shelf and slope, and the deep-ocean floor. The continental shelf and slope are part of the continental crust, but may extend far into the ocean. Sloping quite gently to a depth of about 140 metres, the continental shelf is covered in sandy deposits shaped by waves and tidal currents. At the edge of the continental shelf, the seabed slopes down to the abyssal plain, which lies at an average depth of about 3,800 metres. On this deep-ocean floor is a layer of sediment made up of clays, fine oozes formed from the remains of tiny sea creatures, and occasional mineral-rich deposits. Echo-sounding and remote sensing from satellites has revealed that the abyssal plain is divided by a system of mountain ranges, far bigger than any on land – the mid-ocean ridge. Here, magma (molten rock) wells up from the Earth's interior and solidifies, widening the ocean floor (see pp. 58-59). As the ocean floor spreads, volcanoes that have formed over hot spots in the crust move away from their magma source; they become extinct and are increasingly submerged and eroded. Volcanoes eroded below sea level remain as seamounts (underwater mountains). In warm waters, a volcano that projects above the ocean surface often acquires a fringing coral reef, which may develop into an atoll as the volcano becomes submerged.

CONTINENTAL-SHELF FLOOR

Bedrock exposed by tidal scour

Shoreline

Parallel strip of coarse material left by strong tidal current

Sand deposited in wavy pattern by weaker currents

Irregular patches of fine sand deposited by weakest currents

FEATURES OF THE OCEAN FLOOR

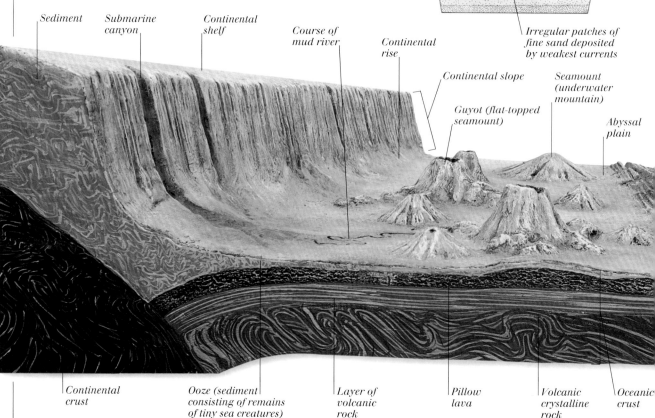

Sediment

Submarine canyon

Continental shelf

Course of mud river

Continental rise

Continental slope

Seamount (underwater mountain)

Guyot (flat-topped seamount)

Abyssal plain

Continental crust

Ooze (sediment consisting of remains of tiny sea creatures)

Layer of volcanic rock

Pillow lava

Volcanic crystalline rock

Oceanic crust

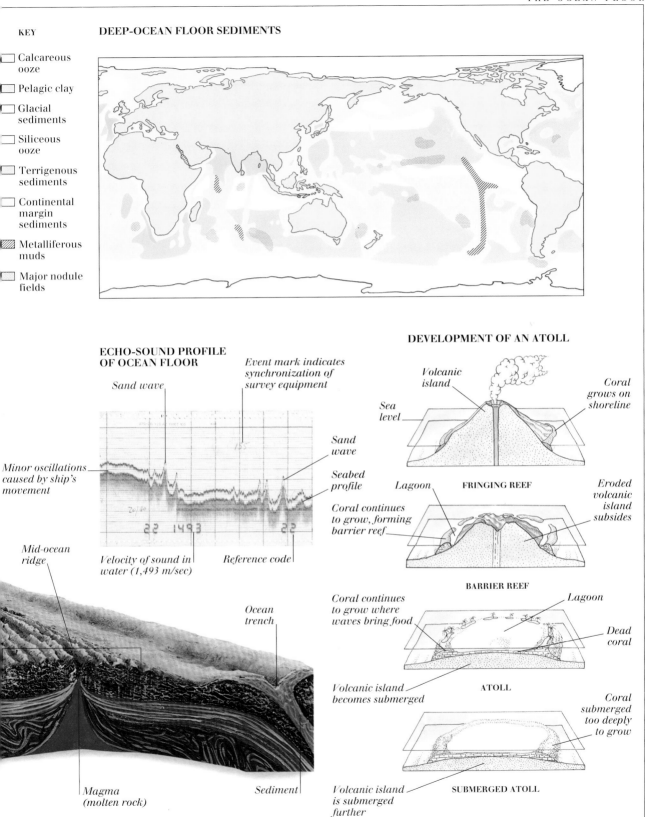

KEY

- Calcareous ooze
- Pelagic clay
- Glacial sediments
- Siliceous ooze
- Terrigenous sediments
- Continental margin sediments
- Metalliferous muds
- Major nodule fields

DEEP-OCEAN FLOOR SEDIMENTS

ECHO-SOUND PROFILE OF OCEAN FLOOR

Sand wave

Event mark indicates synchronization of survey equipment

Minor oscillations caused by ship's movement

Sand wave

Seabed profile

Velocity of sound in water (1,493 m/sec)

Reference code

Mid-ocean ridge

Ocean trench

Magma (molten rock)

Sediment

DEVELOPMENT OF AN ATOLL

Volcanic island

Sea level

Coral grows on shoreline

FRINGING REEF

Lagoon

Coral continues to grow, forming barrier reef

Eroded volcanic island subsides

BARRIER REEF

Coral continues to grow where waves bring food

Lagoon

Dead coral

Volcanic island becomes submerged

ATOLL

Coral submerged too deeply to grow

Volcanic island is submerged further

SUBMERGED ATOLL

The atmosphere

JET STREAM

THE EARTH IS SURROUNDED BY ITS ATMOSPHERE, a blanket of gases that enables life to exist on the planet. This layer has no definite outer edge, gradually becoming thinner until it merges into space, but over 80 per cent of atmospheric gases are held by gravity within about 20 kilometres of the Earth's surface. The atmosphere blocks out much harmful ultraviolet solar radiation, and insulates the Earth against extremes of temperature by limiting both incoming solar radiation and the escape of re-radiated heat into space. This natural balance may be distorted by the greenhouse effect, as gases such as carbon dioxide have built up in the atmosphere, trapping more heat. Close to the Earth's surface, differences in air temperature and pressure cause air to circulate between the equator and poles. This circulation, together with the Coriolis force, gives rise to the prevailing surface winds and the high-level jet streams.

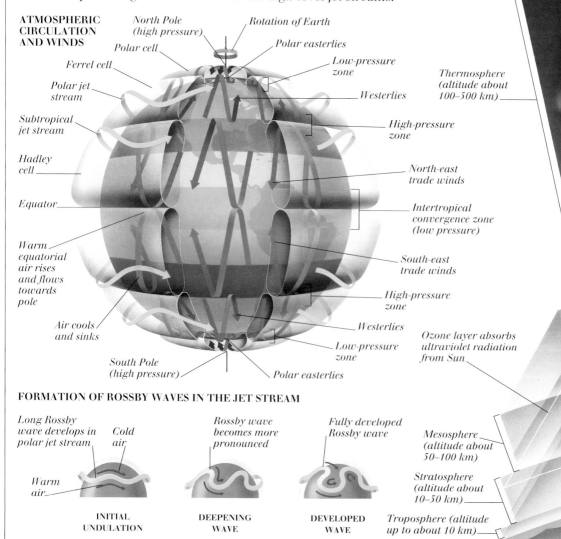

ATMOSPHERIC CIRCULATION AND WINDS

Exosphere (altitude above about 500 km)

Corona

North Pole (high pressure)

Rotation of Earth

Polar easterlies

Polar cell

Ferrel cell

Low-pressure zone

Polar jet stream

Thermosphere (altitude about 100–500 km)

Subtropical jet stream

Westerlies

High-pressure zone

Hadley cell

North-east trade winds

Equator

Intertropical convergence zone (low pressure)

Warm equatorial air rises and flows towards pole

South-east trade winds

High-pressure zone

Air cools and sinks

Westerlies

South Pole (high pressure)

Low-pressure zone

Polar easterlies

Ozone layer absorbs ultraviolet radiation from Sun

FORMATION OF ROSSBY WAVES IN THE JET STREAM

Long Rossby wave develops in polar jet stream

Cold air

Rossby wave becomes more pronounced

Fully developed Rossby wave

Mesosphere (altitude about 50–100 km)

Warm air

Stratosphere (altitude about 10–50 km)

INITIAL UNDULATION

DEEPENING WAVE

DEVELOPED WAVE

Troposphere (altitude up to about 10 km)

STRUCTURE OF THE ATMOSPHERE

GLOBAL WARMING

Solar radiation re-radiated as heat

Some re-radiated heat escapes into space

Sun

Some re-radiated heat reflected back to Earth

Incoming solar radiation

Earth

Atmosphere

NATURALLY MODERATED GREENHOUSE EFFECT

Meteor (shooting star) burns up as it passes through atmosphere

Less re-radiated heat escapes

Solar radiation re-radiated as heat

More re-radiated heat reflected back to Earth

Surface temperature rises

Aurora

"Greenhouse gases" accumulate in atmosphere

Incoming solar radiation

UNBALANCED GREENHOUSE EFFECT

14% of incoming solar radiation absorbed by atmosphere

7% of incoming solar radiation reflected by atmosphere

COMPOSITION OF THE LOWER ATMOSPHERE

24% of incoming solar radiation reflected by clouds

Other elements less than 0.1%

Cosmic rays (high-energy particles from space) penetrate to stratosphere

Argon 0.93%

Oxygen 21%

Some absorbed heat re-radiated by atmosphere

4% of incoming solar radiation reflected by oceans and land

Nitrogen 78%

51% of incoming solar radiation absorbed by Earth's surface

Some absorbed heat re-radiated by clouds

Weather

WEATHER IS DEFINED AS THE ATMOSPHERIC CONDITIONS at a particular time and place; climate is the average weather conditions for a given region over time. Weather is assessed in terms of temperature, wind, cloud cover, and precipitation, such as rain or snow. Fine weather is associated with high-pressure areas, where air is sinking. Cloudy, wet, changeable weather is common in low-pressure zones with rising, unstable air. Such conditions occur at temperate latitudes, where warm air meets cool air along the polar fronts. Here, spiralling low-pressure cells known as depressions (mid-latitude cyclones) often form. A depression usually contains a sector of warmer air, beginning at a warm front and ending at a cold front. If the two fronts merge, forming an occluded front, the warm air is pushed upwards. An extreme form of low-pressure cell is a hurricane (also called a typhoon or tropical cyclone), which brings torrential rain and exceptionally strong winds.

TYPES OF OCCLUDED FRONT

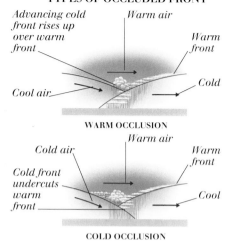

Advancing cold front rises up over warm front

Warm air

Warm front

Cool air

Cold

WARM OCCLUSION

Cold air

Warm air

Warm front

Cold front undercuts warm front

Cool

COLD OCCLUSION

TYPES OF CLOUD

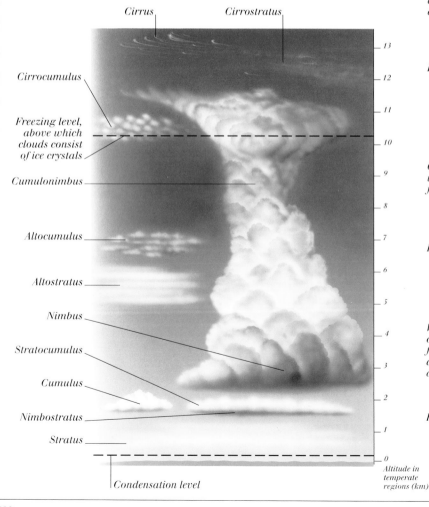

Cirrus

Cirrostratus

Cirrocumulus

Freezing level, above which clouds consist of ice crystals

Cumulonimbus

Altocumulus

Altostratus

Nimbus

Stratocumulus

Cumulus

Nimbostratus

Stratus

Condensation level

13
12
11
10
9
8
7
6
5
4
3
2
1
0

Altitude in temperate regions (km)

FORMS OF PRECIPITATION

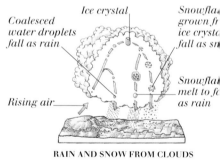

Water droplets less than 0.5 mm in diameter fall as drizzle

Water drop coalesce form raindr 0.5–5.0 mm diame

Rising air

RAIN FROM CLOUDS NOT REACHING FREEZING LEVEL

Coalesced water droplets fall as rain

Ice crystal

Snowfla grown fr ice cryst fall as sn

Rising air

Snowfla melt to f as rain

RAIN AND SNOW FROM CLOUDS REACHING FREEZING LEVEL

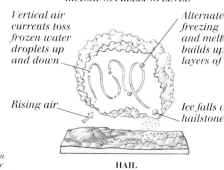

Vertical air currents toss frozen water droplets up and down

Alternate freezing and melt builds up layers of

Rising air

Ice falls hailstone

HAIL

STRUCTURE OF A HURRICANE

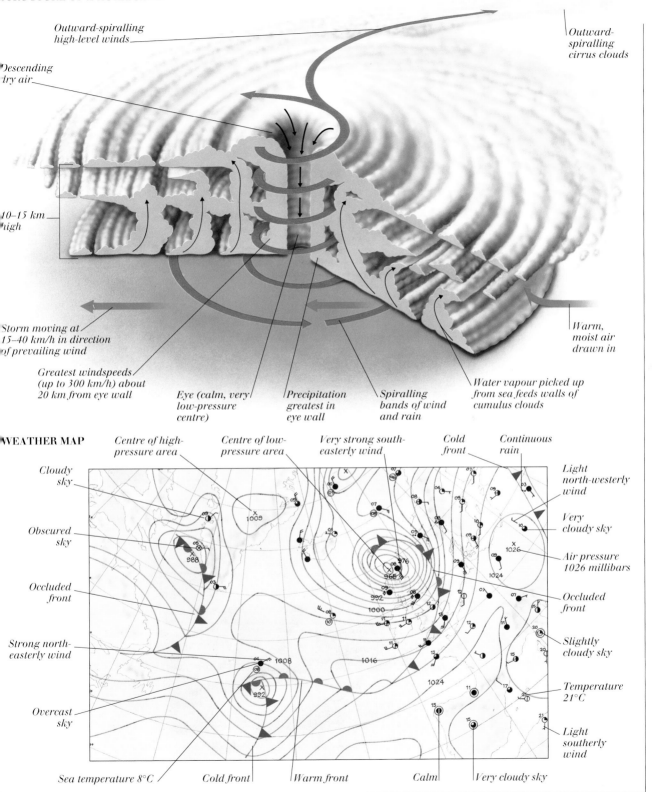

Outward-spiralling
high-level winds

Outward-
spiralling
cirrus clouds

Descending
dry air

10–15 km
high

Storm moving at
15–40 km/h in direction
of prevailing wind

Warm,
moist air
drawn in

Greatest windspeeds
(up to 300 km/h) about
20 km from eye wall

Eye (calm, very
low-pressure
centre)

Precipitation
greatest in
eye wall

Spiralling
bands of wind
and rain

Water vapour picked up
from sea feeds walls of
cumulus clouds

WEATHER MAP

Centre of high-
pressure area

Centre of low-
pressure area

Very strong south-
easterly wind

Cold
front

Continuous
rain

Cloudy
sky

Light
north-westerly
wind

Obscured
sky

Very
cloudy sky

Air pressure
1026 millibars

Occluded
front

Occluded
front

Strong north-
easterly wind

Slightly
cloudy sky

Temperature
21°C

Overcast
sky

Light
southerly
wind

Sea temperature 8°C

Cold front

Warm front

Calm

Very cloudy sky

503

Physics and Chemistry

The variety of matter

**PLANT AND INSECT
(LIVING MATTER)**

MATTER IS ANYTHING THAT HAS A MASS. It includes everything from natural substances, such as minerals or living organisms, to synthetic materials. Matter can exist in three distinct states – solid, liquid, and gas. A solid is rigid and retains its shape. A liquid is fluid, has a definite volume, and will take the shape of its container. A gas (also fluid) fills a space, so its volume will be the same as the volume of its container. Most substances can exist as a solid, a liquid, or a gas: the state is determined by temperature. At very high temperatures, matter becomes plasma, often considered to be a fourth state of matter. All matter is composed of microscopic particles, such as atoms and molecules (see pp. 308-309). The arrangement and interactions of these particles give a substance its physical and chemical properties, by which matter can be identified. There is a huge variety of matter because particles can arrange themselves in countless ways, in one substance or by mixing with others. Natural glass, for example, seems to be a solid but is, in fact, a supercool liquid: the atoms are not locked into a pattern and can flow. Pure substances known as elements (see p. 310) combine to form compounds or mixtures. Mixtures called colloids are made up of larger particles of matter suspended in a solid, liquid, or gas, while a solution is one substance dissolved in another.

TYPES OF COLLOID

HAIR GEL (SOLID IN LIQUID)

**SHAVING FOAM
(AIR IN LIQUID)**

**MIST
(LIQUID IN GAS)**

EXAMPLES OF MATTER

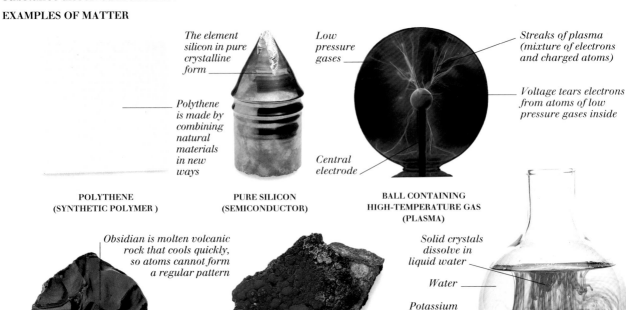

The element silicon in pure crystalline form

Polythene is made by combining natural materials in new ways

**POLYTHENE
(SYNTHETIC POLYMER)**

**PURE SILICON
(SEMICONDUCTOR)**

Low pressure gases

Central electrode

Streaks of plasma (mixture of electrons and charged atoms)

Voltage tears electrons from atoms of low pressure gases inside

**BALL CONTAINING
HIGH-TEMPERATURE GAS
(PLASMA)**

Obsidian is molten volcanic rock that cools quickly, so atoms cannot form a regular pattern

**OBSIDIAN
(NATURAL GLASS)**

Azurite is found naturally with deposits of copper ore

**AZURITE
(CRYSTALLINE MINERAL)**

Solid crystals dissolve in liquid water

Water

Potassium permanganate crystals

**POTASSIUM PERMANGANATE AND WATER
(SOLUTION)**

STATES OF MATTER

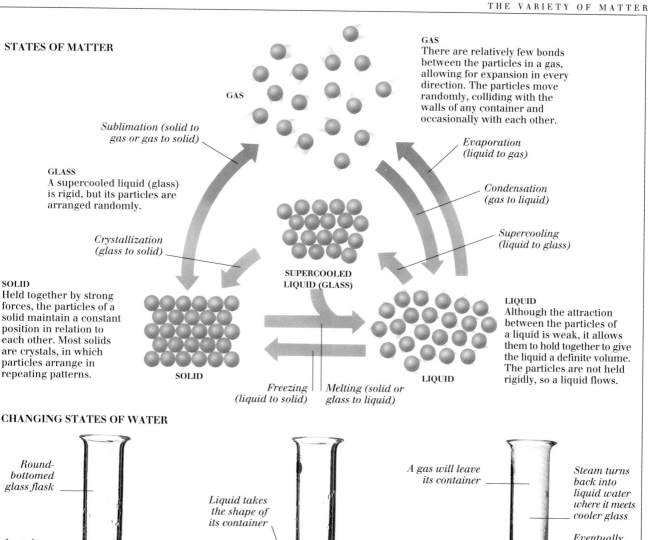

GAS
There are relatively few bonds between the particles in a gas, allowing for expansion in every direction. The particles move randomly, colliding with the walls of any container and occasionally with each other.

GAS

Sublimation (solid to gas or gas to solid)

Evaporation (liquid to gas)

GLASS
A supercooled liquid (glass) is rigid, but its particles are arranged randomly.

Condensation (gas to liquid)

Crystallization (glass to solid)

Supercooling (liquid to glass)

SUPERCOOLED LIQUID (GLASS)

SOLID
Held together by strong forces, the particles of a solid maintain a constant position in relation to each other. Most solids are crystals, in which particles arrange in repeating patterns.

SOLID

LIQUID
Although the attraction between the particles of a liquid is weak, it allows them to hold together to give the liquid a definite volume. The particles are not held rigidly, so a liquid flows.

LIQUID

Freezing (liquid to solid) *Melting (solid or glass to liquid)*

CHANGING STATES OF WATER

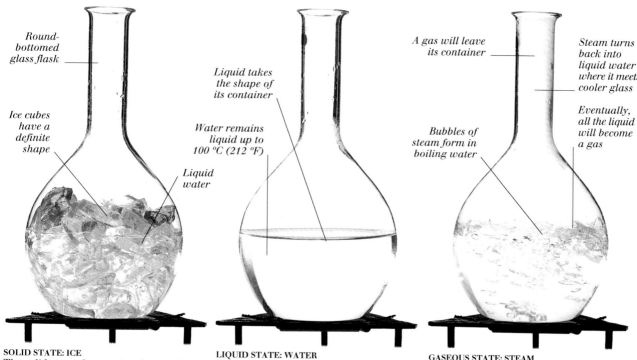

Round-bottomed glass flask

Ice cubes have a definite shape

Liquid water

Liquid takes the shape of its container

Water remains liquid up to 100 °C (212 °F)

A gas will leave its container

Bubbles of steam form in boiling water

Steam turns back into liquid water where it meets cooler glass

Eventually, all the liquid will become a gas

SOLID STATE: ICE
The solid state of water, ice, forms when liquid water is cooled sufficiently. Ice cubes are rigid, with a definite shape and volume.

LIQUID STATE: WATER
When the temperature of a substance rises above its freezing point, it melts to become a liquid. Ice changes to water.

GASEOUS STATE: STEAM
Above its boiling point, a substance will become a gas. When heated sufficiently, liquid water turns to steam, a colourless gas.

Atoms and molecules

(see pp. 310-311)

ATOMS ARE THE smallest individual parts of an element (see pp. 310-311). They are tiny, with diameters in the order of one ten-thousand-millionth of a metre (10^{-10} m). Two or more atoms join together (bond) to form a molecule of a substance known as a compound. For example, when atoms of the elements hydrogen and fluorine join together, they form a molecule of the compound hydrogen fluoride. So molecules are the smallest individual parts of a compound. Atoms themselves are not indivisible – they possess an internal structure. At their centre is a dense nucleus, consisting of protons, which have a positive electric charge (see p. 316), and neutrons, which are uncharged. Around the nucleus are the negatively charged electrons. It is the electrons that give a substance most of its physical and chemical properties. They do not follow definite paths around the nucleus. Instead, electrons are said to be found within certain regions, called orbitals. These are arranged around the nucleus in "shells", each containing electrons of a particular energy. For example, the first shell (1) can hold up to two electrons, in a so-called s-orbital (1s). The second shell (2) can hold up to eight electrons, in s-orbitals (2s) and p-orbitals (2p). If an atom loses an electron, it becomes a positive ion (cation). If an electron is gained, an atom becomes a negative ion (anion). Ions of opposite charges will attract and join together, in a type of bonding known as ionic bonding. In covalent bonding, the atoms bond by sharing their electrons in what become molecular orbitals.

FALSE-COLOUR IMAGE OF ACTUAL GOLD ATOMS

ATOMIC ORBITALS

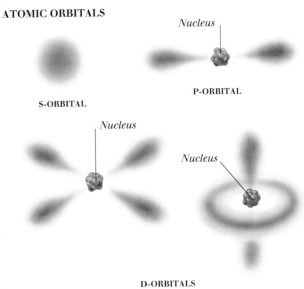

Nucleus

S-ORBITAL

P-ORBITAL

Nucleus

Nucleus

D-ORBITALS

MOLECULAR ORBITALS

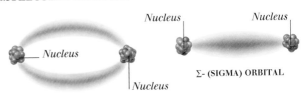

Nucleus

Nucleus

Nucleus

Nucleus

π- (PI) ORBITAL

Σ- (SIGMA) ORBITAL

Nucleus

SP³-HYBRID ORBITAL

EXAMPLE OF IONIC BONDING

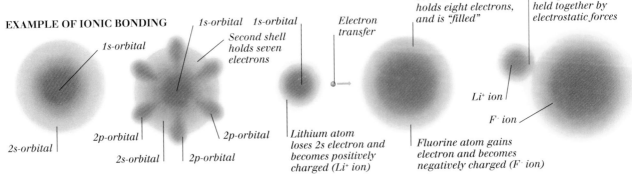

1s-orbital

1s-orbital   1s-orbital

Second shell holds seven electrons

Electron transfer

Second shell now holds eight electrons, and is "filled"

Charged atoms (ions) held together by electrostatic forces

2s-orbital

2p-orbital

2s-orbital   2p-orbital

2p-orbital

Lithium atom loses 2s electron and becomes positively charged (Li⁺ ion)

Fluorine atom gains electron and becomes negatively charged (F⁻ ion)

Li⁺ ion

F⁻ ion

1. NEUTRAL LITHIUM ATOM (Li)

NEUTRAL FLUORINE ATOM (F)

2. ELECTRON TRANSFER

3. IONIC BONDING: LITHIUM FLUORIDE MOLECULE (LiF)

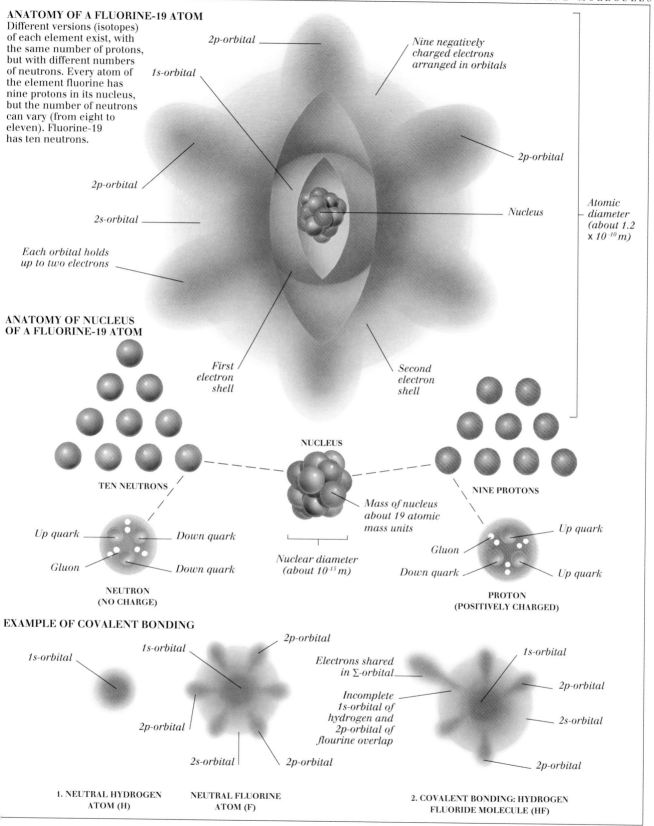

ANATOMY OF A FLUORINE-19 ATOM

Different versions (isotopes) of each element exist, with the same number of protons, but with different numbers of neutrons. Every atom of the element fluorine has nine protons in its nucleus, but the number of neutrons can vary (from eight to eleven). Fluorine-19 has ten neutrons.

2p-orbital

1s-orbital

Nine negatively charged electrons arranged in orbitals

2p-orbital

2p-orbital

Nucleus

2s-orbital

Each orbital holds up to two electrons

Atomic diameter (about 1.2 × 10⁻¹⁰ m)

First electron shell

Second electron shell

ANATOMY OF NUCLEUS OF A FLUORINE-19 ATOM

NUCLEUS

TEN NEUTRONS

NINE PROTONS

Mass of nucleus about 19 atomic mass units

Up quark

Down quark

Gluon

Down quark

NEUTRON (NO CHARGE)

Nuclear diameter (about 10⁻¹⁵ m)

Up quark

Gluon

Down quark

Up quark

PROTON (POSITIVELY CHARGED)

EXAMPLE OF COVALENT BONDING

1s-orbital

1s-orbital

2p-orbital

2p-orbital

2s-orbital

2p-orbital

Electrons shared in Σ-orbital

Incomplete 1s-orbital of hydrogen and 2p-orbital of flourine overlap

1s-orbital

2p-orbital

2s-orbital

2p-orbital

1. NEUTRAL HYDROGEN ATOM (H)

NEUTRAL FLUORINE ATOM (F)

2. COVALENT BONDING: HYDROGEN FLUORIDE MOLECULE (HF)

309

The periodic table

AN ELEMENT is a substance that consists of atoms of one type only. The 92 elements that occur naturally, and the 17 elements created artificially, are often arranged into a chart called the periodic table. Each element is defined by its atomic number – the number of protons in the nucleus of each of its atoms (it is also the number of electrons present). Atomic number increases along each row (period) and down each column (group). The shape of the table is determined by the way in which electrons arrange themselves around the nucleus: the positioning of elements in order of increasing atomic number brings together atoms with a similar pattern of orbiting electrons (orbitals). These appear in blocks. Electrons occupy shells of a certain energy (see pp. 308-309). Periods are ordered according to the filling of successive shells with electrons, while groups reflect the number of electrons in the outer shell (valency electrons). These outer electrons are important – they decide the chemical properties of the atom. Elements that appear in the same group have similar properties because they have the same number of electrons in their outer shell. Elements in Group 0 have "filled shells", where the outer shell holds its maximum number of electrons, and are stable. Atoms of Group I elements have just one electron in their outer shell. This makes them unstable – and ready to react with other substances.

METALS AND NON-METALS

Elements at the left-hand side of each period are metals. Metals easily lose electrons and form positive ions. Non-metals, on the right of a period, tend to become negative ions. Semi-metals, which have properties of both metals and non-metals, are between the two.

TYPES OF ELEMENT KEY:

- Alkali metals
- Alkaline earth metals
- Transition metals
- Lanthanides (rare earths)
- Actinides
- Poor metals
- Semi-metals
- Non-metals
- Noble gases

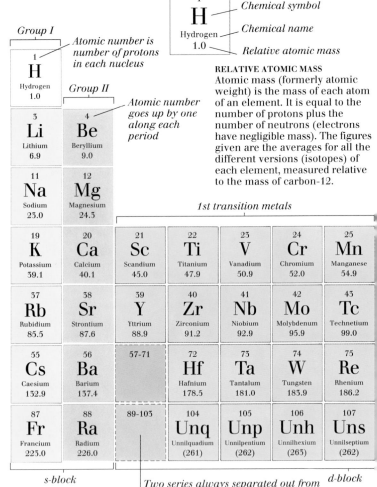

Atomic number is number of protons in each nucleus

1
H
Hydrogen
1.0

Atomic number — Atomic number
Chemical symbol — Chemical symbol
Chemical name — Chemical name
Relative atomic mass — Relative atomic mass

RELATIVE ATOMIC MASS

Atomic mass (formerly atomic weight) is the mass of each atom of an element. It is equal to the number of protons plus the number of neutrons (electrons have negligible mass). The figures given are the averages for all the different versions (isotopes) of each element, measured relative to the mass of carbon-12.

Group I

1
H
Hydrogen
1.0

Group II

Atomic number goes up by one along each period

Group I	Group II	1st transition metals				
3 **Li** Lithium 6.9	4 **Be** Beryllium 9.0					
11 **Na** Sodium 23.0	12 **Mg** Magnesium 24.3					
19 **K** Potassium 39.1	20 **Ca** Calcium 40.1	21 **Sc** Scandium 45.0	22 **Ti** Titanium 47.9	23 **V** Vanadium 50.9	24 **Cr** Chromium 52.0	25 **Mn** Manganese 54.9
37 **Rb** Rubidium 85.5	38 **Sr** Strontium 87.6	39 **Y** Yttrium 88.9	40 **Zr** Zirconium 91.2	41 **Nb** Niobium 92.9	42 **Mo** Molybdenum 95.9	43 **Tc** Technetium 99.0
55 **Cs** Caesium 132.9	56 **Ba** Barium 137.4	57-71	72 **Hf** Hafnium 178.5	73 **Ta** Tantalum 181.0	74 **W** Tungsten 183.9	75 **Re** Rhenium 186.2
87 **Fr** Francium 223.0	88 **Ra** Radium 226.0	89-103	104 **Unq** Unnilquadium (261)	105 **Unp** Unnilpentium (262)	106 **Unh** Unnilhexium (263)	107 **Uns** Unnilseptium (262)

s-block

Two series always separated out from the table to give it a coherent shape

d-block

Soft, silvery, and highly reactive metal

SODIUM: GROUP 1 METAL

Silvery, reactive metal

MAGNESIUM: GROUP 2 METAL

Hard, silvery metal

CHROMIUM: 1ST TRANSITION METAL

Radioactive metal

PLUTONIUM: ACTINIDE SERIES METAL

57 **La** Lanthanum 138.9	58 **Ce** Cerium 140.1	59 **Pr** Praseodymium 140.9	60 **Nd** Neodymium 144.2
89 **Ac** Actinium 227.0	90 **Th** Thorium 232.0	91 **Pa** Protactinium 231.0	92 **U** Uranium 238.0

DIAMOND

ALLOTROPES OF CARBON
Some elements exist in more than one form – these are known as allotropes. Carbon powder, graphite, and diamond are allotropes of carbon. They all consist of carbon atoms, but have very different physical properties.

Bright yellow crystal

SULPHUR:
GROUP 6 SOLID NON-METAL

IODINE:
GROUP 7
SOLID NON-METAL

Purple-black solid turns to gas easily

Group 0

GRAPHITE

CARBON POWDER

Boron and carbon groups

Nitrogen and oxygen groups

Halogens

					2 **He** Helium 4.0	*Period*

Group III | *Group IV* | *Group V* | *Group VI* | *Group VII*

Group III	Group IV	Group V	Group VI	Group VII	Group 0	
5 **B** Boron 10.8	6 **C** Carbon 12.0	7 **N** Nitrogen 14.0	8 **O** Oxygen 16.0	9 **F** Fluorine 19.0	10 **Ne** Neon 20.2	*Short period*
13 **Al** Aluminium 27.0	14 **Si** Silicon 28.1	15 **P** Phosphorus 31.0	16 **S** Sulphur 32.1	17 **Cl** Chlorine 35.5	18 **Ar** Argon 40.0	

2nd transition metals

3rd transition metals

26 **Fe** Iron 55.9	27 **Co** Cobalt 58.9	28 **Ni** Nickel 58.7	29 **Cu** Copper 63.5	30 **Zn** Zinc 65.4	31 **Ga** Gallium 69.7	32 **Ge** Germanium 72.6	33 **As** Arsenic 74.9	34 **Se** Selenium 79.0	35 **Br** Bromine 79.9	36 **Kr** Krypton 83.8	*Long period*
44 **Ru** Ruthenium 101.0	45 **Rh** Rhodium 102.9	46 **Pd** Palladium 106.4	47 **Ag** Silver 107.9	48 **Cd** Cadmium 112.4	49 **In** Indium 114.8	50 **Sn** Tin 118.7	51 **Sb** Antimony 121.8	52 **Te** Tellurium 127.6	53 **I** Iodine 126.9	54 **Xe** Xenon 131.3	
76 **Os** Osmium 190.2	77 **Ir** Iridium 192.2	78 **Pt** Platinum 195.1	79 **Au** Gold 197.0	80 **Hg** Mercury 200.6	81 **Tl** Thallium 204.4	82 **Pb** Lead 207.2	83 **Bi** Bismuth 209.0	84 **Po** Polonium 210.0	85 **At** Astatine 210.0	86 **Rn** Radon 222.0	
108 **Uno** Unniloctium (265)	109 **Une** Unnilennium (266)										

d-block

p-block

Atomic mass is estimated, as element exists fleetingly

Shiny semi-metal

Unreactive, colourless gas glows red in discharge tube

NOBLE GASES
Group 0 contains elements that have a filled (complete) outer shell of electrons, which means the atoms do not need to lose or gain electrons by bonding with other atoms. This makes them stable and they do not easily form ions or react with other elements. Noble gases are also called rare or inert gases.

Yellow, unreactive precious metal

Soft, shiny, reactive metal

GOLD:
3RD TRANSITION METAL

TIN:
GROUP 4 POOR METAL

ANTIMONY:
GROUP 5 SEMI-METAL

NEON:
GROUP 0
COLOURLESS GAS

61 **Pm** Promethium 147.0	62 **Sm** Samarium 150.4	63 **Eu** Europium 152.0	64 **Gd** Gadolinium 157.3	65 **Tb** Terbium 158.9	66 **Dy** Dysprosium 162.5	67 **Ho** Holmium 164.9	68 **Er** Erbium 167.3	69 **Tm** Thulium 168.9	70 **Yb** Ytterbium 173.0	71 **Lu** Lutetium 175.0
93 **Np** Neptunium 237.0	94 **Pu** Plutonium 242.0	95 **Am** Americium 243.0	96 **Cm** Curium 247.0	97 **Bk** Berkelium 247.0	98 **Cf** Californium 251.0	99 **Es** Einsteinium 254.0	100 **Fm** Fermium 253.0	101 **Md** Mendelevium 256.0	102 **No** Nobelium 254.0	103 **Lr** Lawrencium 257.0

f-block

Chemical reactions

A CHEMICAL REACTION TAKES PLACE whenever bonds between atoms are broken or made. In each case, atoms or groups of atoms rearrange, making new substances (products) from the original ones (reactants). Reactions happen naturally, or can be made to happen; they may take years, or only an instant. Some of the main types are shown here. A reaction usually involves a change in energy (see pp. 314-315). In a burning reaction, for example, the making of new bonds between atoms releases energy as heat and light. This type of reaction, in which heat is given off, is an exothermic reaction. Many reactions, like burning, are irreversible, but some can take place in either direction, and are said to be reversible. Reactions can be used to form solids from solutions: in a double decomposition reaction, two compounds in solution break down and re-form into two new substances, often creating a precipitate (insoluble solid); in displacement, an element (eg. copper) displaces another element (eg. silver) from a solution. The rate (speed) of a reaction is determined by many different factors, such as temperature, and the size and shape of the reactants. To describe and keep track of reactions, internationally recognized chemical symbols and equations are used. Reactions are also used in the laboratory to identify matter. An experiment with candle wax, for example, demonstrates that it contains carbon and hydrogen.

SALT FORMATION (ACID ON METAL)

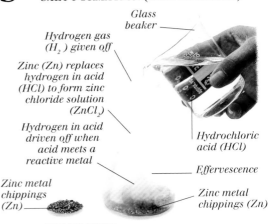

Glass beaker

Hydrogen gas (H_2) given off

Zinc (Zn) replaces hydrogen in acid (HCl) to form zinc chloride solution ($ZnCl_2$)

Hydrogen in acid driven off when acid meets a reactive metal

Hydrochloric acid (HCl)

Effervescence

Zinc metal chippings (Zn)

Zinc metal chippings (Zn)

THE REACTION
Hydrochloric acid added to zinc produces zinc chloride and hydrogen.
$$Zn + 2HCl \rightarrow ZnCl_2 + H_2$$

DISPLACEMENT

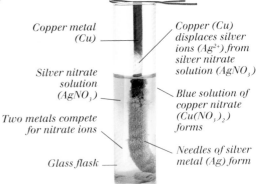

Copper metal (Cu)

Copper (Cu) displaces silver ions (Ag^{2+}) from silver nitrate solution ($AgNO_3$)

Silver nitrate solution ($AgNO_3$)

Blue solution of copper nitrate ($Cu(NO_3)_2$) forms

Two metals compete for nitrate ions

Needles of silver metal (Ag) form

Glass flask

THE REACTION
Copper metal added to silver nitrate solution produces copper nitrate and silver metal.
$$Cu + 2AgNO_3 \rightarrow Cu(NO_3)_2 + 2Ag$$

BURNING MATTER

Ammonium dichromate (($NH_4)_2Cr_2O_7$)

In this burning reaction, atoms form simpler substances and give off heat and light

Flame

Ammonium dichromate (($NH_4)_2Cr_2O_7$) converts to chromium oxide (Cr_2O_3)

Nitrogen monoxide (NO) and water vapour (H_2O) given off as colourless gases

THE REACTION
When lit, ammonium dichromate combines with oxygen from air.
$$(NH_4)_2Cr_2O_7 + O_2 \rightarrow Cr_2O_3 + 4H_2O + 2NO$$

A REVERSIBLE REACTION

Flat-bottomed glass flask

Potassium chromate solution (K_2CrO_4)

Bright yellow solution contains potassium and chromate ions

1. THE REACTANT
Potassium chromate dissolves in water to form potassium ions and chromate ions.
$$K_2CrO_4 \rightarrow 2K^+ + CrO_4^{2-}$$

Pipette

Hydrochloric acid (HCl) added in drops

Acid causes reaction to take place

Chromate ions converted to orange dichromate ions

Potassium dichromate (KCr_2O_7) forms

2. THE REACTION
Addition of hydrochloric acid changes chromate ions into dichromate ions.
$$2CrO_4^{2-} \rightarrow Cr_2O_7^{2-}$$

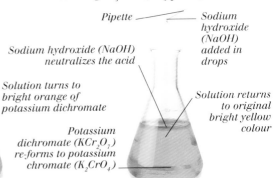

Pipette

Sodium hydroxide (NaOH) added in drops

Sodium hydroxide (NaOH) neutralizes the acid

Solution turns to bright orange of potassium dichromate

Solution returns to original bright yellow colour

Potassium dichromate (KCr_2O_7) re-forms to potassium chromate (K_2CrO_4)

3. REVERSING
Addition of sodium hydroxide changes dichromate ions back into chromate ions.
$$Cr_2O_7^{2-} \rightarrow 2CrO_4^{2-}$$

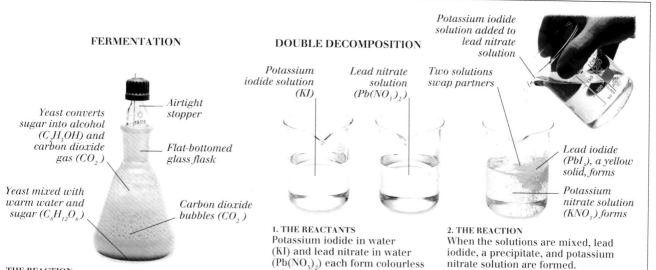

FERMENTATION

Yeast converts sugar into alcohol (C_2H_5OH) and carbon dioxide gas (CO_2)

Airtight stopper

Flat-bottomed glass flask

Yeast mixed with warm water and sugar ($C_6H_{12}O_6$)

Carbon dioxide bubbles (CO_2)

THE REACTION
Yeast converts sugar and warm water into alcohol and carbon dioxide.
$C_6H_{12}O_6 \rightarrow 2C_2H_5OH + 2CO_2$

DOUBLE DECOMPOSITION

Potassium iodide solution (KI)

Lead nitrate solution ($Pb(NO_3)_2$)

Two solutions swap partners

Potassium iodide solution added to lead nitrate solution

Lead iodide (PbI_2), a yellow solid, forms

Potassium nitrate solution (KNO_3) forms

1. THE REACTANTS
Potassium iodide in water (KI) and lead nitrate in water ($Pb(NO_3)_2$) each form colourless solutions.

2. THE REACTION
When the solutions are mixed, lead iodide, a precipitate, and potassium nitrate solution are formed.
$2KI + Pb(NO_3)_2 \rightarrow PbI_2 + 2KNO_3$

TESTING CANDLE WAX, AN ORGANIC COMPOUND

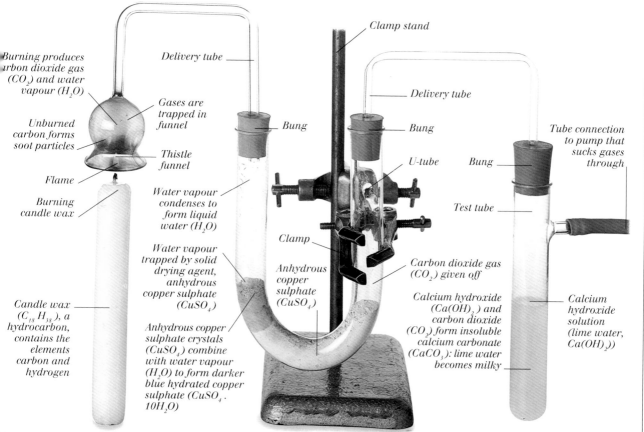

Clamp stand

Delivery tube

Burning produces carbon dioxide gas (CO_2) and water vapour (H_2O)

Delivery tube

Gases are trapped in funnel

Bung

Bung

Tube connection to pump that sucks gases through

Unburned carbon forms soot particles

U-tube

Bung

Thistle funnel

Flame

Water vapour condenses to form liquid water (H_2O)

Burning candle wax

Water vapour trapped by solid drying agent, anhydrous copper sulphate ($CuSO_4$)

Clamp

Anhydrous copper sulphate ($CuSO_4$)

Carbon dioxide gas (CO_2) given off

Test tube

Candle wax ($C_{18}H_{38}$), a hydrocarbon, contains the elements carbon and hydrogen

Anhydrous copper sulphate crystals ($CuSO_4$) combine with water vapour (H_2O) to form darker blue hydrated copper sulphate ($CuSO_4$. $10H_2O$)

Calcium hydroxide ($Ca(OH)_2$) and carbon dioxide (CO_2) form insoluble calcium carbonate ($CaCO_3$): lime water becomes milky

Calcium hydroxide solution (lime water, $Ca(OH)_2$)

1. THE BURNING REACTION
Burning wax produces carbon dioxide gas and water vapour.
$2C_{18}H_{38} + 55O_2 \rightarrow 36CO_2 + 38H_2O$

2. TESTING FOR WATER VAPOUR
A solid drying agent traps water vapour, proving the presence of hydrogen in the candle wax.
$CuSO_4 + 10H_2O \rightarrow CuSO_4 . 10H_2O$

3. TESTING FOR CARBON DIOXIDE
Calcium hydroxide in solution reacts with carbon dioxide, forming a carbonate and turning milky.
$Ca(OH)_2 + CO_2 \rightarrow CaCO_3 + H_2O$

Energy

ANYTHING THAT HAPPENS – from a pin-drop to an explosion – requires energy. Energy is the capacity for "doing work" (making something happen). Various forms of energy exist, including light, heat, sound, electrical, chemical, nuclear, kinetic, and potential energies. The Law of Conservation of Energy states that the total amount of energy in the Universe is fixed – energy cannot be created or destroyed. It means that energy can only change from one form to another (energy transfer). For example, potential energy is energy that is "stored", and can be used in the future. An object gains potential energy when it is lifted; as the object is released, potential energy changes into the energy of motion (kinetic energy). During transference, some of the energy converts into heat. A combined heat and power station can put some of the otherwise "waste" heat to useful effect in local schools and housing. Most of the Earth's energy is provided by the Sun, in the form of electromagnetic radiation (see pp. 316-317). Some of this energy transfers to plant and animal life, and ultimately to fossil fuels, where it is stored in chemical form. Our bodies obtain energy from the food we eat, while energy needed for other tasks, such as heating and transport, can be obtained by burning fossil fuels – or by harnessing natural forces like wind or moving water – to generate electricity. Another source is nuclear power, where energy is released by reactions in the nucleus of an atom. All energy is measured by the international unit, the joule (J). As a guide, one joule is about equal to the amount of energy needed to lift an apple one metre.

SANKEY DIAGRAM SHOWING ENERGY FLOW IN A COAL-FIRED COMBINED HEAT AND POWER STATION

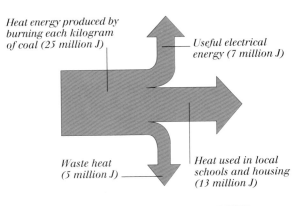

Heat energy produced by burning each kilogram of coal (25 million J)

Useful electrical energy (7 million J)

Waste heat (5 million J)

Heat used in local schools and housing (13 million J)

CROSS-SECTION OF HYDROELECTRIC POWER STATION WITH FRANCIS TURBINE

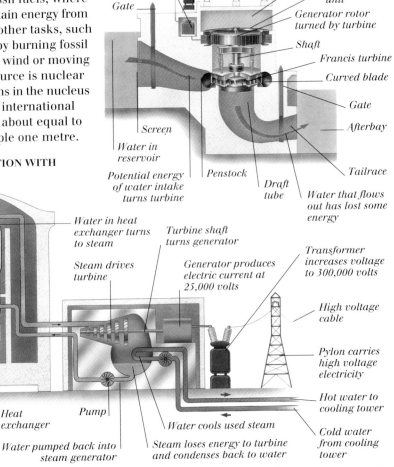

Transformer
Insulator
High voltage cable
Switch gear including circuit braker
Bushing
Rotor house
Gate
Generator unit
Generator rotor turned by turbine
Shaft
Francis turbine
Curved blade
Gate
Afterbay
Screen
Water in reservoir
Potential energy of water intake turns turbine
Penstock
Draft tube
Tailrace
Water that flows out has lost some energy

CROSS-SECTION OF NUCLEAR POWER STATION WITH PRESSURIZED WATER REACTOR

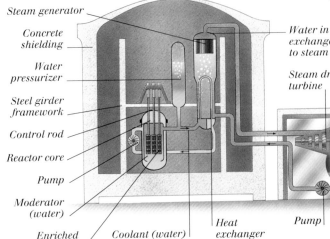

Steam generator
Concrete shielding
Water pressurizer
Steel girder framework
Control rod
Reactor core
Pump
Moderator (water)
Enriched uranium fuel
Coolant (water) takes heat from reactor core to heat exchanger
Heat exchanger
Water pumped back into steam generator
Pump
Water in heat exchanger turns to steam
Steam drives turbine
Turbine shaft turns generator
Generator produces electric current at 25,000 volts
Steam loses energy to turbine and condenses back to water
Water cools used steam
Transformer increases voltage to 300,000 volts
High voltage cable
Pylon carries high voltage electricity
Hot water to cooling tower
Cold water from cooling tower

ENERGY SYSTEMS

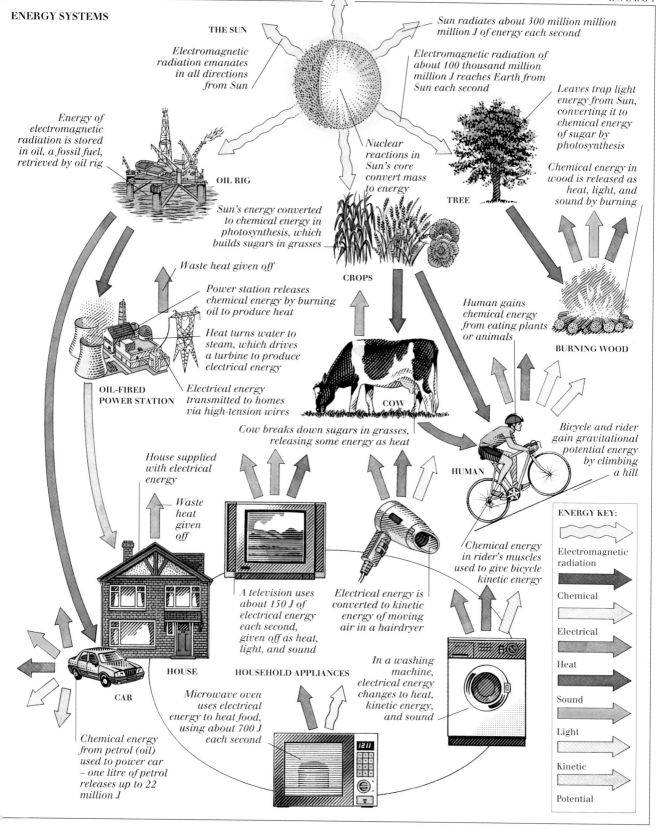

THE SUN

Electromagnetic radiation emanates in all directions from Sun

Sun radiates about 300 million million million J of energy each second

Electromagnetic radiation of about 100 thousand million million J reaches Earth from Sun each second

Leaves trap light energy from Sun, converting it to chemical energy of sugar by photosynthesis

Energy of electromagnetic radiation is stored in oil, a fossil fuel, retrieved by oil rig

OIL RIG

Nuclear reactions in Sun's core convert mass to energy

TREE

Chemical energy in wood is released as heat, light, and sound by burning

Sun's energy converted to chemical energy in photosynthesis, which builds sugars in grasses

Waste heat given off

Power station releases chemical energy by burning oil to produce heat

Heat turns water to steam, which drives a turbine to produce electrical energy

Electrical energy transmitted to homes via high-tension wires

OIL-FIRED POWER STATION

CROPS

Human gains chemical energy from eating plants or animals

BURNING WOOD

Cow breaks down sugars in grasses, releasing some energy as heat

COW

Bicycle and rider gain gravitational potential energy by climbing a hill

House supplied with electrical energy

Waste heat given off

HUMAN

Chemical energy in rider's muscles used to give bicycle kinetic energy

ENERGY KEY:

Electromagnetic radiation

Chemical

Electrical

Heat

Sound

Light

Kinetic

Potential

A television uses about 150 J of electrical energy each second, given off as heat, light, and sound

Electrical energy is converted to kinetic energy of moving air in a hairdryer

In a washing machine, electrical energy changes to heat, kinetic energy, and sound

HOUSE

HOUSEHOLD APPLIANCES

Microwave oven uses electrical energy to heat food, using about 700 J each second

CAR

Chemical energy from petrol (oil) used to power car – one litre of petrol releases up to 22 million J

Electricity and magnetism

ELECTRICAL EFFECTS result from an imbalance of electric charge. There are two types of electric charge, named positive (carried by protons) and negative (carried by electrons). If charges are opposite (unlike), they attract one another, while like charges repel. Forces of attraction and repulsion (electrostatic forces) exist between any two charged particles. Matter is normally uncharged, but if

LIGHTNING

electrons are gained, an object will gain an overall negative charge; if they are removed, it becomes positive. Objects with an overall negative or positive charge are said to have an imbalance of charge, and exert the same forces as individual negative and positive charges. On this larger scale, the forces will always act to regain the balance of charge. This causes static electricity. Lightning, for example, is produced by clouds discharging a huge excess of negative electrons. If charges are "free" – in a wire or material that allows electrons to pass through it – the forces cause a flow of charge called an electric current. Some substances exhibit the strange phenomenon of magnetism – which also produces attractive and repulsive forces. Magnetic substances consist of small regions called domains. Normally unmagnetized, they can be magnetized by being placed in a magnetic field. Magnetism and electricity are inextricably linked, a fact put to use in motors and generators.

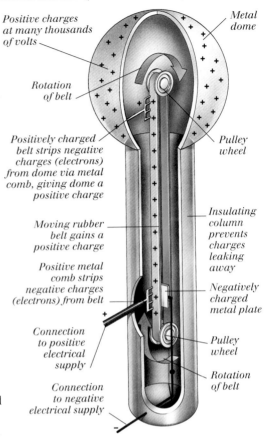

Positive charges at many thousands of volts

Metal dome

Rotation of belt

Positively charged belt strips negative charges (electrons) from dome via metal comb, giving dome a positive charge

Pulley wheel

Moving rubber belt gains a positive charge

Insulating column prevents charges leaking away

Positive metal comb strips negative charges (electrons) from belt

Negatively charged metal plate

Connection to positive electrical supply

Pulley wheel

Rotation of belt

Connection to negative electrical supply

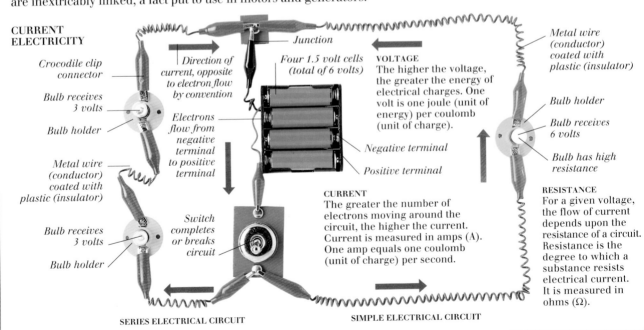

CURRENT ELECTRICITY

Crocodile clip connector

Bulb receives 3 volts

Bulb holder

Metal wire (conductor) coated with plastic (insulator)

Bulb receives 3 volts

Bulb holder

Direction of current, opposite to electron flow by convention

Junction

Electrons flow from negative terminal to positive terminal

Switch completes or breaks circuit

Four 1.5 volt cells (total of 6 volts)

VOLTAGE
The higher the voltage, the greater the energy of electrical charges. One volt is one joule (unit of energy) per coulomb (unit of charge).

Negative terminal

Positive terminal

CURRENT
The greater the number of electrons moving around the circuit, the higher the current. Current is measured in amps (A). One amp equals one coulomb (unit of charge) per second.

Metal wire (conductor) coated with plastic (insulator)

Bulb holder

Bulb receives 6 volts

Bulb has high resistance

RESISTANCE
For a given voltage, the flow of current depends upon the resistance of a circuit. Resistance is the degree to which a substance resists electrical current. It is measured in ohms (Ω).

SERIES ELECTRICAL CIRCUIT

SIMPLE ELECTRICAL CIRCUIT

MAGNETIC FIELDS AND FORCES

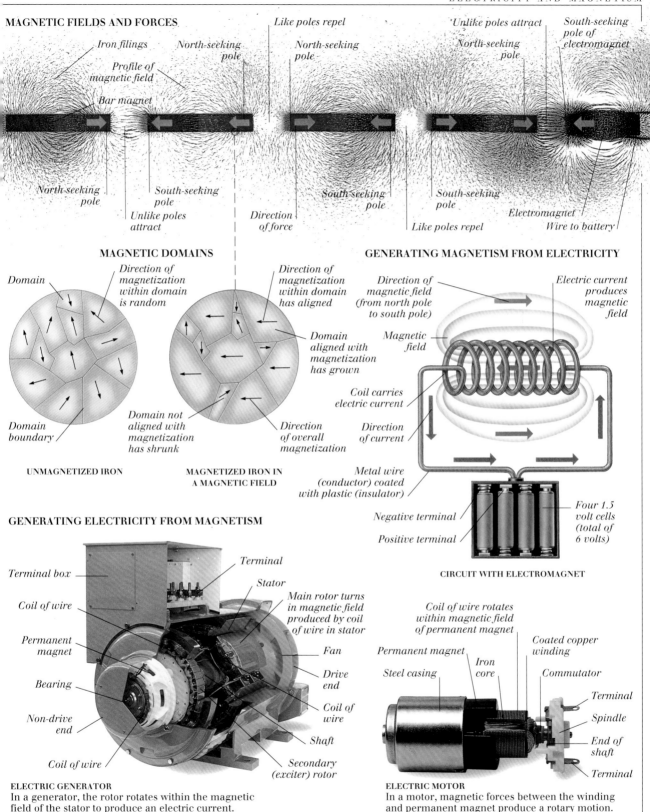

Iron filings

Profile of magnetic field

North-seeking pole

Bar magnet

North-seeking pole

South-seeking pole

Unlike poles attract

Like poles repel

North-seeking pole

South-seeking pole

Direction of force

Like poles repel

Unlike poles attract

North-seeking pole

South-seeking pole

Electromagnet

South-seeking pole of electromagnet

Wire to battery

MAGNETIC DOMAINS

Domain

Direction of magnetization within domain is random

Domain boundary

UNMAGNETIZED IRON

Direction of magnetization within domain has aligned

Domain aligned with magnetization has grown

Domain not aligned with magnetization has shrunk

Direction of overall magnetization

MAGNETIZED IRON IN A MAGNETIC FIELD

GENERATING MAGNETISM FROM ELECTRICITY

Direction of magnetic field (from north pole to south pole)

Electric current produces magnetic field

Magnetic field

Coil carries electric current

Direction of current

Metal wire (conductor) coated with plastic (insulator)

Negative terminal

Positive terminal

Four 1.5 volt cells (total of 6 volts)

CIRCUIT WITH ELECTROMAGNET

GENERATING ELECTRICITY FROM MAGNETISM

Terminal box

Coil of wire

Permanent magnet

Bearing

Non-drive end

Coil of wire

Terminal

Stator

Main rotor turns in magnetic field produced by coil of wire in stator

Fan

Drive end

Coil of wire

Shaft

Secondary (exciter) rotor

ELECTRIC GENERATOR
In a generator, the rotor rotates within the magnetic field of the stator to produce an electric current.

Coil of wire rotates within magnetic field of permanent magnet

Permanent magnet

Steel casing

Iron core

Coated copper winding

Commutator

Terminal

Spindle

End of shaft

Terminal

ELECTRIC MOTOR
In a motor, magnetic forces between the winding and permanent magnet produce a rotary motion.

317

Light

INFRA-RED IMAGE
OF A HOUSE

LIGHT IS A FORM OF ENERGY. It is a
type of electromagnetic radiation, like X-
rays or radio waves. All electromagnetic
radiation is produced by electric charges
(see pp. 316-317): it is caused by the effects
of oscillating electric and magnetic fields as they travel
through space. Electromagnetic radiation is considered to
have both wave and particle properties. It can be thought
of as a wave of electricity and magnetism. In that case,
the difference between the various forms of
radiation is their wavelength. Radiation can
also be said to consist of particles, or packets
of energy, called photons. The difference
between light and X-rays, for instance, is
the amount of energy that each photon
carries. The complete range of radiation is
referred to as the electromagnetic spectrum,
extending from low energy, long wavelength
radio waves to high energy, short wavelength
gamma rays. Light is the only part of the
electromagnetic spectrum that is visible.
White light from the Sun is made up of all
the visible wavelengths of radiation, which
can be seen when it is separated by using a
prism. Light, like all forms of electromagnetic
radiation, can be reflected (bounced back)
and refracted (bent). Different parts of the
electromagnetic spectrum are produced in
different ways. Sometimes visible light –
and infra-red radiation – is generated by the
vibrating particles of warm or hot objects.
The emission of light in this way is called
incandescence. Light can also be produced
by fluorescence, a phenomenon in which
electrons gain and lose energy within atoms.

MAXWELLIAN DIAGRAM OF ELECTROMAGNETIC RADIATION AS WAVES

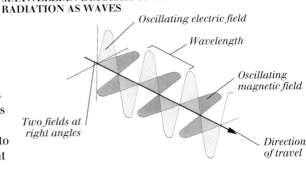

Oscillating electric field

Wavelength

Oscillating
magnetic field

Two fields at
right angles

Direction
of travel

ELECTROMAGNETIC RADIATION AS PARTICLES

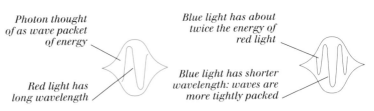

Photon thought
of as wave packet
of energy

Red light has
long wavelength

Blue light has about
twice the energy of
red light

Blue light has shorter
wavelength: waves are
more tightly packed

PHOTON OF RED LIGHT

PHOTON OF BLUE LIGHT

SPLITTING WHITE LIGHT INTO THE SPECTRUM

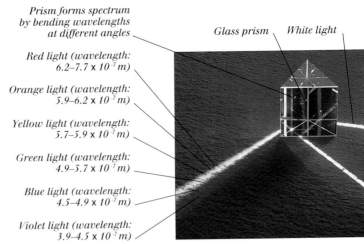

Prism forms spectrum
by bending wavelengths
at different angles

Glass prism

White light

Red light (wavelength:
$6.2–7.7 \times 10^{-7}$ m)

Orange light (wavelength:
$5.9–6.2 \times 10^{-7}$ m)

Yellow light (wavelength:
$5.7–5.9 \times 10^{-7}$ m)

Green light (wavelength:
$4.9–5.7 \times 10^{-7}$ m)

Blue light (wavelength:
$4.5–4.9 \times 10^{-7}$ m)

Violet light (wavelength:
$3.9–4.5 \times 10^{-7}$ m)

THE ELECTROMAGNETIC SPECTRUM

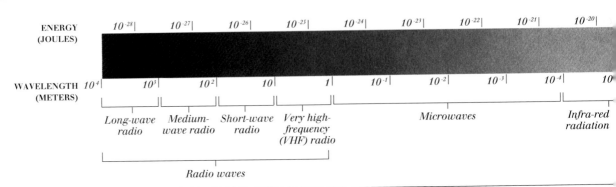

| ENERGY (JOULES) | 10^{-28} | 10^{-27} | 10^{-26} | 10^{-25} | 10^{-24} | 10^{-23} | 10^{-22} | 10^{-21} | 10^{-20} |

| WAVELENGTH (METERS) | 10^4 | 10^3 | 10^2 | 10 | 1 | 10^{-1} | 10^{-2} | 10^{-3} | 10^{-4} | 10 |

Long-wave radio   Medium-wave radio   Short-wave radio   Very high-frequency (VHF) radio   Microwaves   Infra-red radiation

Radio waves

ARTIFICIAL LIGHT SOURCES

FLUORESCENT TUBE

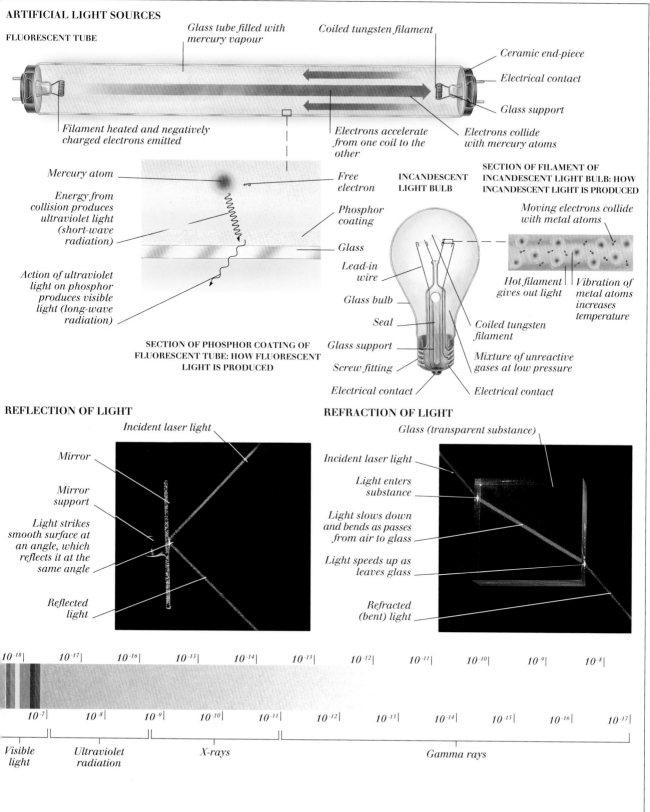

Glass tube filled with mercury vapour

Coiled tungsten filament

Ceramic end-piece

Electrical contact

Glass support

Filament heated and negatively charged electrons emitted

Electrons accelerate from one coil to the other

Electrons collide with mercury atoms

Mercury atom

Energy from collision produces ultraviolet light (short-wave radiation)

Action of ultraviolet light on phosphor produces visible light (long-wave radiation)

Free electron

Phosphor coating

Glass

INCANDESCENT LIGHT BULB

SECTION OF FILAMENT OF INCANDESCENT LIGHT BULB: HOW INCANDESCENT LIGHT IS PRODUCED

Moving electrons collide with metal atoms

Hot filament gives out light

Vibration of metal atoms increases temperature

Lead-in wire

Glass bulb

Seal

Glass support

Screw fitting

Electrical contact

Coiled tungsten filament

Mixture of unreactive gases at low pressure

Electrical contact

SECTION OF PHOSPHOR COATING OF FLUORESCENT TUBE: HOW FLUORESCENT LIGHT IS PRODUCED

REFLECTION OF LIGHT

Incident laser light

Mirror

Mirror support

Light strikes smooth surface at an angle, which reflects it at the same angle

Reflected light

REFRACTION OF LIGHT

Glass (transparent substance)

Incident laser light

Light enters substance

Light slows down and bends as passes from air to glass

Light speeds up as leaves glass

Refracted (bent) light

10^{-18} | 10^{-17} | 10^{-16} | 10^{-15} | 10^{-14} | 10^{-13} | 10^{-12} | 10^{-11} | 10^{-10} | 10^{-9} | 10^{-8} |

10^{-7} | 10^{-8} | 10^{-9} | 10^{-10} | 10^{-11} | 10^{-12} | 10^{-13} | 10^{-14} | 10^{-15} | 10^{-16} | 10^{-17} |

Visible light

Ultraviolet radiation

X-rays

Gamma rays

Force and motion

FORCES ARE PUSHES OR PULLS that change the motion of objects. To make a stationary object move, or a moving object stop, a force is needed. A force is also required to change the speed or direction of an object. This change in speed or direction is known as acceleration. Acceleration depends on the size (magnitude) of the force, and on the mass of the object. The effects of forces were first summarized by Isaac Newton in his three laws of motion. The international unit of force, named after him, is the newton (N), which is approximately equal to the weight of one apple. Gravity – the force of attraction between any two masses – can be measured using a newton meter (spring balance). Forces are put to useful effect in machines. A simple machine, such as a wheel and axle, is a device that changes the size or direction of an applied force. It allows an applied force (the effort) to produce another force (the load). A lever uses a bar that turns on a fulcrum to exert force. In all simple machines, there is a relationship between force and distance. A small force (in a compound pulley, for instance) moves through a large distance to lift a heavy object a small distance. This is called the Law of Simple Machines.

SIMPLE MACHINES

Single-pulley system (simple pulley)

Pulley wheel

Simple pulley only changes direction of a force

Effort is the same size as the load (10 N) and is pulled the same distance

One rope attached to load

Load of 10 N

Two-pulley system (simple pulley)

Pulley wheel

Effort is half the load (5 N), but the rope must be pulled twice the distance

Two ropes share the force and distance

Pulley wheel

Load of 10 N

Four-pulley system (compound pulley)

Two pulley wheels

Effort is one quarter of the load (2.5 N), but the rope must be pulled four times the distance

Four ropes share the force and distance

SIMPLE AND COMPOUND PULLEYS

Two pulley wheels

Load of 10 N

NEWTON METERS (SPRING BALANCES)

Weight is measured using a spring

When weight pulls downwards, pointer moves along scale and measures force

Weight is 10 N

Weight is 20 N

Mass of 1 kg

Mass of 2 kg

WEIGHT AND MASS
The "mass" of an object is a measure of the quantity of matter that it possesses. Mass is usually measured in grams (g) or kilograms (kg). The "weight" of an object is the force exerted on the object's mass by gravity. Since weight is a force, its unit is the newton (N).

Wheel and axle multiplies the effort

Force is transmitted to the wheels by the chain

Pedal

Crank

Effort, provided by cyclist's muscles, is smaller than the load, but moves through a greater distance

A larger force, the load, is produced at the axle

WHEEL AND AXLE

A screw, acting like a wedge wrapped around a shaft, multiplies the effort

Effort, a turning force supplied through a screwdriver

Pitch (the angle of the screw thread)

The smaller the angle of pitch, the less force is required, but more turns are needed to move it through a greater distance

A larger force, the load, pulls the screw into wood

SCREW

Effort pushes axe into wood

A larger force, the load, moves through a smaller distance to push wood apart

Axe blade has wedge shape

Wedge multiplies effort

WEDGE

NEWTON'S THREE LAWS OF MOTION

NEWTON'S FIRST LAW
When no force acts on a body, it will
continue in a state of rest or uniform motion.

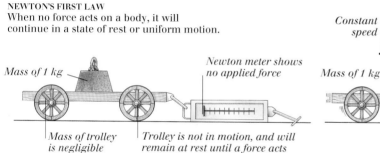

Mass of 1 kg

*Newton meter shows
no applied force*

*Mass of trolley
is negligible*

*Trolley is not in motion, and will
remain at rest until a force acts*

NO FORCE, NO ACCELERATION: STATE OF REST

*Constant
speed*

Mass of 1 kg

*Newton meter
shows no
applied force*

*Trolley is in motion, and will continue at a
constant speed in a straight line until a force acts*

NO FORCE, NO ACCELERATION: UNIFORM MOTION

NEWTON'S SECOND LAW
When a force acts on a body, the motion of the body will change. The size of the change
will depend upon the mass of the object and the magnitude of the applied force.

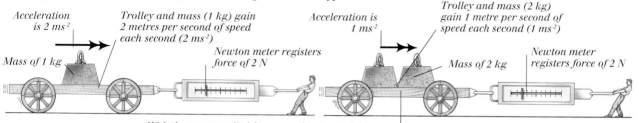

*Acceleration
is 2 ms^{-2}*

*Trolley and mass (1 kg) gain
2 metres per second of speed
each second (2 ms^{-2})*

Mass of 1 kg

*Newton meter registers
force of 2 N*

*Acceleration is
1 ms^{-2}*

*Trolley and mass (2 kg)
gain 1 metre per second of
speed each second (1 ms^{-2})*

Mass of 2 kg

*Newton meter
registers force of 2 N*

*With the same applied force, an object with 2 kg mass
accelerates at half the rate of object with 1 kg mass*

FORCE AND ACCELERATION: SMALL MASS, LARGE ACCELERATION　　**FORCE AND ACCELERATION: LARGE MASS, SMALL ACCELERATION**

NEWTON'S THIRD LAW
If one object exerts a force on another, an equal and opposite force,
called the reaction force, is applied by the second object on the first.

*Newton meters pull on each other with
equal and opposite forces*

*Acceleration: the trolley and
mass accelerate at 2 ms^{-2}*

*Newton meter registers
force of 2 N to the left*

*Newton meter registers
force of 2 N to the right*

Mass of 1 kg

*Person experiences
a reaction force*

ACTION AND REACTION

THREE CLASSES OF LEVER

*Fulcrum,
between effort
and load*

Effort

*Load is greater
than effort, but
moves through
smaller distance*

CLASS 1 LEVER
Pliers consist of two class 1 levers.

Fulcrum

*Load,
between effort
and fulcrum*

*Effort is smaller than load, but
moves through greater distance*

CLASS 2 LEVER
Nutcrackers consist of two class 2 levers.

*Load is applied
at open end*

*Effort forces
tongs together*

*Load is smaller
than effort, but
moves through
greater distance*

*Effort, between
fulcrum and load*

Fulcrum

CLASS 3 LEVER
Tongs consist of two class 3 levers.

RAIL AND ROAD

Steam locomotives

WAGONS THAT ARE PULLED along tracks have been used to transport material since the 16th century, but these trains were drawn by men or horses until the invention of the steam locomotive. Steam locomotives enabled the basic railway system to realize its true potential. In 1804, Richard Trevithick built the world's first working steam locomotive in South Wales. It was not entirely successful, but it encouraged others to develop new designs. By 1829, the British engineer Robert Stephenson had built the "Rocket", considered to be the forerunner of the modern locomotive. The "Rocket" was a self-sufficient unit, carrying coal to heat the boiler and a water supply for generating steam. Steam passed from the boiler to force the pistons back and forth, and this movement turned the driving wheels, propelling the train forwards. Used steam was then expelled in characteristic "chuffs". Later steam locomotives, like "Ellerman Lines" and the "Mallard", worked in a similar way, but on a much larger scale. The simple design and reliability of steam locomotives ensured that they changed very little in 120 years of use, before being replaced from the 1950s by more efficient diesel and electric power (see pp. 326-329).

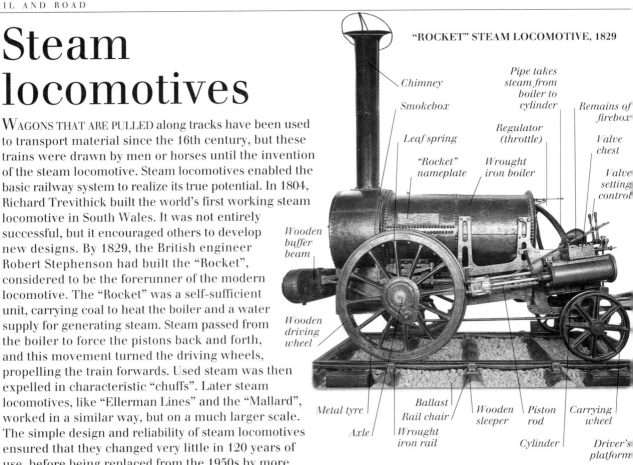

"ROCKET" STEAM LOCOMOTIVE, 1829

Chimney
Smokebox
Leaf spring
"Rocket" nameplate
Pipe takes steam from boiler to cylinder
Regulator (throttle)
Wrought iron boiler
Remains of firebox
Valve chest
Valve setting control
Wooden buffer beam
Wooden driving wheel
Metal tyre
Axle
Ballast
Rail chair
Wrought iron rail
Wooden sleeper
Piston rod
Cylinder
Carrying wheel
Driver's platform
Stay

"ELLERMAN LINES", 1949 (CUTAWAY VIEW)

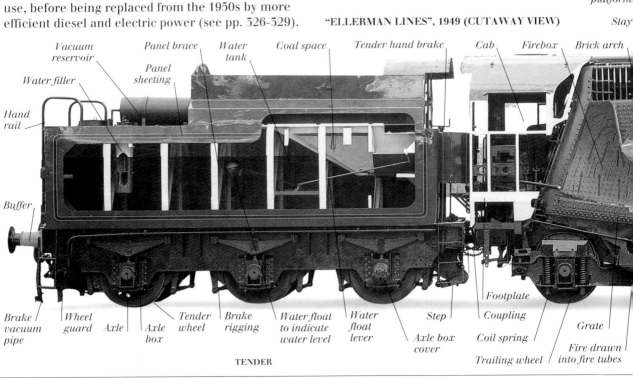

Vacuum reservoir
Water filler
Hand rail
Panel brace
Panel sheeting
Water tank
Coal space
Tender hand brake
Cab
Firebox
Brick arch
Buffer
Brake vacuum pipe
Wheel guard
Axle
Axle box
Tender wheel
Brake rigging
Water float to indicate water level
Water float lever
Step
Axle box cover
Footplate
Coupling
Coil spring
Trailing wheel
Grate
Fire drawn into fire tubes

TENDER

CAB INTERIOR OF "MALLARD" EXPRESS STEAM LOCOMOTIVE, 1938

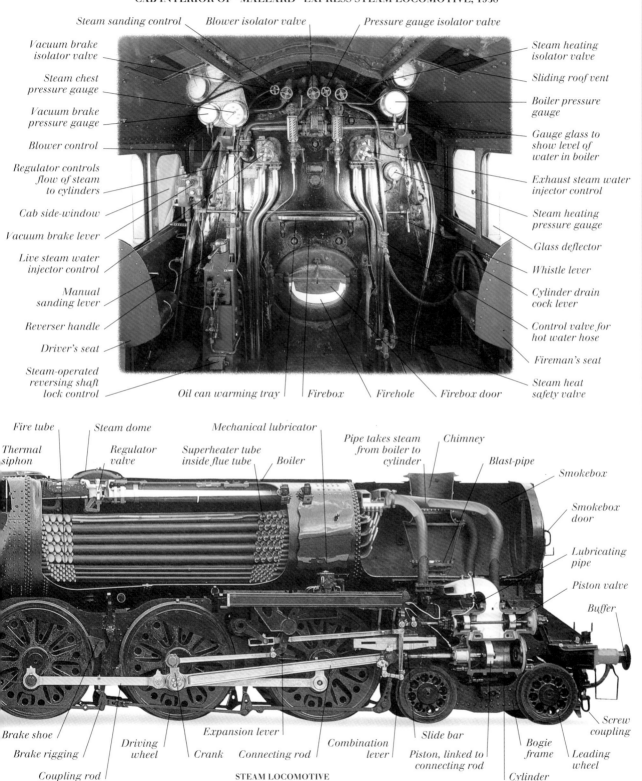

Steam sanding control

Blower isolator valve

Pressure gauge isolator valve

Vacuum brake isolator valve

Steam heating isolator valve

Steam chest pressure gauge

Sliding roof vent

Vacuum brake pressure gauge

Boiler pressure gauge

Blower control

Gauge glass to show level of water in boiler

Regulator controls flow of steam to cylinders

Exhaust steam water injector control

Cab side-window

Steam heating pressure gauge

Vacuum brake lever

Glass deflector

Live steam water injector control

Whistle lever

Manual sanding lever

Cylinder drain cock lever

Reverser handle

Control valve for hot water hose

Driver's seat

Fireman's seat

Steam-operated reversing shaft lock control

Steam heat safety valve

Oil can warming tray

Firebox

Firehole

Firebox door

Fire tube

Steam dome

Mechanical lubricator

Pipe takes steam from boiler to cylinder

Chimney

Thermal siphon

Regulator valve

Superheater tube inside flue tube

Boiler

Blast-pipe

Smokebox

Smokebox door

Lubricating pipe

Piston valve

Buffer

Brake shoe

Expansion lever

Slide bar

Screw coupling

Brake rigging

Driving wheel

Crank

Combination lever

Bogie frame

Leading wheel

Connecting rod

Piston, linked to connecting rod

Coupling rod

Cylinder

STEAM LOCOMOTIVE

Diesel trains

RUDOLF DIESEL FIRST DEMONSTRATED the diesel engine in
Germany in 1898, but it was not until the 1940s that diesel
locomotives were successfully established on both passenger
and freight services, in the US. Early diesel locomotives like
the "Union Pacific" were more expensive to build than steam
locomotives, but were more efficient and cheaper to operate,
especially where oil was plentiful. One feature of diesel engines
is that the power output cannot be coupled directly to the wheels.
To convert the mechanical energy produced by diesel engines,
a transmission system is needed. Almost all diesel locomotives
have electric transmissions, and are known as "diesel-electric"
locomotives. The diesel engine works by drawing air into the
cylinders and compressing it to increase its temperature; a small
quantity of diesel fuel is then injected into it. The resulting
combustion drives the generator (more recently an alternator)
to produce electricity, which is fed to electric motors connected
to the wheels. Diesel-electric locomotives are essentially
electric locomotives that carry their own power plants, and
are used worldwide today. The "Deltic" diesel-electric
locomotive, similar to the one shown here, replaced
classic express steam locomotives, and ran
at speeds up to 160 kph (100 mph).

**FRONT VIEW OF "UNION PACIFIC"
DIESEL-ELECTRIC LOCOMOTIVE, 1950s**

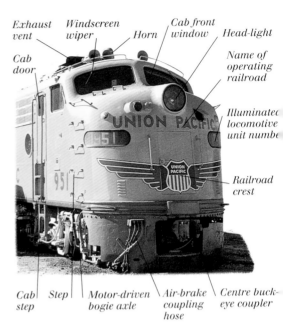

PROTOTYPE "DELTIC" DIESEL-ELECTRIC LOCOMOTIVE, 1956

DIESEL ENGINE OF BRITISH RAIL CLASS 20 DIESEL-ELECTRIC LOCOMOTIVE

EXAMPLES OF FREIGHT CARS

BOX CAR

HOPPER CAR

REFRIGERATOR CAR

LIVESTOCK CAR

FLAT CAR WITH BULKHEADS

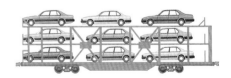

AUTOMOBILE CAR

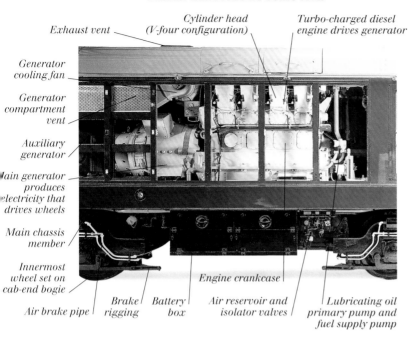

Exhaust vent

Cylinder head (V-four configuration)

Turbo-charged diesel engine drives generator

Generator cooling fan

Generator compartment vent

Auxiliary generator

Main generator produces electricity that drives wheels

Main chassis member

Innermost wheel set on cab-end bogie

Air brake pipe

Brake rigging

Battery box

Engine crankcase

Air reservoir and isolator valves

Lubricating oil primary pump and fuel supply pump

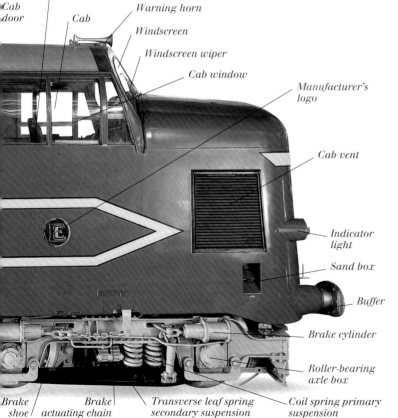

Cab door

Driver's seat

Cab

Warning horn

Windscreen

Windscreen wiper

Cab window

Manufacturer's logo

Cab vent

Indicator light

Sand box

Buffer

Brake cylinder

Roller-bearing axle box

Brake shoe

Brake actuating chain

Transverse leaf spring secondary suspension

Coil spring primary suspension

Electric and high-speed trains

THE FIRST ELECTRIC LOCOMOTIVE ran in 1879 in Berlin, Germany. In Europe, electric trains developed as a more efficient alternative to the steam locomotive and diesel-electric power. Like diesels, electric trains employ electric motors to drive the wheels but, unlike diesels, the electricity is generated externally at a power station. Electric current is picked up either from a catenary (overhead cable) via a pantograph, or from a third rail. Since it does not carry its own power-generating equipment, an electric locomotive has a better power-to-weight ratio and greater acceleration than its diesel-electric equivalent. This makes electric trains suitable for urban routes with many stops. They are also faster, quieter, and less polluting. The latest electric French TGV (Train à Grande Vitesse) reaches 300 kph (186 mph); other trains, like the London to Paris and Brussels "Eurostar", can run at several voltages and operate between different countries. Simpler electric trains perform special duties – the "People Mover" at Gatwick Airport in Britain runs between terminals.

HOW ALTERNATING CURRENT (AC) ELECTRIC TRAINS WORK

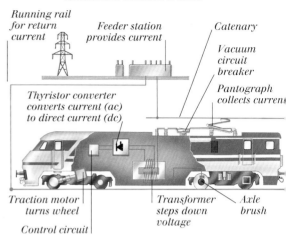

Running rail for return current

Feeder station provides current

Catenary

Vacuum circuit breaker

Pantograph collects current

Thyristor converter converts current (ac) to direct current (dc)

Traction motor turns wheel

Control circuit

Transformer steps down voltage

Axle brush

FRONT VIEW OF PARIS METRO

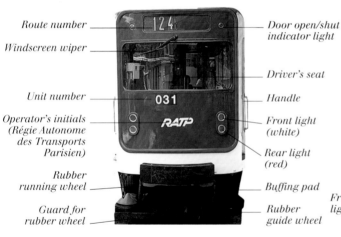

Route number

Windscreen wiper

Unit number

Operator's initials (Régie Autonome des Transports Parisien)

Rubber running wheel

Guard for rubber wheel

Door open/shut indicator light

Driver's seat

Handle

Front light (white)

Rear light (red)

Buffing pad

Rubber guide wheel

FRONT VIEW OF ITALIAN STATE RAILWAYS CLASS 402 ELECTRIC LOCOMOTIVE

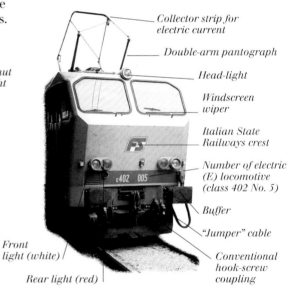

Collector strip for electric current

Double-arm pantograph

Head-light

Windscreen wiper

Italian State Railways crest

Number of electric (E) locomotive (class 402 No. 5)

Buffer

"Jumper" cable

Conventional hook-screw coupling

Front light (white)

Rear light (red)

SIDE VIEW OF GATWICK EXPRESS "PEOPLE MOVER"

Pneumatic rubber wheel

Concrete track

Automatic door

No driver (train controlled by central computer)

"EUROSTAR" MULTI-VOLTAGE ELECTRIC TRAIN

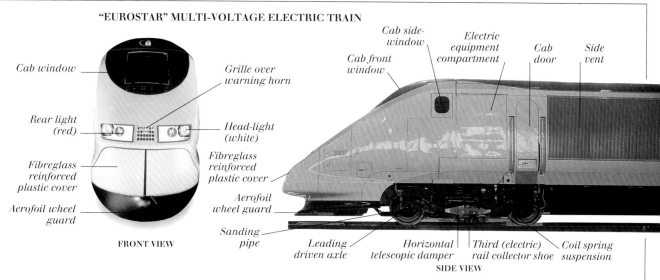

Cab window

Rear light (red)

Head-light (white)

Grille over warning horn

Fibreglass reinforced plastic cover

Aerofoil wheel guard

FRONT VIEW

Cab side-window

Cab front window

Electric equipment compartment

Cab door

Side vent

Fibreglass reinforced plastic cover

Aerofoil wheel guard

Sanding pipe

Leading driven axle

Horizontal telescopic damper

Third (electric) rail collector shoe

Coil spring suspension

SIDE VIEW

TGV ELECTRIC HIGH-SPEED TRAIN

Luggage rack

Reading light

Double-glazed and tinted side-window

Sliding curtain

Seat

Main overhead lighting

Automatic electric carriage end door

Antimacassar

Headrest

Armrest

Centre gangway

INTERIOR OF TGV

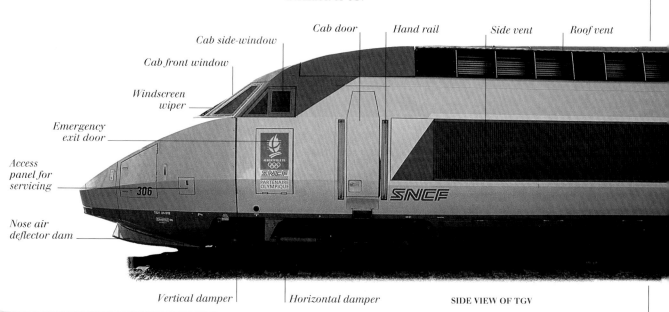

Cab side-window

Cab front window

Windscreen wiper

Emergency exit door

Access panel for servicing

Nose air deflector dam

Cab door

Hand rail

Side vent

Roof vent

Vertical damper

Horizontal damper

SIDE VIEW OF TGV

Train equipment

MODERN RAILWAY TRACK consists of two parallel steel rails clipped on to a support called a sleeper. Sleepers are usually made of reinforced concrete, although wood and steel are still used. The distance between the inside edges of the rails is the track gauge. It evolved in Britain, which uses a gauge of 1,435 mm (4 ft 8½ in), known as the standard gauge. As engineering grew more sophisticated, narrower gauges were adopted because they cost less to build. The loading gauge, which is equally important, determines the size of the largest loaded vehicle that may pass through tunnels and under bridges with adequate clearance. Safe train operation relies on following a signalling system. At first, signalling was based on a simple time interval between trains, but it now depends on maintaining a safe distance between successive trains travelling in the same direction. Most modern signals are colour lights, but older mechanical semaphore signals are still used. On the latest high-speed lines, train drivers receive control instructions by electronic means. Signalling depends on reliable control of the train by effective braking. For fast, modern trains, which have considerable momentum, it is essential that each vehicle in the train can be braked by the driver or by a train control system, such as Automatic Train Protection (ATP). Braking is achieved by the brake shoe acting on the wheel rim (rim brakes), by disc brakes, or, increasingly, by electrical braking.

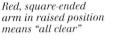

MECHANICAL SEMAPHORE SIGNAL

Red, square-ended arm in raised position means "all clear"

Red glass

Green glass

Actuating lever system

Motor operating "home" stop signal

Green glass

Yellow glass

Yellow, "distant" warning arm in horizontal position means "caution"

Tubular steel post

Ladder

Electrical relay box

FOUR-ASPECT COLOUR LIGHT SIGNAL

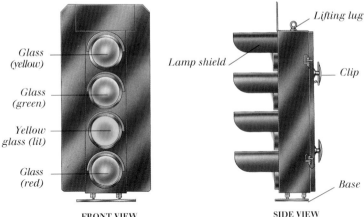

Glass (yellow)

Glass (green)

Yellow glass (lit)

Glass (red)

Lamp shield

Lifting lug

Clip

Base

FRONT VIEW

SIDE VIEW

HOW A MODERN MAIN-LINE SIGNALLING SYSTEM WORKS

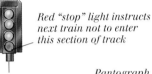

Red "stop" light instructs next train not to enter this section of track

Green "all clear" light instructs train B to proceed into this section of track

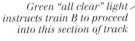

Green "all clear" light instructs train B to proceed into this section of track

Green "all clear" light instructs train B to proceed into this section of track

Pantograph

Catenary

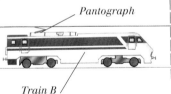

Train B

Track

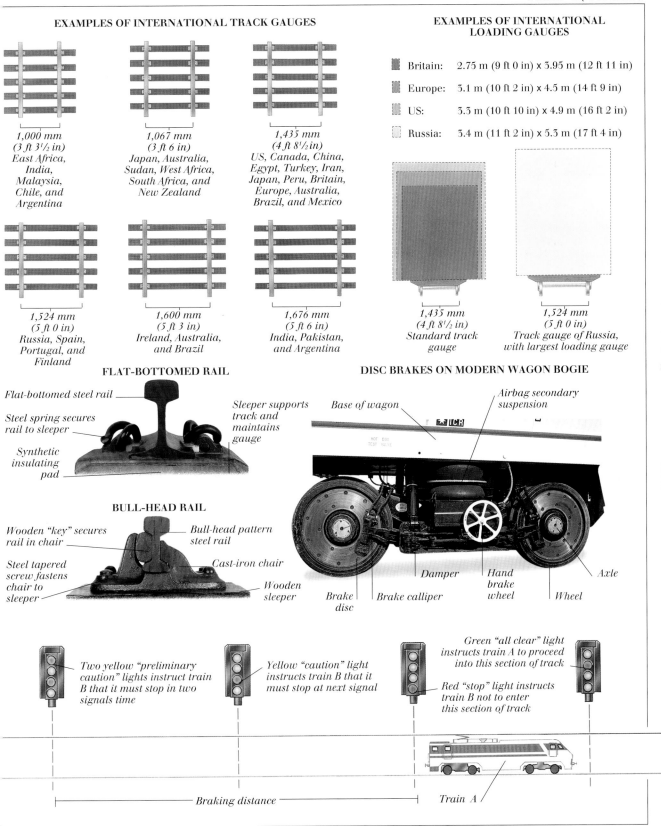

EXAMPLES OF INTERNATIONAL TRACK GAUGES

1,000 mm
(3 ft 3½ in)
*East Africa,
India,
Malaysia,
Chile, and
Argentina*

1,067 mm
(3 ft 6 in)
*Japan, Australia,
Sudan, West Africa,
South Africa, and
New Zealand*

1,435 mm
(4 ft 8½ in)
*US, Canada, China,
Egypt, Turkey, Iran,
Japan, Peru, Britain,
Europe, Australia,
Brazil, and Mexico*

1,524 mm
(5 ft 0 in)
*Russia, Spain,
Portugal, and
Finland*

1,600 mm
(5 ft 3 in)
*Ireland, Australia,
and Brazil*

1,676 mm
(5 ft 6 in)
*India, Pakistan,
and Argentina*

EXAMPLES OF INTERNATIONAL LOADING GAUGES

Britain: 2.75 m (9 ft 0 in) x 3.95 m (12 ft 11 in)

Europe: 3.1 m (10 ft 2 in) x 4.5 m (14 ft 9 in)

US: 3.3 m (10 ft 10 in) x 4.9 m (16 ft 2 in)

Russia: 3.4 m (11 ft 2 in) x 5.5 m (17 ft 4 in)

1,435 mm
(4 ft 8½ in)
*Standard track
gauge*

1,524 mm
(5 ft 0 in)
*Track gauge of Russia,
with largest loading gauge*

FLAT-BOTTOMED RAIL

Flat-bottomed steel rail

Steel spring secures rail to sleeper

Synthetic insulating pad

Sleeper supports track and maintains gauge

BULL-HEAD RAIL

Wooden "key" secures rail in chair

Steel tapered screw fastens chair to sleeper

Bull-head pattern steel rail

Cast-iron chair

Wooden sleeper

DISC BRAKES ON MODERN WAGON BOGIE

Base of wagon

Airbag secondary suspension

Damper

Hand brake wheel

Axle

Wheel

Brake disc

Brake calliper

Two yellow "preliminary caution" lights instruct train B that it must stop in two signals time

Yellow "caution" light instructs train B that it must stop at next signal

Green "all clear" light instructs train A to proceed into this section of track

Red "stop" light instructs train B not to enter this section of track

Braking distance

Train A

Trams and buses

METROLINK TRAM,
MANCHESTER,
BRITAIN

AS CITY POPULATIONS exploded in the 1800s, there was an urgent need for mass transportation. Trams were an early solution. The first trams, like buses, were horse-drawn, but in 1881, electric street tramways appeared in Berlin, Germany. Electric trams soon became widespread throughout Europe and North America. Trams run on rails along a fixed route, using electric motors that receive power from overhead cables. As road networks developed, motorized buses offered a flexible alternative to trams. By the 1930s, they had replaced tram systems in many cities. City buses typically have doors at both front and rear to make loading and unloading easier. Double-decker designs are popular, occupying the same amount of street space as single-decker buses but able to transport twice the number of people. Buses are also commonly used for inter-city travel and touring. Tour buses have reclining seats, large windows, luggage space, and toilets. Recently, as city traffic has become increasingly congested, many city planners have designed new tram routes to run alongside bus routes as part of an integrated transport system.

EARLY TRAM, c.1900

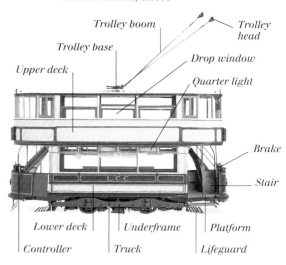

Trolley boom

Trolley base

Trolley head

Drop window

Upper deck

Quarter light

Brake

Stair

Lower deck

Underframe

Platform

Controller

Truck

Lifeguard

MCW METROBUS, LONDON, BRITAIN

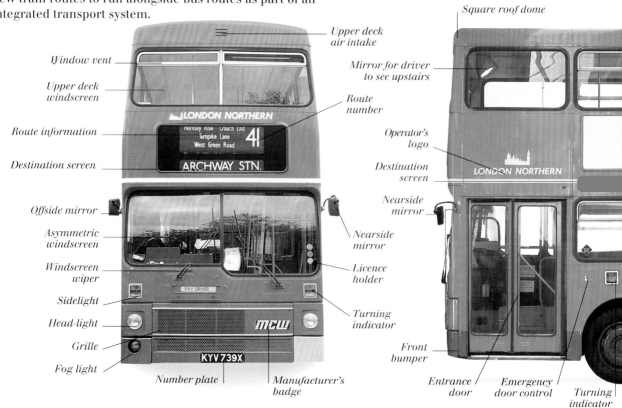

Window vent

Upper deck windscreen

Route information

Destination screen

Offside mirror

Asymmetric windscreen

Windscreen wiper

Sidelight

Head-light

Grille

Fog light

Number plate

Manufacturer's badge

Upper deck air intake

Route number

Nearside mirror

Licence holder

Turning indicator

LONDON NORTHERN

Hornsey Rise · Crouch End
Turnpike Lane
West Green Road

41

ARCHWAY STN.

PAY DRIVER

mcw

KYV 739X

Square roof dome

Mirror for driver to see upstairs

Operator's logo

Destination screen

Nearside mirror

Front bumper

Entrance door

Emergency door control

Turning indicator

LONDON NORTHERN

FRONT VIEW

SINGLE-DECKER BUS, NEW YORK, US

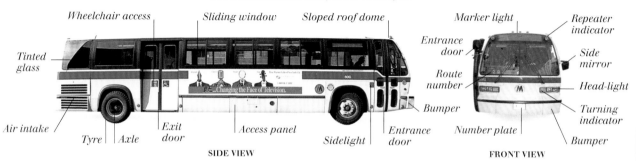

Wheelchair access

Sliding window

Sloped roof dome

Tinted glass

Air intake

Tyre

Axle

Exit door

Access panel

Sidelight

Entrance door

SIDE VIEW

Marker light

Repeater indicator

Entrance door

Side mirror

Route number

Head-light

Bumper

Turning indicator

Number plate

Bumper

FRONT VIEW

DOUBLE-DECKER TOUR BUS, PARIS, FRANCE

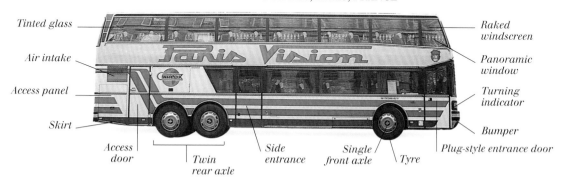

Tinted glass

Air intake

Access panel

Skirt

Access door

Twin rear axle

Side entrance

Single front axle

Tyre

Plug-style entrance door

Bumper

Turning indicator

Panoramic window

Raked windscreen

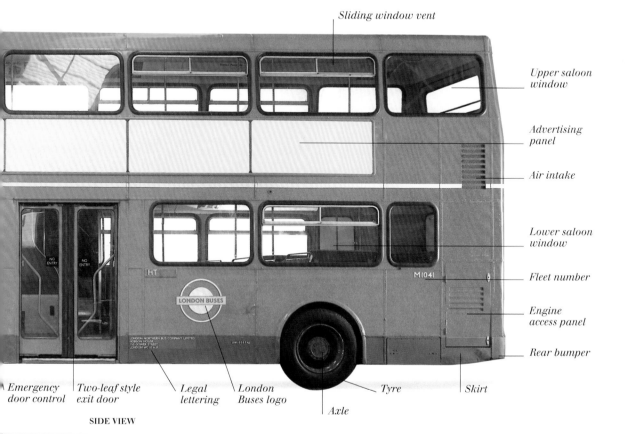

Sliding window vent

Upper saloon window

Advertising panel

Air intake

Lower saloon window

Fleet number

Engine access panel

Rear bumper

Skirt

Emergency door control

Two-leaf style exit door

Legal lettering

London Buses logo

Axle

Tyre

SIDE VIEW

The first cars

THE EARLIEST ROAD VEHICLE powered by an engine, the Cugnot steam traction engine, was built in 1770. More practical steam carriages, such as the Bordino, were available in the early 19th century, but they were heavy and cumbersome. Restrictive laws and the introduction of railways, faster and able to carry more passengers, saw the decline of "cars" powered by steam. It was not until 1860 that the first practical power unit for road vehicles was developed, with the invention of the internal combustion engine by the Belgian Etienne Lenoir. By around 1890, Karl Benz and Gottlieb Daimler in Germany, and Albert de Dion and Armand Peugeot in France were building cars for sale to the public. These early cars, despite being primitive, expensive, and produced in limited numbers, heralded the age of the motor car.

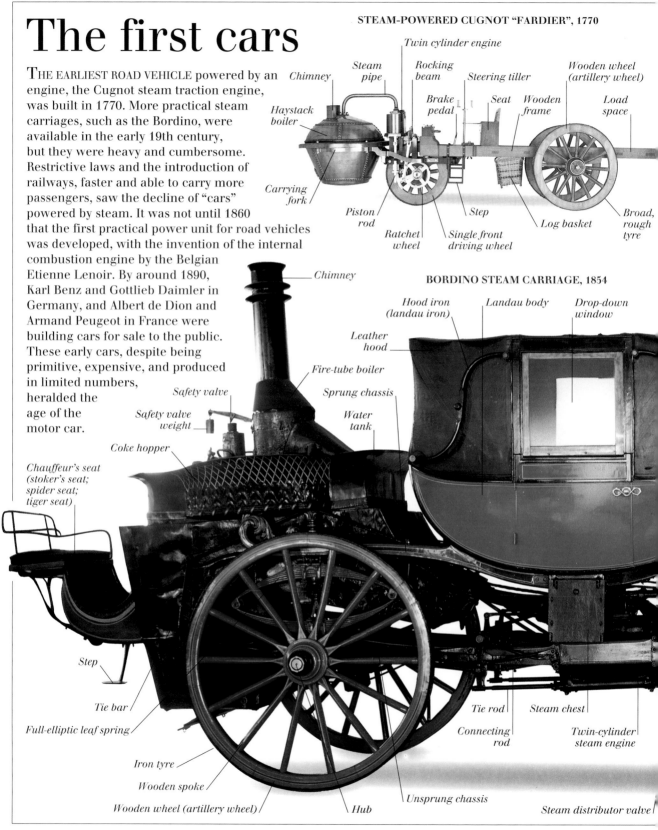

STEAM-POWERED CUGNOT "FARDIER", 1770

Chimney
Steam pipe
Twin cylinder engine
Rocking beam
Steering tiller
Wooden wheel (artillery wheel)
Brake pedal
Seat
Wooden frame
Load space
Haystack boiler
Carrying fork
Piston rod
Ratchet wheel
Single front driving wheel
Step
Log basket
Broad, rough tyre

BORDINO STEAM CARRIAGE, 1854

Chimney
Hood iron (landau iron)
Landau body
Drop-down window
Leather hood
Fire-tube boiler
Sprung chassis
Water tank
Safety valve
Safety valve weight
Coke hopper
Chauffeur's seat (stoker's seat; spider seat; tiger seat)
Step
Tie bar
Full-elliptic leaf spring
Iron tyre
Wooden spoke
Wooden wheel (artillery wheel)
Hub
Tie rod
Steam chest
Connecting rod
Twin-cylinder steam engine
Unsprung chassis
Steam distributor valve

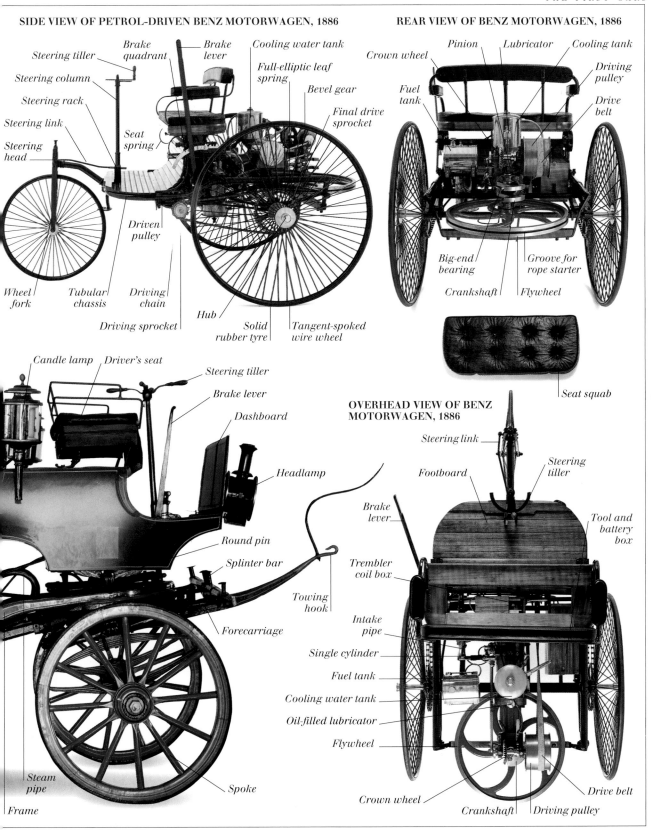

SIDE VIEW OF PETROL-DRIVEN BENZ MOTORWAGEN, 1886

Steering tiller

Brake quadrant

Brake lever

Cooling water tank

Full-elliptic leaf spring

Bevel gear

Steering column

Steering rack

Steering link

Seat spring

Final drive sprocket

Steering head

Driven pulley

Wheel fork

Tubular chassis

Driving chain

Driving sprocket

Hub

Solid rubber tyre

Tangent-spoked wire wheel

REAR VIEW OF BENZ MOTORWAGEN, 1886

Crown wheel

Pinion

Lubricator

Cooling tank

Fuel tank

Driving pulley

Drive belt

Big-end bearing

Groove for rope starter

Crankshaft

Flywheel

Seat squab

OVERHEAD VIEW OF BENZ MOTORWAGEN, 1886

Candle lamp

Driver's seat

Steering tiller

Brake lever

Dashboard

Steering link

Footboard

Steering tiller

Headlamp

Brake lever

Tool and battery box

Round pin

Splinter bar

Trembler coil box

Towing hook

Intake pipe

Forecarriage

Single cylinder

Fuel tank

Cooling water tank

Oil-filled lubricator

Flywheel

Steam pipe

Spoke

Frame

Crown wheel

Crankshaft

Driving pulley

Drive belt

Elegance and utility

DURING THE FIRST DECADE OF THE 20TH CENTURY, the motorist who could afford it had a choice of some of the finest cars ever made. These handbuilt cars were powerful and luxurious, using the finest woods, leathers, and cloths, and bodywork made to the customer's individual requirements; some had six-cylinder engines as big as 15 litres. The price of such cars was several times that of an average house, and their yearly running costs were also very high. As a result, basic, utilitarian cars became popular. Costing perhaps one-tenth of the price of a luxury car, these cars had very little trim and often had only single-cylinder engines.

1904 OLDSMOBILE SINGLE-CYLINDER ENGINE

Oil bottle dripfeed
Crankcase
Starting handle bracket
Exhaust pipe
Cylinder head
Cylinder
Starter cog
Carburettor
Engine timing gear
Crankshaft
Flywheel
Gear band

FRONT VIEW OF 1906 RENAULT

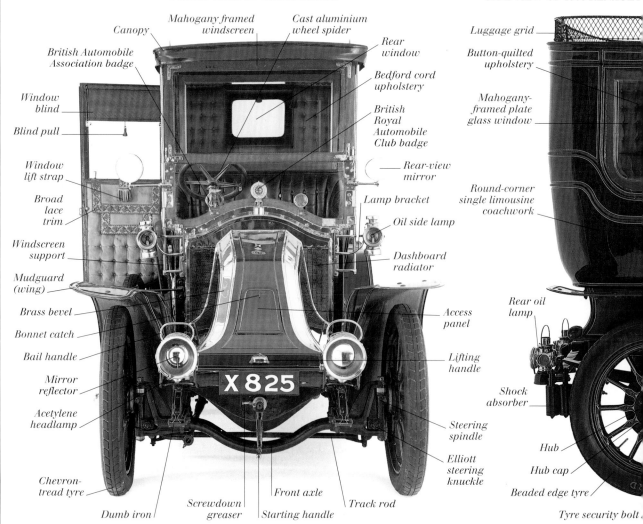

Canopy
Mahogany framed windscreen
Cast aluminium wheel spider
Rear window
British Automobile Association badge
Bedford cord upholstery
Window blind
British Royal Automobile Club badge
Blind pull
Window lift strap
Rear-view mirror
Broad lace trim
Lamp bracket
Oil side lamp
Windscreen support
Dashboard radiator
Mudguard (wing)
Brass bevel
Access panel
Bonnet catch
Bail handle
Lifting handle
Mirror reflector
Acetylene headlamp
Steering spindle
Chevron-tread tyre
Elliott steering knuckle
Dumb iron
Screwdown greaser
Front axle
Starting handle
Track rod

SIDE VIEW OF 1906 RENAULT

Luggage grid
Button-quilted upholstery
Mahogany-framed plate glass window
Round-corner single limousine coachwork
Rear oil lamp
Shock absorber
Hub
Hub cap
Beaded edge tyre
Tyre security bolt

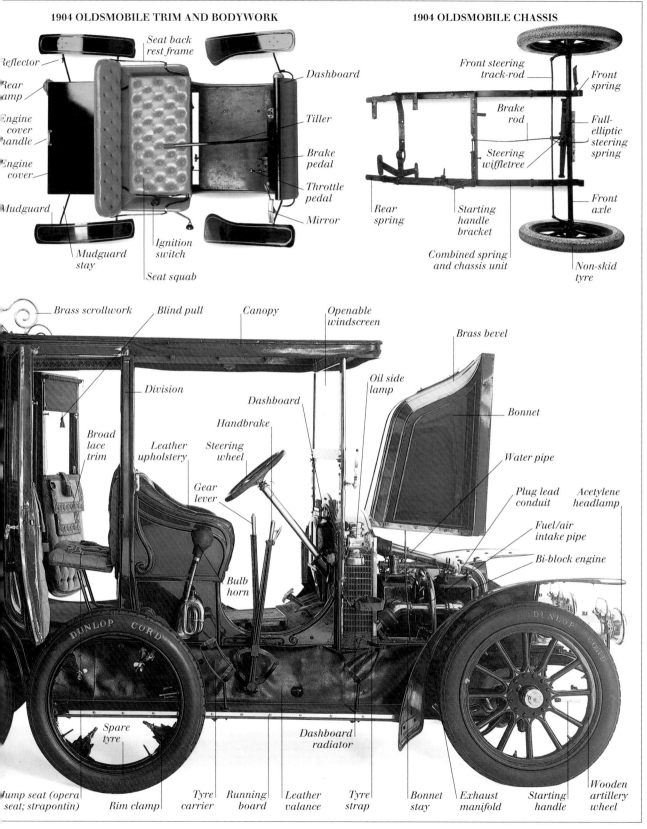

1904 OLDSMOBILE TRIM AND BODYWORK

Reflector

Rear lamp

Engine cover handle

Engine cover

Mudguard

Seat back rest frame

Dashboard

Tiller

Brake pedal

Throttle pedal

Mirror

Mudguard stay

Ignition switch

Seat squab

1904 OLDSMOBILE CHASSIS

Front steering track-rod

Brake rod

Steering wiffletree

Rear spring

Starting handle bracket

Combined spring and chassis unit

Front spring

Full-elliptic steering spring

Front axle

Non-skid tyre

Brass scrollwork

Blind pull

Canopy

Openable windscreen

Brass bevel

Oil side lamp

Division

Dashboard

Bonnet

Broad lace trim

Handbrake

Leather upholstery

Steering wheel

Gear lever

Water pipe

Plug lead conduit

Acetylene headlamp

Fuel/air intake pipe

Bi-block engine

Bulb horn

Spare tyre

Dashboard radiator

Jump seat (opera seat; strapontin)

Rim clamp

Tyre carrier

Running board

Leather valance

Tyre strap

Bonnet stay

Exhaust manifold

Starting handle

Wooden artillery wheel

DUNLOP CORD

DUNLOP CORD

Mass-production

THE FIRST CARS WERE HAND-ASSEMBLED from individually built parts, a time-consuming procedure that required skilled mechanics and made cars very expensive. This problem was solved, in America, by a Detroit car manufacturer named Henry Ford; he introduced mass-production by using standardized parts, and later combined these with a moving production line. The work was brought to the workers, each of whom performed one simple task in the construction process as the chassis moved along the line. The first mass-produced car, the Ford Model T, was launched in 1908 and was available in a limited range of body styles and colours. However, when the production line was introduced in 1914, the colour range was cut back; the Model T became available, as Henry Ford said, in "any colour you like, so long as it's black". Ford cut the production time for a car from several days to about 12 hours, and eventually to minutes, making cars much cheaper than before. As a result, by 1920 half the cars in the world were Model T Fords.

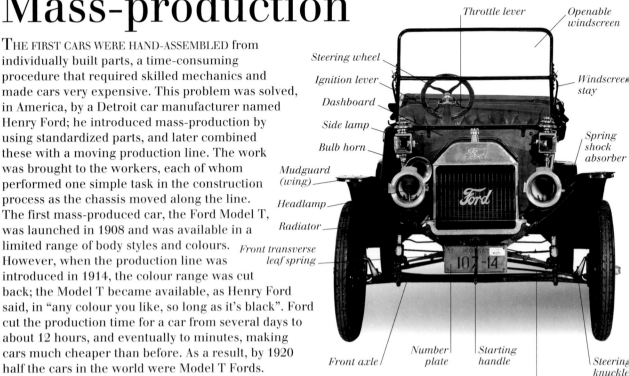

STAGES OF FORD MODEL T PRODUCTION

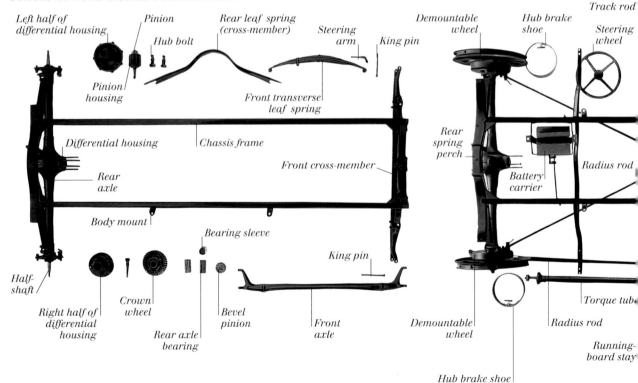

SIDE VIEW OF 1913 FORD MODEL T

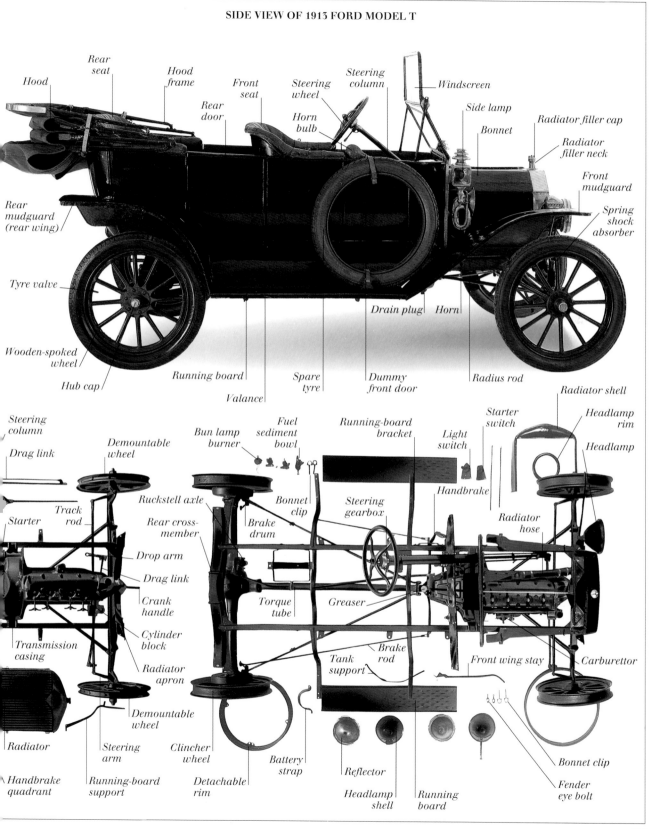

Hood

Rear seat

Hood frame

Front seat

Steering wheel

Horn bulb

Steering column

Windscreen

Rear door

Side lamp

Bonnet

Radiator filler cap

Radiator filler neck

Front mudguard

Rear mudguard (rear wing)

Spring shock absorber

Tyre valve

Wooden-spoked wheel

Hub cap

Running board

Valance

Spare tyre

Drain plug

Horn

Dummy front door

Radius rod

Radiator shell

Steering column

Drag link

Demountable wheel

Bun lamp burner

Fuel sediment bowl

Running-board bracket

Light switch

Starter switch

Headlamp rim

Headlamp

Starter

Track rod

Ruckstell axle

Rear cross-member

Bonnet clip

Steering gearbox

Handbrake

Radiator hose

Drop arm

Brake drum

Drag link

Crank handle

Cylinder block

Radiator apron

Demountable wheel

Torque tube

Greaser

Brake rod

Tank support

Front wing stay

Carburettor

Transmission casing

Radiator

Steering arm

Running-board support

Clincher wheel

Detachable rim

Battery strap

Reflector

Headlamp shell

Running board

Bonnet clip

Fender eye bolt

Handbrake quadrant

The "people's car"

THE MOST POPULAR CAR in the history of car manufacture is the Volkswagen Beetle, originally called the KdF Wagen. The car was developed in Germany in the 1930s by Dr. Ferdinand Porsche. At that time, Germany had only half the number of cars of Britain or France, and Adolf Hitler took a personal interest in the development of the Volkswagen ("people's car"). The intention was to provide a new industry, new jobs, and a car so cheap that anyone in work could afford it. Dr. Porsche designed a car that was cheap to build and run; its rear-mounted, air-cooled engine cut down the number of parts needed and also reduced weight. However, few civilians managed to obtain the Beetle before the outbreak of the Second World War in 1939. After the war, the Beetle proved so popular that eventually more than 20 million were sold.

CUSTOMIZED VOLKSWAGEN BEETLE

FLAT-FOUR CYLINDER ARRANGEMENT

Fuel tank
Steering tie-rod
Fuel tank sender unit
Fuel filler neck
Windscreen-wiper motor assembly
Steering box assembly
Steering idler
Frame head
Anti-roll bar
Suspension strut
Brake back plate
Track control arm
Pedal cluster
Dust shroud
Strut insert (shock absorber)
Gear lever knob
Front suspension top mount
Rear lamp
Air scoop
Quarter light
Bonnet
Seat mount
Front road spring
Handbrake
Front suspension top mount
Floor pan (platform chassis)
Indicator
Torsion bar cover
Rear brake drum
Trailing arm
Pressed steel wheel
Fuel filler cap
Tail pipe
Tyre
Counterweight
Piston
Rear shock absorber
Drive shaft
Sports wheel
Transaxle (gearbox and final drive)
Heat exchanger
Clutch and flywheel
Starter motor
Crankshaft
Flat-four engine
Connecting rod (con-rod)
Air filter
Tail pipe
Big end

**BODY SHELL OF
VOLKSWAGEN BEETLE**

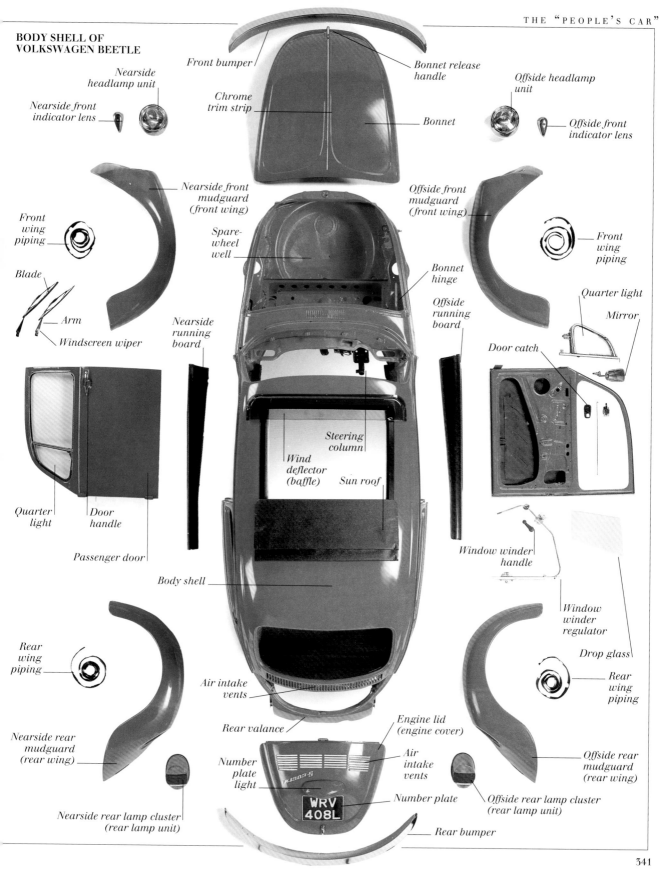

Front bumper

Bonnet release
handle

Nearside
headlamp unit

Offside headlamp
unit

Nearside front
indicator lens

Chrome
trim strip

Bonnet

Offside front
indicator lens

Nearside front
mudguard
(front wing)

Offside front
mudguard
(front wing)

Front
wing
piping

Spare-
wheel
well

Front
wing
piping

Bonnet
hinge

Quarter light

Blade

Mirror

Offside
running
board

Arm

Nearside
running
board

Door catch

Windscreen wiper

Steering
column

Wind
deflector
(baffle)

Sun roof

Quarter
light

Door
handle

Window winder
handle

Passenger door

Window
winder
regulator

Body shell

Drop glass

Rear
wing
piping

Rear
wing
piping

Air intake
vents

Nearside rear
mudguard
(rear wing)

Rear valance

Engine lid
(engine cover)

Air
intake
vents

Offside rear
mudguard
(rear wing)

Number
plate
light

Offside rear lamp cluster
(rear lamp unit)

Number plate

Nearside rear lamp cluster
(rear lamp unit)

WRV
408L

Rear bumper

Early engines

STEAM AND ELECTRICITY were used to power cars until early this century, but neither power source was ideal. Electric cars had to stop frequently to recharge their heavy batteries, and steam cars gave smooth power delivery but were too complicated for the average motorist to use. A rival power source, the internal combustion engine, was invented in 1860 by Etienne Lenoir (see pp. 334-335). This engine converted the force of a controlled explosion into rotary motion, to turn the wheels of a vehicle. Early variations on this basic model included sleeve valves, separately cast cylinders, and the two-stroke combustion cycle. Today, many internal combustion engines, including the Wankel rotary and diesels (see pp. 346-347), use the four-stroke cycle, first demonstrated by Nikolaus Otto in 1876. The Otto cycle, often described as "suck, squeeze, bang, blow", has proved the best method of ensuring that the engine turns over smoothly and that exhaust emissions are controllable.

TROJAN TWO-STROKE ENGINE, 1927

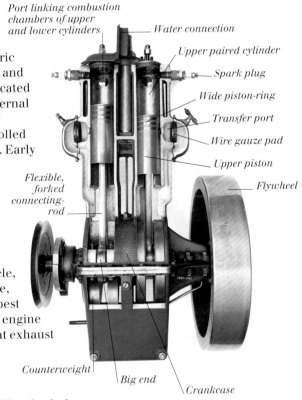

Port linking combustion chambers of upper and lower cylinders

Water connection

Upper paired cylinder

Spark plug

Wide piston-ring

Transfer port

Wire gauze pad

Upper piston

Flywheel

Flexible, forked connecting-rod

Counterweight

Big end

Crankcase

BERSEY ELECTRIC CAB, 1896

Mounting for tray of 40 batteries

Housing for electric motors

SECTIONED WHITE STEAM CAR, 1903

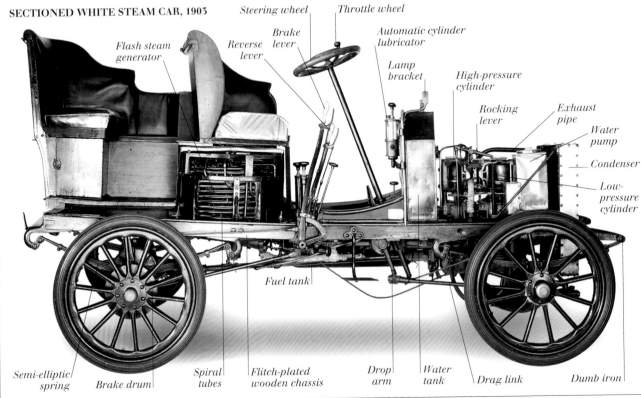

Steering wheel

Throttle wheel

Brake lever

Reverse lever

Automatic cylinder lubricator

Flash steam generator

Lamp bracket

High-pressure cylinder

Rocking lever

Exhaust pipe

Water pump

Condenser

Low-pressure cylinder

Fuel tank

Semi-elliptic spring

Brake drum

Spiral tubes

Flitch-plated wooden chassis

Drop arm

Water tank

Drag link

Dumb iron

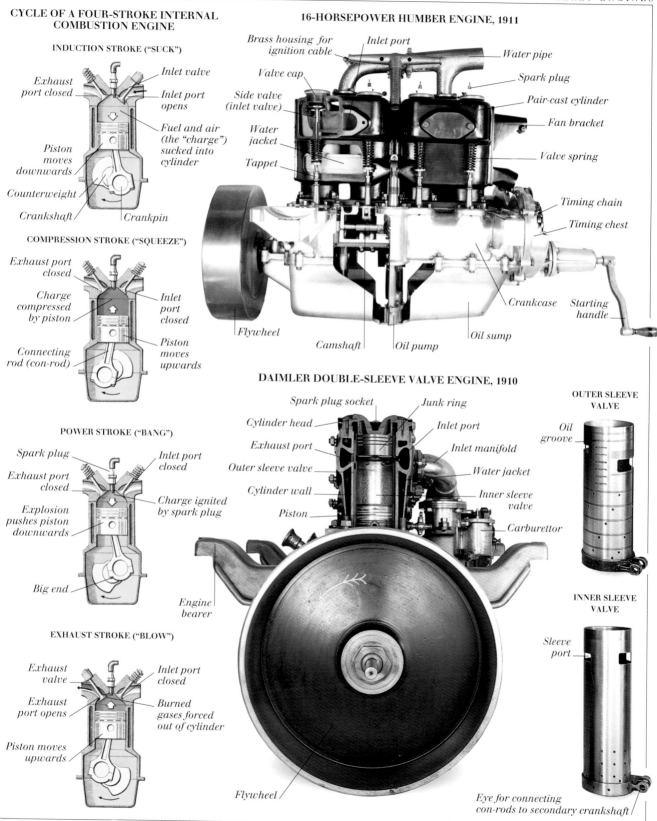

CYCLE OF A FOUR-STROKE INTERNAL COMBUSTION ENGINE

INDUCTION STROKE ("SUCK")

Exhaust port closed
Inlet valve
Inlet port opens
Fuel and air (the "charge") sucked into cylinder
Piston moves downwards
Counterweight
Crankshaft
Crankpin

COMPRESSION STROKE ("SQUEEZE")

Exhaust port closed
Charge compressed by piston
Inlet port closed
Piston moves upwards
Connecting rod (con-rod)

POWER STROKE ("BANG")

Spark plug
Inlet port closed
Exhaust port closed
Charge ignited by spark plug
Explosion pushes piston downwards
Big end

EXHAUST STROKE ("BLOW")

Exhaust valve
Inlet port closed
Exhaust port opens
Burned gases forced out of cylinder
Piston moves upwards

16-HORSEPOWER HUMBER ENGINE, 1911

Brass housing for ignition cable
Inlet port
Water pipe
Valve cap
Spark plug
Side valve (inlet valve)
Pair-cast cylinder
Water jacket
Fan bracket
Tappet
Valve spring
Timing chain
Timing chest
Flywheel
Camshaft
Oil pump
Oil sump
Crankcase
Starting handle

DAIMLER DOUBLE-SLEEVE VALVE ENGINE, 1910

Spark plug socket
Junk ring
Cylinder head
Inlet port
Exhaust port
Inlet manifold
Outer sleeve valve
Water jacket
Cylinder wall
Inner sleeve valve
Piston
Carburettor
Engine bearer
Flywheel

OUTER SLEEVE VALVE

Oil groove

INNER SLEEVE VALVE

Sleeve port
Eye for connecting con-rods to secondary crankshaft

Modern engines

TODAY'S PETROL ENGINE WORKS on the same basic principles as the first car engines of a century ago, although it has been greatly refined. Modern engines, often made from special metal alloys, are much lighter than earlier engines. Computerized ignition systems, fuel injectors, and multi-valve cylinder heads achieve a more efficient combustion of the fuel/air mixture (the charge) so that less fuel is wasted. As a result of this greater efficiency, the power and performance of a modern engine are increased, and the level of pollution in the exhaust gases is reduced. Exhaust pollution levels today are also lowered by the increasing use of special filters called catalytic converters, which absorb many exhaust pollutants. The need to produce ever more efficient engines means that it can take up to seven years to develop a new engine for a family car, at a cost of many millions of pounds.

FRONT VIEW OF A FORD COSWORTH V6 12-VALVE

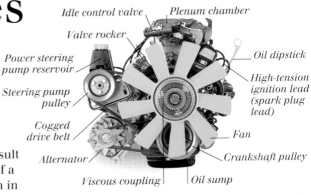

Idle control valve
Valve rocker
Power steering pump reservoir
Steering pump pulley
Cogged drive belt
Alternator
Viscous coupling
Plenum chamber
Oil dipstick
High-tension ignition lead (spark plug lead)
Fan
Crankshaft pulley
Oil sump

FRONT VIEW OF A FORD COSWORTH V6 24-VALVE

Idle control valve
Exhaust gas recirculation valve
Steering pump drive pulley
Belt tensioner
Alternator cooling fan
Oil sump
Plenum chamber
Camshaft timing gear
Camshaft chain
Air conditioning pump
Drive belt
Crankshaft pulley

SECTIONED VIEW OF A JAGUAR STRAIGHT 6

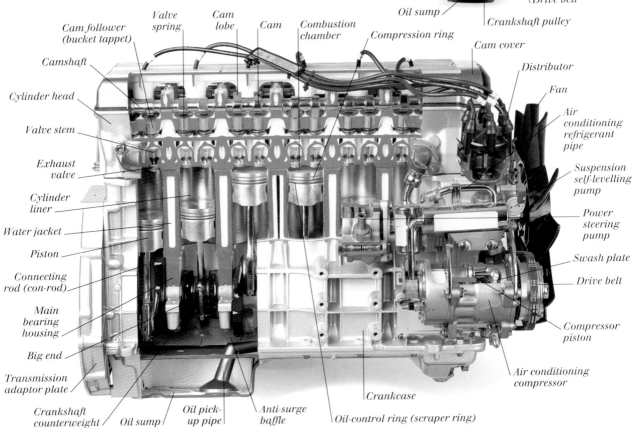

Cam follower (bucket tappet)
Valve spring
Cam lobe
Cam
Combustion chamber
Compression ring
Cam cover
Camshaft
Distributor
Cylinder head
Fan
Valve stem
Air conditioning refrigerant pipe
Exhaust valve
Suspension self-levelling pump
Cylinder liner
Power steering pump
Water jacket
Piston
Swash plate
Connecting rod (con-rod)
Drive belt
Main bearing housing
Compressor piston
Big end
Transmission adaptor plate
Air conditioning compressor
Crankshaft counterweight
Oil sump
Oil pick-up pipe
Anti-surge baffle
Crankcase
Oil-control ring (scraper ring)

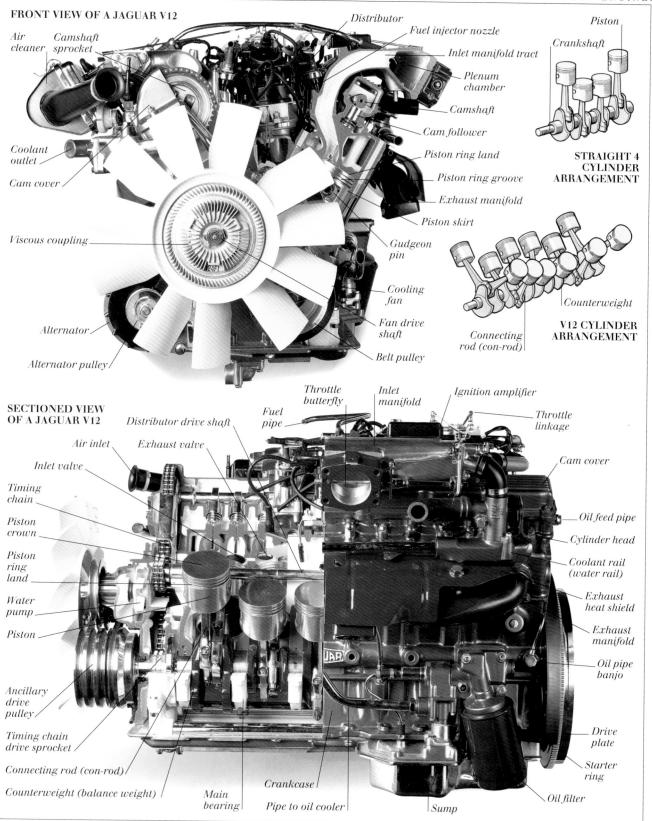

FRONT VIEW OF A JAGUAR V12

Air cleaner

Camshaft sprocket

Distributor

Fuel injector nozzle

Piston

Crankshaft

Inlet manifold tract

Plenum chamber

Camshaft

Cam follower

Piston ring land

Piston ring groove

Exhaust manifold

Piston skirt

Gudgeon pin

Cooling fan

Fan drive shaft

Belt pulley

Coolant outlet

Cam cover

Viscous coupling

Alternator

Alternator pulley

STRAIGHT 4 CYLINDER ARRANGEMENT

Counterweight

Connecting rod (con-rod)

V12 CYLINDER ARRANGEMENT

SECTIONED VIEW OF A JAGUAR V12

Throttle butterfly

Inlet manifold

Ignition amplifier

Throttle linkage

Fuel pipe

Distributor drive shaft

Air inlet

Exhaust valve

Inlet valve

Cam cover

Timing chain

Piston crown

Piston ring land

Water pump

Piston

Oil feed pipe

Cylinder head

Coolant rail (water rail)

Exhaust heat shield

Exhaust manifold

Oil pipe banjo

Ancillary drive pulley

Timing chain drive sprocket

Connecting rod (con-rod)

Counterweight (balance weight)

Main bearing

Pipe to oil cooler

Crankcase

Sump

Drive plate

Starter ring

Oil filter

Alternative engines

THE MOST COMMON TYPE OF ALTERNATIVE ENGINE is the diesel engine, which, instead of igniting the compressed fuel/air mixture with a spark, uses compression alone, heating the mixture to the point where it explodes. A diesel engine's fuel consumption is low in comparison with similarly sized piston engines, despite its heavier, reinforced moving parts and cylinder block. Another type of engine is the rotary-combustion, first successfully developed by Felix Wankel in the 1950s. Its two trilobate (three-sided) rotors revolve in housings shaped in a fat figure-of-eight. The four sequences of the four-stroke cycle, which occur consecutively in a piston engine, occur simultaneously in a rotary engine, producing power in a continuous stream.

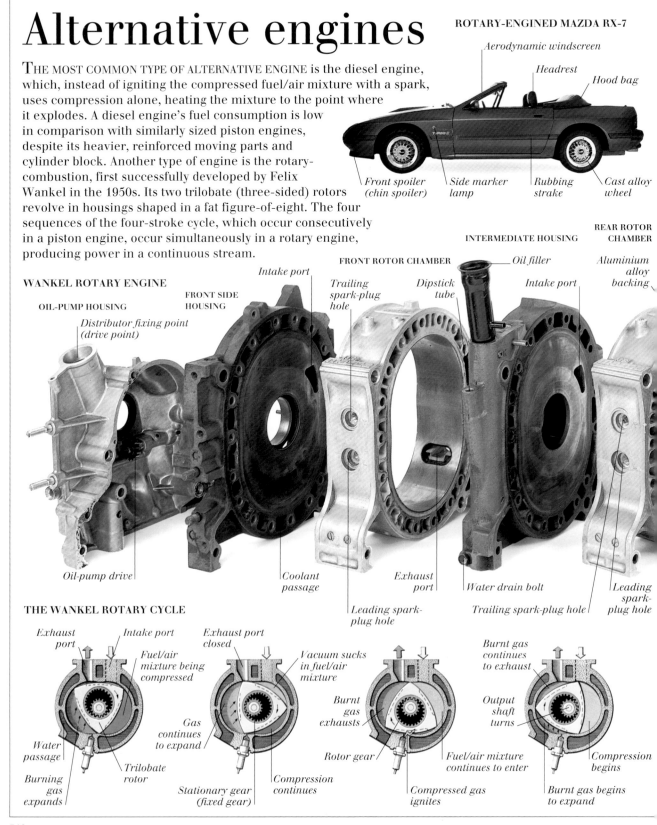

ROTARY-ENGINED MAZDA RX-7

Aerodynamic windscreen

Headrest

Hood bag

Front spoiler (chin spoiler)

Side marker lamp

Rubbing strake

Cast alloy wheel

WANKEL ROTARY ENGINE

OIL-PUMP HOUSING

FRONT SIDE HOUSING

Intake port

FRONT ROTOR CHAMBER

Trailing spark-plug hole

Dipstick tube

INTERMEDIATE HOUSING

Oil filler

Intake port

REAR ROTOR CHAMBER

Aluminium alloy backing

Distributor fixing point (drive point)

Oil-pump drive

Coolant passage

Exhaust port

Leading spark-plug hole

Water drain bolt

Trailing spark-plug hole

Leading spark-plug hole

THE WANKEL ROTARY CYCLE

Exhaust port

Intake port

Fuel/air mixture being compressed

Water passage

Burning gas expands

Trilobate rotor

Gas continues to expand

Stationary gear (fixed gear)

Exhaust port closed

Vacuum sucks in fuel/air mixture

Burnt gas exhausts

Rotor gear

Compression continues

Compressed gas ignites

Fuel/air mixture continues to enter

Burnt gas continues to exhaust

Output shaft turns

Compression begins

Burnt gas begins to expand

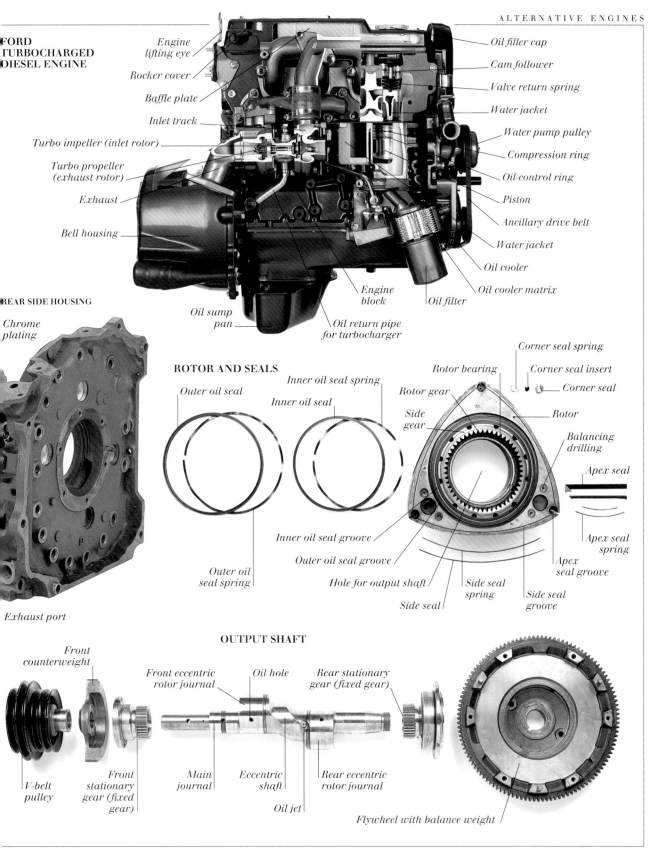

FORD TURBOCHARGED DIESEL ENGINE

Engine lifting eye

Rocker cover

Baffle plate

Inlet track

Turbo impeller (inlet rotor)

Turbo propeller (exhaust rotor)

Exhaust

Bell housing

Oil filler cap

Cam follower

Valve return spring

Water jacket

Water pump pulley

Compression ring

Oil-control ring

Piston

Ancillary drive belt

Water jacket

Oil cooler

Oil cooler matrix

Oil filter

Engine block

Oil sump pan

Oil return pipe for turbocharger

REAR SIDE HOUSING

Chrome plating

Exhaust port

ROTOR AND SEALS

Outer oil seal

Inner oil seal spring

Inner oil seal

Rotor bearing

Rotor gear

Side gear

Corner seal spring

Corner seal insert

Corner seal

Rotor

Balancing drilling

Apex seal

Inner oil seal groove

Outer oil seal groove

Outer oil seal spring

Hole for output shaft

Side seal

Side seal spring

Side seal spring

Apex seal groove

Side seal groove

Apex seal

OUTPUT SHAFT

Front counterweight

Front eccentric rotor journal

Oil hole

Rear stationary gear (fixed gear)

V-belt pulley

Front stationary gear (fixed gear)

Main journal

Eccentric shaft

Oil jet

Rear eccentric rotor journal

Flywheel with balance weight

Bodywork

THE BODY OF A MODERN mass-produced car is built on the monocoque (single-shell) principle, in which the roof, side panels, and floor are welded into a single integral unit. This bodyshell protects and supports the car's internal parts. Steel and glass are used to construct the bodyshell, creating a unit that is both light and strong. Its lightness helps to conserve energy, while its strength protects the occupants. Modern bodywork is designed with the aid of computers, which are used to predict factors such as aerodynamic efficiency and impact-resistance. High-technology is also employed on the production line, where robots are used to assemble, weld, and paint the body.

RENAULT LOGO

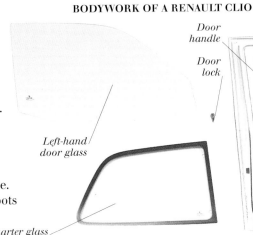

Door handle

Door lock

Left-hand door glass

Left-hand quarter glass

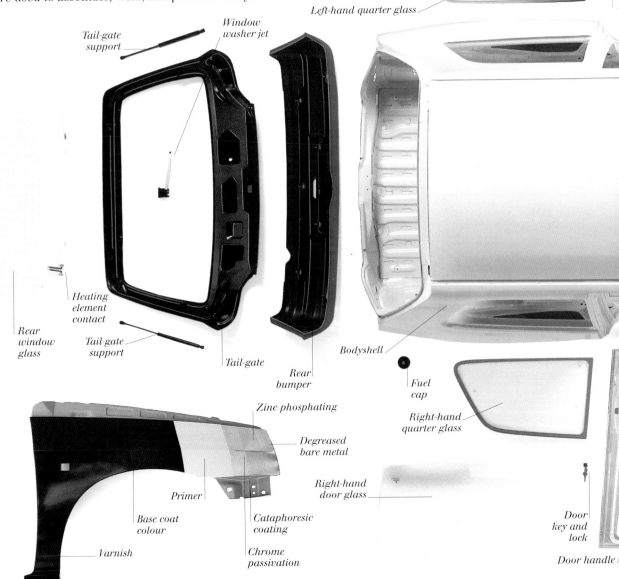

Tail-gate support

Window washer jet

Tail-gate support

Heating element contact

Rear window glass

Tail-gate support

Tail-gate

Rear bumper

Bodyshell

Fuel cap

Right-hand quarter glass

Zinc phosphating

Degreased bare metal

Right-hand door glass

Primer

Base coat colour

Cataphoresic coating

Chrome passivation

Varnish

Door key and lock

Door handle

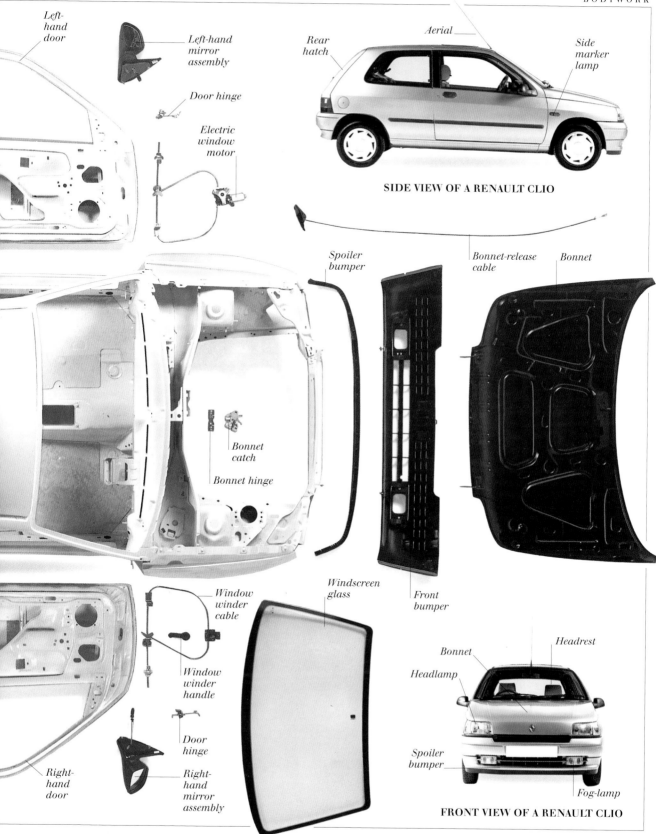

Left-hand door

Left-hand mirror assembly

Door hinge

Electric window motor

Rear hatch

Aerial

Side marker lamp

SIDE VIEW OF A RENAULT CLIO

Spoiler bumper

Bonnet-release cable

Bonnet

Bonnet catch

Bonnet hinge

Window winder cable

Window winder handle

Windscreen glass

Front bumper

Door hinge

Right-hand door

Right-hand mirror assembly

Bonnet

Headrest

Headlamp

Spoiler bumper

Fog-lamp

FRONT VIEW OF A RENAULT CLIO

Mechanical components

A TYPICAL MODERN CAR has several thousand individual mechanical components. These are assembled to form the car's various mechanical systems: engine and exhaust, transmission, steering, suspension, and brakes. To ensure that each system functions properly, components are manufactured to extremely fine tolerances – to within a five-hundredth of a millimetre (about one ten-thousandth of an inch) in some cases.

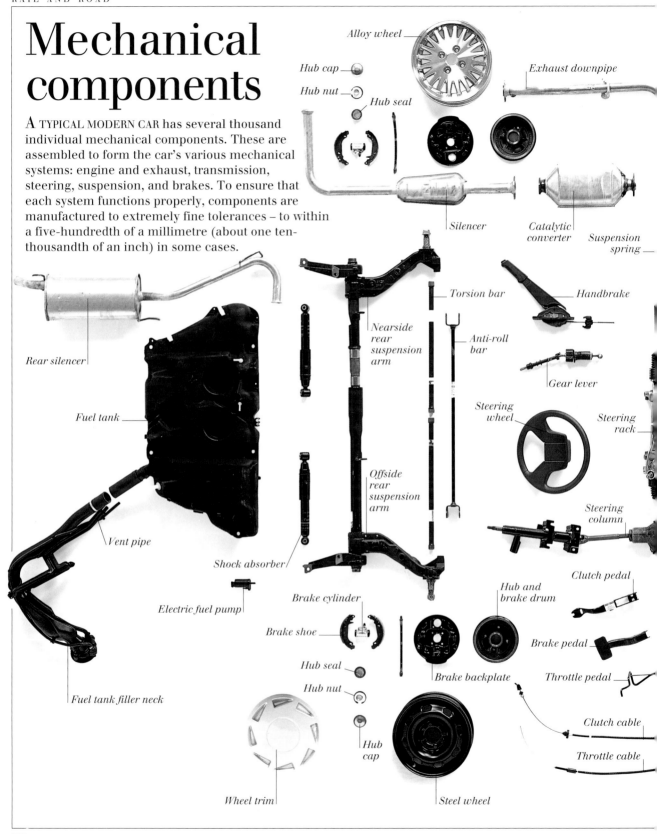

Alloy wheel

Hub cap

Hub nut

Hub seal

Exhaust downpipe

Silencer

Catalytic converter

Suspension spring

Rear silencer

Torsion bar

Handbrake

Nearside rear suspension arm

Anti-roll bar

Gear lever

Steering wheel

Steering rack

Fuel tank

Offside rear suspension arm

Steering column

Vent pipe

Shock absorber

Clutch pedal

Hub and brake drum

Brake cylinder

Electric fuel pump

Brake shoe

Hub seal

Hub nut

Brake backplate

Brake pedal

Throttle pedal

Fuel tank filler neck

Clutch cable

Throttle cable

Hub cap

Wheel trim

Steel wheel

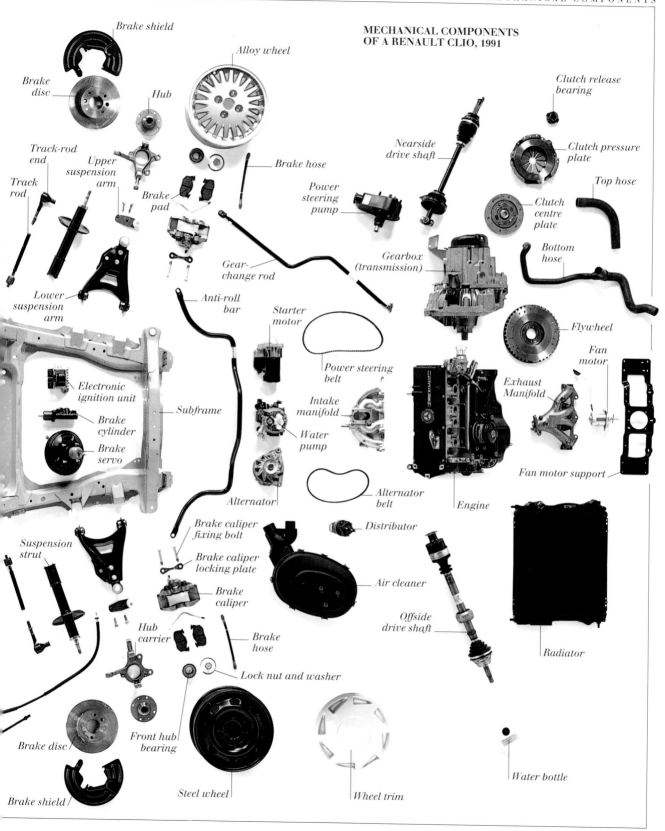

**MECHANICAL COMPONENTS
OF A RENAULT CLIO, 1991**

Brake shield

Alloy wheel

Clutch release
bearing

Brake
disc

Hub

Nearside
drive shaft

Clutch pressure
plate

Track-rod
end

Brake hose

Top hose

Upper
suspension
arm

Brake
pad

Power
steering
pump

Clutch
centre
plate

Track
rod

Gearbox
(transmission)

Bottom
hose

Gear-
change rod

Lower
suspension
arm

Anti-roll
bar

Starter
motor

Flywheel

Fan
motor

Power steering
belt

Exhaust
Manifold

Electronic
ignition unit

Subframe

Intake
manifold

Brake
cylinder

Water
pump

Fan motor support

Brake
servo

Alternator
belt

Alternator

Engine

Radiator

Suspension
strut

Brake caliper
fixing bolt

Distributor

Brake caliper
locking plate

Air cleaner

Brake
caliper

Offside
drive shaft

Hub
carrier

Brake
hose

Lock nut and washer

Brake disc

Front hub
bearing

Brake shield

Steel wheel

Wheel trim

Water bottle

Car trim

A MODERN CAR HAS TWO TYPES OF TRIM, according to the materials used: hard (chrome and plastics) and soft (upholstery materials). Safety and comfort are priorities in the trim's design: seats help the occupants to maintain a comfortable posture, rubber seals keep out dirt and moisture, and headlamps light the way. Older cars had interior or leather panelling cut and fitted by craftsmen; modern cars use precisely moulded plastics and seat fabrics cut by robot-controlled lasers to reduce costs and production time. Doors are now trimmed off the production line so that complex wiring can be built in.

TRIM OF A RENAULT CLIO, 1991

Rear quarter trim panel

Inner roof trim

Roof seal

Quarter trim panel

Quarter panel moulding

Rear seat belt

Centre seat belt

Rear tyre

Split, folding rear seat assembly

Rear shelf

Rear seat belt stalk (catch)

Gear lever surround

Tail-gate trim

Rear wiper blade

Tail-gate seal

Rear wiper arm

Rear shelf radio speaker

Rear shelf radio speaker

Number plate lamp

Rear indicator and stop lamp assembly

Rear wheel embellisher (wheel trim)

Untrimmed headrest

Rear seat belt

Quarter panel moulding

Rear tyre

Quarter trim panel

HALOGEN HEADLAMP BULB

SPOTLAMP BULB

Filament

MARKER LAMP BULB

Filament

Rear quarter trim panel

Roof seal

FESTOON BULB

Inner roof trim

Contact

Bayonet fixing

Contact

Contact

Roof moulding

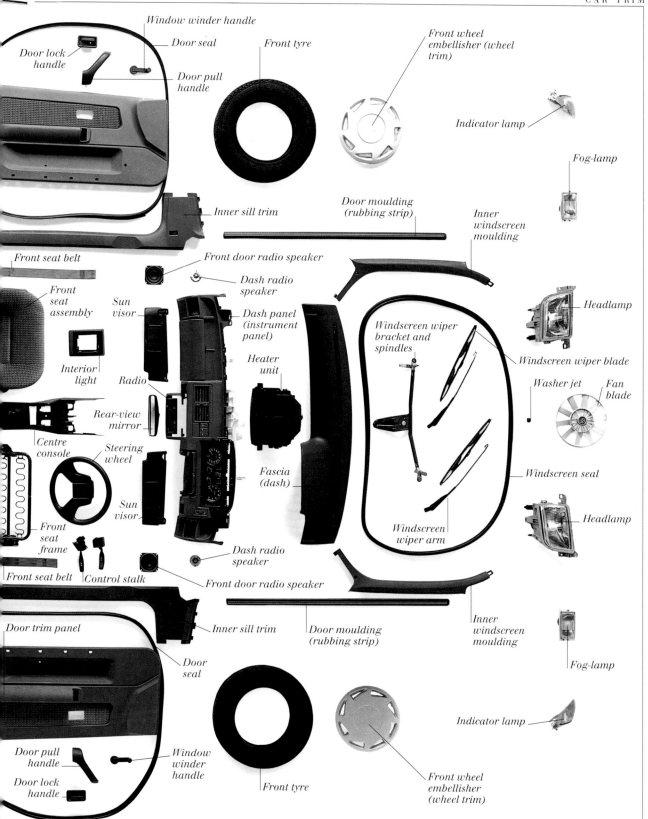

Window winder handle

Door seal

Door lock handle

Door pull handle

Front tyre

Front wheel embellisher (wheel trim)

Indicator lamp

Fog-lamp

Inner sill trim

Door moulding (rubbing strip)

Inner windscreen moulding

Front seat belt

Front door radio speaker

Dash radio speaker

Front seat assembly

Sun visor

Dash panel (instrument panel)

Heater unit

Windscreen wiper bracket and spindles

Headlamp

Windscreen wiper blade

Interior light

Radio

Washer jet

Fan blade

Rear-view mirror

Centre console

Steering wheel

Sun visor

Fascia (dash)

Windscreen seal

Front seat frame

Dash radio speaker

Headlamp

Front seat belt

Control stalk

Front door radio speaker

Windscreen wiper arm

Door trim panel

Inner sill trim

Door moulding (rubbing strip)

Inner windscreen moulding

Door seal

Fog-lamp

Door pull handle

Window winder handle

Door lock handle

Front tyre

Front wheel embellisher (wheel trim)

Indicator lamp

Hybrid car

THERE HAVE BEEN SEVERAL proposed alternatives
to conventional petrol- or diesel-powered cars,
including cars that use solar or battery power. The
object is to lower harmful emissions and conserve
natural resources. One of the alternatives already
in production is the hybrid car. A hybrid vehicle uses
two or more fuels. Examples include diesel-electric
trains and mopeds. The latter combine the power
of a petrol engine with pedal power. In a hybrid car,
petrol consumption is reduced by the provision of
additional power by an electric motor during
acceleration. The motor is driven by power from
on-board batteries that are recharged by an engine-
driven generator when the car is decelerating or
cruising. Some hybrid cars transfer energy from the
wheels to a flywheel during braking. The flywheel
drives the generator, which recharges the batteries.

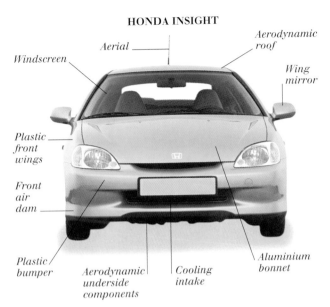

HONDA INSIGHT

Aerial

Aerodynamic roof

Windscreen

Wing mirror

Plastic front wings

Front air dam

Plastic bumper

Aerodynamic underside components

Cooling intake

Aluminium bonnet

SIDE VIEW OF 1-LITRE VTEC ENGINE

Motor power cables

Air-intake duct

Ignition coils

Coolant pipe

Electric motor housing

Lightweight plastic intake manifold

Lightweight magnesium alloy oil sump pan

Oil filter

Air conditioning compressor

Engine drive belt

FRONT VIEW OF 1-LITRE VTEC ENGINE

Dipstick

Rocker cover

Ignition coils

Water pump

Belt tensioner

Air conditioning compressor

Crankshaft pulley

Drive belt

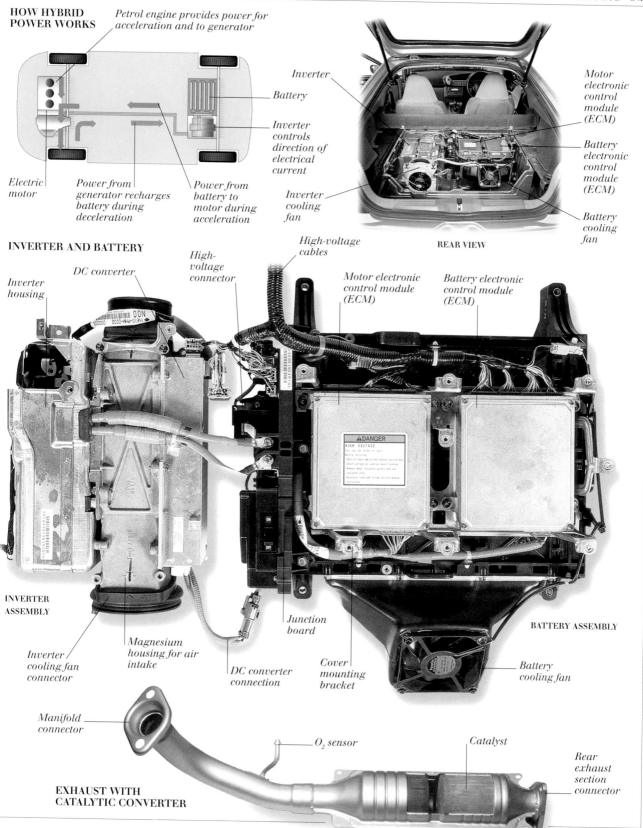

HOW HYBRID POWER WORKS

Petrol engine provides power for acceleration and to generator

Inverter

Battery

Inverter controls direction of electrical current

Inverter cooling fan

Electric motor

Power from generator recharges battery during deceleration

Power from battery to motor during acceleration

Motor electronic control module (ECM)

Battery electronic control module (ECM)

Battery cooling fan

REAR VIEW

INVERTER AND BATTERY

High-voltage cables

Inverter housing

DC converter

High-voltage connector

Motor electronic control module (ECM)

Battery electronic control module (ECM)

⚠ DANGER
HIGH VOLTAGE

INVERTER ASSEMBLY

BATTERY ASSEMBLY

Inverter cooling fan connector

Magnesium housing for air intake

DC converter connection

Junction board

Cover mounting bracket

Battery cooling fan

Manifold connector

O₂ sensor

Catalyst

Rear exhaust section connector

EXHAUST WITH CATALYTIC CONVERTER

Racing cars

SINCE MOTORING BEGAN, racing cars have been a major focus of innovation in car design. Features that are now commonplace, such as disc brakes, turbochargers, and even safety belts, were used first on competition cars. Research into racing cars has contributed to a new understanding of engine performance, aerodynamics, and tyre adhesion, and has led to the development of ultra-light materials such as carbon-fibre for car bodies. A modern McLaren Formula One car has a low, streamlined body and an open cockpit but, unlike its forerunner, it also has front and rear wings that push the wheels firmly on to the track, huge tyres for extra grip, and electronic sensors that continually relay information to the pits about the car's performance.

72° V10 ENGINE

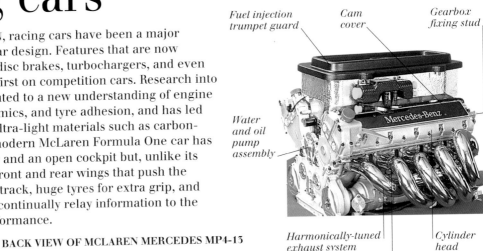

Fuel injection trumpet guard

Cam cover

Gearbox fixing stud

Water and oil pump assembly

Mercedes-Benz

Harmonically-tuned exhaust system

Cylinder head

Stressed cylinder block

BACK VIEW OF MCLAREN MERCEDES MP4-13

Upper flap

Grooved racing tyre

Warning light

Half-shaft

Rear wing end-plate

One-piece side pod and engine cover

Side pod air outlet

West

BRIDGESTONE

BRIDGESTONE

Diffuser

Exhaust pipe

Differential

SIDE VIEW OF MCLAREN MERCEDES MP4-13

Rear wing end-plate

LOCTITE

CAMOZZI

WARSTEINE

BRIDGEST

Alloy wheel

Wheel nut

BRIDGESTONE

POTENZA

ENKEI

Winglet

Engine cover

Head rest

Engine air intake

On-board TV mini-camera

Hakkinen

BOSS
HUGO BOSS

Mobil 1

E

Mercedes-Benz

West

West

Side pod

OVERHEAD VIEW OF MCLAREN MERCEDES MP4-13

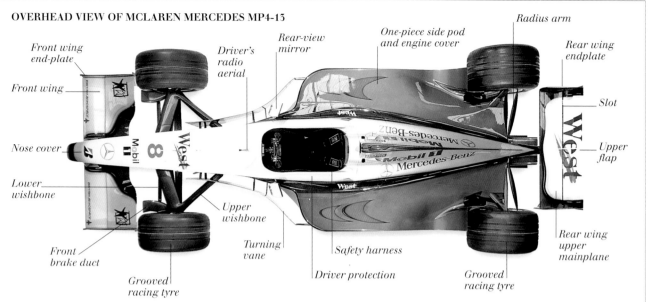

Front wing
end-plate

Front wing

Nose cover

Lower
wishbone

Front
brake duct

Grooved
racing tyre

Driver's
radio
aerial

Rear-view
mirror

One-piece side pod
and engine cover

Radius arm

Rear wing
endplate

Slot

Upper
flap

West

Rear wing
upper
mainplane

Upper
wishbone

Turning
vane

Safety harness

Driver protection

Grooved
racing tyre

FRONT VIEW OF MCLAREN MERCEDES MP4-13

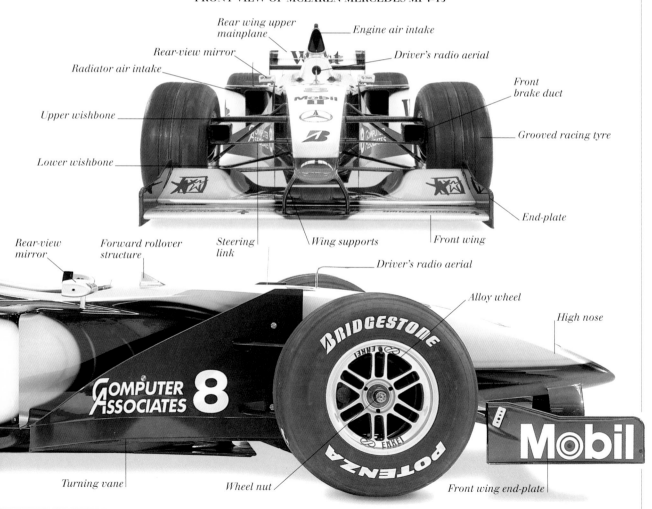

Rear wing upper
mainplane

Engine air intake

Rear-view mirror

Driver's radio aerial

Radiator air intake

Front
brake duct

Upper wishbone

Grooved racing tyre

Lower wishbone

End-plate

Rear-view
mirror

Forward rollover
structure

Steering
link

Wing supports

Front wing

Driver's radio aerial

Alloy wheel

High nose

COMPUTER
ASSOCIATES 8

BRIDGESTONE

POTENZA

Mobil

Turning vane

Wheel nut

Front wing end-plate

Bicycle anatomy

THE BICYCLE IS A TWO-WHEELED, light-weight machine, which is propelled by human power. It is efficient, cheap, easily manufactured, and one of the world's most popular forms of transport. The first pedal-driven bicycle was built in Scotland in 1839. Since then the basic design – of a frame, wheels, brakes, handlebars, and saddle – has been gradually improved, with the addition of a chain, gear system, and pneumatic tyres (tyres inflated with air). The recent invention of the mountain bike (all-terrain bike) has been an important development. With its strong, rugged frame, wide tyres, and 21 gears, a mountain bike enables riders to reach rough and hilly areas that were previously inaccessible to cyclists.

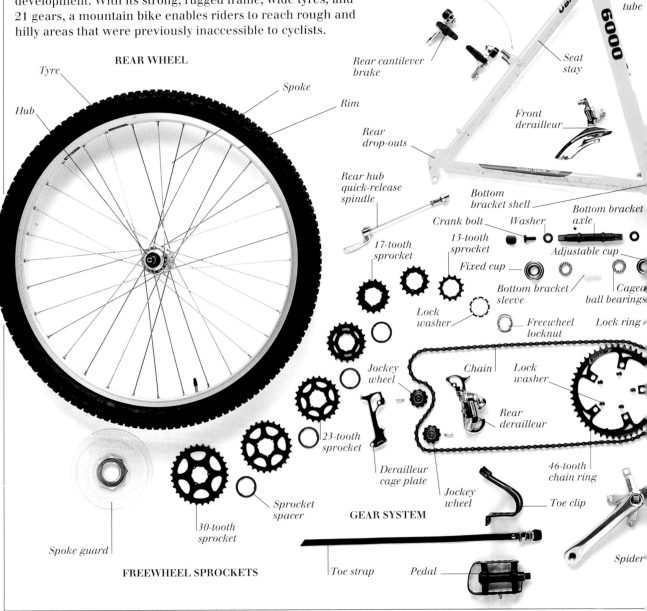

Saddle

Seat post

Cable guide

Seat post quick-release bolt

Straddle wire

Seat tube

Rear cantilever brake

Seat stay

Front derailleur

REAR WHEEL

Tyre

Spoke

Rim

Hub

Rear drop-outs

Rear hub quick-release spindle

Bottom bracket shell

Bottom bracket axle

Crank bolt

Washer

13-tooth sprocket

17-tooth sprocket

Adjustable cup

Fixed cup

Bottom bracket sleeve

Caged ball bearings

Lock washer

Freewheel locknut

Lock ring

Jockey wheel

Chain

Lock washer

23-tooth sprocket

Rear derailleur

Derailleur cage plate

Jockey wheel

46-tooth chain ring

Toe clip

Sprocket spacer

GEAR SYSTEM

30-tooth sprocket

Spider

Spoke guard

FREEWHEEL SPROCKETS

Toe strap

Pedal

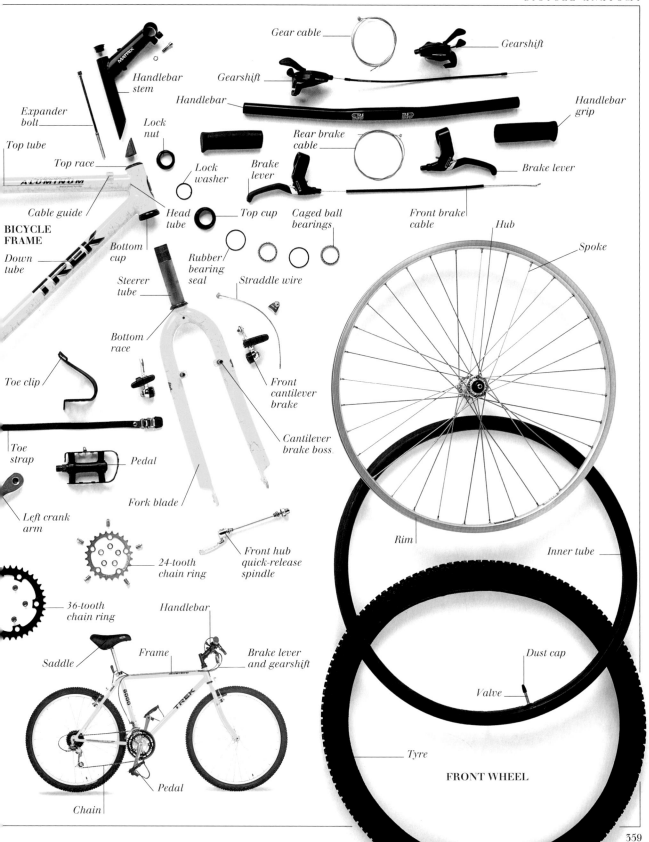

Gear cable

Gearshift

Gearshift

Handlebar

Handlebar
stem

Expander
bolt

Top tube

Lock
nut

Top race

Lock
washer

Rear brake
cable

Brake
lever

Handlebar
grip

Brake lever

Cable guide

Head
tube

Top cup

Caged ball
bearings

Front brake
cable

Hub

Spoke

BICYCLE
FRAME

Down
tube

Bottom
cup

Rubber
bearing
seal

Straddle wire

Steerer
tube

Bottom
race

Toe clip

Front
cantilever
brake

Cantilever
brake boss

Rim

Inner tube

Toe
strap

Pedal

Left crank
arm

Fork blade

Front hub
quick-release
spindle

24-tooth
chain ring

36-tooth
chain ring

Handlebar

Saddle

Frame

Brake lever
and gearshift

Dust cap

Valve

Pedal

Tyre

FRONT WHEEL

Chain

Bicycles

ALTHOUGH ALL BICYCLES are made up of the same basic components, they can vary greatly in design. A racing bike, such as the Eddy Merckx model, with its light frame and steep head- and seat-angles, is built for speed. Its design forces the rider to adopt the "aerotuck", a crouched, aerodynamic position. While a touring bike resembles the racing bike in many respects, it is designed for comfort and stability on long-distance journeys. Touring bikes are characterized by more relaxed frame angles, heavy chain stays that support the rear panniers, and a long wheelbase (the distance between the wheel axles) for reliable handling. All-round bicycles, known as "hybrids", combine the light weight and speed of sports bikes with the rugged durability of mountain bikes (see pp. 358-359). Bicycles that are not designed for conventional road use include time-trial bikes, which have a short head tube, sloping top tube, "aero" handlebars, and aerodynamic tubing. Most Human Powered Vehicles (HPVs) are recumbents – the rider has a recumbent position – which maximize power output and minimize drag (resistance). Essential to the safety of all riders are helmets, and both front and rear lights; locks protect against theft.

FRONT AND REAR LIGHTS

HELMET

Hard outer shell

Red rear light

Air vent

White front light

Polystyrene padding

Quick-release strap

EDDY MERCKX RACING BICYCLE

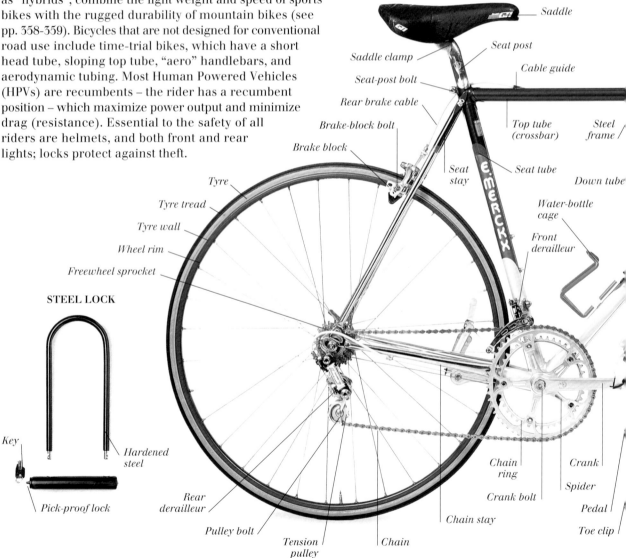

Saddle

Saddle clamp

Seat post

Cable guide

Seat-post bolt

Rear brake cable

Top tube (crossbar)

Steel frame

Brake-block bolt

Brake block

Seat stay

Seat tube

Down tube

Tyre

Tyre tread

Water-bottle cage

Tyre wall

Front derailleur

Wheel rim

Freewheel sprocket

STEEL LOCK

Key

Hardened steel

Chain ring

Crank

Spider

Crank bolt

Pedal

Pick-proof lock

Rear derailleur

Chain stay

Toe clip

Pulley bolt

Tension pulley

Chain

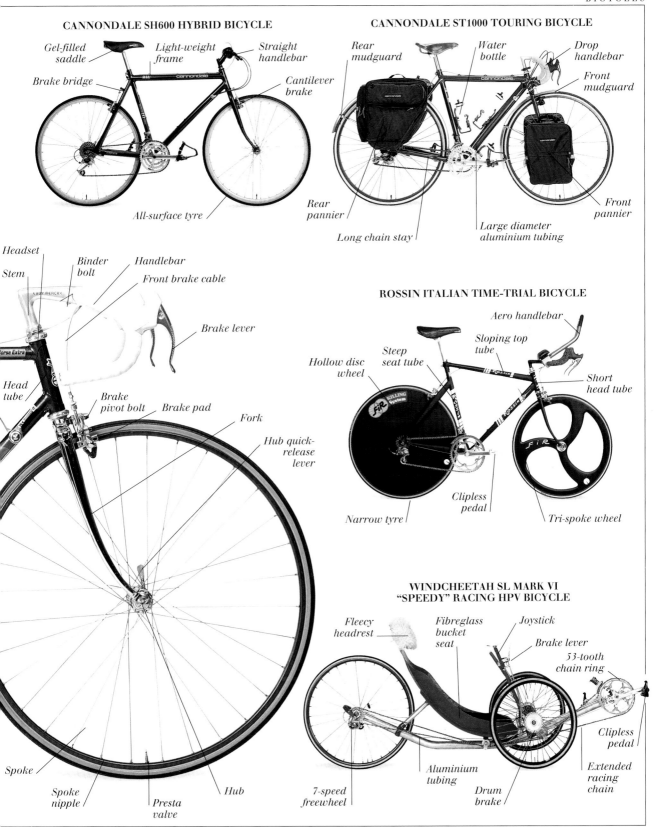

CANNONDALE SH600 HYBRID BICYCLE

Gel-filled saddle

Light-weight frame

Straight handlebar

Brake bridge

Cantilever brake

All-surface tyre

CANNONDALE ST1000 TOURING BICYCLE

Rear mudguard

Water bottle

Drop handlebar

Front mudguard

Rear pannier

Front pannier

Long chain stay

Large diameter aluminium tubing

Headset

Binder bolt

Handlebar

Stem

Front brake cable

Brake lever

Head tube

Brake pivot bolt

Brake pad

Fork

Hub quick-release lever

ROSSIN ITALIAN TIME-TRIAL BICYCLE

Aero handlebar

Sloping top tube

Steep seat tube

Hollow disc wheel

Short head tube

Clipless pedal

Narrow tyre

Tri-spoke wheel

Spoke

Spoke nipple

Presta valve

Hub

WINDCHEETAH SL MARK VI "SPEEDY" RACING HPV BICYCLE

Fleecy headrest

Fibreglass bucket seat

Joystick

Brake lever

53-tooth chain ring

Aluminium tubing

Clipless pedal

7-speed freewheel

Drum brake

Extended racing chain

The motorcycle

THE MOTORCYCLE HAS EVOLVED from a motorized cycle – a basic bicycle with an engine – into a sophisticated, high-performance machine. In 1901, the Werner brothers established the most viable location for the engine by positioning it low in the centre of the chassis (see pp. 364-365): the new Werner became the basis for the modern motorcycle. Motorcycles are used for many purposes – for commuting, delivering messages, touring, and racing – and different machines have been developed according to the demands of different types of riders. The Vespa scooter, for instance, which is small-wheeled, economical, and easy-to-ride, was designed to meet the needs of the commuter. Sidecars provided transport for the family until the arrival of cheap cars caused their popularity to decline. Enthusiast riders generally favour larger capacity machines that are capable of greater performance and offer more comfort. Four-cylinder machines have been common since the Honda CB750 appeared in 1969. Despite advances in motorcycle technology, many riders are attracted to the traditional looks of motorcycles like the twin-cylinder Harley-Davidson. The Harley-Davidson Glides exploit the style of the classic American V-twin engine, where the cylinders are placed in a V-formation.

1901 WERNER MOTORCYCLE

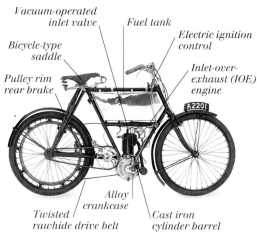

Vacuum-operated inlet valve
Fuel tank
Bicycle-type saddle
Electric ignition control
Pulley rim rear brake
Inlet-over-exhaust (IOE) engine
A2201
Alloy crankcase
Twisted rawhide drive belt
Cast iron cylinder barrel

1988 HARLEY-DAVIDSON FLHS ELECTRA GLIDE

1965 BMW R/60 WITH 1952 STEIB CHAIR

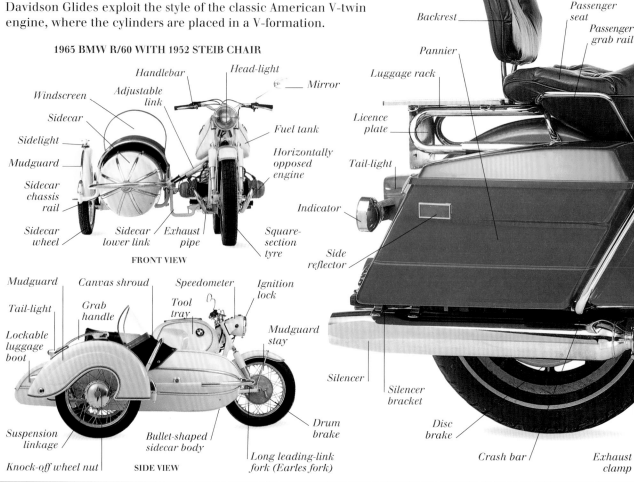

Handlebar
Head-light
Mirror
Windscreen
Adjustable link
Sidecar
Fuel tank
Sidelight
Horizontally opposed engine
Mudguard
Sidecar chassis rail
Sidecar wheel
Sidecar lower link
Exhaust pipe
Square-section tyre

FRONT VIEW

Backrest
Passenger seat
Passenger grab rail
Pannier
Luggage rack
Licence plate
Tail-light
Indicator
Side reflector

Mudguard
Canvas shroud
Speedometer
Ignition lock
Tail-light
Grab handle
Tool tray
Mudguard stay
Lockable luggage boot
Silencer
Silencer bracket
Suspension linkage
Bullet-shaped sidecar body
Drum brake
Disc brake
Knock-off wheel nut
SIDE VIEW
Long leading-link fork (Earles fork)
Crash bar
Exhaust clamp

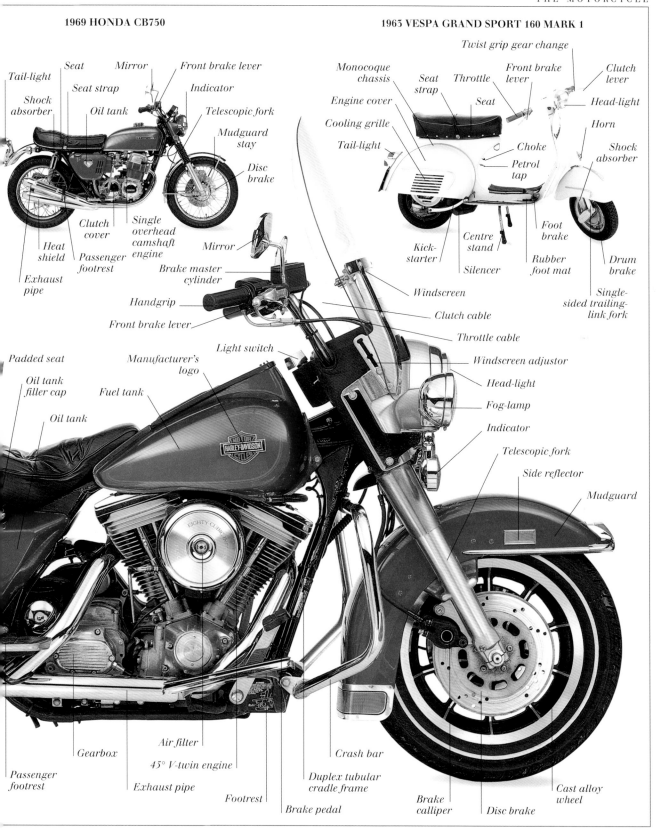

1969 HONDA CB750

Tail-light
Seat
Mirror
Front brake lever
Shock absorber
Seat strap
Indicator
Oil tank
Telescopic fork
Mudguard stay
Disc brake
Clutch cover
Single overhead camshaft engine
Mirror
Heat shield
Passenger footrest
Exhaust pipe
Brake master cylinder
Handgrip
Front brake lever

1963 VESPA GRAND SPORT 160 MARK 1

Twist grip gear change
Monocoque chassis
Seat strap
Throttle
Front brake lever
Clutch lever
Engine cover
Seat
Head-light
Cooling grille
Horn
Tail-light
Choke
Shock absorber
Petrol tap
Kick-starter
Centre stand
Silencer
Rubber foot mat
Foot brake
Drum brake
Single-sided trailing-link fork
Windscreen
Clutch cable
Throttle cable

Padded seat
Manufacturer's logo
Light switch
Windscreen adjustor
Oil tank filler cap
Fuel tank
Head-light
Oil tank
Fog-lamp
Indicator
Telescopic fork
Side reflector
Mudguard
Passenger footrest
Gearbox
Air filter
45° V-twin engine
Exhaust pipe
Footrest
Crash bar
Duplex tubular cradle frame
Brake pedal
Brake calliper
Disc brake
Cast alloy wheel

The motorcycle chassis

THE MOTORCYCLE CHASSIS is the main "body" of the motorcycle, to which the engine is attached. Consisting of the frame, wheels, suspension, and brakes, the chassis performs various functions. The frame, which is built from steel or alloy, keeps the wheels in line to maintain the handling of the motorcycle, and serves as a structure for mounting other components. The engine and gearbox unit is bolted into place, while items such as the seat, the mudguards, and the fairing are more easily removable. Suspension cushions the rider from irregularities in the road surface. In most suspension systems, coil springs controlled by an oil damper separate the main mass of the motorcycle from the wheels. At the front, the spring and damper are usually incorporated in a telescopic fork; the rear employs a pivoted swingarm. The suspension also helps to retain maximum contact between the tyres and the road, necessary to effective braking and steering. Drum brakes were common until the 1970s, but modern motorcycles use disc brakes, which are more powerful.

1985 HONDA VF750 WITH BODYWORK

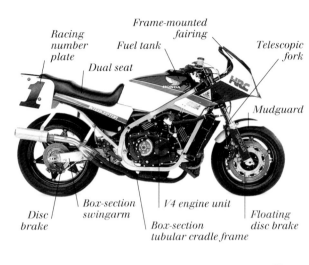

Racing number plate
Frame-mounted fairing
Fuel tank
Telescopic fork
Dual seat
Mudguard
Disc brake
Box-section swingarm
V4 engine unit
Box-section tubular cradle frame
Floating disc brake

1985 HONDA VF750 WITH BODYWORK REMOVED

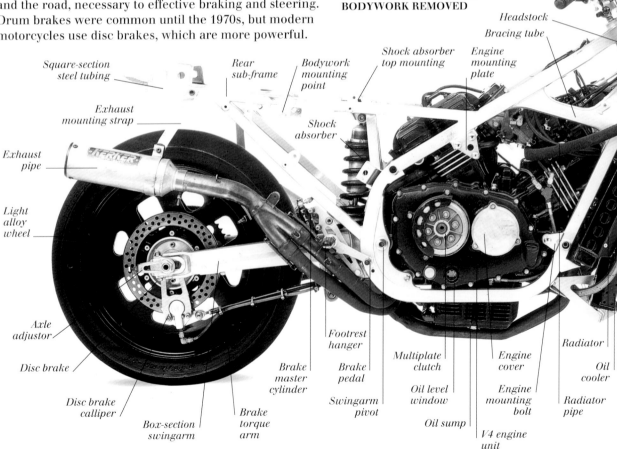

Brake master cylinder
Headstock
Bracing tube
Shock absorber top mounting
Engine mounting plate
Square-section steel tubing
Rear sub-frame
Bodywork mounting point
Exhaust mounting strap
Shock absorber
Exhaust pipe
Light alloy wheel
Axle adjustor
Disc brake
Disc brake calliper
Box-section swingarm
Brake torque arm
Brake master cylinder
Footrest hanger
Brake pedal
Swingarm pivot
Multiplate clutch
Oil level window
Oil sump
Engine cover
Engine mounting bolt
V4 engine unit
Radiator
Oil cooler
Radiator pipe

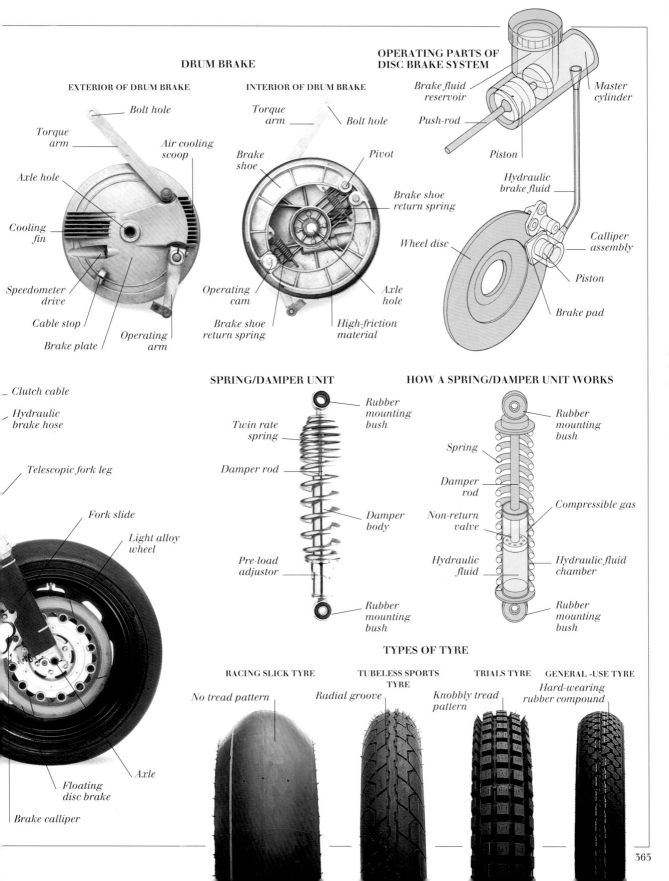

DRUM BRAKE

EXTERIOR OF DRUM BRAKE

Bolt hole

Torque arm

Air cooling scoop

Axle hole

Cooling fin

Speedometer drive

Cable stop

Brake plate

Operating arm

INTERIOR OF DRUM BRAKE

Torque arm

Bolt hole

Brake shoe

Pivot

Brake shoe return spring

Operating cam

Brake shoe return spring

Axle hole

High-friction material

OPERATING PARTS OF DISC BRAKE SYSTEM

Brake fluid reservoir

Master cylinder

Push-rod

Piston

Hydraulic brake fluid

Wheel disc

Calliper assembly

Piston

Brake pad

Clutch cable

Hydraulic brake hose

Telescopic fork leg

Fork slide

Light alloy wheel

Floating disc brake

Axle

Brake calliper

SPRING/DAMPER UNIT

Rubber mounting bush

Twin rate spring

Damper rod

Damper body

Pre-load adjustor

Rubber mounting bush

HOW A SPRING/DAMPER UNIT WORKS

Rubber mounting bush

Spring

Damper rod

Non-return valve

Hydraulic fluid

Compressible gas

Hydraulic fluid chamber

Rubber mounting bush

TYPES OF TYRE

RACING SLICK TYRE

No tread pattern

TUBELESS SPORTS TYRE

Radial groove

TRIALS TYRE

Knobbly tread pattern

GENERAL-USE TYRE

Hard-wearing rubber compound

Motorcycle engines

MOTORCYCLE ENGINES must be light-weight and compact, and have a good power output. They have between one and six cylinders, can be cooled by air or water, and the capacity of the combustion chamber varies from 49cc (cubic centimetres) to 1500cc. Two types of internal combustion engine are common: the four-stroke, which is used in cars (see pp. 342-343), and the two-stroke. A basic two-stroke engine has only three moving parts – the crankshaft, the connecting rod, and the piston – but the power output is high. The engine fires every two strokes (rather than every four), giving a "power stroke" every revolution (see p. 343). Power is conveyed from the engine to the rear wheel by the transmission system. This usually consists of a clutch, a gearbox, and a final drive system. Clutches are multiplate devices, which run in oil. Gearboxes have five or six speeds and are operated by foot pedal. Shaft and belt drive systems are used in some cases, but chain drive to the rear wheel is most common.

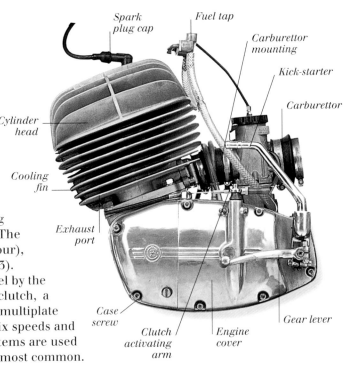

Spark plug cap
Fuel tap
Carburettor mounting
Kick-starter
Carburettor
Cylinder head
Cooling fin
Exhaust port
Case screw
Clutch activating arm
Engine cover
Gear lever

TRANSMISSION SYSTEM

GEARBOX

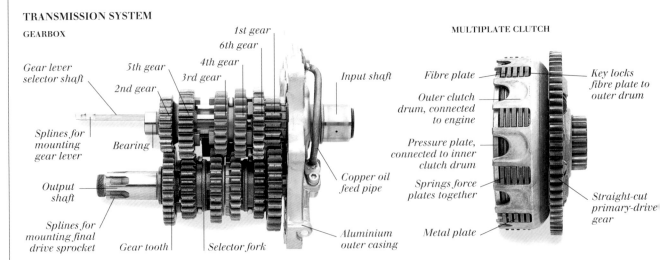

1st gear
6th gear
4th gear
3rd gear
5th gear
2nd gear
Gear lever selector shaft
Splines for mounting gear lever
Bearing
Output shaft
Splines for mounting final drive sprocket
Gear tooth
Selector fork
Input shaft
Copper oil feed pipe
Aluminium outer casing

MULTIPLATE CLUTCH

Fibre plate
Outer clutch drum, connected to engine
Pressure plate, connected to inner clutch drum
Springs force plates together
Metal plate
Key locks fibre plate to outer drum
Straight-cut primary-drive gear

MODERN "O RING" DRIVE CHAIN

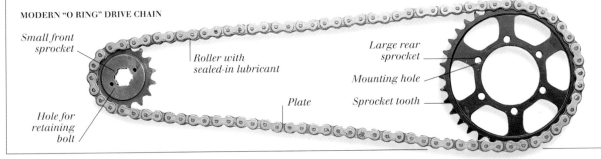

Small front sprocket
Roller with sealed-in lubricant
Large rear sprocket
Mounting hole
Sprocket tooth
Plate
Hole for retaining bolt

VELOCETTE OVERHEAD VALVE (OHV) ENGINE

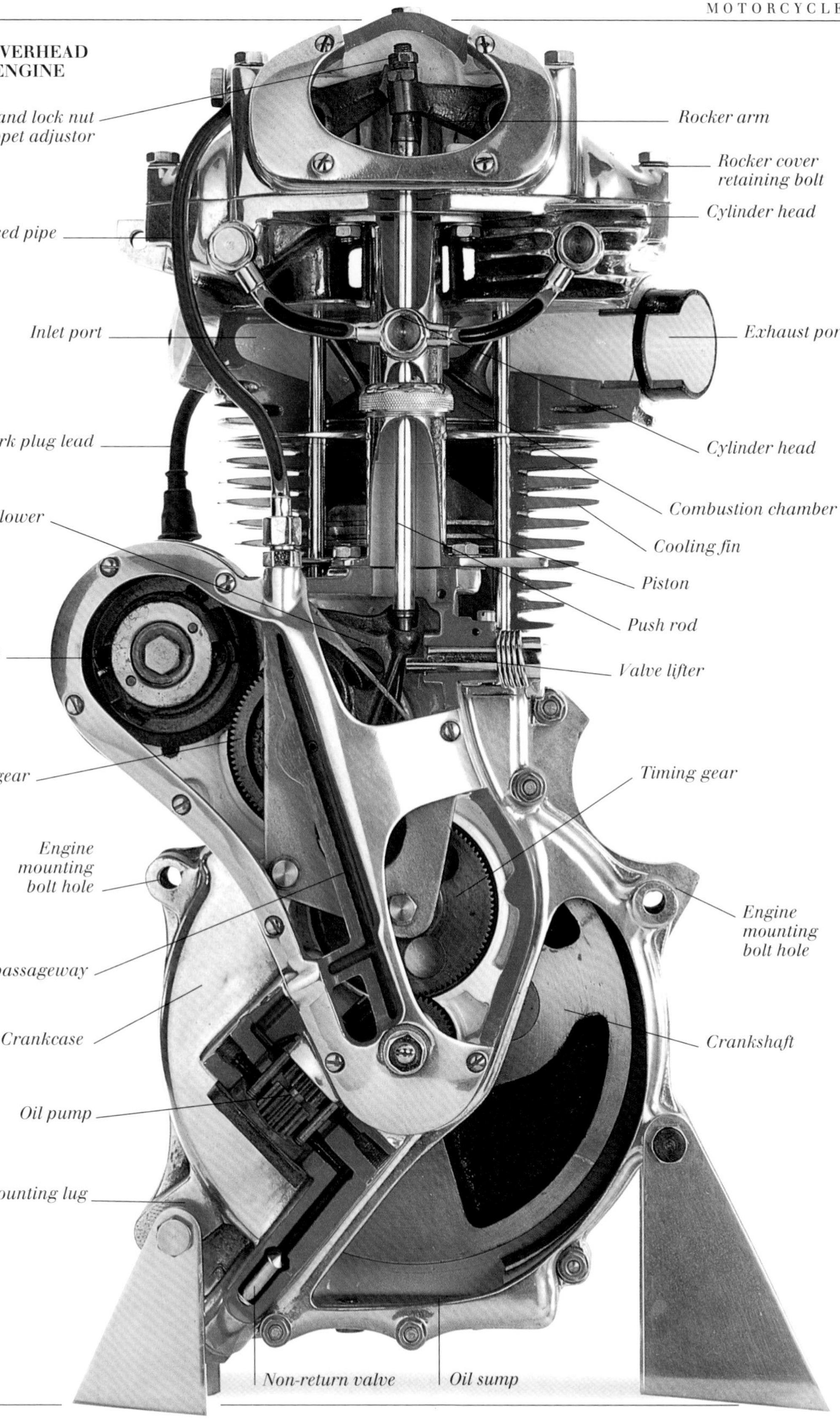

Screw and lock nut tappet adjustor

Oil feed pipe

Inlet port

Spark plug lead

Cam follower

Magneto drive

Camshaft gear

Engine mounting bolt hole

Oil passageway

Crankcase

Oil pump

Mounting lug

Rocker arm

Rocker cover retaining bolt

Cylinder head

Exhaust port

Cylinder head

Combustion chamber

Cooling fin

Piston

Push rod

Valve lifter

Timing gear

Engine mounting bolt hole

Crankshaft

Non-return valve

Oil sump

Competition motorcycles

THERE ARE MANY TYPES of motorcycle sport and in each, a specialist machine has evolved to perform to specific requirements. Races take place on roads or tracks or "off-road", in fields, dirt tracks, and even the desert. "Grand Prix" world championships in road-racing are contested by three classes: 125cc, 250cc two-strokes; the top class of 500cc two-strokes; and 900cc four-stroke machines. The latest racing sidecars have more in common with racing cars than motorcycles. The rider and passenger operate within an all-enclosing, aerodynamic fairing. The Suzuki RGV500 shown here, like other Grand Prix machines, carries advertising, which helps to cover the cost of developing motorcycle technology. In Speedway, which originated in the US in 1902, motorcycles operate without brakes or a gearbox. Off-road competition motorcycles have less emphasis on high power output. In Motocross, for example, which is held on rough terrain, they must have high ground clearance, flexible long-travel suspension, and tyres with a chunky tread pattern.

1992 HUSQVARNA MOTOCROSS TC610

Throttle cable
Hand protector
Flexible plastic mudguard
Telescopic fork
Plastic guard
Axle
Knobbly tyre
Disc brake
Brake calliper
Handlebar brace
Radiator air vent
Long seat
Racing number
Light-weight exhaust system
Overhead camshaft engine
Gear lever
Shock absorber
Alloy swingarm
Shock absorber linkage
Disc brake

1992 SUZUKI RGV500
SIDE VIEW

Exhaust pipe
Racing number
Air vent
One-piece seat and tail unit
Minimal seat padding
Shock absorber
Arched alloy swingarm

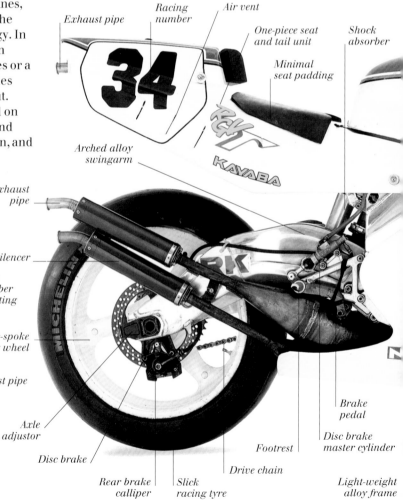

Exhaust pipe
Vent
Handlebar
Footrest
Rear brake pedal
Drive chain
Wide, slick tyre

REAR VIEW

Exhaust pipe
Silencer
Shock absorber mounting
Three-spoke alloy wheel
Exhaust pipe
Axle adjustor
Disc brake
Rear brake calliper
Slick racing tyre
Drive chain
Footrest
Brake pedal
Disc brake master cylinder
Light-weight alloy frame

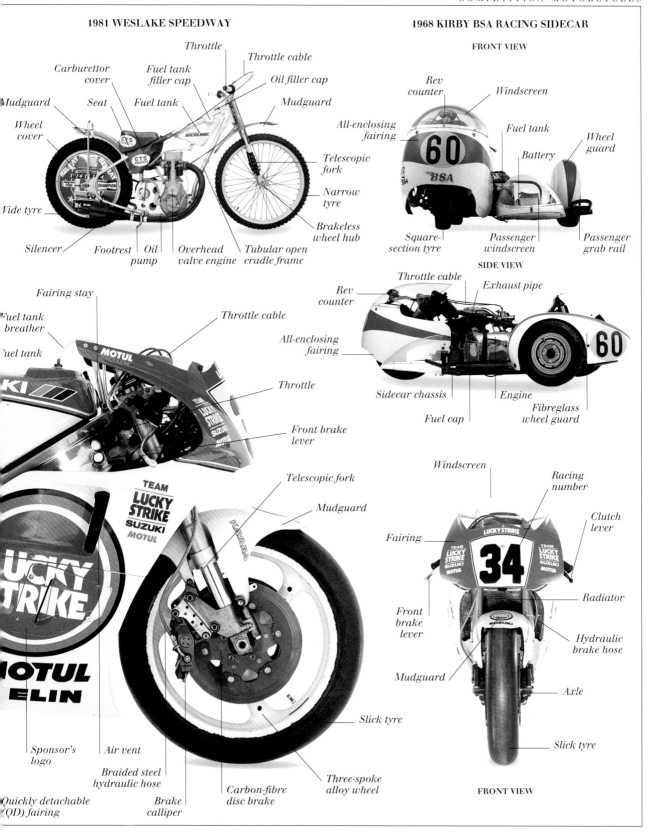

1981 WESLAKE SPEEDWAY

Throttle

Throttle cable

Carburettor cover

Fuel tank filler cap

Oil filler cap

Mudguard

Seat

Fuel tank

Mudguard

Wheel cover

Telescopic fork

Narrow tyre

Vide tyre

Brakeless wheel hub

Silencer

Footrest

Oil pump

Overhead valve engine

Tubular open cradle frame

Fairing stay

Throttle cable

Fuel tank breather

Fuel tank

Throttle

Front brake lever

Telescopic fork

Mudguard

Sponsor's logo

Air vent

Braided steel hydraulic hose

Brake calliper

Carbon-fibre disc brake

Three-spoke alloy wheel

Slick tyre

Quickly detachable (QD) fairing

1968 KIRBY BSA RACING SIDECAR

FRONT VIEW

Rev counter

Windscreen

All-enclosing fairing

Fuel tank

Battery

Wheel guard

60

BSA

Square-section tyre

Passenger windscreen

Passenger grab rail

SIDE VIEW

Throttle cable

Exhaust pipe

Rev counter

All-enclosing fairing

60

Sidecar chassis

Engine

Fibreglass wheel guard

Fuel cap

Windscreen

Racing number

Clutch lever

Fairing

34

Front brake lever

Radiator

Hydraulic brake hose

Mudguard

Axle

Slick tyre

FRONT VIEW

Sea and Air

Ships of Greece and Rome

ROMAN ANCHOR

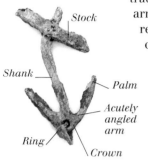

Stock

Shank

Palm

Acutely angled arm

Ring

Crown

IN THE EXPANSIVE EMPIRES OF GREECE AND ROME, powerful fleets were needed for battle, trade, and communication. Greek galleys were powered by a sail and many oars. A new armament, the embolos (ram), was fitted on to the galley bow. As ramming duels required fast and manoeuvrable boats, extra rows of oarsmen were added, culminating in the trireme. During the fifth and fourth centuries B.C., the trireme dominated the Mediterranean. It was powered by 170 oarsmen, rowing with one oar each. The oarsmen were ranged on three levels, as the model opposite shows. The trireme also carried archers and soldiers for boarding. Galleys were pulled out of the water when not in use, and were kept in dockyard ship-sheds. The merchant ships of the Greeks and Romans were mighty vessels too. The full-bodied Roman corbita, for example, could hold up to 400 tons and carried a cargo of spices, gems, silk, and animals. The construction of these boats was based on a stout hull with planking secured by mortice and tenon. Some of these ships embarked on long voyages, sailing even as far as India. To make them easier to steer, corbitas set a fore sail called an "artemon". It flew from a forward-leaning mast that was a forerunner of the long bowsprits carried by the great clipper ships of the 19th century.

ATTIC VASE SHOWING A GALLEY

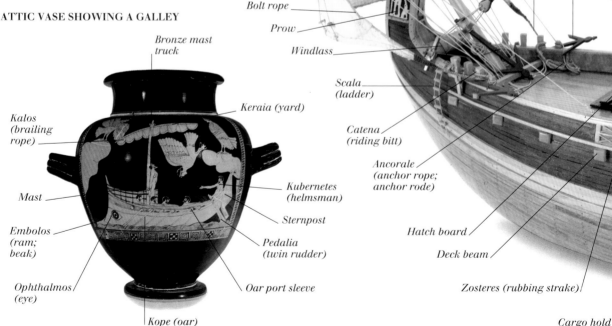

Double halyard   **ROMAN CORBITA**

Bullseye

Fore mast

Antenna (yard)

Buntline

Brace

Artemon (fore sail)

Oculus (eye)

Tabling

Bolt rope

Prow

Windlass

Scala (ladder)

Catena (riding bitt)

Ancorale (anchor rope; anchor rode)

Hatch board

Deck beam

Zosteres (rubbing strake)

Cargo hold

Roband (rope band)

Ceruchi (lift)

Heraldic device

Ring

Ruden (brail line)

Fore stay

Anchor

Sheet

Bronze mast truck

Keraia (yard)

Kalos (brailing rope)

Mast

Embolos (ram; beak)

Ophthalmos (eye)

Kope (oar)

Kubernetes (helmsman)

Sternpost

Pedalia (twin rudder)

Oar port sleeve

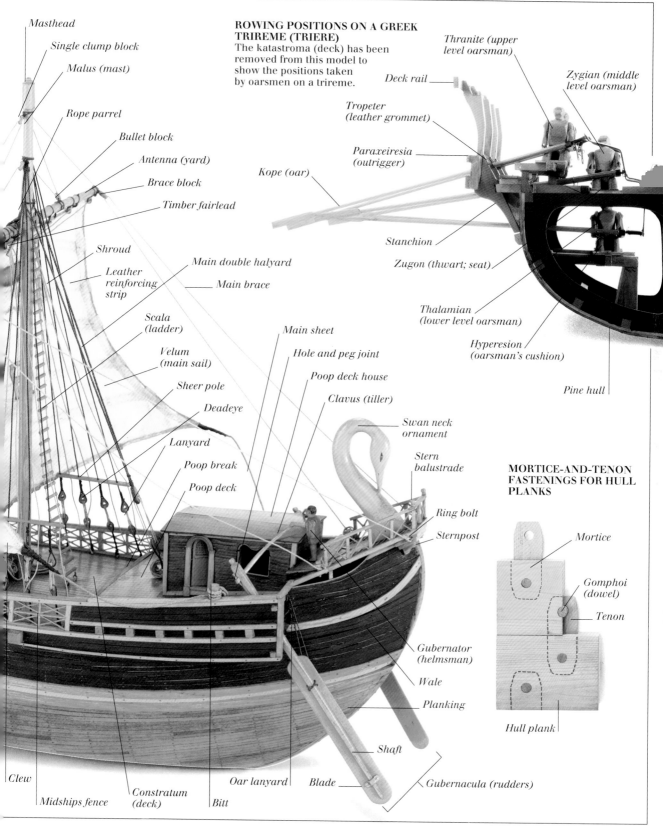

ROWING POSITIONS ON A GREEK TRIREME (TRIERE)
The katastroma (deck) has been removed from this model to show the positions taken by oarsmen on a trireme.

Masthead

Single clump block

Malus (mast)

Rope parrel

Bullet block

Antenna (yard)

Brace block

Timber fairlead

Shroud

Leather reinforcing strip

Scala (ladder)

Velum (main sail)

Sheer pole

Deadeye

Lanyard

Poop break

Poop deck

Main double halyard

Main brace

Main sheet

Hole and peg joint

Poop deck house

Clavus (tiller)

Thranite (upper level oarsman)

Zygian (middle level oarsman)

Deck rail

Tropeter (leather grommet)

Paraxeiresia (outrigger)

Kope (oar)

Stanchion

Zugon (thwart; seat)

Thalamian (lower level oarsman)

Hyperesion (oarsman's cushion)

Pine hull

Swan neck ornament

Stern balustrade

Ring bolt

Sternpost

Gubernator (helmsman)

Wale

Planking

Shaft

MORTICE-AND-TENON FASTENINGS FOR HULL PLANKS

Mortice

Gomphoi (dowel)

Tenon

Hull plank

Clew

Midships fence

Constratum (deck)

Bitt

Oar lanyard

Blade

Gubernacula (rudders)

Viking ships

IN THE DARK AGES and early medieval times, the longships of Scandinavia were one of the most feared sights for people of northern Europe. The Vikings launched raids from Scandinavia every summer in longships equipped with a single steering oar on the right, or "steerboard", side (hence "starboard"). A longship had one row of oars on each side and a single sail. The hull had clinker (overlapping) planks. Prowheads adorned fighting ships during campaigns of war. The sailing longship was also used for local coastal travel. The karv below was probably built as transport for an important family, while the smaller faering (top right) was a rowing boat only. The fleet of William of Normandy that invaded England in 1066 owed much to the Viking boatbuilding tradition, and has been depicted in the Bayeux Tapestry (above). Seals used by port towns and royal courts through the ages provide an excellent record of contemporary ship design. The seal opposite shows how ships changed from the Viking period to the end of the Middle Ages. The introduction of the fighting platform – the castle – and the addition of extra masts and sails changed the character of the medieval ship. Note also that the steering oar has been replaced by a centred rudder.

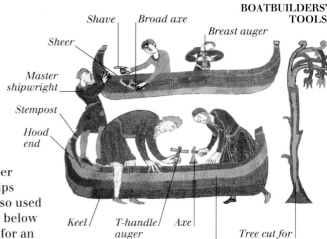

BOATBUILDERS' TOOLS

Shave
Broad axe
Breast auger
Sheer
Master shipwright
Stempost
Hood end
Keel
T-handle auger
Axe
Strake
Tree cut for planking
Roband
Leather diagonal reinforcement
Square sail of homespun yarn
Leech (leach)

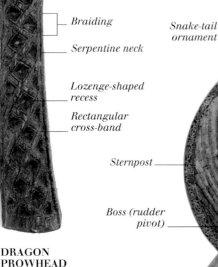

Zoomorphic head
Eye
Tooth
Braiding
Serpentine neck
Lozenge-shaped recess
Rectangular cross-band

DRAGON PROWHEAD

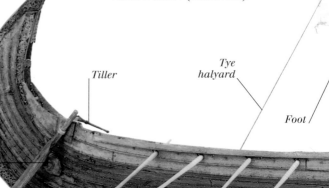

Snake-tail ornament

VIKING KARV (COASTER)

Tye halyard
Foot
Tiller
Sternpost
Boss (rudder pivot)
Steering oar (side rudder)
Oar
Starboard (steerboard) side
Keel

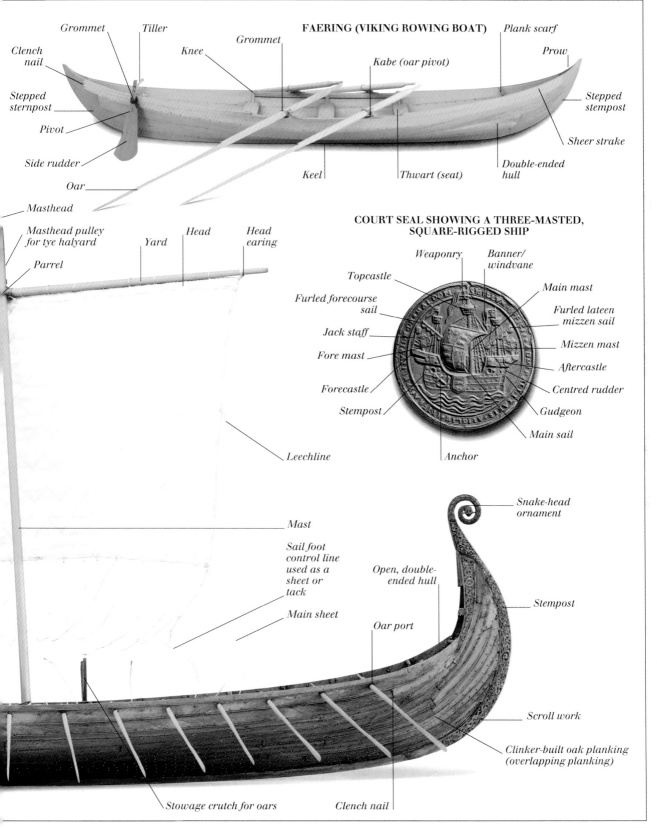

FAERING (VIKING ROWING BOAT)

Grommet

Tiller

Clench nail

Knee

Grommet

Plank scarf

Prow

Kabe (oar pivot)

Stepped sternpost

Stepped sternpost

Pivot

Side rudder

Oar

Keel

Thwart (seat)

Sheer strake

Double-ended hull

Masthead

Masthead pulley for tye halyard

Yard

Head

Head earing

Parrel

COURT SEAL SHOWING A THREE-MASTED, SQUARE-RIGGED SHIP

Weaponry

Banner/ windvane

Topcastle

Main mast

Furled forecourse sail

Furled lateen mizzen sail

Jack staff

Mizzen mast

Fore mast

Aftercastle

Forecastle

Centred rudder

Stempost

Gudgeon

Main sail

Leechline

Anchor

Mast

Snake-head ornament

Sail foot control line used as a sheet or tack

Open, double-ended hull

Stempost

Main sheet

Oar port

Scroll work

Clinker-built oak planking (overlapping planking)

Stowage crutch for oars

Clench nail

Medieval warships and traders

FROM THE 16TH CENTURY, SHIPS WERE BUILT WITH A NEW FORM OF HULL, constructed from carvel (edge-to-edge) planking. Warships of the time, like King Henry VIII of England's Mary Rose, boasted awesome fire power. This ship carried both long-range cannon in bronze, and short-range, anti-personnel guns in iron. Elsewhere, ships took on a multiformity of shapes. Dhows transported slaves from East Africa to Arabia, their fore-and-aft rigged lateen sails allowing them to sail close to the wind around the lands of the Indian Ocean. The Chinese sailed to East Africa and Arabia in junks, trading goods that were carried in watertight compartments. New astronomical tools helped medieval sailors to find their way. Cross-staves and astrolabes were used to measure the altitude of the sun or stars. One of a choice of four cross-pieces was slid up or down the staff of the cross-stave – which was graduated in degrees of altitude – until its top aligned with the celestial body and its base with the horizon. The sighting rule of the astrolabe was simply lined up with a known body, and its altitude read from marks on the metal disc. With sundials, the sailor could use the shadow of the sun to show the time of day.

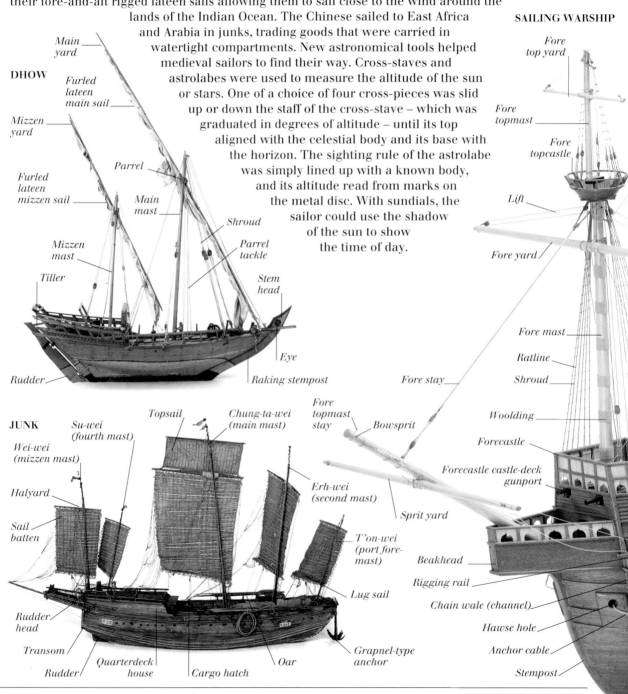

DHOW

Main yard
Furled lateen main sail
Mizzen yard
Furled lateen mizzen sail
Parrel
Main mast
Mizzen mast
Tiller
Shroud
Parrel tackle
Stem head
Eye
Rudder
Raking stempost

JUNK

Su-wei (fourth mast)
Wei-wei (mizzen mast)
Halyard
Sail batten
Rudder head
Transom
Rudder
Quarterdeck house
Cargo hatch
Topsail
Chung-ta-wei (main mast)
Erh-wei (second mast)
T'on-wei (port fore-mast)
Lug sail
Oar
Grapnel-type anchor

SAILING WARSHIP

Fore top yard
Fore topmast
Fore topcastle
Lift
Fore yard
Fore mast
Ratline
Shroud
Fore stay
Woolding
Forecastle
Fore topmast stay
Bowsprit
Sprit yard
Forecastle castle-deck gunport
Beakhead
Rigging rail
Chain wale (channel)
Hawse hole
Anchor cable
Stempost

Main topgallant mast

Main topgallant yard

Main topmast topcastle

Main top yard

Mizzen topmast

Mizzen top yard

Main topmast stay

Mizzen topcastle

Main topmast

Lift

Main topcastle

Bonaventure top yard

Lift

Bonaventure topmast

Main yard

Parrel

30 degree cross-piece

Tye

Bonaventure topcastle

Jeer

Brace

Bonaventure yard

Main stay

Bonaventure mast

Mizzen mast

Aftercastle

Mizzen yard

Main mast

Swifting tackle

Aftercastle castle-deck gunport

Outrigger

Pivot

Upper deck gunport

Chain wale (channel)

Lid

Deadeye

Gangway

Gun carriage

Transom

Rudder

Sternpost

Keel

Blindage (removable archery screen)

Wale

Main deck gunport

Carvel planking

Port bower anchor

CROSS-STAVE (CROSS-STAFF)

90 degree cross-piece (transversary)

Clamp

Boxwood staff

60 degree cross-piece

Altitude scale in degrees and minutes

Ocular end

10 degree cross-piece (dutch shoe)

SUNDIAL

Style of the gnomon (edge)

Needle

Gnomon

Hour line

Dial

ASTROLABE

Swivel suspension ring

Graduated ring

Scale of degrees

Pivot

Alidade (sighting rule)

Bottom ballast

Scribed arc decoration

The expansion of sail

By THE 18TH CENTURY, SAILING SHIPS had become fast and effective floating fortresses. The navies of the north European powers competed with each other by building heavily-armed fighting ships called "men-of-war". The distinctive round stern of the ship below, with its open gallery, balcony, and elaborate wood carving is typical of the period. Hulls around this time were semicircular in cross section, although many boat designers were soon to return to the V-shaped hulls used by the Vikings. Ships of the period carried more sail than ever before. A labyrinth of rigging supported the masts and yards from which the profusion of square sails were set. Ships grew higher, as extra masts were fitted above the lower mast, and the bowsprit became longer to allow the ship to carry staysails, spritsails, and jibsails. Ships went into battle in single file, so that broadsides from the multiple decks of guns would have maximum effect. Ships were classified by rates, the rating of a vessel depending on how many guns it had. A first rate ship had more than 100 guns. The guns fired solid round shot, usually made of iron.

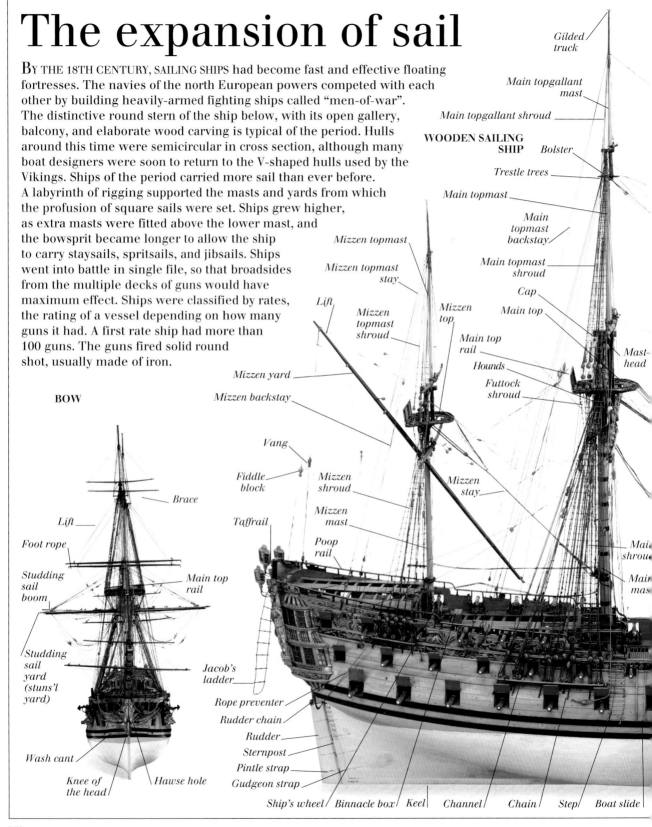

WOODEN SAILING SHIP

Gilded truck

Main topgallant mast

Main topgallant shroud

Bolster

Trestle trees

Main topmast

Main topmast backstay

Main topmast shroud

Cap

Main top

Mast-head

Main top rail

Hounds

Futtock shroud

Mizzen topmast

Mizzen topmast stay

Lift

Mizzen topmast shroud

Mizzen top

Mizzen yard

Mizzen backstay

Vang

Fiddle block

Mizzen shroud

Mizzen mast

Mizzen stay

Mai[n] shrou[d]

Mai[n] mas[t]

BOW

Brace

Lift

Foot rope

Studding sail boom

Main top rail

Studding sail yard (stuns'l yard)

Taffrail

Poop rail

Jacob's ladder

Rope preventer

Rudder chain

Rudder

Sternpost

Pintle strap

Gudgeon strap

Wash cant

Knee of the head

Hawse hole

Ship's wheel

Binnacle box

Keel

Channel

Chain

Step

Boat slide

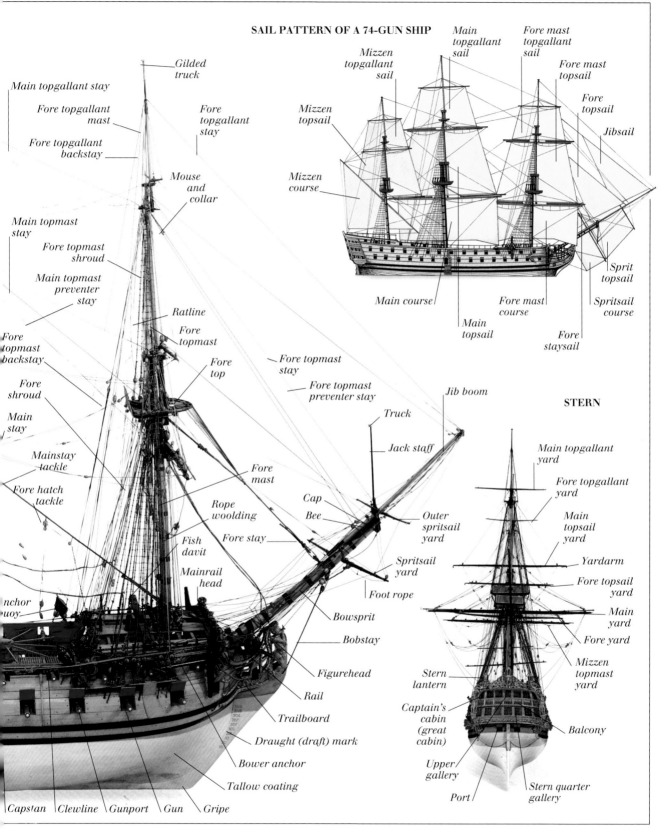

SAIL PATTERN OF A 74-GUN SHIP

Main topgallant sail

Fore mast topgallant sail

Mizzen topgallant sail

Fore mast topsail

Mizzen topsail

Fore topsail

Mizzen course

Jibsail

Gilded truck

Main topgallant stay

Fore topgallant mast

Fore topgallant stay

Fore topgallant backstay

Main topmast stay

Mouse and collar

Fore topmast shroud

Main topmast preventer stay

Main course

Fore mast course

Main topsail

Sprit topsail

Fore staysail

Spritsail course

Fore topmast backstay

Ratline

Fore topmast

Main stay

Fore topmast stay

Fore top

Fore shroud

Fore topmast preventer stay

Main stay

Truck

Jib boom

STERN

Mainstay tackle

Jack staff

Main topgallant yard

Fore hatch tackle

Fore mast

Fore topgallant yard

Fore mast

Cap

Main topsail yard

Fish davit

Rope woolding

Bee

Outer spritsail yard

Yardarm

Mainrail head

Fore stay

Spritsail yard

Fore topsail yard

Foot rope

Main yard

Anchor buoy

Bowsprit

Fore yard

Bobstay

Mizzen topmast yard

Figurehead

Stern lantern

Rail

Captain's cabin (great cabin)

Balcony

Trailboard

Draught (draft) mark

Upper gallery

Bower anchor

Stern quarter gallery

Tallow coating

Port

Capstan   Clewline   Gunport   Gun   Gripe

A ship of the line

THE 74-GUN WOODEN SHIP WAS A MAINSTAY of British and French battlefleets in the late 18th and early 19th centuries. This "ship of the line" was heavy enough to fight with the most potent of rivals, yet nimble too. The length of such a ship was determined by the number of guns required for each deck, allowing enough room for crews to man them. The gun deck was about 52 m (170 ft) long. The decks had to be very strong to carry the weight of the guns. The deck planks have been removed on the vessel pictured below, to show just how close together the beams had to be to make the hull strong enough. Only timber with a perfect grain was used. The upper deck was open at the waist, but afore and abaft were officers' cabins. The forecastle and quarterdeck carried light guns and acted as platforms for working rigging and for reconnaissance. The ship's longboats (launches) were carried on booms between the gangways.

LONGBOAT

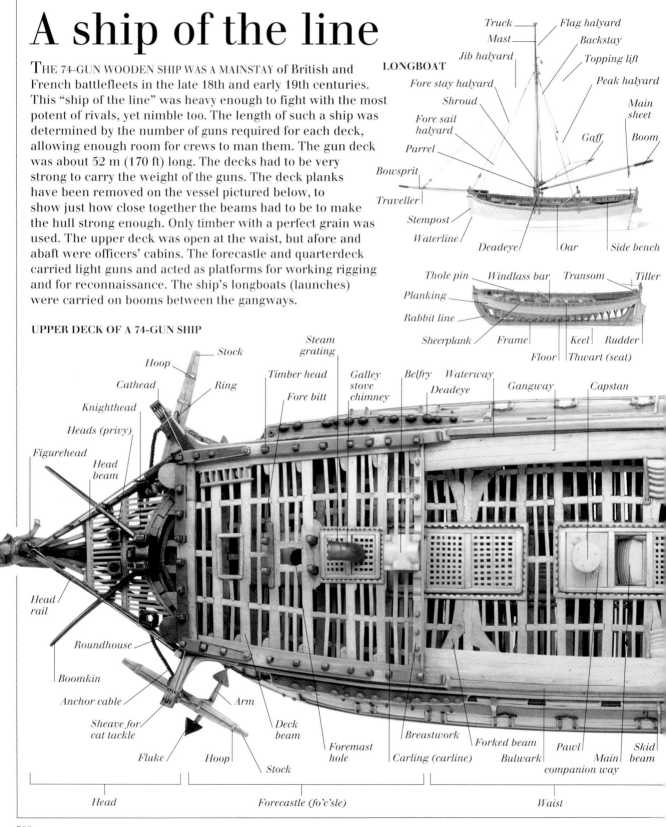

UPPER DECK OF A 74-GUN SHIP

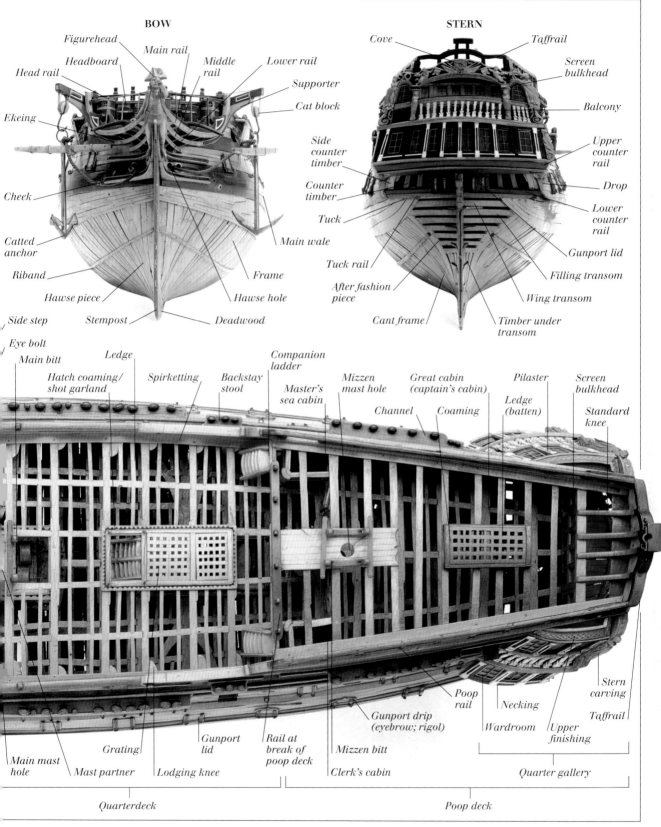

BOW

Figurehead

Headboard

Main rail

Middle rail

Lower rail

Head rail

Supporter

Ekeing

Cat block

Cheek

Catted anchor

Riband

Main wale

Hawse piece

Frame

Side step

Hawse hole

Stempost

Deadwood

Eye bolt

STERN

Cove

Taffrail

Screen bulkhead

Balcony

Side counter timber

Upper counter rail

Counter timber

Drop

Tuck

Lower counter rail

Tuck rail

Gunport lid

After fashion piece

Filling transom

Wing transom

Cant frame

Timber under transom

Main bitt

Ledge

Spirketting

Backstay stool

Companion ladder

Master's sea cabin

Mizzen mast hole

Great cabin (captain's cabin)

Pilaster

Screen bulkhead

Hatch coaming/ shot garland

Channel

Coaming

Ledge (batten)

Standard knee

Stern carving

Poop rail

Taffrail

Gunport drip (eyebrow; rigol)

Necking

Wardroom

Upper finishing

Main mast hole

Grating

Gunport lid

Rail at break of poop deck

Mizzen bitt

Clerk's cabin

Mast partner

Lodging knee

Quarter gallery

Quarterdeck

Poop deck

Rigging

MOST SAILING SHIPS HAVE TWO TYPES OF RIGGING. Standing rigging – kept taut by rigging screws or old-fashioned lanyards and deadeyes – refers to the ropes, wires, and chains that support the masts and yards (horizontal spars). Running rigging, which includes types of block and tackle, halyards, and sheets, is used to hoist, lower, or trim sails.

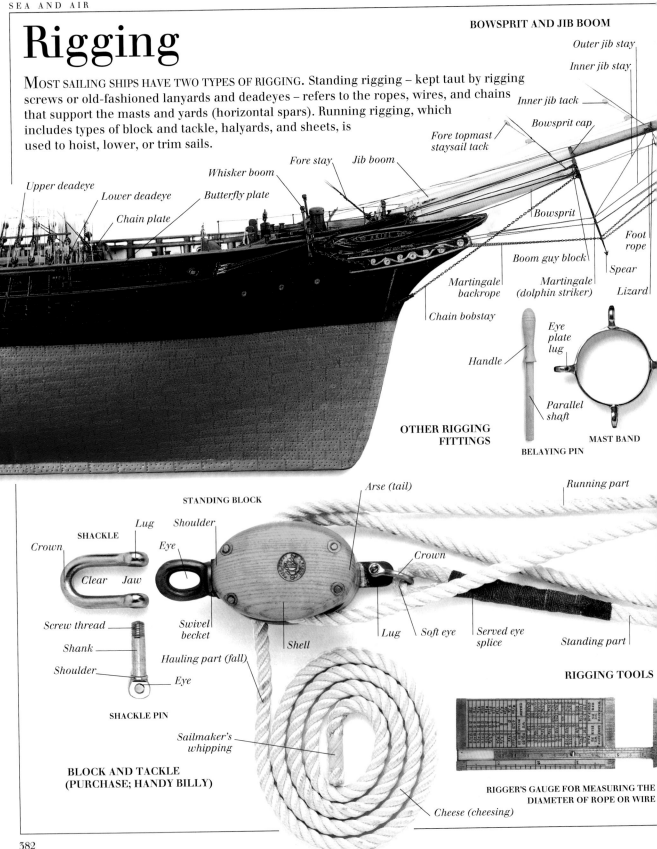

BOWSPRIT AND JIB BOOM

Outer jib stay

Inner jib stay

Inner jib tack

Bowsprit cap

Fore topmast staysail tack

Fore stay

Jib boom

Whisker boom

Butterfly plate

Upper deadeye

Lower deadeye

Chain plate

Bowsprit

Foot rope

Boom guy block

Martingale backrope

Martingale (dolphin striker)

Spear

Lizard

Chain bobstay

Eye plate lug

Handle

OTHER RIGGING FITTINGS

Parallel shaft

BELAYING PIN

MAST BAND

Arse (tail)

Running part

STANDING BLOCK

Shoulder

SHACKLE

Lug

Eye

Crown

Crown

Clear

Jaw

Soft eye

Served eye splice

Standing part

Swivel becket

Lug

Shell

Screw thread

Shank

Shoulder

Eye

Hauling part (fall)

RIGGING TOOLS

SHACKLE PIN

Sailmaker's whipping

BLOCK AND TACKLE (PURCHASE; HANDY BILLY)

RIGGER'S GAUGE FOR MEASURING THE DIAMETER OF ROPE OR WIRE

Cheese (cheesing)

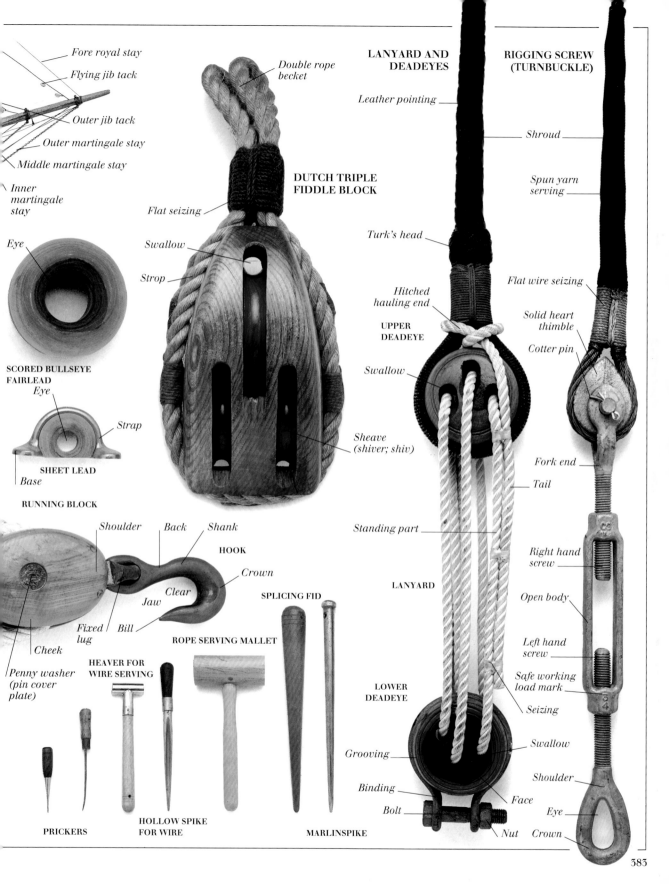

Fore royal stay

Flying jib tack

Outer jib tack

Outer martingale stay

Middle martingale stay

Inner martingale stay

Eye

SCORED BULLSEYE FAIRLEAD

Eye

Strap

SHEET LEAD

Base

RUNNING BLOCK

Shoulder   *Back*   *Shank*

HOOK

Crown

Clear

Jaw

Fixed lug   *Bill*

Cheek

Penny washer (pin cover plate)

HEAVER FOR WIRE SERVING

ROPE SERVING MALLET

SPLICING FID

PRICKERS

HOLLOW SPIKE FOR WIRE

MARLINSPIKE

Double rope becket

DUTCH TRIPLE FIDDLE BLOCK

Flat seizing

Swallow

Strop

LANYARD AND DEADEYES

RIGGING SCREW (TURNBUCKLE)

Leather pointing

Shroud

Spun yarn serving

Turk's head

Flat wire seizing

Hitched hauling end

UPPER DEADEYE

Solid heart thimble

Cotter pin

Swallow

Sheave (shiver; shiv)

Fork end

Tail

Standing part

Right hand screw

LANYARD

Open body

Left hand screw

LOWER DEADEYE

Safe working load mark

Seizing

Grooving

Swallow

Binding

Shoulder

Bolt

Face

Eye

Nut   *Crown*

385

Sails

PARREL BEADS

THERE ARE TWO MAIN TYPES OF SAIL, often used in combination. Square sails are driving sails. They are usually attached by parrels to yards, square to the mast to catch the following wind. On fore-and-aft sails, such as lateen and lug sails, the luff (leading edge) usually abuts a mast or a stay. The head of the sail may abut a gaff, and the foot a boom. Around the world, a great range of rigs (sail patterns), such as the ketch, lugger, and schooner, have evolved to suit local needs. Sails are made from strips of cloth, cut to give the sail a belly and strong enough to resist the most violent of winds. Cotton and flax are the traditional sail materials, but synthetic fabrics are now commonly used.

SECTION OF A SAIL

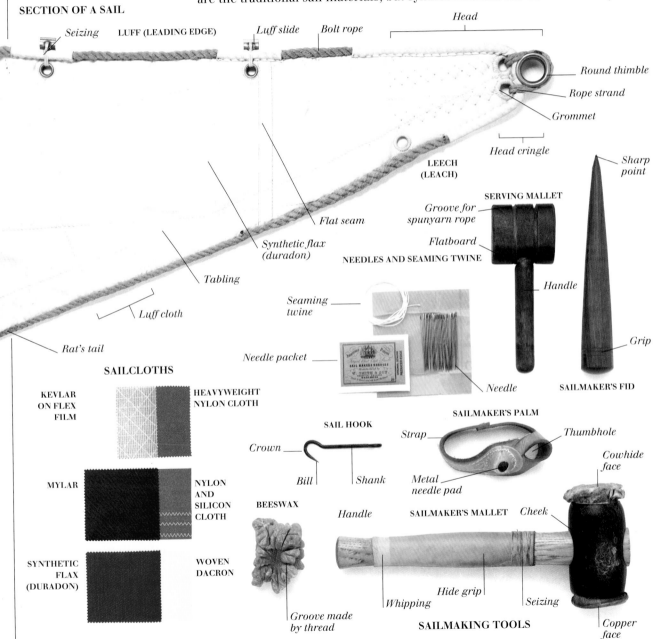

Seizing   LUFF (LEADING EDGE)   Luff slide   Bolt rope   Head

Round thimble

Rope strand

Grommet

Head cringle

LEECH (LEACH)

Flat seam

Synthetic flax (duradon)

Tabling

Luff cloth

Rat's tail

SAILCLOTHS

KEVLAR ON FLEX FILM

HEAVYWEIGHT NYLON CLOTH

MYLAR

NYLON AND SILICON CLOTH

SYNTHETIC FLAX (DURADON)

WOVEN DACRON

SERVING MALLET

Sharp point

Groove for spunyarn rope

Flatboard

Handle

Grip

SAILMAKER'S FID

NEEDLES AND SEAMING TWINE

Seaming twine

Needle packet

Needle

SAIL HOOK

Crown

Bill   Shank

SAILMAKER'S PALM

Strap   Thumbhole

Metal needle pad

Cowhide face

BEESWAX

Groove made by thread

SAILMAKER'S MALLET

Handle

Cheek

Whipping   Hide grip   Seizing

Copper face

SAILMAKING TOOLS

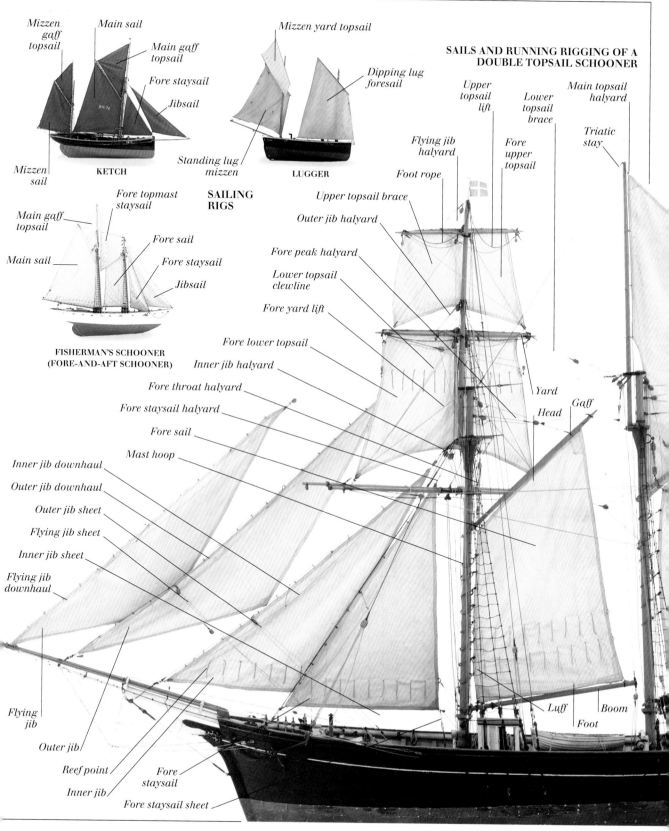

Mizzen gaff topsail

Main sail

Main gaff topsail

Fore staysail

Jibsail

Mizzen sail

KETCH

Mizzen yard topsail

Dipping lug foresail

Standing lug mizzen

LUGGER

SAILING RIGS

Main gaff topsail

Fore topmast staysail

Fore sail

Fore staysail

Jibsail

Main sail

**FISHERMAN'S SCHOONER
(FORE-AND-AFT SCHOONER)**

**SAILS AND RUNNING RIGGING OF A
DOUBLE TOPSAIL SCHOONER**

Upper topsail lift

Lower topsail brace

Main topsail halyard

Flying jib halyard

Fore upper topsail

Triatic stay

Foot rope

Upper topsail brace

Outer jib halyard

Fore peak halyard

Lower topsail clewline

Fore yard lift

Fore lower topsail

Inner jib halyard

Fore throat halyard

Fore staysail halyard

Fore sail

Mast hoop

Inner jib downhaul

Outer jib downhaul

Outer jib sheet

Flying jib sheet

Inner jib sheet

Flying jib downhaul

Yard

Head

Gaff

Flying jib

Outer jib

Reef point

Inner jib

Fore staysail

Fore staysail sheet

Luff

Boom

Foot

Mooring and anchoring

FOR LARGE VESSELS IN OPEN WATER, ANCHORAGE IS ESSENTIAL. By holding a ship securely to the seabed, an anchor prevents the vessel from being at the mercy of wave, tide, and current. The earliest anchors were nothing more than stones. In later years, many anchors had a standard design, much like the Admiralty pattern anchor shown on this page. The Danforth anchor is somewhat different. It has particularly deep flukes to give it great holding power. On large sailing ships, anchors were worked by teams of sailors. They turned the drum of a capstan by pushing on bars slotted into the revolving cylinder. This, in turn, lifted or lowered the anchor chain. In calm harbours and estuaries, ships can moor (make fast) without using anchors. Berthing ropes can be attached to bollards both inboard and on the quayside. Berthing ropes are joined to each other by bends, like those opposite.

STONE ANCHOR (KILLICK)

Rope hole

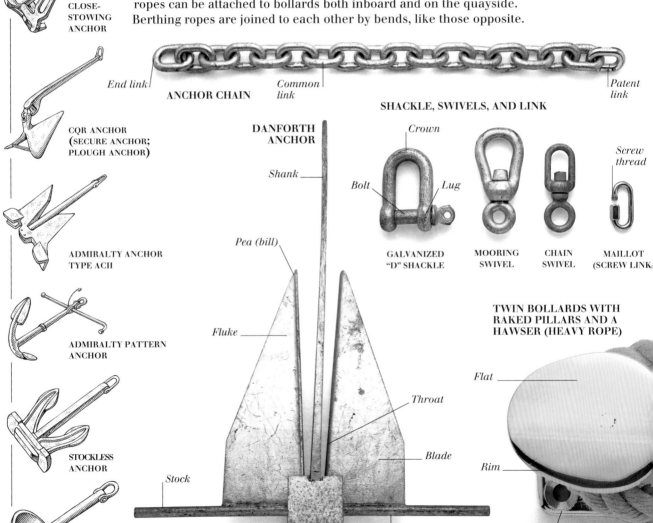

TYPES OF ANCHOR

CLOSE-STOWING ANCHOR

CQR ANCHOR (SECURE ANCHOR; PLOUGH ANCHOR)

ADMIRALTY ANCHOR TYPE ACII

ADMIRALTY PATTERN ANCHOR

STOCKLESS ANCHOR

MUSHROOM ANCHOR (PERMANENT MOORING ANCHOR)

ANCHOR CHAIN

End link

Common link

Patent link

SHACKLE, SWIVELS, AND LINK

Crown

Bolt

Lug

Screw thread

GALVANIZED "D" SHACKLE

MOORING SWIVEL

CHAIN SWIVEL

MAILLOT (SCREW LINK

DANFORTH ANCHOR

Shank

Pea (bill)

Fluke

Throat

Blade

Stock

Tripping palm

Crown

TWIN BOLLARDS WITH RAKED PILLARS AND A HAWSER (HEAVY ROPE)

Flat

Rim

Base

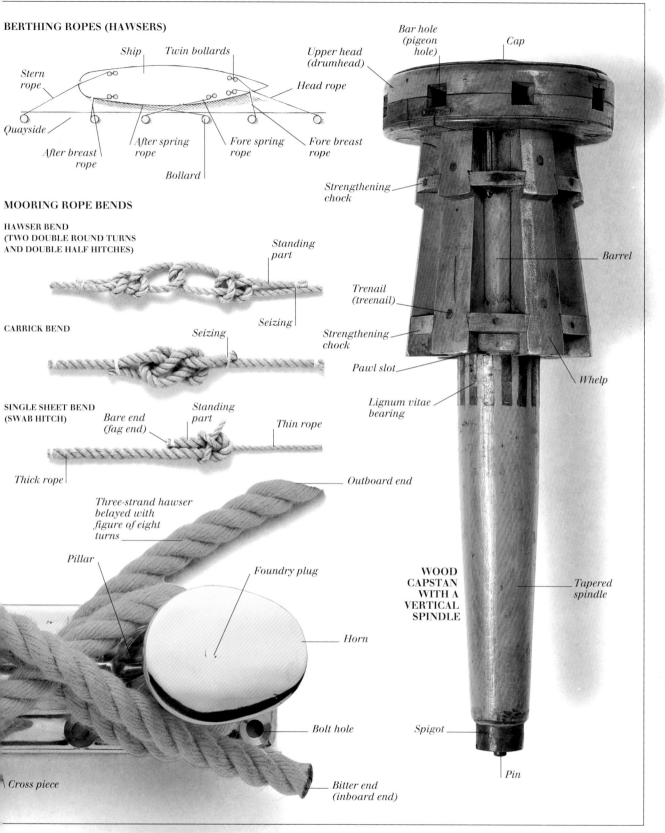

BERTHING ROPES (HAWSERS)

Stern rope

Ship

Twin bollards

Upper head (drumhead)

Head rope

Quayside

After breast rope

After spring rope

Fore spring rope

Fore breast rope

Bollard

MOORING ROPE BENDS

HAWSER BEND (TWO DOUBLE ROUND TURNS AND DOUBLE HALF HITCHES)

Standing part

Seizing

Seizing

CARRICK BEND

Seizing

SINGLE SHEET BEND (SWAB HITCH)

Bare end (fag end)

Standing part

Thin rope

Thick rope

Three-strand hawser belayed with figure of eight turns

Outboard end

Pillar

Foundry plug

Horn

Bolt hole

Cross piece

Bitter end (inboard end)

Bar hole (pigeon hole)

Cap

Strengthening chock

Trenail (treenail)

Barrel

Strengthening chock

Pawl slot

Whelp

Lignum vitae bearing

WOOD CAPSTAN WITH A VERTICAL SPINDLE

Tapered spindle

Spigot

Pin

387

Ropes and knots

ALL KINDS OF ROPES ARE USED AT SEA, from thin twines and yarns to thick hawsers. Synthetic fibres have been developed specifically for use at sea. Nylon ropes stretch, and so are ideal for anchoring; polypropylene has little stretch, so is ideal for halyards and sheets. Different types of knots are used for different purposes. Knots that join two ropes are called bends; hitches join a rope to another object; and bowlines produce an eye (loop) in the end of a rope. Ropes can be joined by splicing (unravelling the ends and weaving them together) or seizing (lashing the ropes together side by side).

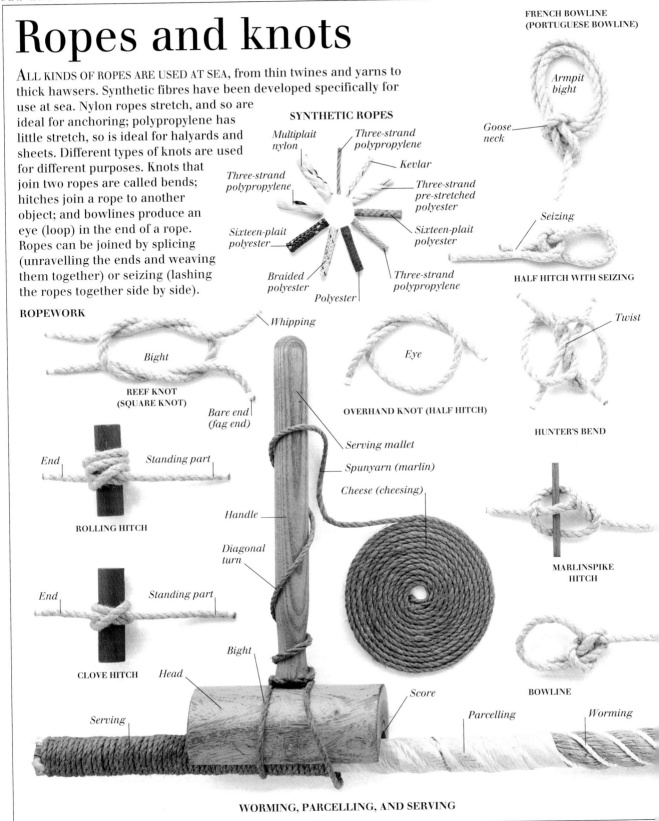

FRENCH BOWLINE (PORTUGUESE BOWLINE)

Armpit bight

Goose neck

Seizing

HALF HITCH WITH SEIZING

SYNTHETIC ROPES

Multiplait nylon

Three-strand polypropylene

Kevlar

Three-strand polypropylene

Three-strand pre-stretched polyester

Sixteen-plait polyester

Sixteen-plait polyester

Braided polyester

Three-strand polypropylene

Polyester

ROPEWORK

Whipping

Bight

REEF KNOT (SQUARE KNOT)

Bare end (fag end)

Eye

OVERHAND KNOT (HALF HITCH)

Twist

HUNTER'S BEND

End *Standing part*

ROLLING HITCH

Serving mallet

Spunyarn (marlin)

Cheese (cheesing)

Handle

Diagonal turn

MARLINSPIKE HITCH

End *Standing part*

CLOVE HITCH

Head

Bight

Score

BOWLINE

Serving

Parcelling

Worming

WORMING, PARCELLING, AND SERVING

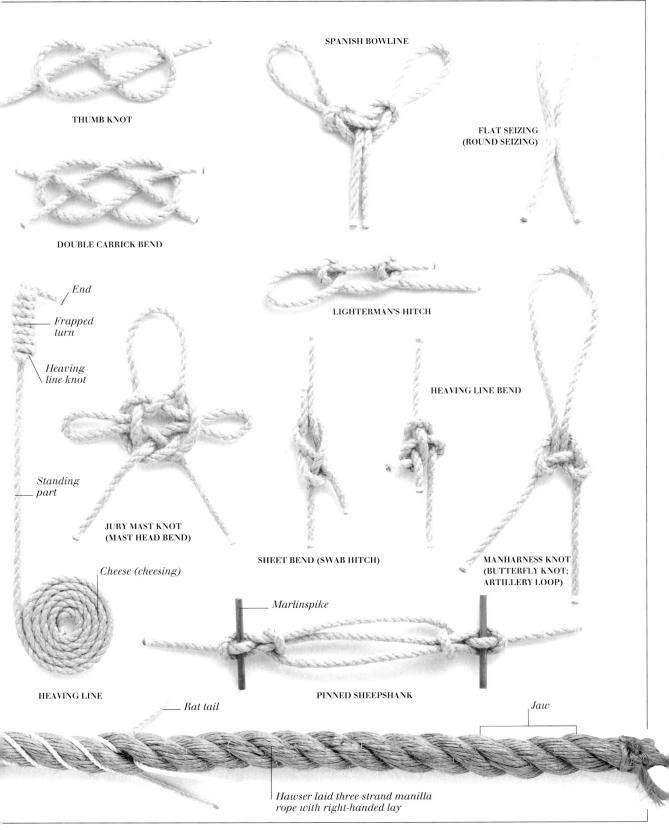

THUMB KNOT

SPANISH BOWLINE

**FLAT SEIZING
(ROUND SEIZING)**

DOUBLE CARRICK BEND

LIGHTERMAN'S HITCH

End

*Frapped
turn*

*Heaving
line knot*

HEAVING LINE BEND

*Standing
part*

**JURY MAST KNOT
(MAST HEAD BEND)**

SHEET BEND (SWAB HITCH)

**MANHARNESS KNOT
(BUTTERFLY KNOT;
ARTILLERY LOOP)**

Cheese (cheesing)

Marlinspike

HEAVING LINE

PINNED SHEEPSHANK

Rat tail

Jaw

*Hawser laid three-strand manilla
rope with right-handed lay*

Paddle wheels and propellers

THE INVENTION OF THE STEAM ENGINE IN THE 18TH CENTURY made mechanically driven ships fitted with paddle wheels or propellers a viable alternative to sails. Paddle wheels have fixed or feathered floats, and the model shown below features both types. Feathered floats give more propulsive power than fixed floats because they are almost upright at all times in the water. Paddle wheels were superseded by the propeller on ocean-going vessels in the mid-19th century. Propellers are more efficient, work better in rough water, and are less vulnerable in collisions. The first propellers were two-bladed but later three- and four-bladed versions are more powerful; the shape and pitch of blades have also been refined over the years. At the beginning of the 18th century, tillers were superseded on many larger ships by the ship's wheel as a means of steering.

SHIP'S WHEEL

King spoke handle

Handle

Spoke

Rim plate

Felloe (rim section)

Maker's name

Nave plate

Nave

PADDLE WHEEL WITH FIXED FLOATS

Wrist pin

Limb

Fixed float

Hub

Deck beam

OSCILLATING STEAM ENGINE

Slip eccentric for slide valve

Ahead/astern controls

Main crank

Slide valve

THREE-BLADED PROPELLER

Blade

Tapered shaft hole

Hub

Keyway

Strut

Frame

Piston rod (tail rod)

Stuffing box

Oscillating cylinder

Bottom plate (bedplate)

Slide valve rod

Control platform

PROPELLER ACTION

Propeller blade tip trace

Pitch

Propeller diameter

Blade

Hub

Propeller hub trace

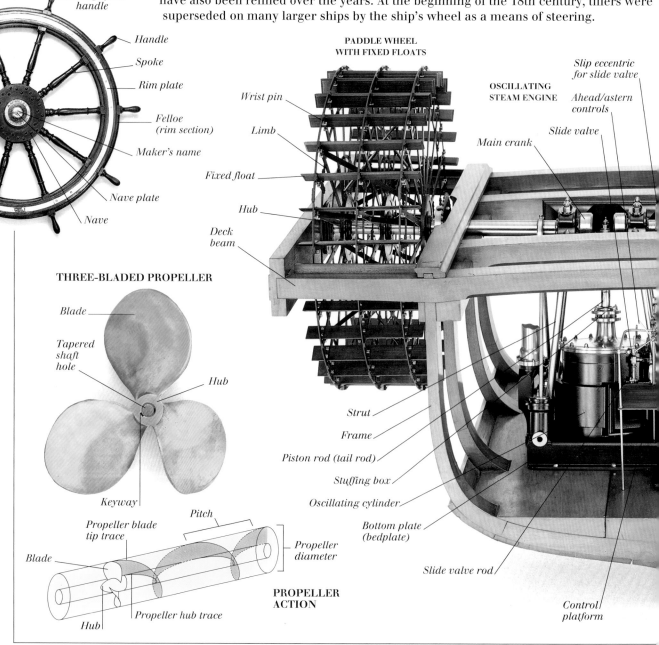

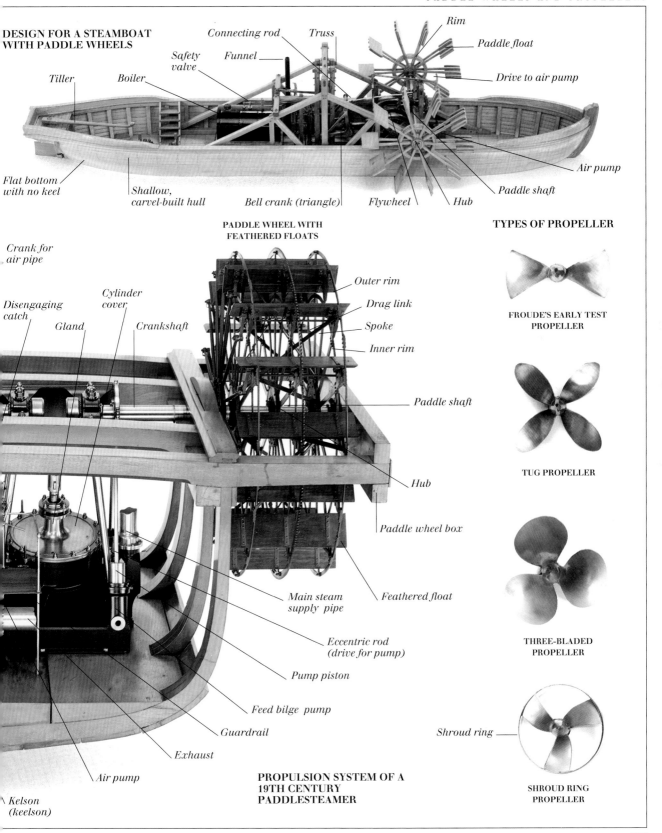

**DESIGN FOR A STEAMBOAT
WITH PADDLE WHEELS**

Rim

Connecting rod

Truss

Paddle float

Safety
valve

Funnel

Drive to air pump

Tiller

Boiler

Flat bottom
with no keel

Shallow,
carvel-built hull

Bell crank (triangle)

Flywheel

Hub

Air pump

Paddle shaft

TYPES OF PROPELLER

**PADDLE WHEEL WITH
FEATHERED FLOATS**

Crank for
air pipe

Outer rim

Drag link

Spoke

Inner rim

Cylinder
cover

Disengaging
catch

Gland

Crankshaft

Paddle shaft

**FROUDE'S EARLY TEST
PROPELLER**

Hub

TUG PROPELLER

Paddle wheel box

Main steam
supply pipe

Feathered float

**THREE-BLADED
PROPELLER**

Eccentric rod
(drive for pump)

Pump piston

Feed bilge pump

Guardrail

Shroud ring

Exhaust

Air pump

**PROPULSION SYSTEM OF A
19TH CENTURY
PADDLESTEAMER**

**SHROUD RING
PROPELLER**

Kelson
(keelson)

Anatomy of an iron ship

IRON PARTS WERE USED IN THE HULLS OF WOODEN SHIPS AS EARLY AS 1675, often in the same form as the wooden parts that they replaced. Eventually, as on the tea clipper Cutty Sark (below), iron rigging was found to be stronger than the traditional rope. The first "ironclads" were warships whose wooden hulls were protected by iron armour plates. Later ironclads actually had iron hulls. The model opposite is based on the British warship HMS Warrior, launched in 1860, the first battleship built entirely of iron. The plan of the iron paddlesteamer (bottom), built somewhat later, shows that this vessel was a sailing ship; but it also boasted a steam propulsion plant amidships that turned two side paddlewheels. Early iron hulls were made from plates that were painstakingly rivetted together (as below), but by the 20th century vessels began to be welded together, whole sections at a time. The Second World War "liberty ship" was one of the first of these "production-line vessels".

TEA CLIPPER

Steel yard

Iron wire stay

Steel lower mast

Steel bowsprit

Wooden planking with copper sheathing

Forged iron anchor

RIVETTED PLATES

Pan head rivet

Plate

Button head rivet (snap head)

Seam

LIBERTY SHIP

Gun section

Accommodation section

Cargo derrick

Weld line

Stern section

Midships section

Cargo hold

Bow section

PLAN OF AN IRON PADDLESTEAMER

Steering position

Steering gear

Stern

Vertical frame ladder

Mast step

Rudder

Rudder post

Heel of rudder post

Mizzen mast

Poop deck

Lounge

Guardrail

Deck lantern

Binnacle

Main mast

State room

Steam whistle

After funnel

Skylight

Crankshaft

Guardrail

Eccentric

Paddle wheel

Connecting rod

Bar keel

Afterpeak

Cabin

Tank

Main mast step

Donkey boiler

Box boiler

Foundation

Reversing wheel

Bottom plate

Side lever

Cylinder

Stern framing

**CUTAWAY SECTION
OF AN "IRONCLAD"**

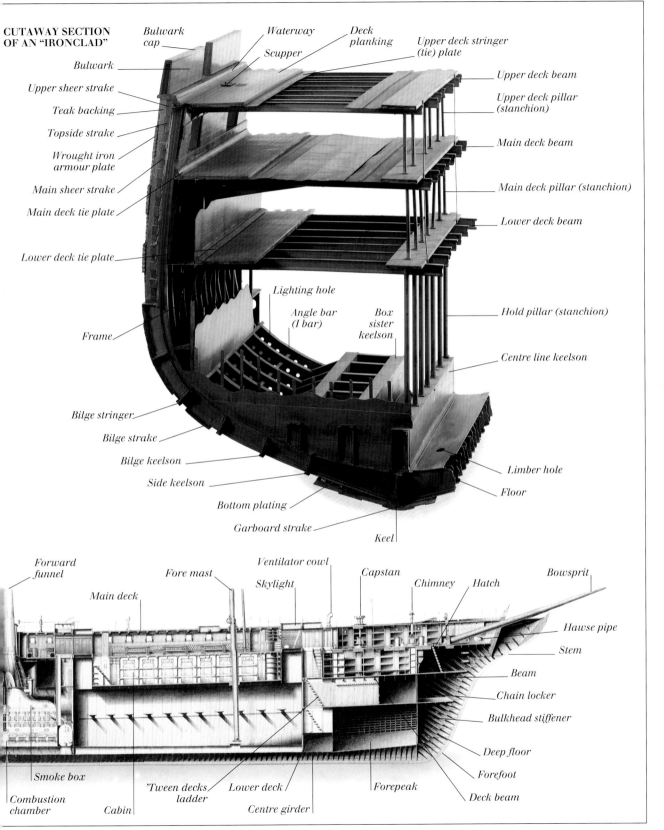

Bulwark
cap

Waterway

Deck
planking

Upper deck stringer
(tie) plate

Scupper

Bulwark

Upper sheer strake

Teak backing

Topside strake

Wrought iron
armour plate

Main sheer strake

Main deck tie plate

Lower deck tie plate

Frame

Bilge stringer

Bilge strake

Bilge keelson

Side keelson

Bottom plating

Garboard strake

Keel

Lighting hole

Angle bar
(I bar)

Box
sister
keelson

Upper deck beam

Upper deck pillar
(stanchion)

Main deck beam

Main deck pillar (stanchion)

Lower deck beam

Hold pillar (stanchion)

Centre line keelson

Limber hole

Floor

Forward
funnel

Fore mast

Ventilator cowl

Capstan

Bowsprit

Main deck

Skylight

Chimney

Hatch

Hawse pipe

Stem

Beam

Chain locker

Bulkhead stiffener

Deep floor

Forefoot

Forepeak

Smoke box

Combustion
chamber

Cabin

'Tween decks
ladder

Lower deck

Centre girder

Deck beam

393

The battleship

IN THE EARLY YEARS OF THE 20TH CENTURY, sea warfare –
attacking enemy vessels or defending a ship – was
revolutionized by the introduction of Dreadnought-type
battleships like the Brazilian vessel below. These new
ships combined the latest advances in steam
propulsion, gunnery, and armour plating. The gun
turret was designed to fire shells over huge distances.
It was protected by armour 30 cm (12 in) thick. The
measurements given for the guns of this ship refer
to the bore diameter. Where "weight" is quoted, this
is the weight of the shell that the gun fires. Torpedoes –
as portrayed on the upper cigarette card (right) – were
self-propelled underwater missiles, often steered by gyro-
control. Depth charges were designed in the First World
War for use against submerged U-boats. They are
canisters filled with explosives that are detonated
by depth-sensitive pistols. The lower cigarette
card shows depth charges being fired by
a "thrower", fired from a torpedo tube,
and rolled from the stern. Ship's shields
were fitted to warships from the late
19th century onwards. The shield
shown opposite depicts a
traditional ship's cannon.

20TH CENTURY WEAPONRY

Torpedo tube   Warhead

Sight

TORPEDOES

DEPTH
CHARGES

Side-thrown
canister

Stern-rolled
canister

Torpedo-fired
canister

BRAZILIAN BATTLESHIP

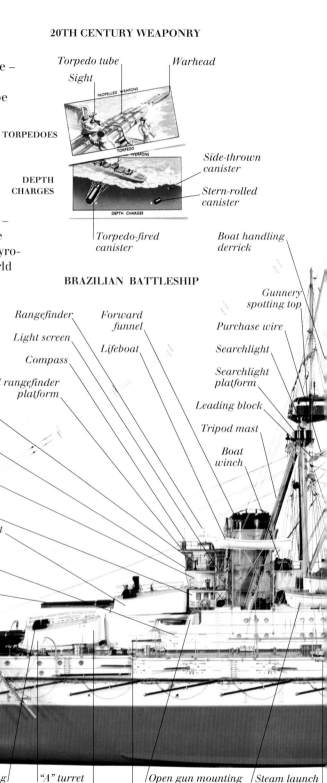

Rangefinder

Forward
funnel

Light screen

Lifeboat

Compass

Compass and rangefinder
platform

Ship's wheel

Navigating bridge

Conning tower

Captain's shelter/
chart house

Weather shutter
for gun

"F" turret

30 cm (12 in)
gun

Skylight

Arms of
Brazil

Jack staff

Boat handling
derrick

Gunnery
spotting top

Purchase wire

Searchlight

Searchlight
platform

Leading block

Tripod mast

Boat
winch

Stem
(false ram bow)

Porthole

Belt
armour

Forward
accommodation
ladder

Sighting
hood

"A" turret

Turret barbette

Open gun mounting

12 cm (4.7 in) gun

Steam launch

Guest boat boom

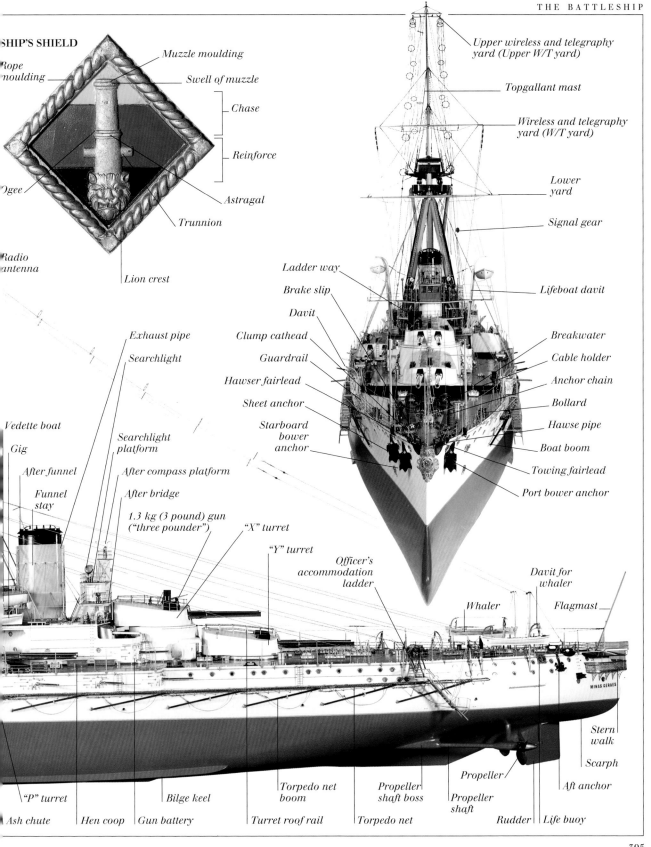

SHIP'S SHIELD

Rope moulding

Muzzle moulding

Swell of muzzle

Chase

Reinforce

Ogee

Astragal

Trunnion

Lion crest

Radio antenna

Upper wireless and telegraphy yard (Upper W/T yard)

Topgallant mast

Wireless and telegraphy yard (W/T yard)

Lower yard

Signal gear

Lifeboat davit

Breakwater

Cable holder

Anchor chain

Bollard

Hawse pipe

Boat boom

Towing fairlead

Port bower anchor

Ladder way

Brake slip

Davit

Clump cathead

Guardrail

Hawser fairlead

Sheet anchor

Starboard bower anchor

Exhaust pipe

Searchlight

Searchlight platform

After compass platform

After bridge

1.3 kg (3 pound) gun ("three pounder")

"X" turret

"Y" turret

Officer's accommodation ladder

Davit for whaler

Whaler

Flagmast

Vedette boat

Gig

After funnel

Funnel stay

Stern walk

Scarph

Aft anchor

"P" turret

Ash chute

Hen coop

Bilge keel

Gun battery

Torpedo net boom

Turret roof rail

Propeller shaft boss

Torpedo net

Propeller shaft

Propeller

Rudder

Life buoy

Frigates and submarines

FROM THE MID-19TH CENTURY, ARMOURED SHIPS provided a new challenge to enemy craft. In response, huge revolving gun turrets were developed. These could fire in any direction, could be loaded from the breech very rapidly, and, instead of cannonballs, they discharged exploding shells. Modern fighting ships, like the frigate, combine heavy ship-borne armament with light helicopter weaponry. Submarines function below the surface of the sea. Their speed and ability to fire missiles from under water are their major assets. The nuclear submarine can stay under water for several years without refuelling.

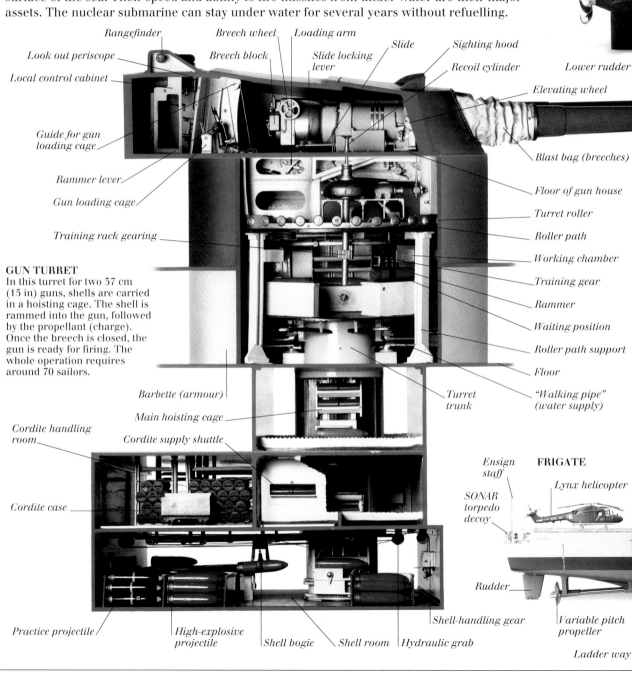

Stabilizer fin

Aft hydroplane

Propeller

Lower rudder

Rangefinder

Look out periscope

Local control cabinet

Breech wheel

Breech block

Loading arm

Slide locking lever

Slide

Sighting hood

Recoil cylinder

Elevating wheel

Guide for gun loading cage

Rammer lever

Gun loading cage

Training rack gearing

Blast bag (breeches)

Floor of gun house

Turret roller

Roller path

Working chamber

Training gear

Rammer

Waiting position

Roller path support

Floor

"Walking pipe" (water supply)

GUN TURRET
In this turret for two 37 cm (15 in) guns, shells are carried in a hoisting cage. The shell is rammed into the gun, followed by the propellant (charge). Once the breech is closed, the gun is ready for firing. The whole operation requires around 70 sailors.

Barbette (armour)

Main hoisting cage

Cordite handling room

Cordite supply shuttle

Cordite case

Turret trunk

Ensign staff

FRIGATE

SONAR torpedo decoy

Lynx helicopter

Rudder

Variable pitch propeller

Practice projectile

High-explosive projectile

Shell bogie

Shell room

Shell-handling gear

Hydraulic grab

Ladder way

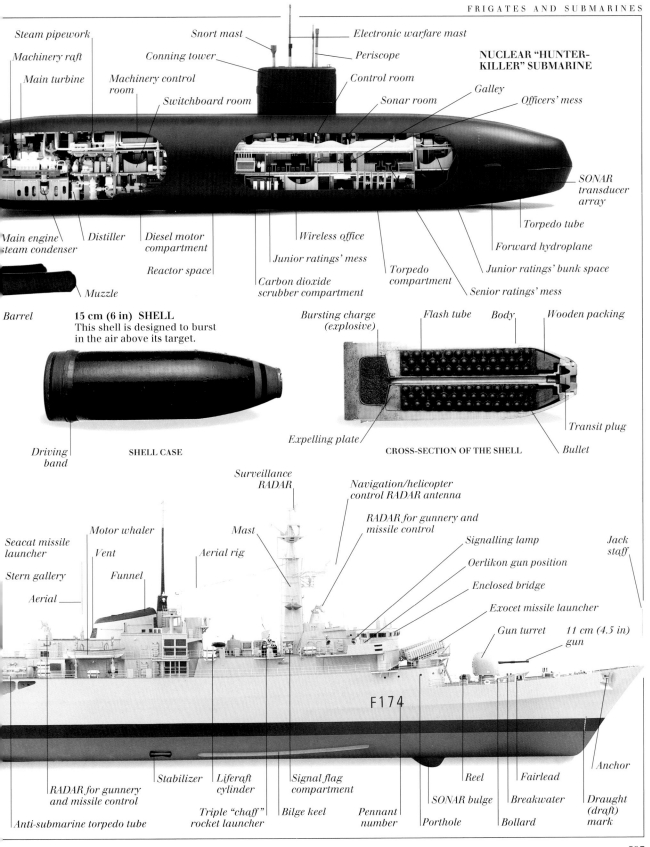

Steam pipework

Machinery raft

Main turbine

Machinery control room

Switchboard room

Snort mast

Electronic warfare mast

Conning tower

Periscope

Control room

Sonar room

Galley

NUCLEAR "HUNTER-KILLER" SUBMARINE

Officers' mess

SONAR transducer array

Main engine steam condenser

Distiller

Muzzle

Diesel motor compartment

Reactor space

Barrel

Wireless office

Junior ratings' mess

Carbon dioxide scrubber compartment

Torpedo compartment

Torpedo tube

Forward hydroplane

Junior ratings' bunk space

Senior ratings' mess

15 cm (6 in) SHELL
This shell is designed to burst in the air above its target.

Bursting charge (explosive)

Flash tube

Body

Wooden packing

Transit plug

Driving band

SHELL CASE

Expelling plate

CROSS-SECTION OF THE SHELL

Bullet

Surveillance RADAR

Navigation/helicopter control RADAR antenna

RADAR for gunnery and missile control

Signalling lamp

Jack staff

Seacat missile launcher

Motor whaler

Vent

Mast

Aerial rig

Oerlikon gun position

Enclosed bridge

Stern gallery

Funnel

Exocet missile launcher

Aerial

Gun turret

11 cm (4.5 in) gun

F174

Anchor

RADAR for gunnery and missile control

Stabilizer

Liferaft cylinder

Signal flag compartment

Reel

Fairlead

Breakwater

Draught (draft) mark

Anti-submarine torpedo tube

Triple "chaff" rocket launcher

Bilge keel

Pennant number

SONAR bulge

Porthole

Bollard

Pioneers of flight

FLIGHT HAS FASCINATED MANKIND for centuries, and countless unsuccessful flying machines have been designed. The first successful flight was made by the French Montgolfier brothers in 1783, when they flew a balloon over Paris. The next major advance was the development of gliders, notably by the Englishman Sir George Cayley, who in 1845 designed the first glider to make a sustained flight, and by the German Otto Lilienthal, who became known as the world's first pilot because he managed to achieve controlled flights. However, powered flight did not become a practical possibility until the invention of lightweight, petrol-driven internal combustion engines at the end of the 19th century. Then, in 1903, the American brothers Orville and Wilbur Wright made the first powered flight in their Wright Flyer biplane, which used a four-cylinder, petrol-driven engine. Aircraft design advanced rapidly, and in 1909 the Frenchman Louis Blériot made his pioneering flight across the English Channel (see pp. 400-401). The American Glenn Curtiss also achieved several "firsts" in his Model-D Pusher and its variants, most notably winning the world's first competition for airspeed at Reims in 1909.

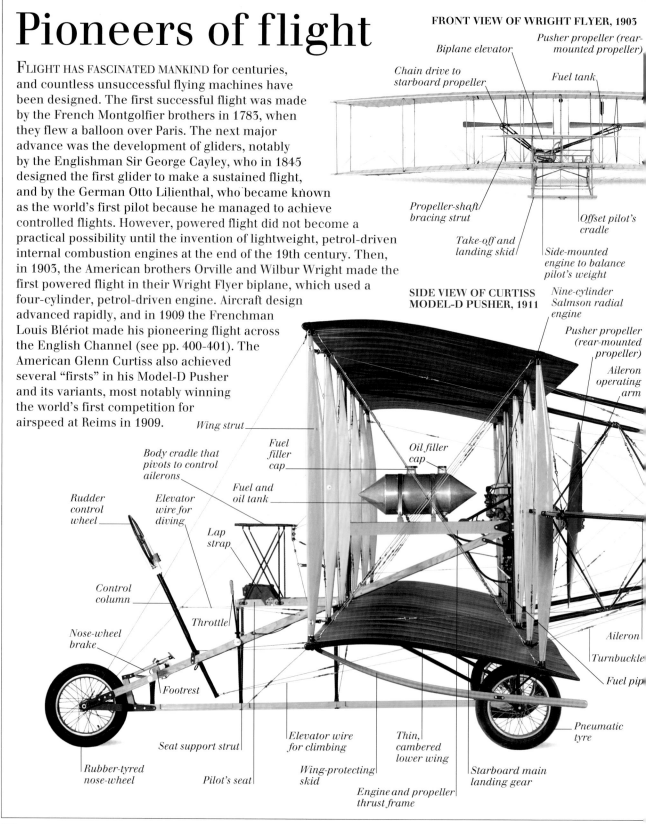

FRONT VIEW OF WRIGHT FLYER, 1903

Biplane elevator

Chain drive to starboard propeller

Pusher propeller (rear-mounted propeller)

Fuel tank

Propeller-shaft bracing strut

Take-off and landing skid

Offset pilot's cradle

Side-mounted engine to balance pilot's weight

SIDE VIEW OF CURTISS MODEL-D PUSHER, 1911

Nine-cylinder Salmson radial engine

Pusher propeller (rear-mounted propeller)

Aileron operating arm

Wing strut

Body cradle that pivots to control ailerons

Fuel filler cap

Oil filler cap

Rudder control wheel

Elevator wire for diving

Fuel and oil tank

Lap strap

Control column

Throttle

Nose-wheel brake

Footrest

Aileron

Turnbuckle

Fuel pip

Pneumatic tyre

Rubber-tyred nose-wheel

Seat support strut

Pilot's seat

Elevator wire for climbing

Wing-protecting skid

Thin, cambered lower wing

Engine and propeller thrust frame

Starboard main landing gear

SIDE VIEW OF WRIGHT FLYER, 1903

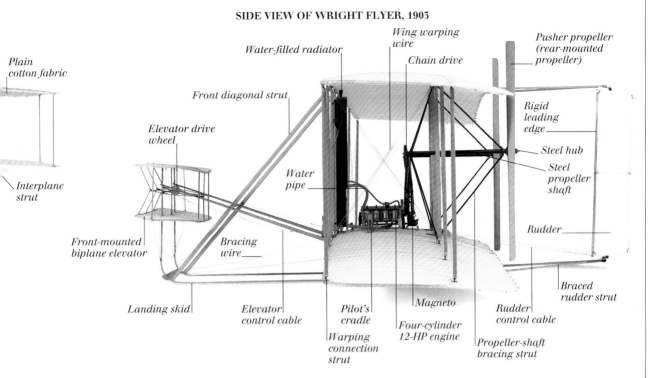

Plain cotton fabric

Interplane strut

Water-filled radiator

Wing warping wire

Chain drive

Pusher propeller (rear-mounted propeller)

Front diagonal strut

Rigid leading edge

Elevator drive wheel

Steel hub

Steel propeller shaft

Water pipe

Rudder

Front-mounted biplane elevator

Bracing wire

Braced rudder strut

Landing skid

Elevator control cable

Pilot's cradle

Magneto

Rudder control cable

Warping connection strut

Four-cylinder 12-HP engine

Propeller-shaft bracing strut

Softwood strut

Tailplane

Elevator control wire

Laminated wooden boom

Rudder bracing wire

Rudder

Elevator operating arm

Curtiss

Elevator

FRONT VIEW OF CURTISS MODEL-D PUSHER, 1911

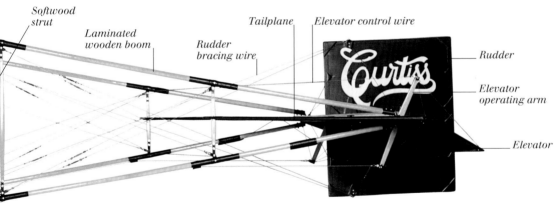

Rudder control wheel

Fuel and oil tank

Nine-cylinder Salmson radial engine

Elevator operating arm

Anti-lift wire

Starboard aileron

Aileron operating arm

Carved interplane strut

Port aileron

Wing-protecting skid

Wing-protecting skid

Lift wire

Control column

Seat beam

Footrest

Axle

Main landing gear lateral brace

Tubular steel leg

Interplane strut pin-jointed to front spar

Early monoplanes

RUMPLER MONOPLANE, 1908

MONOPLANES HAVE ONE WING on each side of the fuselage. The principal disadvantage of this arrangement in early, wooden-framed aircraft was that single wings were weak and required strong wires to brace them to king-posts above and below the fuselage. However, single wings also had advantages: they experienced less drag than multiple wings, allowing greater speed; they also made aircraft more manoeuvrable because single wings were easier to warp (twist) than double wings, and warping the wings was how pilots controlled the roll of early aircraft. By 1912, the French pilot Louis Blériot had used a monoplane to make the first flight across the English Channel, and the Briton Robert Blackburn and the Frenchman Armand Deperdussin had proved the greater speed of monoplanes. However, a spate of crashes caused by broken wings discouraged monoplane production, except in Germany, where all-metal monoplanes were developed in 1917. The wings of all-metal monoplanes did not need strengthening by struts or bracing wires, but despite this, such planes were not widely adopted until the 1930s.

FRONT VIEW OF BLACKBURN MONOPLANE, 1912

Taut fabric

Carved wooden propeller

King-post

Hub bolted to propeller

Nose-ring

Pilot's viewing aperture

Gnome seven-cylinder rotary engine

Exhaust valve push-rod

Elevator hinge

Elevator

Landing gear rear cross-member

Wheel fairing

Rubber-sprung wheel

Landing gear front strut

Tailskid

Axle

Landing skid

Landing gear rear strut

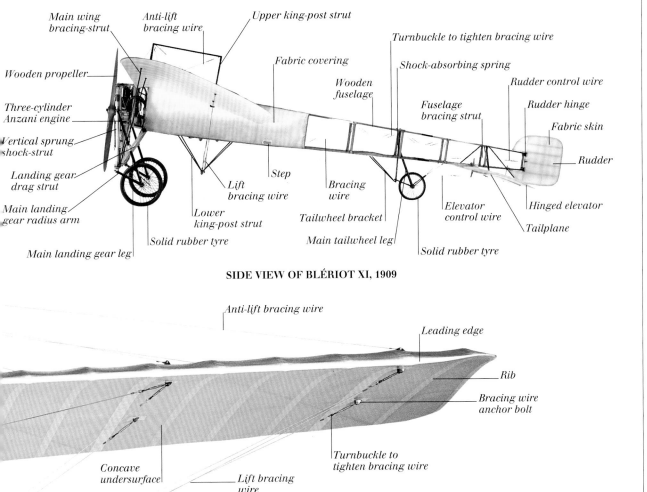

Main wing bracing-strut

Anti-lift bracing wire

Upper king-post strut

Wooden propeller

Fabric covering

Turnbuckle to tighten bracing wire

Shock-absorbing spring

Three-cylinder Anzani engine

Wooden fuselage

Rudder control wire

Rudder hinge

Fuselage bracing strut

Fabric skin

Vertical sprung shock-strut

Landing gear drag strut

Rudder

Main landing gear radius arm

Step

Lift bracing wire

Bracing wire

Elevator control wire

Hinged elevator

Main landing gear leg

Solid rubber tyre

Lower king-post strut

Tailwheel bracket

Main tailwheel leg

Solid rubber tyre

Tailplane

SIDE VIEW OF BLÉRIOT XI, 1909

Anti-lift bracing wire

Leading edge

Rib

Bracing wire anchor bolt

Concave undersurface

Lift bracing wire

Turnbuckle to tighten bracing wire

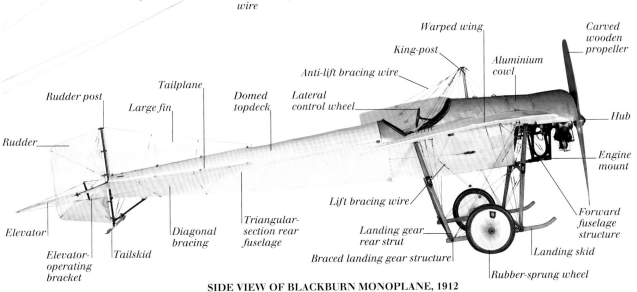

Warped wing

Carved wooden propeller

King-post

Aluminium cowl

Anti-lift bracing wire

Rudder post

Tailplane

Domed topdeck

Lateral control wheel

Large fin

Hub

Rudder

Engine mount

Elevator

Diagonal bracing

Triangular-section rear fuselage

Lift bracing wire

Landing gear rear strut

Forward fuselage structure

Elevator-operating bracket

Tailskid

Braced landing gear structure

Landing skid

Rubber-sprung wheel

SIDE VIEW OF BLACKBURN MONOPLANE, 1912

Biplanes and triplanes

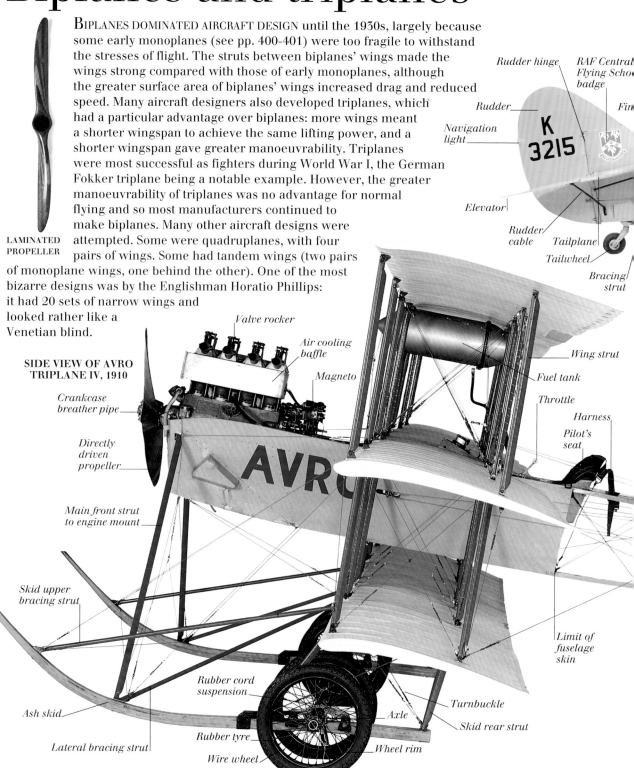

BIPLANES DOMINATED AIRCRAFT DESIGN until the 1930s, largely because some early monoplanes (see pp. 400-401) were too fragile to withstand the stresses of flight. The struts between biplanes' wings made the wings strong compared with those of early monoplanes, although the greater surface area of biplanes' wings increased drag and reduced speed. Many aircraft designers also developed triplanes, which had a particular advantage over biplanes: more wings meant a shorter wingspan to achieve the same lifting power, and a shorter wingspan gave greater manoeuvrability. Triplanes were most successful as fighters during World War I, the German Fokker triplane being a notable example. However, the greater manoeuvrability of triplanes was no advantage for normal flying and so most manufacturers continued to make biplanes. Many other aircraft designs were attempted. Some were quadruplanes, with four pairs of wings. Some had tandem wings (two pairs of monoplane wings, one behind the other). One of the most bizarre designs was by the Englishman Horatio Phillips: it had 20 sets of narrow wings and looked rather like a Venetian blind.

LAMINATED PROPELLER

Rudder hinge

RAF Central Flying School badge

Rudder

Navigation light

K 3215

Fin

Elevator

Rudder cable

Tailplane

Tailwheel

Bracing strut

SIDE VIEW OF AVRO TRIPLANE IV, 1910

Valve rocker

Air cooling baffle

Magneto

Wing strut

Fuel tank

Throttle

Harness

Pilot's seat

Crankcase breather pipe

Directly driven propeller

Main front strut to engine mount

AVRO

Skid upper bracing strut

Limit of fuselage skin

Ash skid

Rubber cord suspension

Axle

Turnbuckle

Skid rear strut

Lateral bracing strut

Rubber tyre

Wheel rim

Wire wheel

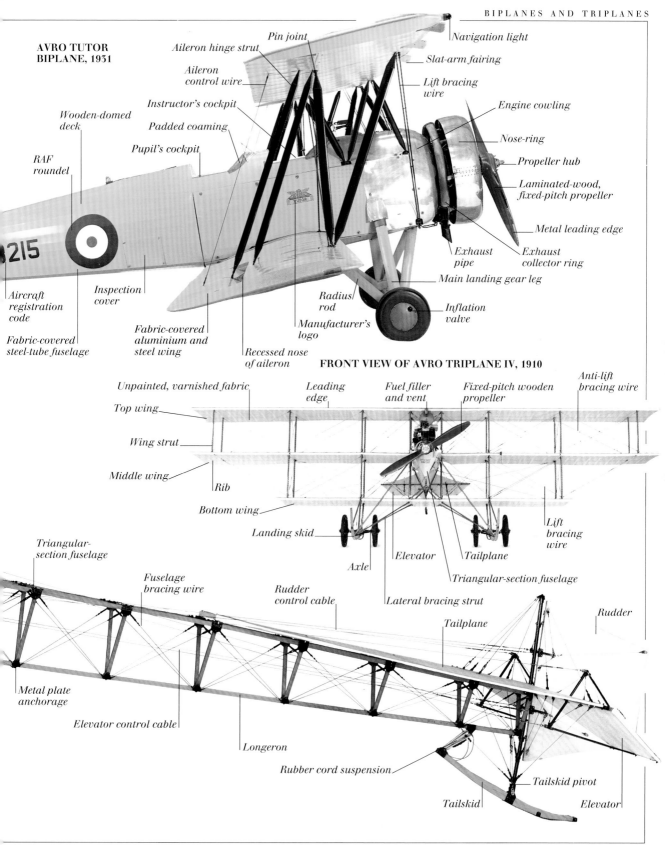

**AVRO TUTOR
BIPLANE, 1931**

Pin joint

Aileron hinge strut

Aileron
control wire

Instructor's cockpit

Padded coaming

Pupil's cockpit

Wooden-domed
deck

RAF
roundel

Navigation light

Slat-arm fairing

Lift bracing
wire

Engine cowling

Nose-ring

Propeller hub

Laminated-wood,
fixed-pitch propeller

Metal leading edge

Exhaust
collector ring

Exhaust
pipe

Main landing gear leg

Inflation
valve

215

Radius
rod

Manufacturer's
logo

Recessed nose
of aileron

Aircraft
registration
code

Fabric-covered
steel-tube fuselage

Inspection
cover

Fabric-covered
aluminium and
steel wing

FRONT VIEW OF AVRO TRIPLANE IV, 1910

Unpainted, varnished fabric

Top wing

Wing strut

Middle wing

Rib

Bottom wing

Leading
edge

Fuel filler
and vent

Fixed-pitch wooden
propeller

Anti-lift
bracing wire

Landing skid

Axle

Elevator

Tailplane

Triangular-section fuselage

Lateral bracing strut

Lift
bracing
wire

Triangular-
section fuselage

Fuselage
bracing wire

Rudder
control cable

Tailplane

Rudder

Metal plate
anchorage

Elevator control cable

Longeron

Rubber cord suspension

Tailskid

Tailskid pivot

Elevator

World War I aircraft

FLYING HELMET

W‌HEN WORLD WAR I STARTED in 1914, the main purpose of military aircraft was reconnaissance. The British-built BE 2, of which the BE 2B was a variant, was well-suited to this duty; it was very stable in flight, allowing the occupants to study the terrain, take photographs, and make notes. The BE 2 was also one of the first aircraft to drop bombs. One of the biggest problems for aircraft designers during the war was mounting machine-guns. On aircraft that had front-mounted propellers, the field of fire was restricted by the propeller and other parts of the aircraft. The problem was solved in 1915 by the Dutchman Anthony Fokker, who designed an interrupter gear that prevented a machine-gun from firing when a propeller blade passed in front of the barrel. The German LVG CVI had a forward-firing gun to the right of the engine, as well as a rear-cockpit gun, and a bombing capability. It was one of the most versatile aircraft of the war.

PORT WINGS FROM A BE 2B

Interplane-strut attachment

Intermediate leading-edge rib

Airspeed-indicator tube

Leading edge

Wingtip

Airspeed-indicator tube

Main rib

Root

Interplane strut

Trailing edge

Airspeed pitot tube

Interplane-strut attachment

Upper side of lower wing

Attachment lug

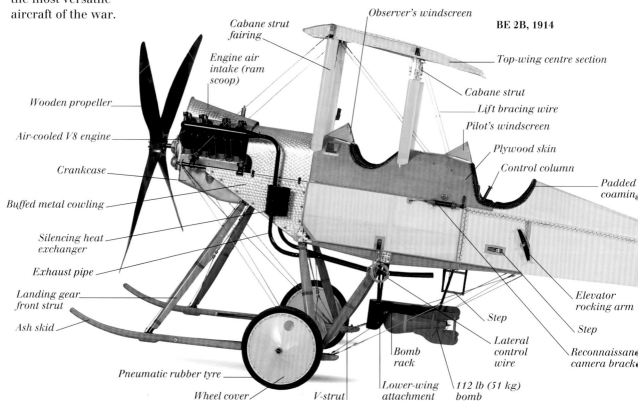

BE 2B, 1914

Observer's windscreen

Cabane strut fairing

Engine air intake (ram scoop)

Top-wing centre section

Cabane strut

Lift bracing wire

Pilot's windscreen

Wooden propeller

Air-cooled V8 engine

Plywood skin

Control column

Crankcase

Padded coamin

Buffed metal cowling

Silencing heat exchanger

Exhaust pipe

Landing gear front strut

Elevator rocking arm

Ash skid

Step

Step

Lateral control wire

Reconnaissanc camera brack

Pneumatic rubber tyre

Bomb rack

112 lb (51 kg) bomb

Wheel cover

V-strut

Lower-wing attachment

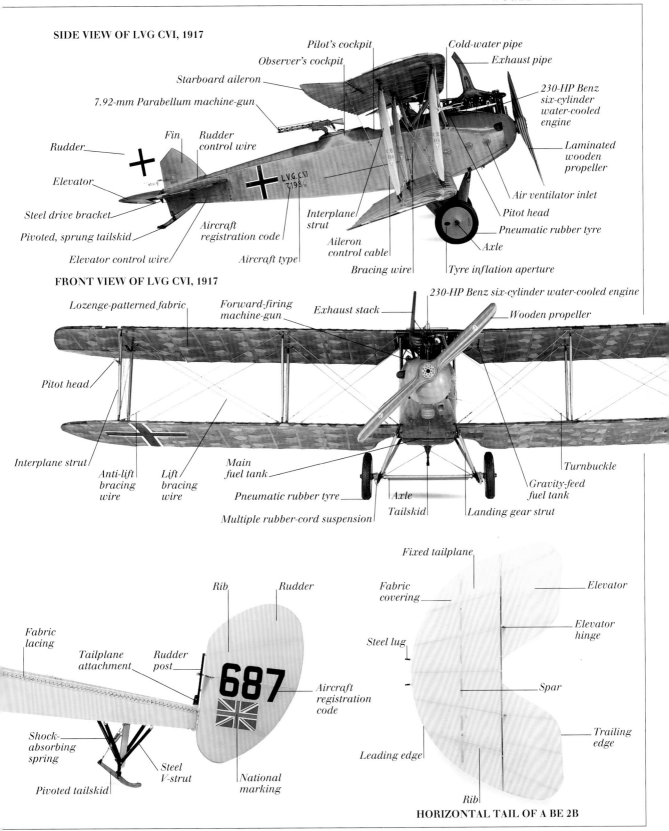

SIDE VIEW OF LVG CVI, 1917

Pilot's cockpit

Observer's cockpit

Cold-water pipe

Exhaust pipe

Starboard aileron

7.92-mm Parabellum machine-gun

230-HP Benz
six-cylinder
water-cooled
engine

Fin

Rudder
control wire

Rudder

Elevator

Laminated
wooden
propeller

Steel drive bracket

Air ventilator inlet

Pivoted, sprung tailskid

Pitot head

Aircraft
registration code

Interplane
strut

Pneumatic rubber tyre

Elevator control wire

Aileron
control cable

Axle

Aircraft type

Bracing wire

Tyre inflation aperture

FRONT VIEW OF LVG CVI, 1917

230-HP Benz six-cylinder water-cooled engine

Lozenge-patterned fabric

Forward-firing
machine-gun

Exhaust stack

Wooden propeller

Pitot head

Interplane strut

Anti-lift
bracing
wire

Lift
bracing
wire

Main
fuel tank

Turnbuckle

Gravity-feed
fuel tank

Pneumatic rubber tyre

Axle

Tailskid

Landing gear strut

Multiple rubber-cord suspension

Fixed tailplane

Rib

Rudder

Fabric
covering

Elevator

Fabric
lacing

Tailplane
attachment

Rudder
post

Steel lug

Elevator
hinge

687

Aircraft
registration
code

Spar

Shock-
absorbing
spring

Steel
V-strut

Trailing
edge

Pivoted tailskid

National
marking

Leading edge

Rib

HORIZONTAL TAIL OF A BE 2B

Early passenger aircraft

FRONT VIEW OF LOCKHEED ELECTRA, 1934

UNTIL THE 1930s, most passenger aircraft were biplanes, with two pairs of wings and a wooden or metal framework covered with fabric or, sometimes, plywood. Such aircraft were restricted to low speeds and low altitudes because of the drag on their wings. Many had an open cockpit, situated behind or in front of an enclosed – but unpressurized – cabin that carried a maximum of ten people. The passengers usually sat in wicker chairs that were not bolted to the floor, and the journey could be bumpy when flying through turbulence. Warm clothing, and ear plugs to reduce the effects of prolonged noise, were often required. During the 1930s, powerful, streamlined, all-metal monoplanes, such as the Lockheed Electra shown here, became widespread. By 1939, the advent of pressurized cabins allowed fast flights at high altitudes, where there is less turbulence. Flying boats were still necessary on many routes until 1945 because of inadequate runways and the frequency of emergency sea-landings. World War II, however, resulted in enough good runways being built for land-planes to become standard on all major airline routes.

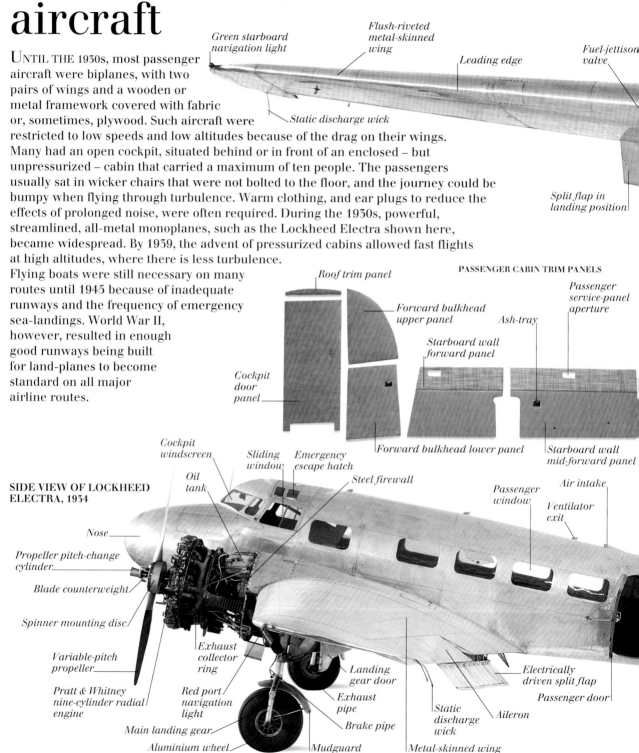

Green starboard navigation light

Flush-riveted metal-skinned wing

Leading edge

Fuel-jettison valve

Static discharge wick

Split flap in landing position

PASSENGER CABIN TRIM PANELS

Roof trim panel

Forward bulkhead upper panel

Passenger service-panel aperture

Ash-tray

Starboard wall forward panel

Cockpit door panel

Forward bulkhead lower panel

Starboard wall mid-forward panel

SIDE VIEW OF LOCKHEED ELECTRA, 1934

Cockpit windscreen

Sliding window

Emergency escape hatch

Oil tank

Steel firewall

Air intake

Passenger window

Ventilator exit

Nose

Propeller pitch-change cylinder

Blade counterweight

Spinner mounting disc

Variable-pitch propeller

Exhaust collector ring

Pratt & Whitney nine-cylinder radial engine

Red port navigation light

Landing gear door

Exhaust pipe

Electrically driven split flap

Passenger door

Main landing gear

Brake pipe

Static discharge wick

Aileron

Aluminium wheel

Mudguard

Metal-skinned wing

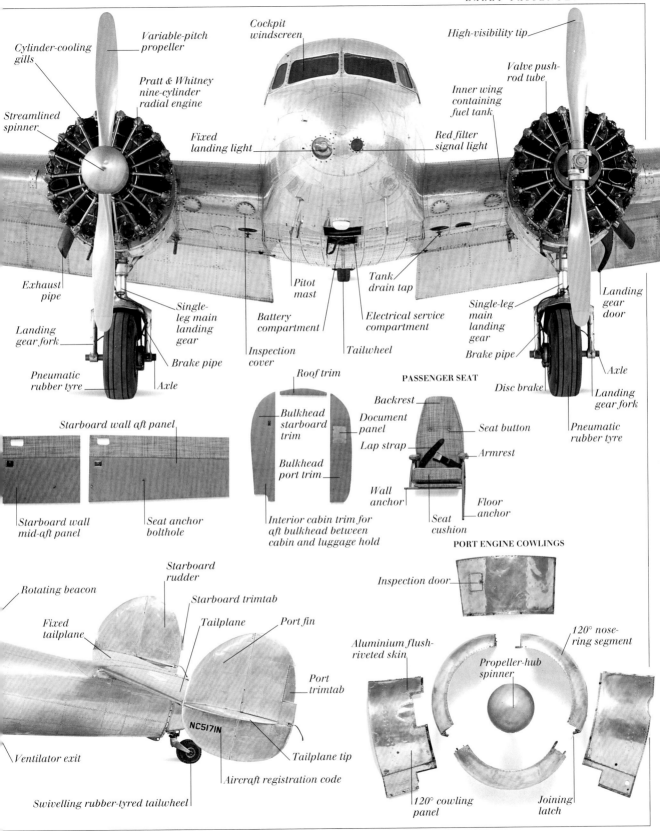

Cylinder-cooling gills

Variable-pitch propeller

Cockpit windscreen

High-visibility tip

Pratt & Whitney nine-cylinder radial engine

Valve push-rod tube

Streamlined spinner

Inner wing containing fuel tank

Fixed landing light

Red filter signal light

Exhaust pipe

Single-leg main landing gear

Landing gear door

Landing gear fork

Pitot mast

Battery compartment

Tank drain tap

Electrical service compartment

Single-leg main landing gear

Pneumatic rubber tyre

Brake pipe

Axle

Inspection cover

Tailwheel

Brake pipe

Axle

Disc brake

Landing gear fork

Pneumatic rubber tyre

Roof trim

PASSENGER SEAT

Starboard wall aft panel

Bulkhead starboard trim

Backrest

Document panel

Seat button

Lap strap

Armrest

Bulkhead port trim

Starboard wall mid-aft panel

Seat anchor bolthole

Wall anchor

Floor anchor

Seat cushion

Interior cabin trim for aft bulkhead between cabin and luggage hold

PORT ENGINE COWLINGS

Rotating beacon

Starboard rudder

Inspection door

Starboard trimtab

Fixed tailplane

Tailplane

Port fin

120° nose-ring segment

Aluminium flush-riveted skin

Propeller-hub spinner

Port trimtab

Ventilator exit

NC517IN

Tailplane tip

Swivelling rubber-tyred tailwheel

Aircraft registration code

Port trimtab

120° cowling panel

Joining latch

407

World War II aircraft

WHEN WORLD WAR II began in 1939, air forces had already replaced most of their fabric-skinned biplanes with all-metal, stressed-skin monoplanes. Aircraft played a far greater role in military operations during World War II than ever before. The wide range of aircraft duties, and the introduction of radar tracking and guidance systems, put pressure on designers to improve aircraft performance. The main areas of improvement were speed, range, and engine power. Bombers became larger and more powerful – converting from two to four engines – in order to carry a heavier bomb load; the US B-17 Flying Fortress could carry up to 6.2 tonnes (6.1 tons) of bombs over a distance of about 3,200 km (2,000 miles). Some aircraft increased their range by using drop tanks (fuel tanks that were jettisoned when empty to reduce drag). Fighters needed speed and manoeuvrability: the Hawker Tempest shown here had a maximum speed of 700 kph (435 mph), and was one of the few Allied aircraft capable of catching the German jet-powered V1 "flying bomb". By 1944, Britain had introduced its first turbojet-powered aircraft, the Gloster Meteor fighter, and Germany had introduced the fastest fighter in the world, the turbojet-powered Me 262, which had a maximum speed of 868 kph (540 mph).

PROPELLER

High-visibility yellow tip

Light-alloy propeller spinner

Variable-pitch aluminium-alloy blade

COMPONENTS OF A HAWKER TEMPEST MARK V, c.1943

Radiator-access cowling

Lower side-cowling

Upper side-cowling

STARBOARD ENGINE COWLINGS

Cowling fastener

Propeller governor

2,400-HP Napier Sabre 24-cylinder engine

Cartridge starter

Radiator header tank

Propeller drive shaft

Distributor

Ejector exhaust

Magneto

Starter motor

Engine top cowling

Cowling fastener

Upper side-cowling

Lower side-cowling

Radiator-access cowling

PORT ENGINE COWLINGS

SECTIONED B-17G FLYING FORTRESS BOMBER, c.1943

VHF aerial

Fin

Rudder

Astronavigation dome

Oxygen bottle

Upper gun turret

Radio operator's seat

Ammunition belt

Dorsal fin

Hand-held gun

First pilot's seat

1,000 lb (454 kg) bomb

Ammunition box

"Cheyenne-type" tail-gun turret

Plastic nose

Waist gun

Tail gunner's compartment

Bomb aimer's viewing panel

HF radio aerial

Navigator's seat

Ammunition feed

Entrance door

Retracted tailwheel

Ammunition feed

Chin gun turret

Bomb door

Sperry ball gun turret

Oxygen bottle

Direction-finding-aerial fairing

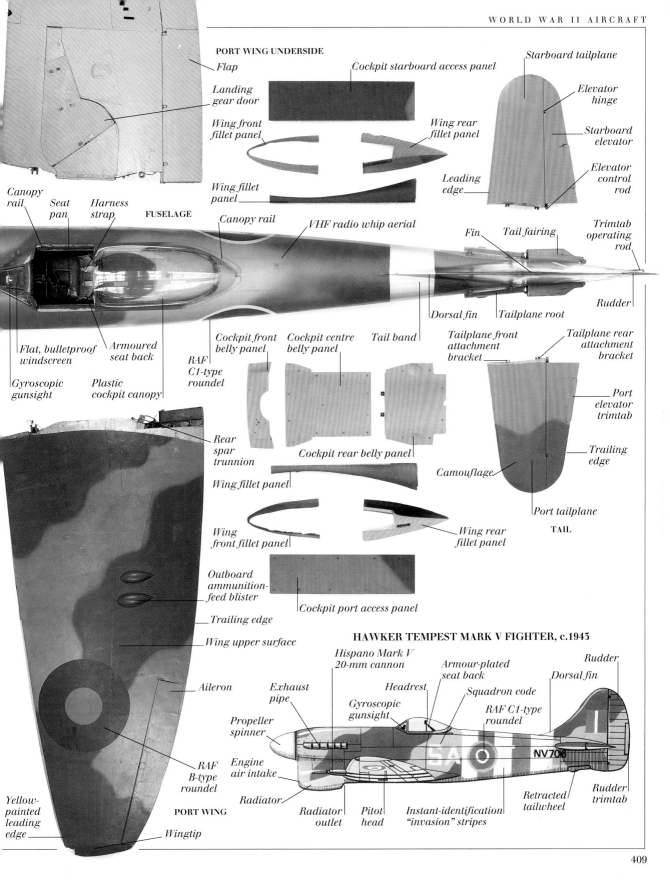

PORT WING UNDERSIDE

Flap

Landing gear door

Wing front fillet panel

Wing fillet panel

Cockpit starboard access panel

Wing rear fillet panel

Leading edge

Starboard tailplane

Elevator hinge

Starboard elevator

Elevator control rod

FUSELAGE

Canopy rail

Seat pan

Harness strap

Canopy rail

VHF radio whip aerial

Fin

Tail fairing

Trimtab operating rod

Rudder

Flat, bulletproof windscreen

Armoured seat back

Gyroscopic gunsight

Plastic cockpit canopy

RAF C1-type roundel

Cockpit front belly panel

Cockpit centre belly panel

Tail band

Dorsal fin

Tailplane root

Tailplane front attachment bracket

Tailplane rear attachment bracket

Port elevator trimtab

Trailing edge

Rear spar trunnion

Cockpit rear belly panel

Camouflage

Port tailplane

TAIL

Wing fillet panel

Wing front fillet panel

Wing rear fillet panel

Outboard ammunition-feed blister

Trailing edge

Wing upper surface

Cockpit port access panel

HAWKER TEMPEST MARK V FIGHTER, c.1943

Aileron

RAF B-type roundel

Yellow-painted leading edge

Wingtip

PORT WING

Hispano Mark V 20-mm cannon

Exhaust pipe

Gyroscopic gunsight

Propeller spinner

Engine air intake

Radiator

Radiator outlet

Pitot head

Headrest

Armour-plated seat back

Squadron code

RAF C1-type roundel

Rudder

Dorsal fin

NV708

Instant-identification "invasion" stripes

Retracted tailwheel

Rudder trimtab

SA

Modern piston aero-engines

MID WEST TWO-STROKE, THREE-CYLINDER ENGINE

PISTON ENGINES today are used mainly to power the vast numbers of light aircraft and microlights, as well as crop-sprayers and crop-dusters, small helicopters, and fire-bombers (which dump water on large fires). Virtually all heavier aircraft are now powered by jet engines. Modern piston aero-engines work on the same basic principles as the engine used by the Wright brothers in the first powered flight in 1903. However, today's engines are more sophisticated than earlier engines. For example, modern aero-engines may use a two-stroke or a four-stroke combustion cycle; they may have from one to nine air- or water-cooled cylinders, which may be arranged horizontally, in-line, in V formation, or radially; and they may drive the aircraft's propeller either directly or through a reduction gearbox. One of the more unconventional types of modern aero-engine is the rotary engine shown here, which has a trilobate (three-sided) rotor spinning in a chamber shaped like a fat figure-of-eight.

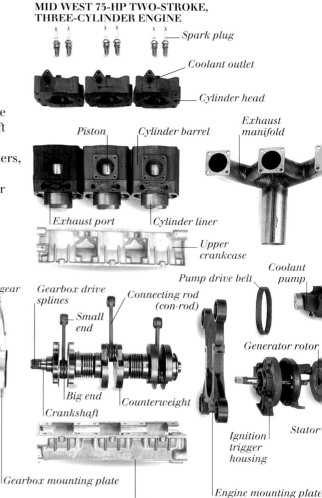

- Spark plug
- Coolant outlet
- Cylinder head
- Exhaust manifold
- Piston
- Cylinder barrel
- Exhaust port
- Cylinder liner
- Upper crankcase
- Coolant pump
- Pump drive belt
- Reduction gearbox
- Driven gear
- Propeller drive flange
- Gearbox drive splines
- Connecting rod (con-rod)
- Small end
- Generator rotor
- Torsional vibration damper
- Sprag clutch
- Big end
- Counterweight
- Crankshaft
- Stator
- Ignition trigger housing
- Gearbox mounting plate
- Lower crankcase
- Engine mounting plate

ROTOR AND HOUSINGS OF A MID WEST SINGLE-ROTOR ENGINE

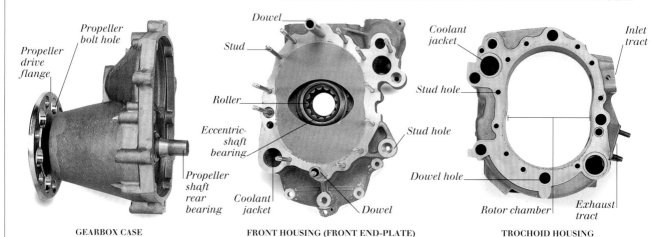

- Propeller bolt hole
- Propeller drive flange
- Dowel
- Stud
- Roller
- Eccentric-shaft bearing
- Propeller shaft rear bearing
- Coolant jacket
- Dowel
- Coolant jacket
- Inlet tract
- Stud hole
- Stud hole
- Dowel hole
- Rotor chamber
- Exhaust tract

GEARBOX CASE

FRONT HOUSING (FRONT END-PLATE)

TROCHOID HOUSING

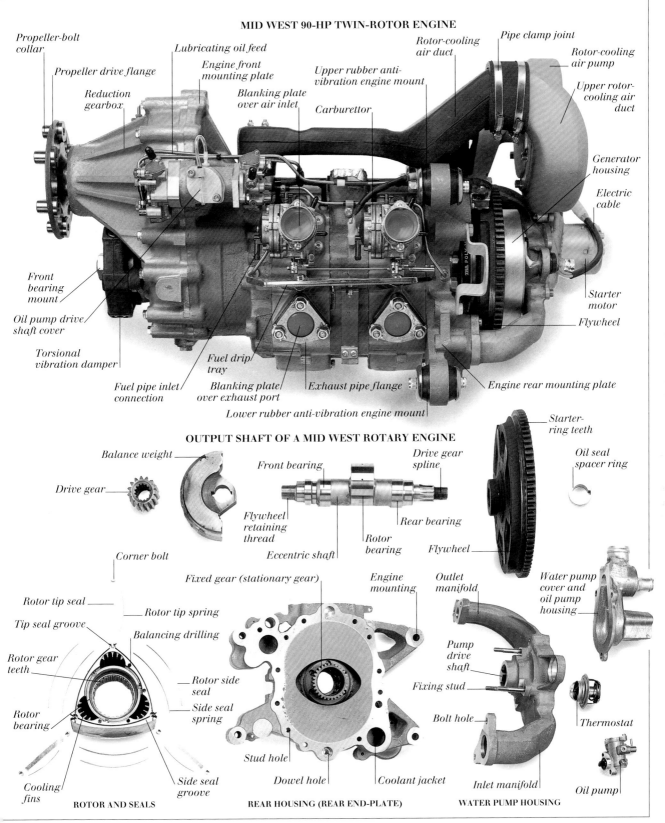

MID WEST 90-HP TWIN-ROTOR ENGINE

Propeller-bolt collar

Propeller drive flange

Reduction gearbox

Lubricating oil feed

Engine front mounting plate

Blanking plate over air inlet

Carburettor

Upper rubber anti-vibration engine mount

Rotor-cooling air duct

Pipe clamp joint

Rotor-cooling air pump

Upper rotor-cooling air duct

Generator housing

Electric cable

Starter motor

Flywheel

Engine rear mounting plate

Lower rubber anti-vibration engine mount

Exhaust pipe flange

Blanking plate over exhaust port

Fuel drip tray

Fuel pipe inlet connection

Torsional vibration damper

Oil pump drive shaft cover

Front bearing mount

OUTPUT SHAFT OF A MID WEST ROTARY ENGINE

Balance weight

Drive gear

Front bearing

Drive gear spline

Flywheel retaining thread

Eccentric shaft

Rotor bearing

Rear bearing

Flywheel

Starter-ring teeth

Oil seal spacer ring

Corner bolt

Rotor tip seal

Tip seal groove

Rotor gear teeth

Rotor bearing

Cooling fins

Rotor tip spring

Balancing drilling

Rotor side seal

Side seal spring

Side seal groove

ROTOR AND SEALS

Fixed gear (stationary gear)

Engine mounting

Stud hole

Dowel hole

Coolant jacket

REAR HOUSING (REAR END-PLATE)

Outlet manifold

Pump drive shaft

Fixing stud

Bolt hole

Inlet manifold

Water pump cover and oil pump housing

Thermostat

Oil pump

WATER PUMP HOUSING

Modern jetliners 1

MODERN JETLINERS HAVE ENABLED ordinary people to travel to places where once only the wealthy could afford to go. Compared with the first jetliners (which were introduced in the 1940s), modern ones are much quieter, burn fuel more efficiently, and produce less air pollution. These advances are largely due to the replacement of turbojet engines with turbofan engines (see pp. 418-419). The greater power of turbofan engines at low speeds enables modern jetliners to carry more fuel and passengers than turbojet aircraft; a modern Boeing 747-400 (popularly known as a "jumbo jet") can fly 400 people for 13,700 km (8,500 miles) without needing to refuel. Jetliners fly at high altitudes, typically cruising at 8,000-11,000 m (26,000-36,000 ft), where they can use fuel efficiently and usually avoid bad weather. The pilot always controls the aircraft during take-off and landing, but at other times the aircraft is usually controlled by an autopilot. Autopilots are complex on-board mechanisms that detect deviations from an aircraft's route and make appropriate adjustments to the flight controls. Flight decks are also equipped with radars that warn pilots of approaching hazards, such as mountain ranges, bad weather, and other aircraft.

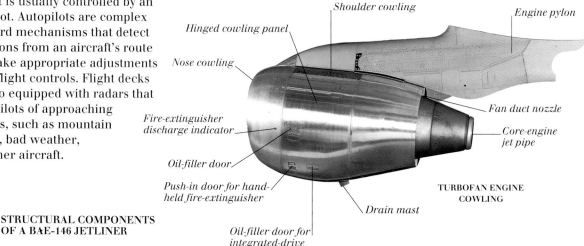

Shoulder cowling

Engine pylon

Hinged cowling panel

Nose cowling

Fan duct nozzle

Fire-extinguisher discharge indicator

Core-engine jet pipe

Oil-filler door

Push-in door for hand-held fire-extinguisher

Drain mast

TURBOFAN ENGINE COWLING

STRUCTURAL COMPONENTS OF A BAE-146 JETLINER

Oil-filler door for integrated-drive generator

FUSELAGE NOSE-SECTION

FUSELAGE MID-SECTION

Electrically heated, birdproof windscreen

Side window

Anchor for open door

Rain gutter

Hinge

Peephole

Finger recess

Static air-pressure plate

Forward main door aperture

VHF omni-range and instrument-landing-system aerials

Light-alloy door frame

Passenger window aperture

Main external operating handle

Multiple-pinned lock

Floor level

Radome

Toilet service connector

Anchor for open door

Air temperature probe

Stall warning vane

Pitot head for dynamic air pressure

FORWARD MAIN DOOR

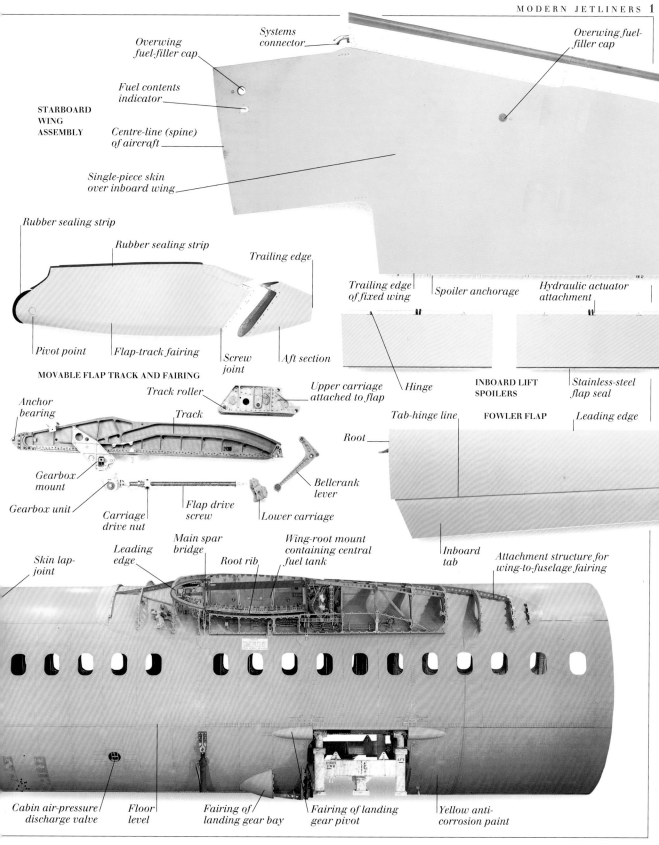

STARBOARD
WING
ASSEMBLY

Overwing
fuel-filler cap

Systems
connector

Overwing fuel-
filler cap

Fuel contents
indicator

Centre-line (spine)
of aircraft

Single-piece skin
over inboard wing

Rubber sealing strip

Rubber sealing strip

Trailing edge

Trailing edge
of fixed wing

Spoiler anchorage

Hydraulic actuator
attachment

Pivot point

Flap-track fairing

Screw
joint

Aft section

Hinge

INBOARD LIFT
SPOILERS

Stainless-steel
flap seal

MOVABLE FLAP TRACK AND FAIRING

Track roller

Upper carriage
attached to flap

Tab-hinge line

FOWLER FLAP

Leading edge

Anchor
bearing

Track

Root

Gearbox
mount

Bellcrank
lever

Gearbox unit

Carriage
drive nut

Flap drive
screw

Lower carriage

Inboard
tab

Skin lap-
joint

Leading
edge

Main spar
bridge

Root rib

Wing-root mount
containing central
fuel tank

Attachment structure for
wing-to-fuselage fairing

Cabin air-pressure
discharge valve

Floor
level

Fairing of
landing gear bay

Fairing of landing
gear pivot

Yellow anti-
corrosion paint

Modern jetliners 2

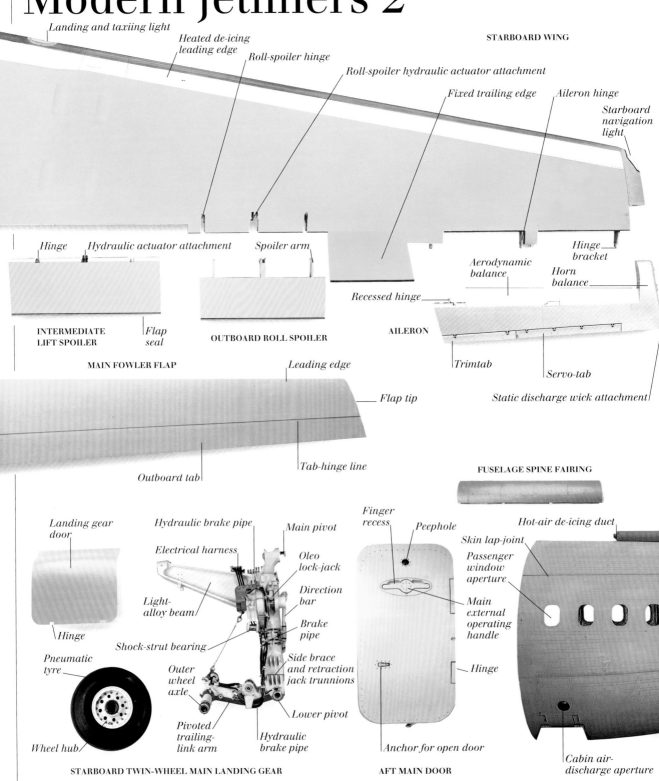

Landing and taxiing light

Heated de-icing
leading edge

Roll-spoiler hinge

Roll-spoiler hydraulic actuator attachment

STARBOARD WING

Fixed trailing edge

Aileron hinge

Starboard
navigation
light

Hinge   Hydraulic actuator attachment   Spoiler arm

Aerodynamic
balance

Hinge
bracket

Horn
balance

Recessed hinge

INTERMEDIATE
LIFT SPOILER

Flap
seal

OUTBOARD ROLL SPOILER

AILERON

Trimtab

Servo-tab

MAIN FOWLER FLAP

Leading edge

Flap tip

Static discharge wick attachment

Tab-hinge line

FUSELAGE SPINE FAIRING

Outboard tab

Finger
recess

Peephole

Hot-air de-icing duct

Landing gear
door

Hydraulic brake pipe

Main pivot

Skin lap-joint

Passenger
window
aperture

Electrical harness

Oleo
lock-jack

Light-
alloy beam

Direction
bar

Main
external
operating
handle

Brake
pipe

Shock-strut bearing

Pneumatic
tyre

Outer
wheel
axle

Side brace
and retraction
jack trunnions

Hinge

Lower pivot

Wheel hub

Pivoted
trailing-
link arm

Hydraulic
brake pipe

Anchor for open door

Cabin air-
discharge aperture

STARBOARD TWIN-WHEEL MAIN LANDING GEAR

AFT MAIN DOOR

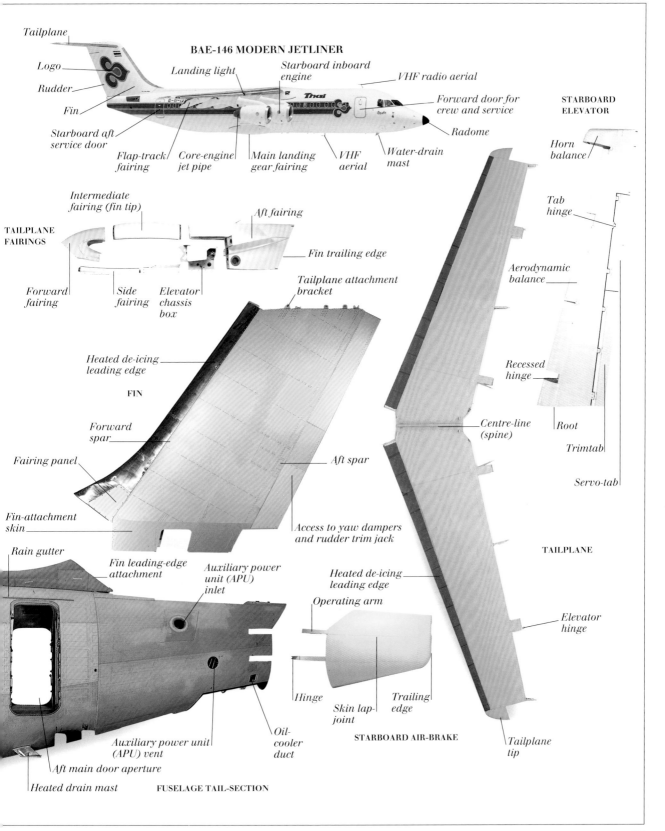

BAE-146 MODERN JETLINER

Tailplane

Logo

Rudder

Fin

Starboard aft
service door

Flap-track
fairing

Core-engine
jet pipe

Main landing
gear fairing

Landing light

Starboard inboard
engine

VHF aerial

Water-drain
mast

VHF radio aerial

Forward door for
crew and service

Radome

STARBOARD
ELEVATOR

Horn
balance

Tab
hinge

Aerodynamic
balance

Recessed
hinge

Root

Trimtab

Servo-tab

TAILPLANE FAIRINGS

Intermediate
fairing (fin tip)

Aft fairing

Fin trailing edge

Forward
fairing

Side
fairing

Elevator
chassis
box

Tailplane attachment
bracket

Heated de-icing
leading edge

FIN

Forward
spar

Fairing panel

Fin-attachment
skin

Aft spar

Access to yaw dampers
and rudder trim jack

Centre-line
(spine)

TAILPLANE

Rain gutter

Fin leading-edge
attachment

Auxiliary power
unit (APU)
inlet

Heated de-icing
leading edge

Operating arm

Elevator
hinge

Auxiliary power unit
(APU) vent

Oil-
cooler
duct

Hinge

Skin lap-
joint

Trailing
edge

Tailplane
tip

Aft main door aperture

Heated drain mast

FUSELAGE TAIL-SECTION

STARBOARD AIR-BRAKE

415

Supersonic jetliners

**COMPUTER-
DESIGNED SST**

SUPERSONIC AIRCRAFT FLY FASTER than the speed of sound (Mach 1). There are many supersonic military aircraft, but only two supersonic passenger-carrying aircraft (also called SSTs, or supersonic transports) have been produced: the Russian Tu-144, and Concorde, produced jointly by Britain and France. The Tu-144 was withdrawn in 1978, after only seven months in service. Concorde has remained in service since 1976, with a break for modifications from July 2000 until October 2001. Its features include a droop nose, which is lowered during take-off and landing to aid visibility from the cockpit, and the pumping of fuel between forward and aft trim tanks to help stabilize the aircraft. Concorde has a narrow fuselage and short-span wings to reduce drag during supersonic flight. Its noisy turbojet engines with afterburners enable it to carry 100 passengers at a cruising speed of Mach 2 at 15,000-18,000 m (50,000-60,000 ft). Once an aircraft is flying faster than Mach 1, it produces a continuous air-pressure wave, which is heard as a "sonic boom".

Strake

Fin

Standby
pitot head

Starboard
outboard
engine air-intake

Inboard
elevon-
jack
fairing

Nose-
gear
leg

FRONT VIEW OF CONCORDE

Toilets

Electrothermal
de-icing panel

Starboard
forward trim tank

Overhead hand-baggage bin

Passenger
accommodation

Seat
attachment
rail

**OVERHEAD VIEW
OF CONCORDE**

Underfloor air-
conditioning duct

Life-raft

VHF
aerial

Variable
nozzle

Leading edge

Wardrobe

Forward galley

Additional crew's seat

Aluminium-alloy layers
and insulation

Third pilot's
seat

Erosion-
resistant
radome

Cockpit
windscreen

Retractable
visor

Lateral bracing strut

Telescopic strut

Port
forward
trim tank

"A" frame

Nose-
gear
leg

Steering
actuator

Standby
flight-control
hydraulic jack

Plug-type
passenger
door

Nose-gear
door

Machined
skin panel

Weather
radar

Captain's
seat

Upper
rudder

Fin

Multi-ply
high-pressure
tyre

Visor jack

Droop-
nose hinge

Cockpit air-
conditioning
duct

Dorsal fin

Emergency exit

Pivoted
retractable frame

Tail cone

G-BOAG

Aft door

Elevon (combined elevator and aileron)

Hot-section steel and titanium skin

Engine cowling

Landing gear door

Bogie main landing gear

SECTIONED VIEW OF CONCORDE

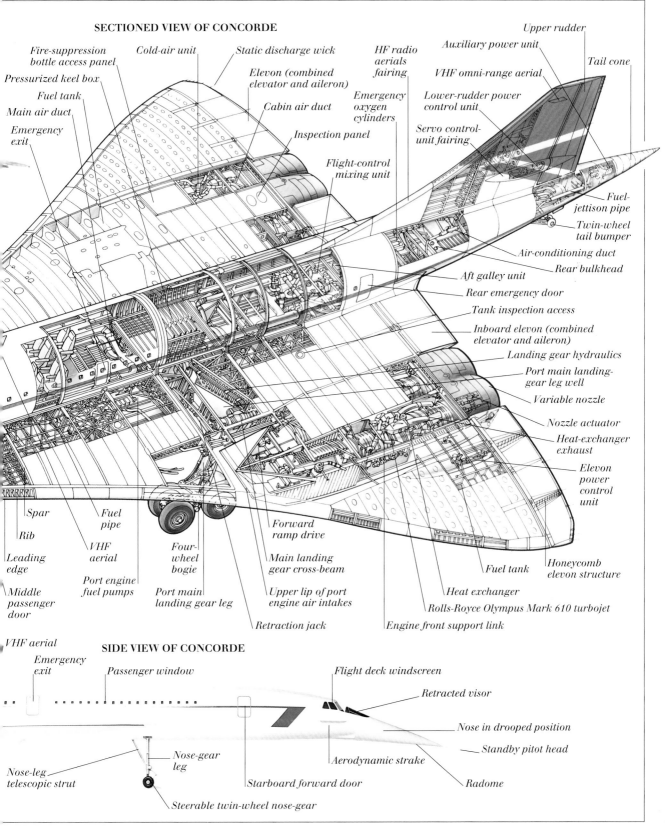

Fire-suppression bottle access panel

Pressurized keel box

Fuel tank

Main air duct

Emergency exit

Cold-air unit

Static discharge wick

Elevon (combined elevator and aileron)

Cabin air duct

Inspection panel

Flight-control mixing unit

HF radio aerials fairing

Emergency oxygen cylinders

Auxiliary power unit

VHF omni-range aerial

Lower-rudder power control unit

Servo control-unit fairing

Upper rudder

Tail cone

Fuel-jettison pipe

Twin-wheel tail bumper

Air-conditioning duct

Rear bulkhead

Aft galley unit

Rear emergency door

Tank inspection access

Inboard elevon (combined elevator and aileron)

Landing gear hydraulics

Port main landing-gear leg well

Variable nozzle

Nozzle actuator

Heat-exchanger exhaust

Elevon power control unit

Spar

Rib

Leading edge

Middle passenger door

Fuel pipe

VHF aerial

Port engine fuel pumps

Four-wheel bogie

Port main landing gear leg

Retraction jack

Forward ramp drive

Main landing gear cross-beam

Upper lip of port engine air intakes

Engine front support link

Fuel tank

Heat exchanger

Rolls-Royce Olympus Mark 610 turbojet

Honeycomb elevon structure

VHF aerial

Emergency exit

SIDE VIEW OF CONCORDE

Passenger window

Flight deck windscreen

Retracted visor

Nose in drooped position

Standby pitot head

Nose-leg telescopic strut

Nose-gear leg

Aerodynamic strake

Starboard forward door

Radome

Steerable twin-wheel nose-gear

Jet engines

JET ENGINES ARE USED BY MOST MILITARY and heavy aircraft, and by many helicopters. The simplest type of jet engine, or gas turbine, is the turbojet. It works by continuously burning a mixture of fuel and air in a combustion chamber to produce a jet of hot exhaust gas that is expelled through a nozzle to produce thrust. The hot gas also spins turbine blades, which, in turn, spin the blades of an air compressor; the compressor forces air into the combustion chamber. Many of the fastest aircraft use turbojets, with additional booster units called afterburners, but their use is restricted by their high noise emission. Most jetliners use turbofan jet engines, which are quieter. An enormous fan, driven by a low-pressure turbine, feeds some air into the compressor but feeds most of it through bypass ducts to join the exhaust jetstream in the tail cone. The bypass stream produces most of the thrust. Many smaller, propeller-driven aircraft use turboprop jet engines, in which the engine powers a propeller.

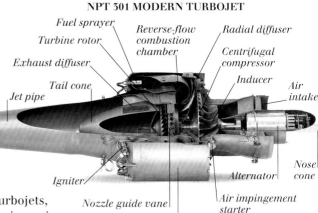

NPT 301 MODERN TURBOJET

Fuel sprayer
Reverse-flow combustion chamber
Radial diffuser
Turbine rotor
Centrifugal compressor
Exhaust diffuser
Inducer
Tail cone
Air intake
Jet pipe
Exhaust nozzle
Nose cone
Igniter
Alternator
Nozzle guide vane
Air impingement starter
Combustion chamber casing

Temperature and pressure sensor

Low-pressure fan

Inlet cone (rotating spinner)

Pressure line

Fancase with special structure to contain broken fan

Electronic engine control and airframe interface connector

Electronic engine control (EEC) unit

Compressor front bearing

Engine front mount

Electrical wiring harness

Fuel and oil heat exchanger

Oil filter

Compressor air-bleed connection

Plenum ring for hot anti-icing air

Flow splitter

Gearbox bevel drive

Integral oil tank

High-pressure compressor

Combustion chamber

Fuel manifold

High-pressure turbine

Fuel nozzle

Centrifugal compressor

Fan duct

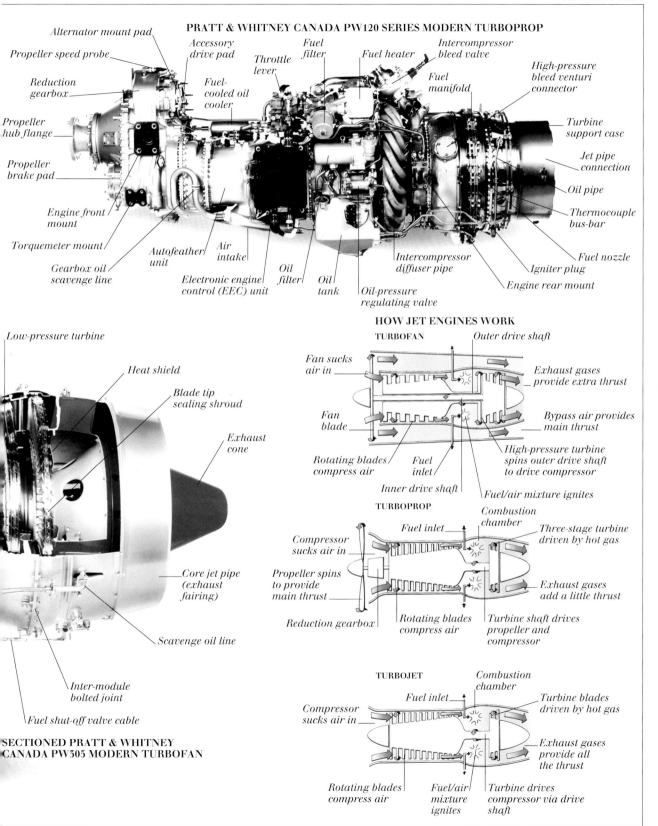

PRATT & WHITNEY CANADA PW120 SERIES MODERN TURBOPROP

Alternator mount pad
Propeller speed probe
Reduction gearbox
Propeller hub flange
Propeller brake pad
Engine front mount
Torquemeter mount
Gearbox oil scavenge line
Autofeather unit
Electronic engine control (EEC) unit
Air intake
Oil filter
Oil tank
Oil-pressure regulating valve
Accessory drive pad
Throttle lever
Fuel-cooled oil cooler
Fuel filter
Fuel heater
Fuel manifold
Fuel nozzle
Igniter plug
Engine rear mount
Intercompressor diffuser pipe
Intercompressor bleed valve
High-pressure bleed venturi connector
Turbine support case
Jet pipe connection
Oil pipe
Thermocouple bus-bar

HOW JET ENGINES WORK

TURBOFAN
Fan sucks air in
Fan blade
Rotating blades compress air
Fuel inlet
Inner drive shaft
Outer drive shaft
Exhaust gases provide extra thrust
Bypass air provides main thrust
High-pressure turbine spins outer drive shaft to drive compressor
Fuel/air mixture ignites

TURBOPROP
Compressor sucks air in
Propeller spins to provide main thrust
Reduction gearbox
Rotating blades compress air
Fuel inlet
Combustion chamber
Three-stage turbine driven by hot gas
Exhaust gases add a little thrust
Turbine shaft drives propeller and compressor

TURBOJET
Compressor sucks air in
Rotating blades compress air
Fuel inlet
Fuel/air mixture ignites
Combustion chamber
Turbine blades driven by hot gas
Exhaust gases provide all the thrust
Turbine drives compressor via drive shaft

Low-pressure turbine
Heat shield
Blade tip sealing shroud
Exhaust cone
Core jet pipe (exhaust fairing)
Scavenge oil line
Inter-module bolted joint
Fuel shut-off valve cable

SECTIONED PRATT & WHITNEY CANADA PW305 MODERN TURBOFAN

Modern military aircraft

MODERN MILITARY AIRCRAFT ARE AMONG THE MOST SOPHISTICATED and expensive products of the 21st century. Fighters need computer-operated controls for manoeuvrability, powerful engines, and effective air-to-air weapons. Most modern fighters also have guided missiles, radar, and passive, infra-red sensors. These developments enable today's fighters to engage in combat with adversaries that are outside visual range. Bombers carry a large weapon load and enough fuel for long-range flights. A few military aircraft, such as the Tornado and the F-14 Tomcat, have variable-sweep ("swing") wings. During take-off and landing their wings are fully extended, but for high-speed flight and low-level attacks the wings are pivoted fully back. A recent development is the "stealth" bomber, which is designed to absorb or deflect enemy radar in order to remain undetected. Earlier bombers, such as the Tornado, use terrain-following radars to fly so close to the ground that they avoid enemy radar detection.

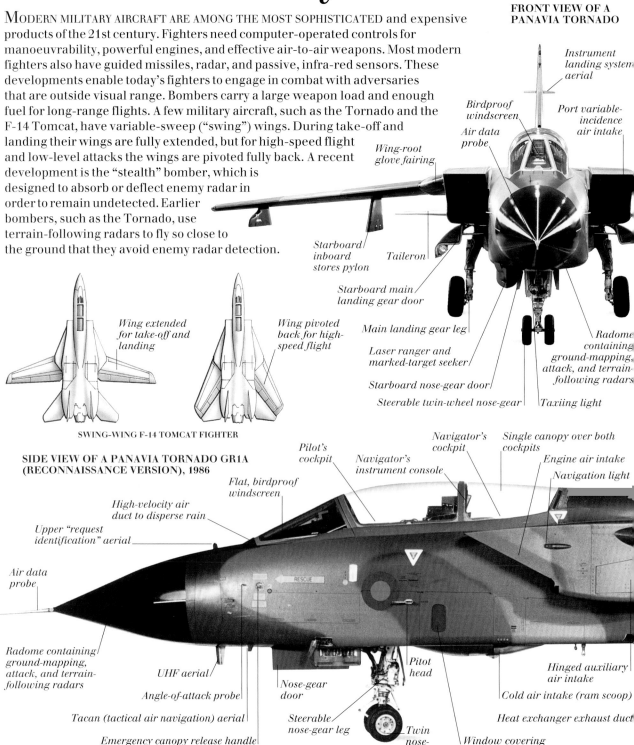

FRONT VIEW OF A PANAVIA TORNADO

Instrument landing system aerial

Birdproof windscreen

Air data probe

Port variable-incidence air intake

Wing-root glove fairing

Starboard inboard stores pylon

Taileron

Starboard main landing gear door

Main landing gear leg

Laser ranger and marked-target seeker

Starboard nose-gear door

Steerable twin-wheel nose-gear

Radome containing ground-mapping, attack, and terrain-following radars

Taxiing light

Wing extended for take-off and landing

Wing pivoted back for high-speed flight

SWING-WING F-14 TOMCAT FIGHTER

SIDE VIEW OF A PANAVIA TORNADO GR1A (RECONNAISSANCE VERSION), 1986

High-velocity air duct to disperse rain

Flat, birdproof windscreen

Pilot's cockpit

Navigator's instrument console

Navigator's cockpit

Single canopy over both cockpits

Engine air intake

Navigation light

Upper "request identification" aerial

Air data probe

Radome containing ground-mapping, attack, and terrain-following radars

UHF aerial

Angle-of-attack probe

Tacan (tactical air navigation) aerial

Emergency canopy release handle

Nose-gear door

Steerable nose-gear leg

Pitot head

Twin nose-wheel

Window covering infra-red reconnaissance camera

Hinged auxiliary air intake

Cold air intake (ram scoop)

Heat exchanger exhaust duct

NORTHROP B-2 ("STEALTH" BOMBER), 1989

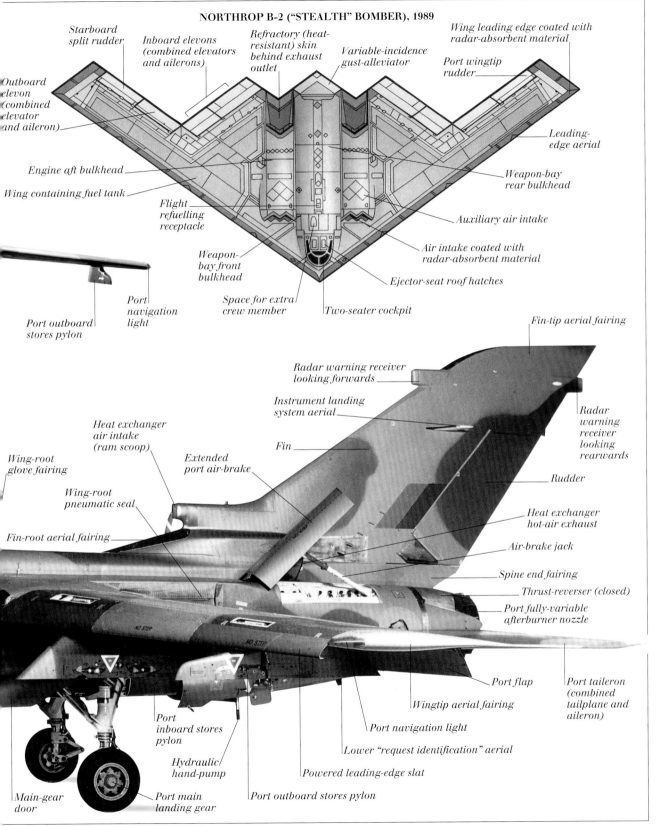

Starboard
split rudder

Inboard elevons
(combined elevators
and ailerons)

Refractory (heat-
resistant) skin
behind exhaust
outlet

Variable-incidence
gust-alleviator

Wing leading edge coated with
radar-absorbent material

Port wingtip
rudder

Outboard
elevon
(combined
elevator
and aileron)

Leading-
edge aerial

Engine aft bulkhead

Wing containing fuel tank

Weapon-bay
rear bulkhead

Flight
refuelling
receptacle

Auxiliary air intake

Air intake coated with
radar-absorbent material

Weapon-
bay front
bulkhead

Ejector-seat roof hatches

Space for extra
crew member

Two-seater cockpit

Port navigation
light

Port outboard
stores pylon

Fin-tip aerial fairing

Radar warning receiver
looking forwards

Instrument landing
system aerial

Radar
warning
receiver
looking
rearwards

Heat exchanger
air intake
(ram scoop)

Extended
port air-brake

Fin

Rudder

Wing-root
glove fairing

Heat exchanger
hot-air exhaust

Wing-root
pneumatic seal

Air-brake jack

Fin-root aerial fairing

Spine end fairing

Thrust-reverser (closed)

Port fully-variable
afterburner nozzle

Port
inboard stores
pylon

Port flap

Port taileron
(combined
tailplane and
aileron)

Hydraulic
hand-pump

Wingtip aerial fairing

Port navigation light

Lower "request identification" aerial

Main-gear
door

Port main
landing gear

Port outboard stores pylon

Powered leading-edge slat

Helicopters

BELL 47G-3B1

HELICOPTERS USE ROTATING BLADES for lift, propulsion, and steering. The first machine to achieve sustained, controlled flight using rotating blades was the autogiro built in the 1920s by the Spaniard Juan de la Cierva. His machine had unpowered blades above the fuselage that relied on the flow of air to rotate them and provide lift as the autogiro was driven forwards by a conventional propeller. Then, in 1939, the Russian-born American Igor Sikorsky produced his VS-300, the forerunner of modern helicopters. Its engine-driven blades provided lift, propulsion, and steering. It could take off vertically, hover, and fly in any direction, and had a tail rotor to prevent the helicopter body from spinning. The introduction of gas turbine jet engines to helicopters in 1955 produced quieter, safer, and more powerful machines. Because of their versatility in flight, helicopters are today used for many purposes, including crop-spraying, traffic surveillance, and transporting crews to deep-sea oil rigs, as well as acting as gunships, air ambulances, and air taxis.

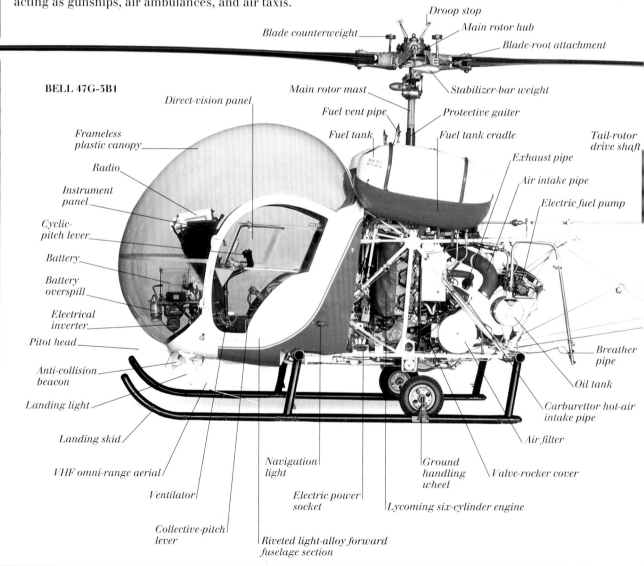

BELL 47G-3B1

Droop stop
Blade counterweight
Main rotor hub
Blade-root attachment
Main rotor mast
Stabilizer-bar weight
Fuel vent pipe
Protective gaiter
Direct-vision panel
Fuel tank
Fuel tank cradle
Tail-rotor drive shaft
Frameless plastic canopy
Exhaust pipe
Radio
Air intake pipe
Instrument panel
Electric fuel pump
Cyclic-pitch lever
Battery
Battery overspill
Electrical inverter
Pitot head
Breather pipe
Anti-collision beacon
Oil tank
Landing light
Carburettor hot-air intake pipe
Landing skid
Air filter
VHF omni-range aerial
Navigation light
Ground handling wheel
Valve-rocker cover
Ventilator
Electric power socket
Lycoming six-cylinder engine
Collective-pitch lever
Riveted light-alloy forward fuselage section

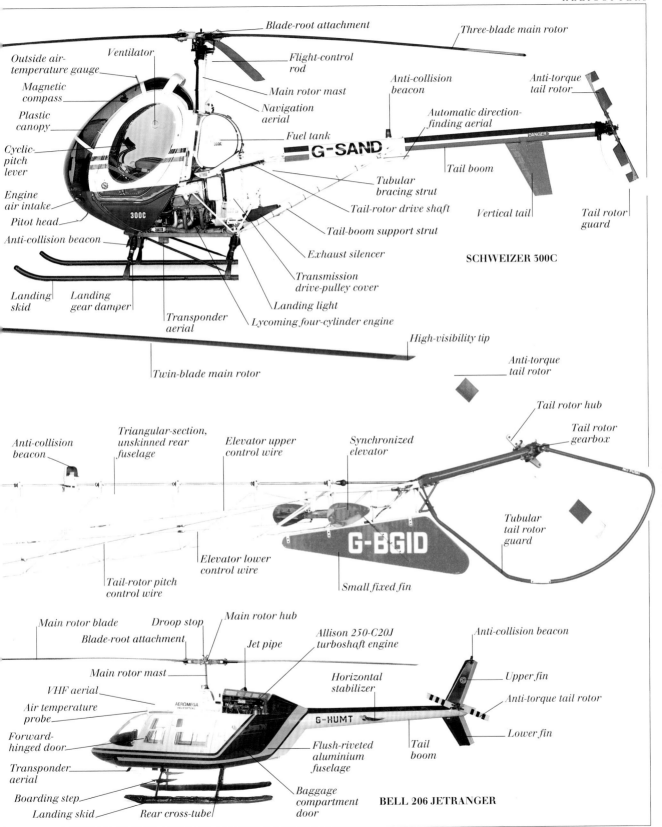

Blade-root attachment

Three-blade main rotor

Outside air-
temperature gauge

Ventilator

Flight-control
rod

Anti-collision
beacon

Anti-torque
tail rotor

Magnetic
compass

Main rotor mast

Automatic direction-
finding aerial

Plastic
canopy

Navigation
aerial

Cyclic-
pitch
lever

Fuel tank

G-SAND

DANGER

Engine
air intake

Tubular
bracing strut

Tail boom

Pitot head

Tail-rotor drive shaft

Anti-collision beacon

300C

Tail-boom support strut

Vertical tail

Tail rotor
guard

Exhaust silencer

SCHWEIZER 300C

Transmission
drive-pulley cover

Landing
skid

Landing
gear damper

Landing light

Transponder
aerial

Lycoming four-cylinder engine

High-visibility tip

Twin-blade main rotor

Anti-torque
tail rotor

Tail rotor hub

Anti-collision
beacon

Triangular-section,
unskinned rear
fuselage

Elevator upper
control wire

Synchronized
elevator

Tail rotor
gearbox

G-BGID

Tubular
tail rotor
guard

Elevator lower
control wire

Tail-rotor pitch
control wire

Small fixed fin

Main rotor blade

Droop stop

Main rotor hub

Allison 250-C20J
turboshaft engine

Anti-collision beacon

Blade-root attachment

Jet pipe

Main rotor mast

Horizontal
stabilizer

Upper fin

VHF aerial

AEROMEGA

Anti-torque tail rotor

Air temperature
probe

G-HUMT

Lower fin

Forward-
hinged door

Tail
boom

Flush-riveted
aluminium
fuselage

Transponder
aerial

Boarding step

Baggage
compartment
door

BELL 206 JETRANGER

Landing skid

Rear cross-tube

Light aircraft

Port wingtip

LIGHT AIRCRAFT, SUCH AS THE ARV SUPER 2 shown here, are small, lightweight, and of simple construction. More than a million have been built since World War I, mainly for recreational use by private owners. Virtually all light aircraft have piston engines, most of which are air-cooled, although some are liquid-cooled. Open cockpits, almost universal in the 1920s, have today been replaced by enclosed cabins. The cabins of high-wing aircraft have one or two doors, whereas those of low-wing aircraft usually have a sliding or hinged canopy. Most modern light aircraft are made of aluminium alloy, although some are made of wood or of fibre-reinforced materials. Light aircraft today also usually have navigational instruments, an electrical system, cabin heating, wheel brakes, and a two-way radio.

Aileron mass balance

Aileron torque tube

Port aileron

PORT MAIN LANDING GEAR

Inner tube

Tyre

Hub

Brake disc

Stub axle

Landing gear leg

Brake mount

Brake pipe

Hydraulic brake calliper

Dorsal fin

TAILPLANE AND RUDDER

Elevator

Rudder tip fairing

Rudder mass balance

Fin tip fairing

Rudder

Fin

Rear fuselage top skin

Rear attachment-bracket for wing

REAR FUSELAGE

Longeron

Frame

Battery box

Diaphragm

Side skin

Elevator trimtab

Drive pillar

Attachment plate

Rear fuselage bottom skin

"Skin-grip" pin

CONTROL RODS AND CABLES

Coolant outlet

Aluminium radiator

Air scoop

Coolant inlet

Elevator push-rod

Elevator push-rod

Rocking elevator arm

Aileron torque tube

Flap torque tube

Aileron rod

Flap drive-rod

Rudder cable

Flap drive-rod

Tailplane

SIDE VIEW OF ARV SUPER 2

Spinner

Canopy

Wing

Communications aerial

Fin

Dorsal fin

Navigational aerial

Rudder

Engine cowling

Elevator

STARBOARD MAIN LANDING GEAR

Brake calliper

Brake mount

Brake pipe

Landing gear leg

G-BNHB

Nose-gear

Step

Venturi for instruments

Main landing gear

Radiator

Wing strut

Tailskid

Tailplane

Aircraft registration code

Brake disc

Inner tube

Stub axle

Tyre

Hub

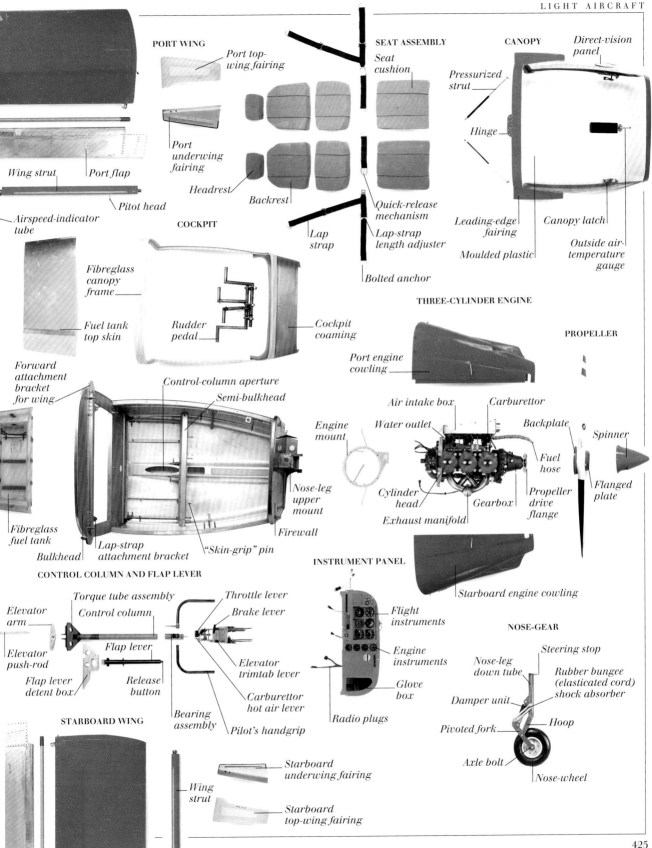

PORT WING

Port top-wing fairing

SEAT ASSEMBLY

Seat cushion

CANOPY

Direct-vision panel

Pressurized strut

Hinge

Port underwing fairing

Wing strut

Port flap

Pitot head

Airspeed-indicator tube

Headrest

Backrest

Lap strap

Quick-release mechanism

Lap-strap length adjuster

Bolted anchor

Leading-edge fairing

Canopy latch

Moulded plastic

Outside air-temperature gauge

COCKPIT

Fibreglass canopy frame

Fuel tank top skin

Rudder pedal

Cockpit coaming

Forward attachment bracket for wing

Control-column aperture

Semi-bulkhead

Engine mount

THREE-CYLINDER ENGINE

Port engine cowling

PROPELLER

Air intake box

Carburettor

Water outlet

Backplate

Spinner

Cylinder head

Fuel hose

Nose-leg upper mount

Firewall

Gearbox

Propeller drive flange

Flanged plate

Exhaust manifold

Fibreglass fuel tank

Bulkhead

Lap-strap attachment bracket

"Skin-grip" pin

Starboard engine cowling

INSTRUMENT PANEL

CONTROL COLUMN AND FLAP LEVER

Torque tube assembly

Throttle lever

Brake lever

Flight instruments

Elevator arm

Control column

Engine instruments

NOSE-GEAR

Steering stop

Elevator push-rod

Flap lever

Elevator trimtab lever

Glove box

Nose-leg down tube

Rubber bungee (elasticated cord) shock absorber

Flap lever detent box

Release button

Carburettor hot air lever

Radio plugs

Damper unit

STARBOARD WING

Bearing assembly

Pilot's handgrip

Pivoted fork

Hoop

Axle bolt

Nose-wheel

Wing strut

Starboard underwing fairing

Starboard top-wing fairing

Gliders, hang-gliders, and microlights

MODERN GLIDERS ARE AMONG the most graceful and aerodynamically efficient of all aircraft. Unpowered but with a large wingspan (up to about 25 m, or 82 ft), gliders use currents of hot, rising air (thermals) to stay aloft, and a rudder, elevators, and ailerons for control. Modern gliders have achieved flights of more than 1,450 km (900 miles) and altitudes above 15,000 m (49,000 ft). Hang-gliders consist of a simple frame across which rigid or flexible material is stretched to form the wings. The pilot is suspended below the wings in a harness or body-bag and, gripping a triangular A-frame, steers by shifting weight from side to side. Like gliders, hang-gliders rely on thermals for lift. Microlights are basically powered hang-gliders. A small engine and an open fibreglass car (trike), which can hold a crew of two, are suspended beneath a stronger version of a hang-glider frame; the frame may have rigid or flexible wings. Microlight pilots, like hang-glider pilots, steer by shifting their weight against an A-frame. Microlights can reach speeds of up to 160 kph (100 mph).

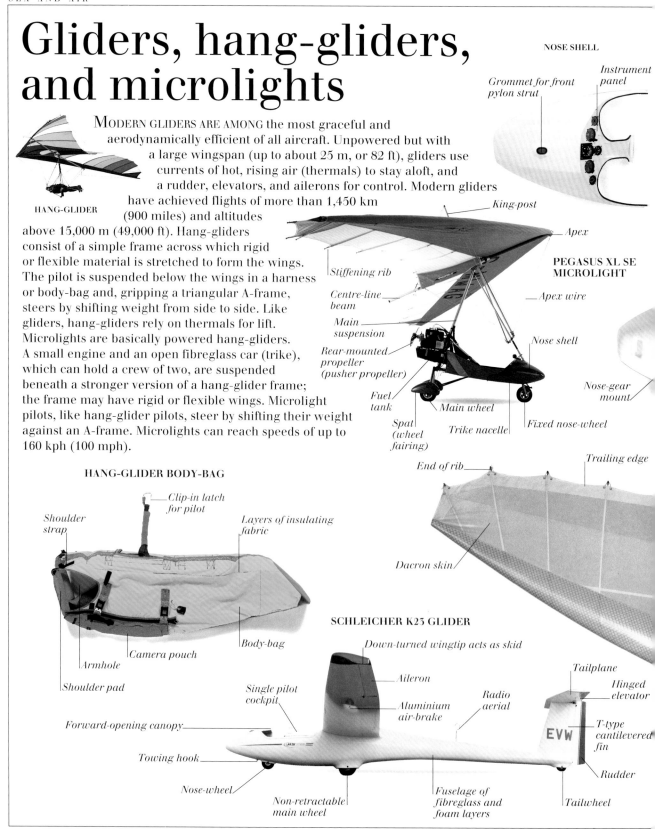

HANG-GLIDER

NOSE SHELL

Grommet for front pylon strut

Instrument panel

King-post

Apex

PEGASUS XL SE MICROLIGHT

Apex wire

Stiffening rib

Centre-line beam

Main suspension

Nose shell

Rear-mounted propeller (pusher propeller)

Nose-gear mount

Fuel tank

Main wheel

Spat (wheel fairing)

Trike nacelle

Fixed nose-wheel

End of rib

Trailing edge

HANG-GLIDER BODY-BAG

Clip-in latch for pilot

Shoulder strap

Layers of insulating fabric

Dacron skin

Armhole

Camera pouch

Body-bag

Shoulder pad

SCHLEICHER K23 GLIDER

Down-turned wingtip acts as skid

Single pilot cockpit

Aileron

Tailplane

Radio aerial

Hinged elevator

Forward-opening canopy

Aluminium air-brake

T-type cantilevered fin

Towing hook

EVW

Rudder

Nose-wheel

Non-retractable main wheel

Fuselage of fibreglass and foam layers

Tailwheel

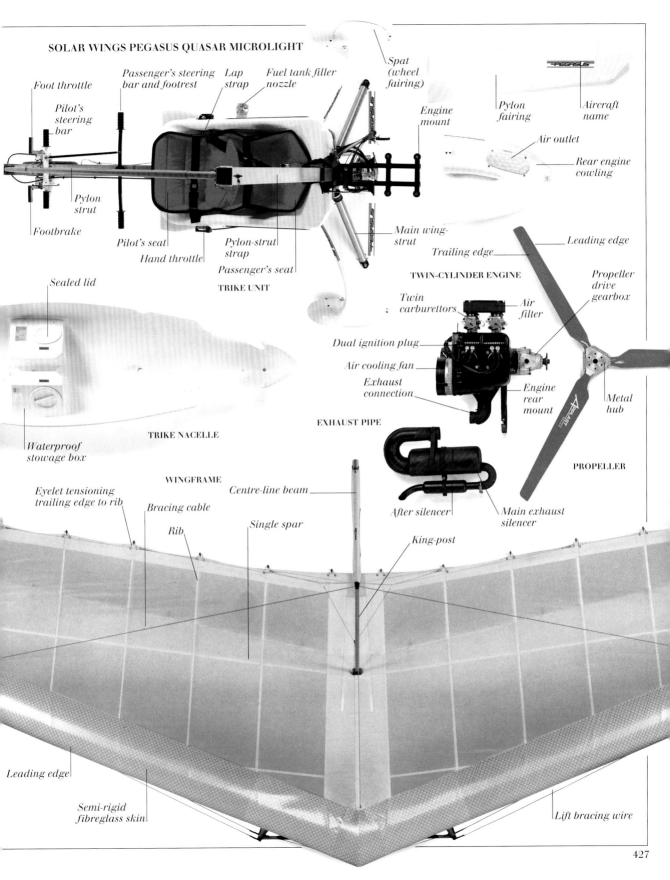

SOLAR WINGS PEGASUS QUASAR MICROLIGHT

Foot throttle

Pilot's steering bar

Passenger's steering bar and footrest

Lap strap

Fuel tank filler nozzle

Spat (wheel fairing)

Engine mount

Pylon fairing

Aircraft name

Air outlet

Rear engine cowling

Pylon strut

Footbrake

Pilot's seat

Hand throttle

Pylon-strut strap

Passenger's seat

Main wing-strut

Trailing edge

Leading edge

TRIKE UNIT

TWIN-CYLINDER ENGINE

Propeller drive gearbox

Twin carburettors

Air filter

Dual ignition plug

Air cooling fan

Sealed lid

Exhaust connection

Engine rear mount

Metal hub

TRIKE NACELLE

EXHAUST PIPE

Waterproof stowage box

PROPELLER

WINGFRAME

Centre-line beam

Eyelet tensioning trailing edge to rib

Bracing cable

Rib

Single spar

King-post

After silencer

Main exhaust silencer

Leading edge

Semi-rigid fibreglass skin

Lift bracing wire

427

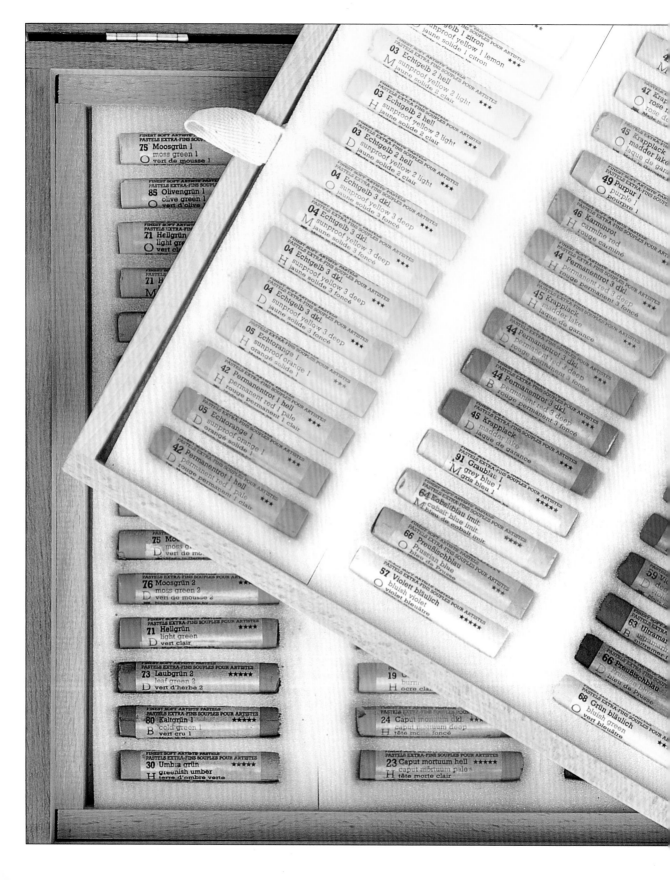

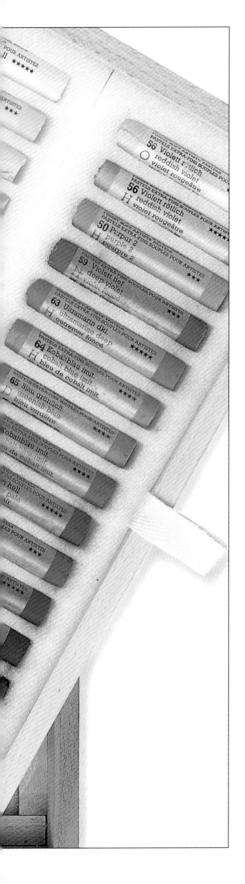

THE VISUAL ARTS

Drawing

DRAWINGS CAN BE FINISHED WORKS OF ART, or preparatory studies for paintings and other visual arts. They can be made using a wide variety of drawing instruments such as pencils, graphite sticks, chalks, charcoal, pens and inks, and silver wires. The most common drawing instrument is the graphite pencil. A graphite pencil consists of a thin rod of graphite mixed with clay, encased in wood. Charcoal is one of the oldest drawing instruments. It is produced by firing twigs of willow, vine, or other woods at high temperatures in airtight containers. Erasers can be used to rub out marks made by drawing materials such as graphite pencils or charcoal, or to achieve a particular effect – such as smudging. Fixative is often applied – using a mouth diffuser or aerosol spray fixative – to prevent smudging once a drawing is finished. Silver lines can be produced by drawing silver wire across specially prepared paper – a technique known as silverpoint. The lines are permanent and cannot be erased. In time the silver lines oxidize and turn brown.

FIXATIVE AND MOUTH DIFFUSER

Hinge

Liquid fixative consisting of dissolved resin

Fixative is sucked into tube and sprayed on to drawing

DRAWING INSTRUMENTS

2B GRAPHITE PENCIL

Medium-soft, light line

8B GRAPHITE PENCIL

Very soft, dark line

SILVER WIRE IN A METAL HOLDER

DRAWING BOARD

Drawing board

Paper

Drawing clip

ERASERS

Hard texture

PLASTIC ERASER

Soft texture

PUTTY ERASER

CHALK, CRAYON, AND CHARCOAL

Calcite (calcium carbonate) mixed with pigment

BLUE CHALK

Iron oxide mixed with chalk

SANGUINE CRAYON

Carbonized wood

WILLOW CHARCOAL

DRAWING MATERIALS

Graphite stick

Bulldog clip

Coloured pencil

Dip pen

Pencil sharpener

Sketch book

Ink bottle

Silver lines
oxidize to a
light brown
colour

Vanishing
point located
on head of
man riding
rearing horse

Figures drawn
in ink on top
of lines

Lines of
squared
pavement slabs
recede toward
a single
vanishing
point

Line drawn
in silverpoint
using a rule

EXAMPLE OF A SILVERPOINT DRAWING
The Adoration of the Magi, Leonardo da Vinci, 1481
Pen and ink over silverpoint on paper
16.5 x 29.2 cm (6½ x 11½ in)

Complex perspective
drawing done as a
preparatory study
for a painting

Paper prepared
with size (glue)
and pigment

Handmade, tinted
paper

One of a series
of drawings
recording
London during
1944–1945

Charcoal lines
softened by
rubbing and
smudging

Broad charcoal
mark

Charcoal
gives strong,
expressive lines

Lines rapidly
drawn on site

EXAMPLE OF A CHARCOAL DRAWING
St. Paul's and the River, David Bomberg, 1945
Charcoal on paper
50.8 x 65.8 cm (20 x 25⅛ in)

Tempera

ILLUMINATED MANUSCRIPT

THE TERM TEMPERA is applied to any paint in which pigment is tempered (mixed) with a water-based binding medium – usually egg yolk. Egg tempera is applied to a smooth surface such as vellum (for illuminated manuscripts) or more commonly to hardwood panels prepared with gesso – a mixture of chalk and size (glue). Hog hair brushes are used to apply the gesso. A layer of gesso grosso (coarse gesso) is followed by successive layers of gesso sotile (fine gesso) that are sanded between coats to provide a smooth, yet absorbent ground. The paint is applied with fine sable brushes in thin layers, using light brushstrokes. Tempera dries quickly to form a tough skin with a satin sheen. The luminous white surface of the gesso combined with the overlaid paint produces the brilliant crispness and rich colours particular to this medium. Egg tempera paintings are frequently gilded with gold. Leaves of finely beaten gold are applied to a bole (reddish-brown clay) base and polished by burnishing.

MATERIALS FOR GILDING

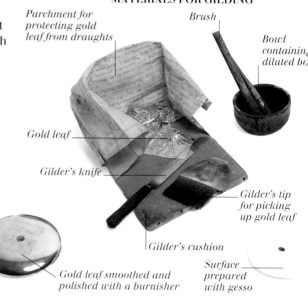

Parchment for protecting gold leaf from draughts

Brush

Bowl containing diluted bo[...]

Gold leaf

Gilder's knife

Gilder's tip for picking up gold leaf

Gilder's cushion

Surface prepared with gesso

Gold leaf smoothed and polished with a burnisher

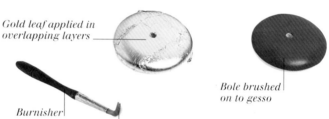

Gold leaf applied in overlapping layers

Bole brushed on to gesso

Burnisher

Agate tip

MATERIALS FOR TEMPERA PANEL PAINTING

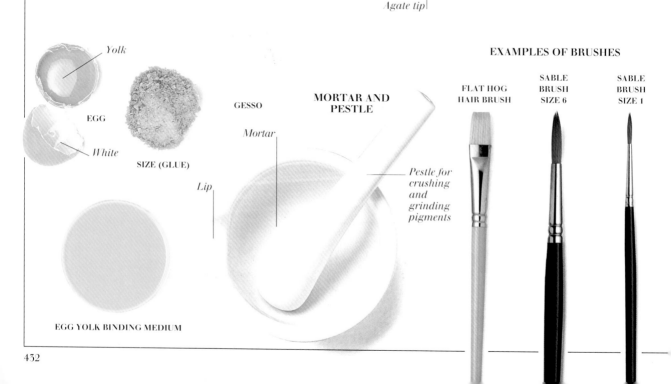

Yolk

EGG

White

SIZE (GLUE)

GESSO

Lip

MORTAR AND PESTLE

Mortar

Pestle for crushing and grinding pigments

EXAMPLES OF BRUSHES

FLAT HOG HAIR BRUSH

SABLE BRUSH SIZE 6

SABLE BRUSH SIZE 1

EGG YOLK BINDING MEDIUM

EXAMPLE OF A TEMPERA PAINTING
Presentation in the Temple, Ambrogio Lorenzetti, 1342
Tempera on wood, 257 x 168 cm (8 ft 5⅛ in x 5 ft 6⅛ in)

*Altarpiece
commissioned for
Siena Cathedral, Italy*

*Textured gold ornament made
by punching motifs into the
gilded surface*

*The red tinge of
the bole is just
visible beneath
the gold*

*Edge of a sheet
of gold leaf*

*Crisp edge
characteristic of
tempera painting*

*Vine black used
to create the
dim cathedral
interior*

*Highlights on
the beard made
by applying thin
layers of white
over dried paint*

*Red drapery
painted in
vermilion*

*Raised right hand
and pointing finger
is the gesture of
prophecy*

*Receding floor
tiles create the
impression of
depth*

*Patch of discoloured
varnish, left from
last cleaning*

VERDACCIO

**VERMILION AND
LEAD WHITE**

VERMILION

**RED EARTH
(IRON OXIDE)**

EXAMPLES OF PIGMENTS

MALACHITE

**ULTRAMARINE
LAPIS LAZULI**

VINE BLACK

LEAD TIN YELLOW

*Warm flesh
tones achieved
by layering
vermilion and
white over an
undercoat of
verdaccio*

*Ultramarine
lapis lazuli, as
costly as gold,
was reserved for
significant
figures such as
the Virgin Mary*

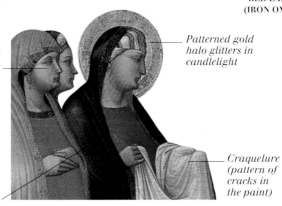

*Patterned gold
halo glitters in
candlelight*

*Craquelure
(pattern of
cracks in
the paint)*

**DETAIL FROM "PRESENTATION
IN THE TEMPLE"**

Fresco

FRESCO IS A METHOD OF WALL PAINTING. In buon fresco (true fresco), pigments are mixed with water and applied to an intonaco (layer of fresh, damp lime-plaster). The intonaco absorbs and binds the pigments as it dries making the picture a permanent part of the wall surface. The intonaco is applied in sections called giornate (daily sections). The size of each giornata depends on the artist's estimate of how much can be painted before the plaster sets. The junctions between giornate are sometimes visible on a finished fresco. The range of colours used in buon fresco are limited to lime-resistant pigments such as earth colours (below). Slaked lime (burnt lime mixed with water), bianco di San Giovanni (slaked lime that has been partly exposed to air), and chalk can be used to produce fresco whites. In fresco secco (dry fresco), pigments are mixed with a binding medium and applied to dry plaster. The pigments are not completely absorbed into the plaster and may flake off over time.

CROSS-SECTION SHOWING FRESCO LAYERS

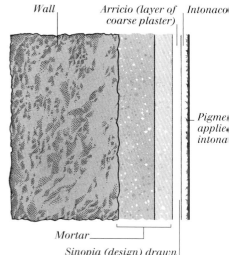

Wall

Arricio (layer of coarse plaster)

Intonaco

Pigment applied intona

Mortar

Pigment applied intona

Sinopia (design) drawn on surface of arricio

EXAMPLES OF EARTH COLOUR PIGMENTS

RAW UMBER

RED EARTH (IRON OXIDE)

GREEN EARTH

RAW SIENNA

EXAMPLES OF FRESCO BRUSHES

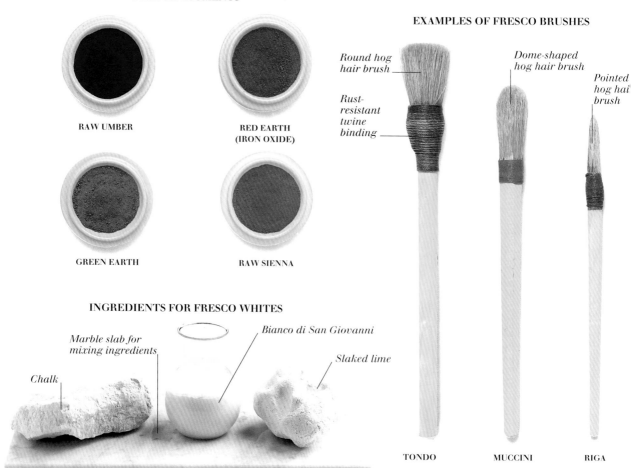

Round hog hair brush

Rust-resistant twine binding

Dome-shaped hog hair brush

Pointed hog hair brush

INGREDIENTS FOR FRESCO WHITES

Marble slab for mixing ingredients

Bianco di San Giovanni

Slaked lime

Chalk

TONDO

MUCCINI

RIGA

EXAMPLE OF A FRESCO
The Expulsion of the Merchants from the Temple, Giotto, c.1306
Fresco, 200 x 185 cm (78 x 72 in)

One of a series of frescoes in the Arena Chapel, Padua, Italy

Temple acts as a backdrop for the action

Patches of azurite blue have turned green due to reaction with carbon dioxide

Bianco di San Giovanni often used for fresco whites

Gold leaf applied to apostle's halo

Hairline junction between giornate is visible

Green earth pigment applied to robe

Red earth pigment applied in buon fresco has retained rich hue

Child painted on top of apostle's robe

Azurite blue applied in fresco secco has flaked off to reveal the plaster beneath

Dry, matt surface characteristic of buon fresco

Paint applied in buon fresco to child's face

White dove represents the Holy Ghost

Paint applied in fresco secco to child's body has flaked off

Sinopia (design) sketched in red earth

DETAIL FROM "THE EXPULSION"

Artist has to finish giornata before plaster dries

Junction between giornate

A fresco was generally worked in zones from the top down

Area with little detail can be painted quickly, allowing a larger giornata to be completed

Highly detailed area takes a longer time to paint, restricting the size of the giornata

GIORNATE (DAILY SECTIONS) IN "THE EXPULSION"

435

Oils

OIL PAINTS ARE MADE BY MIXING and grinding pigment with a drying vegetable oil such as linseed oil. The paint can be applied to many different surfaces and textures – the most common being canvas. Before painting, the canvas is stretched on a wooden frame and its surface is prepared with layers of size (glue) and primer. The two main types of brushes used in oil painting are stiff hog hair bristle brushes – generally used for covering large areas; and soft hair brushes made from sable or synthetic material – generally used for fine detail. Other tools, including painting knives, can also be used to achieve different effects. Oil paint can be applied thickly (a technique known as impasto), or can be thinned down using a solvent – such as turpentine or white spirit. Varnishes are sometimes applied to finished paintings to protect their surface and to give them a matt or gloss finish.

KIDNEY-SHAPED PALETTE

DAMMAR RESIN VARNISH

Crystals are dissolved and applied to painting to protect its surface

COMMERCIAL OIL PAINTS

CADMIUM RED

Lightfast opaque colour

ULTRAMARINE

Transparent colour

LINSEED OIL

Oil derived from seeds of flax plant

EXAMPLES OF PIGMENTS

CADMIUM RED

CERULEAN BLUE

DOUBLE DIPPER (PALETTE ATTACHMENT)

Screw-top lid

Container for storing solvent or drying oil

EXAMPLES OF BRUSHES

SYNTHETIC BRUSH

SABLE BRUSH

HOG HAIR BRISTLE BRUSHES

Flat hog hair brush

Flat hog hair brush

Filbert hog hair brush

Filbert hog hair brush

Round hog hair brush

Long, wooden handle

Protective plastic case

EQUIPMENT FOR MAKING OIL PAINT

Airtight jar for storing paint

Palette knife for mixing drying oil and pigment

PAINTING KNIVES

TROWEL-SHAPED PAINTING KNIFE

DIAMOND-SHAPED PAINTING KNIFE

Blade

Blade

Glass muller for grinding drying oil and pigment

Glass slab with abrasive surface

Cranked, steel shank

Cranked, steel shank

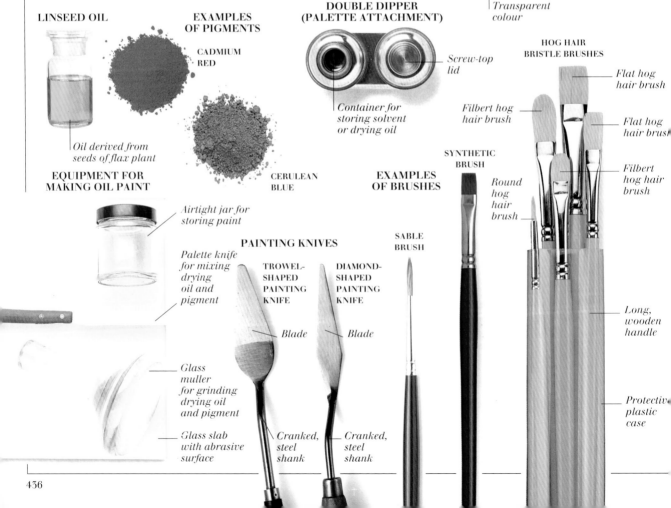

EXAMPLE OF AN OIL PAINTING
Fritillarias, Vincent van Gogh, 1886
Oil on canvas, 73.5 x 60.5 cm (29 x 24 in)

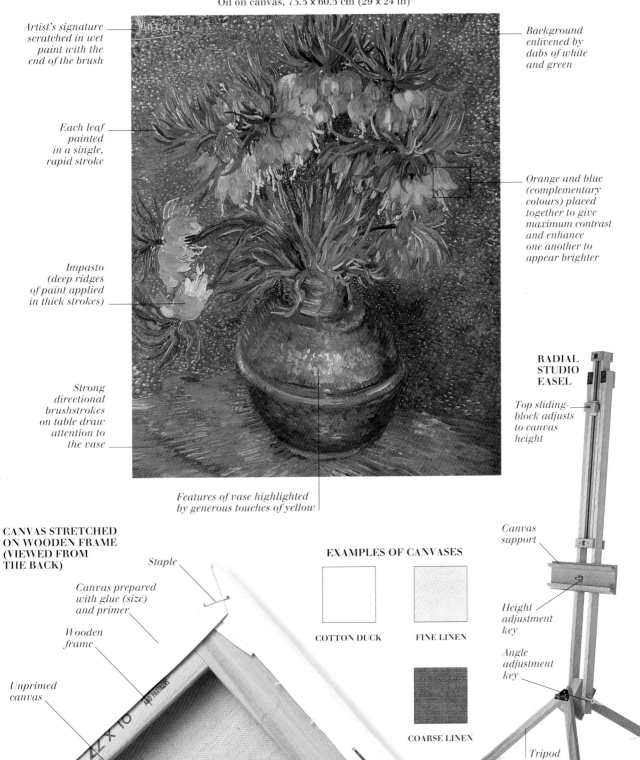

*Artist's signature
scratched in wet
paint with the
end of the brush*

*Each leaf
painted
in a single,
rapid stroke*

*Impasto
(deep ridges
of paint applied
in thick strokes)*

*Strong
directional
brushstrokes
on table draw
attention to
the vase*

*Background
enlivened by
dabs of white
and green*

*Orange and blue
(complementary
colours) placed
together to give
maximum contrast
and enhance
one another to
appear brighter*

*Features of vase highlighted
by generous touches of yellow*

**RADIAL
STUDIO
EASEL**

*Top sliding-
block adjusts
to canvas
height*

*Canvas
support*

*Height
adjustment
key*

*Angle
adjustment
key*

Tripod

CANVAS STRETCHED ON WOODEN FRAME (VIEWED FROM THE BACK)

Staple

*Canvas prepared
with glue (size)
and primer*

*Wooden
frame*

*Unprimed
canvas*

EXAMPLES OF CANVASES

COTTON DUCK

FINE LINEN

COARSE LINEN

Watercolour

WATERCOLOUR PAINT IS MADE OF GROUND PIGMENT mixed with a water-soluble binding medium, usually gum arabic. It is usually applied to paper using soft hair brushes such as sable, goat hair, squirrel, and synthetic brushes. Watercolours are often diluted and applied as overlaying washes (thin, transparent layers) to build up depth of colour. Washes can be laid in a variety of ways to create a range of different effects. For example, a wet-in-wet wash can be achieved by laying a wash on top of another wet wash. The two washes blend together to give a fused effect. Sponges are used to modify washes by soaking up paint so that areas of pigment are lightened or removed from the paper. Watercolours can also be applied undiluted – a technique known as dry brush – to create a broken-colour effect. Watercolours are generally transparent and allow light to reflect from the surface of the paper through the layers of paint to give a luminous effect. They can be thickened and made opaque by adding body colour (Chinese white).

*Natural sap
from acacia tree*

NATURAL SPONGE

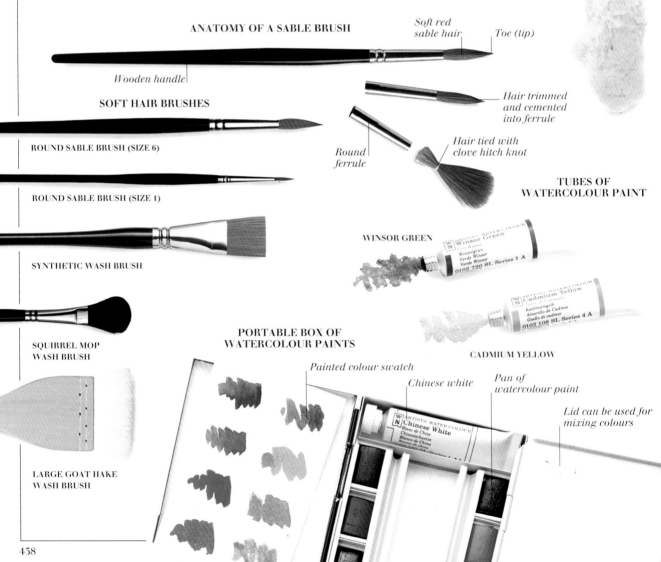

ANATOMY OF A SABLE BRUSH

*Soft red
sable hair*

Toe (tip)

Wooden handle

SOFT HAIR BRUSHES

*Hair trimmed
and cemented
into ferrule*

ROUND SABLE BRUSH (SIZE 6)

*Round
ferrule*

*Hair tied with
clove hitch knot*

ROUND SABLE BRUSH (SIZE 1)

TUBES OF
WATERCOLOUR PAINT

WINSOR GREEN

SYNTHETIC WASH BRUSH

*Winsor Green
Winsorgrün
Verde Winsor
0102 720 SL Series 1 A*

*Cadmium Yellow
Kadmiumgelb
Amarillo de Cadmio
Giallo di cadmio
0102 108 SL Series 4 A*

SQUIRREL MOP
WASH BRUSH

PORTABLE BOX OF
WATERCOLOUR PAINTS

CADMIUM YELLOW

Painted colour swatch

Chinese white

*Pan of
watercolour paint*

*Chinese White
Blanc de Chine
Chinesischweiss
Blanco de China*

*Lid can be used for
mixing colours*

LARGE GOAT HAKE
WASH BRUSH

EXAMPLE OF A WATERCOLOUR
Burning of the Houses of Parliament, Turner, 1834
Watercolour on paper, 29.2 x 44.5 cm (11½ x 17½ in)

Transparent washes laid on top of each other to create tonal depth

Transparent washes allow light to reflect off the surface of the paper to give a luminous effect

Highlight scratched out with a scalpel

Paper shows through thin wash to give flames added highlight

Crowd painted with thin strokes laid over a pale wash

Undiluted paint applied, then partly washed out, to create the impression of water

EXAMPLES OF WATERCOLOUR PAPERS

SMOOTH-TEXTURED PAPER

MEDIUM-TEXTURED PAPER

ROUGH-TEXTURED PAPER

EXAMPLES OF WASHES

WASH OVER DRY BRUSH
Wash laid over paint applied with dry brush gives two-tone effect

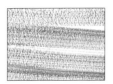

GRADED WASH
Strong wash applied to tilted paper gives graded effect

DRY BRUSH
Undiluted paint dragged across surface of paper gives broken effect

WET-IN-WET
Two diluted washes left to run together to give fused effect

COLOUR WHEEL OF WATERCOLOUR PAINTS

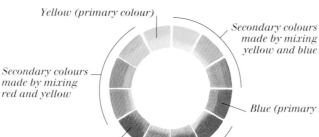

Yellow (primary colour)

Secondary colours made by mixing yellow and blue

Secondary colours made by mixing red and yellow

Blue (primary colour)

Red (primary colour)

Secondary colours made by mixing blue and red

Pastels

PASTELS ARE STICKS OF PIGMENT made by mixing ground pigment with chalk and a binding medium, such as gum arabic. They vary in hardness depending on the proportion of the binding medium to the chalk. Soft pastel – the most common form of pastel – contains just enough binding medium to hold the pigment in stick form. Pastels can be applied directly to any support (surface) with sufficient tooth (texture). When a pastel is drawn over a textured surface, the pigment crumbles and lodges in the fibres of the support. Pastel marks have a particular soft, matt quality and are suitable for techniques such as blending, scumbling, and feathering. Blending is a technique of rubbing and fusing two or more colours on the support using fingers or various tools such as tortillons (paper stumps), soft hair brushes, putty erasers, and soft bread. Scumbling is a technique of building up layers of pastel colours. The side or blunted tip of a soft pastel is lightly drawn over an underpainted area so that patches of the colour beneath show through. Feathering is a technique of applying parallel strokes of colour with the point of a pastel, usually over an existing layer of pastel colour. A thin spray of fixative can be applied – using a mouth diffuser (see pp. 430-431) or aerosol spray fixative – to a finished pastel painting, or in between layers of colour, to prevent smudging.

EQUIPMENT FOR MAKING PASTELS

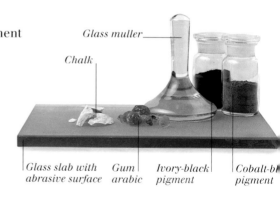

Glass muller

Chalk

Glass slab with abrasive surface

Gum arabic

Ivory-black pigment

Cobalt-b[l]ue pigment

EXAMPLES OF SOFT PASTELS

COBALT-BLUE HALF PASTEL

VERMILION HALF PASTEL

OLIVE-GREEN FULL PASTEL

MAUVE FULL PASTEL

BOXED PASTEL SET

EQUIPMENT USED WITH PASTELS

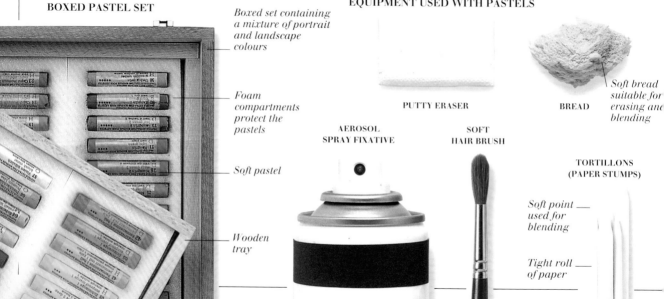

Boxed set containing a mixture of portrait and landscape colours

Foam compartments protect the pastels

Soft pastel

Wooden tray

PUTTY ERASER

AEROSOL SPRAY FIXATIVE

SOFT HAIR BRUSH

BREAD

Soft bread suitable for erasing and blending

TORTILLONS (PAPER STUMPS)

Soft point used for blending

Tight roll of paper

EXAMPLE OF A PASTEL PAINTING
Woman Drying her Neck, Edgar Degas, c.1898
Pastel on cardboard, 62.5 x 65.5 cm (24½ x 25½ in)

Pastels applied directly to support

Colours are blended together using fingers or tools such as tortillons

Built up layers of pastel

Rich colour of fabric created by overlaying yellows and oranges

Broken colours, characteristic of scumbling technique

Toned colour of paper visible beneath thinly applied pastels

Pure bright colours laid side by side produce strong contrasts

DETAIL FROM "WOMAN DRYING HER NECK"

Feathering technique used to produce skin tones

EXAMPLES OF TEXTURED PAPERS AND PASTEL BOARDS

WATERCOLOUR PAPER (ROUGH TEXTURE)

GLASS PAPER

WATERCOLOUR PAPER (MEDIUM TEXTURE)

INGRES PAPER

FLOCKED PASTEL BOARD

CANSON PAPER

EXAMPLES OF COLOURED AND TINTED PAPERS

Acrylics

ACRYLIC PAINT IS MADE BY MIXING PIGMENT with a synthetic resin. It can be thinned with water but dries to become water insoluble. Acrylics are applied to many surfaces, such as paper and acrylic-primed board and canvas. A variety of brushes, painting knives, rollers, air-brushes, plastic scrapers, and other tools are used in acrylic painting. The versatility of acrylics makes them suitable for a wide range of techniques. They can be used opaquely or – by adding water – in a transparent, watercolour style. Acrylic mediums can be added to the paint to adjust its consistency for special effects such as glazing and impasto (ridges of paint applied in thick strokes) or to make it more matt or glossy. Acrylics are quick-drying, which allows layers of paint to be applied on top of each other almost immediately.

EXAMPLES OF BRUSHES

Sable brush

Hog hair sash brush

Synthetic hog hair brush

Synthetic sable brush

Hog hair brush

Goat hair brush

Synthetic wash brush

Ox hair brush

EXAMPLES OF PAINTS USED IN ACRYLICS

Azo yellow

Phthalo green

Cerulean blue

Phthalo blue

Quinacridone red

Titanium white

Pad of disposable paper palettes

Yellow ochre

Burnt umber

Burnt sienna

PAINTING TOOLS

Flexible, plastic blade

Stippled effect achieved using thick paint

PLASTIC PAINTING KNIFE

Striated effect

Glue spreader

Credit card

Paint spread evenly

PLASTIC SCRAPERS

Plastic handle

Blended tones

Nozzle

Paint cup

Main lever

AIR-BRUSH

SPONGE ROLLER

Uniform tone

Air hose

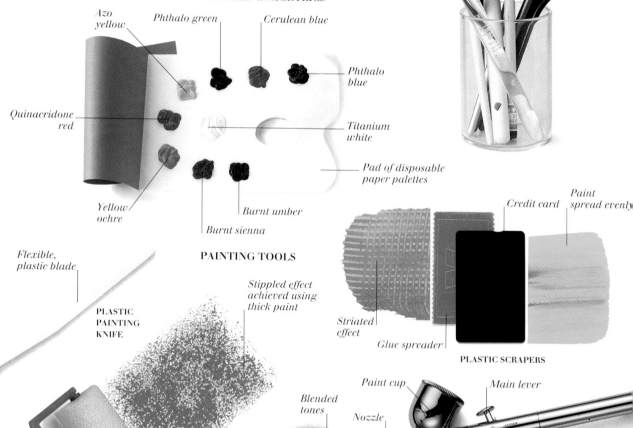

EXAMPLE OF AN ACRYLIC PAINTING
A Bigger Splash, David Hockney, 1967
Acrylic on canvas, 242.5 x 243.8 cm (95½ x 96 in)

Paint applied evenly using a roller

Cotton duck canvas support (surface)

Flatness of rollered areas enhanced by adding gel medium to the paint

Masking tape stuck on to canvas to define main shapes, and paint applied within these areas using a roller

Thin strip of pool edge left unpainted

Splash painted using thicker paint and small brush

Imprecise edge on end of spring board where paint has seeped under masking tape

EXAMPLES OF ACRYLIC PAINTS AND TECHNIQUES

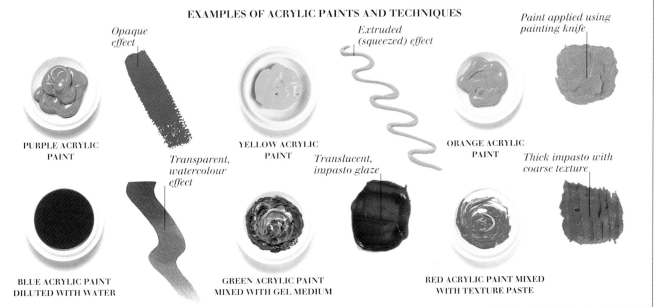

Opaque effect

Extruded (squeezed) effect

Paint applied using painting knife

PURPLE ACRYLIC PAINT

YELLOW ACRYLIC PAINT

ORANGE ACRYLIC PAINT

Transparent, watercolour effect

Translucent, impasto glaze

Thick impasto with coarse texture

BLUE ACRYLIC PAINT DILUTED WITH WATER

GREEN ACRYLIC PAINT MIXED WITH GEL MEDIUM

RED ACRYLIC PAINT MIXED WITH TEXTURE PASTE

Calligraphy

CALLIGRAPHY IS BEAUTIFULLY FORMED LETTERING. The term applies to written text and illumination (the decoration of manuscripts using gold leaf and colour). The essential materials needed to practise calligraphy are a writing tool, ink, and a writing surface. Quills are among the oldest writing tools. They are usually made from goose or turkey feathers, and are noted for their flexibility and ability to produce fine lines. A quill point, however, is not very durable and constant recutting and trimming is required. The most commonly used writing instrument in western calligraphy is a detachable, metal nib held in a penholder. The metal nib is very durable, and there are a wide range of different types. Particular types of nibs – such as copperplate, speedball, and roundhand nibs – are used for specific styles of lettering. Some nibs have integral ink reservoirs and others have reservoirs that are detachable. Brushes are also used for writing, and for filling in outlined letters and painting decoration. Other writing tools used in calligraphy are fountain pens, felt-tip pens, rotring pens, and reed pens. Calligraphy inks may come in liquid form, or as a solid ink stick. Ink sticks are ground down in distilled water to form a liquid ink. The most common writing surfaces for calligraphy are good quality, smooth -surfaced papers. To achieve the best writing position, the calligrapher places the paper on a drawing board set at an angle.

EQUIPMENT USED IN BRUSH LETTERING

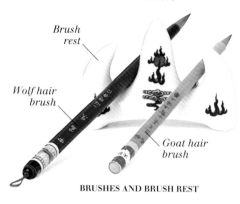

Brush rest

Wolf hair brush

Goat hair brush

BRUSHES AND BRUSH REST

Liquid ink made by grinding down ink stick in distilled water

Solid carbon ink stick

Ink stone

INK STICK AND STONE

Feather

PENS, NIBS, AND BRUSHES USED IN CALLIGRAPHY

PENHOLDER

FELT-TIP PEN

AUTOMATICPEN

REED PEN

SQUARE SABLE BRUSH

POINTED SABLE BRUSH

COPPERPLATE NIB

SPEEDBALL NIB

ROUNDHAND NIB AND DETACHABLE INK RESERVOIR

GOAT HAIR BRUSH

WOLF HAIR BRUSH

Feather stripped for better handling

Barrel

FOUNTAIN PEN AND INK

Bottle of permanent black ink

Barrel

Clip

Nib

Outer cap

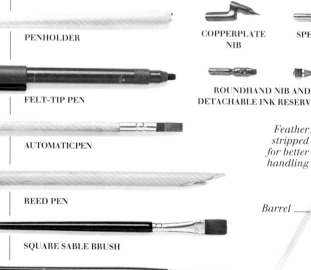

Hand-cut point

GOOSE-FEATHER QUILL

EXAMPLES OF LETTERING STYLES

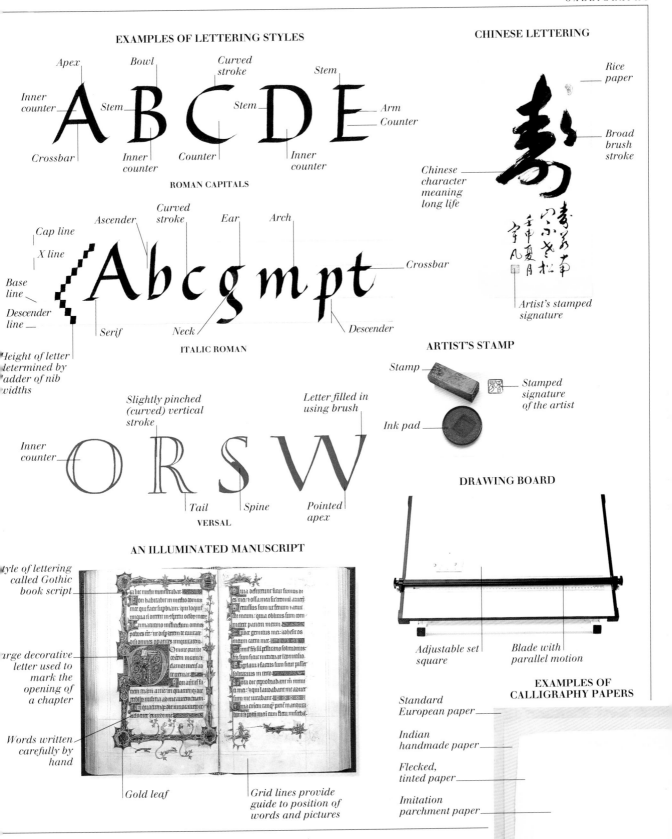

Apex
Bowl
Curved stroke
Stem
Inner counter
Stem
Stem
Arm
Counter
Crossbar
Inner counter
Counter
Inner counter

ROMAN CAPITALS

Ascender
Curved stroke
Ear
Arch
Cap line
X line
Crossbar
Base line
Descender line
Serif
Neck
Descender
Height of letter determined by ladder of nib widths

ITALIC ROMAN

Inner counter
Slightly pinched (curved) vertical stroke
Letter filled in using brush
Tail
Spine
Pointed apex

VERSAL

AN ILLUMINATED MANUSCRIPT

Style of lettering called Gothic book script
Large decorative letter used to mark the opening of a chapter
Words written carefully by hand
Gold leaf
Grid lines provide guide to position of words and pictures

CHINESE LETTERING

Rice paper
Broad brush stroke
Chinese character meaning long life
Artist's stamped signature

ARTIST'S STAMP

Stamp
Stamped signature of the artist
Ink pad

DRAWING BOARD

Adjustable set square
Blade with parallel motion

EXAMPLES OF CALLIGRAPHY PAPERS

Standard European paper
Indian handmade paper
Flecked, tinted paper
Imitation parchment paper

Printmaking 1

PRINTS ARE MADE BY FOUR BASIC printing processes – intaglio, lithographic, relief, and screen. In intaglio printing, lines are engraved or etched into the surface of a metal plate. Lines are engraved by hand using sharp metal tools. They are etched by corroding the metal plate with acid, using acid-resistant ground to protect the areas not to be etched. The plate is then inked and wiped, leaving the grooves filled with ink and the surface clean. Dampened paper is laid over the plate, and both paper and plate are passed through the rollers of an etching press. The pressure of the rollers forces the paper into the grooves, so that it takes up the ink, leaving an impression on the paper. Lithographic printing is based on the antipathy between grease and water. An image is drawn on a surface – usually a stone or metal plate – with a greasy medium, such as tusche (lihographic ink). The greasy drawing is fixed on to the plate by applying an acidic solution, such as gum arabic. The surface is then dampened and rolled with ink. The ink adheres only to the greasy areas and is repelled by the water. Paper is laid on the plate and pressure is applied by means of a press. In relief printing, the non-printing areas of a wood or linoleum block are cut away using gouges, knives, and other tools. The printing areas are left raised in relief and are rolled with ink. Paper is laid on the inked block and pressure is applied by means of a press or by burnishing (rubbing) the back of the paper. The most common forms of relief printing are woodcut, wood engraving, and linocut. In screen printing, the printing surface is a mesh stretched across a wooden frame. A stencil is applied to the mesh to seal the non-printing areas and ink is scraped through the mesh to produce an image.

THE FOUR MAIN PRINTING PROCESSES

Paper
Printed image
Engraved or etched image
Metal plate
Inked area

INTAGLIO

Printed image
Paper
Damp surface rejects ink
Ink adheres to greasy image
Image drawn on stone with greasy medium

LITHOGRAPHIC

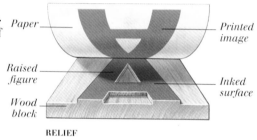

Paper
Printed image
Raised figure
Inked surface
Wood block

RELIEF

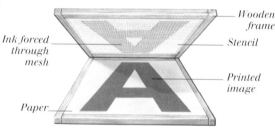

Wooden frame
Stencil
Ink forced through mesh
Printed image
Paper

SCREEN

LEATHER INK DABBER

EQUIPMENT USED IN INTAGLIO PRINTING

ROCKER   SCRIBER   ROULETTE   SCRAPER   BURNISHER   CLAMP

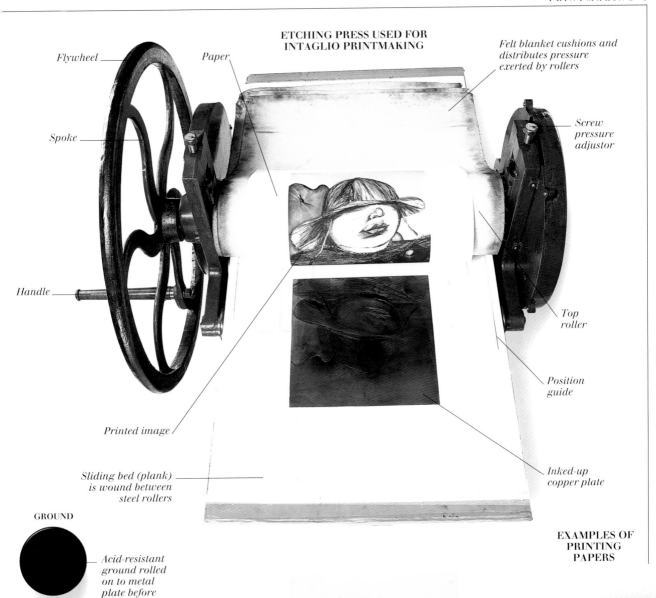

**ETCHING PRESS USED FOR
INTAGLIO PRINTMAKING**

Flywheel

Spoke

Paper

*Felt blanket cushions and
distributes pressure
exerted by rollers*

*Screw
pressure
adjustor*

Handle

*Top
roller*

*Position
guide*

Printed image

*Inked-up
copper plate*

*Sliding bed (plank)
is wound between
steel rollers*

GROUND

*Acid-resistant
ground rolled
on to metal
plate before
etching*

**EXAMPLES OF
PRINTING
PAPERS**

GROUND ROLLER

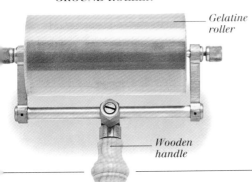

*Gelatine
roller*

*Wooden
handle*

EXAMPLE OF AN INTAGLIO PRINT
Annie with a Sun Hat, Jock McFadyen, 1993
Etched copper plate, 41 x 40 cm (16 x 15¾ in)

Printmaking 2

EXAMPLE OF A LITHOGRAPHIC STONE AND PRINT

Crown Gateway 2, Mandy Bonnell, 1987
Lithograph, 50 x 40 cm (19½ x 15¾ in)

IMAGE DRAWN ON STONE

LITHOGRAPIC PRINT

EXAMPLE OF A SCREEN PRINT

Sea Change, Patrick Hughes, 1992
Screen print, 77 x 94.5 cm (30 x 37 in)

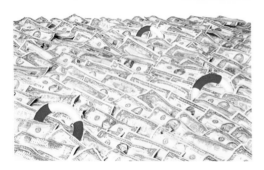

SCREEN AND SQUEEGEE

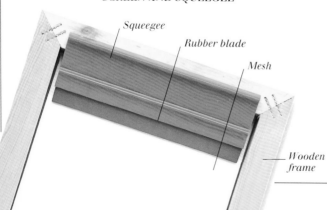

Squeegee

Rubber blade

Mesh

Wooden frame

EQUIPMENT USED IN LITHOGRAPHIC PRINTING

CRAYON AND HOLDER

LITHOGRAPHIC PENCIL

TUSCHE (LITHOGRAPHIC INK) PEN

ERASING STICK

EXPANDABLE SPONGE

TUSCHE (LITHOGRAPHIC INK) STICK

RUBBING INK

INK ROLLER

MILD ACIDIC SOLUTION

GUM ARABIC SOLUTION

WATER-BASED SCREEN PRINTING INKS

BLUE ACRYLIC INK

RED ACRYLIC INK

BROWN TEXTILE INK

EQUIPMENT USED IN RELIEF PRINTING

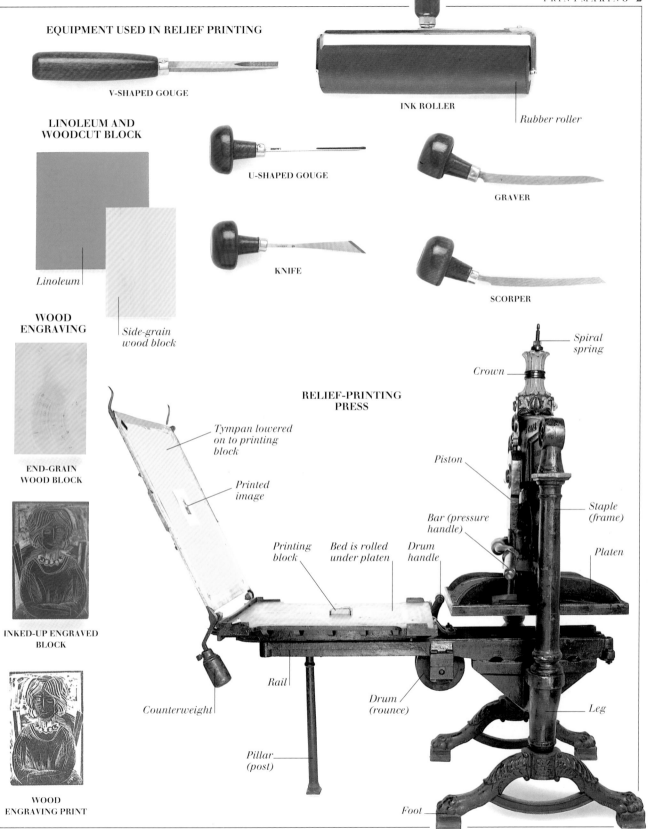

V-SHAPED GOUGE

INK ROLLER

Rubber roller

LINOLEUM AND WOODCUT BLOCK

U-SHAPED GOUGE

GRAVER

Linoleum

KNIFE

SCORPER

WOOD ENGRAVING

Side-grain wood block

END-GRAIN WOOD BLOCK

INKED-UP ENGRAVED BLOCK

WOOD ENGRAVING PRINT

RELIEF-PRINTING PRESS

Spiral spring

Crown

Tympan lowered on to printing block

Piston

Printed image

Bar (pressure handle)

Staple (frame)

Printing block

Bed is rolled under platen

Drum handle

Platen

Rail

Drum (rounce)

Leg

Counterweight

Pillar (post)

Foot

Mosaic

MOSAIC IS THE ART OF MAKING patterns and pictures from tesserae (small, coloured pieces of glass, marble, and other materials). Different materials are cut into tesserae using different tools. Smalti (glass enamel) and marble are cut into pieces using a hammer and a hardy (a pointed blade) embedded in a log. Vitreous glass is cut into pieces using a pair of nippers. Mosaics can be made using a direct or indirect method. In the direct method, the tesserae are laid directly into a bed of cement–based adhesive. In the indirect method, the design is drawn in reverse on paper or cloth. The tesserae are then stuck face-down on the paper or cloth using water-soluble glue. Adhesive is spread with a trowel on to a solid surface – such as a wall – and the back of the mosaic is laid into the adhesive. Finally, the paper or cloth is soaked off to reveal the mosaic. Gaps between tesserae can be filled with grout. Grout is forced into gaps by dragging a grouting squeegee across the face of the mosaic. Mosaics are usually used to decorate walls and floors, but they can also be applied to smaller objects.

EQUIPMENT FOR BREAKING MARBLE

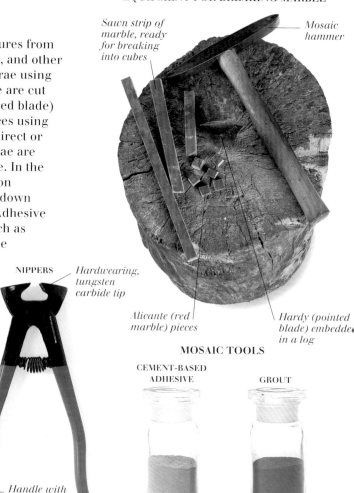

Sawn strip of marble, ready for breaking into cubes

Mosaic hammer

Alicante (red marble) pieces

Hardy (pointed blade) embedded in a log

NIPPERS

Hardwearing, tungsten carbide tip

Handle with rubber grip

MOSAIC TOOLS

CEMENT-BASED ADHESIVE

GROUT

SMALTI (GLASS ENAMEL)

RED SMALTI

EXAMPLE OF A MOSAIC (DIRECT METHOD)
Seascape, Tessa Hunkin, 1993
Smalti mosaic on board
80 cm (31½ in) diameter

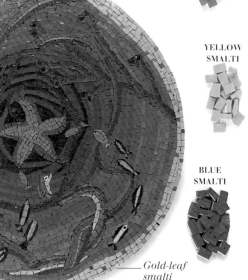

Gold-leaf smalti

YELLOW SMALTI

BLUE SMALTI

TROWEL

Notch

Wooden handle

Steel blade

Wooden handle

GROUTING SQUEEGEE

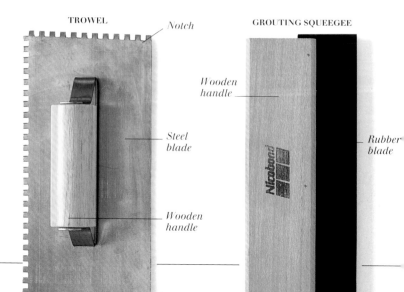

Wooden handle

Rubber blade

Nicobond

STAGES IN THE CREATION OF A MOSAIC (INDIRECT METHOD)

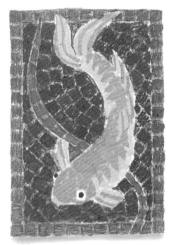

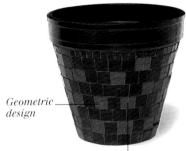

Geometric design

Grout

COLOUR SKETCH
A colour sketch is drawn
in oil pastel to give a clear
impression of how the finished
mosaic will look.

REVERSE IMAGE
Tesserae are glued face-down
on reverse image on paper.
Mosaic is then attached to solid
surface and paper is removed.

MOSAIC MOSQUE DESIGN

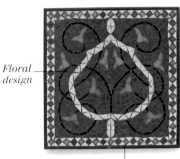

Floral design

Geometric border

*Gold tessera
with ripple
finish*

*Andamenti
(line along
which tesserae
are laid)*

VITREOUS GLASS

*Gold tessera
placed upside-
down*

**GREEN VITREOUS
GLASS WITH GOLD LEAF**

**RED VITREOUS
GLASS**

*Plain
finish*

*Grout fills
the gaps
between the
tesserae*

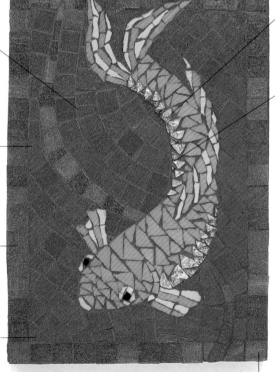

*Ripple
finish*

SHEETS OF VITREOUS GLASS

*Mosaic
mounted
on board*

*Vitreous
glass cut into
triangular
shape with
nippers*

**BLUE VITREOUS
GLASS**

FINISHED MOSAIC
Goldfish, Tessa Hunkin, 1993
Vitreous glass mosaic on board
35.5 x 25.5 cm (14 x 10 in)

*Border of square
vitreous glass*

Sculpture 1

THE TWO TRADITIONAL METHODS OF MAKING SCULPTURE are carving and modelling. A carved sculpture is made by cutting away the surplus from a block of hard material such as stone, marble, or wood. The tools used for carving vary according to the material being carved. Heavy steel points, claws, and chisels that are struck with a lump hammer are generally used for stone and marble. Sharp gouges and chisels that are struck with a wooden mallet are used for wood. Sculptures formed from hard materials are generally finished by filing with rasps, rifflers, and other abrasive implements. Modelling is a process by which shapes are built up, using malleable materials such as clay, plaster, and wax. The material is cut with wire-ended tools and modelled with the fingers or a variety of hardwood and metal implements. For large or intricate modelled sculptures an armature (frame), made from metal or wood, is used to provide internal support. Sculptures formed in soft materials may harden naturally or can be made more durable by firing in a kiln. Modelled sculptures are often first designed in wax or another material to be cast later in a metal (see pp. 454-455) such as bronze. The development of many new materials in the 20th century has enabled sculptors to experiment with new techniques such as construction (joining preformed pieces of material such as machine components, mirrors, and furniture) and kinetic (mobile) sculpture.

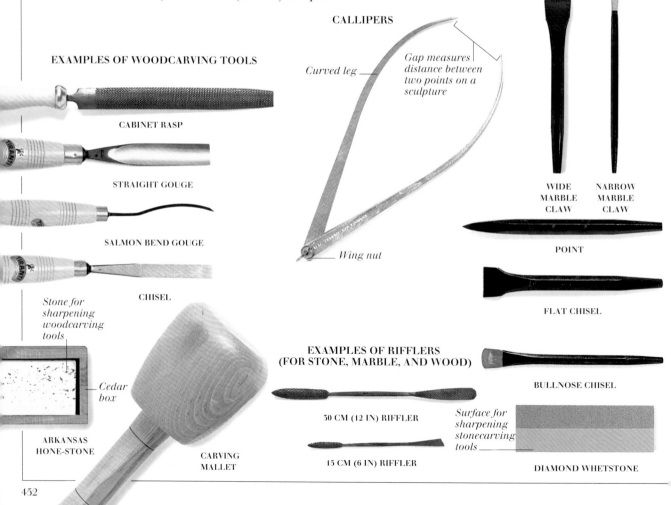

EXAMPLES OF MARBLE CARVING TOOLS

1.1 kg (2½ lb) iron head

Ash handle

LUMP HAMMER

EXAMPLES OF WOODCARVING TOOLS

CABINET RASP

STRAIGHT GOUGE

SALMON BEND GOUGE

CHISEL

Stone for sharpening woodcarving tools

Cedar box

ARKANSAS HONE-STONE

CARVING MALLET

CALLIPERS

Curved leg

Gap measures distance between two points on a sculpture

Wing nut

WIDE MARBLE CLAW

NARROW MARBLE CLAW

POINT

FLAT CHISEL

BULLNOSE CHISEL

EXAMPLES OF RIFFLERS (FOR STONE, MARBLE, AND WOOD)

30 CM (12 IN) RIFFLER

15 CM (6 IN) RIFFLER

Surface for sharpening stonecarving tools

DIAMOND WHETSTONE

*Tiny holes along
the hairline made
with a point*

**DETAIL OF
SLAVE'S HEAD**

*Soft skin texture tooled
with a fine-toothed
marble claw*

EXAMPLE OF A CARVED WOOD SCULPTURE
Mary Magdalene, Donatello, 1454-1455
Poplar wood, height 188 cm (6 ft 2 in)

EXAMPLE OF A CARVED MARBLE SCULPTURE
The Rebel Slave, Michelangelo, 1513-1516
Marble, height 213 cm (7ft)

*Hair worked
with a narrow
claw*

*Delicately
modelled
hand carved
with a chisel*

*Hair
highlighted
with gold
leaf*

*Translucent white
marble, quarried at
Carrara, Italy*

*Figure cut
from single
length of
poplar*

*Deep
ridges of
hair cut
with a
gouge*

*Surface rubbed
smooth with
rifflers and
pumice*

*Strut gives added
support to long
slender limb*

*Wood prepared
with gesso
(chalk and glue)
and painted*

*Base scored with
jagged parallel
cuts made with
point and lump
hammer*

*Series of tiny
punch holes,
made with a
fine point,
outline the
form*

*Foot carved in
deep relief*

*Rough surface
made by driving
a point into the
marble at an
oblique angle*

*The dimensions of the marble block
determine the size of the sculpture*

DETAIL OF SLAVE'S FOOT

Sculpture 2

EXAMPLES OF MODELLING TOOLS

WIRE-ENDED CUTTING TOOL

CURVED MOULDING TOOL

SPATULA-ENDED WAX MODELLING TOOL

ROUNDED WAX MODELLING TOOL

EXAMPLES OF BRONZE FINISHING TOOLS

HOOKED RIFFLER

POINTED RIFFLER

SPIRIT LAMP (FOR HEATING WAX MODELLING TOOLS)

Wick

Brass holder

Glass bowl

Methylated spirit

STAGES IN THE LOST-WAX METHOD OF CASTING
Based on Mars, Giambologna, c.1546

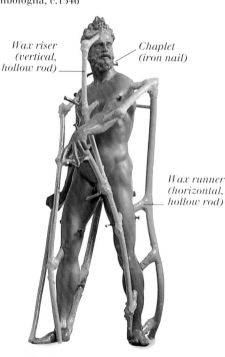

Wax-covered wire armature

Wax riser (vertical, hollow rod)

Chaplet (iron nail)

Wax runner (horizontal, hollow rod)

ORIGINAL MODEL
An original, solid wax model is made and preserved so that numerous replicas can be cast.

HOLLOW WAX FIGURE IS CAST
A new, hollow wax model is cast from the original model. It is filled with a plaster core that is held in place with nails. Wax runners and risers are attached.

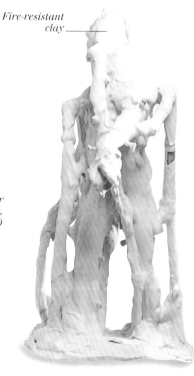

Fire-resistant clay

FIGURE IS BAKED IN CASTING MOULD
The model is encased in clay and baked. The wax melts away (through the channels made by the wax rods) and is replaced by molten bronze.

MODELLING STAND AND ARMATURE

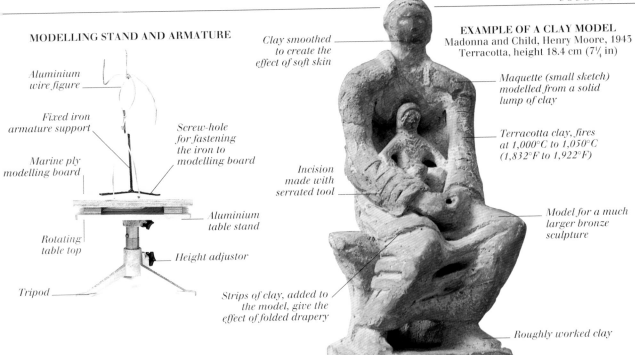

Aluminium wire figure

Fixed iron armature support

Marine ply modelling board

Rotating table top

Tripod

Screw-hole for fastening the iron to modelling board

Aluminium table stand

Height adjustor

EXAMPLE OF A CLAY MODEL
Madonna and Child, Henry Moore, 1943
Terracotta, height 18.4 cm (7¼ in)

Clay smoothed to create the effect of soft skin

Incision made with serrated tool

Strips of clay, added to the model, give the effect of folded drapery

Maquette (small sketch) modelled from a solid lump of clay

Terracotta clay, fires at 1,000°C to 1,050°C (1,832°F to 1,922°F)

Model for a much larger bronze sculpture

Roughly worked clay

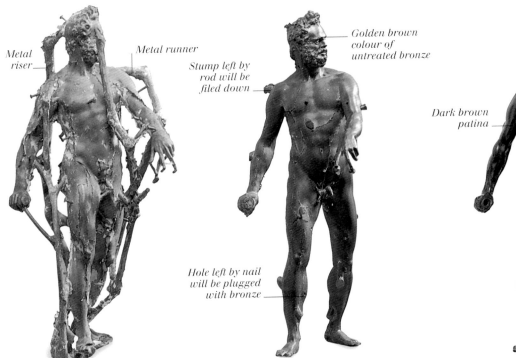

Metal riser

Metal runner

Golden brown colour of untreated bronze

Stump left by rod will be filed down

Dark brown patina

Hole left by nail will be plugged with bronze

STATUE IS STRIPPED OF CLAY
When the bronze has cooled, the clay mould is broken open to reveal the bronze statue with solid metal runners and risers.

STATUE IS FINISHED
The nails are pulled out and a large hole is made to remove the plaster core. When the metal rods have been sawn off, the sculpture is filed to refine the surface.

STATUE IS CLEANED
Finally the work is cleaned and polished. An artificial patina (colouring) is achieved by treating the surface with chemicals.

ARCHITECTURE

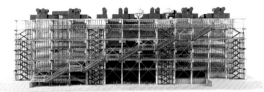

Ancient Egypt

THE CIVILIZATION OF THE ANCIENT EGYPTIANS (which lasted from about 3100 BC until it was finally absorbed into the Roman empire in 30 BC) is famous for its temples and tombs. Egyptian temples were often huge and geometric, like the Temple of Amon-Re (below and right). They were usually decorated with hieroglyphs (sacred characters used for picture-writing) and painted reliefs depicting gods, Pharaohs (kings), and queens. Tombs were particularly important to the Egyptians, who believed that the dead were resurrected in the after-life. The tombs were often decorated – as, for example, the surround of the false door opposite – in order to give comfort to the dead. The best-known ancient Egyptian tombs are the pyramids, which were designed to symbolize the rays of the sun. Many of the architectural forms used by the ancient Egyptians were later adopted by other civilizations; for example, columns and capitals were later used by the ancient Greeks (see pp. 460-461) and ancient Romans (see pp. 462-465).

Cornice decorated with cavetto moulding

Campaniform (open papyrus) capital

Architrave

Papyrus-bud capital

Socle

Side aisle

Central nave

Side aisle

Horus, the sun-god

Architrave

Stone slab forming flat roof of side aisle

SIDE VIEW OF HYPOSTYLE HALL, TEMPLE OF AMON-RE, KARNAK, EGYPT, c.1290 BC

Kepresh crown with disc

Chons, the moon-god

Amon-Re, king of the gods

Hathor, the sky-goddess

Papyrus motif

Cartouche (oval border) containing the titles of the Pharaoh (king)

Socle

Aisle running north-south

LIMESTONE FALSE DOOR WITH HIEROGLYPHS, TOMB OF KING TJETJI, GIZA, EGYPT, c.2400 BC

Hieroglyph representing a house

Lintel

Disc representing sun or light

Eroded image of Tjetji

Limestone stela (slab)

Hoe-shaped hieroglyph representing "mr" sound

Head of false door

Image of Tjetji's wife

Image of Tjetji's daughter

PLANT CAPITAL OF THE PTOLEMAIC-ROMAN PERIOD, EGYPT, 332-30 BC

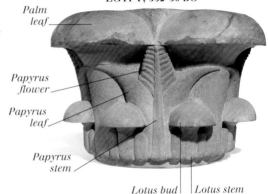

Palm leaf

Papyrus flower

Papyrus leaf

Papyrus stem

Lotus bud   *Lotus stem*

Cornice decorated with cavetto moulding

Bead moulding

Trellis window

Rectangular pier decorated with hieroglyphs

Elevated roof of central nave

Clerestory

Disc representing sun or light

Architrave

Square abacus

Papyrus-bud capital

Papyriform column

Shaft

Scene depicting a Pharaoh (king) paying homage to the god Amon-Re

Central nave

ANCIENT EGYPTIAN BUILDING DECORATION

DECORATED WINDOW, MEDINET HABU, EGYPT, C.1198 BC

ROPE AND PATERAE DECORATION

CAPITAL WITH THE HEAD OF THE SKY-GODDESS HATHOR, TEMPLE OF ISIS, PHILAE, EGYPT, 285-47 BC

LOTUS AND PAPYRUS FRIEZE DECORATION

Ancient Greece

THE CLASSICAL TEMPLES OF ANCIENT GREECE were built according to the belief that certain forms and proportions were pleasing to the gods. There were three main ancient Greek architectural orders (styles), which can be distinguished by the decoration and proportions of their columns, capitals (column tops), and entablatures (structures resting on the capitals). The oldest is the Doric order, which dates from the seventh century BC and was used mainly on the Greek mainland and in the western colonies, such as Sicily and southern Italy. The Temple of Neptune, shown here, is a classic example of this order. It is hypaethral (roofless) and peripteral (surrounded by a single row of columns). About a century later, the more decorative Ionic order developed on the Aegean Islands. Features of this order include volutes (spiral scrolls) on capitals and acroteria (pediment ornaments). The Corinthian order was invented in Athens in the fifth century BC and is typically identified by an acanthus leaf on the capitals. This order was later widely used in ancient Roman architecture.

CAPITALS OF THE THREE ORDERS OF ANCIENT GREEK ARCHITECTURE

DORIC CAPITAL, THE PROPYLAEUM (GATEWAY), THE ACROPOLIS, ATHENS, GREECE, 449 BC

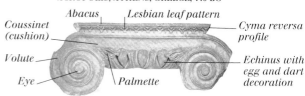

IONIC CAPITAL, THE PROPYLAEUM (GATEWAY), TEMPLE OF ATHENA POLIAS, PRIENE, GREECE, c.334 BC

CORINTHIAN CAPITAL FROM A STOA (PORTICO), PROBABLY FROM ASIA MINOR

TEMPLE OF NEPTUNE, PAESTUM, ITALY, c.460 BC

PLAN OF THE TEMPLE OF NEPTUNE, PAESTUM

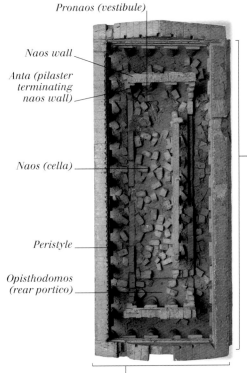

Pronaos (vestibule)

Naos wall

Anta (pilaster terminating naos wall)

Naos (cella)

Peristyle

Opisthodomos (rear portico)

Pteron (external colonnade)

Hexastyle pteron (colonnade of six columns)

ANCIENT GREEK BUILDING DECORATION

Volute

FACADE, TREASURY OF ATREUS, MYCENAE, GREECE, 1350-1250 BC

Meander

FRETWORK, PARTHENON, ATHENS, GREECE, 447-436 BC

ACROTERION, TEMPLE OF APHAIA, AEGINA, GREECE, 490 BC

Griffon (gryphon)

Raking cornice

ANTEFIXA, TEMPLE OF APHAIA, AEGINA, GREECE, 490 BC

Palmette

Volute

Regula (short fillet beneath taenia)

Eaves

Cornice

Frieze

Architrave

Capital

Shaft

Crepidoma (stepped base)

Entasis (slight curve of a column)

Intercolumniation

Fluting

Ancient Rome 1

IN THE EARLY PERIOD OF THE ROMAN EMPIRE extensive use was made of ancient Greek architectural ideas, particularly those of the Corinthian order (see pp. 460-461). As a result, many early Roman buildings – such as the Temple of Vesta (opposite) – closely resemble ancient Greek buildings. A distinctive Roman style began to evolve in the first century AD. This style developed the interiors of buildings (the Greeks had concentrated on the exterior) by using arches, vaults, and domes inside the buildings, and by ornamenting internal walls. Many of these features can be seen in the Pantheon. Exterior columns were often used for decorative, rather than structural, purposes, as in the Colosseum and the Porta Nigra (see pp. 464-465). Smaller buildings had timber frames with wattle-and-daub walls, as in the mill (see pp. 464-465). Roman architecture remained influential for many centuries, with some of its principles being used in the 11th century in Romanesque buildings (see pp. 468-469) and also in the 15th and 16th centuries in Renaissance buildings (see pp. 474-477).

FESTOON, TEMPLE OF VESTA, TIVOLI, ITALY, C.80 BC

RICHLY DECORATED ROMAN OVUM

INTERIOR OF THE PANTHEON, ROME, ITALY, 118-c.128

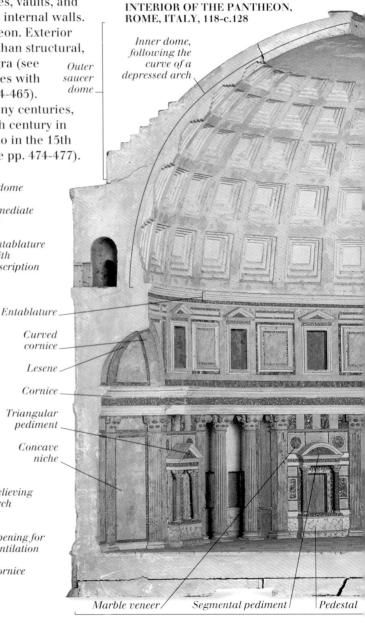

Inner dome, following the curve of a depressed arch

Outer saucer dome

Entablature

Curved cornice

Lesene

Cornice

Triangular pediment

Concave niche

Relieving arch

Opening for ventilation

Cornice

Marble veneer / Segmental pediment / Pedestal

FRONT VIEW OF THE PANTHEON

Oculus

Series of concentric, step-like rings

Outer saucer dome

Intermediate block

Dentil ornament

Engaged pediment

Entablature with inscription

Raking cornice

Pediment

Rotunda

Octastyle portico (eight-column portico)

SIDE VIEW OF THE PANTHEON

Entablature

Intermediate block

Upper cornice

Pitched roof

Eaves

Colonnade

Ornamental band decorated with festoons

Attached fluted pilaster

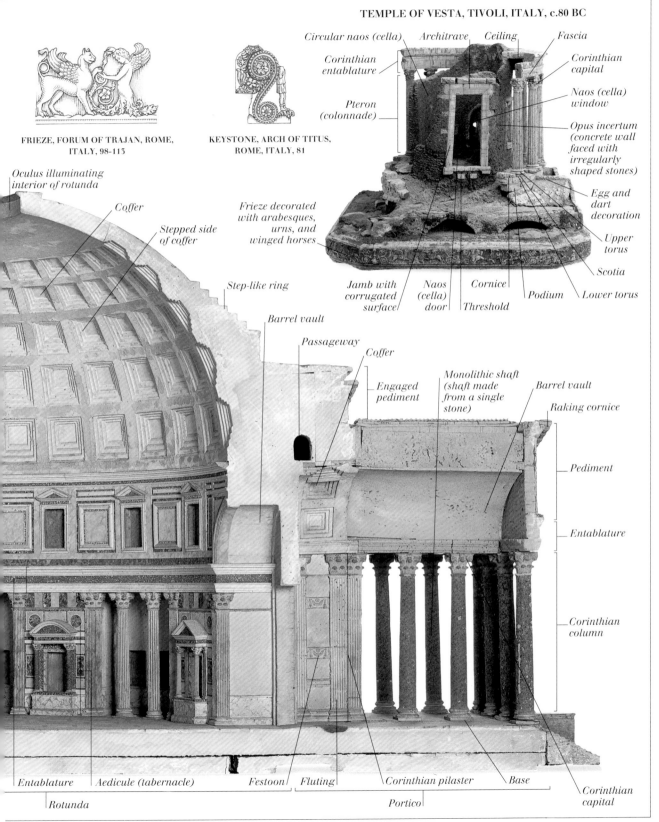

FRIEZE, FORUM OF TRAJAN, ROME, ITALY, 98-115

KEYSTONE, ARCH OF TITUS, ROME, ITALY, 81

TEMPLE OF VESTA, TIVOLI, ITALY, c.80 BC

Circular naos (cella)

Architrave

Ceiling

Fascia

Corinthian entablature

Corinthian capital

Pteron (colonnade)

Naos (cella) window

Opus incertum (concrete wall faced with irregularly shaped stones)

Egg and dart decoration

Upper torus

Scotia

Jamb with corrugated surface

Naos (cella) door

Cornice

Podium

Lower torus

Threshold

Oculus illuminating interior of rotunda

Coffer

Stepped side of coffer

Frieze decorated with arabesques, urns, and winged horses

Step-like ring

Barrel vault

Passageway

Coffer

Engaged pediment

Monolithic shaft (shaft made from a single stone)

Barrel vault

Raking cornice

Pediment

Entablature

Corinthian column

Entablature

Aedicule (tabernacle)

Festoon

Fluting

Corinthian pilaster

Base

Corinthian capital

Rotunda

Portico

Ancient Rome 2

SIDE VIEW OF A ROMAN MILL

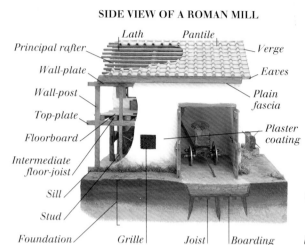

Principal rafter
Lath
Pantile
Verge
Wall-plate
Eaves
Wall-post
Plain fascia
Top-plate
Floorboard
Plaster coating
Intermediate floor-joist
Sill
Stud
Foundation
Grille
Joist
Boarding

FRONT VIEW OF A ROMAN MILL, 1ST CENTURY BC

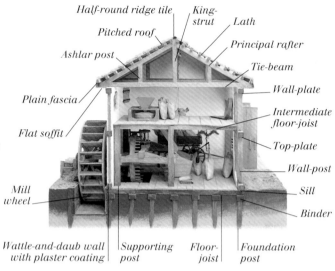

Half-round ridge tile
King-strut
Lath
Pitched roof
Principal rafter
Ashlar post
Tie-beam
Plain fascia
Wall-plate
Flat soffit
Intermediate floor-joist
Top-plate
Wall-post
Sill
Mill wheel
Binder
Wattle-and-daub wall with plaster coating
Supporting post
Floor-joist
Foundation post

THE COLOSSEUM (FLAVIAN AMPHITHEATRE), ROME, ITALY, 70-82

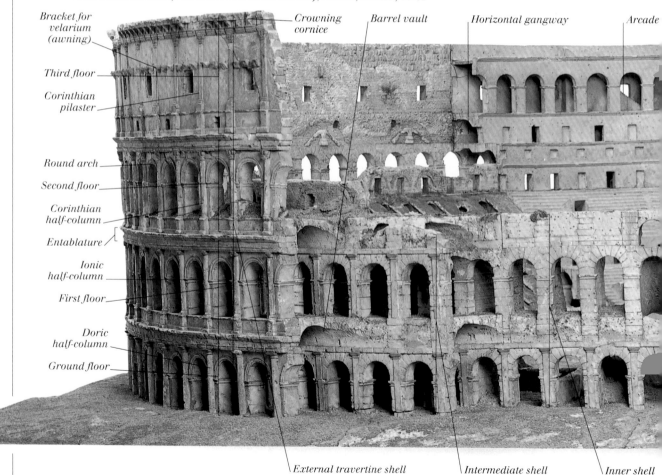

Bracket for velarium (awning)
Crowning cornice
Barrel vault
Horizontal gangway
Arcade
Third floor
Corinthian pilaster
Round arch
Second floor
Corinthian half-column
Entablature
Ionic half-column
First floor
Doric half-column
Ground floor
External travertine shell
Intermediate shell
Inner shell

PORTA NIGRA, TRIER, GERMANY, c.240-260

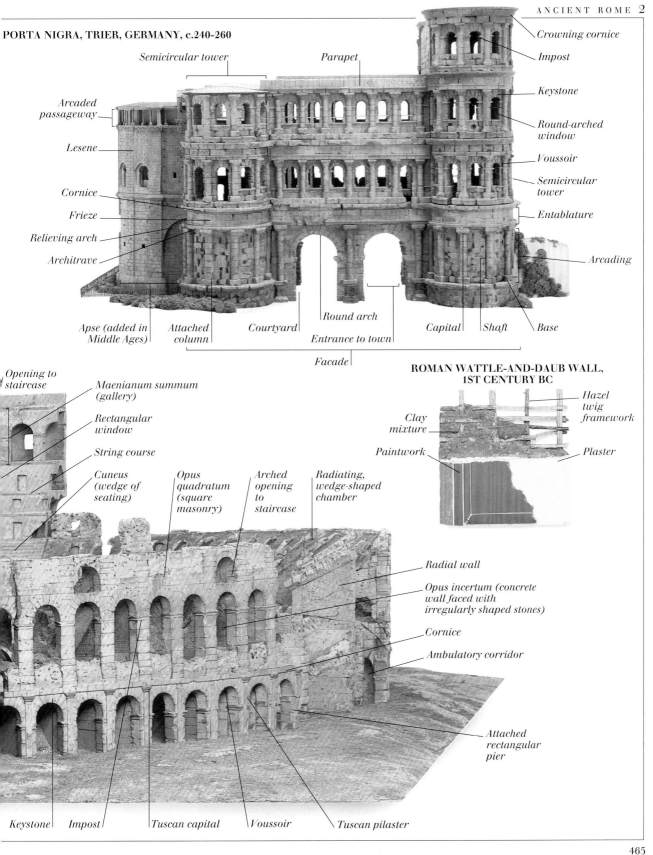

Crowning cornice

Impost

Semicircular tower

Parapet

Keystone

Arcaded passageway

Round-arched window

Lesene

Voussoir

Semicircular tower

Cornice

Entablature

Frieze

Relieving arch

Architrave

Arcading

Apse (added in Middle Ages)

Attached column

Courtyard

Round arch

Entrance to town

Capital

Shaft

Base

Facade

ROMAN WATTLE-AND-DAUB WALL, 1ST CENTURY BC

Opening to staircase

Maenianum summum (gallery)

Hazel twig framework

Rectangular window

Clay mixture

String course

Paintwork

Plaster

Cuneus (wedge of seating)

Opus quadratum (square masonry)

Arched opening to staircase

Radiating, wedge-shaped chamber

Radial wall

Opus incertum (concrete wall faced with irregularly shaped stones)

Cornice

Ambulatory corridor

Attached rectangular pier

Keystone

Impost

Tuscan capital

Voussoir

Tuscan pilaster

Medieval castles and houses

WARFARE WAS COMMON IN EUROPE in the Middle Ages, and many monarchs and nobles built castles as a form of defence. Typical medieval castles have outer walls surrounding a moat. Inside the moat is a bailey (courtyard), protected by a chemise (jacket-wall). The innermost and strongest part of a medieval castle is the keep. There are two main types of keep: towers called donjons, such as the Tour de César and Coucy-le-Château, and rectangular keeps ("hall-keeps"), such as the Tower of London. Castles were often guarded by salients (projecting fortifications), like those of the Bastille. Medieval houses typically had timber cruck (tent-like) frames, wattle-and-daub walls, and pitched roofs, like those on medieval London Bridge (opposite).

DONJON, TOUR DE CESAR, PROVINS, FRANCE, 12TH CENTURY

Oculus
Loophole
Conical spire
Flying buttress
Hexahedral hall
Semicircular turret
Fireplace
Bailey
Embrasure
Chemise (jacket-wall)
Plain impost
Battlements (crenellations)
Hemispherical cupola
Gallery
Squinch
Vaulted room
Main entrance
Staircase to chemise (jacket-wall)
Depressed cupola
Vaulted staircase
Motte

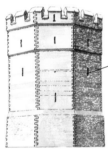

Loophole

SALIENT, CAERNARVON CASTLE, BRITAIN, 1283-1323

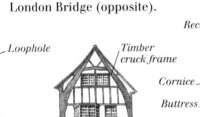

Timber cruck frame

CRUCK-FRAMED HOUSE, BRITAIN, c.1200

Blind, rounded relieving arch
Tetrahedral spire
Rectangular turret
Quoin
Cornice
Buttress
Round-arched window with twin openings
Merlon
Crenel
Battlements (crenellations)
Loophole
Wooden staircase leading to entrance above ground level
Timber-framed house
Cruck frame
Paling

TOWER OF LONDON, BRITAIN, FROM 1070

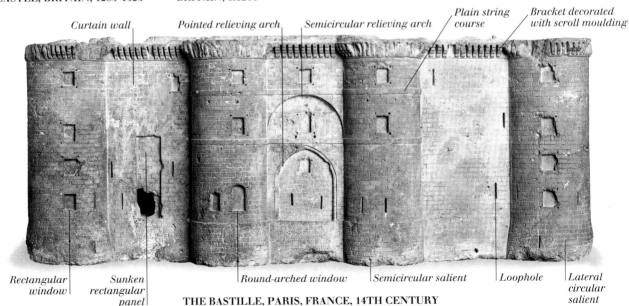

Curtain wall
Pointed relieving arch
Semicircular relieving arch
Plain string course
Bracket decorated with scroll moulding

Rectangular window
Sunken rectangular panel
Round-arched window
Semicircular salient
Loophole
Lateral circular salient

THE BASTILLE, PARIS, FRANCE, 14TH CENTURY

MEDIEVAL LONDON BRIDGE, BRITAIN, 1176 (WITH 14TH-CENTURY BATTLEMENTED BUILDING, NONESUCH HOUSE, AND TWO-TOWERED GATE)

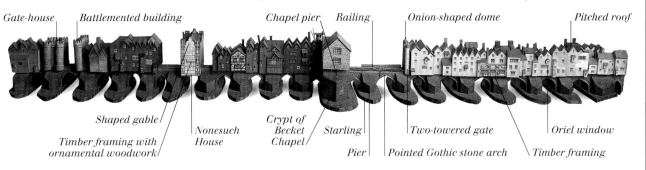

Gate-house
Battlemented building
Chapel pier
Railing
Onion-shaped dome
Pitched roof

Shaped gable
Nonesuch House
Crypt of Becket Chapel
Starling
Two-towered gate
Oriel window

Timber framing with ornamental woodwork
Pier
Pointed Gothic stone arch
Timber framing

DONJON, COUCY-LE-CHATEAU, AISNE, FRANCE, 1225-1245

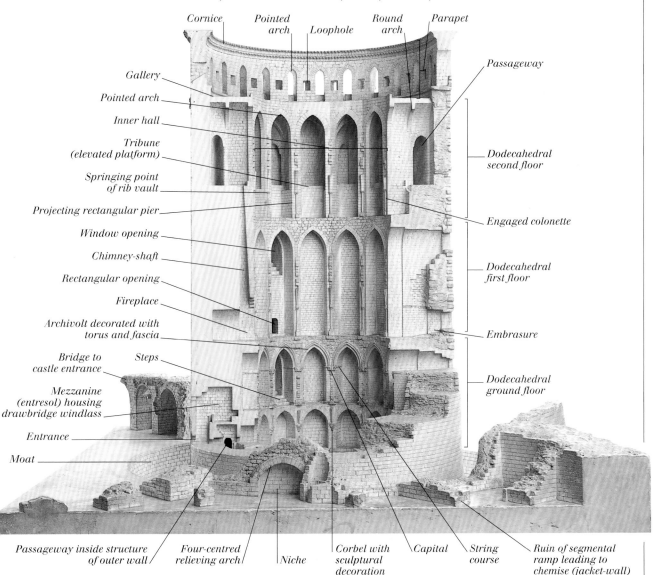

Cornice
Pointed arch
Loophole
Round arch
Parapet

Gallery
Passageway

Pointed arch
Inner hall
Tribune (elevated platform)
Springing point of rib vault
Projecting rectangular pier
Dodecahedral second floor

Engaged colonette

Window opening
Chimney-shaft
Rectangular opening
Fireplace
Dodecahedral first floor

Archivolt decorated with torus and fascia
Embrasure

Bridge to castle entrance
Steps
Dodecahedral ground floor

Mezzanine (entresol) housing drawbridge windlass

Entrance

Moat

Passageway inside structure of outer wall
Four-centred relieving arch
Niche
Corbel with sculptural decoration
Capital
String course
Ruin of segmental ramp leading to chemise (jacket-wall)

Medieval churches

DURING THE MIDDLE AGES, large numbers of churches were built in Europe. European churches of this period typically have high vaults supported by massive piers and columns. In the 10th century, the Romanesque style developed. Romanesque architects adopted many Roman or early Christian architectural ideas, such as cross-shaped ground-plans – like that of Angoulême Cathedral (opposite) – and the basilican system of a nave with a central vessel and side aisles. In the mid-12th century, flying buttresses and pointed vaults appeared. These features later became widely used in Gothic architecture (see pp. 470-471). Bagneux Church (opposite) has both styles: a Romanesque tower, and a Gothic nave and choir.

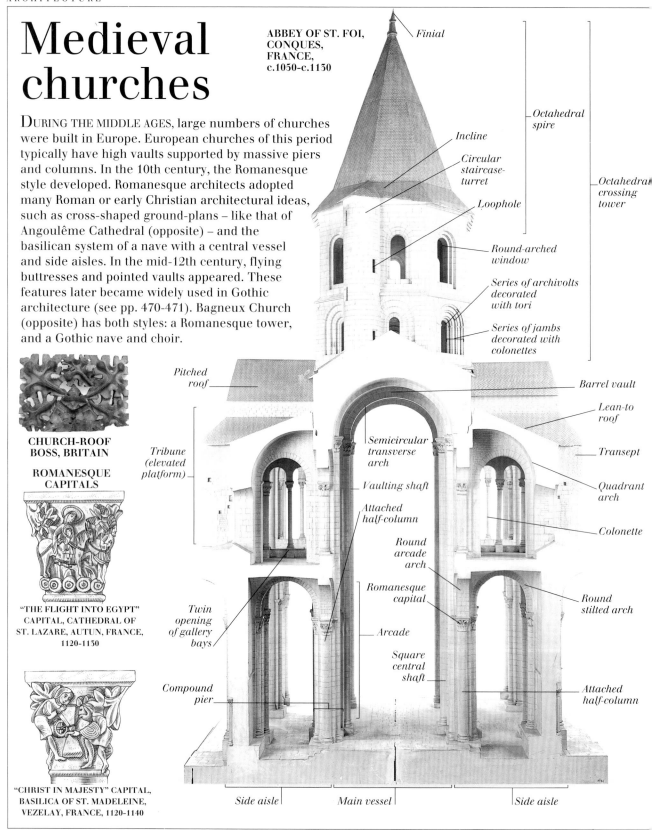

CHURCH-ROOF BOSS, BRITAIN

ROMANESQUE CAPITALS

"THE FLIGHT INTO EGYPT" CAPITAL, CATHEDRAL OF ST. LAZARE, AUTUN, FRANCE, 1120-1130

"CHRIST IN MAJESTY" CAPITAL, BASILICA OF ST. MADELEINE, VEZELAY, FRANCE, 1120-1140

Finial

Octahedral spire

Incline

Circular staircase-turret

Loophole

Octahedral crossing tower

Round-arched window

Series of archivolts decorated with tori

Series of jambs decorated with colonettes

Pitched roof

Barrel vault

Lean-to roof

Tribune (elevated platform)

Semicircular transverse arch

Transept

Vaulting shaft

Quadrant arch

Attached half-column

Colonette

Round arcade arch

Romanesque capital

Round stilted arch

Arcade

Twin opening of gallery bays

Compound pier

Square central shaft

Attached half-column

Side aisle

Main vessel

Side aisle

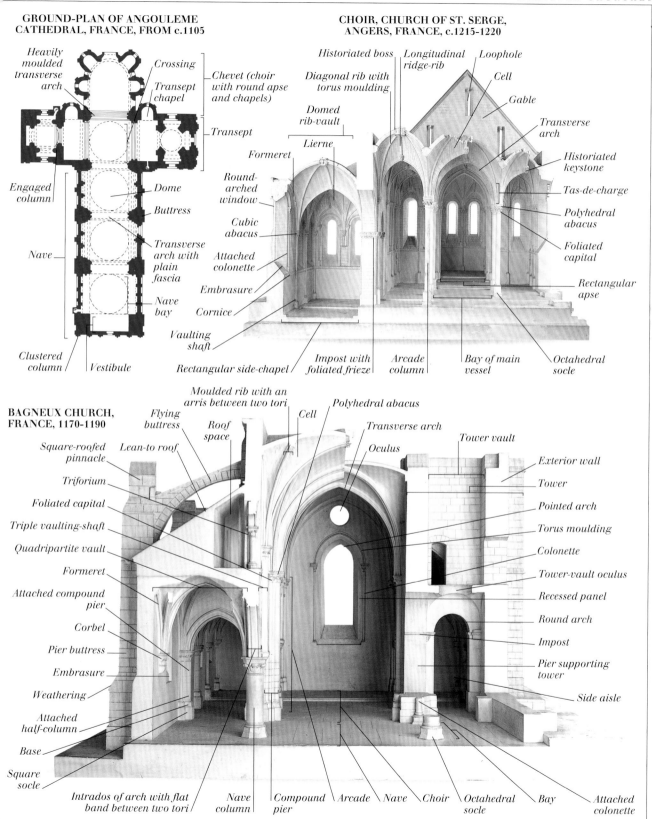

GROUND-PLAN OF ANGOULEME CATHEDRAL, FRANCE, FROM c.1105

Heavily moulded transverse arch

Crossing

Transept chapel

Chevet (choir with round apse and chapels)

Transept

Engaged column

Dome

Buttress

Transverse arch with plain fascia

Nave

Nave bay

Clustered column

Vestibule

CHOIR, CHURCH OF ST. SERGE, ANGERS, FRANCE, c.1215-1220

Historiated boss

Longitudinal ridge-rib

Loophole

Cell

Diagonal rib with torus moulding

Gable

Domed rib-vault

Transverse arch

Lierne

Formeret

Historiated keystone

Round-arched window

Tas-de-charge

Cubic abacus

Polyhedral abacus

Attached colonette

Foliated capital

Embrasure

Rectangular apse

Cornice

Vaulting shaft

Rectangular side-chapel

Impost with foliated frieze

Arcade column

Bay of main vessel

Octahedral socle

BAGNEUX CHURCH, FRANCE, 1170-1190

Moulded rib with an arris between two tori

Flying buttress

Roof space

Cell

Polyhedral abacus

Transverse arch

Tower vault

Square-roofed pinnacle

Lean-to roof

Oculus

Exterior wall

Triforium

Tower

Foliated capital

Pointed arch

Triple vaulting-shaft

Torus moulding

Quadripartite vault

Colonette

Formeret

Tower-vault oculus

Attached compound pier

Recessed panel

Corbel

Round arch

Pier buttress

Impost

Embrasure

Pier supporting tower

Weathering

Side aisle

Attached half-column

Base

Square socle

Intrados of arch with flat band between two tori

Nave column

Compound pier

Arcade

Nave

Choir

Octahedral socle

Bay

Attached colonette

Gothic 1

GOTHIC STAINED
GLASS WITH FOLIATED
SCROLL MOTIF, ON
WOODEN FORM

GOTHIC BUILDINGS are characterized by rib vaults, pointed or lancet arches, flying buttresses, decorative tracery and gables, and stained-glass windows. Typical Gothic buildings include the Cathedrals of Salisbury and old St. Paul's in England, and Notre Dame de Paris in France (see pp. 472-473). The Gothic style developed out of Romanesque architecture in France (see pp. 468-469) in the mid-12th century, and then spread throughout Europe. The decorative elements of Gothic architecture became highly developed in buildings of the English Decorated style (late 13th-14th century) and the French Flamboyant style (15th-16th century). These styles are exemplified by the tower of Salisbury Cathedral and the staircase in the Church of St. Maclou (see pp. 472-473), respectively. In both of these styles, embellishments such as ballflowers and curvilinear (flowing) tracery were used liberally. The English Perpendicular style (late 14th-15th century), which followed the Decorated style, emphasized the vertical and horizontal elements of a building. A notable feature of this style is the hammer-beam roof.

GROUND-PLAN OF SALISBURY CATHEDRAL

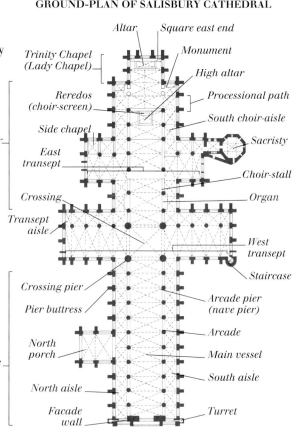

Altar
Square east end
Trinity Chapel (Lady Chapel)
Monument
High altar
Reredos (choir-screen)
Processional path
Side chapel
South choir-aisle
Choir
Sacristy
East transept
Choir-stall
Crossing
Organ
Transept aisle
West transept
Staircase
Crossing pier
Arcade pier (nave pier)
Pier buttress
Arcade
North porch
Main vessel
Nave
South aisle
North aisle
Facade wall
Turret

GOTHIC TORUS WITH BALLFLOWERS

Limestone block

Block members carved into rolls

Block members cut polygonally

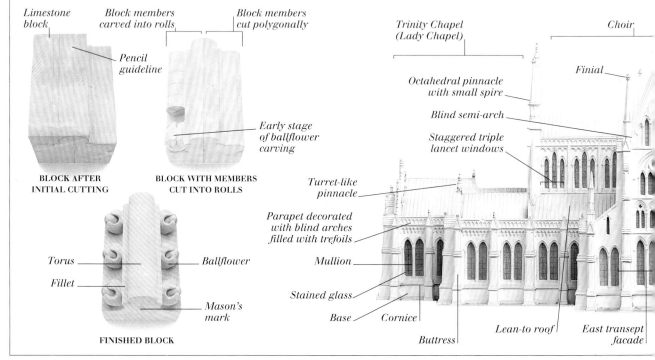

Pencil guideline

Early stage of ballflower carving

BLOCK AFTER INITIAL CUTTING

BLOCK WITH MEMBERS CUT INTO ROLLS

Torus
Ballflower
Fillet
Mason's mark

FINISHED BLOCK

Trinity Chapel (Lady Chapel)

Choir

Octahedral pinnacle with small spire

Finial

Blind semi-arch

Staggered triple lancet windows

Turret-like pinnacle

Parapet decorated with blind arches filled with trefoils

Mullion

Stained glass

Base
Cornice

Buttress

Lean-to roof

East transept facade

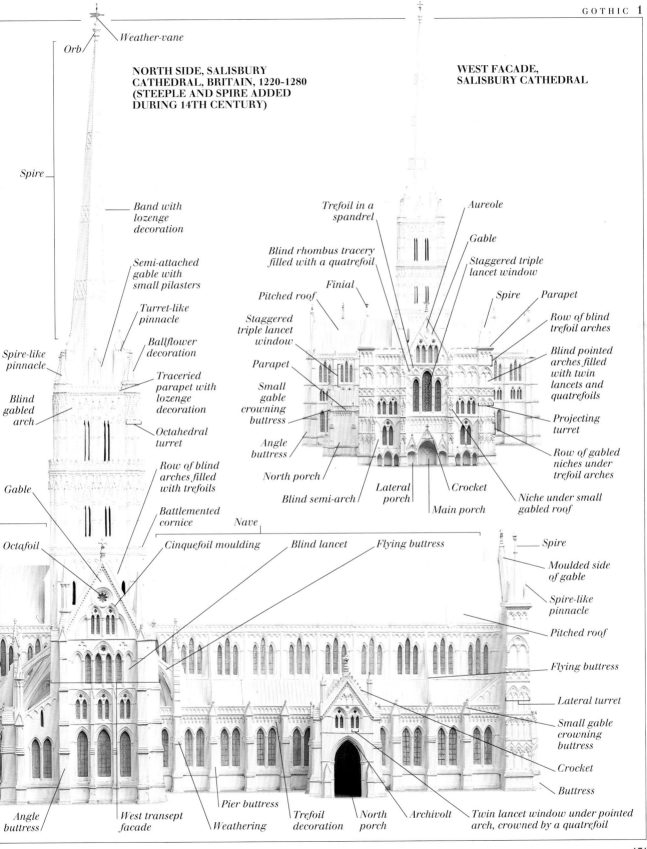

Weather-vane

Orb

**NORTH SIDE, SALISBURY
CATHEDRAL, BRITAIN, 1220–1280
(STEEPLE AND SPIRE ADDED
DURING 14TH CENTURY)**

**WEST FACADE,
SALISBURY CATHEDRAL**

Spire

Band with
lozenge
decoration

Semi-attached
gable with
small pilasters

Turret-like
pinnacle

Ballflower
decoration

Spire-like
pinnacle

Traceried
parapet with
lozenge
decoration

Octahedral
turret

Blind
gabled
arch

Gable

Row of blind
arches filled
with trefoils

Octafoil

Battlemented
cornice

Cinquefoil moulding

Trefoil in a
spandrel

Aureole

Gable

Blind rhombus tracery
filled with a quatrefoil

Staggered triple
lancet window

Finial

Pitched roof

Spire

Parapet

Staggered
triple lancet
window

Row of blind
trefoil arches

Parapet

Blind pointed
arches filled
with twin
lancets and
quatrefoils

Small
gable
crowning
buttress

Angle
buttress

Projecting
turret

North porch

Blind semi-arch

Lateral
porch

Crocket

Row of gabled
niches under
trefoil arches

Main porch

Niche under small
gabled roof

Nave

Blind lancet

Flying buttress

Spire

Moulded side
of gable

Spire-like
pinnacle

Pitched roof

Flying buttress

Lateral turret

Small gable
crowning
buttress

Crocket

Buttress

Angle
buttress

West transept
facade

Pier buttress

Weathering

Trefoil
decoration

North
porch

Archivolt

Twin lancet window under pointed
arch, crowned by a quatrefoil

471

Gothic 2

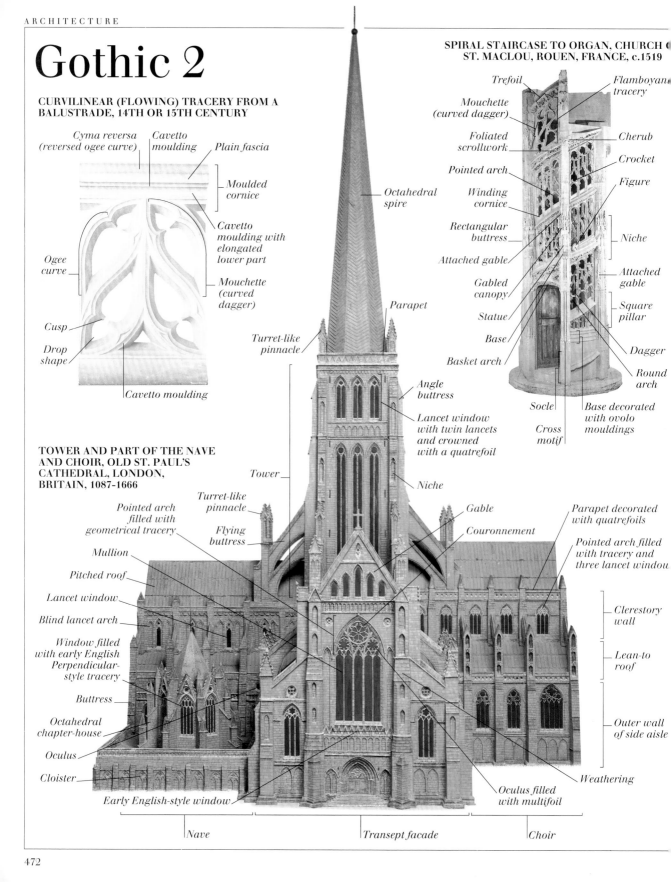

CURVILINEAR (FLOWING) TRACERY FROM A BALUSTRADE, 14TH OR 15TH CENTURY

Cyma reversa (reversed ogee curve)

Cavetto moulding

Plain fascia

Moulded cornice

Cavetto moulding with elongated lower part

Ogee curve

Mouchette (curved dagger)

Cusp

Drop shape

Cavetto moulding

TOWER AND PART OF THE NAVE AND CHOIR, OLD ST. PAUL'S CATHEDRAL, LONDON, BRITAIN, 1087-1666

Pointed arch filled with geometrical tracery

Mullion

Pitched roof

Lancet window

Blind lancet arch

Window filled with early English Perpendicular-style tracery

Buttress

Octahedral chapter-house

Oculus

Cloister

Early English-style window

Turret-like pinnacle

Flying buttress

Tower

Octahedral spire

Parapet

Turret-like pinnacle

Angle buttress

Lancet window with twin lancets and crowned with a quatrefoil

Niche

Gable

Couronnement

Oculus filled with multifoil

Weathering

Parapet decorated with quatrefoils

Pointed arch filled with tracery and three lancet window

Clerestory wall

Lean-to roof

Outer wall of side aisle

Nave

Transept facade

Choir

SPIRAL STAIRCASE TO ORGAN, CHURCH ST. MACLOU, ROUEN, FRANCE, c.1519

Trefoil

Mouchette (curved dagger)

Foliated scrollwork

Pointed arch

Winding cornice

Rectangular buttress

Attached gable

Gabled canopy

Statue

Base

Basket arch

Flamboyant tracery

Cherub

Crocket

Figure

Niche

Attached gable

Square pillar

Dagger

Round arch

Socle

Cross motif

Base decorated with ovolo mouldings

SPIRE AND TRANSEPT ROOF, CATHEDRAL OF NOTRE DAME DE PARIS, FRANCE, c.1163-1250

Ridge

Common rafter

Architrave of window zone, also acting as collar-beam

Principal

Attached baluster

Attached column

Strut

Raised surface

Hammer-post

Bevelled edge

Arched brace

Wooden panel

Hammer-beam

Gothic window tracery

Collar-beam decorated with pearl motif

Gothic window

Arched brace

Arched brace

Brace

Bracket

Impost

Rafter

Straight brace

Beam

Gable

Round arch

Pinnacle

Oculus

Blind trefoil

Lancet arch

Trefoil arch

Cusp

Quatrefoil

Colonette

Pointed arch

Lesene

Lancet arch

Balustrade

Mullion

Triangular cornice

Geometrical tracery

Cornice with chamfered edge

Trefoil arch

Balustrade

Stud

Upper collar

Scissor brace

Ridge-board

Principal rafter

Common rafter

Octahedral spire

Roof truss of nave and transept

TRUSS OF HAMMER-BEAM ROOF, THE UPPER FRATER (LATER BLACKFRIARS' PLAYHOUSE), LONDON, BRITAIN, PROBABLY 14TH CENTURY

TYPICAL GOTHIC FEATURES

FLYING BUTTRESS OVER SIDE AISLES, MILAN CATHEDRAL, ITALY, C.1385-1485

GARGOYLE, HORSLEY CHURCH, DERBYSHIRE, BRITAIN, C.1450

Vertical strut

Intermediate collar

Raised valley-rafter

Beam

Jack-rafter

Clasped purlin

Lower collar

Scissor-beam

King-post

Tie-beam

Queen-post

Passing brace

HAMMER-BEAM ROOF, CHURCH OF ST. BOTOLPH, TRUNCH, NORFOLK, BRITAIN, 1360-1380

Renaissance 1

THE RENAISSANCE was a European movement – lasting roughly from the 14th century to the mid-17th century – in which the arts and sciences underwent great changes. In architecture, these changes were marked by a return to the classical forms and proportions of ancient Roman buildings. The Renaissance originated in Italy, and the buildings most characteristic of its style can be found there, such as the Palazzo Strozzi shown here. Mannerism is a branch of the Renaissance style that distorts the classical forms; an example is the Laurentian Library staircase. As the Renaissance style spread to other European countries, many of its features were incorporated into the local architecture; for example, the Château de Montal in France (see pp. 476-477) incorporates aedicules (tabernacles).

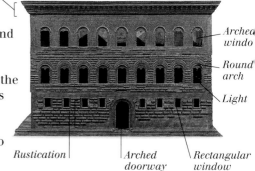

Crowning cornice

Arched window

Round arch

Light

Rustication

Arched doorway

Rectangular window

SIDE VIEW OF PALAZZO STROZZI, FLORENCE, ITALY, 1489 (BY G. DA SANGALLO, B. DA MAIANO, AND CRONACA)

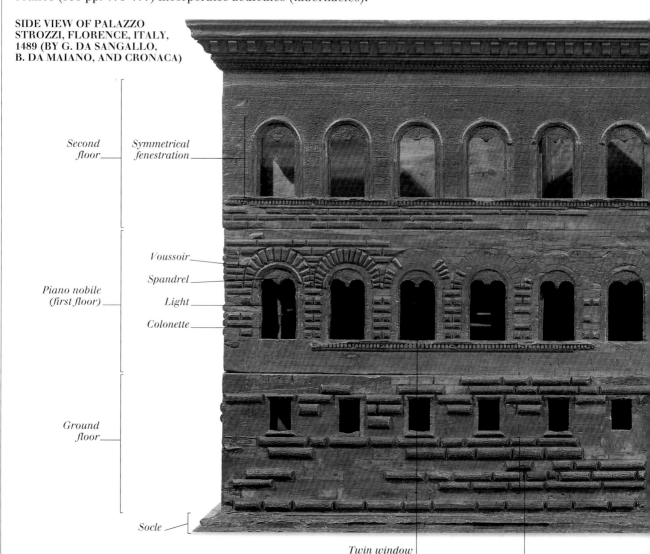

Second floor

Symmetrical fenestration

Voussoir

Spandrel

Light

Colonette

Piano nobile (first floor)

Ground floor

Socle

Twin window under round arch

Rustication

DETAILS FROM ITALIAN RENAISSANCE BUILDINGS

PANEL FROM DRUM OF DOME,
FLORENCE CATHEDRAL, 1420-1436

COFFERING IN DOME,
PAZZI CHAPEL,
FLORENCE, 1429-1461

STAIRCASE,
LAURENTIAN LIBRARY,
FLORENCE, 1559

PORTICO, VILLA ROTUNDA,
VICENZA, 1567-1569

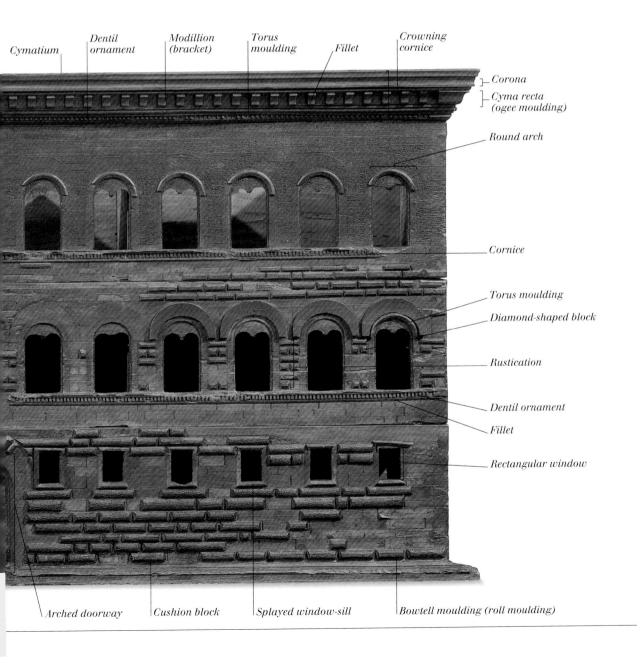

Cymatium

Dentil ornament

Modillion (bracket)

Torus moulding

Fillet

Crowning cornice

Corona

Cyma recta (ogee moulding)

Round arch

Cornice

Torus moulding

Diamond-shaped block

Rustication

Dentil ornament

Fillet

Rectangular window

Arched doorway

Cushion block

Splayed window-sill

Bowtell moulding (roll moulding)

Renaissance 2

**DETAILS FROM
EUROPEAN
RENAISSANCE
BUILDINGS**

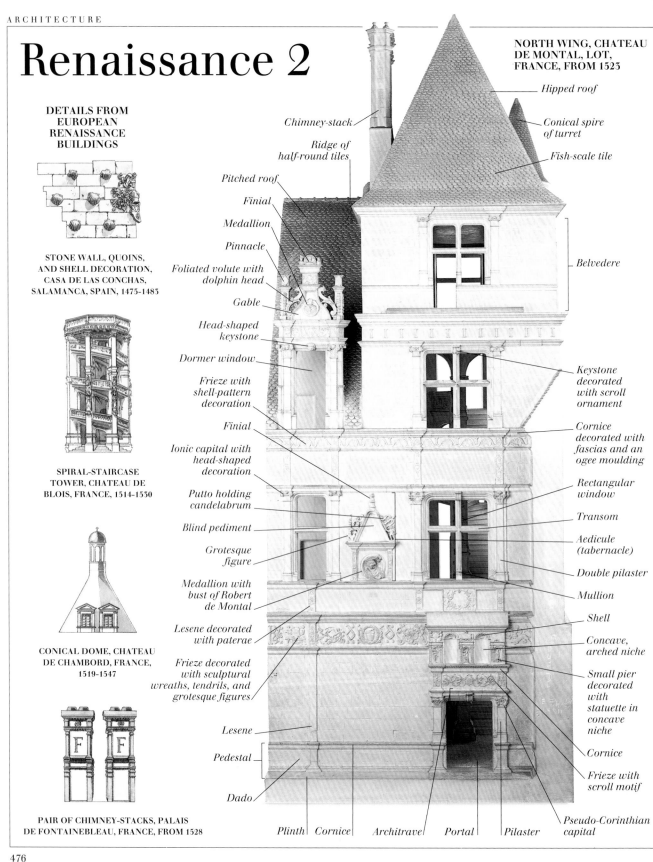

STONE WALL, QUOINS,
AND SHELL DECORATION,
CASA DE LAS CONCHAS,
SALAMANCA, SPAIN, 1475-1483

SPIRAL-STAIRCASE
TOWER, CHATEAU DE
BLOIS, FRANCE, 1514-1530

CONICAL DOME, CHATEAU
DE CHAMBORD, FRANCE,
1519-1547

PAIR OF CHIMNEY-STACKS, PALAIS
DE FONTAINEBLEAU, FRANCE, FROM 1528

Chimney-stack

Ridge of
half-round tiles

Pitched roof

Finial

Medallion

Pinnacle

Foliated volute with
dolphin head

Gable

Head-shaped
keystone

Dormer window

Frieze with
shell-pattern
decoration

Finial

Ionic capital with
head-shaped
decoration

Putto holding
candelabrum

Blind pediment

Grotesque
figure

Medallion with
bust of Robert
de Montal

Lesene decorated
with paterae

Frieze decorated
with sculptural
wreaths, tendrils, and
grotesque figures

Lesene

Pedestal

Dado

Hipped roof

Conical spire
of turret

Fish-scale tile

Belvedere

Keystone
decorated
with scroll
ornament

Cornice
decorated with
fascias and an
ogee moulding

Rectangular
window

Transom

Aedicule
(tabernacle)

Double pilaster

Mullion

Shell

Concave,
arched niche

Small pier
decorated
with
statuette in
concave
niche

Cornice

Frieze with
scroll motif

Pseudo-Corinthian
capital

Plinth   Cornice   Architrave   Portal   Pilaster

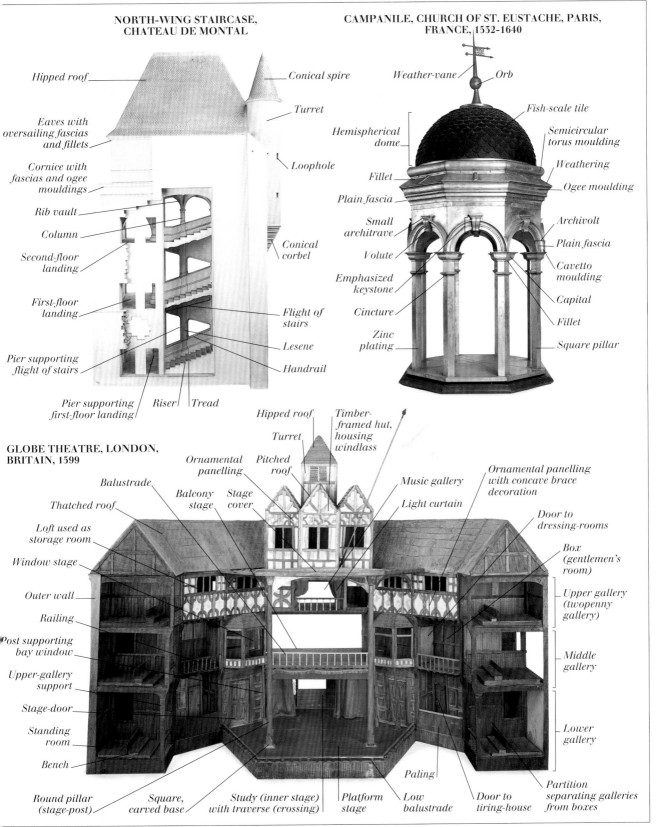

NORTH-WING STAIRCASE, CHATEAU DE MONTAL

Hipped roof

Eaves with oversailing fascias and fillets

Cornice with fascias and ogee mouldings

Rib vault

Column

Second-floor landing

First-floor landing

Pier supporting flight of stairs

Pier supporting first-floor landing

Riser

Tread

Conical spire

Turret

Loophole

Conical corbel

Flight of stairs

Lesene

Handrail

CAMPANILE, CHURCH OF ST. EUSTACHE, PARIS, FRANCE, 1552-1640

Weather-vane

Orb

Hemispherical dome

Fillet

Plain fascia

Small architrave

Volute

Emphasized keystone

Cincture

Zinc plating

Fish-scale tile

Semicircular torus moulding

Weathering

Ogee moulding

Archivolt

Plain fascia

Cavetto moulding

Capital

Fillet

Square pillar

GLOBE THEATRE, LONDON, BRITAIN, 1599

Balustrade

Thatched roof

Loft used as storage room

Window stage

Outer wall

Railing

Post supporting bay window

Upper-gallery support

Stage-door

Standing room

Bench

Round pillar (stage-post)

Square, carved base

Ornamental panelling

Balcony stage

Stage cover

Pitched roof

Hipped roof

Turret

Timber-framed hut, housing windlass

Music gallery

Light curtain

Ornamental panelling with concave brace decoration

Door to dressing-rooms

Box (gentlemen's room)

Upper gallery (twopenny gallery)

Middle gallery

Lower gallery

Partition separating galleries from boxes

Study (inner stage) with traverse (crossing)

Platform stage

Low balustrade

Paling

Door to tiring-house

Baroque and neoclassical 1

THE BAROQUE STYLE EVOLVED IN THE EARLY 17TH CENTURY in Rome. It is characterized by curved outlines and ostentatious decoration, as can be seen in the Italian church details (right). The baroque style was particularly widely favoured in Italy, Spain, and Germany. It was also adopted in Britain and France, but with adaptations. The British architects Sir Christopher Wren and Nicholas Hawksmoor, for example, used baroque features – such as the concave walls of St. Paul's Cathedral and the curved buttresses of the Church of St. George in the East (see pp. 480-481) – but they did so with restraint. Similarly, the curved buttresses and volutes of the Parisian Church of St. Paul-St. Louis are relatively plain. In the second half of the 17th century, a distinct classical style (known as neoclassicism) developed in northern Europe as a reaction to the excesses of baroque. Typical of this new style were churches such as the Madeleine (a proposed facade is shown below), as well as secular buildings such as the Cirque Napoleon (opposite) and the buildings of the British architect Sir John Soane (see pp. 482-483). In early 18th-century France, an extremely lavish form of baroque developed, known as rococo. The balcony from Nantes (see pp. 482-483) with its twisted ironwork and head-shaped corbels is typical of this style.

SCROLLED BUTTRESS, CHURCH OF ST. MARIA DELLA SALUTE, VENICE, 1631-1682

STATUE OF THE ECSTASY OF ST. THERESA, CHURCH OF ST. MARIA DELLA VITTORIA, ROME, 1645-1652

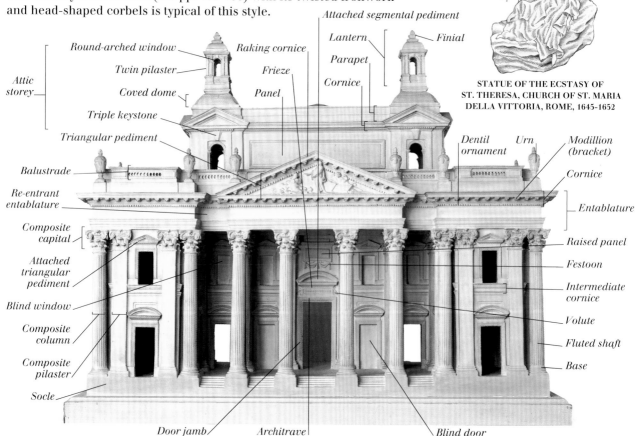

PROPOSED FACADE, THE MADELEINE (NEOCLASSICAL), PARIS, FRANCE, 1764 (BY P. CONTANT D'IVRY)

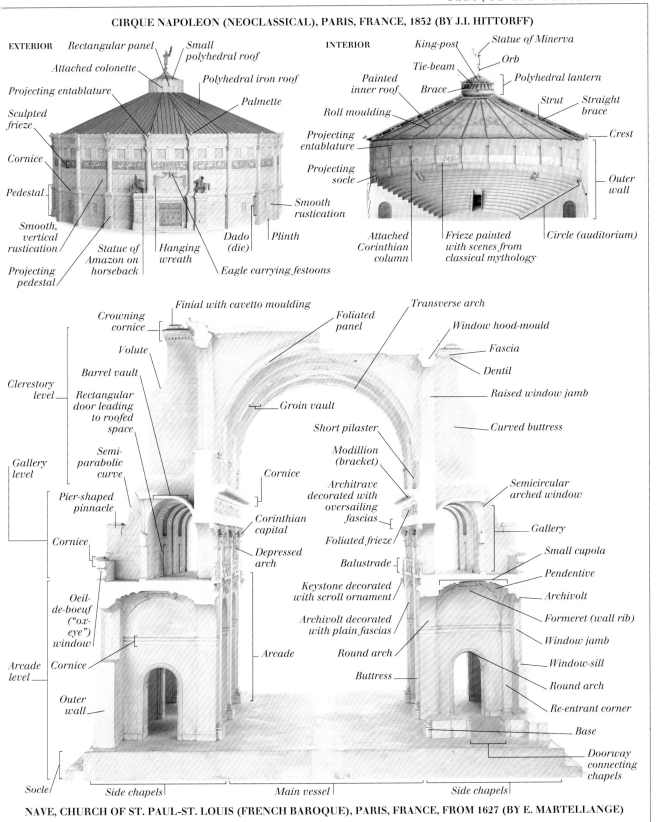

CIRQUE NAPOLEON (NEOCLASSICAL), PARIS, FRANCE, 1852 (BY J.I. HITTORFF)

EXTERIOR

- Rectangular panel
- Small polyhedral roof
- Attached colonette
- Polyhedral iron roof
- Projecting entablature
- Palmette
- Sculpted frieze
- Cornice
- Pedestal
- Smooth rustication
- Smooth, vertical rustication
- Statue of Amazon on horseback
- Hanging wreath
- Dado (die)
- Plinth
- Projecting pedestal
- Eagle carrying festoons

INTERIOR

- King-post
- Statue of Minerva
- Tie-beam
- Orb
- Painted inner roof
- Polyhedral lantern
- Brace
- Strut
- Straight brace
- Roll moulding
- Crest
- Projecting entablature
- Projecting socle
- Outer wall
- Attached Corinthian column
- Frieze painted with scenes from classical mythology
- Circle (auditorium)

- Finial with cavetto moulding
- Transverse arch
- Crowning cornice
- Foliated panel
- Window hood-mould
- Volute
- Fascia
- Barrel vault
- Dentil
- Clerestory level
- Rectangular door leading to roofed space
- Groin vault
- Raised window jamb
- Short pilaster
- Curved buttress
- Semi-parabolic curve
- Modillion (bracket)
- Cornice
- Gallery level
- Architrave decorated with oversailing fascias
- Semicircular arched window
- Pier-shaped pinnacle
- Corinthian capital
- Foliated frieze
- Gallery
- Cornice
- Depressed arch
- Small cupola
- Balustrade
- Pendentive
- Oeil-de-boeuf ("ox-eye") window
- Keystone decorated with scroll ornament
- Archivolt
- Formeret (wall rib)
- Archivolt decorated with plain fascias
- Window jamb
- Cornice
- Arcade
- Round arch
- Window-sill
- Arcade level
- Buttress
- Round arch
- Outer wall
- Re-entrant corner
- Base
- Doorway connecting chapels
- Socle
- Side chapels
- Main vessel
- Side chapels

NAVE, CHURCH OF ST. PAUL-ST. LOUIS (FRENCH BAROQUE), PARIS, FRANCE, FROM 1627 (BY E. MARTELLANGE)

Baroque and neoclassical 2

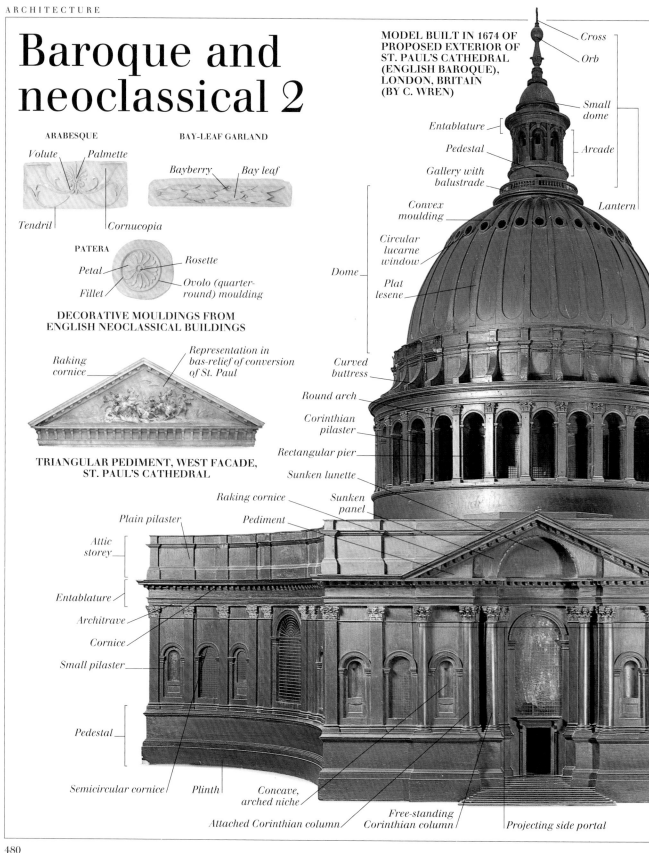

ARABESQUE

Volute
Palmette
Tendril
Cornucopia

BAY-LEAF GARLAND

Bayberry
Bay leaf

PATERA

Petal
Fillet
Rosette
Ovolo (quarter-round) moulding

DECORATIVE MOULDINGS FROM ENGLISH NEOCLASSICAL BUILDINGS

Raking cornice
Representation in bas-relief of conversion of St. Paul

TRIANGULAR PEDIMENT, WEST FACADE, ST. PAUL'S CATHEDRAL

MODEL BUILT IN 1674 OF PROPOSED EXTERIOR OF ST. PAUL'S CATHEDRAL (ENGLISH BAROQUE), LONDON, BRITAIN (BY C. WREN)

Cross
Orb
Small dome
Entablature
Pedestal
Arcade
Gallery with balustrade
Lantern
Convex moulding
Circular lucarne window
Dome
Plat lesene
Curved buttress
Round arch
Corinthian pilaster
Rectangular pier
Sunken lunette
Sunken panel
Raking cornice
Pediment
Plain pilaster
Attic storey
Entablature
Architrave
Cornice
Small pilaster
Pedestal
Semicircular cornice
Plinth
Concave, arched niche
Attached Corinthian column
Free-standing Corinthian column
Projecting side portal

CHURCH OF ST. GEORGE IN THE EAST (ENGLISH BAROQUE), LONDON, BRITAIN, 1714-1734 (BY N. HAWKSMOOR)

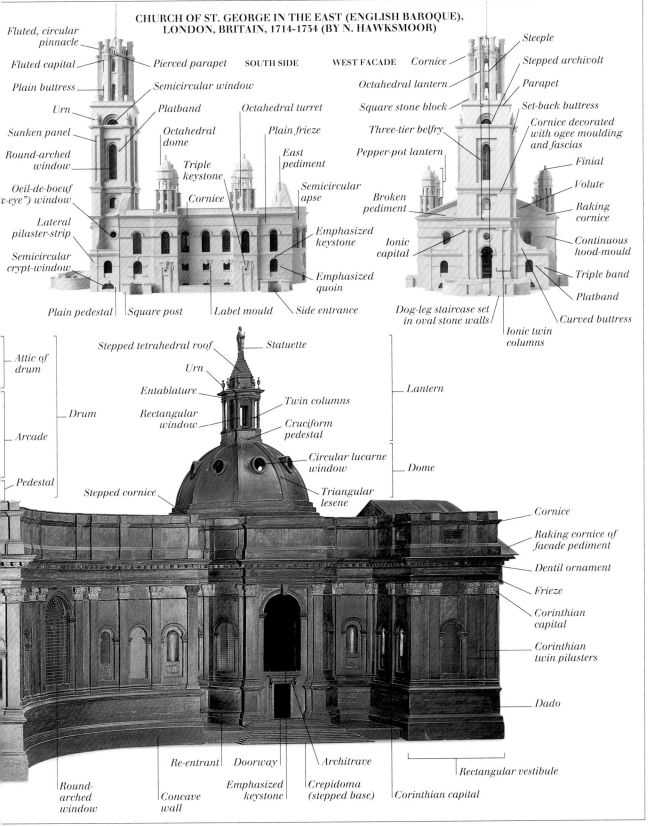

SOUTH SIDE

WEST FACADE

Fluted, circular pinnacle

Fluted capital

Plain buttress

Urn

Sunken panel

Round-arched window

Oeil-de-boeuf ("ox-eye") window

Lateral pilaster-strip

Semicircular crypt-window

Pierced parapet

Semicircular window

Platband

Octahedral dome

Triple keystone

Cornice

Plain pedestal

Square post

Octahedral turret

Plain frieze

East pediment

Semicircular apse

Emphasized keystone

Emphasized quoin

Label mould

Side entrance

Cornice

Octahedral lantern

Square stone block

Three-tier belfry

Pepper-pot lantern

Broken pediment

Ionic capital

Dog-leg staircase set in oval stone walls

Ionic twin columns

Steeple

Stepped archivolt

Parapet

Set-back buttress

Cornice decorated with ogee moulding and fascias

Finial

Volute

Raking cornice

Continuous hood-mould

Triple band

Platband

Curved buttress

Attic of drum

Drum

Arcade

Pedestal

Stepped tetrahedral roof

Urn

Entablature

Rectangular window

Stepped cornice

Statuette

Twin columns

Cruciform pedestal

Circular lucarne window

Triangular lesene

Lantern

Dome

Cornice

Raking cornice of facade pediment

Dentil ornament

Frieze

Corinthian capital

Corinthian twin pilasters

Dado

Round-arched window

Concave wall

Re-entrant

Doorway

Emphasized keystone

Architrave

Crepidoma (stepped base)

Corinthian capital

Rectangular vestibule

Baroque and neoclassical 3

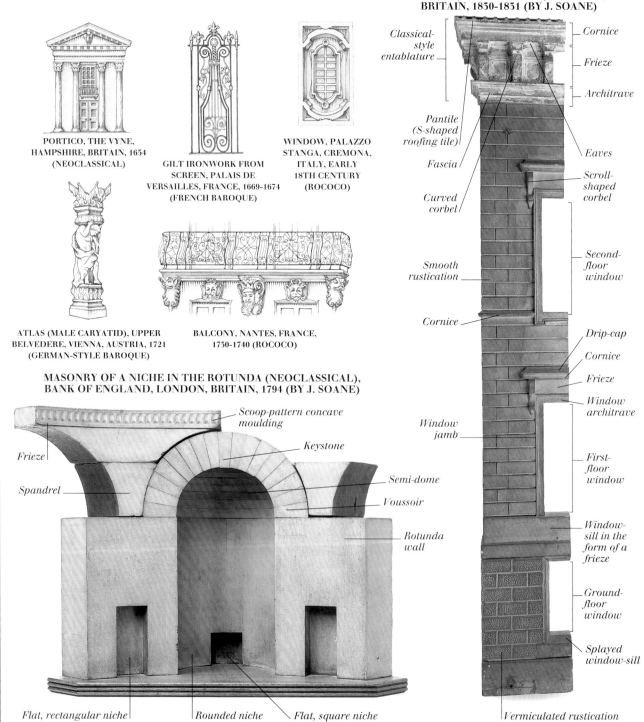

DETAILS FROM BAROQUE, NEOCLASSICAL, AND ROCOCO BUILDINGS

PORTICO, THE VYNE, HAMPSHIRE, BRITAIN, 1654 (NEOCLASSICAL)

GILT IRONWORK FROM SCREEN, PALAIS DE VERSAILLES, FRANCE, 1669-1674 (FRENCH BAROQUE)

WINDOW, PALAZZO STANGA, CREMONA, ITALY, EARLY 18TH CENTURY (ROCOCO)

ATLAS (MALE CARYATID), UPPER BELVEDERE, VIENNA, AUSTRIA, 1721 (GERMAN-STYLE BAROQUE)

BALCONY, NANTES, FRANCE, 1730-1740 (ROCOCO)

MASONRY OF A NICHE IN THE ROTUNDA (NEOCLASSICAL), BANK OF ENGLAND, LONDON, BRITAIN, 1794 (BY J. SOANE)

Scoop-pattern concave moulding

Keystone

Frieze

Spandrel

Semi-dome

Voussoir

Rotunda wall

Flat, rectangular niche

Rounded niche

Flat, square niche

CORNER OF THE NEW STATE PAPER OFFICE (NEOCLASSICAL), LONDON, BRITAIN, 1830-1831 (BY J. SOANE)

Classical-style entablature

Cornice

Frieze

Architrave

Pantile (S-shaped roofing tile)

Fascia

Eaves

Scroll-shaped corbel

Curved corbel

Smooth rustication

Second-floor window

Cornice

Drip-cap

Cornice

Frieze

Window architrave

Window jamb

First-floor window

Window-sill in the form of a frieze

Ground-floor window

Splayed window-sill

Vermiculated rustication

TYRINGHAM HOUSE (NEOCLASSICAL), BUCKINGHAMSHIRE, BRITAIN, 1793-1797 (BY J. SOANE)

**ROOF LEVEL
(ATTIC LEVEL)**

Space for illumination above unroofed central hall

Chimney-stack

Space above unroofed main staircase

Oculus illuminating secondary staircase

Flat roof

Parapet rail

Balustrade

Baluster

Cornice

Attic storey of convex portico

Cornice

**FIRST-FLOOR LEVEL
(CHAMBER FLOOR)**

Upper level of central hall, open to floor below

Main staircase

Secondary staircase

Abacus

Pilaster capital

Triangular pilaster

Attached Tuscan twin pilasters

First-floor storey of convex portico

Window-sill

Bow front

**GROUND-FLOOR LEVEL
(PRINCIPAL FLOOR)**

Withdrawing-room

Central hall

Main staircase

Library and breakfast-room

Water-closet (toilet)

Eating-room

Secondary staircase

Segmented lintel course

Band incised with Greek-style fret ornament

Window-sill

Window architrave

Window jamb

Base

Basement

Plinth

Horizontal rustication

Vestibule (entrance hall)

Ground-floor storey of convex portico

**FACADE OF
TYRINGHAM HOUSE**

Chimney-stack

Rail

Baluster

Parapet

Balustrade

Cornice

Entablature

Voussoir

Capital

Basement window

Shaft

Ionic column

Base

Entrance door

Circular entrance steps

PROSTYLE COLONNADE

Arches and vaults

ARCHES ARE CURVED STRUCTURES used to bridge spans and to support the weight of upper parts of buildings, such as domes, as in St. Paul's Cathedral (below) and the antique temple (opposite). The voussoirs (wedge-shaped blocks) that form an arch (right) support each other and convert the downward force of the weight of the building into an outward force. This outward force is in turn transferred to buttresses, piers, or abutments. A vault is an arched roof or ceiling. There are four main types of vault (opposite). A barrel vault is a single vault, semicircular in cross-section; a groin vault consists of two barrel vaults intersecting at right-angles; a rib vault is a groin vault reinforced by ribs; and a fan vault is a rib vault in which the ribs radiate from the springing point (where the arch begins) like a fan.

PARTS OF AN ARCH

Voussoir
Keystone
Crown
Abutment
Abutment
Keystone
Intrados (soffit)
Extrados
Haunch
Impost
Intrados (soffit)
Abutment
Springing point
Abutment
Span

FRONT

SIDE

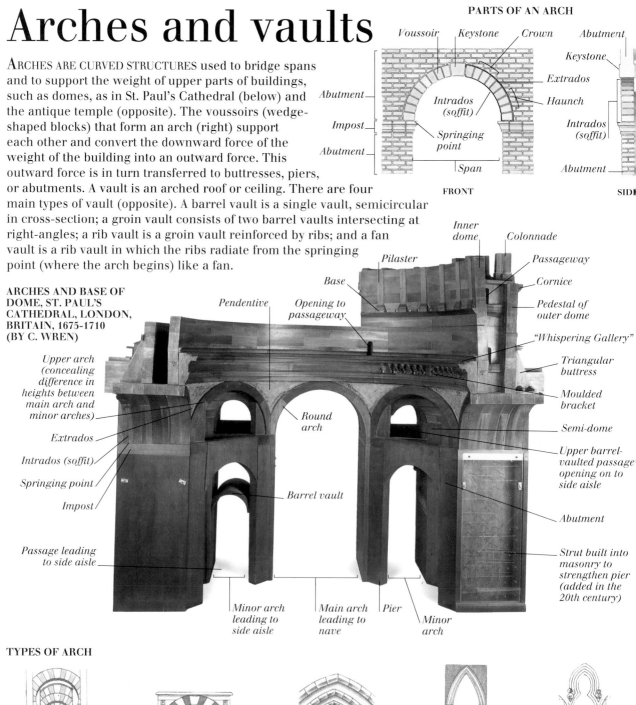

ARCHES AND BASE OF DOME, ST. PAUL'S CATHEDRAL, LONDON, BRITAIN, 1675-1710 (BY C. WREN)

Inner dome
Colonnade
Pilaster
Passageway
Base
Cornice
Pendentive
Opening to passageway
Pedestal of outer dome
"Whispering Gallery"
Upper arch (concealing difference in heights between main arch and minor arches)
Triangular buttress
Moulded bracket
Round arch
Semi-dome
Extrados
Intrados (soffit)
Upper barrel-vaulted passage opening on to side aisle
Springing point
Impost
Barrel vault
Abutment
Passage leading to side aisle
Strut built into masonry to strengthen pier (added in the 20th century)
Minor arch leading to side aisle
Main arch leading to nave
Pier
Minor arch

TYPES OF ARCH

HORSESHOE ARCH (MOORISH ARCH), GREAT MOSQUE, CORDOBA, SPAIN, 785

BASKET ARCH (SEMI-ELLIPTICAL ARCH), PALATINE CHAPEL, AIX-LA-CHAPELLE, FRANCE, 790-798

TUDOR ARCH, TOWER OF LONDON, BRITAIN, C.1086-1097

LANCET ARCH, WESTMINSTER ABBEY, LONDON, BRITAIN, 1503-1519

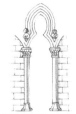

TREFOIL ARCH, BEVERLEY MINSTER, YORKSHIRE, BRITAIN, C.1300

TYPES OF VAULT

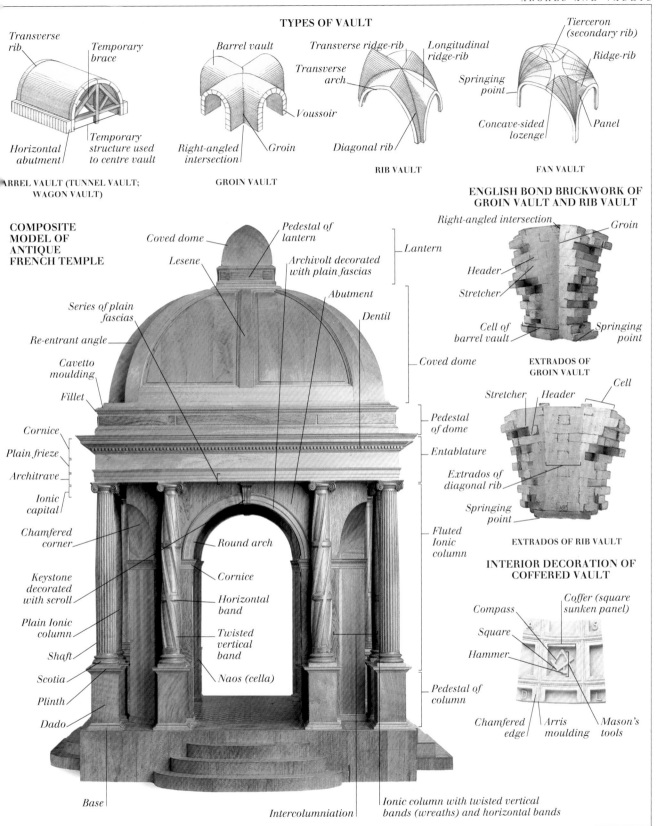

Transverse rib

Temporary brace

Horizontal abutment

Temporary structure used to centre vault

BARREL VAULT (TUNNEL VAULT; WAGON VAULT)

Barrel vault

Voussoir

Right-angled intersection

Groin

GROIN VAULT

Transverse ridge-rib

Transverse arch

Longitudinal ridge-rib

Diagonal rib

RIB VAULT

Tierceron (secondary rib)

Ridge-rib

Springing point

Concave-sided lozenge

Panel

FAN VAULT

COMPOSITE MODEL OF ANTIQUE FRENCH TEMPLE

Coved dome

Lesene

Series of plain fascias

Re-entrant angle

Cavetto moulding

Fillet

Cornice

Plain frieze

Architrave

Ionic capital

Chamfered corner

Keystone decorated with scroll

Plain Ionic column

Shaft

Scotia

Plinth

Dado

Base

Pedestal of lantern

Archivolt decorated with plain fascias

Abutment

Dentil

Round arch

Cornice

Horizontal band

Twisted vertical band

Naos (cella)

Intercolumniation

Lantern

Coved dome

Pedestal of dome

Entablature

Fluted Ionic column

Pedestal of column

Ionic column with twisted vertical bands (wreaths) and horizontal bands

ENGLISH BOND BRICKWORK OF GROIN VAULT AND RIB VAULT

Right-angled intersection

Groin

Header

Stretcher

Cell of barrel vault

Springing point

EXTRADOS OF GROIN VAULT

Stretcher

Header

Cell

Extrados of diagonal rib

Springing point

EXTRADOS OF RIB VAULT

INTERIOR DECORATION OF COFFERED VAULT

Coffer (square sunken panel)

Compass

Square

Hammer

Chamfered edge

Arris moulding

Mason's tools

Domes

A DOME IS A CONVEX ROOF. Domes are categorized according to the shapes of both the base and the section through the centre of the dome. The base may be circular, square, or polygonal (many-sided), depending on the plan of the drum (the walls on which the dome rests). The section of a dome may be the same shape as any arch (see pp. 484-485). Various types of dome are illustrated here: a hemispherical dome, which has a circular base and a semicircular section; a saucer dome, which has a circular base and a segmental (less than a semicircle) section; a polyhedral dome, which is a dome on a polygonal base whose sides meet at the top of the dome; and an onion dome, which has a circular or polygonal base and an ogee-shaped section. Many domes have a lantern (a turret with windows) to provide light inside.

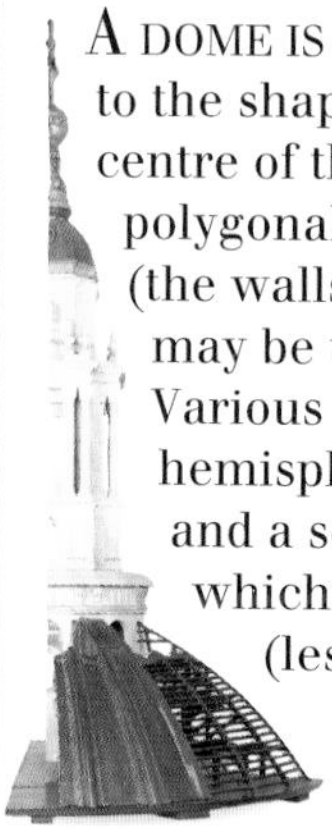

LANTERN AND UPPER DOME TIMBERING, ST. PAUL'S CATHEDRAL

DOME TIMBERING, CHURCH OF THE SORBONNE PARIS, FRANCE, 1635-1642 (BY J. LEMERCIER)

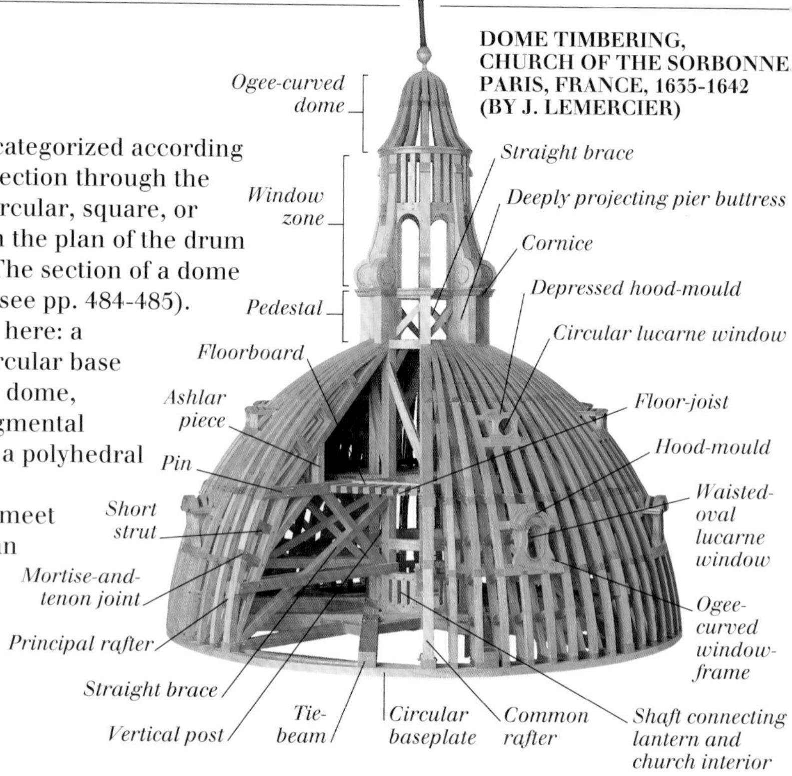

Ogee-curved dome
Window zone
Pedestal
Floorboard
Ashlar piece
Pin
Short strut
Mortise-and-tenon joint
Principal rafter
Straight brace
Vertical post
Tie-beam
Circular baseplate
Common rafter
Straight brace
Deeply projecting pier buttress
Cornice
Depressed hood-mould
Circular lucarne window
Floor-joist
Hood-mould
Waisted-oval lucarne window
Ogee-curved window-frame
Shaft connecting lantern and church interior

ROOF WITH LANTERN AND ONION DOME

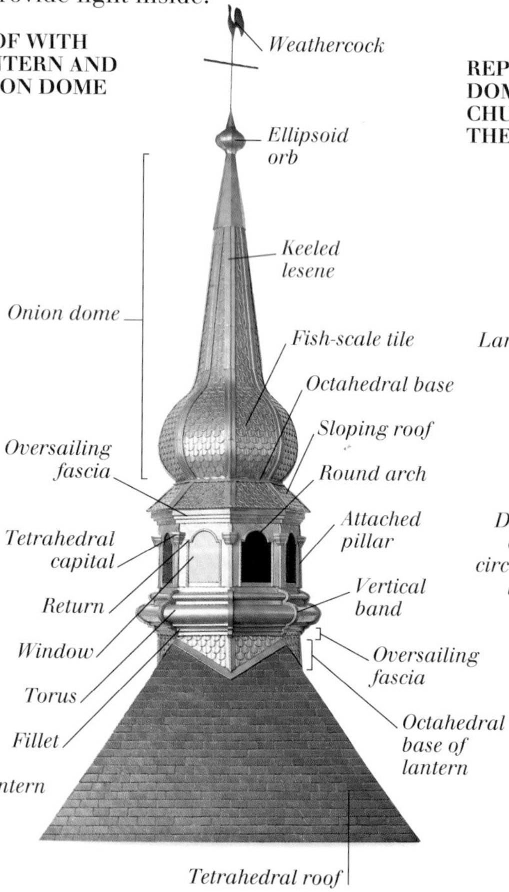

Weathercock
Ellipsoid orb
Keeled lesene
Fish-scale tile
Octahedral base
Sloping roof
Round arch
Attached pillar
Vertical band
Oversailing fascia
Octahedral base of lantern
Onion dome
Oversailing fascia
Tetrahedral capital
Return
Window
Torus
Fillet
Lantern
Tetrahedral roof

REPRESENTATION OF DOME METALLING, CHURCH OF THE SORBONNE

Cross
Orb
Square rib
Astragal
Inverted ovolo (quarter-round)
Fillet
Volute
Plain fascia
Roll moulding
Round-arched window
Buttress
Ovolo (quarter-round)
Volute
Fillet
Cornice
Lantern
Projecting pier buttress
Dome on a circular base
Fish-scale tile
Inverted demi-heart torus moulding
Hood-mould
Waisted-oval lucarne window
Small volute
Gutter
Parapet
Semicircular torus moulding
Small roll
Fillet
Plain fascia
Triple lesene

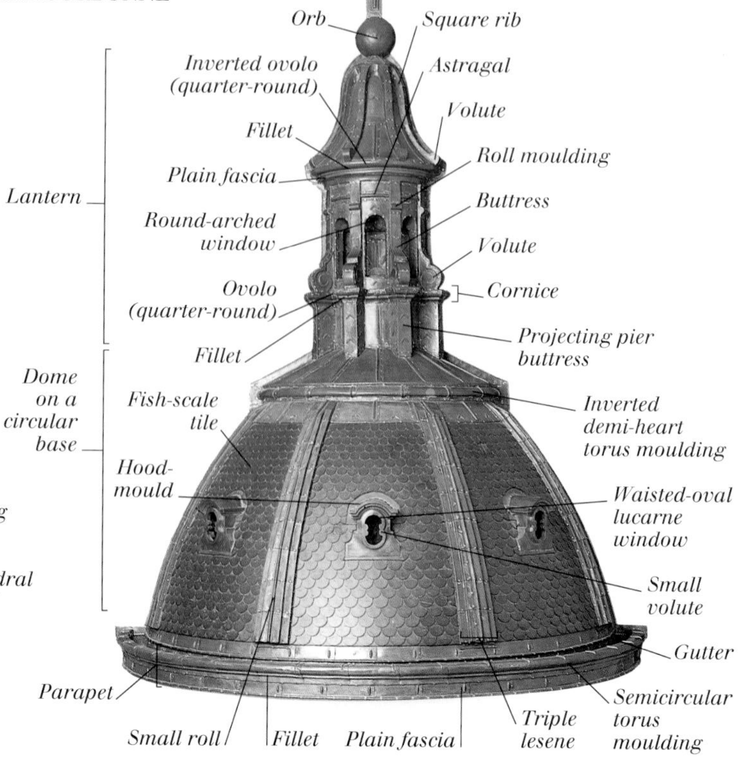

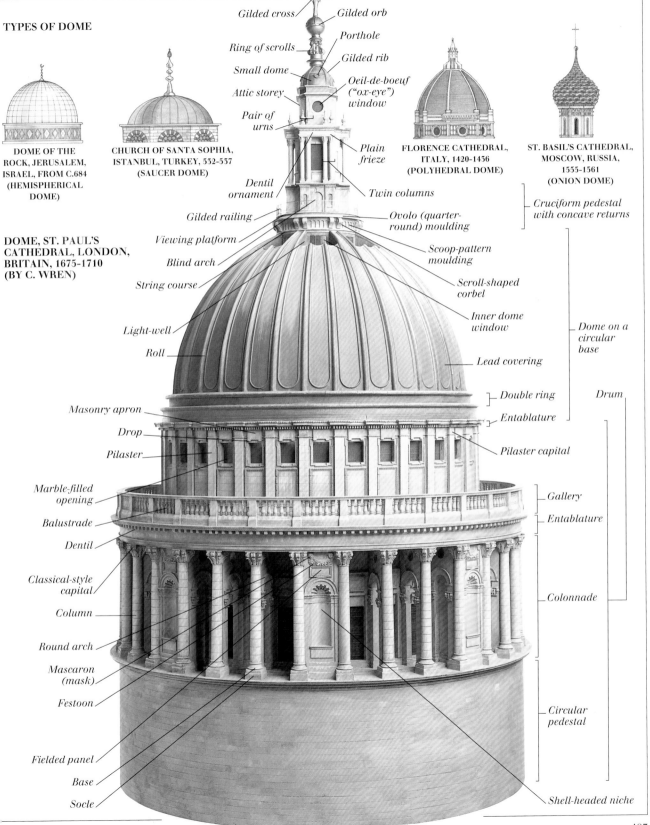

TYPES OF DOME

DOME OF THE ROCK, JERUSALEM, ISRAEL, FROM C.684 (HEMISPHERICAL DOME)

CHURCH OF SANTA SOPHIA, ISTANBUL, TURKEY, 532-537 (SAUCER DOME)

FLORENCE CATHEDRAL, ITALY, 1420-1436 (POLYHEDRAL DOME)

ST. BASIL'S CATHEDRAL, MOSCOW, RUSSIA, 1555-1561 (ONION DOME)

DOME, ST. PAUL'S CATHEDRAL, LONDON, BRITAIN, 1675-1710 (BY C. WREN)

Gilded cross

Gilded orb

Porthole

Ring of scrolls

Gilded rib

Small dome

Oeil-de-boeuf ("ox-eye") window

Attic storey

Pair of urns

Plain frieze

Dentil ornament

Twin columns

Gilded railing

Ovolo (quarter-round) moulding

Viewing platform

Scoop-pattern moulding

Blind arch

Scroll-shaped corbel

String course

Inner dome window

Light-well

Lead covering

Roll

Double ring

Masonry apron

Entablature

Drop

Pilaster capital

Pilaster

Marble-filled opening

Gallery

Balustrade

Entablature

Dentil

Classical-style capital

Column

Colonnade

Round arch

Mascaron (mask)

Festoon

Fielded panel

Base

Circular pedestal

Socle

Shell-headed niche

Cruciform pedestal with concave returns

Dome on a circular base

Drum

Islamic buildings

OPUS SECTILE MOSAIC DESIGN

THE ISLAMIC RELIGION was founded by the prophet Mohammed, who was born in Mecca (in present-day Saudi Arabia) about 570 AD. In the following three centuries, Islam spread from Arabia to North Africa and Spain, as well as to India and much of the rest of Asia. The worldwide influence of Islam remains strong today. Common characteristics of Islamic buildings include ogee arches and roofs, onion domes, and walls decorated with carved stone, paintings, inlays, or mosaics. The most important type of Islamic building is the mosque – the place of worship – which generally has a minaret (tower) from which the muezzin (official crier) calls Muslims to prayer. Most mosques have a mihrab (decorative niche) that indicates the direction of Mecca. As figurative art is not allowed in Islam, buildings are ornamented with geometric and arabesque motifs, and inscriptions (frequently Koranic verses).

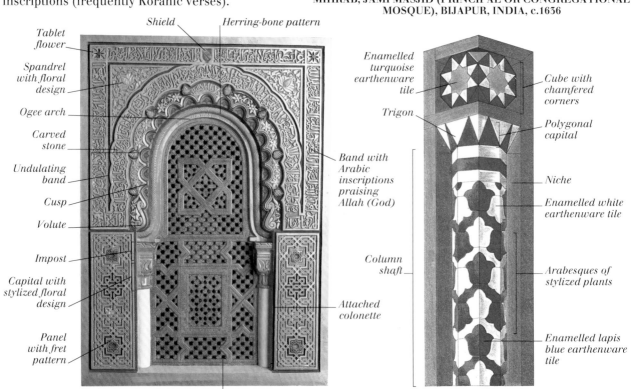

Bud-like onion dome
Depressed arch surrounding mihrab
Painted roof pavilion
Turkish-crescent finial
Lotus-flower pendentive
Arabic inscription
Crest
Painted minaret with censer (incense burner)
Spandrel
Series of recessed arches
Semi-dome
Arched niche within a niche
Mural resembling tomb
Polyhedral niche
Recessed colonettes

MIHRAB, JAMI MASJID (PRINCIPAL OR CONGREGATIONAL MOSQUE), BIJAPUR, INDIA, c.1636

Tablet flower
Shield
Herring-bone pattern
Spandrel with floral design
Ogee arch
Carved stone
Undulating band
Cusp
Volute
Impost
Capital with stylized floral design
Panel with fret pattern
Band with Arabic inscriptions praising Allah (God)
Attached colonette
Jali (latticed screen) with geometrical patterns

ARCH, THE ALHAMBRA, GRANADA, SPAIN, 1333-1354

Enamelled turquoise earthenware tile
Trigon
Cube with chamfered corners
Polygonal capital
Niche
Enamelled white earthenware tile
Column shaft
Arabesques of stylized plants
Enamelled lapis blue earthenware tile

MIHRAB WITH COLUMN, EL-AINYI MOSQUE, CAIRO, EGYPT, 15TH CENTURY

EXAMPLES OF ISLAMIC MOSAICS, EGYPT AND SYRIA

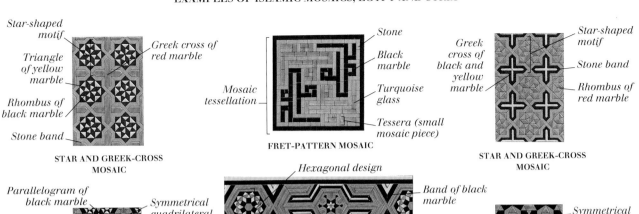

Star-shaped motif

Triangle of yellow marble

Greek cross of red marble

Rhombus of black marble

Stone band

STAR AND GREEK-CROSS MOSAIC

Stone

Black marble

Turquoise glass

Mosaic tessellation

Tessera (small mosaic piece)

FRET-PATTERN MOSAIC

Greek cross of black and yellow marble

Star-shaped motif

Stone band

Rhombus of red marble

STAR AND GREEK-CROSS MOSAIC

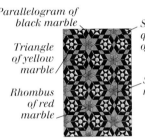

Parallelogram of black marble

Triangle of yellow marble

Rhombus of red marble

Symmetrical quadrilateral of stone

Star-shaped motif

MOSAIC OF HEXAGONS, TRIANGLES, AND SYMMETRICAL QUADRILATERALS

Hexagonal design

Band of black marble

Band of stone

HEXAGON AND BAND MOSAIC

Triangle of turquoise glass

Parallelogram of mother-of-pearl

DANCETTE-PATTERN MOSAIC

Symmetrical quadrilateral of black marble

Triangle of stone

Hexagon of red marble

MOSAIC OF HEXAGONS, TRIANGLES, AND SYMMETRICAL QUADRILATERALS

MARBLE TOMB OF ITIMAD-UD-DAULA, AGRA, INDIA, c.1622-1628

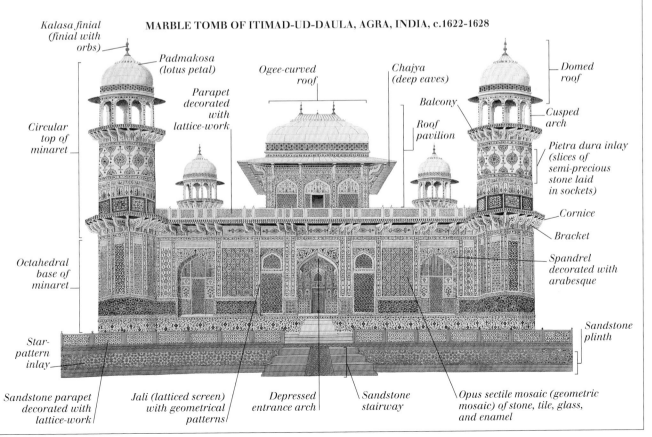

Kalasa finial (finial with orbs)

Padmakosa (lotus petal)

Circular top of minaret

Parapet decorated with lattice-work

Ogee-curved roof

Chajya (deep eaves)

Balcony

Roof pavilion

Domed roof

Cusped arch

Pietra dura inlay (slices of semi-precious stone laid in sockets)

Cornice

Bracket

Spandrel decorated with arabesque

Octahedral base of minaret

Star-pattern inlay

Sandstone parapet decorated with lattice-work

Jali (latticed screen) with geometrical patterns

Depressed entrance arch

Sandstone stairway

Opus sectile mosaic (geometric mosaic) of stone, tile, glass, and enamel

Sandstone plinth

South and east Asia

THE TRADITIONAL ARCHITECTURE of south and east Asia has been profoundly influenced by the spread from India of Buddhism and Hinduism. This influence is shown both by the abundance and by the architectural styles of temples and shrines in the region. Many early Hindu temples consist of rooms carved from solid rock-faces. However, free-standing structures began to be built in southern India from about the eighth century AD. Many were built in the Dravidian style, like the Temple of Virupaksha (opposite) with its characteristic antarala (terraced tower), perforated windows, and numerous arches, pilasters, and carvings. The earliest Buddhist religious monuments were Indian stupas, which consisted of a single hemispherical dome surmounted by a chattravali (shaft) and surrounded by railings with ornate gates. Later Indian stupas and those built elsewhere were sometimes modified; for example, in Sri Lanka, the dome became bell-shaped, and was called a dagoba. Buddhist pagodas, such as the Burmese example (right), are multistoreyed temples, each storey having a projecting roof. The form of these buildings probably derived from the yasti (pointed spire) of the stupa. Another feature of many traditional Asian buildings is their imaginative roof-forms, such as gambrel (mansard) roofs, and roofs with angle-rafters (below).

DETAILS FROM EAST ASIAN BUILDINGS

KASUGA-STYLE ROOF WITH SUMIGI (ANGLE-RAFTERS), KASUGADO SHRINE OF ENJOJI, NARA, JAPAN, 12TH-14TH CENTURY

TERRACES, TEMPLE OF HEAVEN, BEIJING, CHINA, 15TH CENTURY

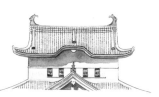

GAMBREL (MANSARD) ROOF WITH UPSWEPT EAVES AND UNDULATING GABLES, HIMEJI CASTLE, HIMEJI, JAPAN, 1608-1609

CORNER CAPITAL WITH ROOF BEAMS, POPCHU-SA TEMPLE, POPCHU-SA, SOUTH KOREA, 17TH CENTURY

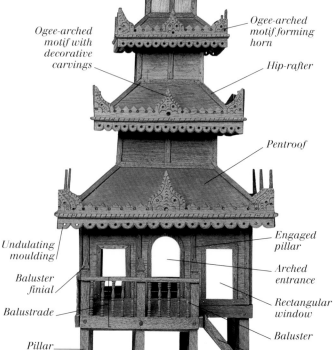

SEVEN-STOREYED PAGODA IN BURMESE STYLE, c.9TH-10TH CENTURY

Gilded band

Gilded iron hti (crown)

Dubika (mast)

Arrow motif

Torus moulding with spiral carving

Decorative eaves board

Ogee-arched motif with decorative carvings

Ogee-arched motif forming horn

Hip-rafter

Pentroof

Engaged pillar

Arched entrance

Rectangular window

Baluster

Straight brace

Pillar

Balustrade

Baluster finial

Undulating moulding

PERFORATED STONE WINDOWS, TEMPLES OF VIRUPAKSHA AND MALLIKARJUNA, PATTADAKAL, INDIA, 8TH CENTURY

Tablet flower

Fret motif

Chain motif

Floral pattern

Sickle motif

Semicircle

Leaf

Scroll motif

DAGOBA STUPA, KANDY, SRI LANKA, c.2ND CENTURY BC–7TH CENTURY AD

Chattra (umbrella)

Hanging ornament

Chattravali (shaft)

Ring with indentations symbolizing chattras

Ornamental metalwork

Yasti (tee; pointed spire)

Harmika (stylized square railing)

Auda (bell-shaped dome)

Trimala (series of three circular courses)

Circular base

SIDE VIEW AND PLAN VIEW, TEMPLE OF VIRUPAKSHA, PATTADAKAL, INDIA, c.746

Stupica (small stupa) of the Dravidian order

Dravidian finial

Blind chataya arch

Perforated window

Gopuram finial (wagon-like finial)

Bracketed capital

Small gopuram (gate-head)

Parapet

Roll cornice

Antarala (terraced tower)

Niche with statue

Gate

Plan view

Panel with bas-relief carving

Pillar

Twin pilasters

Shrine

Niche

Mandapa (pillared hall)

Pradakshina (circumambulatory passage around shrine)

Shrine chamber

Gate

The 19th century

BUILDINGS OF THE 19TH CENTURY are characterized by the use of new materials and by a great diversity of architectural styles. From the end of the 18th century, iron and steel became widely used as alternatives to wood for the framework of buildings, as in the flax-spinning mill shown here. Built in Britain in 1796, this mill exemplifies an architectural style that became common throughout the industrialized world for more than a century. The Industrial Revolution also brought mass-production of building parts – a development that enabled the British architect Sir Joseph Paxton to erect London's Crystal Palace (a building made entirely of iron and glass) in only nine months, ready for the Great Exhibition of 1851. The 19th century saw a widespread revival of older architectural styles. For example, in the USA and Germany, Neo-Greek architecture was fashionable; in Britain and France, Neo-Baroque, Neo-Byzantine, and Neo-Gothic styles (as seen in the Palace of Westminster and Tower Bridge) were dominant.

Cast-iron wall-plate
Machinery space
Pitched roof
Ridge
Verge
Gutter
Cast-iron mortise-and-tenon joint
Anchor-joint
Inverted T-section cast-iron beam
Drain-pipe
Segmentally arched brick vault
End flange
Concrete floor
Tapering part of column
Paved ground floor
Strengthened central column

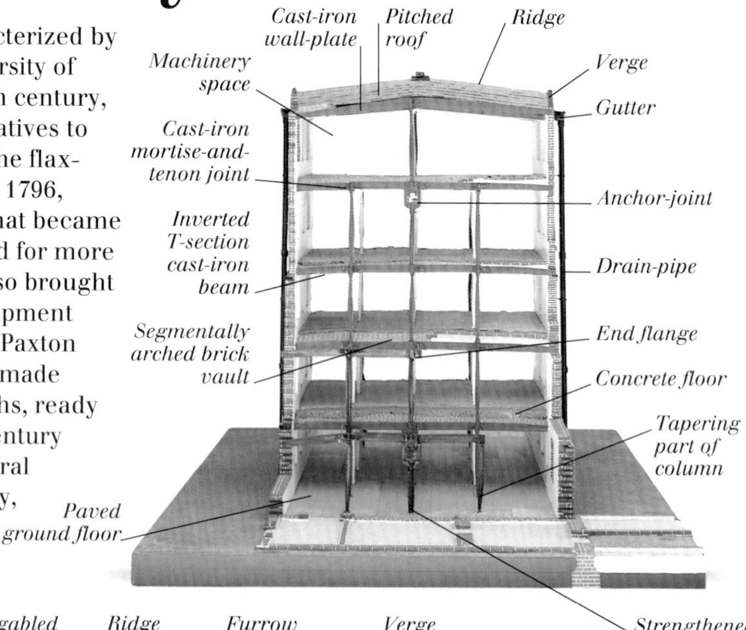

FLAX-SPINNING MILL, SHREWSBURY, BRITAIN, 1796 (BY C. BAGE)

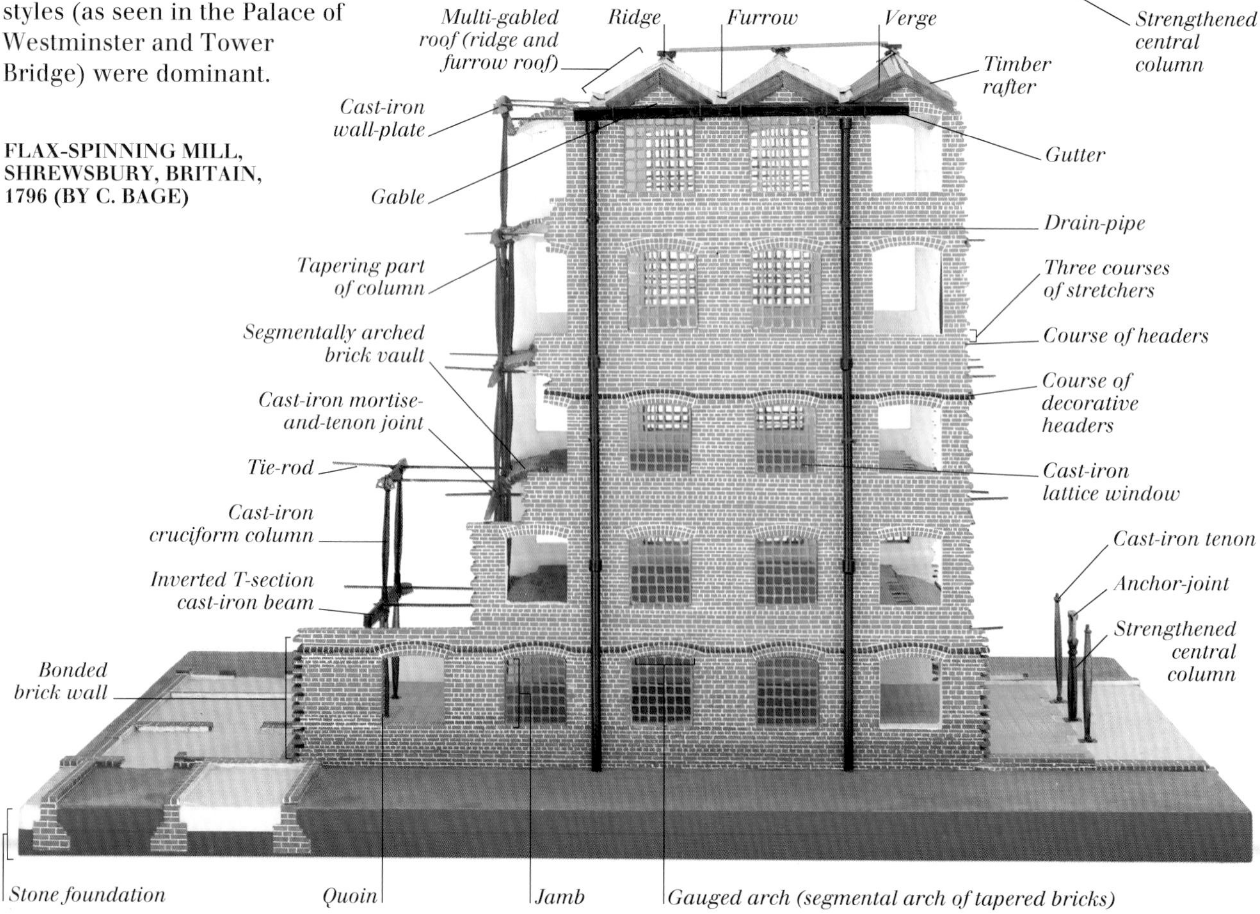

Multi-gabled roof (ridge and furrow roof)
Ridge
Furrow
Verge
Timber rafter
Cast-iron wall-plate
Gable
Gutter
Tapering part of column
Drain-pipe
Three courses of stretchers
Segmentally arched brick vault
Course of headers
Cast-iron mortise-and-tenon joint
Course of decorative headers
Tie-rod
Cast-iron cruciform column
Cast-iron lattice window
Inverted T-section cast-iron beam
Cast-iron tenon
Anchor-joint
Strengthened central column
Bonded brick wall
Stone foundation
Quoin
Jamb
Gauged arch (segmental arch of tapered bricks)

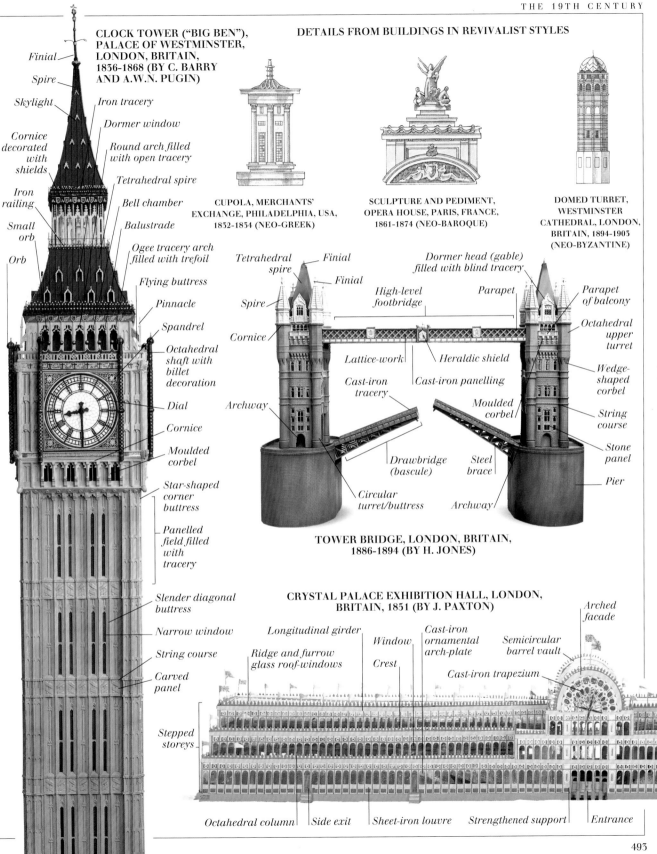

CLOCK TOWER ("BIG BEN"), PALACE OF WESTMINSTER, LONDON, BRITAIN, 1836-1868 (BY C. BARRY AND A.W.N. PUGIN)

Finial
Spire
Skylight
Cornice decorated with shields
Iron railing
Small orb
Orb
Iron tracery
Dormer window
Round arch filled with open tracery
Tetrahedral spire
Bell chamber
Balustrade
Ogee tracery arch filled with trefoil
Flying buttress
Pinnacle
Spandrel
Octahedral shaft with billet decoration
Dial
Cornice
Moulded corbel
Star-shaped corner buttress
Panelled field filled with tracery
Slender diagonal buttress
Narrow window
String course
Carved panel
Stepped storeys

DETAILS FROM BUILDINGS IN REVIVALIST STYLES

CUPOLA, MERCHANTS' EXCHANGE, PHILADELPHIA, USA, 1832-1834 (NEO-GREEK)

SCULPTURE AND PEDIMENT, OPERA HOUSE, PARIS, FRANCE, 1861-1874 (NEO-BAROQUE)

DOMED TURRET, WESTMINSTER CATHEDRAL, LONDON, BRITAIN, 1894-1903 (NEO-BYZANTINE)

Tetrahedral spire
Finial
Spire
Cornice
Archway
Finial
Dormer head (gable) filled with blind tracery
High-level footbridge
Parapet
Lattice-work
Heraldic shield
Cast-iron tracery
Cast-iron panelling
Drawbridge (bascule)
Circular turret/buttress
Moulded corbel
Steel brace
Archway
Parapet of balcony
Octahedral upper turret
Wedge-shaped corbel
String course
Stone panel
Pier

TOWER BRIDGE, LONDON, BRITAIN, 1886-1894 (BY H. JONES)

CRYSTAL PALACE EXHIBITION HALL, LONDON, BRITAIN, 1851 (BY J. PAXTON)

Longitudinal girder
Ridge and furrow glass roof-windows
Window
Crest
Cast-iron ornamental arch-plate
Semicircular barrel vault
Cast-iron trapezium
Arched facade
Octahedral column
Side exit
Sheet-iron louvre
Strengthened support
Entrance

The early 20th century

ARCHITECTURE OF THE EARLY 20TH CENTURY is notable for radical new types of steel-and-glass buildings – particularly skyscrapers – and the widespread use of steel-reinforced concrete. The steel-framed skyscraper was pioneered in Chicago in the 1880s, but did not become widespread until the first decades of the 20th century. As construction techniques were refined, skyscrapers became higher and higher; for example, the Empire State Building (right) of 1929-1931 has 102 storeys. Many buildings of this period were constructed from lightweight concrete slabs, which could be supported by cantilever beams or by pilotis (stilts), as in the Villa Savoye (below). The early 20th century also produced a great variety of architectural styles, some of which are illustrated opposite. Despite their diversity, the styles of this period generally had one thing in common: they were completely new, with few links to past architectural styles. This originality is in marked contrast to 19th-century architecture (see pp. 492-493), much of which was revivalist.

EMPIRE STATE BUILDING, NEW YORK, USA, 1929-193? (BY R. H. SHREVE, T. LAMB, AND A. L. HARMON)

- Radio mast
- Circular lantern
- Art deco splayed seashell form
- Stepped plinth
- Chamfered corner
- Colonnaded storey
- Ornamentation
- Ziggurat-style step-back
- Set-back
- Steel mullion
- Flush window
- Vertical pier
- Regular fenestration
- Solid-panel infill
- Fan-like art deco decoration
- Decorated stone lintel
- Stone structure-line
- Limestone and granite cladding
- Flat roof
- Stepped cornice
- Parapet
- Plinth
- Ground-floor entrance
- Base
- Square bay

VILLA SAVOYE, POISSY, FRANCE, 1929-1931 (BY LE CORBUSIER)

TOP VIEW

- Slab floor
- Fixed table
- Parapet
- Ramp
- Screen
- Handrail
- Window-sill
- Flat roof
- Flat roof
- Curved wall
- Directional skylight
- Terrace
- Raised planting bed

SIDE VIEW

- Terrace
- Cement-rendered wall of lightweight slabs
- Solarium
- Sliding pane of glass
- Mullion
- Piano nobile (first floor)
- Reinforced-concrete pilotis (stilt)
- Rooms for staff
- Ribbon window of long living-room
- Curved glazing
- Covered driveway

MIDWAY GARDENS, CHICAGO, USA, 1914 (BY F. L. WRIGHT)

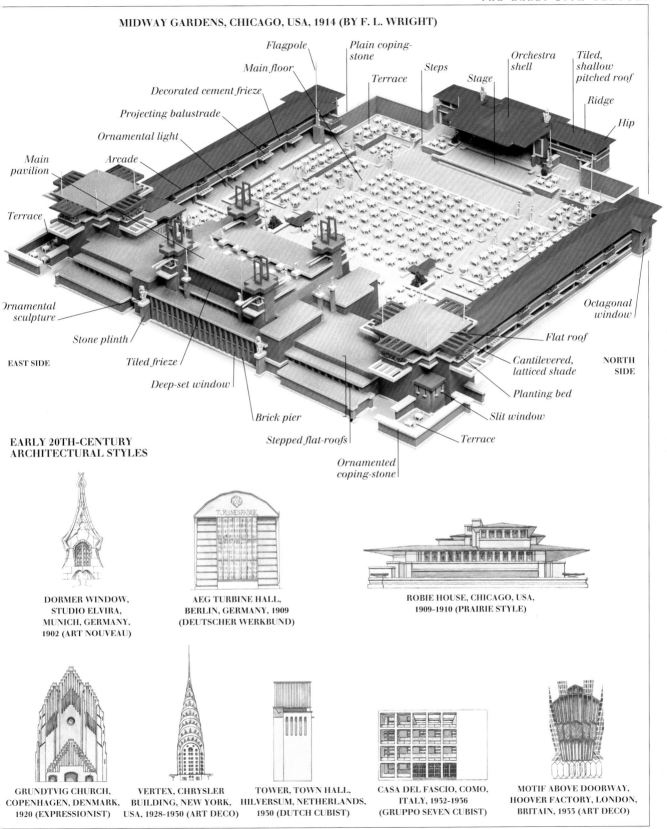

Flagpole

Plain coping-stone

Main floor

Orchestra shell

Tiled, shallow pitched roof

Decorated cement frieze

Terrace

Steps

Stage

Ridge

Projecting balustrade

Hip

Ornamental light

Main pavilion

Arcade

Terrace

Ornamental sculpture

Stone plinth

Tiled frieze

Deep-set window

Brick pier

Stepped flat-roofs

Ornamented coping-stone

Terrace

Slit window

Planting bed

Cantilevered, latticed shade

Flat roof

Octagonal window

EAST SIDE

NORTH SIDE

EARLY 20TH-CENTURY ARCHITECTURAL STYLES

DORMER WINDOW, STUDIO ELVIRA, MUNICH, GERMANY, 1902 (ART NOUVEAU)

AEG TURBINE HALL, BERLIN, GERMANY, 1909 (DEUTSCHER WERKBUND)

ROBIE HOUSE, CHICAGO, USA, 1909-1910 (PRAIRIE STYLE)

GRUNDTVIG CHURCH, COPENHAGEN, DENMARK, 1920 (EXPRESSIONIST)

VERTEX, CHRYSLER BUILDING, NEW YORK, USA, 1928-1930 (ART DECO)

TOWER, TOWN HALL, HILVERSUM, NETHERLANDS, 1930 (DUTCH CUBIST)

CASA DEL FASCIO, COMO, ITALY, 1932-1936 (GRUPPO SEVEN CUBIST)

MOTIF ABOVE DOORWAY, HOOVER FACTORY, LONDON, BRITAIN, 1933 (ART DECO)

Modern buildings 1

**KAWANA HOUSE, JAPAN,
FROM 1987 (BY N. FOSTER)**

ARCHITECTURE SINCE ABOUT THE 1950s is generally known as modern architecture. One of its main influences has been functionalism – a belief that a building's function should be apparent in its design. Both the Centre Georges Pompidou (below and opposite) and the Hong Kong and Shanghai Bank (see pp. 498-499) are functionalist buildings: on each, elements of engineering and the building's services are clearly visible on the outside. In the 1980s, some architects rejected functionalism in favour of post-modernism, in which historical styles – particularly neoclassicism – were revived, using modern building materials and techniques. In many modern buildings, walls are made of glass or concrete hung from a frame, as in the Kawana House (right); this type of wall construction is known as curtain walling. Other modern construction techniques include the intricate interlocking of concrete vaults – as in the Sydney Opera House (see pp. 498-499) – and the use of high-tension beams to create complex roof shapes, such as the paraboloid roof of the Church of St. Pierre de Libreville (see pp. 498-499).

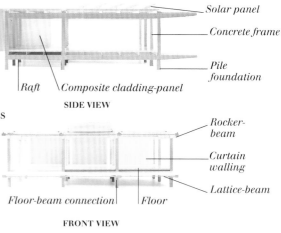

Solar panel

Concrete frame

Pile foundation

Raft   Composite cladding-panel

SIDE VIEW

Rocker-beam

Curtain walling

Lattice-beam

Floor-beam connection   Floor

FRONT VIEW

**SERVICES FACADE, CENTRE GEORGES POMPIDOU,
PARIS, FRANCE, 1977 (BY R. PIANO AND R. ROGERS)**

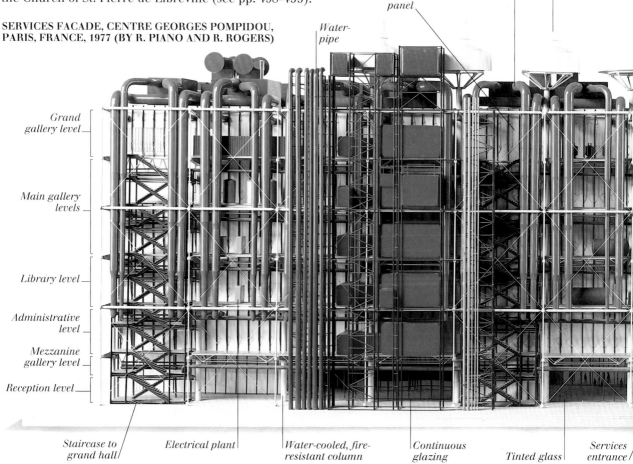

Metal-faced, fire-resistant panel

Air-conditioning duct

Cooling tower

Water-pipe

Grand gallery level

Main gallery levels

Library level

Administrative level

Mezzanine gallery level

Reception level

Staircase to grand hall

Electrical plant

Water-cooled, fire-resistant column

Continuous glazing

Tinted glass

Services entrance

PRINCIPAL FACADE, CENTRE GEORGES POMPIDOU

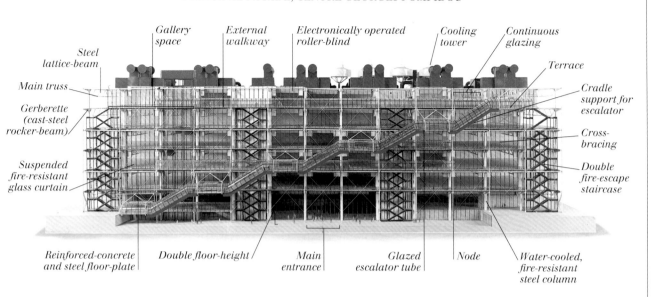

Gallery space

External walkway

Electronically operated roller-blind

Cooling tower

Continuous glazing

Terrace

Steel lattice-beam

Main truss

Gerberette (cast-steel rocker-beam)

Suspended fire-resistant glass curtain

Cradle support for escalator

Cross-bracing

Double fire-escape staircase

Reinforced-concrete and steel floor-plate

Double floor-height

Main entrance

Glazed escalator tube

Node

Water-cooled, fire-resistant steel column

Exposed "plug-in" services

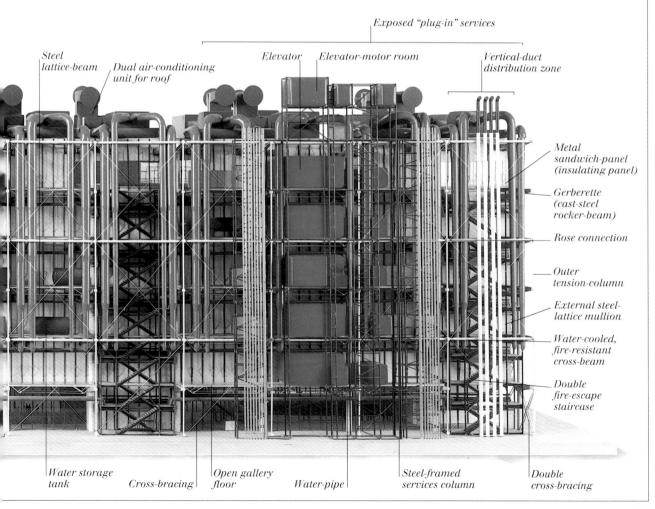

Steel lattice-beam

Dual air-conditioning unit for roof

Elevator

Elevator-motor room

Vertical-duct distribution zone

Metal sandwich-panel (insulating panel)

Gerberette (cast-steel rocker-beam)

Rose connection

Outer tension-column

External steel-lattice mullion

Water-cooled, fire-resistant cross-beam

Double fire-escape staircase

Water storage tank

Cross-bracing

Open gallery floor

Water-pipe

Steel-framed services column

Double cross-bracing

Modern buildings 2

HONG KONG AND SHANGHAI BANK, HONG KONG, 1981-1985 (BY N. FOSTER)

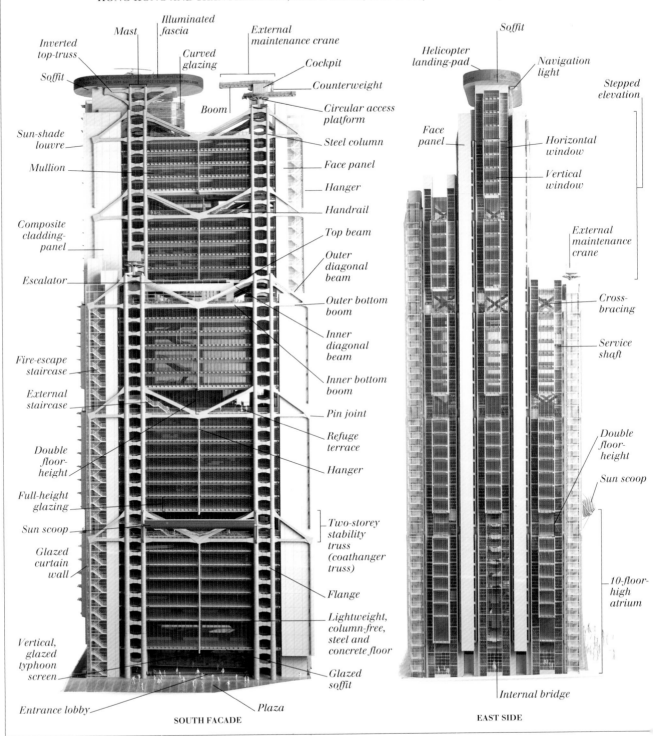

Inverted top-truss

Soffit

Mast

Illuminated fascia

Curved glazing

External maintenance crane

Cockpit

Counterweight

Boom

Circular access platform

Sun-shade louvre

Steel column

Mullion

Face panel

Hanger

Composite cladding-panel

Handrail

Top beam

Escalator

Outer diagonal beam

Outer bottom boom

Inner diagonal beam

Fire-escape staircase

Inner bottom boom

External staircase

Pin joint

Double floor-height

Refuge terrace

Full-height glazing

Hanger

Sun scoop

Two-storey stability truss (coathanger truss)

Glazed curtain wall

Flange

Lightweight, column-free, steel and concrete floor

Vertical, glazed typhoon screen

Glazed soffit

Entrance lobby

Plaza

SOUTH FACADE

Soffit

Helicopter landing-pad

Navigation light

Stepped elevation

Face panel

Horizontal window

Vertical window

External maintenance crane

Cross-bracing

Service shaft

Double floor-height

Sun scoop

10-floor-high atrium

Internal bridge

EAST SIDE

**CHURCH OF ST. PIERRE,
LIBREVILLE, GABON, 1990**

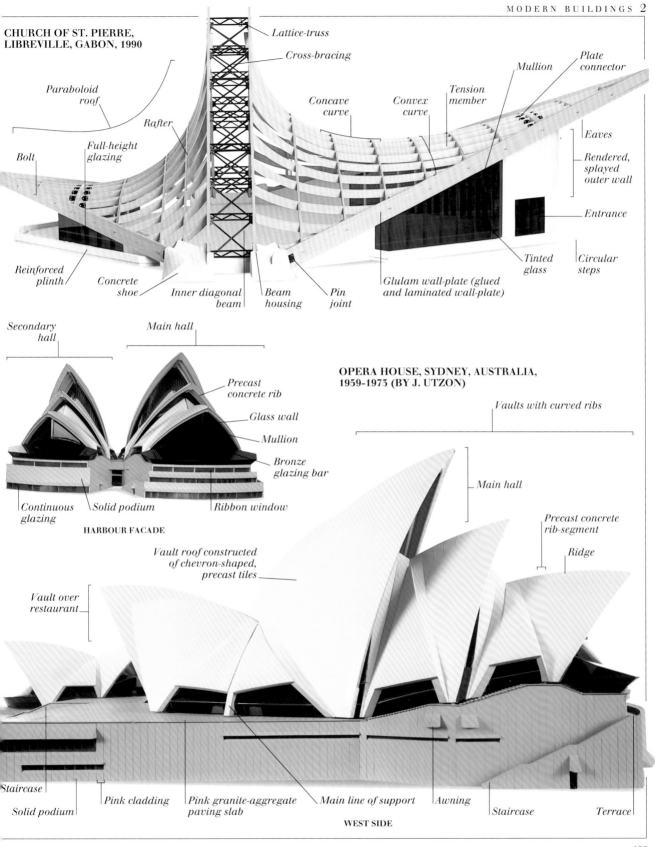

Lattice-truss

Cross-bracing

Concave
curve

Convex
curve

Tension
member

Mullion

Plate
connector

Paraboloid
roof

Rafter

Eaves

Rendered,
splayed
outer wall

Bolt

Full-height
glazing

Entrance

Tinted
glass

Circular
steps

Reinforced
plinth

Concrete
shoe

Inner diagonal
beam

Beam
housing

Pin
joint

Glulam wall-plate (glued
and laminated wall-plate)

Secondary
hall

Main hall

**OPERA HOUSE, SYDNEY, AUSTRALIA,
1959-1973 (BY J. UTZON)**

Vaults with curved ribs

Precast
concrete rib

Glass wall

Mullion

Bronze
glazing bar

Main hall

Precast concrete
rib-segment

Ridge

Continuous
glazing

Solid podium

Ribbon window

HARBOUR FACADE

Vault roof constructed
of chevron-shaped,
precast tiles

Vault over
restaurant

Staircase

Solid podium

Pink cladding

Pink granite-aggregate
paving slab

Main line of support

Awning

Staircase

Terrace

WEST SIDE

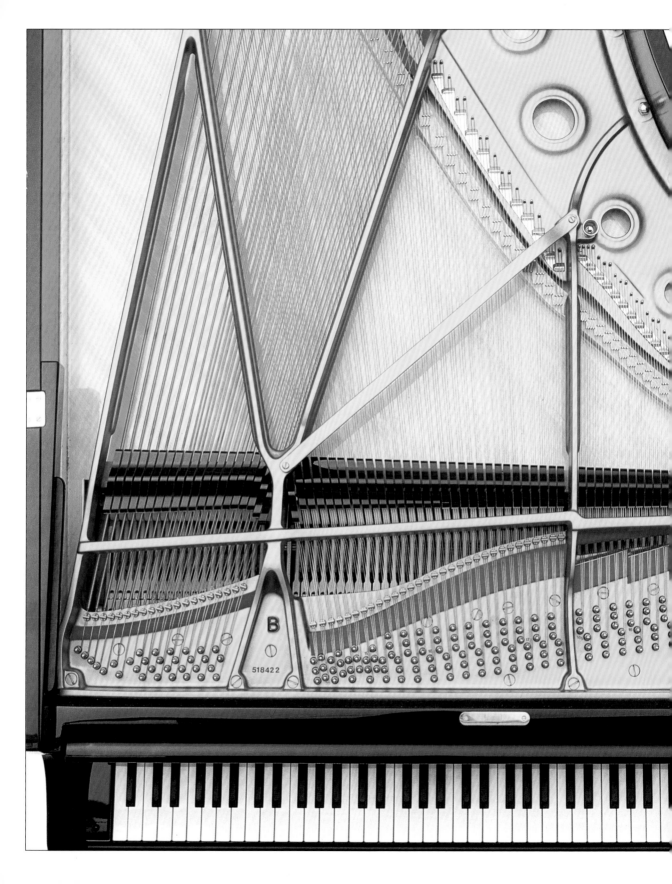

MUSIC

Musical notation

MUSICAL NOTATION IS ANY METHOD by which sounds are written down so that they can be read and performed by others. The present-day conventional system of notation uses a five-line stave (staff) – divided by vertical lines into sections known as bars – on which notes, rests, clefs, key signatures, time signatures, accidentals, and other symbols are written. A note indicates the duration of a sound and, according to its position on the stave, its pitch. Notes can be arranged on the stave in order of pitch to form a scale. A silence in the music is indicated by a rest. The clef, which is placed at the begininng of a stave, fixes the pitch. The key signature, which is placed after the clef, indicates the key. The time signature, placed after the key signature, shows the number of beats in a bar. Accidentals are used to indicate the raising or lowering of the pitch of a note.

ELEMENTS OF MUSICAL NOTATION

CLEFS

Treble (or G) clef

Alto (or C) clef

Bass (or F) clef

TIME SIGNATURES

Six-eight time

Three-four time

Stave (staff)

NOTES

Breve   Minim   Quaver

Semibreve   Crotchet   Semiquaver

RESTS

Breve rest   Minim rest   Quaver rest

Semibreve rest   Crotchet rest   Semiquaver rest

SCALE

C D E F G A B C

ACCIDENTALS

Sharp   Natural   Double sharp

Flat   Double flat   Key signature

Moderately fast and quiet

Tie (bind)

Repeat the previous bar

Treble clef

Bass clef

Four-four time (common time)

Key signature

Alto clef

Treble voice

Alto voice

Tenor voice

Bass voice

Organ part for right hand

Organ part for left hand

Organ pedal line

Instruments of the orchestra written in Italian

Bar line

Bar

Bass clef

Crotchet

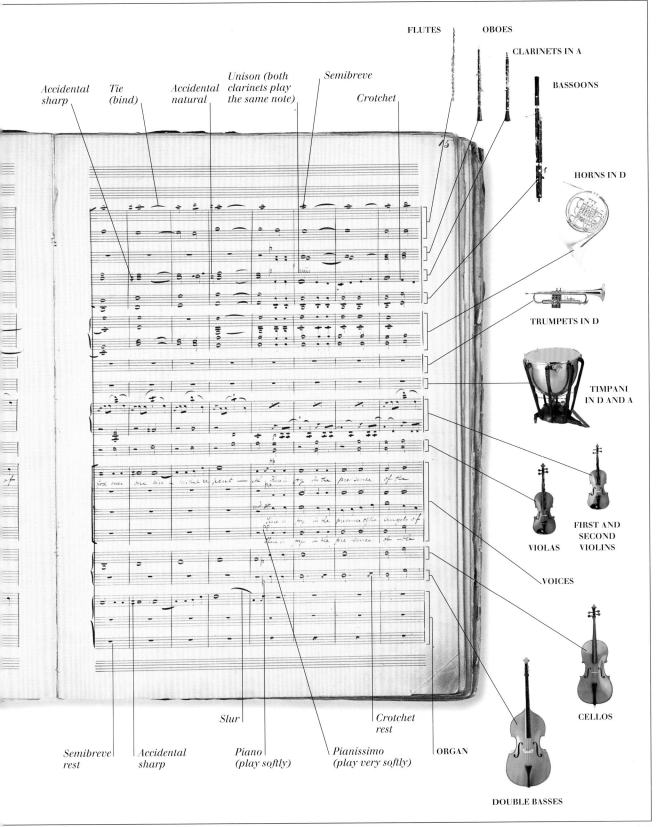

FLUTES

OBOES

CLARINETS IN A

BASSOONS

Accidental sharp

Tie (bind)

Accidental natural

Unison (both clarinets play the same note)

Semibreve

Crotchet

HORNS IN D

TRUMPETS IN D

TIMPANI IN D AND A

FIRST AND SECOND VIOLINS

VIOLAS

VOICES

CELLOS

Semibreve rest

Accidental sharp

Slur

Piano (play softly)

Pianissimo (play very softly)

Crotchet rest

ORGAN

DOUBLE BASSES

Orchestras

AN ORCHESTRA IS A GROUP of musicians that plays music written for a specific combination of instruments. The number and type of instruments included in the orchestra depends on the style of music being played. The modern orchestra (also known as a symphony orchestra) is made up of four sections of instruments – stringed, woodwind, brass, and percussion. The stringed section consists of violins, violas, cellos (violoncellos), double basses, and sometimes a harp (see pp. 510-511). The main instruments of the woodwind section are flutes, oboes, clarinets, and bassoons – the piccolo, cor anglais, bass clarinet, saxophone, and double bassoon (contrabassoon) can also be included if the music requires them (see pp. 508-509). The brass section usually consists of horns, trumpets, trombones, and the tuba (see pp. 506-507). The main instruments of the percussion section are the timpani (see pp. 518-519). The side drum, bass drum, cymbals, tambourine, triangle, tubular bells, xylophone, vibraphone, tam-tam (gong), castanets, and maracas can also be included in the percussion section (see pp. 516-517). The musicians are usually arranged in a semi-circle – strings spread along the front, woodwind and brass in the centre, and percussion at the back. A conductor stands in front of the musicians and controls the tempo (speed) of the music and the overall balance of the sound, ensuring that no instruments are too loud or too soft in relation to the others.

TUBULAR BELLS

TAM-TAM (GONG)

VIBRAPHONE

XYLOPHONE

CASTANETS

TAMBOURINE

TRUMPETS

MARACAS

TRIANGLE

HORNS

CLARINETS

BASS CLARINET

HARP

SAXOPHONE

PICCOLO

SECOND VIOLINS

FIRST VIOLINS

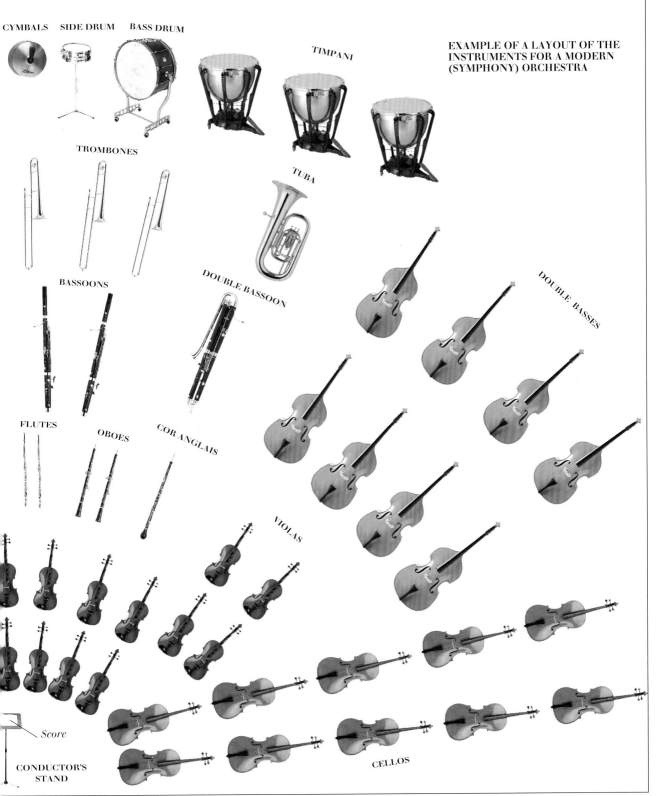

CYMBALS SIDE DRUM BASS DRUM

TIMPANI

EXAMPLE OF A LAYOUT OF THE INSTRUMENTS FOR A MODERN (SYMPHONY) ORCHESTRA

TROMBONES

TUBA

BASSOONS

DOUBLE BASSOON

DOUBLE BASSES

FLUTES

OBOES

COR ANGLAIS

VIOLAS

CELLOS

Score

CONDUCTOR'S STAND

Brass instruments

BUGLE

BRASS INSTRUMENTS ARE WIND INSTRUMENTS that are made of metal, usually brass. Although they appear in many different shapes and sizes, all brass instruments have a mouthpiece, a length of hollow tube, and a flared bell. The mouthpiece of a brass instrument may be cup-shaped, as in the cornet, or cone-shaped, as in the horn. The tube may be wide or narrow, mainly conical, as in the horn and tuba, or mainly cylindrical, as in the trumpet and trombone. The sound of a brass instrument is made by the player's lips vibrating against the mouthpiece, so that the air vibrates in the tube. By changing lip tension, the player can vary the vibrations and produce notes of different pitches. The range of notes produced by a brass instrument can be extended by means of a valve system. Most brass instruments, such as the trumpet, have piston valves that divert the air in the instrument along an extra piece of tubing (known as a valve slide) when pressed down. The total length of the tube is increased and the pitch of the note produced is lowered. Instead of valves, the trombone has a movable slide that can be pushed away from or drawn toward the player. The sound of a brass instrument can also be changed by inserting a mute into the bell of the instrument.

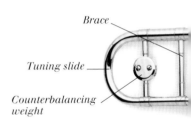

Brace

Tuning slide

Counterbalancing weight

SIMPLIFIED DIAGRAM SHOWING HOW A PISTON VALVE SYSTEM WORKS

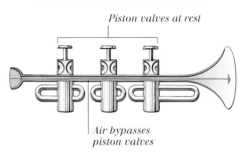

Piston valves at rest

Air bypasses piston valves

PISTON VALVES AT REST

First piston valve pressed down

Second and third piston valves at rest

Air diverted through first valve slide

PISTON VALVE PRESSED DOWN

TRUMPET

Finger button

First piston valve

Spring returns piston valve to rest position

Second piston valve

Third piston valve

Holes divert air into valve slides

Cup-shaped mouthpiece

Mouthpiece receiver

Little finger support

Music stand holder

Narrow, cylindrical tube

Flared bell

Tuning slide

First valve slide

Tuning slide water key

First valve slide thumb hook

Third valve slide finger ring

Third valve slide

Third valve slide water key

Second valve slide

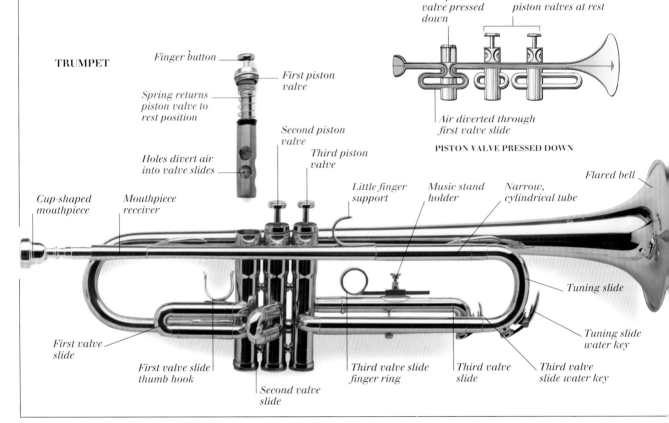

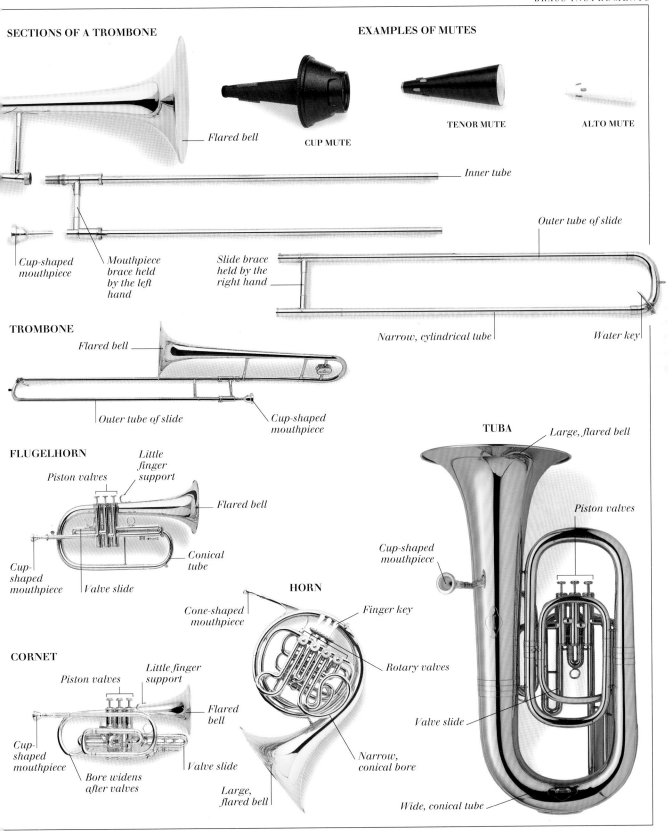

SECTIONS OF A TROMBONE

Flared bell

Inner tube

Outer tube of slide

Cup-shaped mouthpiece

Mouthpiece brace held by the left hand

Slide brace held by the right hand

Narrow, cylindrical tube

Water key

EXAMPLES OF MUTES

CUP MUTE

TENOR MUTE

ALTO MUTE

TROMBONE

Flared bell

Outer tube of slide

Cup-shaped mouthpiece

FLUGELHORN

Little finger support

Piston valves

Flared bell

Cup-shaped mouthpiece

Valve slide

Conical tube

CORNET

Piston valves

Little finger support

Flared bell

Cup-shaped mouthpiece

Bore widens after valves

Valve slide

HORN

Cone-shaped mouthpiece

Finger key

Rotary valves

Narrow, conical bore

Large, flared bell

TUBA

Large, flared bell

Piston valves

Cup-shaped mouthpiece

Valve slide

Wide, conical tube

Woodwind instruments

WOODWIND INSTRUMENTS ARE wind instruments that are generally made of wood, although some are made of metal or plastic. The sound of a woodwind instrument is produced by the vibration of air in a hollow tube. The air is made to vibrate by blowing across a blow hole – as in the flute and piccolo – or by blowing through a single reed – as in the clarinet and saxophone – or a double reed – as in the bassoon, cor anglais, and oboe. The pitch of a woodwind instrument can be changed by opening or closing holes cut into the tube of the instrument.

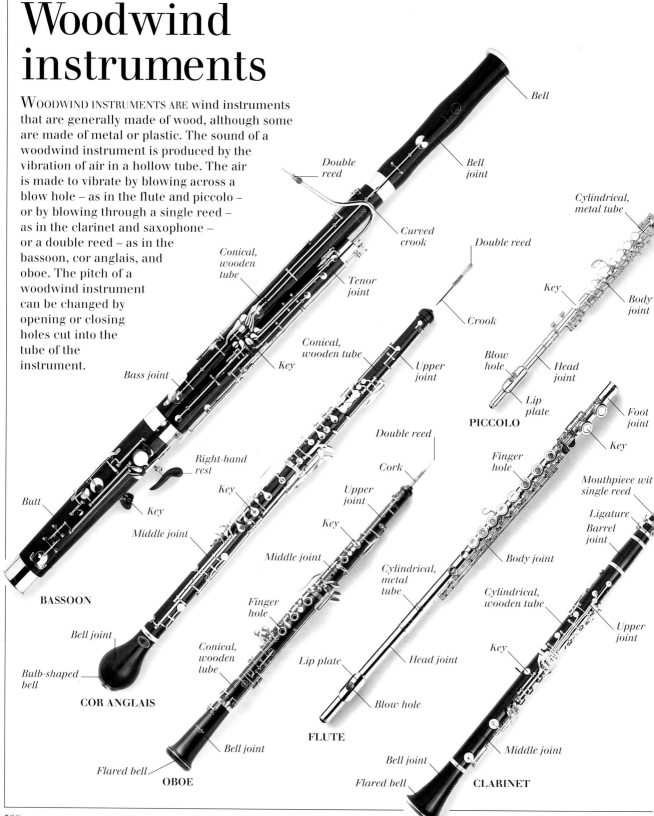

Bell

Double reed

Bell joint

Curved crook

Conical, wooden tube

Tenor joint

Conical, wooden tube

Key

Bass joint

Butt

Key

BASSOON

Right-hand rest

Key

Middle joint

Bell joint

Bulb-shaped bell

COR ANGLAIS

Double reed

Crook

Conical, wooden tube

Upper joint

Key

Middle joint

Finger hole

Conical, wooden tube

Bell joint

Flared bell

OBOE

Double reed

Cork

Upper joint

Key

Cylindrical, metal tube

Finger hole

Lip plate

Blow hole

FLUTE

Head joint

Double reed

Crook

Blow hole

Lip plate

PICCOLO

Cylindrical, metal tube

Key

Head joint

Body joint

Foot joint

Key

Finger hole

Body joint

Mouthpiece with single reed

Ligature

Barrel joint

Cylindrical, wooden tube

Key

Upper joint

Middle joint

Bell joint

Flared bell

CLARINET

TENOR SAXOPHONE

SECTIONS OF A TENOR SAXOPHONE

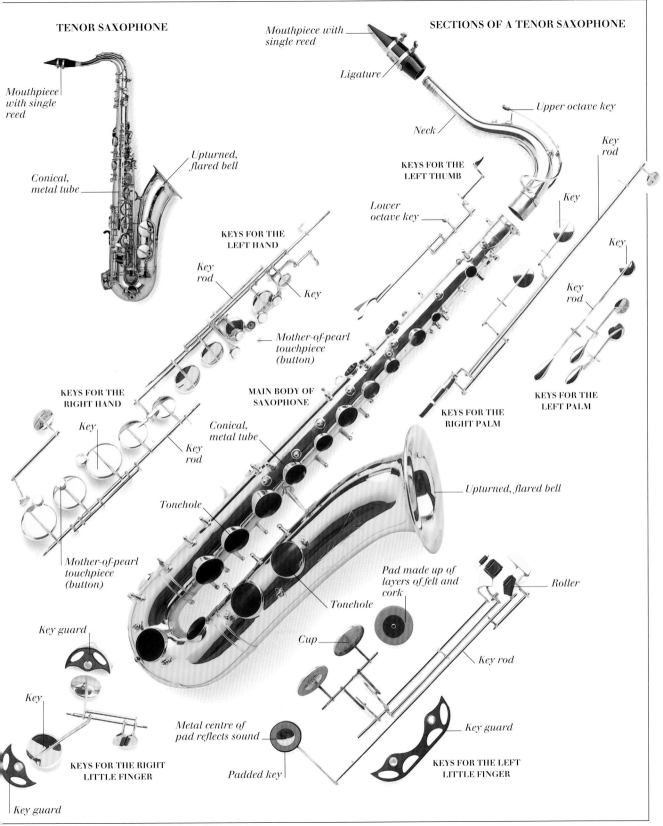

Mouthpiece with single reed

Mouthpiece with single reed

Ligature

Upper octave key

Neck

Key rod

Conical, metal tube

Upturned, flared bell

KEYS FOR THE LEFT THUMB

Lower octave key

Key

KEYS FOR THE LEFT HAND

Key

Key rod

Key rod

Key

Mother-of-pearl touchpiece (button)

MAIN BODY OF SAXOPHONE

KEYS FOR THE RIGHT PALM

KEYS FOR THE LEFT PALM

KEYS FOR THE RIGHT HAND

Key

Conical, metal tube

Key rod

Tonehole

Upturned, flared bell

Mother-of-pearl touchpiece (button)

Tonehole

Pad made up of layers of felt and cork

Roller

Key guard

Cup

Key rod

Key

Metal centre of pad reflects sound

Key guard

KEYS FOR THE RIGHT LITTLE FINGER

Padded key

KEYS FOR THE LEFT LITTLE FINGER

Key guard

Stringed instruments

STRINGED INSTRUMENTS PRODUCE SOUND by the vibration of stretched strings. This may be done by drawing a bow across the strings, as in the violin; or by plucking the strings, as in the harp and guitar (see pp. 512-513). The four modern members of the bowed string family are the violin, viola, cello (violoncello), and double bass. Each consists of a hollow, wooden body, a long neck, and four strings. The bow is a wooden stick with horsehair stretched across its length. The vibrations made by drawing the bow across the strings are transmitted to the hollow body, and this itself vibrates, amplifying and enriching the sound produced. The harp consists of a set of strings of different lengths stretched across a wooden frame. The strings are plucked by the player's thumbs and fingers – except the little finger of each hand – which produces vibrations that are amplified by the harp's soundboard. The pitch of the note produced by any stringed instrument depends on the length, weight, and tension of the string. A shorter, lighter, or tighter string gives a higher note.

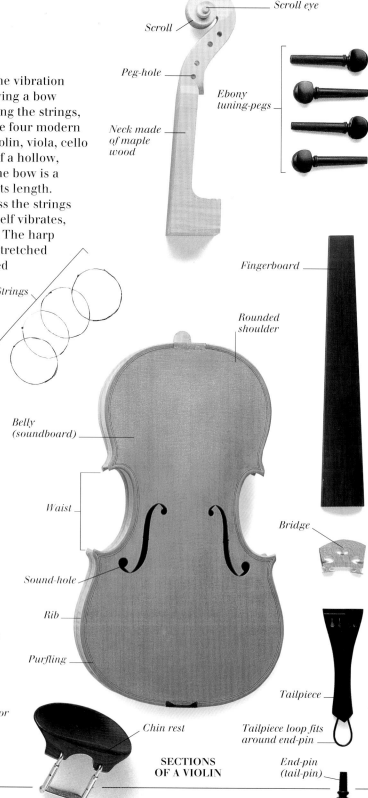

Scroll eye
Scroll
Peg-hole
Ebony tuning-pegs
Neck made of maple wood
Fingerboard
Strings
Rounded shoulder
Belly (soundboard)
Waist
Sound-hole
Rib
Purfling
Bridge
Tailpiece
Chin rest
Tailpiece loop fits around end-pin
End-pin (tail-pin)

SECTIONS OF A VIOLIN

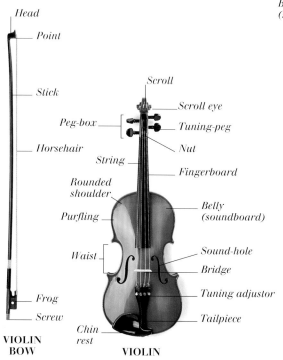

Head
Point
Stick
Horsehair
Scroll
Scroll eye
Peg-box
Tuning-peg
Nut
String
Fingerboard
Rounded shoulder
Belly (soundboard)
Purfling
Waist
Sound-hole
Bridge
Tuning adjustor
Frog
Tailpiece
Screw
Chin rest

VIOLIN BOW

VIOLIN

HARP

Crown

Tuning-peg

Neck (string arm)

Shoulder

String

Soundboard

Pillar

Pedestal

Foot

Pedal

DOUBLE BASS BOW

Head

Point

Inward-curving stick

Horsehair

Frog

Screw

Scroll

Scroll eye

Tuning-pegs at back of peg-box

Nut

Fingerboard

String

Sloping shoulder

VIOLA

Scroll

Tuning-peg

Scroll eye

Peg-box

Nut

ngerboard

ly
undboard)

String

Rounded shoulder

Purfling

aist

Bridge

und-
le

Tuning adjustor

Chin rest

Tailpiece

CELLO (VIOLONCELLO)

Scroll

Scroll eye

Peg-box

Tuning-peg

Nut

Fingerboard

String

Belly (soundboard)

Rounded shoulder

Waist

Sound-hole

Bridge

Tuning adjustor

Tailpiece

Spike

DOUBLE BASS

Belly (soundboard)

Purfling

Waist

Sound-hole

Bridge

Rib

Sound-hole

Tailpiece

Spike

Guitars

THE GUITAR IS A PLUCKED stringed instrument
(see pp. 510-511). There are two types of guitar –
acoustic and electric. Acoustic guitars have hollow
bodies and six or twelve strings. Plucking the strings
produces vibrations that are amplified by their hollow
bodies. Electric guitars usually have solid bodies and
six strings. Pick-ups placed under the strings convert
their vibrations into electronic signals that are magnified
by an amplifier, and sent to a loudspeaker where they are
converted into sounds (see pp. 520-521). Electric bass
guitars are very similar in structure to electric guitars,
and produce sound in the same way, but have four
strings and play bass notes.

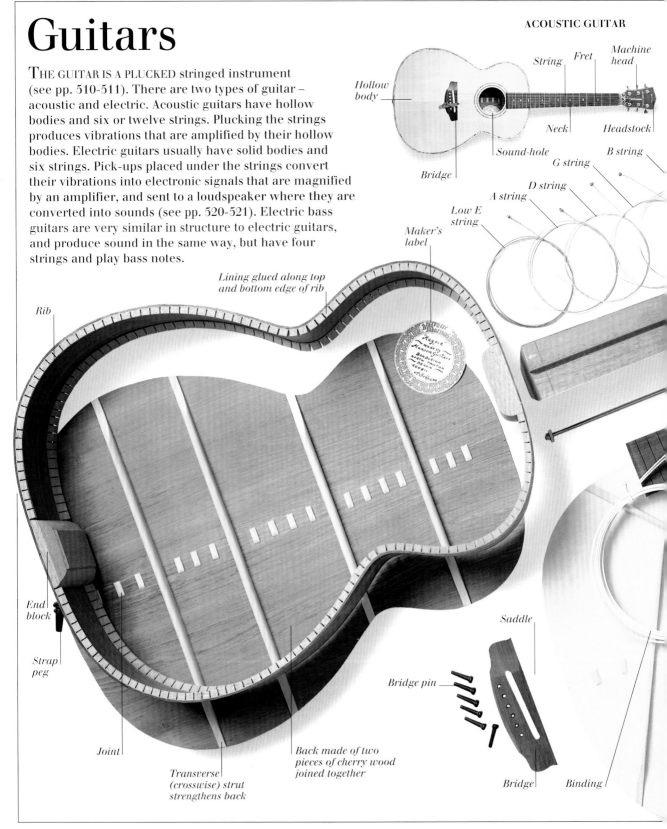

ACOUSTIC GUITAR

Hollow body

String

Fret

Machine head

Neck

Headstock

Sound-hole

B string

Bridge

G string

D string

A string

Low E string

Maker's label

Lining glued along top and bottom edge of rib

Rib

End block

Strap peg

Joint

Transverse (crosswise) strut strengthens back

Back made of two pieces of cherry wood joined together

Bridge pin

Saddle

Bridge

Binding

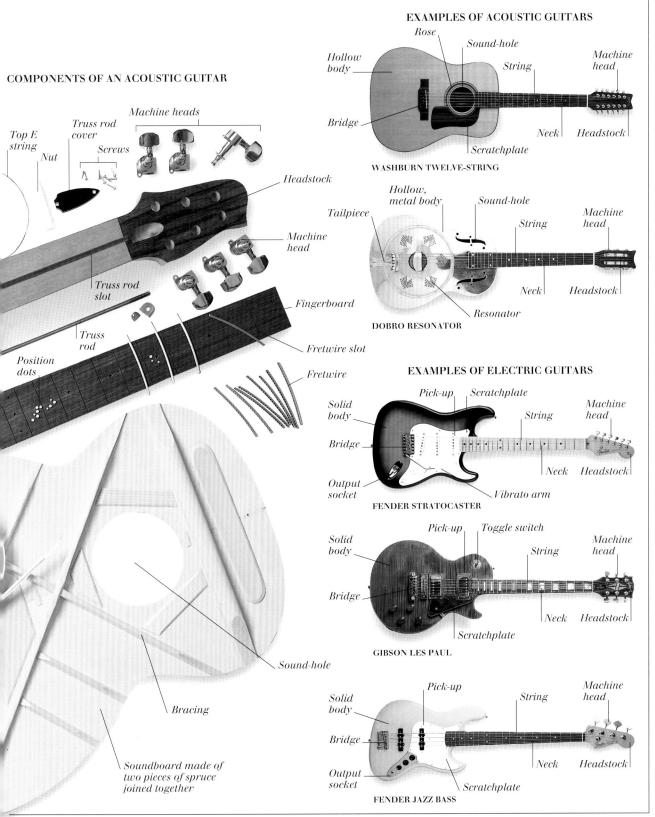

EXAMPLES OF ACOUSTIC GUITARS

Rose
Sound-hole
String
Machine head
Hollow body
Bridge
Neck
Headstock
Scratchplate

WASHBURN TWELVE-STRING

COMPONENTS OF AN ACOUSTIC GUITAR

Machine heads
Truss rod cover
Screws
Top E string
Nut
Headstock
Machine head
Truss rod slot
Truss rod
Fingerboard
Position dots
Fretwire slot
Fretwire
Sound-hole
Bracing
Soundboard made of two pieces of spruce joined together

Hollow, metal body
Tailpiece
Sound-hole
String
Machine head
Neck
Headstock
Resonator

DOBRO RESONATOR

EXAMPLES OF ELECTRIC GUITARS

Pick-up
Scratchplate
Machine head
Solid body
String
Bridge
Neck
Headstock
Output socket
Vibrato arm

FENDER STRATOCASTER

Pick-up
Toggle switch
Machine head
Solid body
String
Bridge
Neck
Headstock
Scratchplate

GIBSON LES PAUL

Pick-up
Machine head
Solid body
String
Bridge
Neck
Headstock
Output socket
Scratchplate

FENDER JAZZ BASS

Keyboard instruments

KEYBOARD INSTRUMENTS are instruments that are sounded by means of a keyboard. The organ and piano are two of the principal members of the keyboard family. The organ consists of pipes which are operated by one or more manuals (keyboards) and a pedal board. The pipes are lined up in rows (known as ranks or registers) on top of a wind chest. The sound of the organ is made when air is admitted into a pipe by pressing a key or pedal. The piano consists of wire strings stretched over a metal frame, and a keyboard and pedals that operate hammers and dampers. The piano frame is either vertical – as in the upright piano – or horizontal – as in the grand piano. When a key is at rest, a damper lies against the string to stop it vibrating. When a key is pressed down, the damper moves away from the string as the hammer strikes it, causing the string to vibrate and sound a note.

ORGAN PIPE

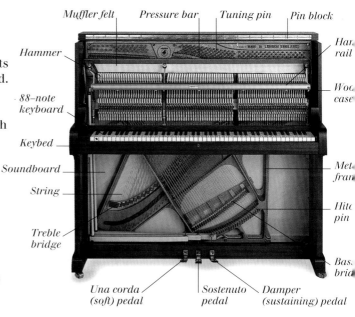

UPRIGHT PIANO

Muffler felt
Pressure bar
Tuning pin
Pin block
Hammer
Har rail
88–note keyboard
Woo case
Keybed
Soundboard
Met fran
String
Hito pin
Treble bridge
Bas bri

Una corda (soft) pedal
Sostenuto pedal
Damper (sustaining) pedal

UPRIGHT PIANO ACTION

KEY AT REST

String
Hammer
Damper lies against string, and stops it vibrating
Hammer rest
Back check
Damper lever
Action lever
Jack
Capstan screw
Key released

KEY PRESSED DOW

String
Hammer strikes string
Damper moves away from string, allowing it to vibrate
Hammer rest
Back check
Action lever
Damper lever
Capstan screw
Jack
Key pressed down

ORGAN CONSOLE

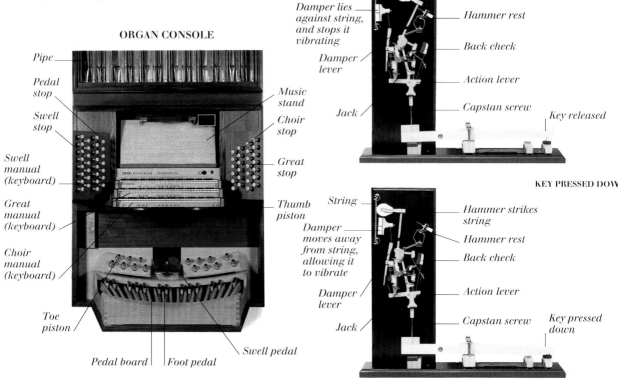

Pipe
Pedal stop
Swell stop
Music stand
Choir stop
Swell manual (keyboard)
Great stop
Great manual (keyboard)
Thumb piston
Choir manual (keyboard)
Toe piston
Pedal board
Foot pedal
Swell pedal

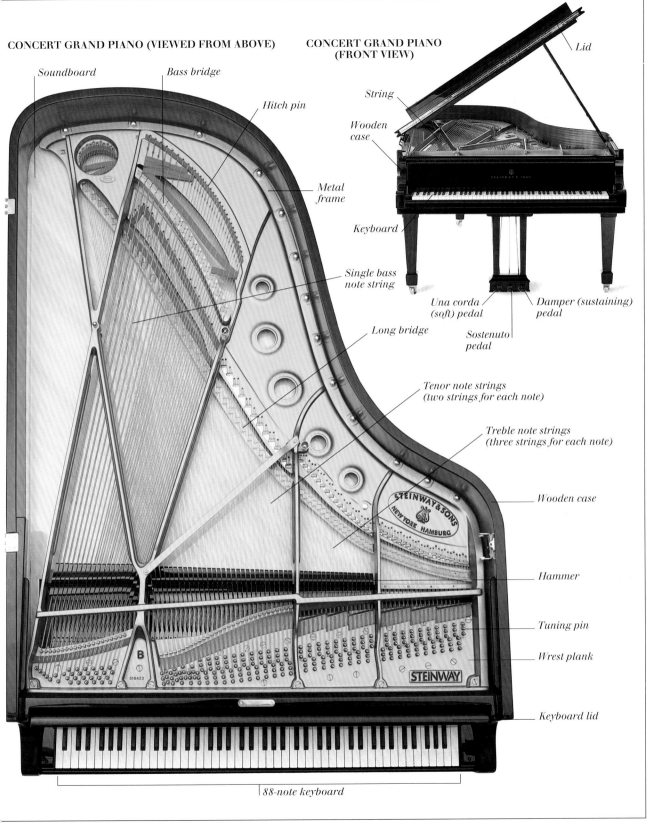

CONCERT GRAND PIANO (VIEWED FROM ABOVE)

CONCERT GRAND PIANO (FRONT VIEW)

Soundboard

Bass bridge

Hitch pin

Lid

String

Wooden case

Metal frame

Keyboard

Single bass note string

Long bridge

Una corda (soft) pedal

Damper (sustaining) pedal

Sostenuto pedal

Tenor note strings (two strings for each note)

Treble note strings (three strings for each note)

Wooden case

Hammer

Tuning pin

Wrest plank

Keyboard lid

STEINWAY

88-note keyboard

Percussion instruments

TEMPLE BLOCKS

PERCUSSION INSTRUMENTS are a large group of instruments that produce sound by being struck, shaken, scraped, or clashed together. Most percussion instruments – such as the tam-tam (gong), cymbals, and maracas – do not have a definite pitch and are used for rhythm and impact, and the distinctive timbre (colour) of their sound. Other percussion instruments – such as the xylophone, vibraphone, and tubular bells – are tuned to a definite pitch and can play melody, harmony, and rhythms. The xylophone and vibraphone each have two rows of bars that are arranged in a similar way to the black and white keys of a piano. Metal tubes are suspended below the bars to amplify the sound. The vibraphone has electrically operated fans that rotate in the tubes and produce a vibrato (wavering pitch) effect.

TUBULAR BELLS

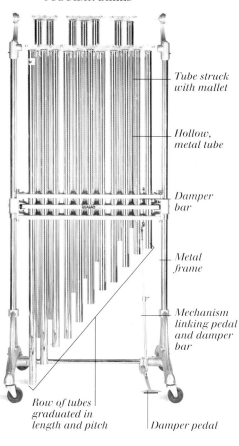

Tube struck with mallet

Hollow, metal tube

Damper bar

Metal frame

Mechanism linking pedal and damper bar

Row of tubes graduated in length and pitch

Damper pedal

EXAMPLES OF BEATERS

SOFT-HEADED BEATER　　*Felt-covered head*

HARD-HEADED BEATER　　*Rosewood head*

Leather-covered head

MALLET

TAM-TAM (GONG)

Tam-tam struck in centre with soft-headed beater

Cord

Metal frame

XYLOPHONE

Row of bars graduated in length and pitch

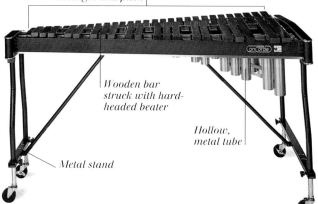

Wooden bar struck with hard-headed beater

Hollow, metal tube

Metal stand

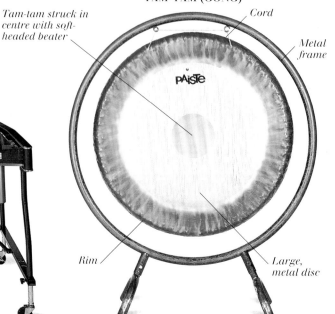

Rim

Large, metal disc

CYMBALS

Leather strap fits around player's hand

Pad protects hands from vibrations

Zildjian

Thin, convex disc of copper and tin alloy

SECTIONS OF A MARACA

Wooden handle

Lead shot

Hollow, wooden head

CLAVES

Hardwood sticks clashed together to give a sharp crack

TRIANGLE

Steel rod bent into triangular shape

Steel beater

CASTANETS

Cord

Hollowed wood

VIBRAPHONE

Row of bars graduated in length and pitch

Metal bar struck with soft-headed beater

MUSSER

Metal frame

Damper pedal

Metal tube containing electrically operated fan that produces vibrato (wavering pitch) effect

Electric cable

Drums

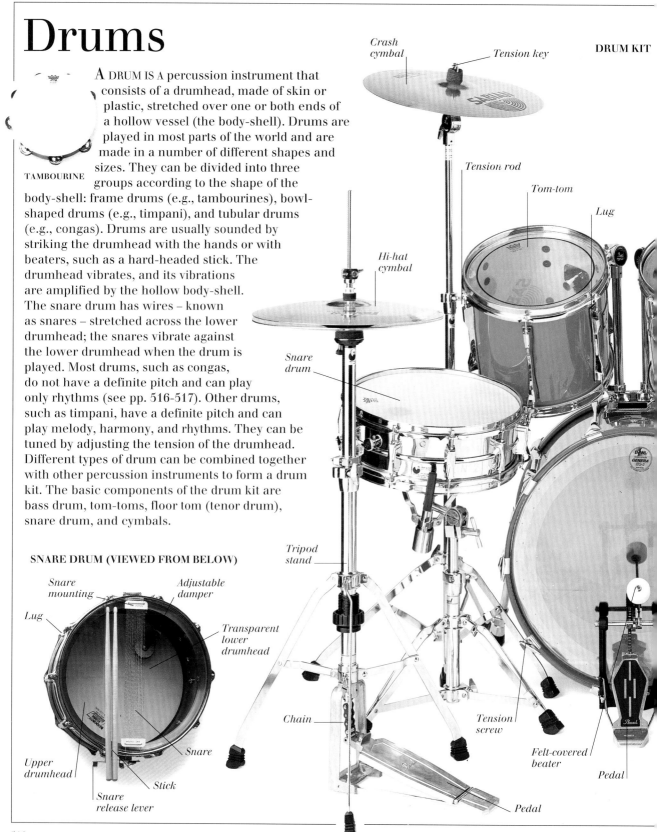

A DRUM IS A percussion instrument that consists of a drumhead, made of skin or plastic, stretched over one or both ends of a hollow vessel (the body-shell). Drums are played in most parts of the world and are made in a number of different shapes and sizes. They can be divided into three groups according to the shape of the body-shell: frame drums (e.g., tambourines), bowl-shaped drums (e.g., timpani), and tubular drums (e.g., congas). Drums are usually sounded by striking the drumhead with the hands or with beaters, such as a hard-headed stick. The drumhead vibrates, and its vibrations are amplified by the hollow body-shell. The snare drum has wires – known as snares – stretched across the lower drumhead; the snares vibrate against the lower drumhead when the drum is played. Most drums, such as congas, do not have a definite pitch and can play only rhythms (see pp. 516-517). Other drums, such as timpani, have a definite pitch and can play melody, harmony, and rhythms. They can be tuned by adjusting the tension of the drumhead. Different types of drum can be combined together with other percussion instruments to form a drum kit. The basic components of the drum kit are bass drum, tom-toms, floor tom (tenor drum), snare drum, and cymbals.

TAMBOURINE

DRUM KIT

Crash cymbal

Tension key

Tension rod

Tom-tom

Lug

Hi-hat cymbal

Snare drum

Tripod stand

Chain

Tension screw

Felt-covered beater

Pedal

Pedal

SNARE DRUM (VIEWED FROM BELOW)

Snare mounting

Adjustable damper

Lug

Transparent lower drumhead

Upper drumhead

Snare

Stick

Snare release lever

EXAMPLES OF BEATERS

Acorn

HARD-HEADED STICK

Taper

SOFT-HEADED STICK

Felt-covered head

WIRE BRUSH

Wire bristles

Ride cymbal

Tension key

Tom-tom

Height adjustment key

Tension rod

Lug

Floor tom (tenor drum)

Tension rod

Lug

Wooden body-shell

Height adjustment key

Leg

Bass drum

Rubber foot

CONGAS

Metal hoop

Drumhead

Tension rod

Wooden body-shell

Tripod stand

Leg

TIMPANUM (KETTLE DRUM)

Drumhead

Tension rod

Tuning gauge

Metal hoop

Copper body-shell

Strut

Crown

Tension rod

Tuning pedal

Castor

Electronic instruments

ELECTRONIC DRUMS

ELECTRONIC INSTRUMENTS generate electronic signals that are magnified by an amplifier, and sent to a loudspeaker where they are converted into sounds. Synthesizers, and other electronic instruments, simulate the characteristic sounds of conventional instruments, and also create entirely new sounds. Most electronic instruments are keyboard instruments, but electronic wind and percussion instruments are also popular. A digital sampler records and stores sounds from musical instruments or other sources. When the sound is played back, the pitch of the original sound can be altered. A keyboard can be connected to the sampler so that a tune can be played using the sampled sounds. With a MIDI (Musical Instrument Digital Interface) system, a computer can be linked with other electronic instruments, such as keyboards and electronic drums, to make sounds together or in sequence. It is also possible, using music software, to compose and play music on a home computer.

Drum pad

Height adjustment key

HOME KEYBOARD

Power button

Volume control

Function display

Memory record button

Tone editor control

Demonstration tune button

Pitch modulator

Multi-accompaniment system control

Tone and rhythm pattern selector

Key

Tripod

SYNTHESIZER

Memory card slot

Joystick

Function display

Edit control

Data entry key pad

Sound structure guide

Volume control

Pitch modulator

Sound selection control

Key

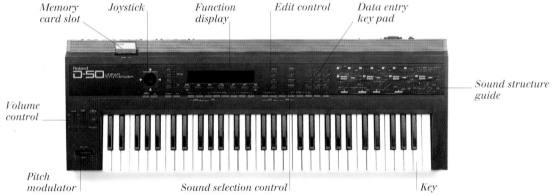

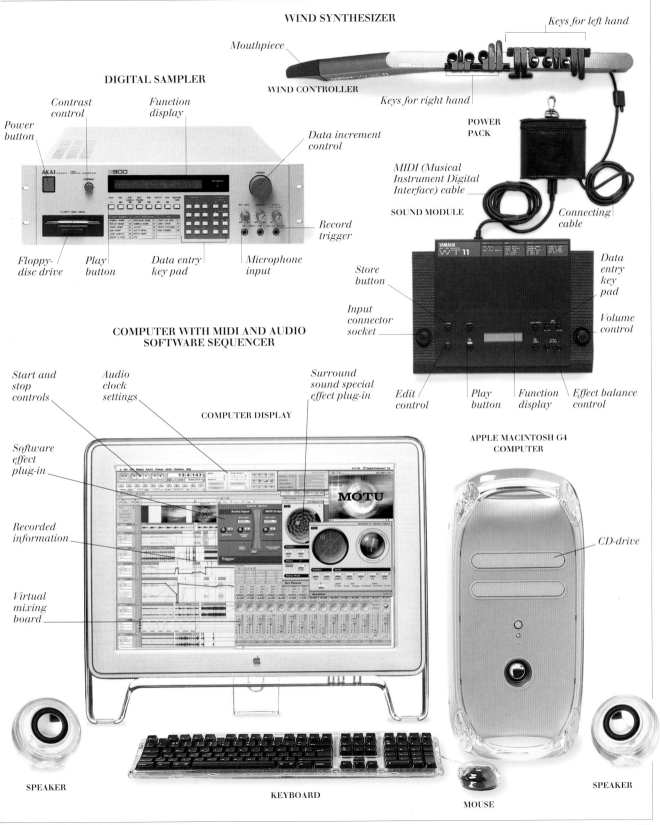

WIND SYNTHESIZER

Keys for left hand

Mouthpiece

WIND CONTROLLER

Keys for right hand

DIGITAL SAMPLER

Contrast control

Function display

Power button

Data increment control

POWER PACK

MIDI (Musical Instrument Digital Interface) cable

SOUND MODULE

Connecting cable

Record trigger

Floppy-disc drive

Play button

Data entry key pad

Microphone input

Store button

Input connector socket

Data entry key pad

Volume control

COMPUTER WITH MIDI AND AUDIO SOFTWARE SEQUENCER

Edit control

Play button

Function display

Effect balance control

Start and stop controls

Audio clock settings

Surround sound special effect plug-in

COMPUTER DISPLAY

APPLE MACINTOSH G4 COMPUTER

Software effect plug-in

MOTU

Recorded information

CD-drive

Virtual mixing board

SPEAKER

KEYBOARD

MOUSE

SPEAKER

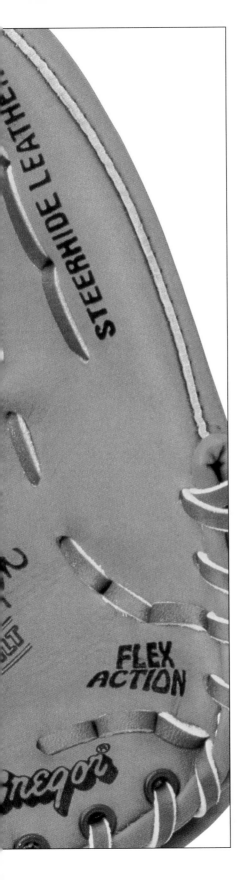

SPORTS

Soccer

GAMES INVOLVING KICKING A BALL have a long history and were recorded in China as early as 300 BC; in medieval Europe, street football was banned as a menace to the public; only in 1863 were the rules established, specifically banning carrying the ball for all players except the goalkeeper, and separating rugby from soccer. Soccer, officially termed association football, is a team sport in which players attempt to score goals by passing and dribbling the ball down the field past opposing defenders, and kicking or heading the ball into the goal net, outwitting the defending goalkeeper. Each team consists of ten outfield players (defenders, midfielders, and strikers) and a goalkeeper. Players from the opposing team may challenge the player in possession of the ball, but an illegal or foul tackle results in a penalty if a foul occurs inside the penalty area or a free kick if outside the penalty area. The round ball used in soccer is more easily controlled than the oval balls used in American, Canadian, and Australian rules football and in rugby. The result is a more "open" or flowing game which is played and watched by millions of people worldwide.

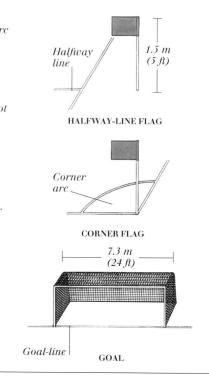

ASSISTANT REFEREE'S FLAG

Lightweight, brightly coloured fabric

Handle with rubber grip

REFEREE'S EQUIPMENT

Red card

Yellow card

Referee's whistle

Stop-watch

PITCH MARKINGS

Halfway line

1.5 m (5 ft)

HALFWAY-LINE FLAG

Corner arc

CORNER FLAG

7.3 m (24 ft)

Goal-line

GOAL

SOCCER PITCH

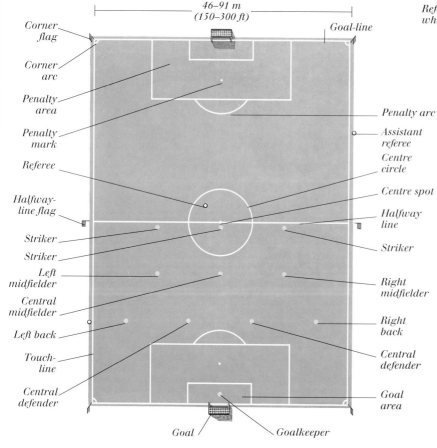

46–91 m (150–300 ft)

Goal-line

Corner flag

Corner arc

Penalty area

Penalty mark

Referee

Halfway-line flag

Striker

Striker

Left midfielder

Central midfielder

Left back

Touch-line

Central defender

Penalty arc

Assistant referee

Centre circle

Centre spot

Halfway line

Striker

Right midfielder

Right back

Central defender

Goal area

Goal

Goalkeeper

GOALKEEPER

Goalkeeper's shirt

Glove

Shin guard

Shorts

Sock

Soccer boot

SOCCER STRIP

Open-neck collar

Lightweight, man-made fabric team shirt

Team logo

Manufacturer's logo

Ribbed welt

Sponsor's logo

MAKING A SOCCER BALL

Hole punched in panel for stitching

Ball size number

Manufacturer's name

Edge cut to fit perfectly

Waxed thread

22–23 cm (8½–9 in)

Needle

Bladder valve

Bladder made from latex rubber

Panels sewn together with ball inside out

Laminated panel

Long cotton sock

Club crest

Synthetic bootlace

Interchangeable nylon stud

Team shorts

SOCCER BOOT

American football

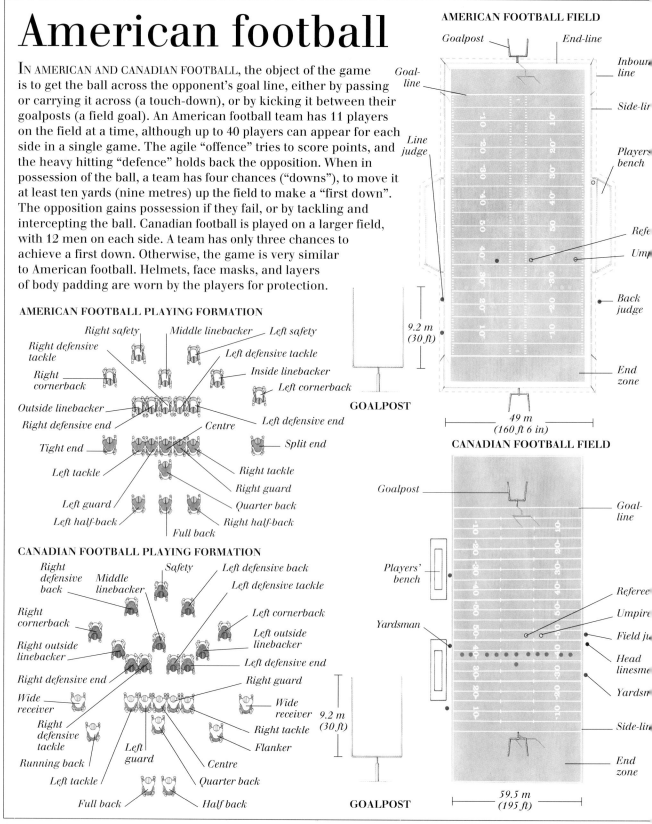

IN AMERICAN AND CANADIAN FOOTBALL, the object of the game is to get the ball across the opponent's goal line, either by passing or carrying it across (a touch-down), or by kicking it between their goalposts (a field goal). An American football team has 11 players on the field at a time, although up to 40 players can appear for each side in a single game. The agile "offence" tries to score points, and the heavy hitting "defence" holds back the opposition. When in possession of the ball, a team has four chances ("downs"), to move it at least ten yards (nine metres) up the field to make a "first down". The opposition gains possession if they fail, or by tackling and intercepting the ball. Canadian football is played on a larger field, with 12 men on each side. A team has only three chances to achieve a first down. Otherwise, the game is very similar to American football. Helmets, face masks, and layers of body padding are worn by the players for protection.

AMERICAN FOOTBALL FIELD

Goalpost
End-line
Goal-line
Inbound line
Side-line
Line judge
Players' bench
Refe
Ump
Back judge
End zone
9.2 m (30 ft)
49 m (160 ft 6 in)

GOALPOST

AMERICAN FOOTBALL PLAYING FORMATION

Right safety
Middle linebacker
Left safety
Right defensive tackle
Left defensive tackle
Right cornerback
Inside linebacker
Left cornerback
Outside linebacker
Right defensive end
Centre
Left defensive end
Tight end
Split end
Left tackle
Right tackle
Right guard
Left guard
Quarter back
Left half-back
Right half-back
Full back

CANADIAN FOOTBALL FIELD

Goalpost
Goal-line
Players' bench
Referee
Umpire
Yardsman
Field ju
Head linesme
Yardsn
Side-lin
End zone
9.2 m (30 ft)
59.5 m (195 ft)

GOALPOST

CANADIAN FOOTBALL PLAYING FORMATION

Right defensive back
Middle linebacker
Safety
Left defensive back
Left defensive tackle
Right cornerback
Left cornerback
Left outside linebacker
Right outside linebacker
Left defensive end
Right defensive end
Right guard
Wide receiver
Wide receiver
Right defensive tackle
Right tackle
Flanker
Running back
Centre
Left guard
Left tackle
Quarter back
Full back
Half back

PLAYER

- Team logo
- Helmet
- Wrist pad
- Player's number
- Thigh pad
- Pants
- Studded shoe

PROTECTIVE EQUIPMENT

28 cm (11 in)

- Painted white ring
- Lace
- Brown pebbled leather

FOOTBALL

HELMET

- Non-breakable plastic
- Rubber-coated plastic
- Shock absorber

Riddell

SHOULDER PAD

BIKE

AIR·LITE

BLUE·LASER 40-42

Chest protector weight up to 2.5 kg (5 lb 8 oz)

BIKE

UPPER ARM PAD

Tie to shoulder pads

BIKE

ELBOW PAD

BIKE

FINGERLESS GLOVE

RIB PADS

Strap ties on to shoulder pad

Tail bone pad

Foam-sponge filling

BIKE AL60

HIP PAD

BIKE AL60

Rigid plastic covering

BIKE AL82

BIKE AL82

THIGH PAD

REFEREE'S SIGNALS

TIME OUT

TOUCH-DOWN OR FIELD GOAL

PERSONAL FOUL

OFFSIDE OR ENCROACHMENT

HOLDING

ILLEGAL MOTION

FIRST DOWN

PASS INTERFERENCE

Screw-in stud

PONY

Fold-over leather tongue

BOOT

PANTS

KNEE PAD

Australian rules and Gaelic football

VARIETIES OF FOOTBALL have developed all over the world and Australian rules football is considered to be one of the roughest versions, allowing full body tackles although participants wear no protective padding. The game is played on a large, oval pitch by two sides, each of 18 players. Players can kick or punch the ball, which is shaped like a rugby ball, but cannot throw it. Running with the ball is permitted, as long as the ball touches the ground at least once every ten metres. The full backs defend two sets of posts. Teams try to score "goals" (six points) between the inner posts or "behinds" (one point) inside the outer posts. Each game has four quarters of 25 minutes, and the team with the most points at the end of the allotted time is the winner. In Gaelic football, an Irish version of soccer (see pp. 524–525), a size 5 soccer ball is used. Each team can have 15 players on the field at a time. Players are allowed to catch, fist, and kick the ball, or dribble it using their hands or feet, but cannot throw it. Teams are awarded three points for getting the ball into the net, and one point for getting it through the posts above the crossbar. Gaelic football is rarely played outside of Ireland.

START OF PLAY

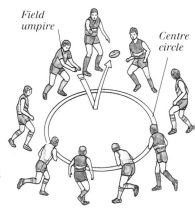

Field umpire

Centre circle

SCORING

GOAL
(6 POINTS)

BEHIND
(1 POINT)

AUSTRALIAN RULES FOOTBALL FIELD

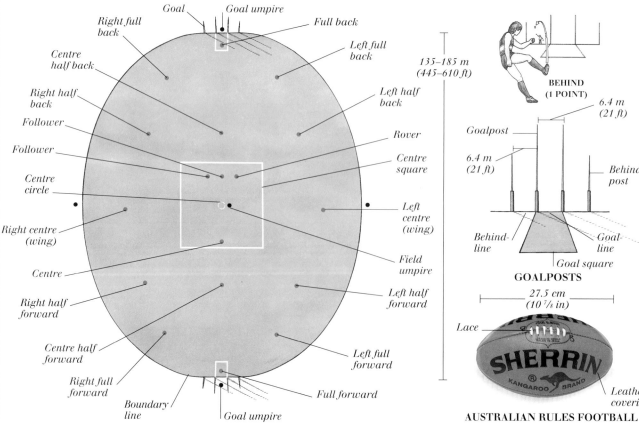

Goal

Goal umpire

Right full back

Full back

Centre half back

Left full back

Right half back

Left half back

Follower

Rover

Follower

Centre square

Centre circle

Left centre (wing)

Right centre (wing)

Field umpire

Centre

Left half forward

Right half forward

Centre half forward

Left full forward

Right full forward

Full forward

Boundary line

Goal umpire

135–185 m
(445–610 ft)

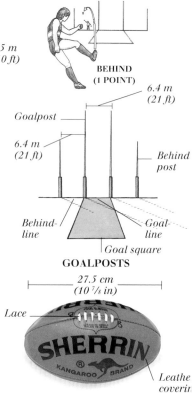

6.4 m
(21 ft)

Goalpost

6.4 m
(21 ft)

Behind post

Behind-line

Goal-line

Goal square

GOALPOSTS

27.5 cm
(10 ⁷/8 in)

Lace

SHERRIN
KANGAROO BRAND

Leather covering

AUSTRALIAN RULES FOOTBALL

AUSTRALIAN RULES FOOTBALL SKILLS

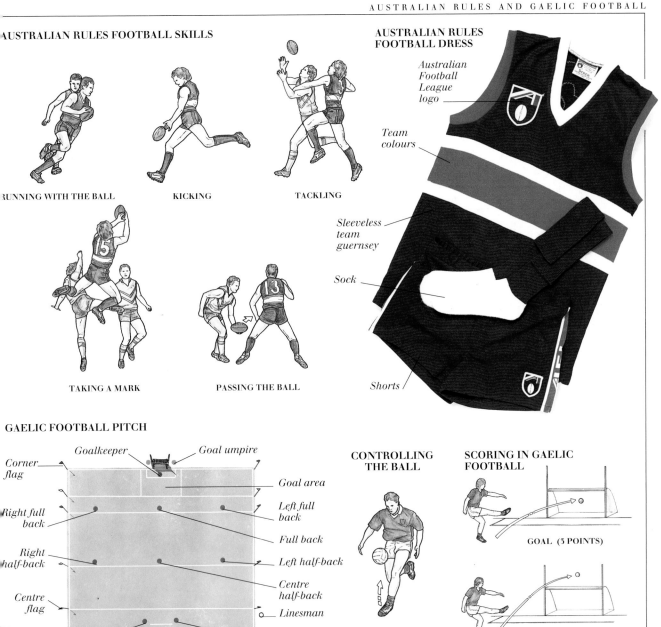

RUNNING WITH THE BALL

KICKING

TACKLING

TAKING A MARK

PASSING THE BALL

AUSTRALIAN RULES FOOTBALL DRESS

Australian Football League logo

Team colours

Sleeveless team guernsey

Sock

Shorts

GAELIC FOOTBALL PITCH

Goalkeeper   *Goal umpire*

Corner flag

Right full back

Right half-back

Centre flag

Linesman

Right midfielder

Referee

Right half-forward

Right full-forward

Full forward

Goal area

Left full back

Full back

Left half-back

Centre half-back

Linesman

Left midfielder

Midfield line

Left half-forward

Centre half-forward

Left full-forward

80–90 m
260–295 ft)

CONTROLLING THE BALL

SCORING IN GAELIC FOOTBALL

GOAL (3 POINTS)

POINT (1 POINT)

22–23 cm
(8 1/2–9 in)

6.4 m
(21ft)

Goalpost

Crossbar

Parallelogram

GOAL

o'neills
all-ireland

GAELIC FOOTBALL

Rugby

RUGBY IS PLAYED WITH AN OVAL BALL, which may be carried, thrown, or kicked. There are two codes of rugby, both played at amateur and professional levels. Rugby Union is played by two teams of 15 players. They can score points in two ways: by placing the ball by hand over the opponents' goal-line (a try, scoring four points) or by kicking it over the crossbar of the opponent's goal (a conversion of a try, scoring two points; a penalty kick, scoring three points; or a drop-kick, scoring three points). Rugby League developed from the Union game but is played by 13 players. In League games, a try scores four points; a conversion scores two points; a drop goal scores one point, and a penalty kick scores two points. Scrummages occur in both codes when play stops following an infringement.

RUGBY UNION SCRUMMAGE

Loose-head prop
Hooker
Tight-head prop
Scrum-half
Flanker
Flanker
Lock forward
Lock forward
Number 8

RUGBY UNION PITCH

Goal
Dead-ball line
Touch in-goal line
Goal-line
5 m line
Scrum-half
10 m line
Loose-head prop
Flanker
Lock forward
Centre
Left wing
Centre
Full back
Touch line
Refere[e]
Hooke[r]
Tight-[head] prop
Touch
Flank[er]
Lock forwar[d]
Right wing
Numb[er]
Fly-ha[lf]
In-goa[l] area

68 m
(225 ft)
maximum

RUGBY UNION GOALPOST

5.5 m (18 ft)
Upright
Crossbar
Protective padding
3 m (9 ft 10 in)

RUGBY LEAGUE SCRUMMAGE

Hooker
Open-side prop
Scrum-half
Blind-side prop
Second-row forward
Second-row forward
Loose forward

RUGBY LEAGUE GOALPOST

5.5 m (18 ft)
Upright
Crossbar
Protective padding

RUGBY LEAGUE PITCH

Goal
Dead-ball line
Touch in-goal
Goal-line
10 m line
Referee
Touch judge
Blind-side prop
Second-row forward
Loose forward
Left wing
Full back
Touch in-goal
Touch-line
Hooke[r]
Open-side pr[op]
Touch
Secon[d] forwa[rd]
Scrum half
Stand-[off] half
Centre
Centre
Right wing

68m
(225 ft)
maximum

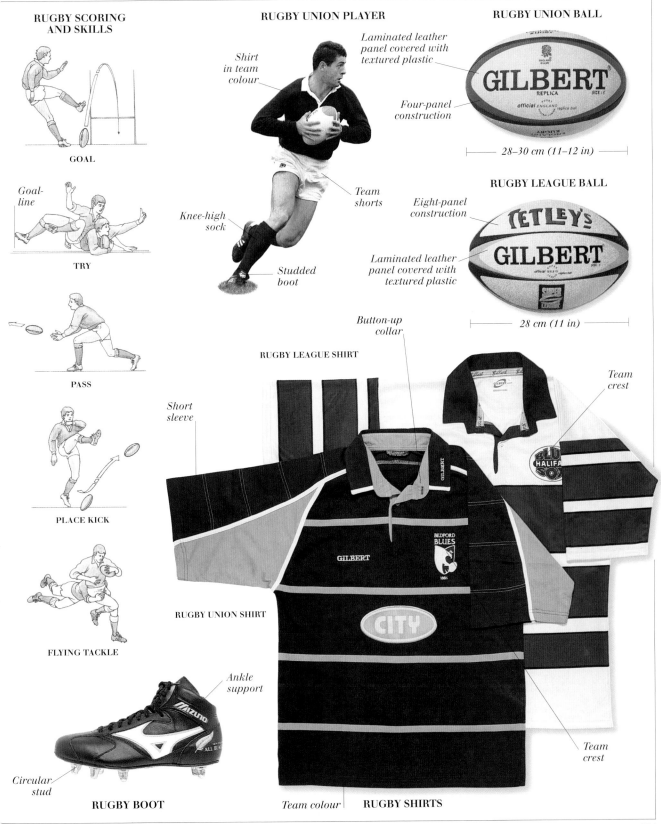

RUGBY SCORING AND SKILLS

GOAL

Goal-line

TRY

PASS

PLACE KICK

FLYING TACKLE

RUGBY UNION PLAYER

Shirt in team colour

Knee-high sock

Team shorts

Studded boot

RUGBY UNION BALL

Laminated leather panel covered with textured plastic

Four-panel construction

28–30 cm (11–12 in)

RUGBY LEAGUE BALL

Eight-panel construction

Laminated leather panel covered with textured plastic

28 cm (11 in)

Button-up collar

RUGBY LEAGUE SHIRT

Team crest

Short sleeve

RUGBY UNION SHIRT

Ankle support

Circular stud

RUGBY BOOT

Team crest

Team colour

RUGBY SHIRTS

Basketball

BASKETBALL IS A BALL GAME for two teams of five players, originally devised in 1890 by James Naismath for the Y.M.C.A. in Springfield, Massachusetts, U.S.A. The object of the game is to take possession of the ball and score points by throwing the ball into the opposing team's basket. A player moves the ball up and down the court by bouncing it along the ground or "dribbling"; the ball may be passed between players by throwing, bouncing, or rolling. Players may not run with or kick the ball, although pivoting on one foot is allowed. The game begins with the referee throwing the ball into the air and a player from each team jumping up to try and "tip" the ball to a team-mate. The length of the game and the number of periods played varies at different levels. There are amateur, professional, and international rules. No game ends in a draw. An extra period of five minutes is played, plus as many extra periods as are necessary to break the tie. In addition to the five players on court, each team has up to seven substitutes, but players may only leave the court with the permission of the referee. Basketball is a non-contact sport and fouls on other players are penalized by a throw-in awarded against the offending team; a free throw at the basket is awarded when a player is fouled in the act of shooting. Basketball is a fast-moving game, requiring both physical and mental coordination. Skilful tactical play matters more than simple physical strength and the agility of the players makes the game an excellent spectator sport.

BASKETBALL SKILLS

CHEST PASS

DRIBBLE

OVERHEAD PASS

LAY-UP SHOT

JUMP SHOT

LONG PASS

INTERNATIONAL BASKETBALL COURT

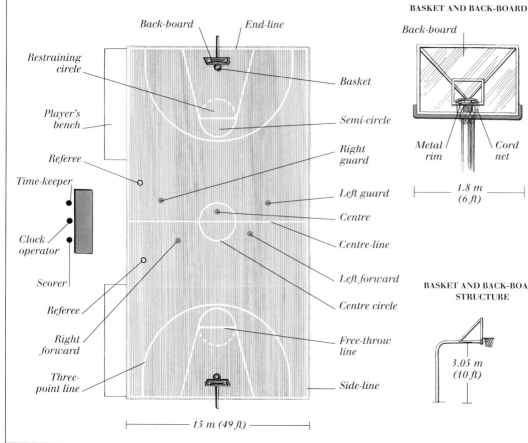

Back-board
End-line
Restraining circle
Player's bench
Referee
Time-keeper
Clock operator
Scorer
Referee
Right forward
Three-point line
Basket
Semi-circle
Right guard
Left guard
Centre
Centre-line
Left forward
Centre circle
Free-throw line
Side-line
15 m (49 ft)

BASKET AND BACK-BOARD

Back-board
Metal rim
Cord net
1.8 m (6 ft)

BASKET AND BACK-BOARD STRUCTURE

3.05 m (10 ft)

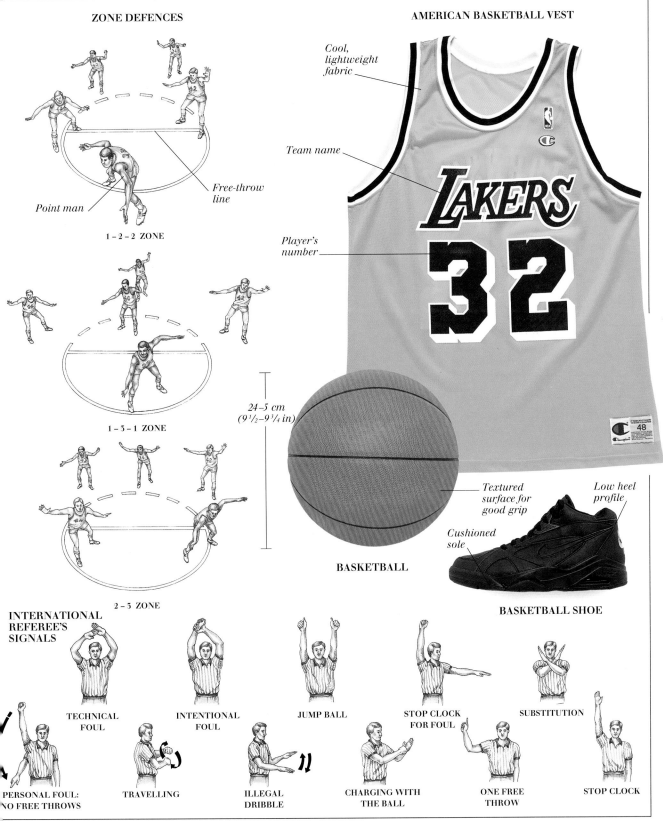

ZONE DEFENCES

Point man

Free-throw line

1 – 2 – 2 ZONE

1 – 3 – 1 ZONE

2 – 3 ZONE

AMERICAN BASKETBALL VEST

Cool, lightweight fabric

Team name

Player's number

LAKERS

32

48

24–5 cm (9½–9¾ in)

Textured surface for good grip

Cushioned sole

BASKETBALL

Low heel profile

BASKETBALL SHOE

INTERNATIONAL REFEREE'S SIGNALS

TECHNICAL FOUL

INTENTIONAL FOUL

JUMP BALL

STOP CLOCK FOR FOUL

SUBSTITUTION

PERSONAL FOUL: NO FREE THROWS

TRAVELLING

ILLEGAL DRIBBLE

CHARGING WITH THE BALL

ONE FREE THROW

STOP CLOCK

Volleyball, netball, and handball

VOLLEYBALL, NETBALL, AND HANDBALL are fast-moving team sports played with balls on courts with a hard surface. In volleyball, the object of the game is to hit the ball over a net strung across the centre of the court so that it touches the ground on the opponent's side. The team of six players can take three hits to direct the ball over the net, although the same player cannot hit the ball twice in a row. Players can hit the ball with their arms, hands or any other part of their upper body. Teams score points only while serving. The first team to score 15 points, with a two-point margin over their opponent, wins the game. Netball is one of the few sports played exclusively by women. Similar to basketball (see pp.532–533), it is played on a slightly larger court with seven players instead of five. A team moves the ball towards the goal by throwing, passing, and catching it with the aim of throwing the ball through the opponents' goal net. Players are confined by their playing position to specific areas of the court. Team handball is one of the world's fastest games. Each side has seven players. A team moves the ball by dribbling, passing, or bouncing it as they run. Players may stop, catch, throw, bounce, or strike the ball with any part of the body above the knees. Each team tries to score goals by directing the ball past the opposition's goalkeeper into the net, which is similar to a soccer net.

VOLLEYBALL SHOTS

OVERHAND SERVE   SPIKE (SMASH)

UNDERHAND SERVE   FOREARM PASS (DIG)

VOLLEYBALL KIT

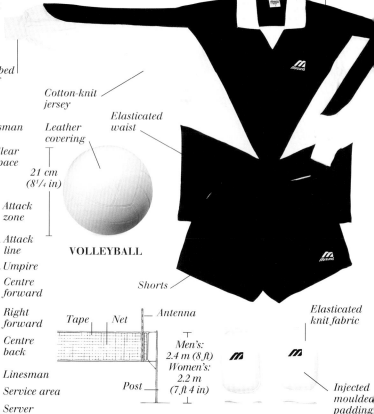

Team colours

Ribbed cuff

Cotton-knit jersey

Elasticated waist

Shorts

Elasticated knit fabric

Injected moulded padding

VOLLEYBALL COURT

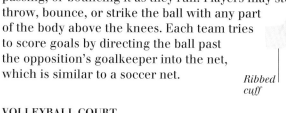

End-line

Linesman

Clear space

Linesman

Side-line

Players' bench

Attack zone

Referee

Attack line

Scorer

Umpire

Net

Centre forward

Left forward

Right forward

Back zone

Centre back

Left back

Linesman

Linesman

Service area

Server

9 m
(29 ft 6 in)

VOLLEYBALL

Leather covering

21 cm
(8¹/₄ in)

VOLLEYBALL NET

Tape   Net   Antenna

Men's:
2.4 m (8 ft)
Women's:
2.2 m
(7 ft 4 in)

Post

KNEE PADS

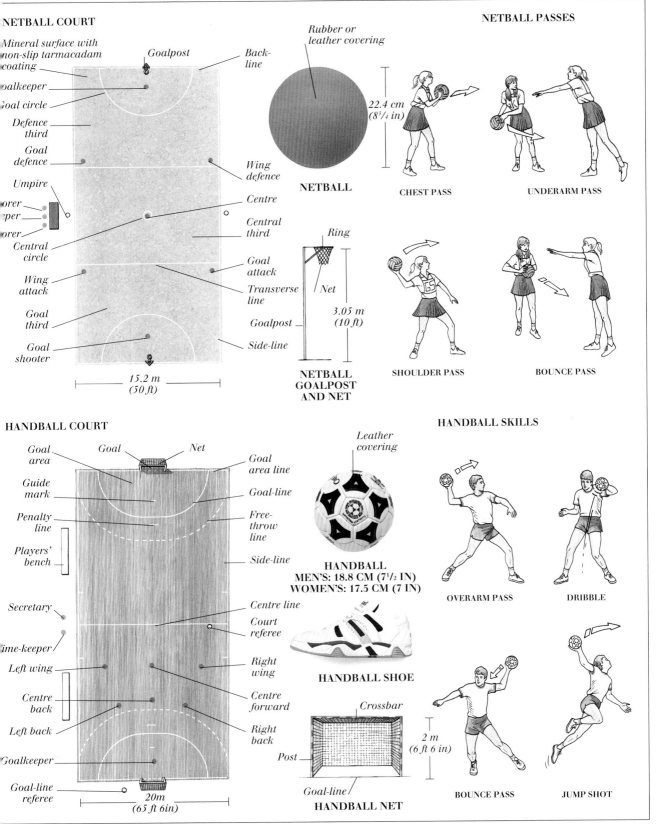

NETBALL COURT

Mineral surface with non-slip tarmacadam coating

Goalkeeper

Goal circle

Defence third

Goal defence

Umpire

orer
eper
orer

Central circle

Wing attack

Goal third

Goal shooter

Goalpost

Back-line

Centre

Central third

Goal attack

Transverse line

Side-line

15.2 m
(50 ft)

NETBALL PASSES

Rubber or leather covering

22.4 cm
(8¾ in)

NETBALL

CHEST PASS

UNDERARM PASS

Ring

Net

3.05 m
(10 ft)

Goalpost

NETBALL GOALPOST AND NET

SHOULDER PASS

BOUNCE PASS

HANDBALL COURT

Goal area

Goal

Net

Guide mark

Penalty line

Players' bench

Secretary

ime-keeper

Left wing

Centre back

Left back

Goalkeeper

Goal-line referee

Goal area line

Goal-line

Free-throw line

Side-line

Centre line

Court referee

Right wing

Centre forward

Right back

20m
(65 ft 6in)

HANDBALL SKILLS

Leather covering

HANDBALL
MEN'S: 18.8 CM (7½ IN)
WOMEN'S: 17.5 CM (7 IN)

OVERARM PASS

DRIBBLE

HANDBALL SHOE

Crossbar

2 m
(6 ft 6 in)

Post

Goal-line

HANDBALL NET

BOUNCE PASS

JUMP SHOT

Baseball

BASEBALL IS A BALL GAME for two teams of nine players. The batter hits the ball thrown by the opposing team's pitcher, into the area between the foul lines. He then runs round all four fixed bases in order to score a run, touching or "tagging" each base in turn. The pitcher must throw the ball at a height between the batter's armpits and knees, a height which is called the "strike zone". A ball pitched in this area that crosses over the "home plate" is called a "strike" and the batter has three strikes in which to try and hit the ball (otherwise he is "struck out"). The fielding team tries to get the batting team out by catching the ball before it bounces, tagging a player of the batting team with the ball who is running between bases, or by tagging a base before the player has reached it. Members of the batting team may stop safely at a base as long as it is not occupied by another member of their team. When the batter runs to first base, his team-mate at first base must run on to second – this is called "force play". A game consists of nine innings and each team will bat once during an inning. When three members of the batting team are out, the teams swap roles. The team with the greatest number of runs wins the game.

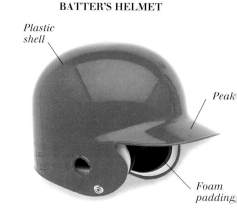

BATTER'S HELMET

Plastic shell

Peak

Foam padding

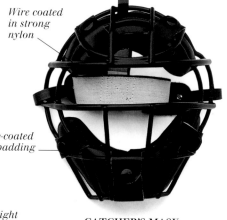

Wire coated in strong nylon

Plastic-coated foam padding

CATCHER'S MASK

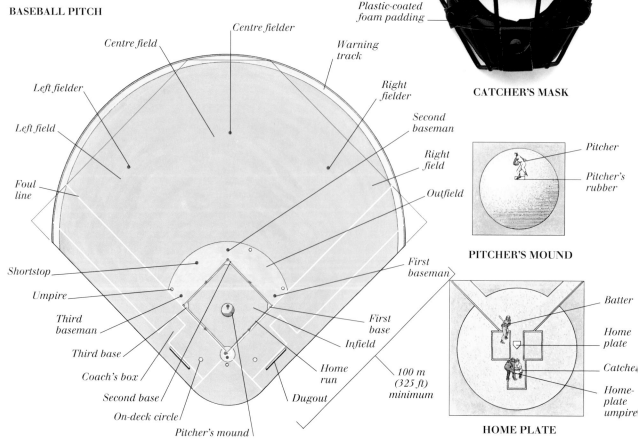

BASEBALL PITCH

Centre field

Centre fielder

Warning track

Left fielder

Right fielder

Left field

Second baseman

Right field

Foul line

Outfield

Shortstop

First baseman

Umpire

First base

Third baseman

Infield

Third base

Coach's box

Home run

Second base

Dugout

On-deck circle

Pitcher's mound

100 m (325 ft) minimum

Pitcher

Pitcher's rubber

PITCHER'S MOUND

Batter

Home plate

Catcher

Home-plate umpire

HOME PLATE

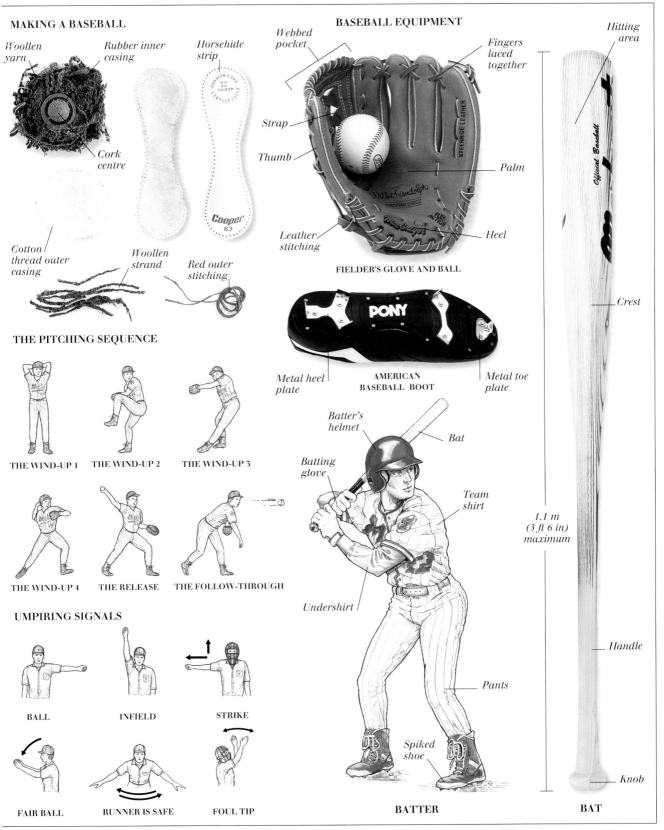

MAKING A BASEBALL

Woollen yarn

Rubber inner casing

Horsehide strip

Cork centre

Cotton thread outer casing

Woollen strand

Red outer stitching

BASEBALL EQUIPMENT

Webbed pocket

Fingers laced together

Strap

Thumb

Palm

Leather stitching

Heel

FIELDER'S GLOVE AND BALL

Metal heel plate

Metal toe plate

PONY

AMERICAN BASEBALL BOOT

THE PITCHING SEQUENCE

THE WIND-UP 1

THE WIND-UP 2

THE WIND-UP 3

THE WIND-UP 4

THE RELEASE

THE FOLLOW-THROUGH

UMPIRING SIGNALS

BALL

INFIELD

STRIKE

FAIR BALL

RUNNER IS SAFE

FOUL TIP

Batter's helmet

Bat

Batting glove

Team shirt

Undershirt

Pants

Spiked shoe

BATTER

Hitting area

Crest

1.1 m (3 ft 6 in) maximum

Handle

Knob

BAT

Cricket

CRICKET IS A BALL GAME PLAYED by two teams of eleven players on a pitch with two sets of three stumps (wickets). The bowler bowls the ball down the pitch to the batsman of the opposing team, who must defend the wicket in front of which he stands. The object of the game is to score as many runs as possible. Runs can be scored individually by running the length of the playing strip, or by hitting a ball which lands outside the boundary ("six"), or which lands inside the boundary but bounces or rolls outside ("four"); the opposing team will bowl and field, attempting to dismiss the batsmen. A batsman can be dismissed in one of several ways: by the bowler hitting the wicket with the ball ("bowled"); by a fielder catching the ball hit by the batsman before it touches the ground ("caught"); by the wicket-keeper or another fielder breaking the wicket while the batsman is attempting a run and is therefore out of his ground ("stumped" or "run out"); by the batsman breaking the wicket with his own bat or body ("hit wicket"); by a part of the batsman's body being hit by a ball that would otherwise have hit the wicket ("leg before wicket" ["lbw"]). A match consists of one or two innings and each innings ends when the tenth batsman of the batting team is out, when a certain number of overs (a series of six balls bowled) have been played, or when the captain of the batting team "declares" ending the innings voluntarily.

CRICKET STROKES

FORWARD DEFENSIVE STROKE

BACKWARD DEFENSIVE STROKE

ON-DRIVE

OFF-DRIVE

PULL

HOOK

SQUARE CUT

LEG GLANCE

POSSIBLE FIELD POSITIONS FOR AN AWAY SWING BOWLER TO A RIGHT-HANDED BATSMAN (IN RED) AND OTHER FIELD POSITIONS

Long on
Long off
Umpire
Boundary line
Bowler
Deep mid-wicket
Non-striking batsman
Mid-on
Extra cover
Silly mid-on
Mid-off
Forward short leg
Silly mid-off
Square leg
Cover
Deep square leg
Point
Square-leg umpire
Gulley
Batsman
Third man
Long leg
Bowler
Leg slip
Second slip
Wicket-keeper
First slip
Fine leg
Sight screen

CRICKET PITCH

Wicket-keeper
Batsman
Wicket
Bowling crease
20 m (66 ft)
Bowler
Return crease
Umpire
Non-striking batsman

CRICKET BALL AND WICKET

Leather skin
Seam
BALL
Bail
WICKET
Stump

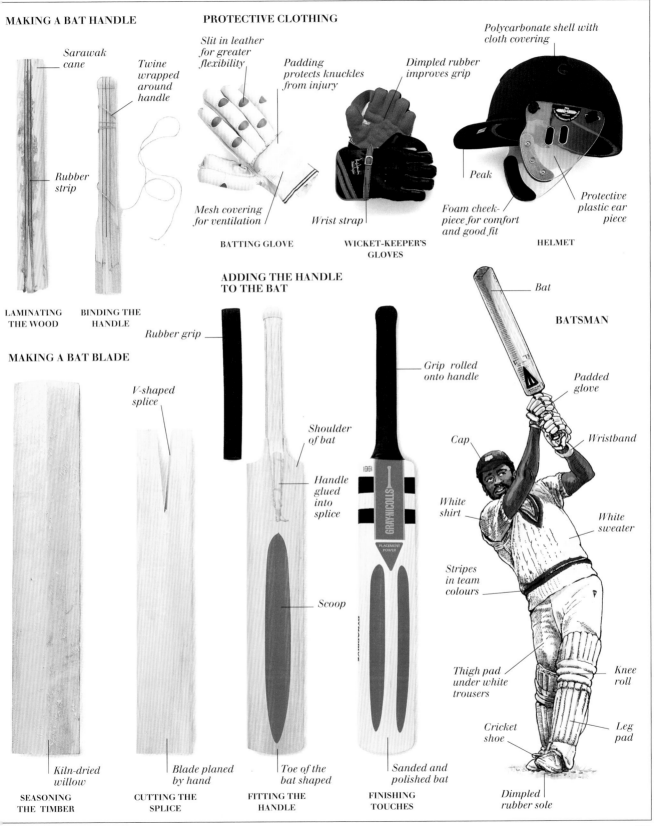

MAKING A BAT HANDLE

Sarawak cane

Twine wrapped around handle

Rubber strip

LAMINATING THE WOOD

BINDING THE HANDLE

MAKING A BAT BLADE

Kiln-dried willow

SEASONING THE TIMBER

V-shaped splice

Blade planed by hand

CUTTING THE SPLICE

PROTECTIVE CLOTHING

Slit in leather for greater flexibility

Padding protects knuckles from injury

Mesh covering for ventilation

BATTING GLOVE

Dimpled rubber improves grip

Wrist strap

WICKET-KEEPER'S GLOVES

Polycarbonate shell with cloth covering

Peak

Foam cheek-piece for comfort and good fit

Protective plastic ear piece

HELMET

ADDING THE HANDLE TO THE BAT

Rubber grip

Grip rolled onto handle

Shoulder of bat

Handle glued into splice

Scoop

Toe of the bat shaped

FITTING THE HANDLE

Sanded and polished bat

FINISHING TOUCHES

Bat

BATSMAN

Padded glove

Cap

Wristband

White shirt

White sweater

Stripes in team colours

Thigh pad under white trousers

Knee roll

Cricket shoe

Leg pad

Dimpled rubber sole

Hockey, lacrosse, and hurling

ALL OVER THE WORLD, TEAM GAMES have evolved which require that a ball be struck or carried, and tossed at the end of a stick. Early forms of these games include hurling, shinty, bandy, and pelota. Hockey is played by men and women: two teams of eleven players try to gain and keep possession of the ball and score goals by using the hockey stick to propel the ball into their opponents' goal net. Skills such as passing, pushing, or hitting the ball by slapping or lifting it in a flicking movement, and shooting at goal are crucial. Hockey is played indoors and outdoors on grass or synthetic pitches. Lacrosse is played internationally as a 12-a-side game for women and as 10-a-side game for men. The women's pitch has no absolute boundaries but the men's pitch has clearly defined side-lines and end-lines. The ball is kept in play by being carried, thrown or batted with the crosse, and rolled or kicked in any direction. In men's and women's lacrosse, play can continue behind the marked goal areas. Similar skills are required in hurling – a Gaelic field game played on the same pitch as Gaelic football (see pp. 528–529), using the same goalposts and net. In hurling, the ball may be struck with or carried on the hurley and, when off the ground, may be struck with the hand or kicked. Goals (three points) are scored when the ball passes between the posts and under the crossbar; one point is scored when it passes between the posts and over the crossbar.

GOALKEEPER'S EQUIPMENT

Face mask

Hard shell

Air vent

HELMET

Stra

Rigid palm

Padded wrist

GAUNTLET

HOCKEY STICK AND BALL

STICK

Handle

Tape

Steam-bent ash head

Blade

Stitched seam

7–7.5 cm (2¹/₄–3 in)

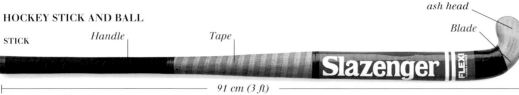

Slazenger FLEXI

91 cm (3 ft)

BALL

HOCKEY FIELD

Centre forward

Inside right

Right wing

Right half

Right back

Side-line

Corner flag

Shooting circle

Goal

Penalty spot

Five yard mark

Goal-line

Inside left

Left wing

Umpire

Centre half

Left half

Left back

Goalkeeper

55 m (180 ft)

Protective overshoe

Padding protect toes against th hard ba

Strap

GOALKEEPER'S KICKER

2.1 m (7 ft)

HOCKEY GOAL

MEN'S LACROSSE FIELD

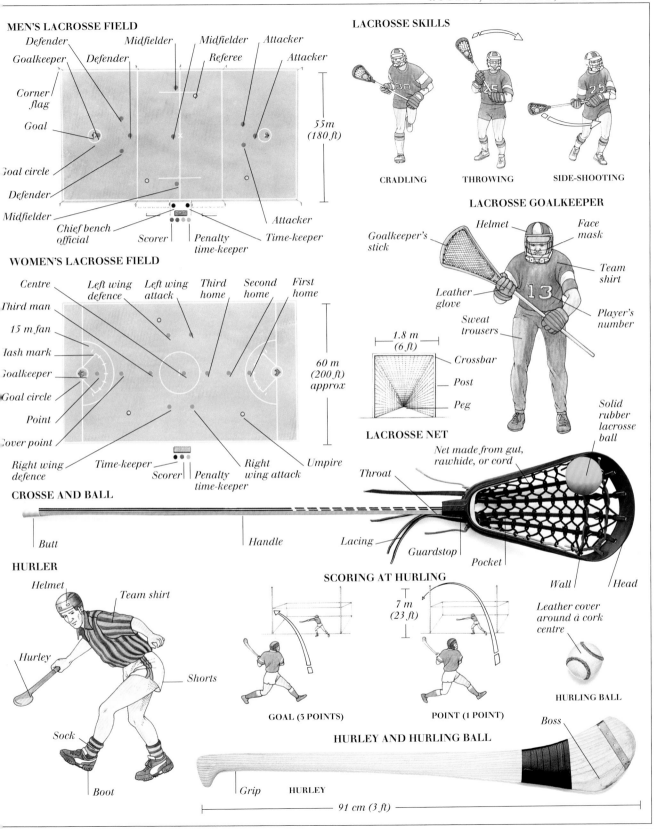

Defender
Goalkeeper
Defender
Midfielder
Midfielder
Referee
Attacker
Attacker
Corner flag
Goal
Goal circle
Defender
Midfielder
Chief bench official
Scorer
Penalty time-keeper
Attacker
Time-keeper
55m (180 ft)

WOMEN'S LACROSSE FIELD

Centre
Third man
15 m fan
Hash mark
Goalkeeper
Goal circle
Point
Cover point
Right wing defence
Time-keeper
Scorer
Penalty time-keeper
Left wing defence
Left wing attack
Third home
Second home
First home
Right wing attack
Umpire
60 m (200 ft) approx

CROSSE AND BALL

Butt
Handle

HURLER

Helmet
Team shirt
Hurley
Shorts
Sock
Boot

LACROSSE SKILLS

CRADLING
THROWING
SIDE-SHOOTING

LACROSSE GOALKEEPER

Goalkeeper's stick
Helmet
Face mask
Team shirt
Leather glove
Sweat trousers
Player's number
13

1.8 m (6 ft)
Crossbar
Post
Peg

LACROSSE NET

Net made from gut, rawhide, or cord
Throat
Lacing
Guardstop
Pocket
Solid rubber lacrosse ball
Wall
Head

SCORING AT HURLING

7 m (23 ft)
GOAL (3 POINTS)
POINT (1 POINT)

Leather cover around a cork centre

HURLING BALL

HURLEY AND HURLING BALL

Boss
Grip   HURLEY
91 cm (3 ft)

Athletics

THE SPORTS that make up athletics are divided into two main groups: track events – which include sprinting, middle, and long distance running, relay running, hurdling, and walking – and field events which require jumping and throwing skills. Contests designed to test the speed, strength, agility, and stamina of athletes were held by the ancient Greeks over 4,000 years ago. However, the abolition of the Olympic Games in 393 AD meant that athletics were neglected until the revival of large-scale competitions in the mid-nineteenth century. Modern stadia offer areas reserved for the long jump, triple jump, and pole vault usually situated outside the running track. The javelin, shot, hammer, and discus are thrown within the track area. Most athletes specialize in one or two events but, in the heptathlon, women compete in seven events, held over two days: 200 m and 800 m races, 100 m hurdles, javelin, shot put, high jump, and long jump. In the decathlon, men compete in ten events over two days: 100 m, 400 m, and 1,500 m races, 110 m hurdles, javelin, discus, shot put, pole vault, high jump, and long jump.

FIELD EVENT EQUIPMENT

Steel wire

Head

Body

Swivel

HAMMER
7 KG (16 LB)

Metal rir

Centi weigh

DISCUS
MEN: 2 KG (4 LB 7 OZ)
WOMEN: 1 KG (2 LB 3 OZ)

Hammer handle

Rubber coating

Shot-pellet filling

12.7 cm
(5 in)

10 cm
(4 in)

MEN'S SHOT
7 KG (16 LB)

WOMEN'S SHOT
4 KG (8 LB 12 OZ)

JAVELIN   Cord grip   Shaft

Tip

Men: 2.6 m (8 ft 6 in)
Women: 2.3 m (7 ft 6 in)

ATHLETICS TRACK AND FIELD

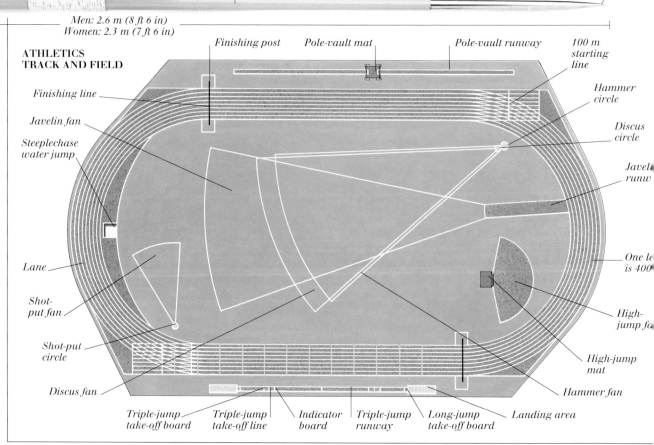

Finishing post
Pole-vault mat
Pole-vault runway
100 m starting line

Finishing line

Javelin fan

Steeplechase water jump

Lane

Shot-put fan

Shot-put circle

Discus fan

Triple-jump take-off board
Triple-jump take-off line
Indicator board
Triple-jump runway
Long-jump take-off board
Landing area

Hammer circle

Discus circle

Javel runw

One l is 400

High-jump fo

High-jump mat

Hammer fan

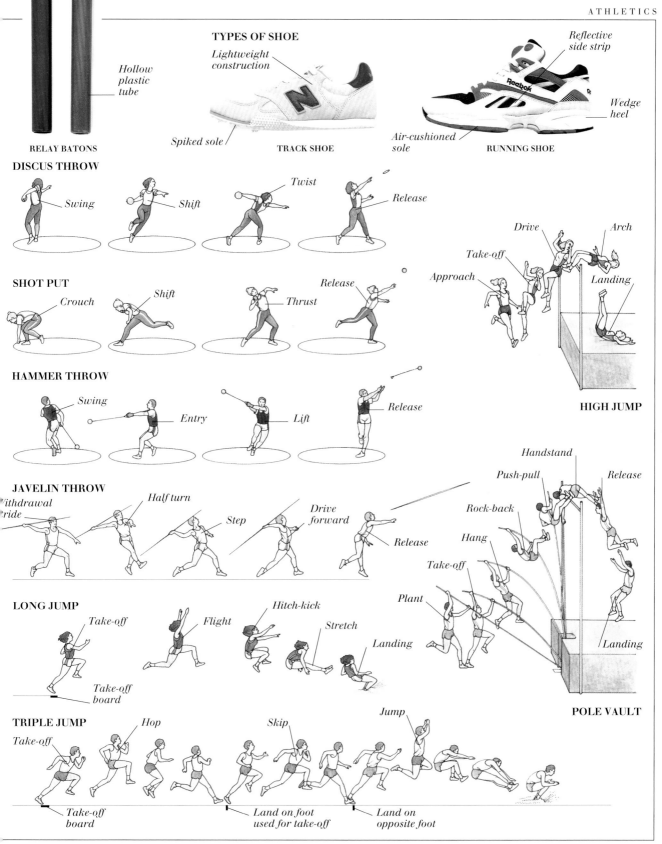

RELAY BATONS

Hollow plastic tube

TYPES OF SHOE

Lightweight construction

Spiked sole

TRACK SHOE

Reflective side strip

Wedge heel

Air-cushioned sole

RUNNING SHOE

DISCUS THROW

Swing · Shift · Twist · Release

SHOT PUT

Crouch · Shift · Thrust · Release

HAMMER THROW

Swing · Entry · Lift · Release

JAVELIN THROW

Withdrawal stride · Half turn · Step · Drive forward · Release

HIGH JUMP

Approach · Take-off · Drive · Arch · Landing

LONG JUMP

Take-off · Flight · Hitch-kick · Stretch · Landing · Take-off board

POLE VAULT

Plant · Take-off · Hang · Rock-back · Push-pull · Handstand · Release · Landing

TRIPLE JUMP

Take-off · Hop · Skip · Jump · Take-off board · Land on foot used for take-off · Land on opposite foot

Racket sports

PROTECTIVE EYEWEAR

THE OBJECT OF ALL RACKET SPORTS is to make shots the opponent cannot return. Games are played by two players (singles) or four players (doubles). Racket shape and size is tailored to each sport, but all rackets are constructed of wood, plastic, aluminium, or high-performance materials such as fibreglass and carbon graphite. Racket strings are usually synthetic, although natural gut is still used. Tennis is played on a court divided by a low net. Opposing players serve alternate games. At least six games must be won to gain a set, and two or sometimes three sets are needed to win a match. Tennis courts may be concrete, grass, clay, or synthetic, each surface requiring a different style of play. Badminton is an indoor sport that is played with light, flexible rackets and a feather shuttlecock on a court with a high net. Players can score points only on their serve. The first to reach 15 points (11 points for women's singles) wins the game. Two games are needed to win a match. Squash and racketball are both played in enclosed courts. One player hits the ball against the front wall, and the other tries to return it before it bounces on the floor more than once. Squash rackets have smaller, rounder heads and stiffer frames than badminton rackets. In America, the game is played on a narrower court than an international court using a much harder ball. Squash games are played to nine points (international) or 15 points (American). In racketball, players use a ball that is larger and bouncier than a squash ball. The racket is thick and sturdy, with a large head, short handle, and a thong that loops around the wrist. Points can be won only when serving, and the first player to reach 21 points wins.

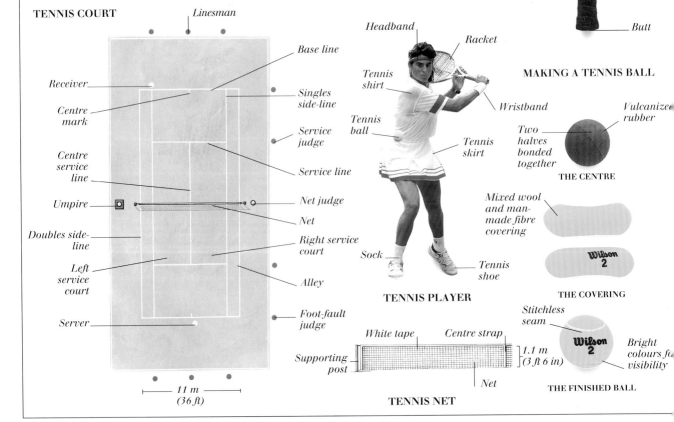

TENNIS RACKET

Synthetic string

Frame

Head

Logo

Throat

Grip

Butt

TENNIS COURT

Linesman

Base line

Receiver

Singles side-line

Centre mark

Service judge

Centre service line

Service line

Umpire

Net judge

Net

Doubles side-line

Right service court

Left service court

Alley

Server

Foot-fault judge

11 m (36 ft)

TENNIS PLAYER

Headband

Racket

Tennis shirt

Wristband

Tennis ball

Tennis skirt

Sock

Tennis shoe

TENNIS NET

White tape

Centre strap

Supporting post

Net

1.1 m (3 ft 6 in)

MAKING A TENNIS BALL

Vulcanized rubber

Two halves bonded together

THE CENTRE

Mixed wool and man-made fibre covering

THE COVERING

Stitchless seam

Bright colours for visibility

THE FINISHED BALL

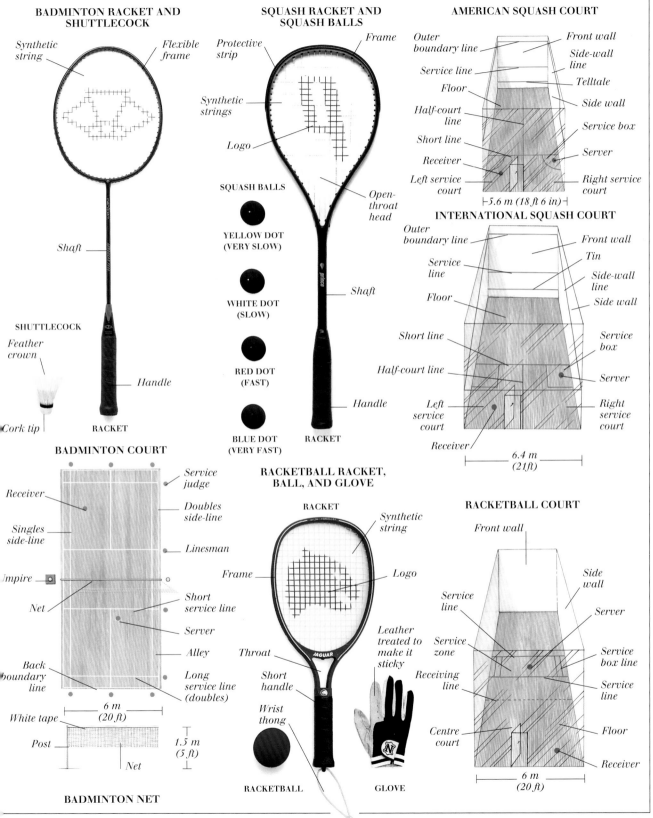

BADMINTON RACKET AND SHUTTLECOCK

Synthetic string

Flexible frame

Shaft

SHUTTLECOCK

Feather crown

Cork tip

Handle

RACKET

SQUASH RACKET AND SQUASH BALLS

Protective strip

Frame

Synthetic strings

Logo

Open-throat head

Shaft

Handle

RACKET

SQUASH BALLS

YELLOW DOT (VERY SLOW)

WHITE DOT (SLOW)

RED DOT (FAST)

BLUE DOT (VERY FAST)

AMERICAN SQUASH COURT

Outer boundary line

Front wall

Service line

Side-wall line

Telltale

Floor

Side wall

Half-court line

Service box

Short line

Server

Receiver

Left service court

Right service court

⊢5.6 m (18 ft 6 in)⊣

INTERNATIONAL SQUASH COURT

Outer boundary line

Front wall

Service line

Tin

Floor

Side-wall line

Side wall

Short line

Service box

Half-court line

Server

Left service court

Right service court

Receiver

6.4 m (21ft)

BADMINTON COURT

Service judge

Receiver

Doubles side-line

Singles side-line

Linesman

Umpire

Short service line

Net

Server

Alley

Back boundary line

Long service line (doubles)

6 m (20 ft)

White tape

Post

1.5 m (5 ft)

Net

BADMINTON NET

RACKETBALL RACKET, BALL, AND GLOVE

RACKET

Synthetic string

Frame

Logo

Leather treated to make it sticky

Throat

Short handle

Wrist thong

RACKETBALL

GLOVE

RACKETBALL COURT

Front wall

Side wall

Service line

Server

Service zone

Service box line

Receiving line

Service line

Centre court

Floor

Receiver

6 m (20 ft)

Golf

THE GAME OF GOLF was first played in Scotland some 400 years ago. Players are required to hit a ball, using a wooden or iron club, from a smooth level point or "teeing ground", down the "fairway", and on to a putting green where the target hole is located. The fairway is a strip of clear land along which there are natural hazards – such as ponds and streams, man-made hazards – such as bunkers (sand-pits), and rough (areas of uncut grass). Championship golf courses have 18 holes. The object of the game is to hit the ball into each hole in turn, and to complete the "round" using as few strokes as possible. Players compete individually or in teams, playing the course together in groups of two, three, or four. The two basic forms of competition are match play and stroke play. In match play, the side winning the majority of holes over a certain number of rounds wins the match. In stroke play, the winner is the player who finishes a certain number of rounds having made the fewest strokes.

GOLF BALL
AND TEE

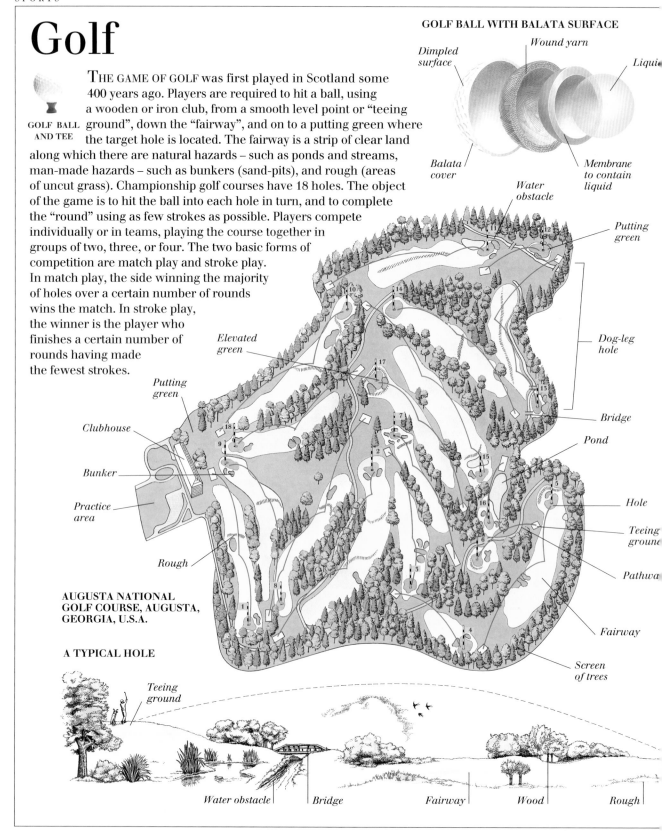

GOLF BALL WITH BALATA SURFACE

Dimpled surface

Wound yarn

Liqui

Balata cover

Membrane to contain liquid

Water obstacle

Putting green

Elevated green

Dog-leg hole

Putting green

Bridge

Clubhouse

Pond

Bunker

Hole

Practice area

Teeing ground

Rough

Pathwa

AUGUSTA NATIONAL GOLF COURSE, AUGUSTA, GEORGIA, U.S.A.

Fairway

Screen of trees

A TYPICAL HOLE

Teeing ground

Water obstacle | Bridge | Fairway | Wood | Rough

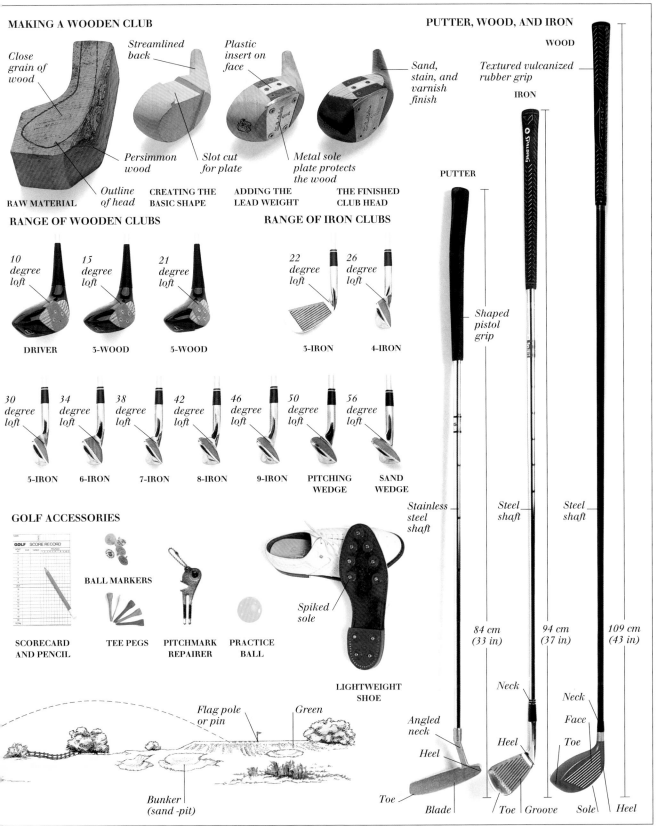

MAKING A WOODEN CLUB

Close grain of wood

Streamlined back

Plastic insert on face

Sand, stain, and varnish finish

Persimmon wood

Slot cut for plate

Metal sole plate protects the wood

Outline of head

RAW MATERIAL

CREATING THE BASIC SHAPE

ADDING THE LEAD WEIGHT

THE FINISHED CLUB HEAD

PUTTER, WOOD, AND IRON

WOOD

Textured vulcanized rubber grip

IRON

PUTTER

RANGE OF WOODEN CLUBS

10 degree loft

15 degree loft

21 degree loft

DRIVER

3-WOOD

5-WOOD

RANGE OF IRON CLUBS

22 degree loft

26 degree loft

3-IRON

4-IRON

30 degree loft

34 degree loft

38 degree loft

42 degree loft

46 degree loft

50 degree loft

56 degree loft

5-IRON

6-IRON

7-IRON

8-IRON

9-IRON

PITCHING WEDGE

SAND WEDGE

Shaped pistol grip

GOLF ACCESSORIES

GOLF SCORE RECORD

BALL MARKERS

Spiked sole

SCORECARD AND PENCIL

TEE PEGS

PITCHMARK REPAIRER

PRACTICE BALL

Stainless steel shaft

Steel shaft

Steel shaft

LIGHTWEIGHT SHOE

84 cm (33 in)

94 cm (37 in)

109 cm (43 in)

Neck

Neck

Face

Flag pole or pin

Green

Angled neck

Heel

Heel

Toe

Toe

Bunker (sand -pit)

Toe

Blade

Toe

Groove

Sole

Heel

547

Archery and shooting

Target shooting and archery evolved as practice for hunting and battle skills. Modern bows, although designed according to the principles of early hunting bows, use laminates, fibreglass, dacron, and carbon, and are equipped with sights and stabilizers. Competitors in target archery shoot over distances of 30 m (100 ft), 50 m (165 ft), 70 m (230 ft), and 90 m (300 ft) for men, and 30 m (100 ft), 50 m (165 ft), 60 m (200 ft), and 70 m (230 ft) for women. The closer the shot is to the centre of the target, the higher the score. The individual scores are added up, and the archer with the highest total wins the competition. Crossbows are used in match competitions over 10 m (33 ft), and 30 m (100 ft). Rifle shooting is divided into three categories: smallbore, bigbore, and air rifle. Contests take place over a variety of distances and further subdivisions are based on the type of shooting position used: prone, kneeling, or standing. The Olympic biathlon combines cross-country skiing and rifle shooting over a course of approximately 20 km (12½ miles). Additional magazines of ammunition are carried in the butt of the rifles. Bigbore rifles fitted with a telescopic sight can be used for hunting and running game target shooting. Pistol shooting events, using rapid-fire pistols, target pistols, and air pistols, take place over 10 m (33 ft), 25 m (82 ft), and 50 m (165 ft) distances. In rapid-fire pistol shooting, a total of 60 shots are fired from a distance of 25 m (83 ft).

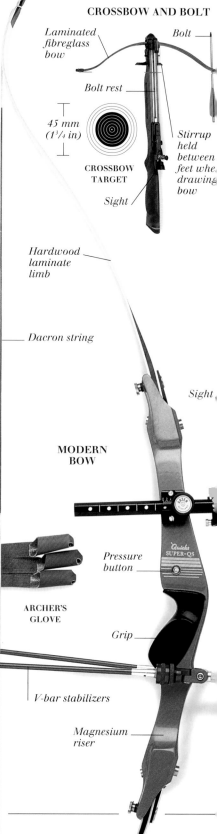

CROSSBOW AND BOLT

Laminated fibreglass bow

Bolt

Bolt rest

45 mm (1¾ in)

CROSSBOW TARGET

Stirrup held between feet when drawing bow

Sight

Hardwood laminate limb

Dacron string

Sight

MODERN BOW

Pressure button

Grip

V-bar stabilizers

Magnesium riser

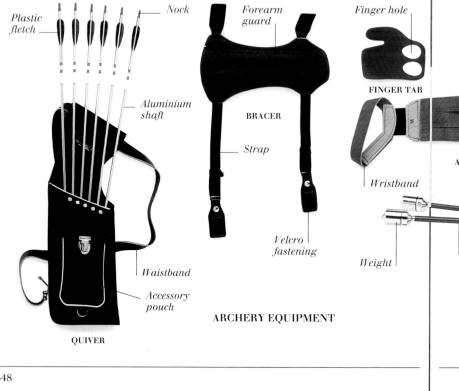

Plastic fletch

Nock

Forearm guard

Finger hole

Aluminium shaft

BRACER

Strap

FINGER TAB

ARCHER'S GLOVE

Wristband

Weight

Velcro fastening

Waistband

Accessory pouch

ARCHERY EQUIPMENT

QUIVER

SMALLBORE BIATHLON RIFLE

Rifle sight without magnifying lens

Fore sight

Barrel

Trigger

5.6 mm (0.22 in) calibre bullet

Trigger guard

Magazine

Extra magazine stored in rifle butt

155 mm (6 in)

SMALLBORE FREE RIFLE TARGET FOR 50 M (165 FT) RANGE

BIGBORE HUNTING RIFLE

Bolt handle

Bolt

Telescopic sight

Open sight

Open sight

7.62 mm (0.3 in) calibre bullet

Sling fixing point

1 m (39 in)

BIGBORE RIFLE TARGET FOR 300 M (1000 FT) RANGE

AIR PISTOL

Wooden grip shaped to fit the hand

Cocking lever and barrel

Piston

155 mm (6 in)

TARGET PISTOL

Back sight

Fore sight

Hammer

Firing pin

Sight pin

197 mm (7¹⁄₄ in)

PISTOL TARGET FOR 18 M (60 FT) RANGE

AIR-PISTOL TARGET FOR 10 M (33 FT) RANGE

Sight ring attachment

Magazine

9 mm (0.35 in) calibre bullet

Trigger

Air-pistol pellet

Nock

FIELD ARROW

Metal tip

Feathering

Wooden shaft

Straw butt

White inner 2 points

Aluminium longrod stabilizer

Blue outer 5 points

Yellow inner 10 points (bull's-eye)

ARCHERY TARGET

Ice hockey

ICE HOCKEY IS PLAYED by two teams of six players on
an ice rink, with a goal net at each end. The object of this
fast, and often dangerous, game is to hit a frozen rubber
puck into the opposing team's net with a ice hockey stick.
The game begins when the referee drops the puck between
the sticks of two players from opposing teams, who "face
off". The rink is divided into three areas: defending, neutral,
and attacking zones. Players may move with the puck and
pass the puck to one another along the ice, but may not
pass it more than two zones across the rink markings.
A goal is scored when the puck entirely crosses the goal-line
between the posts and under the crossbar of the goal.
A team may field up to 20 players although only six players
are allowed on the ice at one time; substitutions occur
frequently. Each game consists of three periods of
20 minutes, divided by breaks of 15 minutes.

GOALKEEPER

- Helmet
- Throat protector
- Butt end
- Pants
- Blocking pad
- Goalkeeper's pad
- Skate
- Goalkeeper's stick
- Face mask
- Team shirt
- Catch glove
- Blade
- Heel
- Blade

ICE HOCKEY RINK

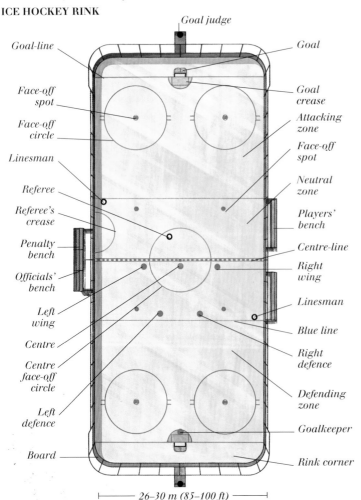

- Goal judge
- Goal-line
- Face-off spot
- Face-off circle
- Linesman
- Referee
- Referee's crease
- Penalty bench
- Officials' bench
- Left wing
- Centre
- Centre face-off circle
- Left defence
- Board
- Goal
- Goal crease
- Attacking zone
- Face-off spot
- Neutral zone
- Players' bench
- Centre-line
- Right wing
- Linesman
- Blue line
- Right defence
- Defending zone
- Goalkeeper
- Rink corner

26–30 m (85–100 ft)

THE FACE-OFF

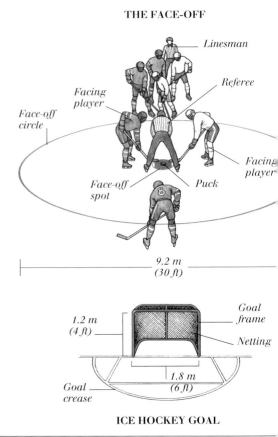

- Face-off circle
- Facing player
- Face-off spot
- Linesman
- Referee
- Facing player
- Puck

9.2 m (30 ft)

- 1.2 m (4 ft)
- Goal frame
- Netting
- 1.8 m (6 ft)
- Goal crease

ICE HOCKEY GOAL

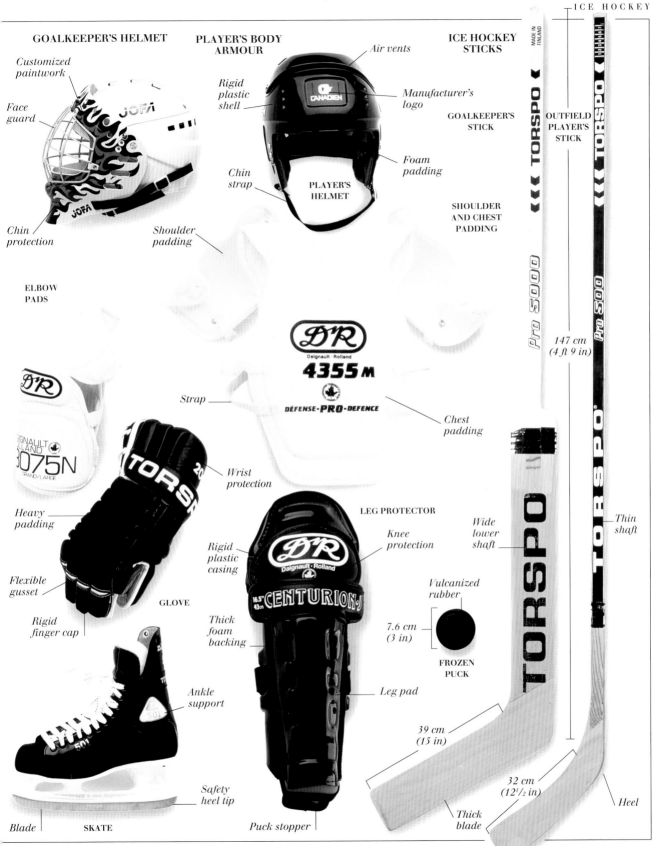

GOALKEEPER'S HELMET

Customized
paintwork

Face
guard

Chin
protection

**PLAYER'S BODY
ARMOUR**

Rigid
plastic
shell

Chin
strap

Shoulder
padding

Air vents

Manufacturer's
logo

Foam
padding

PLAYER'S
HELMET

**ICE HOCKEY
STICKS**

GOALKEEPER'S
STICK

SHOULDER
AND CHEST
PADDING

OUTFIELD
PLAYER'S
STICK

MADE IN
FINLAND

TORSPO

Pro 5000

147 cm
(4 ft 9 in)

TORSPO

Pro 500

ELBOW
PADS

Strap

Chest
padding

Wrist
protection

Heavy
padding

Flexible
gusset

Rigid
finger cap

GLOVE

LEG PROTECTOR

Knee
protection

Rigid
plastic
casing

Thick
foam
backing

Vulcanized
rubber

7.6 cm
(3 in)

FROZEN
PUCK

Wide
lower
shaft

TORSPO

Thin
shaft

Ankle
support

Leg pad

Safety
heel tip

39 cm
(15 in)

32 cm
(12½ in)

Heel

Blade

SKATE

Puck stopper

Thick
blade

Alpine skiing

COMPETITIVE ALPINE SKIING is divided into four disciplines: downhill, slalom, giant slalom, and super-giant slalom (Super-G). Each one tests different skills. In downhill skiing, competitors race down a slope marked out by control flags, known as "gates", and are timed on a single run only. Competitors wear crash helmets, one-piece Lycra suits, and long skis with flattened tips to minimize air resistance. Slalom and giant slalom skiers negotiate a twisting course requiring balance, agility, and quick reactions. Courses are defined by pairs of gates. Racers must pass through each pair of gates to complete the course successfully. Competitors are timed on two runs over different courses, and the skier who completes the courses in the shortest time wins. The equipment and protective guards used by slalom skiers are shown opposite. In Super-G races, competitors ski a single run that combines the technical challenge of slalom with the speed of downhill. The course requires skiers to complete medium-to-long radius turns at high speed, and contain up to two jumps. Clothing is the same as for downhill, but slightly shorter skis are used.

Helmet

Ski goggles

One-piece lycra ski suit

Wrist strap

Ski pole

Basket

Ski boot

Safety binding

Tail

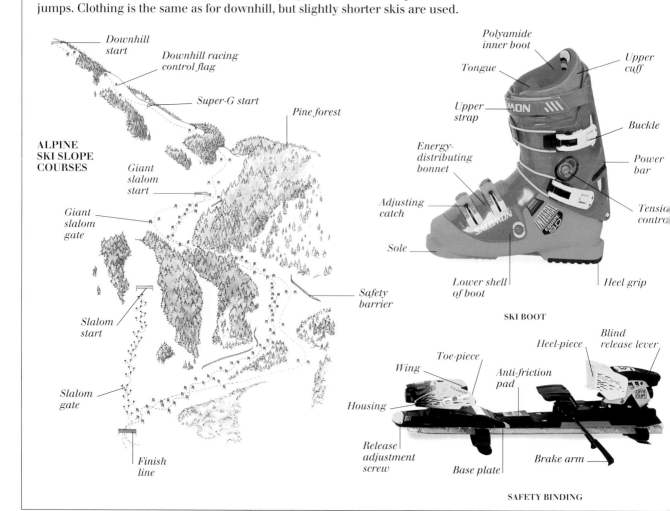

Downhill start

Downhill racing control flag

Super-G start

Pine forest

ALPINE SKI SLOPE COURSES

Giant slalom start

Giant slalom gate

Slalom start

Slalom gate

Finish line

Safety barrier

Polyamide inner boot

Tongue

Upper cuff

Upper strap

Buckle

Energy-distributing bonnet

Power bar

Adjusting catch

Tension contro

Sole

Lower shell of boot

Heel grip

SKI BOOT

Blind release lever

Heel-piece

Toe-piece

Wing

Anti-friction pad

Housing

Release adjustment screw

Base plate

Brake arm

SAFETY BINDING

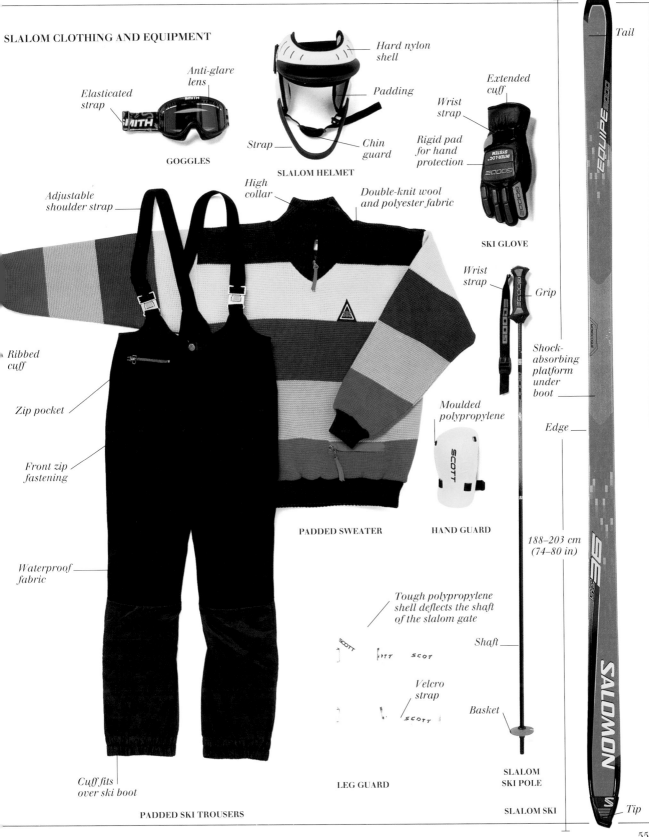

SLALOM CLOTHING AND EQUIPMENT

GOGGLES

Elasticated strap

Anti-glare lens

SLALOM HELMET

Hard nylon shell

Padding

Strap

Chin guard

SKI GLOVE

Extended cuff

Wrist strap

Rigid pad for hand protection

Adjustable shoulder strap

High collar

Double-knit wool and polyester fabric

Ribbed cuff

Zip pocket

Front zip fastening

Waterproof fabric

PADDED SWEATER

Moulded polypropylene

HAND GUARD

Wrist strap

Grip

Shock-absorbing platform under boot

Edge

188–203 cm (74–80 in)

Tail

Tough polypropylene shell deflects the shaft of the slalom gate

Shaft

Velcro strap

Basket

LEG GUARD

SLALOM SKI POLE

SLALOM SKI

Cuff fits over ski boot

PADDED SKI TROUSERS

Tip

Equestrian sports

EQUESTRIAN SPORTS HAVE TAKEN place throughout the world for centuries: events involving mounted horses were recorded in the Olympic Games of 642 BC. Showjumping, however, is a much more recent innovation, and the first competitions were held at the beginning of the 1900s. In this sport, horse and rider must negotiate a course of variable, unfixed obstacles, making as few mistakes as possible. Showjumping fences consist of wooden stands, known as standards or wings, that support planks or poles. Parts of the fence are designed to collapse on impact, preventing injury to the horse and rider. Judges penalise competitors for errors, such as knocking down obstacles, refusing jumps, or deviating from the course. Depending on the type of competition, the rider with the fewest faults, most points, or fastest time wins. There are two basic forms of horse racing – flat races and races with jumps, such as steeplechase or hurdle-races. Thoroughbred horses are used in this sport, as they have great strength and stamina and can achieve speeds of up to 65 kph (40 mph). Jockeys wear "silks" – caps and jackets designed in distinctive colours and patterns which help identify the horses. In harness racing, the horse is driven from a light, two-wheeled carriage called a sulky. Horses are trained to trot and to pace, and different races are held for each of these types of gait. In pacing races, the horses wear hobbles to prevent them from breaking into a trot or gallop. Breeds such as the Standardbred and the French Trotter have been developed especially for this sport.

SHOWJUMPING SADDLE
High cantle
Deep seat
Pommel
Forward-cut flap
Knee roll

SHOWJUMPING FENCES
Standard / Foot / Plank
UPRIGHT PLANKS

Standard / Foot / Pole
UPRIGHT POLES

Back pole / Standard / Foot / Pole
TRIPLE BAR (STAIRCASE)

Standard / Pole / Foot
HOG'S-BACK

Pillar / Wood block pain to resem a br
WALL

Hard hat
Browband
Throat-latch
Rein
Riding jacket
Jodhpurs
Cheek-piece
Showjumping saddle
Running martingale
Hindquarters
Noseband
Dock
Brushing boot
Sheepskin numnah
Girth
Stirrup iron
Riding boot
Hoof
Gaskin
Hock joint
Fetlock joint
Pastern
Coronet

SHOWJUMPING HORSE WITH RIDER

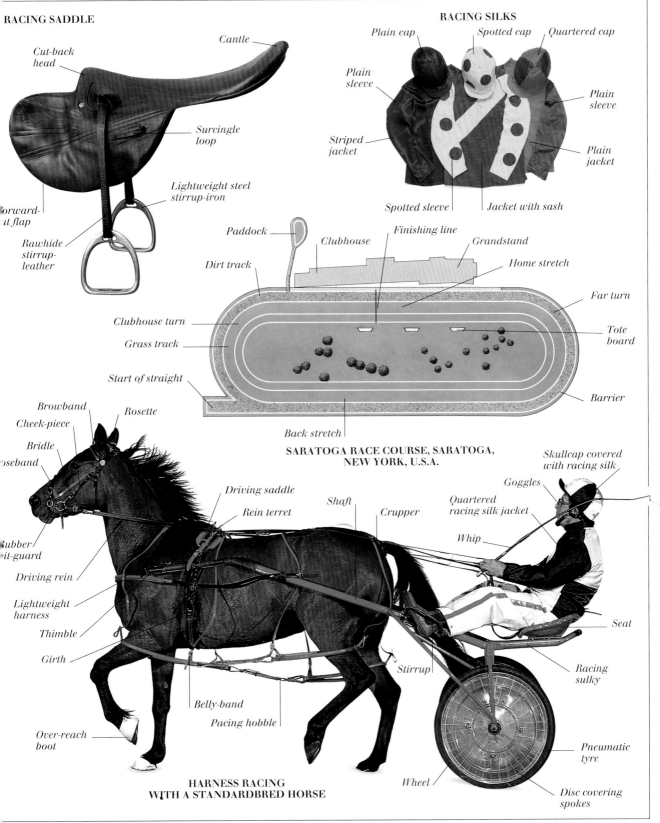

RACING SADDLE

Cantle

Cut-back head

Surcingle loop

Lightweight steel stirrup-iron

Forward-cut flap

Rawhide stirrup-leather

RACING SILKS

Plain cap

Spotted cap

Quartered cap

Plain sleeve

Plain sleeve

Striped jacket

Plain jacket

Spotted sleeve

Jacket with sash

Paddock

Clubhouse

Finishing line

Grandstand

Home stretch

Dirt track

Far turn

Clubhouse turn

Tote board

Grass track

Start of straight

Barrier

Back stretch

SARATOGA RACE COURSE, SARATOGA, NEW YORK, U.S.A.

Browband

Rosette

Cheek-piece

Bridle

Noseband

Rubber bit-guard

Driving rein

Lightweight harness

Thimble

Girth

Over-reach boot

Driving saddle

Rein terret

Shaft

Crupper

Whip

Skullcap covered with racing silk

Goggles

Quartered racing silk jacket

Seat

Racing sulky

Stirrup

Belly-band

Pacing hobble

Wheel

Pneumatic tyre

Disc covering spokes

HARNESS RACING WITH A STANDARDBRED HORSE

Judo and fencing

COMBAT SPORTS ARE BASED ON THE SKILLS used in fighting. In these sports, the competitors may be unarmed – as in judo and boxing – or armed – as in fencing and kendo. Judo is a system of unarmed combat developed in the East. Translated from the Japanese the name means "the gentle way". Students learn how to turn an opponent's force to their own advantage. The usual costume is loose white trousers and a jacket, fastened with a cloth belt. The colour of belt indicates the student's level of expertise, from white-belted novices to the expert "black belts". Competitions take place on a mat or "shiaijo", 9 or 10 m (30 or 33 ft) square in size, bounded by "danger" and "safety" areas to prevent injury. Competitors try to throw, pin, or master their opponent by applying pressure to the arm joints or neck. Judo bouts are strictly monitored, and competitors receive points for superior technique, not for injuring their opponent. Fencing is a combat sport using swords, which takes place on a narrow "piste" 14 m (46 ft) long. Competitors try to touch specific target areas on their opponent with their sword or "foil" while avoiding being touched themselves. The winner is the one who scores the greatest number of hits. Fencers wear clothing made from strong white material, which affords maximum protection while allowing freedom of movement, steel mesh masks with padded bibs to protect the fencer's neck, and a long white glove on their sword hand. Fencing foils do not have sharpened blades, and their tips end in a blunt button to prevent injuries. Three types of swords are used – foils, épées, and sabres. Official foil and épée competitions always use an electric scoring system. The sword tips are connected to lights by a long wire that passes underneath each fencer's jacket. A bulb flashes when a hit is made.

JUDO HOLDS AND THROWS

SIDE FOUR QUARTER HOLD

SINGLE WING

BODY DROP

ONE ARM SHOULDER THROW

SHOULDER WHEEL

SWEEPING LOW THROW

STOMACH THROW

KNEE WHEEL

JUDO KIT

JUDO MAT

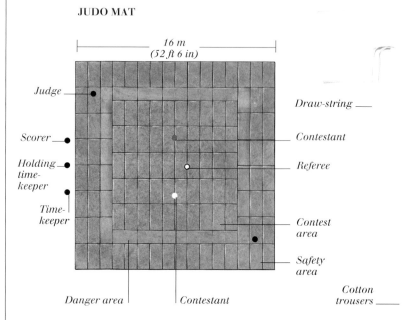

16 m
(52 ft 6 in)

Judge

Scorer

Holding time-keeper

Time-keeper

Draw-string

Contestant

Referee

Contest area

Safety area

Danger area | Contestant

Cotton trousers

Black belt | Heavy-duty cotton jacket

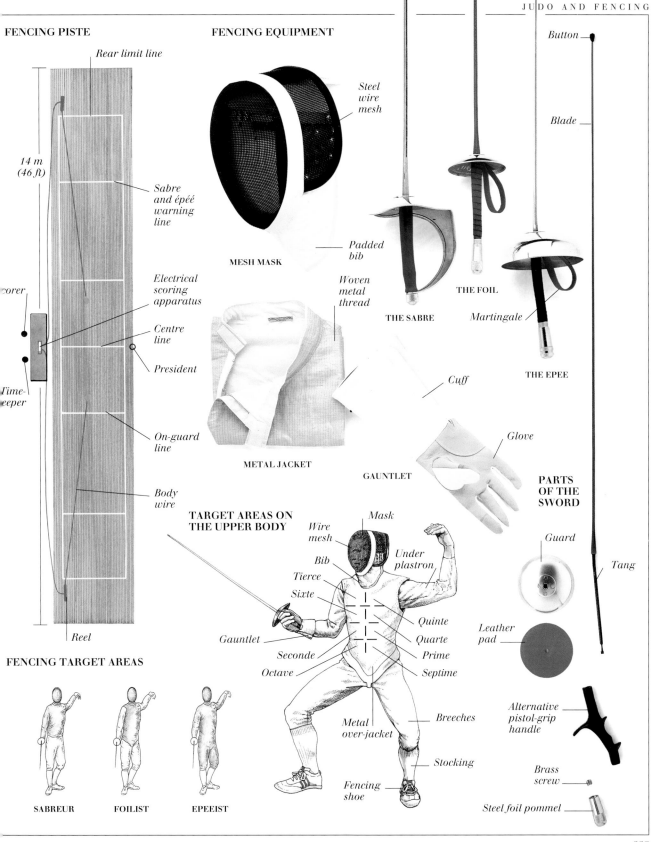

FENCING PISTE

Rear limit line

14 m
(46 ft)

Sabre
and épéé
warning
line

Scorer

Electrical
scoring
apparatus

Centre
line

President

Time-
keeper

On-guard
line

Body
wire

Reel

FENCING TARGET AREAS

SABREUR

FOILIST

EPEEIST

FENCING EQUIPMENT

Steel
wire
mesh

Padded
bib

MESH MASK

Woven
metal
thread

METAL JACKET

THE SABRE

THE FOIL

Martingale

THE EPEE

Cuff

Glove

GAUNTLET

TARGET AREAS ON
THE UPPER BODY

Mask

Wire
mesh

Bib

Tierce

Sixte

Under
plastron

Gauntlet

Quinte

Quarte

Seconde

Prime

Octave

Septime

Metal
over-jacket

Breeches

Stocking

Fencing
shoe

PARTS
OF THE
SWORD

Button

Blade

Guard

Leather
pad

Tang

Alternative
pistol-grip
handle

Brass
screw

Steel foil pommel

Swimming and diving

SWIMMING GOGGLES

SWIMMING WAS INCLUDED in the first modern Olympic Games in 1896 and diving events were added in 1904. Swimming is both an individual and a team sport and races take place over a predetermined distance in one of the four major categories of stroke – freestyle (usually front crawl), butterfly, breaststroke, and backstroke. Competition pools are clearly marked for racing and anti-turbulence lane lines are used to separate the swimmers and help keep the water calm. The first team or individual to finish the race is the winner. Competitive diving is divided into men's and women's springboard and platform (highboard) events. There are six official groups of dives: forward dives, backward dives, armstand dives, twist dives, reverse dives, and inward dives. Competitors perform a set number of dives and after each one a panel of judges awards marks according to the quality of execution and the degree of difficulty.

STYLES OF DIVES

Starting position

Hands above head

Legs fully stretched

Flight

Arched back

Toes pointed

Entry

Feet together

Hands close together

Entry

FORWARD DIVE

BACKWARD DIVE

Latex rubber moulds to shape of head

SWIMWEAR

CAPS

Rubber-covered wire

NOSE CLIP

Moulded rubber

EARPLUG

High neckline

Man-made stretch fabric

Drawstring

High-cut leg

Strong seam

SWIMSUIT

TRUNKS

SWIMMING POOL

Swimmer

Lane number

Starting block

Lane time-keeper

Chief time-keeper

End wall

Placing judge

Starter

Recorder

Side wall

Backstroke marker 15 m (49 ft) from end of pool

Anti-turbulence lane line

Referee

Stroke judge

Backstroke turn indicator 5 m (16 ft) from end of pool

Bottom line

Turning judge

Turning wall

Lane

23 m (75 ft 6 in)

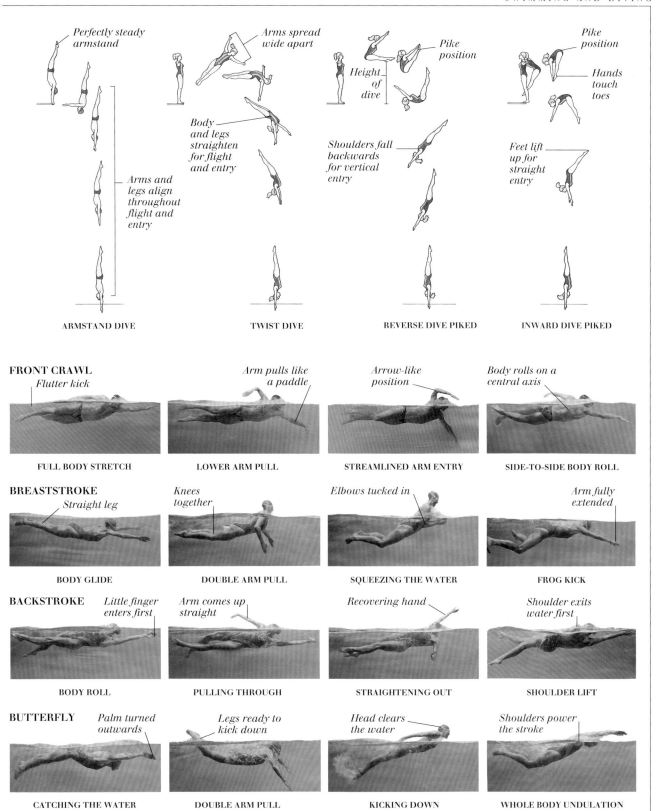

Perfectly steady armstand

Arms and legs align throughout flight and entry

ARMSTAND DIVE

Arms spread wide apart

Body and legs straighten for flight and entry

TWIST DIVE

Pike position

Height of dive

Shoulders fall backwards for vertical entry

REVERSE DIVE PIKED

Pike position

Hands touch toes

Feet lift up for straight entry

INWARD DIVE PIKED

FRONT CRAWL
Flutter kick

FULL BODY STRETCH

Arm pulls like a paddle

LOWER ARM PULL

Arrow-like position

STREAMLINED ARM ENTRY

Body rolls on a central axis

SIDE-TO-SIDE BODY ROLL

BREASTSTROKE
Straight leg

BODY GLIDE

Knees together

DOUBLE ARM PULL

Elbows tucked in

SQUEEZING THE WATER

Arm fully extended

FROG KICK

BACKSTROKE
Little finger enters first

BODY ROLL

Arm comes up straight

PULLING THROUGH

Recovering hand

STRAIGHTENING OUT

Shoulder exits water first

SHOULDER LIFT

BUTTERFLY
Palm turned outwards

CATCHING THE WATER

Legs ready to kick down

DOUBLE ARM PULL

Head clears the water

KICKING DOWN

Shoulders power the stroke

WHOLE BODY UNDULATION

Canoeing, rowing, and sailing

WATERBORNE SPORTS are as varied as the crafts used. There are two disciplines in rowing; sweep rowing, in which each rower has one oar and sculling, in which rowers use two oars. There are a number of different Olympic and competitive rowing events for both men and women. The number of rowers and weight classes vary. Some rowing events use a coxswain; a steersman who does not row but directs the crew. Kayaks and canoes are used in straight sprint and slalom races. Slalom races take place over a course consisting of 20 to 25 gates, including at least six upstream gates. In yacht racing, competitors must complete prescribed courses, organized by the race committees, in the shortest possible time, using sail power only. Olympic events include classes for keel boats, dinghies, and catamarans.

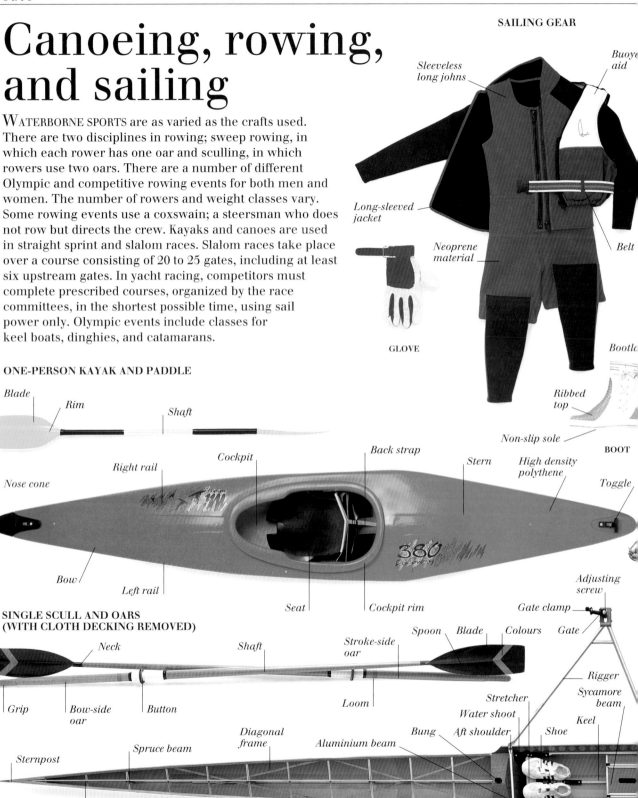

SAILING GEAR

Sleeveless long johns

Buoye aid

Long-sleeved jacket

Neoprene material

Belt

GLOVE

Bootl

Ribbed top

Non-slip sole

BOOT

ONE-PERSON KAYAK AND PADDLE

Blade

Rim

Shaft

Back strap

Stern

High density polythene

Toggle

Right rail

Cockpit

Nose cone

Bow

Left rail

Seat

Cockpit rim

Adjusting screw

Gate clamp

Gate

SINGLE SCULL AND OARS
(WITH CLOTH DECKING REMOVED)

Spoon   Blade   Colours

Neck

Shaft

Stroke-side oar

Rigger

Sycamore beam

Grip

Bow-side oar

Button

Loom

Stretcher

Water shoot

Keel

Shoe

Sternpost

Spruce beam

Diagonal frame

Aluminium beam

Bung   Aft shoulder

Kelson (keelson)

LIFEJACKET

Backstrap/ rescue strap

Reinforced seam

Neck opening

Mast

Whistle

Topping- up valve

Lanyard

Waistband

Standing rigging

Spreader

Bow

SAILING DINGHY

Elastic control line

Boom

Rudder

Mainsheet

Stern

Tiller

Toestrap

Centre-board

Cockpit

Shroud

Jib fairlead

Non-slip deck surface

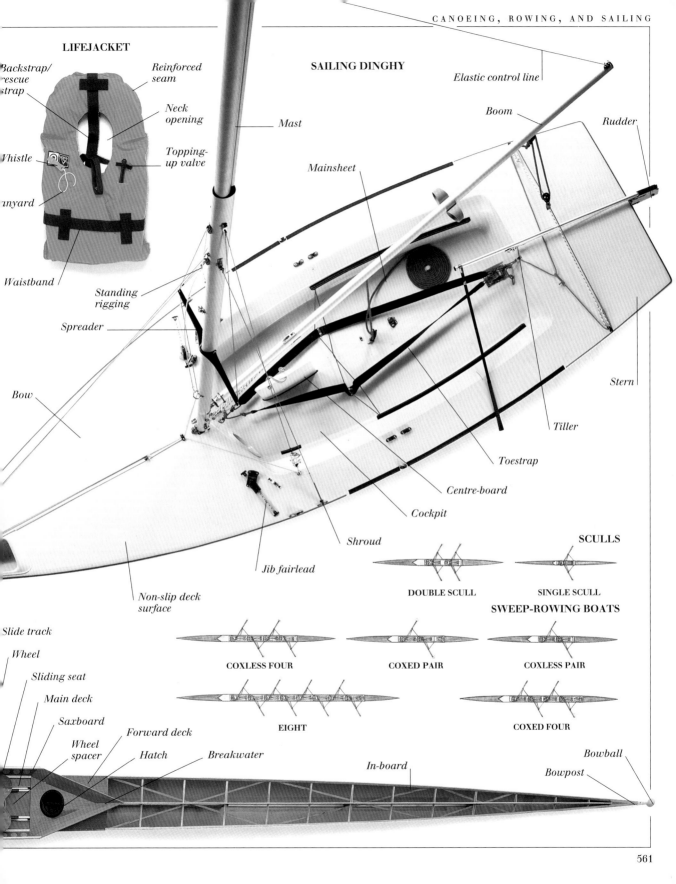

SCULLS

DOUBLE SCULL

SINGLE SCULL

SWEEP-ROWING BOATS

COXLESS FOUR

COXED PAIR

COXLESS PAIR

EIGHT

COXED FOUR

Slide track

Wheel

Sliding seat

Main deck

Saxboard

Wheel spacer

Forward deck

Hatch

Breakwater

In-board

Bowball

Bowpost

Angling

ANGLING MEANS FISHING WITH A ROD, reel, line, and lure. There are several different types of angling: freshwater coarse angling, for members of the carp family and pike; freshwater game angling, for salmon and trout; and sea angling, for sea fish such as flatfish, bass, and mackerel. Anglers use a variety of methods of catching fish. These include bait fishing, in which bait (food to allure the fish) is placed on a hook and cast into the water; fly fishing, in which a natural or artificial fly is used to lure the fish; and spinning, in which a lure that looks like a small fish revolves as it is pulled through the water. The angler uses the rod, reel, and line to cast the lure over the water. The reel controls the line as it spills off the spool and as it is wound back. Weights may be fixed to the line so that it will sink. Swivels are attached to prevent the line from twisting. When a fish bites, the hook must become embedded in its mouth and remain there while the catch is reeled in.

Keeper ring

Drag spindle

Handgrip

Disk drag

Drag washer

Disk spring

Gear retainer

Dual click gear

Retaining screw

Check slide

Check pawl cover

Check pawl

Check spring

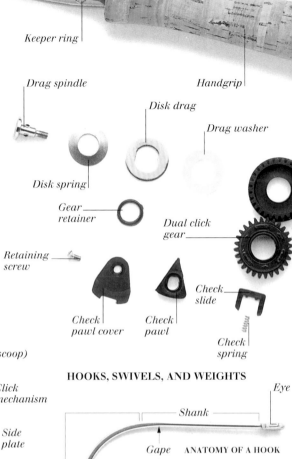

REELS

Spool-release button

Reel foot (reel scoop)

Plate-nut

Click mechanism

Mechanical brake

Side plate

Centrifugal brake

Spool

Handle

Star drag

Level-wind system

MULTIPLIER REEL

Reel foot (reel scoop)

Unskirted spool

Handle

Line

Tension nut (drag adjustment)

Ratchet (anti-reverse device)

Handgrip

Reel

Bail arm

FIXED-SPOOL REEL

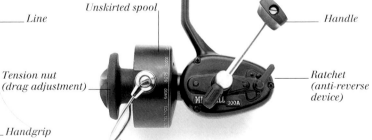

HOOKS, SWIVELS, AND WEIGHTS

Eye

Shank

Gape

ANATOMY OF A HOOK

Bend

Throat

Point

Barb

TREBLE HOOK

ABERDEEN HOOK

REVERSED BEND HOOK

EXAMPLES OF BARREL SWIVELS

HILLMAN ANTI-KINK WEIGHT

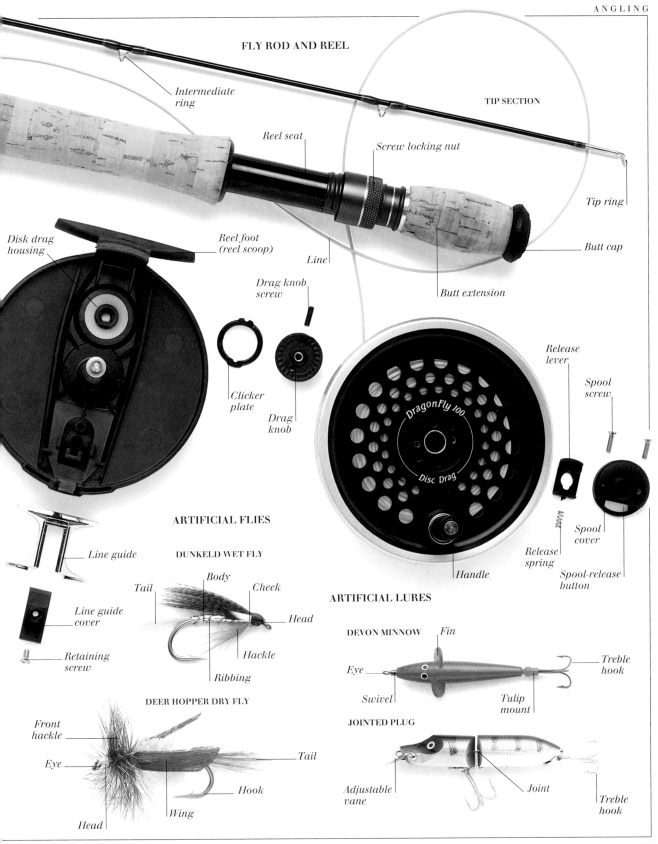

FLY ROD AND REEL

Intermediate ring

TIP SECTION

Reel seat

Screw locking nut

Tip ring

Disk drag housing

Reel foot (reel scoop)

Line

Butt cap

Drag knob screw

Butt extension

Release lever

Spool screw

Clicker plate

DragonFly 100

Disc Drag

Spool cover

Drag knob

Release spring

Spool-release button

Handle

ARTIFICIAL FLIES

Line guide

DUNKELD WET FLY

Body

Tail

Cheek

Line guide cover

Head

ARTIFICIAL LURES

Retaining screw

Hackle

DEVON MINNOW

Fin

Ribbing

Eye

Treble hook

DEER HOPPER DRY FLY

Swivel

Tulip mount

Front hackle

JOINTED PLUG

Eye

Tail

Adjustable vane

Joint

Hook

Treble hook

Wing

Head

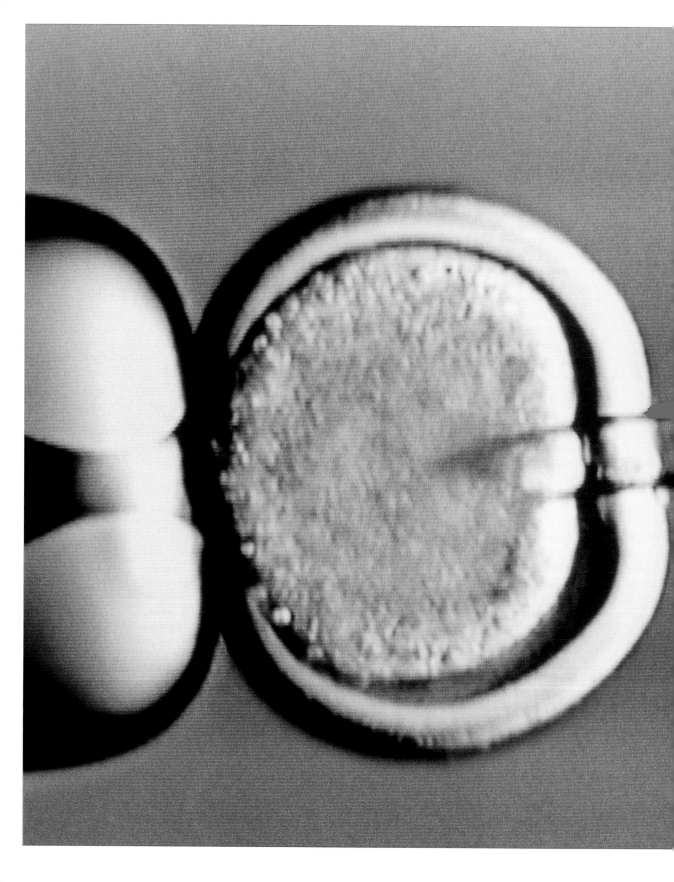

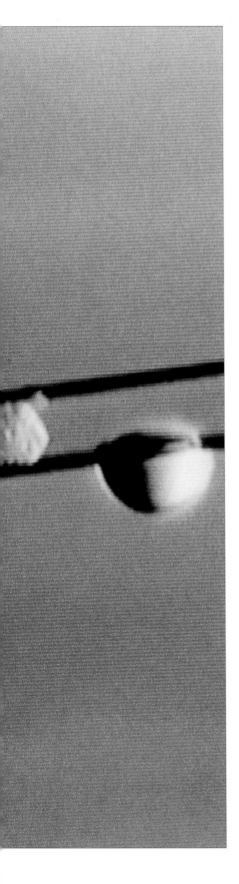

THE MODERN WORLD

Personal computer

PERSONAL COMPUTERS (PCs) fall into two main types: IBM-compatible PCs, known simply as PCs, and Apple Macintosh PCs, known as "Macs". They differ in the way files and programs, and the user's access to them, are organized, and programs must be tailored for each type. However, in most other respects PCs and Macs have much in common. Both contain microchips, or integrated circuits, that store and process data. The "brain" of any PC is a chip known as the central processing unit (CPU), which performs mathematical operations in order to run program instructions and receive, store, and output data. The most powerful CPUs today perform over a billion calculations a second. Data can be input via CDs and other storage media, as well as via modems. Highly portable laptop PCs are also in widespread use. Most PCs are able to communicate with many other devices, from video cameras (see pp. 582–83) to personal digital assistants (see pp. 568–69).

APPLE POWER MAC G4 DUAL PROCESSOR

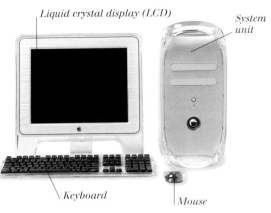

Liquid crystal display (LCD)

System unit

Keyboard

Mouse

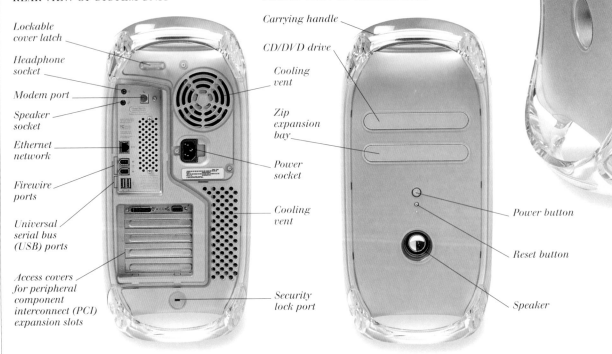

REAR VIEW OF SYSTEM UNIT

Lockable cover latch

Headphone socket

Modem port

Speaker socket

Ethernet network

Firewire ports

Universal serial bus (USB) ports

Access covers for peripheral component interconnect (PCI) expansion slots

Power socket

Security lock port

FRONT VIEW OF SYSTEM UNIT

Carrying handle

CD/DVD drive

Cooling vent

Zip expansion bay

Cooling vent

Power button

Reset button

Speaker

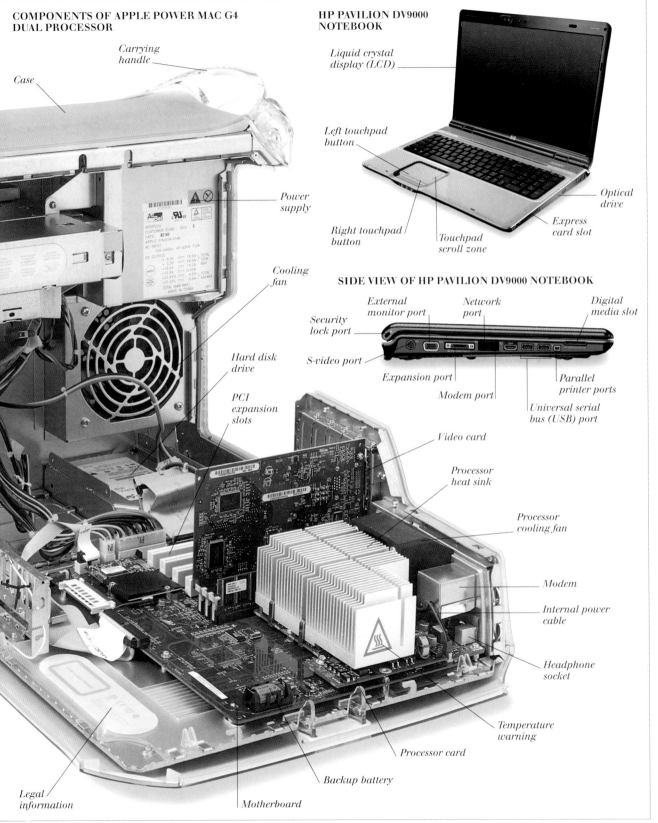

COMPONENTS OF APPLE POWER MAC G4 DUAL PROCESSOR

Carrying handle

Case

Power supply

Cooling fan

Hard disk drive

PCI expansion slots

Legal information

Motherboard

Backup battery

Processor card

HP PAVILION DV9000 NOTEBOOK

Liquid crystal display (LCD)

Left touchpad button

Right touchpad button

Touchpad scroll zone

Optical drive

Express card slot

SIDE VIEW OF HP PAVILION DV9000 NOTEBOOK

External monitor port

Network port

Digital media slot

Security lock port

S-video port

Expansion port

Modem port

Parallel printer ports

Universal serial bus (USB) port

Video card

Processor heat sink

Processor cooling fan

Modem

Internal power cable

Headphone socket

Temperature warning

567

Hand-held computer

PERSONAL DIGITAL ASSISTANTS (PDAs), or hand-held computers, are among the many small electronic devices that were first developed during the last years of the 20th century. Some PDAs have integral keyboards, and these are larger and heavier than their keyboardless counterparts, which can be easily held in one hand. The latter employ a combination of touch-screen technology and handwriting-recognition programs to receive instructions and data. In order to write data into the PDA screen with a stylus, users must usually learn to use a special alphabet that the computer understands. The contents of a PDA's memory need to be regularly backed up on to a PC. Besides basic functions, such as address book, calendar, and note pad, PDAs are increasingly absorbing elements of other devices, such as MP3 players (see pp. 586–587), Global Positioning System (GPS) receivers (see pp. 590–591), and mobile phones (see pp. 588–589). Some can also access email and the Internet. A related product is the e-book reader, which uses "electronic paper" to mimic the appearance of ink and normal paper, providing a more comfortable reading experience. The screen reflects light, as does normal paper, and so can be read comfortably outside in daylight.

PALM M500 PDA

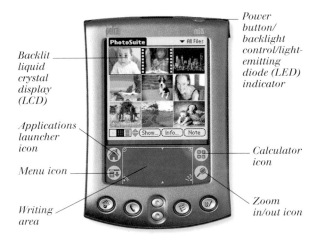

Power button/ backlight control/light-emitting diode (LED) indicator

Backlit liquid crystal display (LCD)

Applications launcher icon

Menu icon

Writing area

Calculator icon

Zoom in/out icon

IREX ILIAD E-BOOK READER

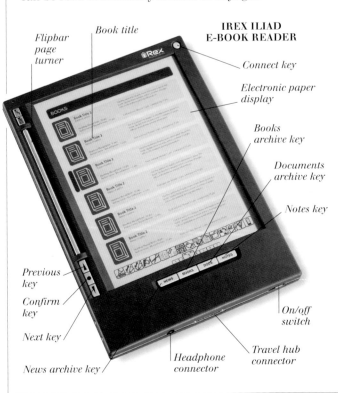

Flipbar page turner

Book title

Connect key

Electronic paper display

Books archive key

Documents archive key

Notes key

Previous key

Confirm key

Next key

News archive key

Headphone connector

On/off switch

Travel hub connector

FRONT CASE

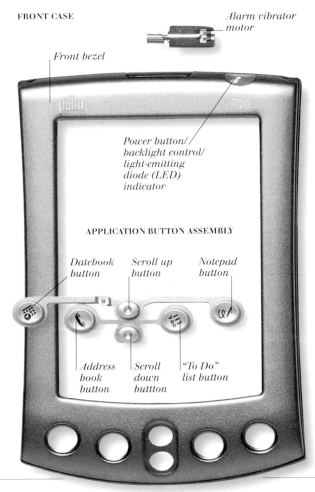

Alarm vibrator motor

Front bezel

Power button/ backlight control/ light-emitting diode (LED) indicator

APPLICATION BUTTON ASSEMBLY

Datebook button

Scroll up button

Notepad button

Address book button

Scroll down buttton

"To Do" list button

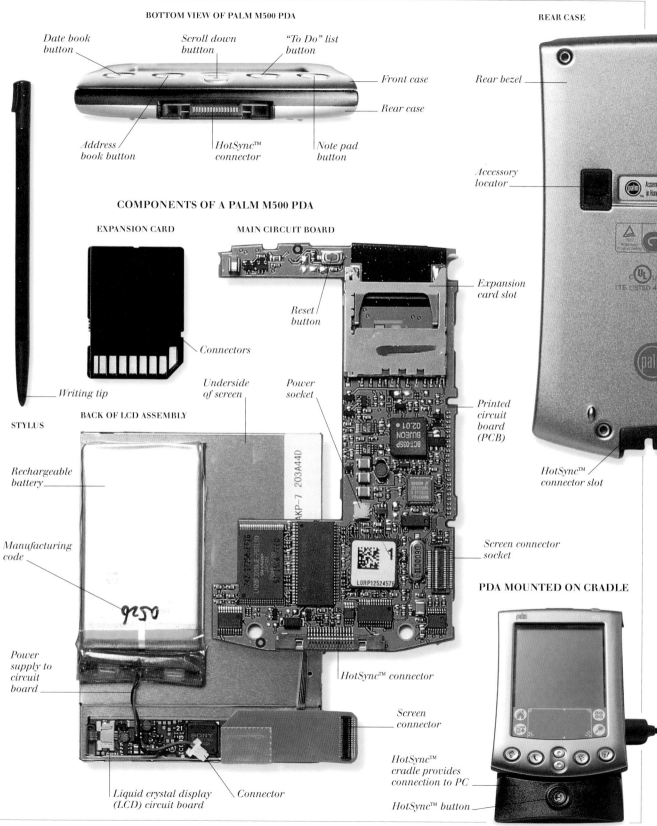

BOTTOM VIEW OF PALM M500 PDA

Date book button

Scroll down butttion

"To Do" list button

Front case

Rear case

Address book button

HotSync™ connector

Note pad button

REAR CASE

Rear bezel

Accessory locator

COMPONENTS OF A PALM M500 PDA

EXPANSION CARD

MAIN CIRCUIT BOARD

Reset button

Connectors

Writing tip

STYLUS

Underside of screen

Power socket

Expansion card slot

Printed circuit board (PCB)

BACK OF LCD ASSEMBLY

Rechargeable battery

Manufacturing code

9250

Power supply to circuit board

HotSync™ connector slot

Screen connector socket

PDA MOUNTED ON CRADLE

HotSync™ connector

Screen connector

HotSync™ cradle provides connection to PC

Liquid crystal display (LCD) circuit board

Connector

HotSync™ button

Flatbed scanner

SCANNERS CONVERT physical images into electronic form, allowing them to be sent over the Internet, displayed on a website, stored on a computer, and manipulated using specialized software. Scanners work by detecting and analysing light reflected from an opaque image, such as a photographic print. Some can also scan photographic transparencies by analysing light that has passed through the image. Flatbed scanners contain a unit, called the scan head, that contains a lamp, mirrors, a lens, and an array of CCDs (Charge-Coupled Devices). The carriage passes beneath the image; the lamp shines light on to or through the original; the mirrors reflect the light on to the lens, which focuses it on to the CCD array. Each CCD detects the brightness of light from a particular pixel (picture element) along a horizontal strip and converts this data into an electric signal. For colour images, the light is usually passed through red, green, and blue filters and then directed to the CCD array so that it can be broken down into its component colours. This information is then converted to digital form. The quality of the image depends on its resolution, measured in dpi (Dots Per Inch).

EPSON PERFECTION 1650 SCANNER

Integrated transparency unit (TPU)

Glass plate

Start button and indicator light

Photo print button

Scan to e-mail button

Scan to Web button

Reflective document mat

Power supply cable

Direct current (DC) inlet

TPU connec port

Lock

Inverter board

Lamp power supply connector

Shield plate

Panel board connector

FILM AND SLIDE HOLDER

35mm-slide holder

35mm film strip holder

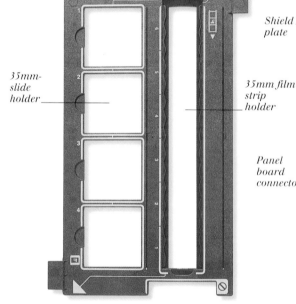

HOW A FLATBED SCANNER WORKS

Original image (photograph or artwork)

Lens focuses light on to CCD array

Glass plate

Lamp

The electronic image is converted to digital form and transmitted to a computer

CCD array builds up electric charges that vary according to the brightness of the light beam

Light beam is reflected from the original to a series of mirrors

Carriage is moved beneath the original by a stepper motor in a rapid series of tiny steps

Cover support

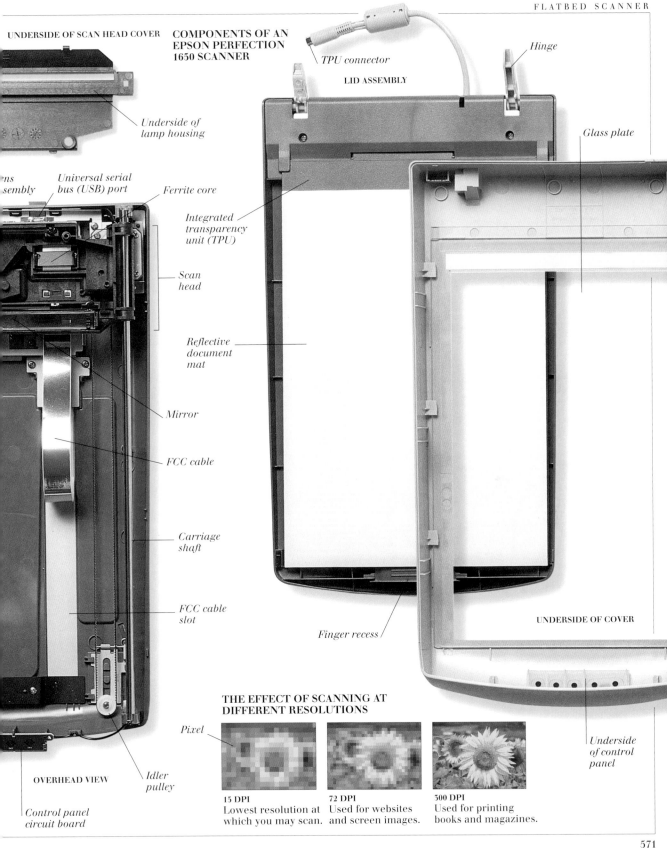

UNDERSIDE OF SCAN HEAD COVER

**COMPONENTS OF AN
EPSON PERFECTION
1650 SCANNER**

TPU connector

Hinge

LID ASSEMBLY

*Underside of
lamp housing*

Glass plate

*ns
ssembly*

*Universal serial
bus (USB) port*

Ferrite core

*Integrated
transparency
unit (TPU)*

*Scan
head*

*Reflective
document
mat*

Mirror

FCC cable

*Carriage
shaft*

*FCC cable
slot*

Finger recess

UNDERSIDE OF COVER

*Underside
of control
panel*

OVERHEAD VIEW

*Idler
pulley*

*Control panel
circuit board*

**THE EFFECT OF SCANNING AT
DIFFERENT RESOLUTIONS**

Pixel

15 DPI
Lowest resolution at
which you may scan.

72 DPI
Used for websites
and screen images.

300 DPI
Used for printing
books and magazines.

571

Airbus 380

**CROSS-SECTION
OF FUSELAGE**

THE AIRBUS A380 WAS CONCEIVED in the early 1990s to compete with, and if possible replace, the Boeing 747. Work began in earnest on what was then called the A3XX in 1994. Its maiden flight was in April 2005. The A380's shape is subtly moulded to minimize drag from its ovoid fuselage. The structure makes extensive use of composite materials, such as thermoplastics and GLARE (aluminium and glass fibre). Its four huge engines, the most powerful ever used on an airliner, are surprisingly quiet. It is claimed that when carrying 550 passengers, the A380 will use only 2.9 litres (⅗ gallon) of fuel per passenger per 100km (60 miles).

INTERIOR VIEW OF BUSINESS CLASS CABIN

Galley area

Personal lighting

Concealed lighting

Storage locker

Window blind

Reclining seat

Seat control panel

Aisle

Folding foot rest

Vertical tailplane

GLARE upper fuselage

Horizontal tailplane

Obstruction light

Swept titanium fan blades

Company logo

Wing landing gear

FRONT VIEW

Split rudder

Jupp-Reese winglet

Upper deck windows

Overwing emergency exit

A380

F-WWOW

Auxiliary Power Unit (APU) exhaust

Horizontal tailplane

Tailcone fairing

Aft door

Belly fairing

Flap track fairings

Body landing gear

SIDE VIEW

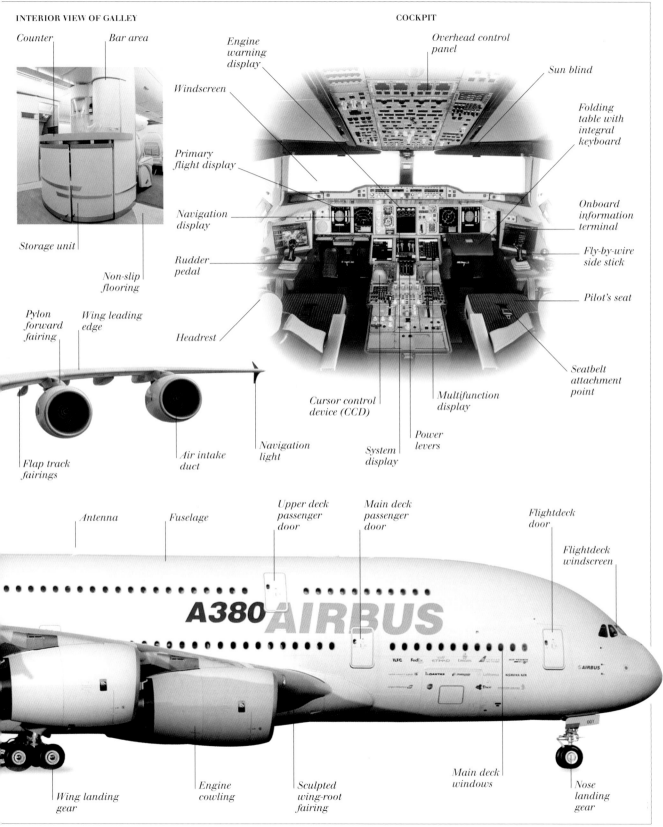

INTERIOR VIEW OF GALLEY

Counter

Bar area

Storage unit

Non-slip flooring

COCKPIT

Engine warning display

Windscreen

Primary flight display

Navigation display

Rudder pedal

Headrest

Overhead control panel

Sun blind

Folding table with integral keyboard

Onboard information terminal

Fly-by-wire side stick

Pilot's seat

Seatbelt attachment point

Cursor control device (CCD)

Multifunction display

Power levers

System display

Pylon forward fairing

Wing leading edge

Flap track fairings

Air intake duct

Navigation light

Antenna

Fuselage

Upper deck passenger door

Main deck passenger door

Flightdeck door

Flightdeck windscreen

A380 AIRBUS

Wing landing gear

Engine cowling

Sculpted wing-root fairing

Main deck windows

Nose landing gear

Inkjet printer

INKJET PRINTERS EXPEL ink droplets from hundreds of tiny jets, or nozzles, on to a medium, such as paper, to print an image. Each droplet corresponds to a single pixel (picture element). Black-and-white printers use only black ink, while colour printers overprint combinations of the printing colours (cyan, yellow, magenta, and black) to create a full colour range. The printhead containing the nozzles moves sideways across the paper, creating a line of pixels, before the paper moves slightly forward so the next line can be printed. Two basic methods are used to eject ink: thermal, in which ink is heated to form an expanding bubble that expels a droplet from the nozzle, and piezoelectric, in which an electric current expands a crystal causing it to push out the ink droplet. The printer shown here can print digital photographs directly from a memory card.

EPSON STYLUS PHOTO 895 COLOUR INKJET PRINTER

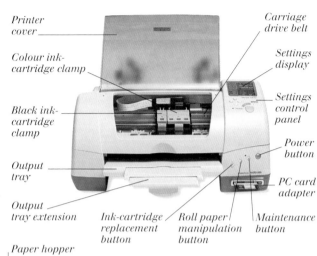

Printer cover
Colour ink-cartridge clamp
Black ink-cartridge clamp
Output tray
Output tray extension
Carriage drive belt
Settings display
Settings control panel
Power button
PC card adapter
Ink-cartridge replacement button
Roll paper manipulation button
Maintenance button

OVERHEAD VIEW WITH OUTER CASING REMOVED

Paper hopper
Head data cable support
Preview monitor socket
Motor assembly
Paper thickness adjust lever
Colour ink-cartridge clamp
Black ink-cartridge clamp
Spur gear
Head data cable
Paper output stacker

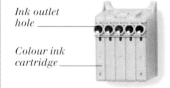

Ink outlet hole
Colour ink cartridge
Ink outlet hole
Black ink cartridge

INK CARTRIDGES

PC CARD ADAPTER

PAPER FEED COMPONENTS

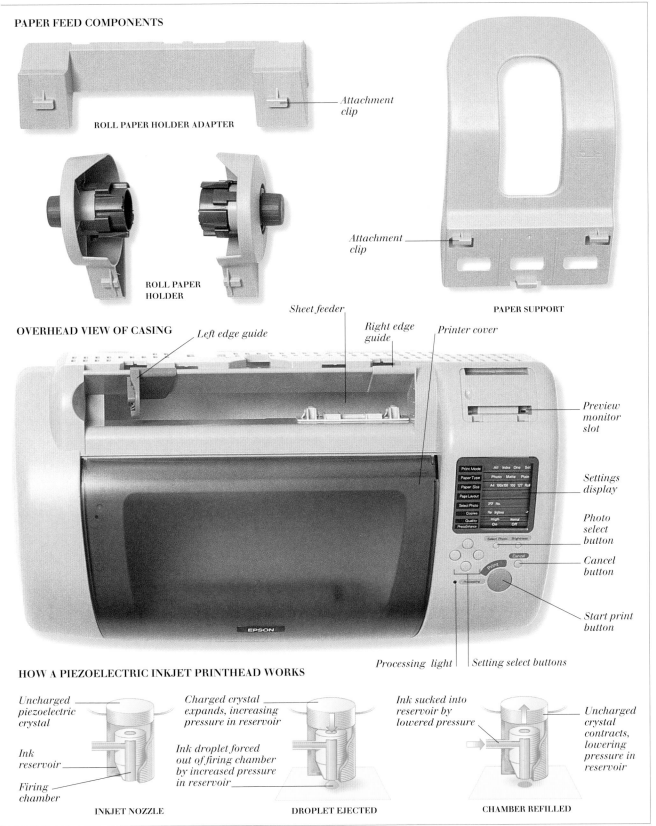

Attachment
clip

ROLL PAPER HOLDER ADAPTER

Attachment
clip

**ROLL PAPER
HOLDER**

PAPER SUPPORT

OVERHEAD VIEW OF CASING

Left edge guide

Sheet feeder

Right edge
guide

Printer cover

Preview
monitor
slot

Print Mode	All	Index	One	Set
Paper Type		Photo	Matte	Plain
Paper Size	A4	100x150	100	127	Roll
Page Layout				
Select Photo		PIF	No.	
Copies			Fle	Brightness
Quality			High	Normal
PhotoEnhance			On	Off

Settings
display

Photo
select
button

Select Photo Brightness

Cancel

Cancel
button

Print

Start print
button

EPSON

Processing light Setting select buttons

HOW A PIEZOELECTRIC INKJET PRINTHEAD WORKS

Uncharged
piezoelectric
crystal

Ink
reservoir

Firing
chamber

INKJET NOZZLE

Charged crystal
expands, increasing
pressure in reservoir

Ink droplet forced
out of firing chamber
by increased pressure
in reservoir

DROPLET EJECTED

Ink sucked into
reservoir by
lowered pressure

Uncharged
crystal
contracts,
lowering
pressure in
reservoir

CHAMBER REFILLED

The Internet

THE INTERNET CONSISTS OF TENS of thousands of computer networks linked together to form one huge global network, allowing any computer on one network to communicate with any computer on another. The two main services used on the Internet are email and the World Wide Web. Email allows text messages to be sent – along with attached computer files, images, or video clips, for example – to other computers on the Internet. The Web consists of billions of pages made up of digital files that are stored on computers across the world and can be viewed using a Web browser. The Web also provides interactive access to various services, for example banking and shopping.

Sender's Internet service provider (ISP) directs message into the Internet

Recipient's ISP receives message and stores it until retrieved by the recipient

Server guides message to its intended destination

Telephone line

HOW EMAIL WORKS

Screen displays email program

EMAIL SENDER

Modem encodes and sends message via the telephone line

EMAIL ADDRESS

User name *Domain name*

anna@merlin.provider.co.uk

Separator *Country code*

Window controls

EMAIL PROGRAM

Delete mail button *Reply button* *New mail button*

Sender's name *Reply all button* *Get mail button*

Search field

Inbox folder

Drafts folder

Sent mail folder

Deleted items folder

Junk mail folder

Personalized mail folder

Message display area

Font menus button

Font colour button

Save as draft button

Add address button

Add attachments button

Chat selector button

Send button

Address options button

Message area

DK (588 messages)

Delete Junk Reply Reply All Forward New Get Mail Search

From	Subject	Date Received	
Kedwell, Laragh	FW: Birds 8D153 templates	6 July 2006	12.26
St Louis, Susan	RE: Templates	6 July 2006	12.26
van Zyl, Miezan	Visual Dictionary	6 July 2006	10.07
Stradins, Ina			
van Zyl, Miezan			
St Louis, Susan			
Gilbert, Richard (DK)			
Farrow, Stephanie			
Upadhyay, Shefali			
St Louis, Susan			
Farrow, Stephanie			
van Zyl, Miezan			
St Louis, Susan			
Upadhyay, Shefali			
Upadhyay, Shefali			
Stradins, Ina			
St Louis, Susan			
Stradins, Ina			
Farrow, Stephanie			
St Louis, Susan			
St Louis, Susan			
van Zyl, Miezan			
Farrow, Stephanie			

New Message

Send Chat Attach Address Fonts Colors Save As Draft

To:
Cc:
Bcc:
Subject:

Signature: None

From: Ina Stradins
Subject: **RE: Bird samples**
Date: 7 July 2006 15:43:2
To: Hugh Schermuly
Return-Path: <Ina.Stradins@uk.d
Received: from punt3.mail.den
Fri, 07 Jul 2006 14:
Received: from [194.217.242.2
1FyrYL-2W2knw-07
Received: from [80.82.96.144]

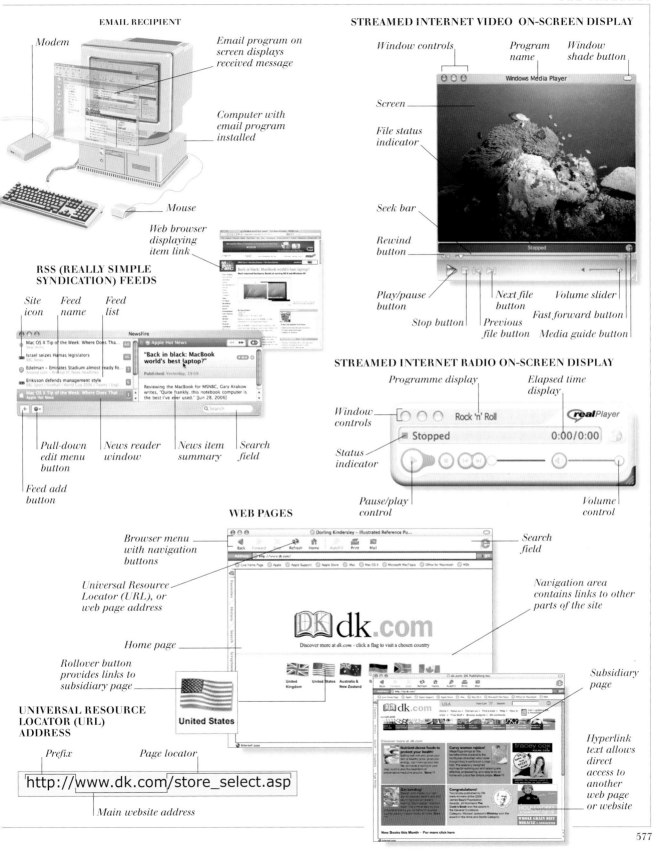

EMAIL RECIPIENT

Modem

Email program on screen displays received message

Computer with email program installed

Mouse

Web browser displaying item link

RSS (REALLY SIMPLE SYNDICATION) FEEDS

Site icon

Feed name

Feed list

Pull-down edit menu button

News reader window

News item summary

Search field

Feed add button

STREAMED INTERNET VIDEO ON-SCREEN DISPLAY

Window controls

Program name

Window shade button

Screen

File status indicator

Seek bar

Rewind button

Play/pause button

Stop button

Previous file button

Next file button

Volume slider

Fast forward button

Media guide button

STREAMED INTERNET RADIO ON-SCREEN DISPLAY

Programme display

Elapsed time display

Window controls

Status indicator

Pause/play control

Volume control

WEB PAGES

Browser menu with navigation buttons

Universal Resource Locator (URL), or web page address

Home page

Rollover button provides links to subsidiary page

Search field

Navigation area contains links to other parts of the site

Subsidiary page

Hyperlink text allows direct access to another web page or website

UNIVERSAL RESOURCE LOCATOR (URL) ADDRESS

Prefix

Page locator

http://www.dk.com/store_select.asp

Main website address

Electronic games

RIDGE RACER, FOR PSP

KAMEO: ELEMENTS OF
POWER, FOR XBOX 360

VIDEO GAMES HAVE BEEN around since the early 1970s. They are played on PCs, arcade machines, on a TV using a home console, and on portable hand-held consoles. Players use devices such as joysticks and control pads with buttons to control movement and action on screen. The latest generation of consoles uses motion sensor technology to allow players to manipulate objects on screen by simply moving the controller. The game itself is stored in the form of digital information on CD, DVD, or microchip – which may be integral or stored in a removable cartridge – or on an internal hard disk. A central processing unit (CPU) (see pp. 566–567) is needed to process commands from the players, while specialized graphics chips are used to process the complex mapping and texturing functions that make modern games appear so realistic.

COMPONENTS OF A SONY PSP

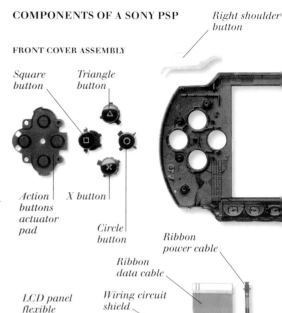

FRONT COVER ASSEMBLY

Square button
Triangle button
Action buttons actuator pad
X button
Circle button
Right shoulder button

Ribbon power cable
Ribbon data cable
Wiring circuit shield
LCD panel flexible wiring circuit

SONY PSP

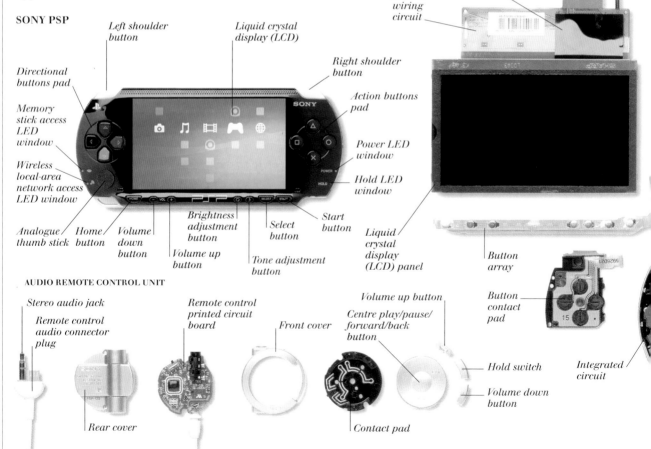

Left shoulder button
Liquid crystal display (LCD)
Right shoulder button
Action buttons pad
Power LED window
Hold LED window
Directional buttons pad
Memory stick access LED window
Wireless local-area network access LED window
Analogue thumb stick
Home button
Volume down button
Volume up button
Brightness adjustment button
Tone adjustment button
Select button
Start button
Liquid crystal display (LCD) panel
Button array
Button contact pad
Integrated circuit

AUDIO REMOTE CONTROL UNIT

Stereo audio jack
Remote control audio connector plug
Remote control printed circuit board
Front cover
Volume up button
Centre play/pause/ forward/back button
Hold switch
Volume down button
Rear cover
Contact pad

HEADPHONE ASSEMBLY

Dual mould top cover

Headphone housing

Left shoulder button

In ear headphone

Piezo speaker

Directional buttons

Directional buttons actuator pad

Analogue thumb stick

Felt washer

Analogue stick printed wire board

BATTERY

SONY
MODEL PSP-110
BATTERY PACK 3.6V

Li-ion

危険

Lithium-ion rechargeable battery

Battery compartment cover

Shoulder button actuator pad

Shoulder button frame

Frame

Integrated circuit

Optical pickup

Internal power connector

WiFi aerial

External power connector

Speaker

Universal Media Disk (UMD) drive traverse motor

UMD drive ribbon cable

REAR PANEL AND CIRCUIT BOARD

Shoulder button contact

Shoulder button ribbon cable

Button contact pad

SONY PLAYSTATION 3

CONSOLE

Analogue control stick

Action buttons pad

CONTROLLER

USB port

Motion sensor on/off button

Select button

Blu-ray drive bay

Directional buttons pad

MICROSOFT XBOX360

Removable hard drive

Cooling vent

CONSOLE

Wireless sensor

Memory unit port

Disc tray

Connect button

"Ring of fire" (online and game status indicator)

Guide button

Action buttons

Directional buttons

CONTROLLER

Digital camera

FOR MORE THAN 200 YEARS, CAMERAS recorded pictures as chemical changes in silver-containing substances, on a strip of flexible, celluloid film. The digital camera records pictures in electronic form. At its heart is a specialized integrated circuit known as a charge-coupled device (CCD). This has millions of micro-units known as pixels. It works in the opposite way to a miniature computer or TV screen. Instead of electric signals making pixels shine, when light hits a pixel it generates a tiny electrical signal, according to the light's colour and brightness. The signals from the CCD's millions of pixels are analogue: they vary continuously in a wave-like fashion. They are converted by a microchip to digital codes of numbers, represented as on-off electronic pulses. The digital signals are processed and fed both to the in-camera memory chip, which holds a temporary version, and the memory stick, which can be removed to download its contents into a computer or television. The rest of the camera is similar to the traditional design.

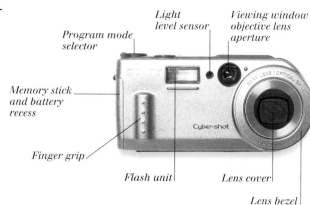

FRONT VIEW OF SONY CYBER-SHOT DSC-P1 DIGITAL CAMERA

Light level sensor

Viewing window objective lens aperture

Program mode selector

Memory stick and battery recess

Finger grip

Flash unit

Lens cover

Lens bezel

Cyber-shot

LENS ZOOM AND FOCUS

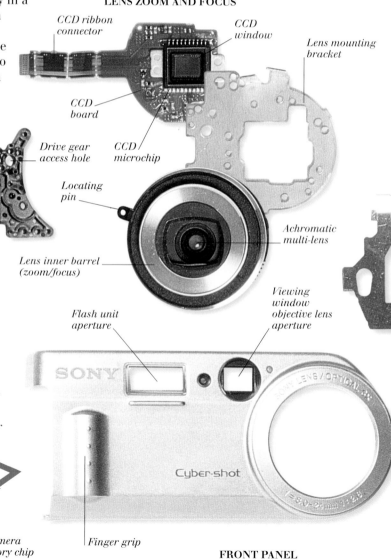

CCD ribbon connector

CCD window

Lens mounting bracket

CCD board

CCD microchip

Drive gear access hole

Locating pin

Achromatic multi-lens

Lens inner barrel (zoom/focus)

Viewing window objective lens aperture

Flash unit aperture

Finger grip

SONY

Cyber-shot

FRONT PANEL

Zoom motor

09BB

Drive pin

HOW A DIGITAL CAMERA WORKS

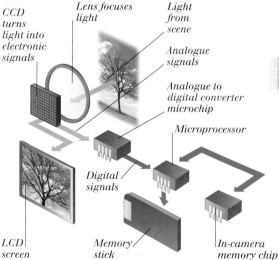

CCD turns light into electronic signals

Lens focuses light

Light from scene

Analogue signals

Analogue to digital converter microchip

Microprocessor

Digital signals

LCD screen

Memory stick

In-camera memory chip

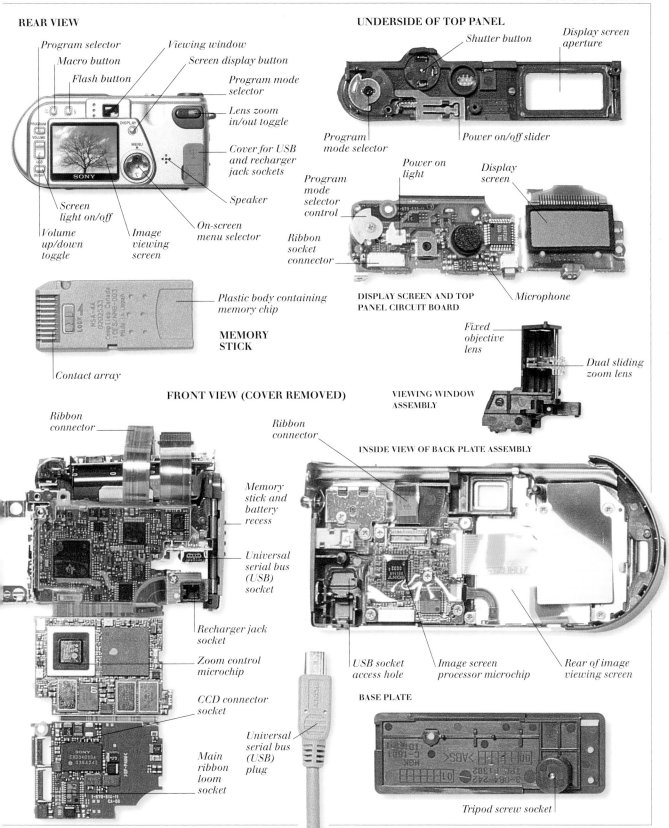

REAR VIEW

Program selector

Macro button

Flash button

Viewing window

Screen display button

Program mode selector

Lens zoom in/out toggle

Cover for USB and recharger jack sockets

Speaker

On-screen menu selector

Image viewing screen

Screen light on/off

Volume up/down toggle

UNDERSIDE OF TOP PANEL

Shutter button

Display screen aperture

Program mode selector

Power on/off slider

Power on light

Display screen

Program mode selector control

Ribbon socket connector

Microphone

DISPLAY SCREEN AND TOP PANEL CIRCUIT BOARD

MEMORY STICK

Plastic body containing memory chip

Contact array

Fixed objective lens

Dual sliding zoom lens

VIEWING WINDOW ASSEMBLY

FRONT VIEW (COVER REMOVED)

Ribbon connector

Ribbon connector

INSIDE VIEW OF BACK PLATE ASSEMBLY

Memory stick and battery recess

Universal serial bus (USB) socket

Recharger jack socket

Zoom control microchip

CCD connector socket

Main ribbon loom socket

Universal serial bus (USB) plug

USB socket access hole

Image screen processor microchip

Rear of image viewing screen

BASE PLATE

Tripod screw socket

Digital video camera

A VIDEO CAMERA, OR CAMCORDER, records a scene as a sequence of 25 still images per second, along with sound. It comprises a camera to capture light from the scene, a viewfinder through which the scene may be viewed, a screen on which the recorded scene may be viewed, charge-coupled devices (CCDs) to convert the visual data into an electric signal, and a means of storing the signal. Digital video cameras convert the signal into digital form – a series of separate measurements of the initial analogue (continuously varying) signal. They record the digital signal on tape, hard disk, or DVD. Digital recordings can be copied accurately, whereas analogue recordings tend to "fade" with each copy.

SONY DIGITAL HANDYCAM

Accessory shoe

Viewfinder

Lock

Power switch

Memory stick slot

Cassette compartment lid

Liquid crystal display (LCD) panel

Battery release

Battery

SCREEN ASSEMBLY

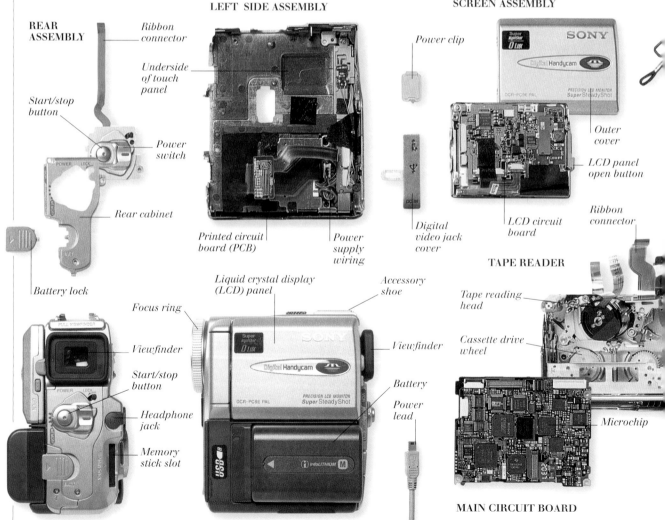

LEFT SIDE ASSEMBLY

REAR ASSEMBLY

Ribbon connector

Underside of touch panel

Start/stop button

Power switch

Rear cabinet

Battery lock

Printed circuit board (PCB)

Power supply wiring

Power clip

Digital video jack cover

Outer cover

LCD panel open button

LCD circuit board

Ribbon connector

TAPE READER

Tape reading head

Cassette drive wheel

Microchip

Liquid crystal display (LCD) panel

Focus ring

Viewfinder

Start/stop button

Headphone jack

Memory stick slot

Accessory shoe

Viewfinder

Battery

Power lead

MAIN CIRCUIT BOARD

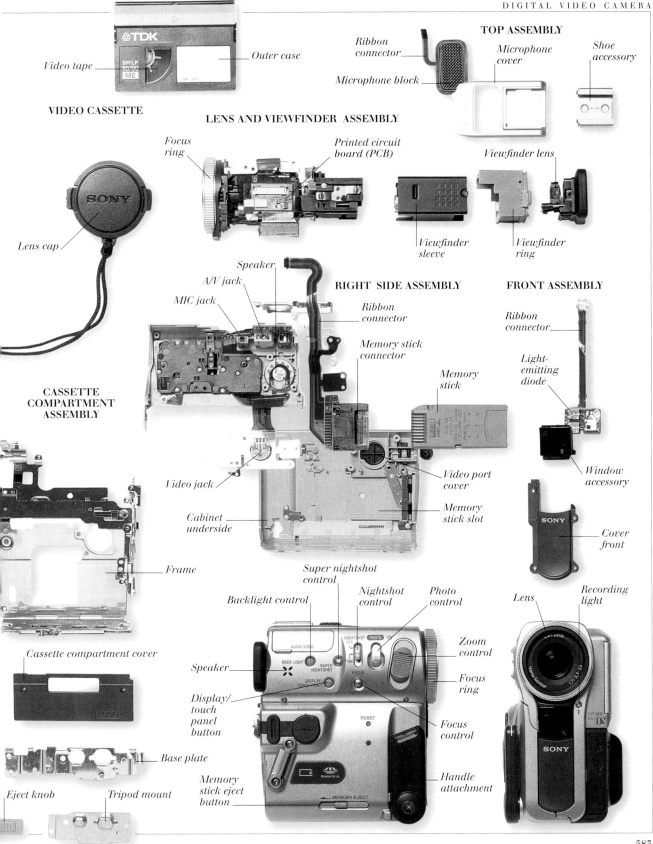

TOP ASSEMBLY

Ribbon connector

Microphone cover

Shoe accessory

Microphone block

Video tape

Outer case

VIDEO CASSETTE

LENS AND VIEWFINDER ASSEMBLY

Focus ring

Printed circuit board (PCB)

Viewfinder lens

Lens cap

Viewfinder sleeve

Viewfinder ring

Speaker

A/V jack

MIC jack

RIGHT SIDE ASSEMBLY

FRONT ASSEMBLY

Ribbon connector

Ribbon connector

Memory stick connector

Light-emitting diode

Memory stick

CASSETTE COMPARTMENT ASSEMBLY

Video jack

Video port cover

Window accessory

Cabinet underside

Memory stick slot

Cover front

Frame

Super nightshot control

Backlight control

Nightshot control

Photo control

Lens

Recording light

Cassette compartment cover

Speaker

Zoom control

Display/ touch panel button

Focus ring

Base plate

Focus control

Eject knob

Tripod mount

Memory stick eject button

Handle attachment

Home cinema

HOME CINEMA REPLICATES a real "movie theatre" using visuals from a plasma wide-screen and surround sound from strategically sited loudspeakers. The source for sound and vision is a DVD (Digital Versatile Disc). Its player uses standard CD (Compact Disc) digital technology, but with a higher density of laser-read microscopic pits – more than 20 billion such pits in multi-level spiral tracks that, stretched out, would extend nearly 40km (25 miles). Emerging technologies include Blu-ray and HD DVD, both of which fit much more data on their discs than standard DVDs, allowing High Definition video files to be stored. It is hard for the human ear to discern the direction of low-pitched sounds, so these emanate from a central bass speaker, often built into or below the screen unit. High-pitched sounds, the direction of which is easier to detect, emanate from mid- and high-frequency speakers positioned around the viewer. Plasma screens use fluorescent tube ("strip-light") technology. Tiny three-cell pixels, each about one millimetre across, contain red, green, and blue phosphor chemicals and a gas mix. Where electric pulses coincide for a split second in the criss-cross matrix of wire electrodes, the gas energizes and emits ultraviolet light, which in turn makes the phosphor glow.

SONY BDZ_S77 BLU-RAY RECORDER

Display panel

Remote control

Control panel and disc tray cover

HOW SURROUND SOUND WORKS

Woofer (bass unit)

Front left sound channel

Rear left sound channel

DVD player under screen

Plasma screen

Front right sound channel

Region of most realistic sound reception

Rear right sound channel

WIDE-SCREEN PLASMA DISPLAY

Mid-grey bezel

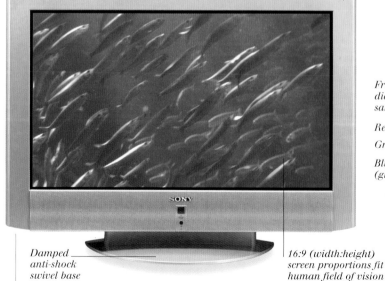

Damped anti-shock swivel base

16:9 (width:height) screen proportions fit human field of vision

HOW A PLASMA SCREEN WORKS

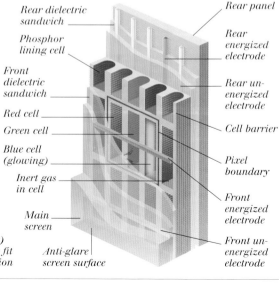

Rear dielectric sandwich

Phosphor lining cell

Front dielectric sandwich

Red cell

Green cell

Blue cell (glowing)

Inert gas in cell

Main screen

Anti-glare screen surface

Rear panel

Rear energized electrode

Rear un-energized electrode

Cell barrier

Pixel boundary

Front energized electrode

Front un-energized electrode

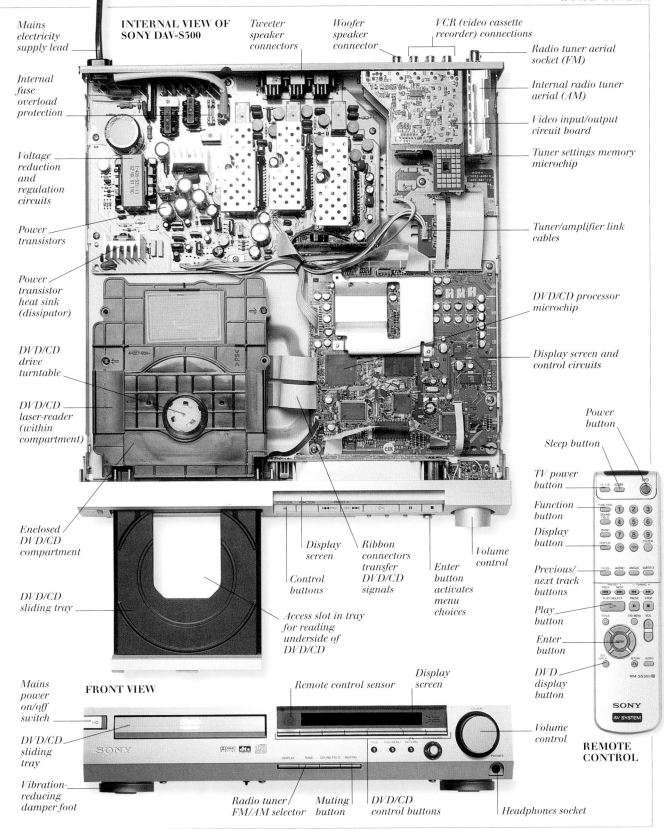

Mains electricity supply lead

INTERNAL VIEW OF SONY DAV-S300

Tweeter speaker connectors

Woofer speaker connector

VCR (video cassette recorder) connections

Radio tuner aerial socket (FM)

Internal fuse overload protection

Internal radio tuner aerial (AM)

Video input/output circuit board

Voltage reduction and regulation circuits

Tuner settings memory microchip

Power transistors

Tuner/amplifier link cables

Power transistor heat sink (dissipator)

DVD/CD processor microchip

DVD/CD drive turntable

Display screen and control circuits

DVD/CD laser-reader (within compartment)

Power button

Sleep button

TV power button

Enclosed DVD/CD compartment

Display screen

Ribbon connectors transfer DVD/CD signals

Enter button activates menu choices

Volume control

Function button

Display button

Previous/ next track buttons

DVD/CD sliding tray

Control buttons

Play button

Access slot in tray for reading underside of DVD/CD

Enter button

DVD display button

Display screen

Mains power on/off switch

FRONT VIEW

Remote control sensor

Volume control

DVD/CD sliding tray

REMOTE CONTROL

Vibration-reducing damper foot

Radio tuner FM/AM selector

Muting button

DVD/CD control buttons

Headphones socket

Personal music and video

THE FIRST BATTERY-DRIVEN PORTABLE source of sound and
music was the transistor radio of the 1950s. In the 1970s, the
magnetic audio cassette tape allowed recordings to be played on
portable tape players. Also, new metal alloys permitted the tiny
but high-power magnets needed for lightweight earphones. In
the 1980s, compact discs brought music into the digital era.
Sony's MD, or minidisc, introduced re-recordable CDs that used
magnetic and optical technology. From the mid 1990s, music
could be stored in all-electronic digital form in a microchip,
usually in the MP3 file format. These files can be transferred
between devices and via the Internet. Today, a variety of
portable media gadgets can record, play, and store video,
photographs, and music in electronic form.

**HARD DISK DRIVE
COMPONENTS**

Platter
separating
ring

Platter
securing
ring

Hard disk
drive platter

HARD DISK DRIVE

Disc spindle
motor

ARCHOS AV500 MOBILE VIDEO RECORDER

Remote
control
infrared
sensor

Head
actuator

Actuator axis

Hard drive
connector

Head position
stepping motor

Accelerate down
button

Play/pause
/resume button

Accelerate
up button

Forward/
reverse,
volume
control, and
directional
buttons

Stop/escape/
off button

Up action
button

Select
action button

Down action
button

Liquid crystal display
(LCD) screen

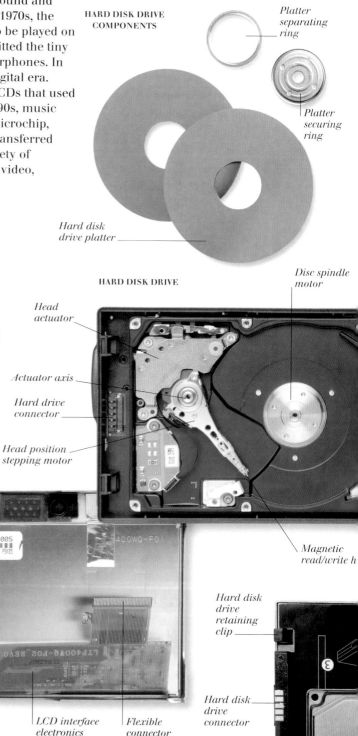

Magnetic
read/write h

Hard disk
drive
retaining
clip

Hard disk
drive
connector

SCREEN AND BUTTON PANELS

LCD interface
electronics

Flexible
connector

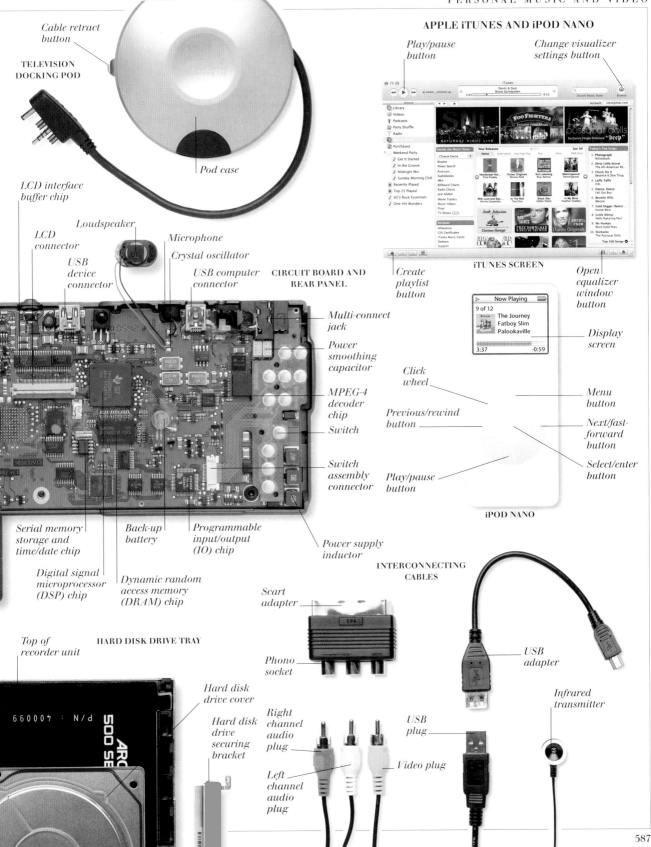

TELEVISION DOCKING POD

Cable retract button

Pod case

APPLE iTUNES AND iPOD NANO

Play/pause button

Change visualizer settings button

iTUNES SCREEN

LCD interface buffer chip

Loudspeaker

LCD connector

Microphone

USB device connector

Crystal oscillator

USB computer connector

CIRCUIT BOARD AND REAR PANEL

Create playlist button

Open equalizer window button

Multi-connect jack

Power smoothing capacitor

MPEG-4 decoder chip

Switch

Switch assembly connector

Now Playing

9 of 12

The Journey
Fatboy Slim
Palookaville

3:37   -0:59

Display screen

Click wheel

Previous/rewind button

Play/pause button

Menu button

Next/fast-forward button

Select/enter button

iPOD NANO

Serial memory storage and time/date chip

Back-up battery

Programmable input/output (IO) chip

Power supply inductor

Digital signal microprocessor (DSP) chip

Dynamic random access memory (DRAM) chip

INTERCONNECTING CABLES

Scart adapter

USB adapter

Top of recorder unit

HARD DISK DRIVE TRAY

Phono socket

Infrared transmitter

Hard disk drive cover

Right channel audio plug

USB plug

Hard disk drive securing bracket

Left channel audio plug

Video plug

587

Mobile and smartphones

IN THE EARLY 1990S, THE MOBILE PHONE (or cellphone) was a rare luxury, but in recent years it has outsold almost every other electrical gadget – as a professional tool, domestic convenience, and even a fashion accessory. Mobile phones have also generally shrunk in size, due to improvements in rechargeable batteries, which now store more electricity for longer in a smaller package, and to smaller, more efficient electronics that use less electricity. A "mobile" is basically a low-power radio receiver-transmitter, plus a tiny microphone to convert sounds into electrical signals, and a small speaker that does the reverse. When the mobile phone is activated, it sends out a radio pulse that is answered by nearby mast transmitter-receivers. The phone locks onto the clearest signal and uses this while within range (the range of each transmitter is known as a cell). The phone continuously monitors signal strength and switches to an alternative transmitter when necessary. The phone's liquid crystal display (LCD) shows numbers, letters, symbols, and colour pictures. Newer models have a larger screen for more complex colour images, and commonly incorporate a camera, radio, and MP3 functionality. Smartphones, which are increasingly widespread, contain additional software and more may be bolted on. Smartphones typically offer Internet and email access, PDA-like functions (see pp. 568–569), and may even contain GPS navigation software.

NOKIA N93

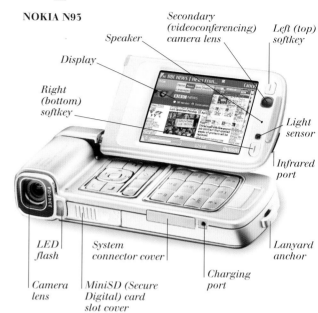

- Speaker
- Display
- Right (bottom) softkey
- Secondary (videoconferencing) camera lens
- Left (top) softkey
- Light sensor
- Infrared port
- LED flash
- System connector cover
- Charging port
- Lanyard anchor
- Camera lens
- MiniSD (Secure Digital) card slot cover

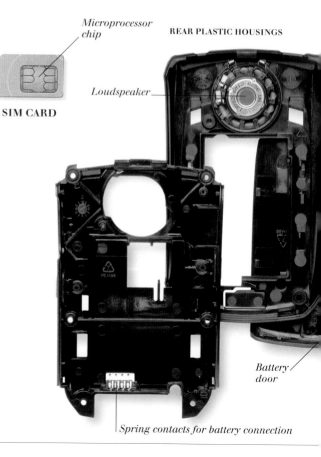

- Microprocessor chip

SIM CARD

REAR PLASTIC HOUSINGS

- Loudspeaker
- Battery door
- Spring contacts for battery connection

BLACKBERRY 8700G

- New message indicator
- Scroll wheel
- Shortcut key
- End key
- Delete key
- Enter key
- Shift key
- Symbol key
- Send/make call key
- Alt key
- Number lock key

HOW A MOBILE PHONE WORKS

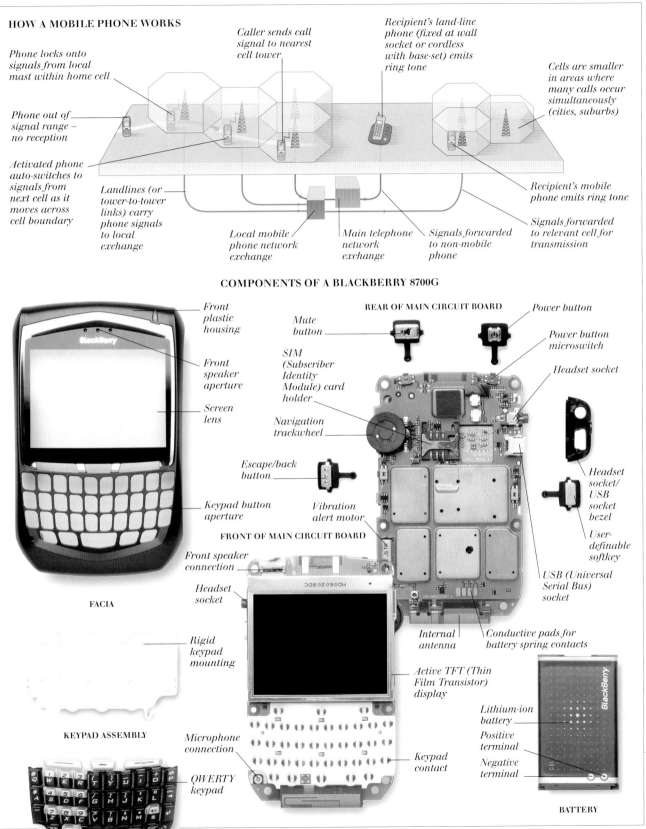

Phone locks onto signals from local mast within home cell

Caller sends call signal to nearest cell tower

Recipient's land-line phone (fixed at wall socket or cordless with base-set) emits ring tone

Cells are smaller in areas where many calls occur simultaneously (cities, suburbs)

Phone out of signal range – no reception

Activated phone auto-switches to signals from next cell as it moves across cell boundary

Landlines (or tower-to-tower links) carry phone signals to local exchange

Local mobile phone network exchange

Main telephone network exchange

Signals forwarded to non-mobile phone

Recipient's mobile phone emits ring tone

Signals forwarded to relevant cell for transmission

COMPONENTS OF A BLACKBERRY 8700G

Front plastic housing

Mute button

REAR OF MAIN CIRCUIT BOARD

Power button

Power button microswitch

Front speaker aperture

SIM (Subscriber Identity Module) card holder

Headset socket

Screen lens

Navigation trackwheel

Escape/back button

Headset socket/ USB socket bezel

Keypad button aperture

Vibration alert motor

User-definable softkey

FRONT OF MAIN CIRCUIT BOARD

USB (Universal Serial Bus) socket

FACIA

Front speaker connection

Headset socket

Internal antenna

Conductive pads for battery spring contacts

Rigid keypad mounting

Active TFT (Thin Film Transistor) display

Lithium-ion battery

Positive terminal

Negative terminal

KEYPAD ASSEMBLY

Microphone connection

QWERTY keypad

Keypad contact

BATTERY

Global positioning system

THE GLOBAL POSITIONING SYSTEM (GPS) is a network of 24 navigation satellites orbiting the Earth that people can use to pinpoint their position. The satellites orbit at a height of 20,000 kilometres (12,500 miles). A GPS receiver picks up signals from any of these satellites that are above the horizon. It uses information in each signal to work out how far away it is from the satellite. It can calculate its position on the Earth's surface when it has information from at least three satellites. A basic GPS receiver shows the latitude and longitude of its position on its screen. A more advanced receiver shows the position on a digital map. Some receivers display extra information, such the distance that has been travelled and the average speed of the vehicle in which the receiver is installed.

Cigarette lighter adapter and speaker cable

Antenna

GARMIN STREET PILOT III GPS

Page key

On/off and screen control button

Enter key

Quit key

Rocker pad

Menu key

Speak key

Liquid crystal display (LCD) screen

Find key

Route key

HOW GPS WORKS

Zoom keys

Satellite 2

Satellite 1

The receiver takes a reading of its distance from two satellites. The receiver is located along the plane where the two resultant spheres meet

IN-CAR MOUNTING BRACKET ASSEMBLY

MOUNTING BRACKET

QUICK-RELEASE BASE

Earth

Satellite 3

A signal from a third satellite defines two positions on that plane. The position on the earth's surface is read as the correct location

Locking lever

Release catch

Ratcheted base

Speaker plug

Power plug

GARMIN GPS V

Adjustable antenna

Power backlight key

Rocker keypad

COMPONENTS OF A GARMIN STREET PILOT III GPS

Data plug

Antenna

Liquid crystal display (LCD) screen

Memory battery

Data plug socket

Main printed circuit board (PCB)

Rear case

USB PROGRAMMER ASSEMBLY

Shielded receiver

Data cartridge

Universal serial bus (USB) programmer

Front case

Liquid crystal display (LCD) assembly

Underside of control pad

SPARE FUSES

591

Vacuum cleaner

IN A CONVENTIONAL VACUUM CLEANER, an electric motor spins a fan that sucks in air carrying dust and debris. The air is forced through tiny pores in a dust bag, trapping most particles. In the 1990s, James Dyson's dual cyclone "bag-less" design did away with the dust bag – and the reduced airflow caused by clogging of its pores. An electrically-driven fan creates a partial vacuum within the machine. Air is forced at more than 100 kilometres per hour past a rotating brush that loosens dirt. The airflow passes along the wand and hose to the outer part of a cylinder-shaped bin. As the air whirls around at 300 kilometres per hour (like a mini-hurricane or cyclone), centrifugal force flings larger particles outwards, to fall to the bin's base. The air then passes through perforations into the cone-shaped, narrower inner bin, where a second cyclone spins even faster, almost 1,000 kilometres per hour, flinging off yet smaller particles. The now almost-clean air exits via two microporous filters.

Wand handle and brushbar controls

Upper wand

Lower wand

Motorized brushbar floor tool

CYCLONE ASSEMBLY

Air intake from hose

Inner cyclone cone

DYSON DC05 MOTORHEAD

Air exit to bin/cyclone cover

Hose electricity connector

Hose slider

WASHABLE PRE-MOTOR FILTER

Microporous filter

Bin upper seal seating

Perforated shroud

Bin handle clip

Hose slider seating

Central retaining screw

Hose electricity supply

Post-motor micropore filter

Filter rim casing

DUST COLLECTION BIN

Inner bin fin

Bin upper seal

Bin base

Bin lower seal

Bin handle

Inner bin dust collection area

Polycarbonate plastic bin body

Bin cover retaining clip

OVERHEAD VIEW OF
DYSON DC05 MOTORHEAD

*Suction
reduction
control*

*On/off and brushbar
motor control*

*Hose cuff
electrical
link*

*Flexible
hose
shrouding*

*Tool or
wand cuff*

*Accessory
holder*

*Electricity connector to
brushbar motor*

Hose base

*Main motor
casing*

*Hinged
bin/cyclone
cover*

*Air intake to
bin/cyclone cover*

*Bin cover
retaining
clip*

dyson

*Bin
cover
handle*

*Motor
air
intake*

*Wheel guard
and flex rewind*

*Main
wheel*

ACCESSORIES

*Tool/
brushbar
connector*

Nozzle

*Textured
scraper*

STAIR TOOL

CREVICE TOOL

*Wand
telescopic
link*

*Brush tool
articulation*

UPHOLSTERY BRUSH

*Flexible
hose
shrouding*

WAND

MOTORIZED
BRUSHBAR
FLOOR TOOL

*Wand/handle
connector*

*Handle
connector*

*Brushbar
drive
motor
cover*

Roller

*Sole plate
roller*

*Brushbar drive
belt cover*

*Rotating
brushbar*

Sole plate

593

Iron and washer-dryer

IN THE DAYS BEFORE WASHING MACHINES, laundry was done by hand – washed in a barrel, squeezed in a roller-mangle, hung on a line, and smoothed with an iron heated on the hob or stove. In the 1880s electrically heated irons were one of the first home electrical appliances. Today's iron still applies heat, sometimes moistened with steam, to dampen and flatten garment fibres. Machines with electric heaters and motors took the strain out of washing from the 1910s. Up to the 1960s, three machines were needed to wash, spin, and dry. Now clothes are swirled in a rotating ribbed tub of hot water, then spun fast to throw off most of the water, before slowly tumbling in electrically heated air to dry – all in one appliance.

FRONT VIEW OF A MIELE WASHER-DRYER

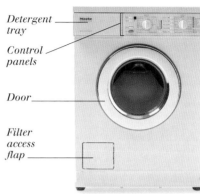

Detergent tray

Control panels

Door

Filter access flap

COMPONENTS OF A STEAM IRON

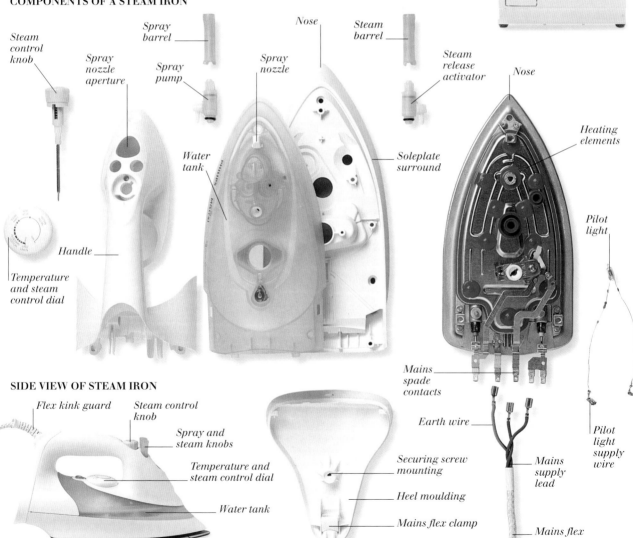

Steam control knob

Spray barrel

Spray nozzle aperture

Spray pump

Spray nozzle

Nose

Steam barrel

Steam release activator

Nose

Water tank

Heating elements

Soleplate surround

Pilot light

Handle

Temperature and steam control dial

Mains spade contacts

Earth wire

Pilot light supply wire

Mains supply lead

SIDE VIEW OF STEAM IRON

Flex kink guard

Steam control knob

Spray and steam knobs

Temperature and steam control dial

Water tank

Soleplate

Securing screw mounting

Heel moulding

Mains flex clamp

Mains flex

COMPONENTS OF A MIELE WASHER-DRYER

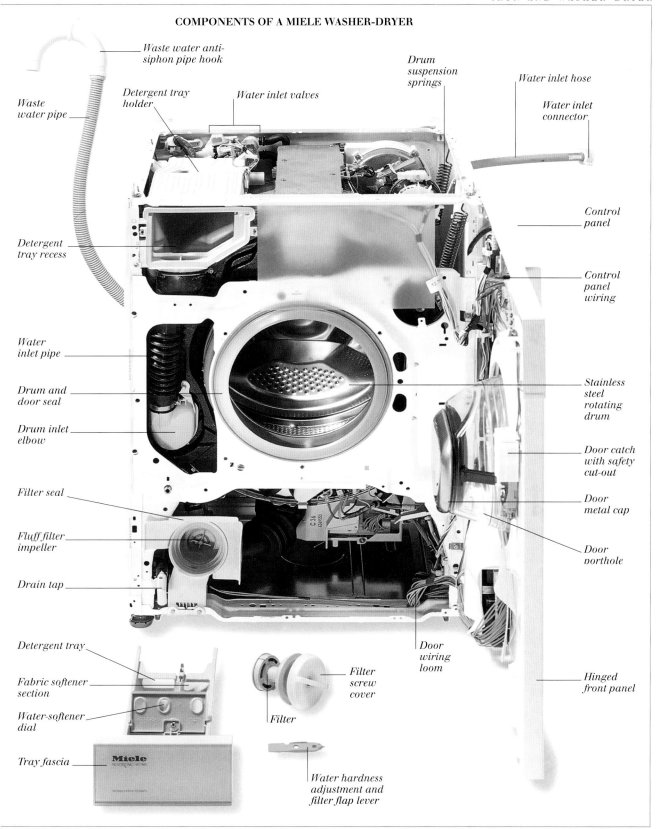

Waste water anti-siphon pipe hook

Drum suspension springs

Water inlet hose

Waste water pipe

Detergent tray holder

Water inlet valves

Water inlet connector

Detergent tray recess

Control panel

Control panel wiring

Water inlet pipe

Drum and door seal

Drum inlet elbow

Stainless steel rotating drum

Door catch with safety cut-out

Filter seal

Door metal cap

Fluff filter impeller

Door porthole

Drain tap

Detergent tray

Door wiring loom

Fabric softener section

Filter screw cover

Hinged front panel

Water-softener dial

Filter

Tray fascia

Miele

Water hardness adjustment and filter flap lever

Microwave combination oven

CONVENTIONAL OVENS use electrically warmed elements or a flame to heat food. In a microwave oven heat energy is created by electromagnetic waves produced by a magnetron and led by waveguides into the oven compartment. These microwaves cannot pass through the compartment's metal casing, being reflected within and spread evenly by a fan. But they do pass through most types of plastic, ceramics, and glass. Therefore platters or containers made from these materials are suitable for use in microwave ovens. A combination oven also has conventional heating elements, to grill and "brown" in the traditional fashion, either alone or in conjunction with microwaves.

MICROWAVE COMBINATION OVEN

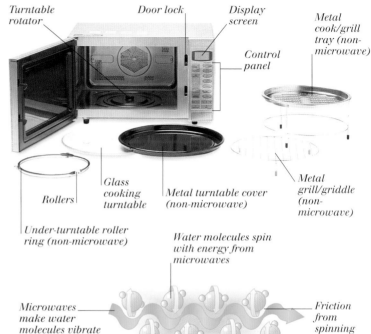

Turntable rotator
Door lock
Display screen
Metal cook/grill tray (non-microwave)
Control panel
Rollers
Glass cooking turntable
Metal turntable cover (non-microwave)
Metal grill/griddle (non-microwave)
Under-turntable roller ring (non-microwave)

HOW MICROWAVES HEAT FOOD

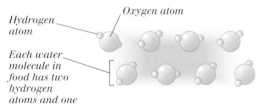

Hydrogen atom
Oxygen atom
Each water molecule in food has two hydrogen atoms and one oxygen atom
Microwaves make water molecules vibrate
Water molecules spin with energy from microwaves
Friction from spinning molecules creates heat

SIDE VIEW OF MICROWAVE COMBINATION OVEN

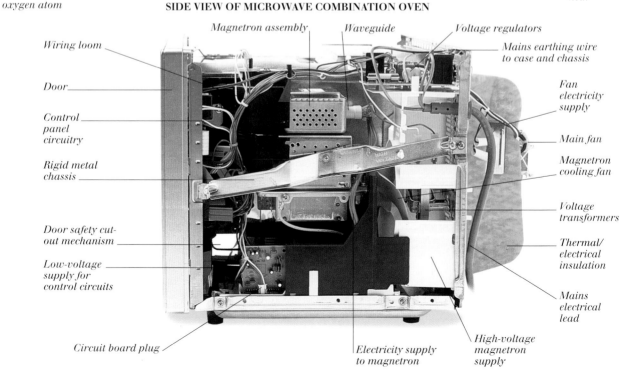

Wiring loom
Door
Control panel circuitry
Rigid metal chassis
Door safety cut-out mechanism
Low-voltage supply for control circuits
Circuit board plug
Magnetron assembly
Waveguide
Voltage regulators
Mains earthing wire to case and chassis
Fan electricity supply
Main fan
Magnetron cooling fan
Voltage transformers
Thermal/electrical insulation
Mains electrical lead
Electricity supply to magnetron
High-voltage magnetron supply

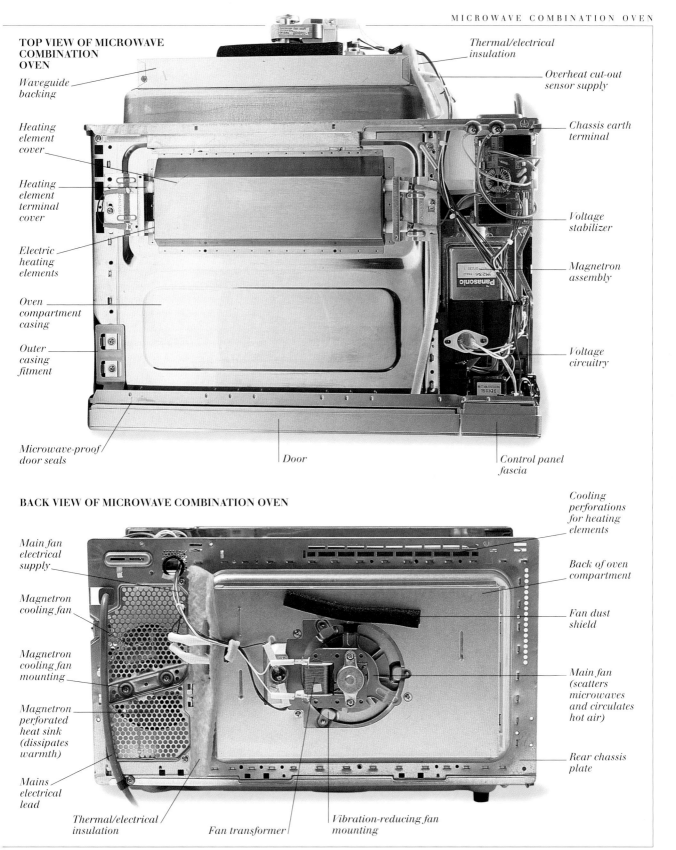

TOP VIEW OF MICROWAVE COMBINATION OVEN

Waveguide backing

Heating element cover

Heating element terminal cover

Electric heating elements

Oven compartment casing

Outer casing fitment

Microwave-proof door seals

Door

Thermal/electrical insulation

Overheat cut-out sensor supply

Chassis earth terminal

Voltage stabilizer

Magnetron assembly

Voltage circuitry

Control panel fascia

BACK VIEW OF MICROWAVE COMBINATION OVEN

Main fan electrical supply

Magnetron cooling fan

Magnetron cooling fan mounting

Magnetron perforated heat sink (dissipates warmth)

Mains electrical lead

Thermal/electrical insulation

Fan transformer

Vibration-reducing fan mounting

Cooling perforations for heating elements

Back of oven compartment

Fan dust shield

Main fan (scatters microwaves and circulates hot air)

Rear chassis plate

Toaster

MOST ELECTRIC TOASTERS not only grill slices of bread, they also pop them up when ready. While the slices rest on a spring-loaded rack, electric heating elements toast the bread. At the same time, a bimetallic strip heats and expands. One of the two metals in this strip expands more quickly than the other, causing the strip to curve. As it bends, it completes an electrical circuit and activates an electromagnet. The magnet attracts a catch, releasing the spring that holds the rack down in the toaster. The elements switch off, and the toasted slices pop up.

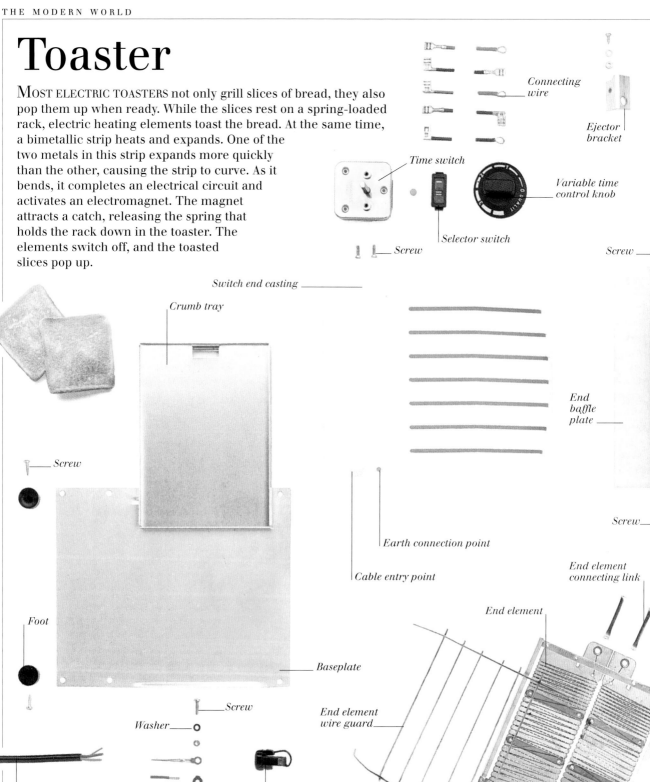

Connecting wire

Ejector bracket

Time switch

Variable time control knob

Selector switch

Screw

Screw

Switch end casting

Crumb tray

End baffle plate

Screw

Screw

Earth connection point

Cable entry point

End element connecting link

End element

Foot

Baseplate

End element wire guard

Washer

Screw

Mains input lead

Cable retaining gland

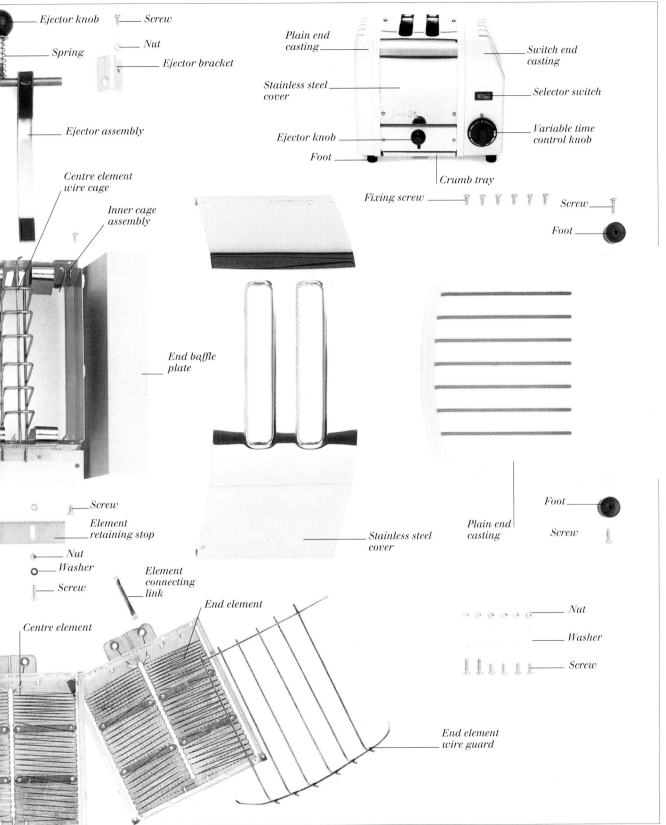

Ejector knob

Screw

Spring

Nut

Ejector bracket

Ejector assembly

Centre element wire cage

Inner cage assembly

End baffle plate

Plain end casting

Switch end casting

Stainless steel cover

Selector switch

Ejector knob

Variable time control knob

Foot

Crumb tray

Fixing screw

Screw

Foot

Stainless steel cover

Plain end casting

Foot

Screw

Screw

Element retaining stop

Nut

Washer

Screw

Element connecting link

End element

Nut

Washer

Screw

Centre element

End element wire guard

Drills

THE ELECTRICALLY POWERED MOTOR OF A POWER DRILL, cooled by a fan, turns a shaft at high speed. The shaft connects, in turn, to a system of gears that rotates a chuck even faster. Clamped by the chuck, a sharp bit cuts out the hole, and at the same time the bit's screw-shaped grooves channel the waste out of the hole. For drilling hard materials, many power drills have a hammer mechanism: when this is operated a ratchet in the gearcase causes the chuck and bit to pound in and out as they drill. A hand drill, although slower and less forceful than a power drill, is easier to control. For cutting wide holes, carpenters often prefer a brace-and-bit. This acts like a lever: the bowed handle of the brace moves a larger distance than the bit, turning the bit with extra force.

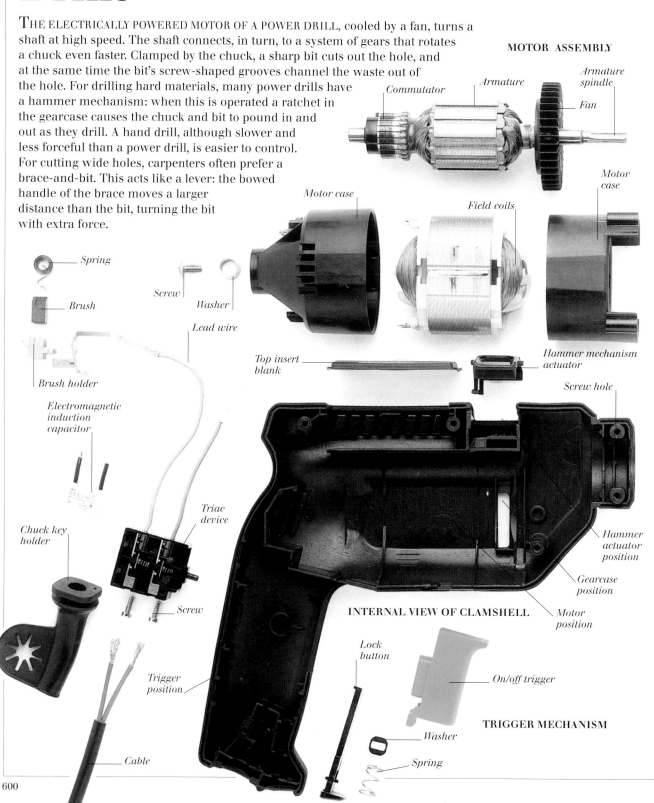

MOTOR ASSEMBLY

Commutator
Armature
Armature spindle
Fan
Motor case

Spring
Brush
Screw
Washer
Lead wire
Brush holder
Motor case
Field coils
Electromagnetic induction capacitor
Top insert blank
Hammer mechanism actuator
Screw hole
Chuck key holder
Triac device
Hammer actuator position
Gearcase position
Screw
INTERNAL VIEW OF CLAMSHELL
Motor position
Trigger position
Lock button
On/off trigger
Washer
TRIGGER MECHANISM
Cable
Spring

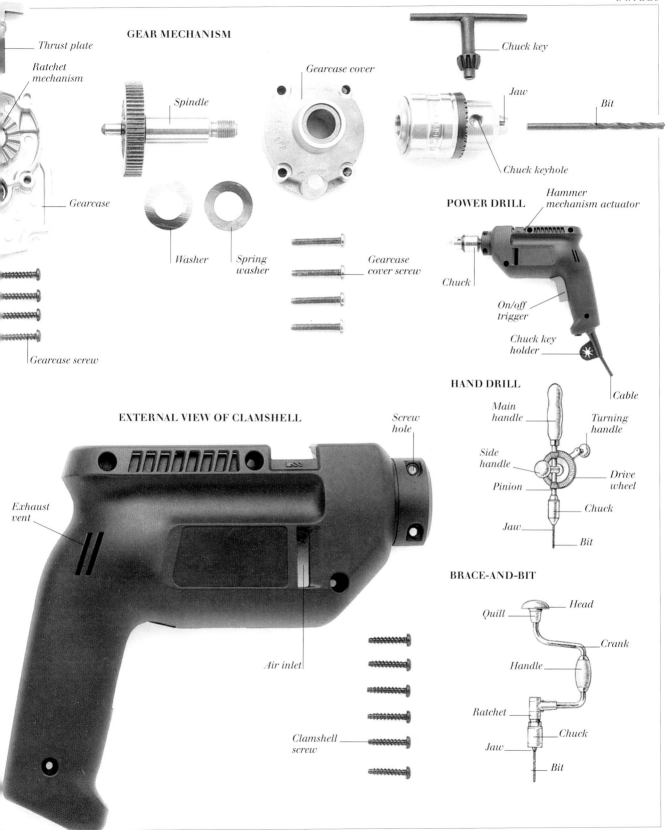

GEAR MECHANISM

Thrust plate

Ratchet mechanism

Spindle

Chuck key

Jaw

Bit

Gearcase cover

Gearcase

Washer

Spring washer

Gearcase cover screw

Chuck keyhole

Gearcase screw

POWER DRILL

Hammer mechanism actuator

Chuck

On/off trigger

Chuck key holder

Cable

HAND DRILL

Main handle

Turning handle

Side handle

Pinion

Drive wheel

Chuck

Jaw

Bit

EXTERNAL VIEW OF CLAMSHELL

Screw hole

Exhaust vent

Air inlet

Clamshell screw

BRACE-AND-BIT

Quill

Head

Crank

Handle

Ratchet

Chuck

Jaw

Bit

House of the future

HOUSES IN THE FUTURE are likely to be more environmentally friendly and energy-efficient than older dwellings, by making better use of materials and intelligent control systems. The Integer house was designed by Cole Thompson Associates, Bree Day Partnership, and Paul Hodgkins Associates, and built in conjunction with the Building Research Establishment in the UK. One of its key features is a large conservatory that warms one side of the house. Extensive use is made of recycled, natural, and renewable materials and energy. The walls are made from timber and insulated with fibre from recycled newspaper; waste water from the bathrooms is saved and used to flush the toilets; and a wind turbine and solar panels contribute some of the electricity requirements. Many elements were prefabricated off site for ease of construction. The Integer house uses only half the energy and a third less water than a traditionally built house.

WALL CONSTRUCTION

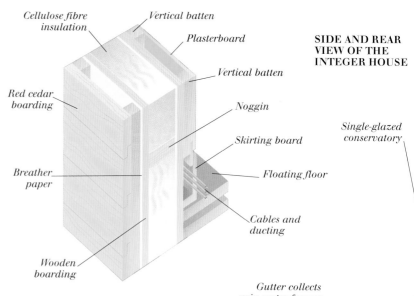

Cellulose fibre insulation

Vertical batten

Plasterboard

Vertical batten

Red cedar boarding

Noggin

Skirting board

Breather paper

Floating floor

Cables and ducting

Wooden boarding

SIDE AND REAR VIEW OF THE INTEGER HOUSE

Single-glazed conservatory

Gutter collects rain water for use in the garden

Composter for recycling kitchen waste

FRONT VIEW OF THE INTEGER HOUSE

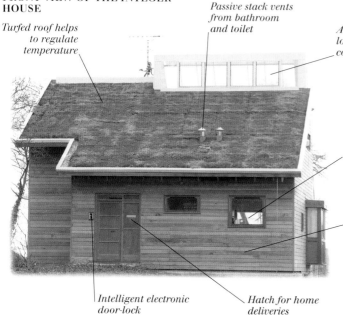

Turfed roof helps to regulate temperature

Passive stack vents from bathroom and toilet

Automatic louvres cool conservatory

Small windows reduce heat loss

Red cedar walls that do not require painting or staining

Intelligent electronic door-lock

Hatch for home deliveries

ROOF CONSTRUCTION

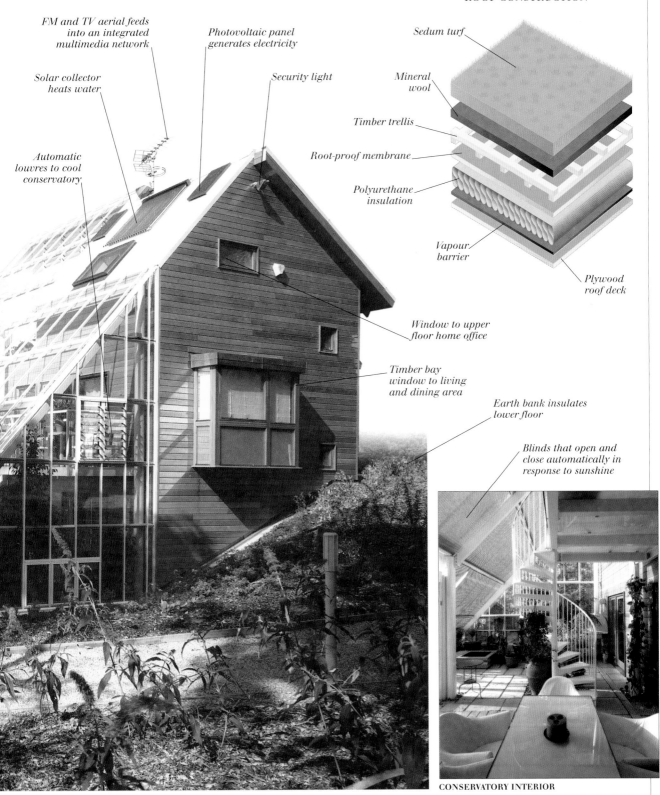

FM and TV aerial feeds
into an integrated
multimedia network

Photovoltaic panel
generates electricity

Solar collector
heats water

Security light

Automatic
louvres to cool
conservatory

Sedum turf

Mineral
wool

Timber trellis

Root-proof membrane

Polyurethane
insulation

Vapour
barrier

Plywood
roof deck

Window to upper
floor home office

Timber bay
window to living
and dining area

Earth bank insulates
lower floor

Blinds that open and
close automatically in
response to sunshine

CONSERVATORY INTERIOR

Renewable energy

RENEWABLE ENERGY COMES from sources that do not become depleted as we use the energy. When a fossil fuel such as coal is burned, it is gone forever, but a renewable source remains available no matter how much is used. The tides, waves, flowing water, sunlight, and the wind are all renewable sources of energy. Wind and water energy are captured by a device called a turbine. The turbine spins and drives an electricity generator. Energy from sunlight, or solar energy, is changed into electricity in two main ways. One uses mirrors to concentrate solar energy and magnify its heating effect which is used to change water into steam to drive turbines. Photovoltaic cells change sunlight directly into electricity. A cell is made from two layers of silicon. One gives out electrons (negative particles) and the other receives them. Sunlight knocks electrons out of atoms where the two layers meet, separating them from the positive particles. The electrons are attracted to one layer of the cell, the positive particles to the other layer. Electrons are naturally attracted to the positive particles, but to come together again, the electrons must flow out of the cell, through an external electric circuit, or load, and back to the other side of the cell, creating a charge. The cell supplies electric current for as long as light keeps falling on it.

VESTAS V47 WIND TURBINE

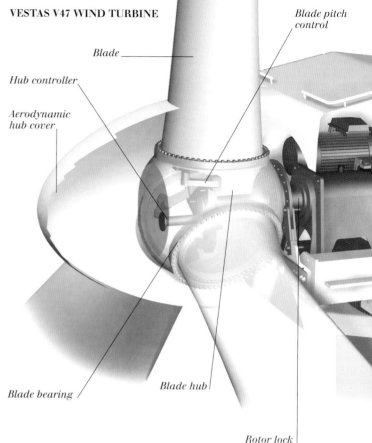

Blade

Blade pitch control

Hub controller

Aerodynamic hub cover

Blade bearing

Blade hub

Rotor lock

TIDAL POWER

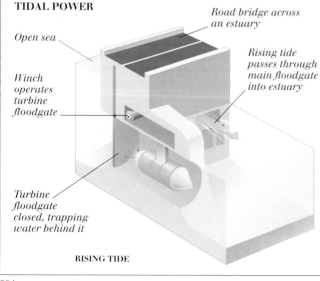

Road bridge across an estuary

Open sea

Rising tide passes through main floodgate into estuary

Winch operates turbine floodgate

Turbine floodgate closed, trapping water behind it

RISING TIDE

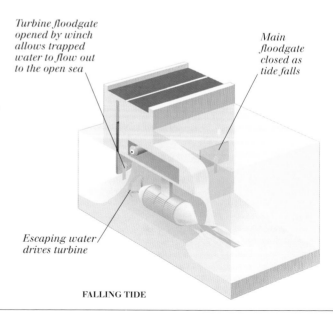

Turbine floodgate opened by winch allows trapped water to flow out to the open sea

Main floodgate closed as tide falls

Escaping water drives turbine

FALLING TIDE

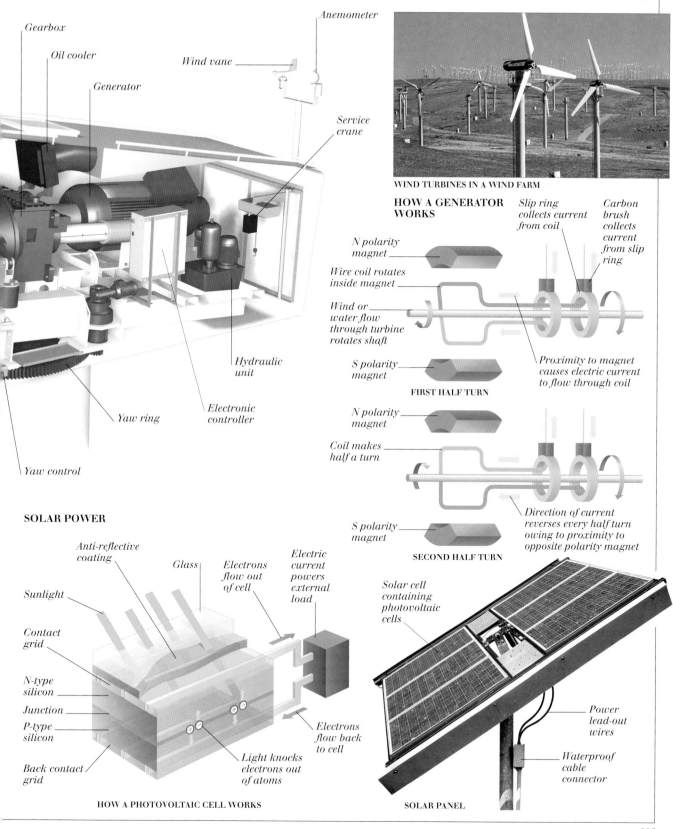

Gearbox

Oil cooler

Generator

Anemometer

Wind vane

Service crane

Hydraulic unit

Yaw ring

Electronic controller

Yaw control

WIND TURBINES IN A WIND FARM

HOW A GENERATOR WORKS

Slip ring collects current from coil

Carbon brush collects current from slip ring

N polarity magnet

Wire coil rotates inside magnet

Wind or water flow through turbine rotates shaft

S polarity magnet

FIRST HALF TURN

Proximity to magnet causes electric current to flow through coil

N polarity magnet

Coil makes half a turn

S polarity magnet

SECOND HALF TURN

Direction of current reverses every half turn owing to proximity to opposite polarity magnet

SOLAR POWER

Anti-reflective coating

Glass

Electrons flow out of cell

Electric current powers external load

Sunlight

Contact grid

Solar cell containing photovoltaic cells

N-type silicon

Junction

P-type silicon

Back contact grid

Light knocks electrons out of atoms

Electrons flow back to cell

Power lead-out wires

Waterproof cable connector

HOW A PHOTOVOLTAIC CELL WORKS

SOLAR PANEL

Cloning technology

IN A LIVING CELL THE GENETIC MATERIAL DNA (deoxyribonucleic acid) contains thousands of units called genes that carry instructions for development, growth, and repair of the living creature. During normal reproduction, half the mother's genetic material contained in an egg cell joins with half the genetic material from the father carried in a sperm cell, to form a unique new genome (set of genes) for a new life. During the early stages of embryo development, the fertilized egg divides into stem cells, which have the potential to become specialized into the hundreds of cell types in a body. Through therapeutic cloning, stem cells can be produced in a laboratory. It is hoped that in the future this technology can be used to grow new tissue that can be transplanted back into the donor to treat illness, without fear of rejection – when the body recognizes a transplanted part as "foreign" because it has different genes, and tries to destroy it. In another form of cloning, performed experimentally using animals, genetic material from a donor animal has been inserted into an egg from another animal that has been emptied of its own genetic material, to produce an animal genetically identical to the donor.

NORMAL REPRODUCTION

Spare cells from egg development

Nucleus with mother's genetic material

Egg cell membrane

Egg cell

Nucleus with mother's genetic material

Polar body (spare genetic material) forms as part of final egg cell division

THERAPEUTIC CLONING

Egg cell with polar body

Zona pellucida (outer casing of egg cell)

"Plug" of zona removed

Fragments of DNA stain as dark "bar code" bands

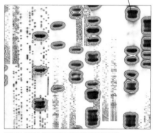

GEL IMAGE SHOWING DNA PROFILE

Suction through micro-pipette holds egg steady

Gentle suction through micro-needle

Micro-needle inserted through egg cell membrane

Zona plug discarded

Polar body removed

Egg genetic material in nucleus removed

Discarded parts no longer needed

Egg cell provides conditions for multiplication

Zona (casing)

Egg cell

Egg cell nucleus containing genetic material

Donor genetic material introduced into egg cell

GENETIC MATERIAL REMOVED FROM EGG

"Enucleated" egg cell (lacks nucleus with genetic material)

Stem cells (unspecialized or undifferentiated cells) collected from donor

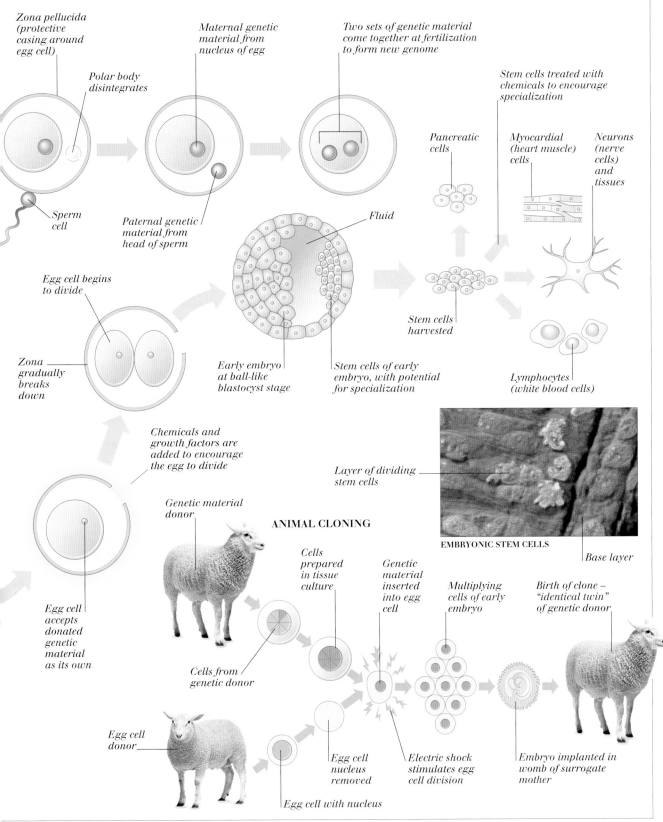

Zona pellucida (protective casing around egg cell)

Polar body disintegrates

Maternal genetic material from nucleus of egg

Two sets of genetic material come together at fertilization to form new genome

Stem cells treated with chemicals to encourage specialization

Pancreatic cells

Myocardial (heart muscle) cells

Neurons (nerve cells) and tissues

Sperm cell

Paternal genetic material from head of sperm

Fluid

Egg cell begins to divide

Zona gradually breaks down

Early embryo at ball-like blastocyst stage

Stem cells of early embryo, with potential for specialization

Stem cells harvested

Lymphocytes (white blood cells)

Chemicals and growth factors are added to encourage the egg to divide

Layer of dividing stem cells

EMBRYONIC STEM CELLS

Base layer

Genetic material donor

ANIMAL CLONING

Cells prepared in tissue culture

Genetic material inserted into egg cell

Multiplying cells of early embryo

Birth of clone – "identical twin" of genetic donor

Egg cell accepts donated genetic material as its own

Cells from genetic donor

Egg cell donor

Egg cell nucleus removed

Egg cell with nucleus

Electric shock stimulates egg cell division

Embryo implanted in womb of surrogate mother

Robots

ROBOTS ARE MACHINES THAT CAN carry out a variety of tasks on their own, with little or no human control. Most robots are mechanical arms used to build things in factories. The end of the robot's arm can be fitted with different tools for gripping, drilling, cutting, welding, and painting. Robot toys have become popular, too. They incorporate sensors that respond to sounds and sometimes touch. Some of them can even understand spoken words. The Aibo robot dog can understand 100 voice commands. Scientists are also trying to create more advanced, human-like robots that can see, hear, learn, and make their own decisions. Cog, a robot that has been progressively developed at the Massachusetts Institute of Technology since the 1990s, is one of these "humanoid" robots.

CAR-BUILDING ROBOTS

Vehicle body

Welding tool

ELEMENTS OF ROBOT ACTION

CENTRAL PROCESSING UNIT (CPU)

Information from sensors

Pre-programmed instructions

Information from sensors interpreted by CPU to modify actions

SENSORS

| LIGHT |
| SOUND |
| TOUCH |
| PROXIMITY |
| SMELL |
| TASTE |

MECHANICAL ACTIONS

INDUSTRIAL ROBOTS

Arm up-down joint

Wrist joints

KAWASAKI INDUSRIAL ROBOT

Arm rotation joint

End effector

Arm out-in joint

Floor-mounted base

Kawasaki

Face light emitting diodes (LEDs)

Mode indicator

Stereo microphone

Movable tail

Rear back sensor and LED

Middle back sensor and LED

Front back sensor and LED

Head distance sensor

Colour 350,000-pixel camera

Mouth

Movable chin touch sensor

Movable ear

SONY AIBO ENTERTAINMENT ROBOT DOG

AIBOne

Infrared chest distance sensor

Paw sensor

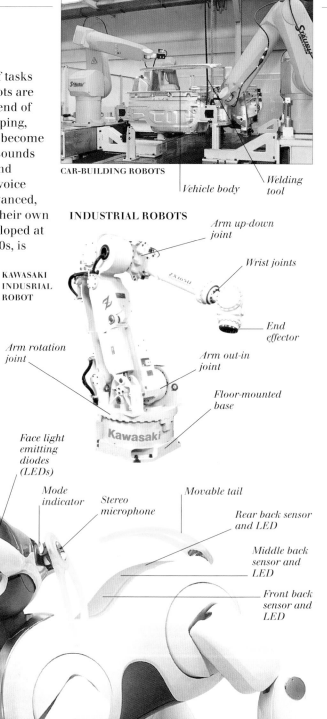

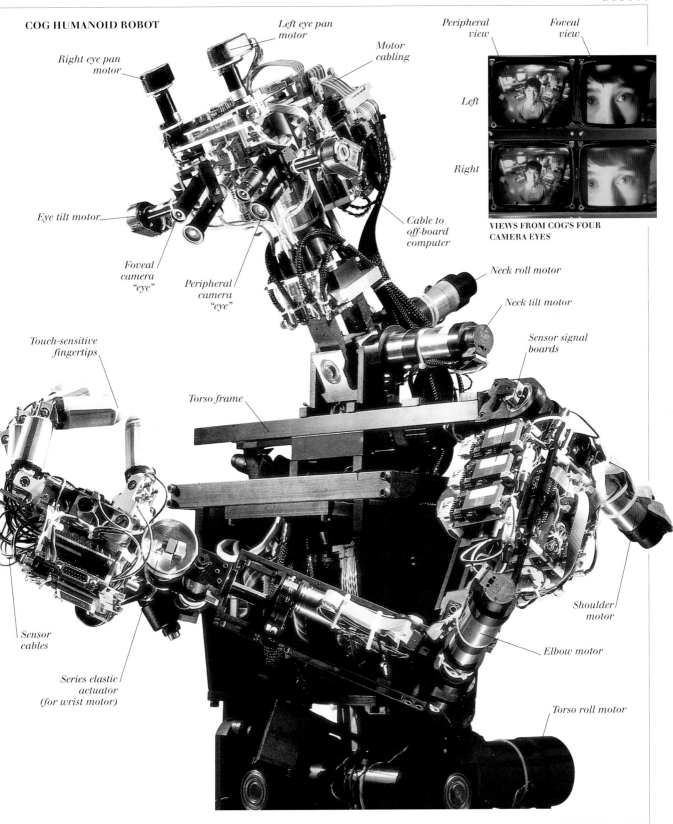

COG HUMANOID ROBOT

Right eye pan motor

Left eye pan motor

Motor cabling

Eye tilt motor

Foveal camera "eye"

Peripheral camera "eye"

Cable to off-board computer

Peripheral view

Foveal view

Left

Right

VIEWS FROM COG'S FOUR CAMERA EYES

Neck roll motor

Neck tilt motor

Sensor signal boards

Touch-sensitive fingertips

Torso frame

Sensor cables

Series elastic actuator (for wrist motor)

Shoulder motor

Elbow motor

Torso roll motor

High-performance microscopes

OPTICAL MICROSCOPES FORM A MAGNIFIED image by using lenses to bend light. Some special-purpose optical microscopes used in industry and research are designed for observing particular materials, such as living cells. They produce magnifications of up to about 1,000. Electron microscopes produce magnifications of as much as 1.5 million. Their images are formed by means of electrons focused by magnetic lenses. There are two main types: scanning electron microscopes (SEMs) scan electrons back and forth across the surface of a specimen; transmission electron microscopes (TEMs) transmit electrons through a thin slice of the specimen.

FEI TECNAI G² TRANSMISSION ELECTRON MICROSCOPE

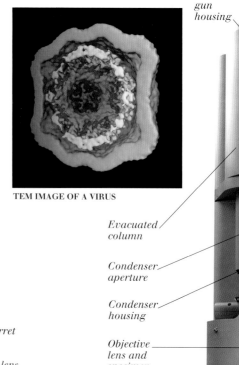

TEM IMAGE OF A VIRUS

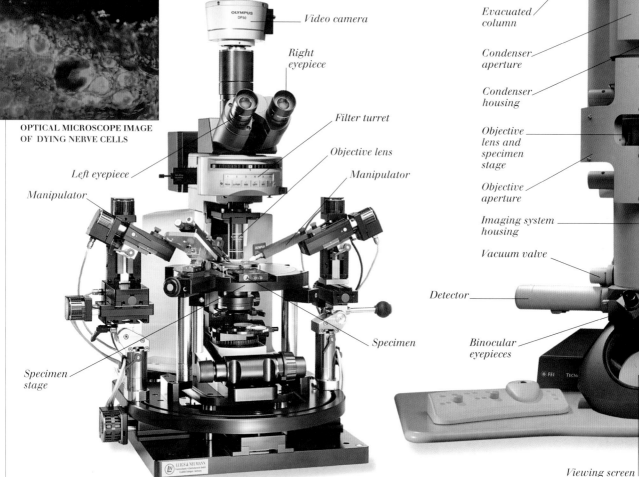

OPTICAL MICROSCOPE IMAGE OF DYING NERVE CELLS

Video camera

Right eyepiece

Filter turret

Objective lens

Manipulator

Left eyepiece

Manipulator

Specimen stage

Specimen

OLYMPUS BX51W1 OPTICAL MICROSCOPE

Electron gun housing

Evacuated column

Condenser aperture

Condenser housing

Objective lens and specimen stage

Objective aperture

Imaging system housing

Vacuum valve

Detector

Binocular eyepieces

Viewing screen

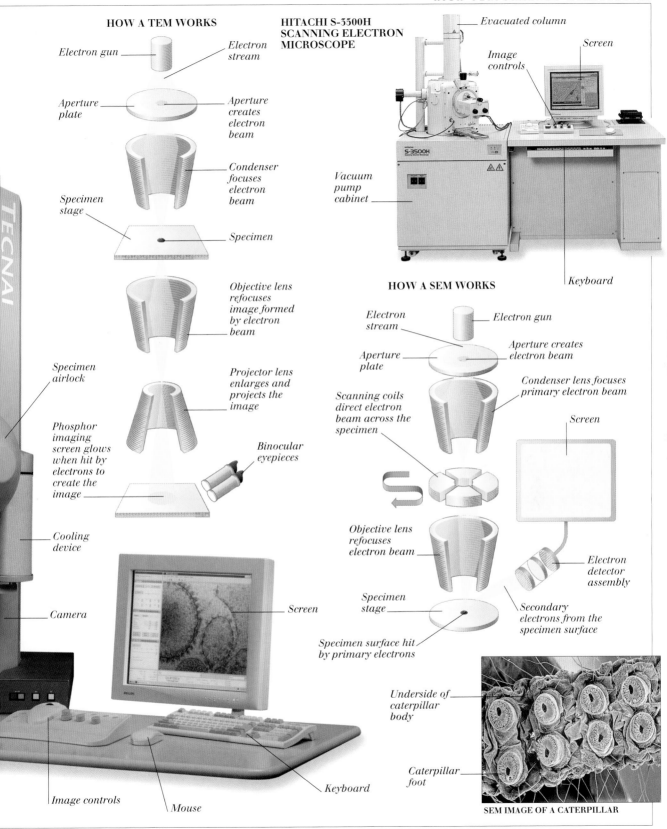

HOW A TEM WORKS

Electron gun

Electron stream

Aperture plate

Aperture creates electron beam

Condenser focuses electron beam

Specimen stage

Specimen

Objective lens refocuses image formed by electron beam

Projector lens enlarges and projects the image

Specimen airlock

Phosphor imaging screen glows when hit by electrons to create the image

Binocular eyepieces

Cooling device

Camera

Screen

Image controls

Mouse

Keyboard

HITACHI S-3500H SCANNING ELECTRON MICROSCOPE

Evacuated column

Image controls

Screen

Vacuum pump cabinet

Keyboard

HOW A SEM WORKS

Electron stream

Electron gun

Aperture plate

Aperture creates electron beam

Scanning coils direct electron beam across the specimen

Condenser lens focuses primary electron beam

Screen

Objective lens refocuses electron beam

Electron detector assembly

Specimen stage

Secondary electrons from the specimen surface

Specimen surface hit by primary electrons

Underside of caterpillar body

Caterpillar foot

SEM IMAGE OF A CATERPILLAR

611

Space telescope

SPACE TELESCOPES ORBIT THE EARTH hundreds of kilometres above the ground, their instruments collecting light from stars and galaxies. Telescopes in space have a clearer view than those on Earth, because they are unaffected by the Earth's atmosphere, which absorbs or distorts much of this radiation. There are a variety of types of space telescopes designed to observe different types of light. The Hubble Space Telescope observes infra-red, ultraviolet, and visible light. It can detect objects that are 100 times fainter than those any telescopes on Earth can see. When this 11,000-kilogram (242-ton), 13-metre (50-foot) long telescope was launched by the Space Shuttle in 1990, it was found that its primary mirror was faulty and its images were blurred. Astronauts fitted extra optics to correct the problem in 1993.

IMAGES TAKEN FROM HUBBLE

Pillar of gas

CONE NEBULA

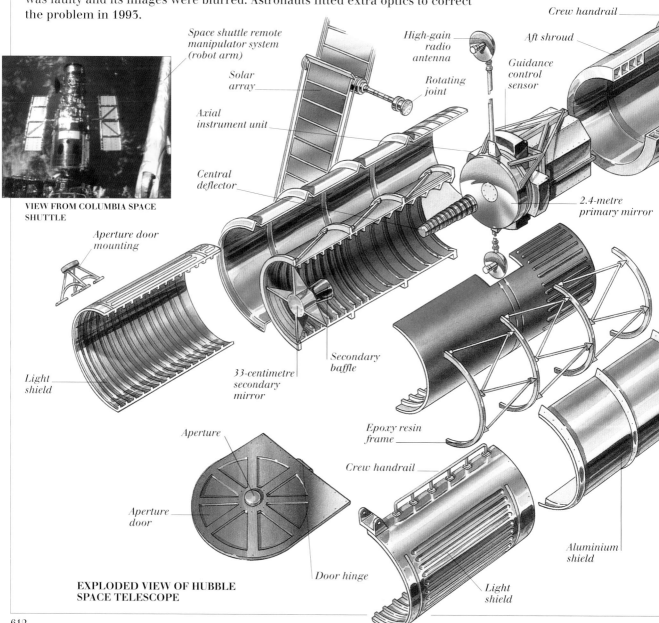

VIEW FROM COLUMBIA SPACE SHUTTLE

Space shuttle remote manipulator system (robot arm)

Solar array

Axial instrument unit

Central deflector

High-gain radio antenna

Rotating joint

Crew handrail

Aft shroud

Guidance control sensor

2.4-metre primary mirror

Aperture door mounting

Light shield

33-centimetre secondary mirror

Secondary baffle

Aperture

Aperture door

Epoxy resin frame

Crew handrail

Door hinge

Light shield

Aluminium shield

EXPLODED VIEW OF HUBBLE SPACE TELESCOPE

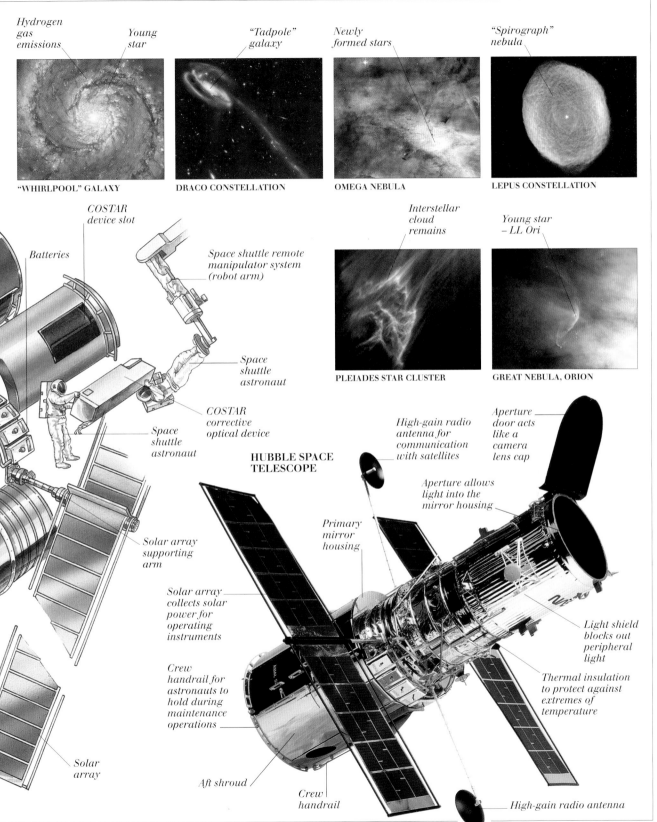

Hydrogen gas emissions

Young star

"WHIRLPOOL" GALAXY

"Tadpole" galaxy

DRACO CONSTELLATION

Newly formed stars

OMEGA NEBULA

"Spirograph" nebula

LEPUS CONSTELLATION

Interstellar cloud remains

Young star – LL Ori

PLEIADES STAR CLUSTER

GREAT NEBULA, ORION

COSTAR device slot

Batteries

Space shuttle remote manipulator system (robot arm)

Space shuttle astronaut

COSTAR corrective optical device

Space shuttle astronaut

HUBBLE SPACE TELESCOPE

High-gain radio antenna for communication with satellites

Aperture door acts like a camera lens cap

Aperture allows light into the mirror housing

Primary mirror housing

Solar array supporting arm

Solar array collects solar power for operating instruments

Crew handrail for astronauts to hold during maintenance operations

Light shield blocks out peripheral light

Thermal insulation to protect against extremes of temperature

Solar array

Aft shroud

Crew handrail

High-gain radio antenna

Probing the Universe

SPACE PROBES HAVE VISITED every planet in the Solar System except Pluto. They take photographs and gather data that cannot be collected using Earth-based equipment. Some probes fly past or orbit around planets or moons, while others land. Two Voyager space probes flew past most of the outer planets in the 1970s and 1980s. Two Viking spacecraft landed on Mars in 1976. The Magellan spacecraft orbited Venus from 1989 and mapped its surface. The Pathfinder spacecraft landed on Mars in 1997 and released a rover vehicle to explore the surface. The Mars Exploration Rover (MER) Mission landed two rovers in 2003. The Cassini space probe reached Saturn in 2004, and in 2005 its mini-probe, Huygens, landed on one of its moons, Titan, and became the first probe to land on a moon of another planet.

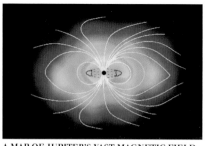

A MAP OF JUPITER'S VAST MAGNETIC FIELD PRODUCED BY CASSINI'S INSTRUMENTS

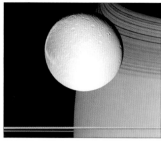

DIONE, ONE OF SATURN'S MOONS, ORBITING ABOVE THE "A" RING

PANORAMIC VIEW OF TITAN TAKEN AS HUYGENS DESCENDED

THE ROCK-STREWN SURFACE OF TITAN, PHOTOGRAPHED BY HUYGENS

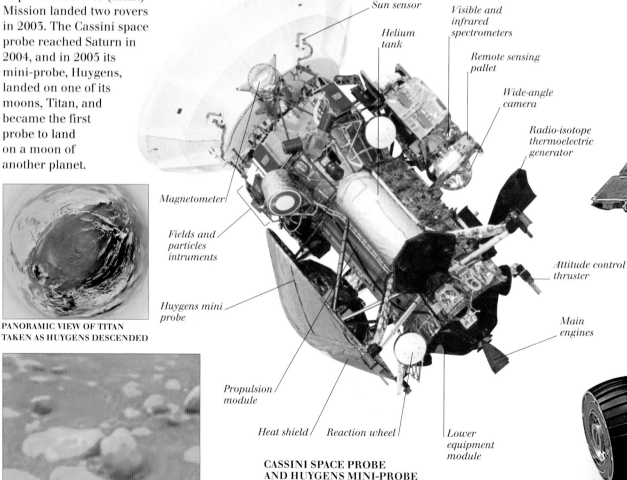

High-gain antenna

Sun sensor

Helium tank

Visible and infrared spectrometers

Remote sensing pallet

Wide-angle camera

Radio-isotope thermoelectric generator

Magnetometer

Fields and particles intruments

Attitude control thruster

Huygens mini probe

Main engines

Propulsion module

Heat shield

Reaction wheel

Lower equipment module

CASSINI SPACE PROBE AND HUYGENS MINI-PROBE

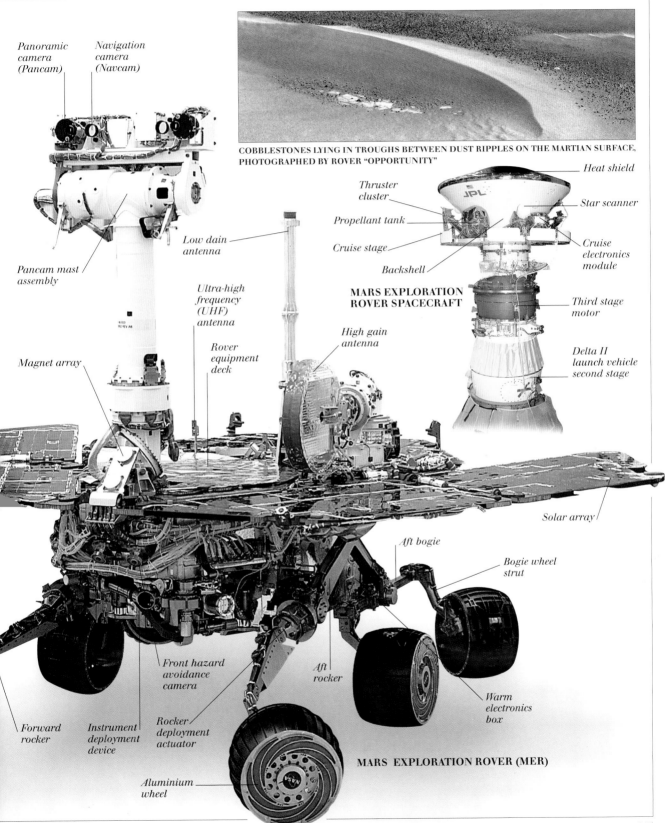

Panoramic
camera
(Pancam)

Navigation
camera
(Navcam)

COBBLESTONES LYING IN TROUGHS BETWEEN DUST RIPPLES ON THE MARTIAN SURFACE,
PHOTOGRAPHED BY ROVER "OPPORTUNITY"

Thruster
cluster

Heat shield

Star scanner

Propellant tank

Cruise stage

Backshell

Cruise
electronics
module

Low dain
antenna

**MARS EXPLORATION
ROVER SPACECRAFT**

Pancam mast
assembly

Ultra-high
frequency
(UHF)
antenna

Third stage
motor

High gain
antenna

Delta II
launch vehicle
second stage

Rover
equipment
deck

Magnet array

Solar array

Aft bogie

Bogie wheel
strut

Front hazard
avoidance
camera

Aft
rocker

Warm
electronics
box

Forward
rocker

Instrument
deployment
device

Rocker
deployment
actuator

MARS EXPLORATION ROVER (MER)

Aluminium
wheel

615

Political map of the world

This map depicts the political boundaries of the world's nations. There are currently 193 independent countries in the world – a marked increase from the 82 that existed in 1950. With the trend towards greater fragmentation, this figure is likely to increase. There are also some 60 overseas dependencies still in existence, with various forms of local administration, but all belonging to a sovereign state. The largest country in the world is the Russian Federation, which covers 17,075,400 sq. km (6,592,800 sq. mi.), while the smallest is the Vatican City, covering 0.44 sq. km (0.17 sq. mi.). Under the Antarctic Treaty of 1959, no countries are permitted territorial claims in Antarctica.

ABBREVIATIONS	
AFGH.	Afghanistan
ALB.	Albania
AUT.	Austria
AZ. OR AZERB.	Azerbaijan
B. & H.	Bosnia & Herzegovina
BELG.	Belgium
BELO.	Belorussia
BOTS.	Botswana
BULG.	Bulgaria
CAMB.	Cambodia
C.A.R.	Central African Republic
CRO.	Croatia
CZ. REP.	Czech Republic
DOM. REP.	Dominican Republic
EST.	Estonia
HUNG.	Hungary
KYRG.	Kyrgyzstan
LAT.	Latvia
LIECH.	Liechtenstein
LITH.	Lithuania
LUX.	Luxemburg
MACED.	Macedonia
MOLD.	Moldavia
NETH.	Netherlands
NETH. ANT.	Netherlands Antilles
PORT.	Portugal
ROM.	Romania
RUSS. FED.	Russian Federation
SERB. & MON.	Serbia & Montenegro
SLVK.	Slovakia
SLVN.	Slovenia
S.M.	San Marino
SWITZ.	Switzerland
TAJ.	Tajikistan
THAI.	Thailand
TURKMEN.	Turkmenistan
U.A.E.	United Arab Emirates
UZBEK.	Uzbekistan
VAT. CITY	Vatican City
ZIMB.	Zimbabwe

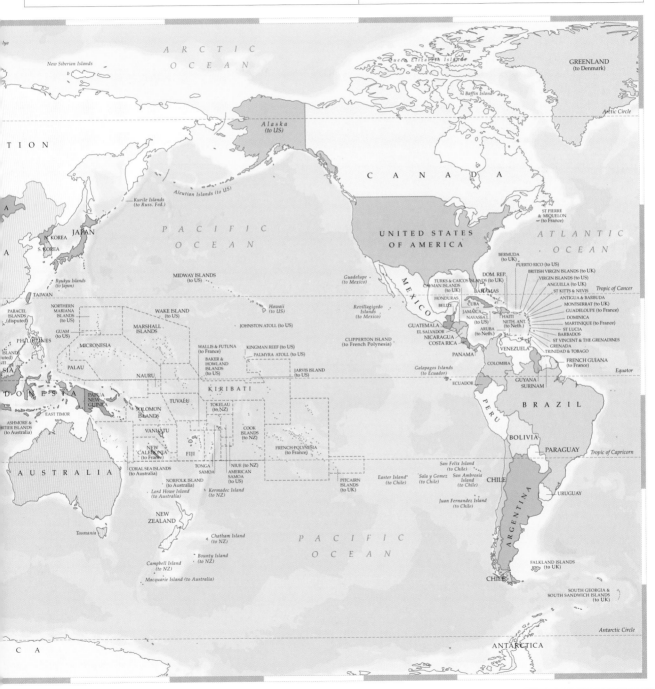

Time zones

The world is divided into 24 time zones, measured in relation to 12 noon Greenwich Mean Time (GMT), on the Greenwich Meridian (0°). Time advances by one hour for every 15° longitude east of Greenwich (and goes back one hour for every 15° west), but the system is adjusted in line with administrative boundaries. Numbers on the map indicate the number of hours that must be added to, or subtracted from GMT to calculate the time in each zone. Thus, eastern USA (–5) is 5 hours behind GMT.

TYPES OF CALENDAR

GREGORIAN
The 365-day Gregorian calendar was introduced by Pope Gregory XIII in 1582 and is now in use throughout most of the Western world. Every four years (leap year) an extra day is added. Below are the names of the months (and number of days).

January (31)	July (31)
February (28, 29 in	August (31)
leap years)	September (30)
March (31)	October (31)
April (30)	November
May (31)	December (31)
June (30)	

JEWISH
The Jewish calendar is a lunar calendar adapted to the solar year. It normally has 12 months but in leap years, which occur seven times in every cycle of 19 years, there are 13 months. The years are reckoned from the Creation (which is placed at 3761 BC); the months are Nisan, Iyyar, Sivan, Thammuz, Ab, Elul, Tishri, Hesvan, Kislev, Tebet, Sebat, and Adar, with an intercalary month (First Adar) being added in leap years.

MUSLIM
The Muslim calendar is based on a year of 12 months, each month beginning roughly at the time of the New Moon. The months are Muharram, Safar, Rabi'I, Rabi'II, Jumada I, Jumada II, Rajab, Sha'ban, Ramadan, Shawwal, Dhu l-Qa'dah, and Dhu l-Hijja.

CHINESE
The Chinese calendar is a lunar calendar, with a year consisting of 12 months. Intercalary months are added to keep the calendar in step with the solar year of 365 days. Months are referred to by a number within a year, but also by animal names that, from ancient times, have been attached to years and hours of the day.

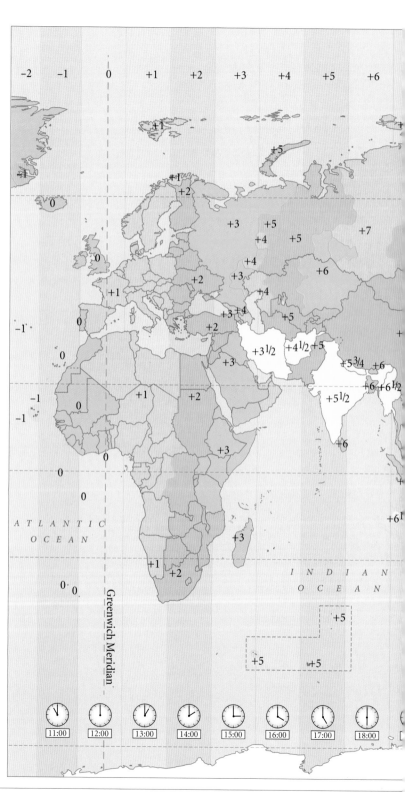

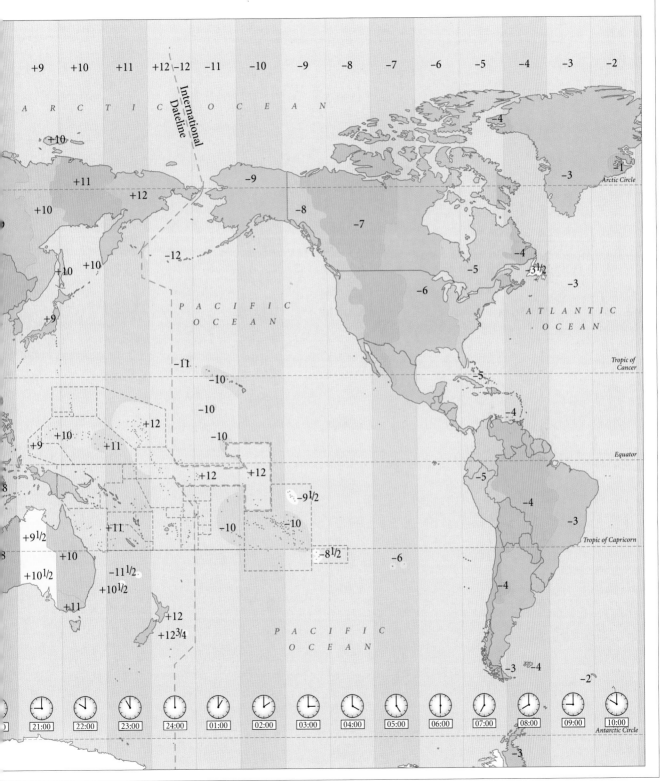

Useful data

ROMAN	ARABIC
I	1
II	2
III	3
IV	4
V	5
VI	6
VII	7
VIII	8
IX	9
X	10
XI	11
XII	12
XIII	13
XIV	14
XV	15
XX	20
XXI	21
XXX	30
XL	40
L	50
LX	60
LXX	70
LXXX	80
XC	90
C	100
CI	101
CC	200
CCC	300
CD	400
D	500
DC	600
DCC	700
DCCC	800
CM	900
M	1,000
MM	2,000

UNITS OF MEASUREMENT

METRIC UNIT	EQUIVALENT
Length	
1 centimetre (cm)	10 millimetres (mm)
1 metre (m)	100 centimetres
1 kilometre (km)	1,000 metres
Mass	
1 kilogram (kg)	1,000 grams (g)
1 tonne (t)	1,000 kilograms
Area	
1 square centimetre (cm²)	100 square millimetres (mm²)
1 square metre (m²)	10,000 square centimetres
1 hectare	10,000 square metres
1 square kilometre (km²)	1,000,000 square metres
Volume	
1 cubic centimetre (cc)	1 millilitre (ml)
1 litre (l)	1,000 millilitres
1 cubic metre (m³)	1,000 litres
Capacity (liquid and dry measures)	
1 centilitre (cl)	10 millilitres (ml)
1 decilitre (dl)	10 centilitres
1 litre (l)	10 decilitres
1 decalitre (dal)	10 litres
1 hectolitre (hi)	10 decalitres
1 kilolitre (kl)	10 hectolitres

IMPERIAL UNIT	EQUIVALENT
Length	
1 foot (ft)	12 inches (in)
1 yard (yd)	3 feet
1 rod (rd)	5.5 yards
1 mile (mi)	1,760 yards
Mass	
1 dram (dr)	27.344 grains (gr)
1 ounce (oz)	16 drams
1 pound (lb)	16 ounces
1 hundredweight (cwt) (long)	112 pounds
1 hundredweight (cwt) (short)	100 pounds
1 ton (long)	2,240 pounds
1 ton (short)	2,000 pounds
Area	
1 square foot (ft²)	144 square inches (in²)
9 square feet	1 square yard (yd²)
1 acre	4,840 square yards
1 square mile	640 acres
Volume	
1 cubic foot	1,728 cubic inches
1 cubic yard	27 cubic feet
Capacity (liquid and dry measures)	
1 fluidram (fl dr)	60 minims (min)
1 fluid ounce (fl oz)	8 fluidrams
1 gill (gi)	5 fluid ounces
1 pint (pt)	4 gills
1 quart (qt)	2 pints
1 gallon (gal)	4 quarts
1 peck (pk)	2 gallons
1 bushel (bu)	4 pecks

METRIC – IMPERIAL CONVERSIONS

TO CONVERT	INTO	MULTIPLY BY
Length		
Centimetres	inches	0.3937
Metres	feet	3.2810
Kilometres	miles	0.6214
Metres	yards	1.0940
Mass		
Grams	ounces	0.0352
Kilograms	pounds	2.2050
Tonnes	long tons	0.9843
Tonnes	short tons	1.1025
Area		
Square centimetres	square inches	0.1550
Square metres	square feet	10.7600
Hectares	acres	2.4710
Square kilometres	square miles	0.3861
Square metres	square yards	1.1960
Volume		
Cubic centimetres	cubic inches	0.0610
Cubic metres	cubic feet	35.3100
Capacity		
Litres	pints	1.7600
Litres	gallons	0.2200

IMPERIAL – METRIC CONVERSIONS

TO CONVERT	INTO	MULTIPLY BY
Length		
Inches	centimetres	2.5400
Feet	metres	0.3048
Miles	kilometres	1.6090
Yards	metres	0.9144
Mass		
Ounces	grams	28.3500
Pounds	kilograms	0.4536
Long tons	tonnes	1.0160
Short tons	tonnes	0.9070
Area		
Square inches	square centimetres	6.4520
Square feet	square metres	0.0929
Acres	hectares	0.4047
Square miles	square kilometres	2.5900
Square yards	square metres	0.8361
Volume		
Cubic inches	cubic centimetres	16.3900
Cubic feet	cubic metres	0.0283
Capacity		
Pints	litres	0.5683
Gallons	litres	4.5460

RULES OF ALGEBRA

EXPRESSION	COMMENTS	EXPRESSION BECOMES
$a + a$	Simple addition	$2a$
$a + b = c + d$	Subtract b from either side	$a = c + d - b$
$ab = cd$	Divide both sides by b	$a = cd \div b$
$(a + b)(c + d)$	Multiplication of bracketed terms	$ac + ad + bc + bd$
$a^2 + ab$	Use parentheses	$a(a + b)$
$(a + b)^2$	Expand brackets	$a^2 + 2ab + b^2$
$a^2 - b^2$	Difference of two squares	$(a + b)(a - b)$
$1/a + 1/b$	Find common denominator	$(a + b)/ab$
$a/b \div c/d$	Dividing by a fraction is the same as multiplying by its reciprocal	$a/b \times d/c$

POWERS OF TEN USED WITH SCIENTIFIC UNITS

FACTOR	NAME	PREFIX	SYMBOL
10^{18}	quintillion	exa-	E
10^{15}	quadrillion	peta-	P
10^{12}	trillion	tera-	T
10^{9}	billion	giga-	G
10^{6}	million	mega-	M
10^{3}	thousand	kilo-	k
10^{2}	hundred	hecto-	h
10^{1}	ten	deca-	da
10^{-1}	one tenth	deci-	d
10^{-2}	one hundredth	centi-	c
10^{-3}	one thousandth	milli-	m
10^{-6}	one millionth	micro-	μ
10^{-9}	one billionth	nano-	n
10^{-12}	one trillionth	pico-	p
10^{-15}	one quadrillionth	femto-	f
10^{-18}	one quintillionth	atto-	a

Note: The American system of numeration for denominations above one million is used in this book. In this system, each of the denominations above one billion (1,000 millions) is 1,000 times the preceding one.

BIOLOGY SYMBOLS

SYMBOL	MEANING
○	female individual (used in inheritance charts)
□	male individual (used in inheritance charts)
♀	female
♂	male
×	crossed with; hybrid
+	wild type
F_1	offspring of the first generation
F_2	offspring of the second generation

TEMPERATURE SCALES

To convert from Celsius (C) to Fahrenheit (F): $F = (C \times 9 \div 5) + 32$
To convert from Fahrenheit to Celsius: $C = (F - 32) \times 5 \div 9$
To convert from Celsius to Kelvin (K): $K = C + 273$
To convert from Kelvin to Celsius: $C = K - 273$

Celsius	-20	-10	0	10	20	30	40	50	60	70	80	90	100
Fahrenheit	-4	14	32	50	68	86	104	122	140	158	176	194	212
Kelvin	253	263	273	283	293	303	313	323	333	343	353	363	373

PHYSICS SYMBOLS

SYMBOL	MEANING
α	alpha particle
β	beta ray
γ	gamma ray; photon
ε	electromotive force
η	efficiency; viscosity
λ	wavelength
μ	micro-; permeability
ν	frequency; neutrino
ρ	density; resistivity
σ	conductivity
c	velocity of light
e	electronic charge

SCIENTIFIC NOTATION

NUMBER	NUMBER BETWEEN 1 AND 10	POWER OF TEN	SCIENTIFIC NOTATION
10	1	10^1	1×10^1
150	1.5	$10^2 (= 100)$	1.5×10^2
274,000,000	2.74	$10^8 (= 100,000,000)$	2.74×10^8
0.0023	2.3	$10^{-3} (= 0.001)$	2.3×10^{-3}

MATHEMATICAL SYMBOLS

SYMBOL	EXPLANATION
+	addition
−	subtraction
×	multiplication
÷	division
=	equals
≠	does not equal
>	greater than
<	less than
≥	greater than or equal to
≤	less than or equal to
∞	infinity
%	per cent
π	pi (3.1416)
°	degree
≈	is approximately equal to
∠	angle
∥	parallel to
Σ	summation
u,u	vectors
f(x)	function
!	factorial
√	square root
$\mathscr{E}$	universal set
$A \cap B$	intersection
$A \cup B$	unison
$A \subset B$	subset
∅	null set

CHEMISTRY SYMBOLS

SYMBOL	MEANING
+	plus; together with
−	single bond
•	single bond; single unpaired electron; two separate parts or compounds regarded as loosely joined
=	double bond
≡	triple bond
R	group
X	halogen atom
Z	atomic number

TRIGONOMETRY

Angle A (degrees)	sin A	cos A	tan A
0	0	1	0
30	1/2	$\sqrt{3}/2$	$1/\sqrt{3}$
45	$1/\sqrt{2}$	$1/\sqrt{2}$	1
60	$\sqrt{3}/2$	1/2	$\sqrt{3}$
90	1	0	∞

Shapes: Plane

Two-dimensional shapes are termed plane (or flat) shapes. Plane shapes constructed with straight sides, as illustrated here, are called polygons. They are categorized according to the number of sides they have – for example, three-sided polygons are known as triangles. A polygon that has sides of equal length and internal angles of equal size, such as a square, is said to be regular.

AREAS AND PERIMETERS

The formulae for calculating the areas and perimeters of simple plane shapes were devised by Classical Greek mathematicians.

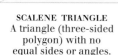

SCALENE TRIANGLE
A triangle (three-sided polygon) with no equal sides or angles.

ISOSCELES TRIANGLE
A triangle with only two sides and two angles equal.

RIGHT-ANGLED TRIANGLE
A triangle with one angle as a right angle (90°).

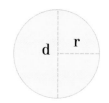

CIRCLE
r = radius
d = diameter = 2 × r

Circumference = 2 × π × r
Area = π × r²
(π = 3.1416)

$$r = \text{radius}$$
$$d = \text{diameter} = 2 \times r$$
$$\text{Circumference} = 2 \times \pi \times r$$
$$\text{Area} = \pi \times r^2$$
$$(\pi = 3.1416)$$

EQUILATERAL TRIANGLE
A regular triangle.
All angles are 60°.

SQUARE
A regular quadrilateral.
All angles are 90°.

RHOMBUS
A quadrilateral with all sides equal and two pairs of equal angles.

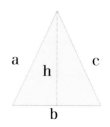

TRIANGLE
Height = h
Sides = a, b, c

Perimeter = a + b + c
Area = ½ × b × h

$$\text{Perimeter} = a + b + c$$
$$\text{Area} = \tfrac{1}{2} \times b \times h$$

RECTANGLE
A quadrilateral with four right angles and opposite sides of equal length.

PARALLELOGRAM
A quadrilateral with two pairs of parallel sides.

TRAPEZIUM
A quadrilateral with one pair of parallel sides.

PENTAGON
A five-sided polygon. A regular pentagon is shown above.

HEXAGON
A six-sided polygon. A regular hexagon is shown above.

OCTAGON
An eight-sided polygon. A regular octagon is shown above.

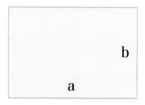

RECTANGLE
Sides = a, b

Perimeter = 2 × (a + b)
Area = a × b

$$\text{Perimeter} = 2 \times (a + b)$$
$$\text{Area} = a \times b$$

Shapes: Solid

Three-dimensional shapes are known as solid shapes, and include spheres, cubes, and pyramids. A solid shape with a polygon at each face is called a polyhedron.

TETRAHEDRON
A four-sided polyhedron. A regular tetrahedron is shown.

CUBE
A regular hexahedron. All sides are equal and all angles are 90°.

OCTAHEDRON
A polyhedron with eight sides.

PRISM
A polyhedron of constant cross-sections in planes perpendicular to its longitudinal axis.

PYRAMID
A polygonal base and triangular sides that meet at a point.

TORUS
A doughnut-like, ring shape.

SPHERE
A round shape, as in a ball or an orange.

HEMISPHERE
Formed when a sphere is cut exactly in half.

SPHEROID
An egg-shaped solid object whose cross-section is a circle or an ellipse.

CONE
An elliptical or circular base with sides tapering to a single point.

RIGHT CYLINDER
A tube-shaped, solid figure. A right cylinder has parallel faces.

HELIX
A twisted curve. The distance moved in one revolution is its pitch.

SURFACE AREAS AND VOLUMES

Volume refers to the amount of space that a solid object occupies. Its surface area is the sum of the area of each of its faces.

CYLINDER
Surface area =
$2 \times \pi \times r \times h + 2\pi r^2$
Volume $= \pi \times r^2 \times h$

Height $= h$
Radius $= r$

CONE
Surface area =
$\pi \times r \times l + \pi r^2$
Volume $= \frac{1}{3} \times \pi \times r^2 \times l$

Height $= h$
Radius $= r$
Side $= l$

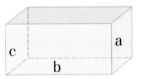

RECTANGULAR BLOCK
Surface area =
$2 (a \times b + b \times c + a \times c)$
Volume $= a \times b \times c$

Sides $= a, b, c$

645

646

657

Acknowledgments

Dorling Kindersley would like to thank (in order of sections):

**The Universe
(consultant editors – Sue Becklake, Gevorkyan Tatyana Alekseyevna):**
John Becklake; the Memorial Museum of Cosmonautics, Moscow; The Cosmos Pavilion, Moscow; The United States Space and Rocket Centre, Alabama; Broadhurst, Clarkson and Fuller Ltd; Susannah Massey

**Prehistoric Earth
(consultant editors – William Lindsay, Martyn Bramwell, Dr Ralph E. Molnar, David Lambert):**
Dr Monty Reid, Andrew Neuman, and the staff of the Royal Tyrrell Museum of Palaeontology, Drumheller, Alberta; Dr Angela Milner and the staff of the Department of Palaeontology, the Natural History Museum, London; Professor W. Ziegler and the staff, in particular Michael Loderstaedt, of the Naturmuseum Senckenburg, Frankfurt; Dr Alexander Liebau, Axel Hunghrebüller, Reiner Schoch, and the staff of the Institut und Museum für Geologie und Paläontologie der Universität, Tübingen; Rupert Wild of the Institut für Paläontologie, Staatliches Museum für Naturkunde, Stuttgart; Dr Scheiber of the Stadtmuseum, Nördlingen; Professor Dr Dietrich Herm of Staatssammlung für Paläontologie und Historische Geologie, München; Dr Michael Keith-Lucas of the Department of Botany, University of Reading; Richard Walker; American Museum of Natural History, New York

**Plants
(consultant editor – Richard Walker):**
Diana Miller; Lawrie Springate; Karen Sidwell; Chris Thody; Michelle End; Susan Barnes and Chris Jones of the EMU Unit of the Natural History Museum, London; Jenny Evans of Kew Gardens, London; Kate Biggs of the Royal Horticultural Society Gardens, Wisley, Surrey; Spike Walker of Microworld Services; Neil Fletcher; John Bryant of Bedgebury Pinetum, Kent; Dean Franklin

**Animals
(consultant editor – Richard Walker):**
David Manning's Animal Ark; Intellectual Animals; Howletts Zoo, Canterbury; John Dunlop; Alexander O'Donnell; Sue Evans of the Royal Veterinary College, London; Dr Geoff Potts and Fred Frettsome of the Marine Biological Association of the United Kingdom, Plymouth; Jeremy Adams of the Booth Museum of Natural History, Brighton; Derek Telling of the Department of Anatomy, University of Bristol; the Natural History Museum, London; Andy Highfield of the Tortoise Trust; Brian Harris of the Aquarium, London Zoo; the Invertebrate Department, London Zoo; Dr Harold McClure of the Yerkes Regional Primate Research Center, Emory University, Atlanta, Georgia; Nielson Lausen of the Harvard Medical School, New England Regional Primates Research

Centre, Southborough, Massachusetts; Dr Paul Hopwood of the Department of Veterinary Anatomy, University of Sydney; Dean Franklin

**The Human Body
(consultant editors – Dr Frances Williams, Dr Fiona Payne, Richard Cummins FRCS):**
Derek Edwards and Dr Martin Collins, British School of Osteopathy; Dr M.C.E. Hutchinson of the Department of Anatomy, United Medical and Dental Schools of Guy's and St Thomas' Hospitals, London. Models – Barry O'Rorke (Bodyline Agency) and Pauline Swaine (MOT Model Agency)

**Geology, Geography, and Meteorology
(consultant editor – Martyn Bramwell):**
Dr John Nudds of the Manchester Museum, Manchester; Dr Alan Wooley and Dr Andrew Clark of the Natural History Museum, London; Graham Bartlett of the National Meteorological Library and Archive, Bracknell; Tony Drake of BP Exploration, Uxbridge; Jane Davies of the Royal Society of Chemistry, Cambridge; Dr Tony Waltham of Nottingham Trent University, Nottingham; staff of the Smithsonian Institute, Washington; staff of the United States Geological Survey, Washington; staff of the National Geographic Society, Washington; staff of Edward Lawrence Associates (Export Ltd), Midhurst; John Farndon; David Lambert

**Rail and Road
Rail (consultant editor – John Coiley)**
Michael Ashworth of the London Transport Museum

Road (consultant editors – David Burgess-Wise, Hugo Wilson)
The National Motor Museum, Beaulieu; Alf Newell of Renault UK Ltd; David Suter of Cheltenham Cutaway Exhibits Ltd; Francesca Riccini of the Science Museum, London. Signore Amadelli of the Museo dell' Automobile Carlo Biscaretti di Ruffia; Paul Bolton of the Mazda MCL Group; Duncan Bradford of Reg Mills Wire Wheels; John and Leslie Brewster of Autocavan; David Burgess-Wise; Trevor Cass of Garrett Turbo Service; John Corbett of The Patrick Collection; Gary Crumpler of Williams Grand Prix Engineering Ltd; Mollie Easterbrooke and Duncan Gough of Overland Ltd; Arthur Fairley of the Vauxhall Motor Company; Paul Foulkes-Halbard of Filching Manor Motor Museum; Frank Gilbert of I. Wilkinson and Son Ltd; Paolo Gratton of Gratton Museum; Colvin Gunn of Gunn and Son; Judy Hogg of Ecurie Bertelli; Milton Holman of Dream Cars; Ian Matthews of IMAT Electronics; Eric Neal of Jaguar Cars Ltd; Paul Niblett, Keith Davidson, Mark Reumel, and David Woolf of Michelin Tyre plc; Doug Nye; Kevin O'Keefe of O'Keefe Cars; Seat UK; Ian Whitley, Raj Johal and Andy Faiers of the Honda Institute; Roger Smith; Jim Stirling of Ironbridge Gorge Museum, Staffordshire; Jon Taylor; Doug Thompson; Martyn Watkins of Ford Motor Company Ltd; John Cattermole, Customer Services Manager at London Northern Buses; F. W. Evans Cycles Ltd; Trek UK Ltd (Bicycle); Sam Grimmer; Colin Uttley

**Physics and Chemistry
(consultant editor – Jack Challoner)**

**Sea and Air
Sea (consultant editors – Geoff Hales and Harvey B. Loomis):**
David Spence, Gillian Hutchinson, David Topliss, Simon Stephens, Robert Baldwin, Jonathan Betts, all of the National Maritime Museum, London; Ian Friel; Simon Turnage of Captain O.M. Watts of London Ltd; Davey and Company Ltd, Great Dunmow; Avon Inflatables Ltd, Llanelli; Musto Ltd, Benfleet; Peter Martin of Spencer Rigging Ltd, Southampton; Peter Rowson of Ratseys Sailmakers, Southampton; Swiftech Ltd, Wallingford; Colin Scattergood of the Barrow Boat Company Ltd, Colchester; Professor J.S. Morrison of the Trireme Trust, Cambridge; The Cutty Sark Maritime Trust; Adrian Daniels of Kelvin Hughes Marine Instruments, London; Arthur Credland of Hull City Council Museums and Art Galleries; The Hull Maritime Society; Gerald Clark; Peter Fitzgerald of the Science Museum, London; Alec Michael of HMB Subwork Ltd, Great Yarmouth, and Ray Ward of the OSEL Group, Great Yarmouth; Richard Bird of UWI, Weybridge; Walker Marine Instruments, Birmingham; The International Sailing Craft Association; The Exeter Maritime Museum; Jane Wilson of the Trinity Lighthouse Company, London; The Imperial War Museum Collections; Thorn Security Ltd; Michael Bach

Air (consultant editor – Bill Gunston):
Aeromega Helicopters, Stapleford; Aero Shopping, London; Avionics Mobile Services Ltd, Watford; Roy Barber and John Chapman of the RAF Museum, Hendon; Mitch Barnes Aviation, London; Mike Beach; British Caledonian Flight Training Ltd; Fred Coates of Helitech (Luton) Ltd; Michael Cuttell and CSE Aviation Ltd, Oxford; Dowty Aerospace Landing Gear, Gloucester; Guy Hartcup of the Airship Association; Anthony Hooley, Chris Walsh, and David Cord of British Aerospace Regional Aircraft Ltd; Ken Huntley of Mid-West Aero Engines Ltd; Imperial War Museum, Duxford; The London Gliding Club, Dunstable; Musée des Ballons, Calvados; Noel Penny Turbines Ltd; Andy Pavey of Aviation Scotland Ltd; Tony Pavey of Thermal Aircraft Developments, London; the Commanding Officer and personnel of RAF St Athan; the Commanding Officer and personnel of RAF Wittering; The Science Museum, London; Ross Sharp of the Science Museum, Wroughton; The Shuttleworth Collection; Skysport Engineering; Mike Smith; Solar Wings Ltd, Marlborough; Julian Temple of Brooklands Museum Trust Ltd; Kelvin Wilson of Flying Start

**Architecture
(consultant editor – Alexandra Kennedy):**
Stephen Cutler for advice and text; Gavin Morgan of the Museum of London, London; Chris Zeuner of the Weald and Downland Museum, Singleton, Sussex; Alan Hills and James Putnam of the British Museum, London; Dr Simon Penn and Michael Thomas of the Avoncroft Museum of Buildings, Bromsgrove,